AF352787

Applied Computing and Artificial Intelligence

Applied Computing and Artificial Intelligence

Editors

Xiang Li
Shuo Zhang
Wei Zhang

MDPI • Basel • Beijing • Wuhan • Barcelona • Belgrade • Manchester • Tokyo • Cluj • Tianjin

Editors
Xiang Li
Xi'an Jiaotong University
Xi'an, China

Shuo Zhang
Northwestern Polytechnical
University
Xi'an, China

Wei Zhang
Shenyang Aerospace
University
Shenyang, China

Editorial Office
MDPI
St. Alban-Anlage 66
4052 Basel, Switzerland

This is a reprint of articles from the Special Issue published online in the open access journal *Mathematics* (ISSN 2227-7390) (available at: https://www.mdpi.com/si/mathematics/Applied_Computing_and_Artificial_Intelligence).

For citation purposes, cite each article independently as indicated on the article page online and as indicated below:

LastName, A.A.; LastName, B.B.; LastName, C.C. Article Title. *Journal Name* **Year**, *Volume Number*, Page Range.

ISBN 978-3-0365-8022-7 (Hbk)
ISBN 978-3-0365-8023-4 (PDF)

Contents

About the Editors . . . . **vii**

Xiang Li, Shuo Zhang and Wei Zhang
Applied Computing and Artificial Intelligence
Reprinted from: *Mathematics* **2023**, *11*, 2309, doi:10.3390/math11102309 . . . . **1**

Jin Qian and Yu Zhan
The Due Date Assignment Scheduling Problem with Delivery Times and Truncated
Sum-of-Processing-Times-Based Learning Effect
Reprinted from: *Mathematics* **2021**, *9*, 3085, doi:10.3390/math9233085 . . . . **5**

Lei Li, Zhong Luo, Fengxia He, Zhaoye Qin, Yuqi Li and Xiaolu Yan
Similitude for the Dynamic Characteristics of Dual-Rotor System with Bolted Joints
Reprinted from: *Mathematics* **2021**, *10*, 3, doi:10.3390/math10010003 . . . . **19**

Xiaobing Yu, Xuejing Wu and Wenguan Luo
Parameter Identification of Photovoltaic Models by Hybrid Adaptive JAYA Algorithm
Reprinted from: *Mathematics* **2022**, *10*, 183, doi:10.3390/math10020183 . . . . **41**

Ying Li and Ye Tang
Design on Intelligent Feature Graphics Based on Convolution Operation
Reprinted from: *Mathematics* **2022**, *10*, 384, doi:10.3390/math10030384 . . . . **69**

Abhijeet Ainapure, Shahin Siahpour, Xiang Li, Faray Majid and Jay Lee
Intelligent Robust Cross-Domain Fault Diagnostic Method for Rotating Machines Using Noisy
Condition Labels
Reprinted from: *Mathematics* **2022**, *10*, 455, doi:10.3390/math10030455 . . . . **85**

Wangying Xu and Xiaobing Yu
Adaptive Guided Spatial Compressive Cuckoo Search for Optimization Problems
Reprinted from: *Mathematics* **2022**, *10*, 495, doi:10.3390/math10030495 . . . . **103**

Xin Wang, Seyed Mehdi Abtahi, Mahmood Chahari and Tianyu Zhao
An Adaptive Neuro-Fuzzy Model for Attitude Estimation and Control of a 3 DOF System
Reprinted from: *Mathematics* **2022**, *10*, 976, doi:10.3390/math10060976 . . . . **131**

Dezhi Hao and Xianwen Gao
Unsupervised Fault Diagnosis of Sucker Rod Pump Using Domain Adaptation with Generated
Motor Power Curves
Reprinted from: *Mathematics* **2022**, *10*, 1224, doi:10.3390/math10081224 . . . . **147**

Jin Qian and Yu Zhan
The Due Window Assignment Problems with Deteriorating Job and Delivery Time
Reprinted from: *Mathematics* **2022**, *10*, 1672, doi:10.3390/math10101672 . . . . **169**

Mercedes Orús-Lacort and Christophe Jouis
Analyzing the Collatz Conjecture Using the Mathematical Complete Induction Method
Reprinted from: *Mathematics* **2022**, *10*, 1972, doi:10.3390/math10121972 . . . . **185**

Zian Lin, Yuanfa Ji, Weibin Liang and Xiyan Sun
Landslide Displacement Prediction Based on Time-Frequency Analysis and LMD-BiLSTM
Model
Reprinted from: *Mathematics* **2022**, *10*, 2203, doi:10.3390/math10132203 . . . . **193**

Jin Qian and Yu Zhan
Single-Machine Group Scheduling Model with Position-Dependent and Job-Dependent
DeJong's Learning Effect
Reprinted from: *Mathematics* **2022**, *10*, 2454, doi:10.3390/math10142454 . . . . **213**

Nannan Xu, Xinze Cui, Xin Wang, Wei Zhang and Tianyu Zhao
An Intelligent Athlete Signal Processing Methodology for Balance Control Ability Assessment
with Multi-Headed Self-Attention Mechanism
Reprinted from: *Mathematics* **2022**, *10*, 2794, doi:10.3390/math10152794 . . . . **223**

Jiapei Peng, Lefa Zhao and Tianyu Zhao
Study on Dynamic Characteristics of a Rotating Sandwich Porous Pre-Twist Blade with a Setting
Angle Reinforced by Graphene Nanoplatelets
Reprinted from: *Mathematics* **2022**, *10*, 2814, doi:10.3390/math10152814 . . . . **239**

Lefa Zhao, Yafei Zhu and Tianyu Zhao
Deep Learning-Based Remaining Useful Life Prediction Method with Transformer Module and
Random Forest
Reprinted from: *Mathematics* **2022**, *10*, 2921, doi:10.3390/math10162921 . . . . **255**

Yue Lu and Gang Mei
A Deep Learning Approach for Predicting Two-Dimensional Soil Consolidation Using
Physics-Informed Neural Networks (PINN)
Reprinted from: *Mathematics* **2022**, *10*, 2949, doi:10.3390/math10162949 . . . . **271**

Wael Etaiwi and Arafat Awajan
SemG-TS: Abstractive Arabic Text Summarization Using Semantic Graph Embedding
Reprinted from: *Mathematics* **2022**, *10*, 3225, doi:10.3390/math10183225 . . . . **289**

**Izaz Raouf, Asif Khan, Salman Khalid, Muhammad Sohail, Muhammad Muzammil Azad
and Heung Soo Kim**
Sensor-Based Prognostic Health Management of Advanced Driver Assistance System for
Autonomous Vehicles: A Recent Survey
Reprinted from: *Mathematics* **2022**, *10*, 3233, doi:10.3390/math10183233 . . . . **311**

Seogu Park, Jinwoo Song, Heung Soo Kim and Donghyeon Ryu
Non-Contact Detection of Delamination in Composite Laminates Coated with a
Mechanoluminescent Sensor Using Convolutional AutoEncoder
Reprinted from: *Mathematics* **2022**, *10*, 4254, doi:10.3390/math10224254 . . . . **337**

Yan Zhang, Jiyuan Tao, Zhixiang Yin and Guoqiang Wang
Improved Large Covariance Matrix Estimation Based on Efficient Convex Combination and Its
Application in Portfolio Optimization
Reprinted from: *Mathematics* **2022**, *10*, 4282, doi:10.3390/math10224282 . . . . **353**

Ahmed Hamza Osman and Hani Moaiteq Aljahdali
Important Arguments Nomination Based on Fuzzy Labeling for Recognizing Plagiarized
Semantic Text
Reprinted from: *Mathematics* **2022**, *10*, 4613, doi:10.3390/math10234613 . . . . **369**

**Fahman Saeed, Muhammad Hussain, Hatim A. Aboalsamh, Fadwa Al Adel and
Adi Mohammed Al Owaifeer**
Designing the Architecture of a Convolutional Neural Network Automatically for Diabetic
Retinopathy Diagnosis
Reprinted from: *Mathematics* **2022**, *10*, 307, doi:10.3390/math11020307 . . . . **391**

About the Editors

Xiang Li

Xiang Li is an Associate Professor with the School of Mechanical Engineering of Xi'an Jiaotong University, China. Before that, he was a postdoctoral fellow at the University of Cincinnati, US, and a visiting scholar at University of California at Merced, US. He received his B.S. and Ph.D. degrees from Tianjin University, China, in 2012 and 2017, respectively.

His research interests include industrial artificial intelligence, industrial big data, machine vision, intelligent fault diagnosis and prognosis, etc. He has published more than 70 research papers in well-known journals, including 17 ESI highly cited papers, 5 ESI hot papers, and 14 ESI research front papers. He has over 5700 citations in Google Scholar, with an H-index of 35. He is the Associate Editor of Expert Systems With Applications. He is also on the editorial boards of Mathematics, IEEE/CAA Journal of Automatica Sinica, Journal of Dynamics, Monitoring and Diagnostics, Machines, and Sensors, among others.

Shuo Zhang

Shuo Zhang is currently an Associate Professor with the School of Mathematics and Statistics, Northwestern Polytechnical University, Xi'an, China. He received his B.S. degree from the Department of Mathematical Science, Shandong Normal University, Jinan, China, in 2011, and his Ph.D. degree from the Department of Mathematics, School of Science, Beijing Jiaotong University, Beijing, China, in 2017. He is the author of more than 50 papers with over 1000 citations. His research interests include neural networks, intelligent control algorithms, and nonlinear dynamics and control.

Wei Zhang

Wei Zhang is an Associate Professor with the School of Aerospace Engineering, Shenyang Aerospace University, China. She received her Ph.D. degree in mechanics from Tianjin University in 2017. She was a visiting scholar with Texas A&M University, US, in 2015. Her research interests include rotor dynamics, deep learning, industrial AI, and squeeze film dampers.

She has published more than 50 research papers in well-known journals, including more than 10 ESI highly cited and hot papers. She has over 3600 citations in Google Scholar. She is on the editorial boards of Measurement, and the Journal of Dynamics, Monitoring and Diagnostics, etc.

 *mathematics*

Editorial

Applied Computing and Artificial Intelligence

Xiang Li [1,*]**, Shuo Zhang** [2] **and Wei Zhang** [3]

[1] School of Mechanical Engineering, Xi'an Jiaotong University, Xi'an 710049, China
[2] School of Mathematics and Statistics, Northwestern Polytechnical University, Xi'an 710072, China; zhangshuo1018@nwpu.edu.cn
[3] School of Aerospace Engineering, Shenyang Aerospace University, Shenyang 110136, China; 1012201003@tju.edu.cn
* Correspondence: lixiang@xjtu.edu.cn

Citation: Li, X.; Zhang, S.; Zhang, W. Applied Computing and Artificial Intelligence. *Mathematics* **2023**, *11*, 2309. https://doi.org/10.3390/math11102309

Received: 5 May 2023
Accepted: 12 May 2023
Published: 15 May 2023

Applied computing and artificial intelligence methods have been attracting growing interest in recent years due to their effectiveness in solving technical problems. The recent developments in applied mathematics have largely led to benefits in many industrial tasks in different fields, including the aerospace industry, manufacturing, transportation, energy, robotics, materials, informatics, etc. The objective of this Special Issue is to present advanced methods in applied computing and artificial intelligence to address the practical challenges in the related areas. The response of the scientific community has been remarkable, and a large number of papers have been submitted. After a careful peer-review process, 22 papers have been accepted and published at a high quality.

The paper by Saeed et al. [1] proposes an approach to building an AutoML data-dependent CNN model (DeepPCANet) customized for DR screening automatically. This approach tackles the limitations of the available annotated DR datasets and the problem of a vast search space and a huge number of parameters in a deep CNN model.

The paper by Osman et al. [2] studies an important arguments nomination technique based on the fuzzy labeling method for identifying plagiarized semantic text. The suggested method matches the text by assigning a value to each phrase within a sentence semantically. Semantic role labeling has several benefits for constructing semantic arguments for each phrase. The approach proposes nominating each argument produced by the fuzzy logic to choose key arguments. It has been determined that not all textual arguments affect text plagiarism.

The paper by Zhang et al. [3] proposes a new estimator, which is a convex combination of the linear shrinkage estimation and the rotation-invariant estimator under the Frobenius norm. They first obtain the optimal parameters by using grid search and cross-validation, and then, they use these optimal parameters to demonstrate the effectiveness and robustness of the proposed estimation in the numerical simulations.

In the paper by Park et al. [4], a method of detecting the delamination of composites using ML sensors is presented. A convolutional autoencoder (CAE) was used to automatically extract the delamination positions from light emission images, which offers better performance compared to edge detection methods.

In the paper by Etaiwi et al. [5], their study proposes a novel semantic graph embedding-based abstractive text summarization technique for the Arabic language, namely SemG-TS. SemG-TS employs a deep neural network to produce the abstractive summary. A set of experiments is conducted to evaluate the performance of SemG-TS and to compare the results to those of a popular baseline word-embedding technique called word2vec. A new dataset was collected for the experiments.

In the paper by Lu et al. [6], they propose a deep learning method using physics-informed neural networks (PINN) to predict the excess pore water pressure of two-dimensional soil consolidation. The proposed deep learning approach can be used to investigate large and complex multidirectional soil consolidation.

Lu et al. [7] propose a deep learning-based method for a balance control ability assessment involving an analysis of the time-series signals from the athletes. The proposed method directly processes the raw data and provides the assessment results, with an end-to-end structure. This straightforward structure facilitates its practical application. A deep learning model is employed to explore the target features with a multi-headed self-attention mechanism, which is a new approach to sports assessments.

Lu et al. [8] study a novel deep learning-based RUL prediction method for the etching system. The transformer module and random forest are integrated in the methodology to identify the health state of the machine and predict its RUL, through training with the complex data of the etching machine's sensors and exploring its underlying features.

The paper authored by Gerogiannis et al. [9] considers the single-group scheduling models with Pegels' and DeJong's learning effect and the single-group scheduling models with Pegels' and DeJong's aging effect. Compared with the classical learning model and aging model for scheduling, the proposed models are more general and realistic. The objective functions are to minimize the total completion time. The polynomial time methods are proposed to solve all the studied problems.

Peng et al. [10] study the vibration of a rotating sandwich pre-twist plate with a setting angle reinforced by graphene nanoplatelets (GPLs). Its core is made of foam metal, and GPLs are added to the surface layers. Supposing that nanofillers are perfectly connected with matrix material, the effective mechanical parameters of the surface layers are calculated by the mixing law and the Halpin–Tsai model, while those of the core layers are determined by the open-cell scheme. The governing equation of the rotating plate is derived by employing the Hamilton principle.

The paper by Lin et al. [11] analyzes the internal relationship between landslide displacement and rainfall, reservoir water level, and landslide state. The maximum information coefficient (MIC) algorithm is used to calculate the intrinsic correlation between each subsequence of landslide displacement and rainfall, reservoir water level, and landslide state. Subsequences of influential factors with high correlation are selected as input variables of the bidirectional long short-term memory (BiLSTM) model to predict each subsequence. Finally, the predicted results of each of the subsequences are added to obtain the final predicted displacement.

In the paper by Orús-Lacort et al. [12], they demonstrate the Collatz conjecture using the mathematical complete induction method. They show that this conjecture is satisfied for the first values of natural numbers, and in analyzing the sequence generated by odd numbers, they can deduce a formula for the general term of the Collatz sequence for any odd natural number n after several iterations. This formula is used in one case that they analyze using the mathematical complete induction method in the process of demonstrating the conjecture.

The paper by Qian et al. [13] considers the single machine scheduling problem with the due window, delivery time and deteriorating job, whose goal is to minimize the window location, window size, earliness, and tardiness. Common due window and slack due window are considered. The delivery time depends on the actual processing time of past sequences. The actual processing time of the job is an increasing function of the start time. Based on the small perturbation technique and adjacent exchange technique, they obtain the propositions of the problems.

Hao et al. [14] present an unsupervised fault diagnosis methodology to leverage the generated MPCs of different working conditions to diagnose the actual unlabeled MPCs. Firstly, the MPCs of six working conditions are generated with an integrated dynamics mathematical model. Secondly, a framework named mechanism-assisted domain adaptation network (MADAN) is proposed to minimize the distribution discrepancy between the generated and actual MPCs.

In the paper by Wang et al. [15], an adaptive neuro-fuzzy integrated system (ANFIS) for satellite attitude estimation and control was developed. The controller was trained with the data provided by an optimal controller. Furthermore, a pulse modulator was used to generate the right ON/OFF commands of the thruster actuator. To evaluate the performance of the proposed controller in closed-loop simulation, an ANFIS observer was also used to estimate the attitude and angular velocities of the satellite using a magnetometer, sun sensor, and gyro data.

In the paper by Xu et al. [16], an adaptive guided spatial compressive CS (AGSCCS)has been proposed. It mainly aims at improving the section of the local search, which helped enhance the exploitation of AGSCCS. The improvements have been implemented in three steps.

The paper by Ainapure et al. [17] proposes a new cross-domain fault diagnosis method with enhanced robustness. Noisy labels are introduced to significantly increase the generalization ability of the data-driven model. A promising diagnosis performance can be obtained with strong noise interference in testing, as in practical cases with low-quality data.

In the paper by Li et al. [18], an image feature-extracted model based on convolution operation is proposed. Parametric tests and effectiveness research are conducted to evaluate the performance of the proposed model. Theoretical and practical research shows that the image-extracted model has a significant effect on the extraction of image features from traditional engraving graphics because the image brightness processing greatly simplifies the process of image feature extraction, and the convolution operation improves the accuracy.

In the paper by Yu et al. [19], a hybrid adaptive algorithm based on JAYA and differential evolution (HAJAYADE) is developed. The HAJAYADE algorithm consists of adaptive JAYA, adaptive DE, and the chaotic perturbation method. Two adaptive coefficients are introduced in adaptive JAYA to balance the local and global search. In adaptive DE, the Rank/Best/1 mutation operator is put forward to boost the exploration and maintain the exploitation. The chaotic perturbation method is applied to reinforce the local search further.

In the paper by Li et al. [20], the scaling relationships for the dual-rotor system with bolted joints are proposed for predicting the responses of full-scale structure, which are developed by generalized and fundamental equations of substructures (shaft, disk, and bolted joints). Different materials between the prototype and model are considered in the derived scaling relationships. Moreover, the effects of bolted joints on the dual-rotor system are analyzed to demonstrate the necessity for considering bolted joints in the similitude procedure. Furthermore, the dynamic characteristics for different working conditions (low-pressure rotor excitation, high-pressure rotor excitation, two frequency excitations, and counter-rotation) are predicted by the scaled model made of relatively cheap material.

Qian et al. [21] consider a single-machine scheduling problem with past-sequence-dependent delivery times and the truncated sum-of-processing-times-based learning effect. The goal is to minimize the total costs that comprise the number of early jobs, the number of tardy jobs and due dates. The due date is a decision variable. There will be corresponding penalties for jobs that are not completed on time.

Raouf et al. [22] propose an extensive review of the main features of ADAS, the types of faults in each different sensor, and the research efforts related to PHM from the published literature. A detailed discussion of the possible shortcomings and commonly occurring defects is summarized for different ADAS components.

As the Guest Editor, I appreciate that the authors contributed their articles to the Special Issue. I would also like to express my gratitude to all reviewers for their valuable comments for significant improvements to the manuscripts. The goal of this Special Issue was to attract quality and novel papers in the field of "Applied Computing and Artificial Intelligence". It is hoped that the published papers will be impactful for international scholars in this field and promote further remarkable research in this area.

Funding: This research received no external funding.

Conflicts of Interest: The authors declare no conflict of interest.

References

1. Saeed, F.; Hussain, M.; Aboalsamh, H.A.; Al Adel, F.; Al Owaifeer, A.M. Designing the Architecture of a Convolutional Neural Network Automatically for Diabetic Retinopathy Diagnosis. *Mathematics* **2023**, *11*, 307. [CrossRef]
2. Osman, A.H.; Aljahdali, H.M. Important Arguments Nomination Based on Fuzzy Labeling for Recognizing Plagiarized Semantic Text. *Mathematics* **2022**, *10*, 4613. [CrossRef]
3. Zhang, Y.; Tao, J.; Yin, Z.; Wang, G. Improved Large Covariance Matrix Estimation Based on Efficient Convex Combination and Its Application in Portfolio Optimization. *Mathematics* **2022**, *10*, 4282. [CrossRef]
4. Park, S.; Song, J.; Kim, H.S.; Ryu, D. Non-Contact Detection of Delamination in Composite Laminates Coated with a Mechanoluminescent Sensor Using Convolutional AutoEncoder. *Mathematics* **2022**, *10*, 4254. [CrossRef]
5. Etaiwi, W.; Awajan, A. SemG-TS: Abstractive Arabic Text Summarization Using Semantic Graph Embedding. *Mathematics* **2022**, *10*, 3225. [CrossRef]
6. Lu, Y.; Mei, G. A Deep Learning Approach for Predicting Two-Dimensional Soil Consolidation Using Physics-Informed Neural Networks (PINN). *Mathematics* **2022**, *10*, 2949. [CrossRef]
7. Xu, N.; Cui, X.; Wang, X.; Zhang, W.; Zhao, T. An Intelligent Athlete Signal Processing Methodology for Balance Control Ability Assessment with Multi-Headed Self-Attention Mechanism. *Mathematics* **2022**, *10*, 2794. [CrossRef]
8. Zhao, L.; Zhu, Y.; Zhao, T. Deep learning-based remaining useful life prediction method with transformer module and random forest. *Mathematics* **2022**, *10*, 2921. [CrossRef]
9. Gerogiannis, V.C. Preface to the Special Issue on "Applications of Fuzzy Optimization and Fuzzy Decision Making". *Mathematics* **2021**, *9*, 3009. [CrossRef]
10. Peng, J.; Zhao, L.; Zhao, T. Study on Dynamic Characteristics of a Rotating Sandwich Porous Pre-Twist Blade with a Setting Angle Reinforced by Graphene Nanoplatelets. *Mathematics* **2022**, *10*, 2814. [CrossRef]
11. Lin, Z.; Ji, Y.; Liang, W.; Sun, X. Landslide Displacement Prediction Based on Time-Frequency Analysis and LMD-BiLSTM Model. *Mathematics* **2022**, *10*, 2203. [CrossRef]
12. Orús-Lacort, M.; Jouis, C. Analyzing the Collatz Conjecture Using the Mathematical Complete Induction Method. *Mathematics* **2022**, *10*, 1972. [CrossRef]
13. Qian, J.; Zhan, Y. The Due Window Assignment Problems with Deteriorating Job and Delivery Time. *Mathematics* **2022**, *10*, 1672. [CrossRef]
14. Hao, D.; Gao, X. Unsupervised Fault Diagnosis of Sucker Rod Pump Using Domain Adaptation with Generated Motor Potheyr Curves. *Mathematics* **2022**, *10*, 1224. [CrossRef]
15. Wang, X.; Abtahi, S.M.; Chahari, M.; Zhao, T. An adaptive neuro-fuzzy model for attitude estimation and control of a 3 DOF system. *Mathematics* **2022**, *10*, 976. [CrossRef]
16. Xu, W.; Yu, X. Adaptive Guided Spatial Compressive Cuckoo Search for Optimization Problems. *Mathematics* **2022**, *10*, 495. [CrossRef]
17. Ainapure, A.; Siahpour, S.; Li, X.; Majid, F.; Lee, J. Intelligent robust cross-domain fault diagnostic method for rotating machines using noisy condition labels. *Mathematics* **2022**, *10*, 455. [CrossRef]
18. Li, Y.; Tang, Y. Design on intelligent feature graphics based on convolution operation. *Mathematics* **2022**, *10*, 384. [CrossRef]
19. Yu, X.; Wu, X.; Luo, W. Parameter identification of photovoltaic models by hybrid adaptive JAYA algorithm. *Mathematics* **2022**, *10*, 183. [CrossRef]
20. Li, L.; Luo, Z.; He, F.; Qin, Z.; Li, Y.; Yan, X. Similitude for the Dynamic Characteristics of Dual-Rotor System with Bolted Joints. *Mathematics* **2022**, *10*, 3. [CrossRef]
21. Qian, J.; Zhan, Y. The due date assignment scheduling problem with delivery times and truncated sum-of-processing-times-based learning effect. *Mathematics* **2021**, *9*, 3085. [CrossRef]
22. Raouf, I.; Khan, A.; Khalid, S.; Sohail, M.; Azad, M.M.; Kim, H.S. Sensor-Based Prognostic Health Management of Advanced Driver Assistance System for Autonomous Vehicles: A Recent Survey. *Mathematics* **2022**, *10*, 3233. [CrossRef]

 *mathematics*

Article

The Due Date Assignment Scheduling Problem with Delivery Times and Truncated Sum-of-Processing-Times-Based Learning Effect

Jin Qian and Yu Zhan *

College of Science, Northeastern University, Shenyang 110819, China; qianjin@mail.neu.edu.cn
* Correspondence: zhanyu@mail.neu.edu.cn

Abstract: This paper considers a single-machine scheduling problem with past-sequence-dependent delivery times and the truncated sum-of-processing-times-based learning effect. The goal is to minimize the total costs that comprise the number of early jobs, the number of tardy jobs and due date. The due date is a decision variable. There will be corresponding penalties for jobs that are not completed on time. Under the common due date, slack due date and different due date, we prove that these problems are polynomial time solvable. Three polynomial time algorithms are proposed to obtain the optimal sequence.

Keywords: scheduling; delivery times; learning effect; common due date; slack due date; different due date

Citation: Qian, J.; Zhan, Y. The Due Date Assignment Scheduling Problem with Delivery Times and Truncated Sum-of-Processing-Times-Based Learning Effect. *Mathematics* **2021**, *9*, 3085. https://doi.org/10.3390/math9233085

Academic Editor: Javier Alcaraz

Received: 28 October 2021
Accepted: 26 November 2021
Published: 30 November 2021

Publisher's Note: MDPI stays neutral with regard to jurisdictional claims in published maps and institutional affiliations.

1. Introduction

Scheduling problems are widely used in manufacturing, logistics, and other practical applications. For a real-word example of our scheduling problems, consider a processing enterprise that has no inventory capacity. As the processing time increases, the processing technology improves. The processing time of the product becomes shorter. The pick-up time of each product is determined by the customer. If the product is produced before the pick-up time or after the pick-up time, an additional delivery fee will be incurred. The delivery price of each early (tardy) job is a fixed charge.

The following three forms of pick-up time are often considered:

(1) All products have a uniform delivery time;
(2) The pick-up time of each product is related to its own processing time and a constant;
(3) Each product has its own independent pick-up time.

The scheduling problem is a very classic discrete combinatorial optimization problem. The methods to solve the scheduling problem mainly include two types: the exact algorithm and approximate algorithm. Exact algorithms mainly include mathematical programming methods, dynamic programming, and branch and bound algorithms. Approximate algorithms mainly include heuristic algorithms and intelligent algorithms. For large-scale non-polynomial time-solvable scheduling problems, intelligent algorithms and machine learning algorithms can be used to solve them. In this paper, a single-machine scheduling problem is considered that contains due dates, the delivery time and learning effect. The actual processing time of a job is a learning function of the previous processing time. The objective function is to minimize the number of early jobs, the number of tardy jobs and due date. Under the common due date, slack due date and different due date, three polynomial time algorithms are proposed to obtain the optimal sequence.

2. Literature Review

In traditional scheduling problems, it is considered that the processing time of jobs is constant. However, in reality, the processing time is often reduced with the increase in workers' skills and abilities. That means the processing time is no longer a constant. In 2011, Cheng et al. developed the branch-and-bound algorithm and simulated an annealing algorithm in order to study the single-machine scheduling problem with a learning effect and truncation processing time [1]. In 2013, Li et al. analyzed the polynomial time algorithm of the single-machine scheduling problem with a truncation processing time [2]. In 2013, Cheng et al. used a genetic algorithm and branch-and-bound algorithm to solve the two-machine flow-shop scheduling problem with a truncated learning function [3]. In 2016, Wu and Wang studied a single-machine scheduling problem with a learning effect and delivery times [4]. In 2017, Wang et al. solved the single-machine scheduling problem with resource allocation and deterioration effects by using the polynomial time algorithm [5]. In 2018, Wu et al. studied a two-stage scheduling problem with a position-based learning effect [6]. In 2018, Yin studied a single-scheduling problem with resource allocation and a learning effect [7]. In 2020, Zhang studied the scheduling problem with the sum-of-processing-times-based learning effect [8]. In 2020, Qian et al. designed a heuristic algorithm to study the single-scheduling problem with release times and a learning factor [9]. In 2020, Zou et al. studied a multi-machine scheduling problem with the sum-of-processing-times-based learning effect [10]. In 2021, Wu et al. studied a flow-shop scheduling problem with a truncated learning function [11].

In the field of scheduling, the delivery time has attracted extensive attention. The extra time required for a completed job to be delivered to the customer is called the *p ast-sequence-dependent (psd)* delivery time. In 2011, Yang et al. studied a single-machine scheduling problem with delivery times and a learning effect [12]. In 2012, Yang et al. studied a single-machine scheduling problem with delivery times and position-dependent processing times [13]. In 2013, Liu studied a scheduling problem with delivery times and deteriorating jobs [14]. In 2014, Zhao et al. studied a single-machine scheduling problem with delivery times and general position-dependent processing times [15]. In 2021, Qian et al. studied a single-machine scheduling problem with delivery times and deteriorating jobs [16].

In actual production scheduling, the jobs often have due dates. If a job is completed ahead of the due date, it will have an earliness cost; if a job is completed behind the due date, it will have a tardiness cost. In 2013, Yin et al. studied a single-machine scheduling problem with a due date, delivery times and learning effect [17]. In 2014, Lu et al. studied a single-machine scheduling problem with a due date, learning effect and resource allocation [18]. In 2015, Li et al. studied a single-machine scheduling problem with a slack due window, learning effect and resource allocation [19]. In 2016, Sun et al. studied a single-machine scheduling problem with a due date and convex resource allocation [20]. In 2019, Geng et al. studied a flow-shop scheduling problem with a common due date, resource allocation and learning effect [21]. In 2020, Liu et al. studied a single-machine scheduling problem with a due date, learning effect and resource allocation [22]. In 2021, Tian studied a single-machine scheduling problem with resource allocation and generalized earliness–tardiness penalties [23]. In 2021, Wang studied a single-machine scheduling problem with proportional setup times and earliness–tardiness penalties [24]. In 1996, Lann et al. studied a single-machine scheduling problem whose goal was to minimize the number of early and tardy jobs [25]. In 2017, Yuan studied a single-machine scheduling problem to minimize the number of tardy jobs [26]. In 2021, Hermelin studied a single-machine scheduling problem to minimize the weighted number of tardy jobs [27].

The problem is described in the Section 3. The research methods are discussed in the Section 4. Discussion of results is in the Section 5. The conclusion is given in the Section 6.

3. Notation and Problem Statement

Some notations used in this paper are introduced in Table 1.

Table 1. Symbol definition.

Symbol	Meaning
n	the number of jobs
p_j	the normal processing time of J_j
$p_{[j]}$	the normal processing time for the jth position
$p_{[j]}^A$	the actual processing time of $J_{[j]}$
$w_{[j]}$	the waiting time of $J_{[j]}$
$C_{[j]}$	the completion time of $J_{[j]}$
$C_{\max}$	the makespan
$q_{[j]}$	the delivery time of $J_{[j]}$
d	the due date
a	the learning index, $a < 0$
r	the delivery rate, $r > 0$
β	the truncation parameter, $0 < \beta < 1$
α, δ, η	the weights
$[j]$	the job arranged at the jth position
CON	the common due date
SLK	the slack due date
DIF	the different due date

Suppose there were n independent jobs $J = \{J_1, \cdots J_n\}$ continuously processed on a single machine. The machine can handle one job at a time. The actual processing time of J_j at the kth position was:

$$p_{j[k]}^A = p_j \max\{(1 + \sum_{i=1}^{k-1} p_{[i]})^a, \beta\}. \tag{1}$$

The delivery time $q_{[j]}$ of $J_{[j]}$ was:

$$q_{[j]} = rw_{[j]} = r \sum_{i=1}^{j-1} p_{[i]}^A, \tag{2}$$

where $w_{[j]} = \sum_{i=1}^{j-1} p_{[i]}^A$. The completion time of $J_{[j]}$:

$$C_{[j]} = w_{[j]} + p_{[j]}^A + q_{[j]}. \tag{3}$$

The common due date, slack due date and different due date were considered in this paper. For the CON model, the due date of each job was the same. For the SLK model, the due date was the sum of the processing time and certain parameter q. For the DIF model, each job had its own due date. The due date was a decision variable. If J_j was an early job, $U_j = 1$, $V_j = 0$. If J_j was a tardy job, $U_j = 0$, $V_j = 1$. By the three-field notation [28], the models could be defined as:

$$1 | p_{j[k]}^A = p_j \max\{(1 + \sum_{i=1}^{k-1} p_{[i]})^a, \beta\}, q_{psd}, CON | \sum_{j=1}^{n} (\alpha U_j + \delta V_j + \eta d), \tag{4}$$

$$1 | p_{j[k]}^A = p_j \max\{(1 + \sum_{i=1}^{k-1} p_{[i]})^a, \beta\}, q_{psd}, SLK | \sum_{j=1}^{n} (\alpha U_j + \delta V_j + \eta q), \tag{5}$$

$$1 | p_{j[k]}^A = p_j \max\{(1 + \sum_{i=1}^{k-1} p_{[i]})^a, \beta\}, q_{psd}, DIF | \sum_{j=1}^{n} (\alpha U_j + \delta V_j + \eta d_j), \tag{6}$$

where q_{psd} represents the past-sequence-dependent delivery times. The following Figure 1 shows the just-in-time common due date scheduling model.

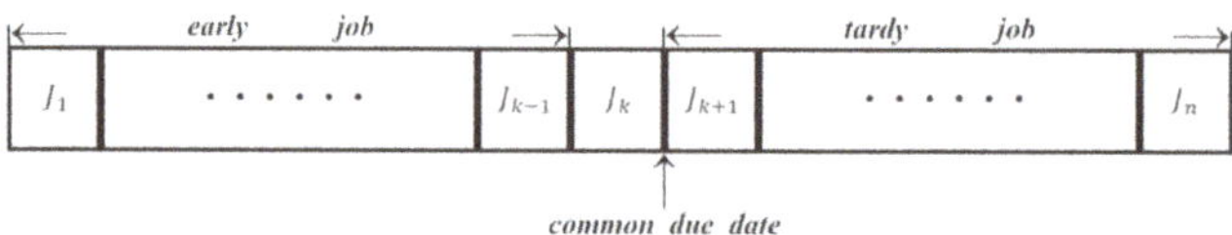

Figure 1. The just-in-time CON scheduling model.

4. Research Method

Lemma 1. *For the* $1|p^A_{j[k]} = p_j \max\{(1 + \sum_{i=1}^{k-1} p_{[i]})^a, \beta\}|C_{\max}$ *problem, an optimal schedule could be obtained by the SPT rule* [4].

Lemma 2. *For the* $1|p^A_{j[k]} = p_j \max\{(1 + \sum_{i=1}^{k-1} p_{[i]})^a, \beta\}, q_{psd}|C_{\max}$ *problem, an optimal schedule could be obtained by the SPT rule* [4].

4.1. The Problem $1|p^A_{j[k]} = p_j \max\{(1 + \sum_{i=1}^{k-1} p_{[i]})^a, \beta\}, q_{psd}, CON| \sum_{j=1}^{n} (\alpha U_j + \delta V_j + \eta d)$

Lemma 3. *For any job sequence, the due date d of the optimal scheduling was the completion time of some job.*

Proof. Suppose that the due date d of the optimal scheduling was not equal to the completion time of some job, i.e., $C_{[h]} < d < C_{[h+1]}$, $0 \le h < n$, $C_{[0]} = 0$. The objective function was:

$$Z = h\alpha + (n - h)\delta + n\eta d. \tag{7}$$

When d was equal to $C_{[h]}$, the objective function was:

$$Z_1 = (h - 1)\alpha + (n - h)\delta + n\eta C_{[h]}, \tag{8}$$

$$Z - Z_1 = \alpha + n\eta(d - C_{[h]}) > 0. \tag{9}$$

Therefore, d was the completion time of some job. $\square$

Lemma 4. *When* $\alpha \ge \delta$, *the due date d was equal to 0.*

Proof. When the due date d was equal to $C_{[h]}$, the objective function was:

$$Z = (h - 1)\alpha + (n - h)\delta + n\eta C_{[h]}. \tag{10}$$

(1) When d was equal to $C_{[h-1]}$, the objective function was:

$$Z_1 = (h - 2)\alpha + (n - h + 1)\delta + n\eta C_{[h-1]}. \tag{11}$$

(2) When d was equal to $C_{[h+1]}$, the objective function was:

$$Z_2 = h\alpha + (n - h - 1)\delta + n\eta C_{[h+1]}.$$

when $\alpha \ge \delta$,

$$Z - Z_1 = \alpha - \delta + n\eta(C_{[h]} - C_{[h-1]}) = \alpha - \delta + n\eta(p_{[h]} + rp_{[h-1]}) > 0, \tag{12}$$

$$Z - Z_2 = -\alpha + \delta + n\eta(C_{[h]} - C_{[h+1]}) = -\alpha + \delta - n\eta(p_{[h+1]} + rp_{[h]}) < 0, \tag{13}$$

$Z_2 > Z > Z_1$. Therefore, the due date d was equal to the start time of the first job. $\square$

For the convenience of proof, we defined two sets: $G_1 = \{J_j | 1 \leq j \leq h\}$, $G_2 = \{J_j | h+1 \leq j \leq n\}$, $d = C_{[h]}$.

Lemma 5. *In the optimal scheduling, the jobs of set G_1 were arranged in an ascending order of normal processing time.*

Proof. There were two adjacent jobs J_u and J_v in the G_1, and J_u was in front of J_v which was at the $(k+1)$th position, $S_1 = \{J_1, \cdots, J_u, J_v, \cdots, J_n\}$. Suppose that the starting time of J_1 was 0, $d = C_{[h]}$, $1 \leq k < h \leq n$. The objective function of S_1 was:

$$Z_1 = (h-1)\alpha + (n-h)\delta + n\eta C_{[h]}(S_1). \tag{14}$$

when J_u and J_v were swapped, the sequence of jobs was $S_2 = \{J_1, \cdots, J_v, J_u, \cdots, J_n\}$. The objective function of S_2 was:

$$Z_2 = (h-1)\alpha + (n-h)\delta + n\eta C_{[h]}(S_2). \tag{15}$$

$$Z_1 - Z_2 = n\eta(C_{[h]}(S_1) - C_{[h]}(S_2)). \tag{16}$$

From $p_u \leq p_v$ and Lemma 2, $Z_1 \leq Z_2$, i.e., the jobs of set G_1 were arranged in an ascending order of normal processing time. $\square$

Lemma 6. *In the optimal scheduling, the jobs of set G_2 were arranged in any order of normal processing time.*

Proof. There were two adjacent jobs J_u and J_v in the G_2, and J_u was in front of J_v which was at the $(k+1)$th position, $S_1 = \{J_1, \cdots, J_u, J_v, \cdots, J_n\}$, $h < k < n$. The objective function of S_1 was:

$$Z_1 = (h-1)\alpha + (n-h)\delta + n\eta C_{[h]}(S_1). \tag{17}$$

when J_u and J_v were swapped, the sequence of jobs was $S_2 = \{J_1, \cdots, J_v, J_u, \cdots, J_n\}$. The objective function of S_2 was:

$$Z_2 = (h-1)\alpha + (n-h)\delta + n\eta C_{[h]}(S_2). \tag{18}$$

$$Z_1 = Z_2. \tag{19}$$

Therefore, the jobs of set G_2 were arranged in any order of normal processing time. $\square$

Lemma 7. *In the optimal scheduling, the processing time of any job in the G_1 was less than the processing time of any job in the G_2.*

Proof. There were two adjacent jobs J_u and J_v, J_u was at the hth position in the G_1, and J_v was at the $(h+1)$th position in the G_2, $S_1 = \{J_1, \cdots, J_u, J_v, \cdots, J_n\}$. The objective function of S_1 was:

$$Z_1 = (h-1)\alpha + (n-h)\delta + n\eta C_{[h]}(S_1). \tag{20}$$

when J_u and J_v were swapped, the sequence of jobs was $S_2 = \{J_1, \cdots, J_v, J_u, \cdots, J_n\}$. The objective function of S_2 was:

$$Z_2 = (h-1)\alpha + (n-h)\delta + n\eta C_{[h]}(S_2). \tag{21}$$

$$Z_1 - Z_2 = n\eta(p_u - p_v)\max\{(1 + \sum_{k=1}^{h-1} p_{[k]})^a, \beta\}. \tag{22}$$

If $p_u \leq p_v$, $Z_1 \leq Z_2$, i.e., the processing time of any job in the G_1 was less than the processing time of any job in the G_2. $\square$

The Algorithm 1 was summarized as follows:

Algorithm 1 $1|p_{j[k]}^A = p_j \max\{(1 + \sum_{i=1}^{k-1} p_{[i]})^a, \beta\}, q_{psd}, CON| \sum_{j=1}^{n}(\alpha U_j + \delta V_j + \eta d)$

Require: $\alpha, \beta, \delta, \eta, a, r, p_j, n$
Ensure: The optimal sequence, d
  1: **First step:** All jobs were sorted by increasing processing time, i.e., $p_1 \leq \cdots \leq p_n$.
  2: **Second step:** When h was from 0 to n, the objective function values were calculated, respectively.
  3: **Last step:** The optimal position of h was determined by the smallest value of the objective function, and the optimal sequence was arrangedn an ascending order of normal processing time.

Theorem 1. *For the problem* $1|p_{j[k]}^A = p_j \max\{(1 + \sum_{i=1}^{k-1} p_{[i]})^a, \beta\}, q_{psd}, CON| \sum_{j=1}^{n}(\alpha U_j + \delta V_j + \eta d)$, *the complexity of the algorithm was* $O(nlogn)$.

Proof. The first step required $O(nlogn)$ time. The second step required $O(n)$ time. The third step was completed in a constant time. Therefore, the complexity of the algorithm was $O(nlogn)$. $\square$

4.2. The Problem $1|p_{j[k]}^A = p_j \max\{(1 + \sum_{i=1}^{k-1} p_{[i]})^a, \beta\}, q_{psd}, SLK| \sum_{j=1}^{n}(\alpha U_j + \delta V_j + \eta q)$

Lemma 8. *For the optimal scheduling, q was equal to* $(1 + r)$ *times the sum of actual processing time for some jobs.*

Proof. Suppose that q was not equal to $(1 + r)$ times the sum of the actual processing time for some jobs, i.e., $(1 + r) \sum_{j=1}^{h-1} p_{[j]}^A < q < (1 + r) \sum_{j=1}^{h} p_{[j]}^A, 1 \leq h \leq n, p_{[0]} = 0$. The objective function was:

$$Z = h\alpha + (n - h)\delta + n\eta q. \tag{23}$$

when $q = (1 + r) \sum_{j=1}^{h-1} p_{[j]}^A$, the objective function was:

$$Z_1 = (h - 1)\alpha + (n - h)\delta + n\eta(1 + r) \sum_{j=1}^{h-1} p_{[j]}^A, \tag{24}$$

$$Z - Z_1 = \alpha + n\eta[q - (1 + r) \sum_{j=1}^{h-1} p_{[j]}^A] > 0. \tag{25}$$

Therefore, q was equal to $(1 + r)$ times the sum of the actual processing time for some jobs. $\square$

Lemma 9. *When $\alpha \geq \delta$, q was equal to 0.*

Proof. When q was equal to $(1 + r) \sum_{j=1}^{h-1} p_{[j]}^A$ for the optimal scheduling, the objective function was:

$$Z = (h - 1)\alpha + (n - h)\delta + n\eta(1 + r) \sum_{j=1}^{h-1} p_{[j]}^A. \tag{26}$$

(1) When $q = (1+r) \sum_{j=1}^{h-2} p_{[j]}^A$, the objective function was

$$Z_1 = (h-2)\alpha + (n-h+1)\delta + n\eta(1+r) \sum_{j=1}^{h-2} p_{[j]}^A. \tag{27}$$

(2) When $q = (1+r) \sum_{j=1}^{h} p_{[j]}^A$, the objective function was

$$Z_2 = h\alpha + (n-h-1)\delta + n\eta(1+r) \sum_{j=1}^{h} p_{[j]}^A. \tag{28}$$

$$Z - Z_1 = \alpha - \delta + n\eta(1+r)p_{[h-1]}^A, \tag{29}$$

$$Z - Z_2 = -\alpha + \delta - n\eta(1+r)p_{[h]}^A. \tag{30}$$

when $\alpha \geq \delta$, $Z_2 > Z > Z_1$. Therefore, q was equal to 0. $\square$

For the convenience of proof, we defined two sets: $G_3 = \{J_j | 1 \leq j \leq h-1\}$, $G_4 = \{J_j | h \leq j \leq n\}$, $q = (1+r) \sum_{j=1}^{h-1} p_{[j]}^A$.

Lemma 10. *In the optimal scheduling, the jobs of set G_3 were arranged in an ascending order of normal processing time.*

Proof. There were two adjacent jobs J_u and J_v in the G_3, and J_u was in front of J_v which was at the $(k+1)$th position, $S_1 = \{J_1, \cdots, J_u, J_v, \cdots, J_n\}$. Suppose that the starting time of J_1 was 0, $q = (1+r) \sum_{j=1}^{h-1} p_{[j]}^A$, $1 \leq k \leq h-2$. The objective function of S_1 was:

$$Z_1 = (h-1)\alpha + (n-h)\delta + n\eta(1+r) \sum_{j=1}^{h-1} p_{[j]}^A(S_1). \tag{31}$$

when J_u and J_v were swapped, the sequence of jobs was $S_2 = \{J_1, \cdots, J_v, J_u, \cdots, J_n\}$. The objective function of S_2 was:

$$Z_2 = (h-1)\alpha + (n-h)\delta + n\eta(1+r) \sum_{j=1}^{h-1} p_{[j]}^A(S_2). \tag{32}$$

$$Z_1 - Z_2 = n\eta(1+r)\left(\sum_{j=1}^{h-1} p_{[j]}^A(S_1) - \sum_{j=1}^{h-1} p_{[j]}^A(S_2) \right). \tag{33}$$

From $p_u \leq p_v$ and Lemma 1, $Z_1 \leq Z_2$, i.e., the jobs of set G_3 were arranged in an ascending order of normal processing time. $\square$

Lemma 11. *In the optimal scheduling, the jobs of set G_4 were arranged in an ascending order of normal processing time.*

Proof. There were two adjacent jobs J_u and J_v in the G_4, and J_u was in front of J_v which was at the $(k+1)$th position, $S_1 = \{J_1, \cdots, J_u, J_v, \cdots, J_n\}$, $h \leq k < n$. The objective function of S_1 was:

$$Z_1 = (h-1)\alpha + (n-h)\delta + n\eta(1+r) \sum_{j=1}^{h-1} p_{[j]}^A(S_1). \tag{34}$$

when J_u and J_v were swapped, the sequence of jobs was $S_2 = \{J_1, \cdots, J_v, J_u, \cdots, J_n\}$. The objective function of S_2 was:

$$Z_2 = (h-1)\alpha + (n-h)\delta + n\eta(1+r)\sum_{j=1}^{h-1} p_{[j]}^A(S_2). \tag{35}$$

$$Z_1 = Z_2. \tag{36}$$

Therefore, the jobs of set G_4 were arranged in any order of normal processing time. $\square$

Lemma 12. *In the optimal scheduling, the processing time of any job in the G_3 was less than the processing time of any job in the G_4.*

Proof. There were two adjacent jobs J_u and J_v, and J_u was at the $(h-1)$th position in the G_3, and J_v was at the hth position in the G_4, $S_1 = \{J_1, \cdots, J_u, J_v, \cdots, J_n\}$. The objective function of S_1 was:

$$Z_1 = (h-1)\alpha + (n-h)\delta + n\eta(1+r)\sum_{j=1}^{h-1} p_{[j]}^A(S_1). \tag{37}$$

when J_u and J_v were swapped, the sequence of jobs was $S_2 = \{J_1, \cdots, J_v, J_u, \cdots, J_n\}$. The objective function of S_2 was:

$$Z_2 = (h-1)\alpha + (n-h)\delta + n\eta(1+r)\sum_{j=1}^{h-1} p_{[j]}^A(S_2). \tag{38}$$

$$Z_1 - Z_2 = n\eta(1+r)(p_u - p_v)\max\{(1 + \sum_{k=1}^{h-2} p_{[k]})^a, \beta\}. \tag{39}$$

If $p_u \leq p_v$, $Z_1 \leq Z_2$, i.e., the processing time of any job in the G_3 was less than the processing time of any job in the G_4. $\square$

The Algorithm 2 was summarized as follows:

Algorithm 2 $1|p_{j[k]}^A = p_j\max\{(1 + \sum_{i=1}^{k-1} p_{[i]})^a, \beta\}, q_{psd}, SLK| \sum_{j=1}^{n}(\alpha U_j + \delta V_j + \eta q)$

Require: $\alpha, \beta, \delta, \eta, a, r, p_j, n$
Ensure: The optimal sequence, q
  1: **First step:** All jobs were sorted by the increasing processing time, i.e., $p_1 \leq \cdots \leq p_n$.
  2: **Second step:** When h was from 0 to n, the objective function values were calculated, respectively.
  3: **Last step:** The optimal position of h was determines by the smallest value of the objective function, and the optimal sequence was arranged in an ascending order of the normal processing time.

Theorem 2. *For the problem* $1|p_{j[k]}^A = p_j\max\{(1 + \sum_{i=1}^{k-1} p_{[i]})^a, \beta\}, q_{psd}, SLK| \sum_{j=1}^{n}(\alpha U_j + \delta V_j + \eta q)$, *the complexity of the algorithm was $O(nlogn)$.*

Proof. The first step required $O(nlogn)$ time. The second step required $O(n)$ time. The third step was completed in a constant time. Therefore, the complexity of the algorithm was $O(nlogn)$. $\square$

4.3. The Problem $1|p_{j[k]}^A = p_j \max\{(1 + \sum\limits_{i=1}^{k-1} p_{[i]})^a, \beta\}, q_{psd}, DIF| \sum\limits_{j=1}^{n} (\alpha U_j + \delta V_j + \eta d_j)$

Lemma 13. *In the optimal scheduling, if $\eta C_j \geq \delta$, the due date d_j of J_j was equal to 0; otherwise, d_j was equal to the completion time of J_j.*

Proof. The objective function was:

$$Z = \sum_{j=1}^{n} Z_j = \sum_{j=1}^{n} (\alpha U_j + \delta V_j + \eta d_j), \tag{40}$$

$$Z_j = \alpha U_j + \delta V_j + \eta d_j. \tag{41}$$

(1) When $C_j > d_j$,

$$Z_j = \delta + \eta d_j. \tag{42}$$

(2) When $C_j = d_j$,

$$Z_j = \eta C_j. \tag{43}$$

(3) When $C_j < d_j$,

$$Z_j = \alpha + \eta d_j > \eta C_j. \tag{44}$$

$$Z_j = \min\{\delta, \eta C_j\}. \tag{45}$$

when $\eta C_j \geq \delta$, d_j was equal to 0; otherwise, d_j was equal to C_j. $\square$

Lemma 14. *In the optimal scheduling, the jobs were sequenced in an increasing order of normal processing time.*

Proof. We considered the job sequence $S_1 = \{J_1, \cdots, J_u, J_v, \cdots, J_n\}$. There were two adjacent jobs J_u and J_v. J_u was at the kth position in the S_1 and J_v was at the $(k+1)$th position in the S_1, $1 \leq k < n$. Z_1 was the objective function of S_1. When J_u and J_v were swapped, the sequence of jobs was $S_2 = \{J_1, \cdots, J_v, J_u, \cdots, J_n\}$. Z_2 was the objective function of S_2.

$$Z_1 - Z_2 = \min\{\delta, \eta C_{[k]}(S_1)\} + \min\{\delta, \eta C_{[k+1]}(S_1)\} - \min\{\delta, \eta C_{[k]}(S_2)\} - \min\{\delta, \eta C_{[k+1]}(S_2)\}. \tag{46}$$

$$C_{[k]}(S_1) = (1+r) \sum_{j=1}^{k-1} p_{[j]}^A + p_u \max\{(1 + \sum_{i=1}^{k-1} p_{[j]})^a, \beta\}, \tag{47}$$

$$C_{[k]}(S_2) = (1+r) \sum_{j=1}^{k-1} p_{[j]}^A + p_v \max\{(1 + \sum_{i=1}^{k-1} p_{[j]})^a, \beta\}, \tag{48}$$

$$C_{[k+1]}(S_1) = (1+r) \sum_{j=1}^{k-1} p_{[j]}^A + (1+r)p_u \max\{(1 + \sum_{i=1}^{k-1} p_{[j]})^a, \beta\} + p_v \max\{(1 + \sum_{i=1}^{k-1} p_{[j]} + p_u)^a, \beta\}, \tag{49}$$

$$C_{[k+1]}(S_2) = (1+r) \sum_{j=1}^{k-1} p_{[j]}^A + (1+r)p_v \max\{(1 + \sum_{i=1}^{k-1} p_{[j]})^a, \beta\} + p_u \max\{(1 + \sum_{i=1}^{k-1} p_{[j]} + p_v)^a, \beta\}. \tag{50}$$

From $p_u \leq p_v$ and Lemma 1, $C_{[k]}(S_1) \leq C_{[k]}(S_2)$, $C_{[k+1]}(S_1) \leq C_{[k+1]}(S_2)$, $Z_1 \leq Z_2$. Therefore, the jobs were sequenced in an increasing order of normal processing time in the optimal scheduling. $\square$

The Algorithm 3 was summarized as follows:

Algorithm 3 $1|p_{j[k]}^{A} = p_j \max\{(1 + \sum\limits_{i=1}^{k-1} p_{[i]})^a, \beta\}, q_{psd}, DIF| \sum\limits_{j=1}^{n} (\alpha U_j + \delta V_j + \eta d_j)$

Require: $\alpha, \beta, \delta, \eta, a, r, p_j, n$
Ensure: The optimal sequence, d_j
  1: **First step:** The optimal sequence was sequenced by an increasing order of normal processing time, i.e., $p_1 \leq \cdots \leq p_n$.
  2: **Last step:** The due date d_j was determined by the relationship between ηC_j and δ.

Theorem 3. *For the problem* $1|p_{j[k]}^{A} = p_j \max\{(1 + \sum\limits_{i=1}^{k-1} p_{[i]})^a, \beta\}, q_{psd}, DIF| \sum\limits_{j=1}^{n} (\alpha U_j + \delta V_j + \eta d_j)$, *the complexity of the algorithm was* $O(nlogn)$.

Proof. The first step required $O(nlogn)$ time. The second step required $O(n)$ time. Therefore, the complexity of the algorithm was $O(nlogn)$. $\square$

5. Discussion of Results

5.1. Numerical Discussion

In this section, we used an example to show the calculation process for three different due dates.

Example 1. *There were five jobs processed sequentially on the same machine. The processing time of each job is shown in the Tables 2–20 below:*
$\alpha = 1, \delta = 2, \eta = 0.2, a = -1, \beta = 0.5, r = 0.1.$

Table 2. Normal processing time.

Job	J_1	J_2	J_3	J_4	J_5
p_j	4	3	5	2	1

Solution 1: $1|p_{j[k]}^{A} = p_j \max\{(1 + \sum\limits_{i=1}^{k-1} p_{[i]})^a, \beta\}, q_{psd}, CON| \sum\limits_{j=1}^{n} (\alpha U_j + \delta V_j + \eta d)$

First step: $p_5 < p_4 < p_2 < p_1 < p_3$. The processing sequence of jobs: $J_5 \to J_4 \to J_2 \to J_1 \to J_3$.

Second step:

(1)   When $h = 0, d = 0, Z = 10$;
(2)   When $h = 1, d = 1, Z = 9$;
(3)   When $h = 2, d = 2.1, Z = 9.1$;
(4)   When $h = 3, d = 3.7, Z = 9.7$;
(5)   When $h = 4, d = 5.85, Z = 10.85$;
(6)   When $h = 5, d = 8.55, Z = 12.55$.

Third step: The optimal due date was 1.

Table 3. Actual processing time.

$p_{[j]}^{A}$	$p_{[1]}^{A}$	$p_{[2]}^{A}$	$p_{[3]}^{A}$	$p_{[4]}^{A}$	$p_{[5]}^{A}$
Value	1	1	1.5	2	2.5

Table 4. Waiting time.

$w_{[j]}$	$w_{[1]}$	$w_{[2]}$	$w_{[3]}$	$w_{[4]}$	$w_{[5]}$
Value	0	1	2	3.5	5.5

Table 5. Delivery time.

$q_{[j]}$	$q_{[1]}$	$q_{[2]}$	$q_{[3]}$	$q_{[4]}$	$q_{[5]}$
Value	0	0.1	0.2	0.35	0.55

Table 6. Completion time.

$C_{[j]}$	$C_{[1]}$	$C_{[2]}$	$C_{[3]}$	$C_{[4]}$	$C_{[5]}$
Value	1	2.1	3.7	5.85	8.55

Solution 2: $1|p_{j[k]}^{A} = p_j \max\{(1 + \sum_{i=1}^{k-1} p_{[i]})^a, \beta\}, q_{psd}, SLK| \sum_{j=1}^{n} (\alpha U_j + \delta V_j + \eta q)$

First step: $p_5 < p_4 < p_2 < p_1 < p_3$. The processing sequence of jobs: $J_5 \rightarrow J_4 \rightarrow J_2 \rightarrow J_1 \rightarrow J_3$.

Second step:

(1)   When $h = 0, q = 0, Z = 8$;
(2)   When $h = 1, q = 1.1, Z = 8.1$;
(3)   When $h = 2, q = 2.2, Z = 8.2$;
(4)   When $h = 3, q = 3.85, Z = 8.85$;
(5)   When $h = 4, q = 6.05, Z = 10.05$,

Third step: The optimal q was 0.

Table 7. Actual processing time.

$p_{[j]}^{A}$	$p_{[1]}^{A}$	$p_{[2]}^{A}$	$p_{[3]}^{A}$	$p_{[4]}^{A}$	$p_{[5]}^{A}$
Value	1	1	1.5	2	2.5

Table 8. Waiting time.

$w_{[j]}$	$w_{[1]}$	$w_{[2]}$	$w_{[3]}$	$w_{[4]}$	$w_{[5]}$
Value	0	1	2	3.5	5.5

Table 9. Delivery time.

$q_{[j]}$	$q_{[1]}$	$q_{[2]}$	$q_{[3]}$	$q_{[4]}$	$q_{[5]}$
Value	0	0.1	0.2	0.35	0.55

Table 10. Completion time.

$C_{[j]}$	$C_{[1]}$	$C_{[2]}$	$C_{[3]}$	$C_{[4]}$	$C_{[5]}$
Value	1	2.1	3.7	5.85	8.55

Table 11. Due date.

$d_{[j]}$	$d_{[1]}$	$d_{[2]}$	$d_{[3]}$	$d_{[4]}$	$d_{[5]}$
Value	1	1	1.5	2	2.5

Table 12. Due date.

$d_{[j]}$	$d_{[1]}$	$d_{[2]}$	$d_{[3]}$	$d_{[4]}$	$d_{[5]}$
Value	2.1	2.1	2.6	3.1	3.6

Table 13. Due date.

$d_{[j]}$	$d_{[1]}$	$d_{[2]}$	$d_{[3]}$	$d_{[4]}$	$d_{[5]}$
Value	3.2	3.2	3.7	4.2	4.7

Table 14. Due date.

$d_{[j]}$	$d_{[1]}$	$d_{[2]}$	$d_{[3]}$	$d_{[4]}$	$d_{[5]}$
Value	4.85	4.85	5.35	5.85	6.35

Table 15. Due date.

$d_{[j]}$	$d_{[1]}$	$d_{[2]}$	$d_{[3]}$	$d_{[4]}$	$d_{[5]}$
Value	7.05	7.05	7.55	8.05	8.55

Solution 3: $1|p_{j[k]}^{A} = p_j \max\{(1 + \sum_{i=1}^{k-1} p_{[i]})^a, \beta\}, q_{psd}, DIF| \sum_{j=1}^{n} (\alpha U_j + \delta V_j + \eta d_j)$

First step: $p_5 < p_4 < p_2 < p_1 < p_3$. The processing sequence of jobs: $J_5 \to J_4 \to J_2 \to J_1 \to J_3$.

Second step: $Z = 2.12$.

Table 16. Due date.

$d_{[j]}$	$d_{[1]}$	$d_{[2]}$	$d_{[3]}$	$d_{[4]}$	$d_{[5]}$
Value	1	2.1	3.7	5.85	8.55

5.2. Extension

In the learning effect scheduling model, the learning index a was less than 0. If $a > 0$, it became the forgetting effect scheduling model.

$$1|p_{j[k]}^{A} = p_j(1 + \sum_{i=1}^{k-1} p_{[i]})^a, q_{psd}, CON(SLK, DIF)| \sum_{j=1}^{n} (\alpha U_j + \delta V_j + \eta d), \tag{51}$$

where $a > 0$. The same method could prove the following conclusions. When $0 < a \leq 1$, the optimal sequence was obtained by the longest processing time order. When $a > 1$, the optimal sequence was obtained by the shortest processing time order. Take Example 1 above as an example to show the algorithmic process of the forgetting effect scheduling model (CON).

Solution 4: $1|p_{j[k]}^{A} = p_j(1 + \sum_{i=1}^{k-1} p_{[i]})^a, q_{psd}, CON| \sum_{j=1}^{n} (\alpha U_j + \delta V_j + \eta d)$, where $a = 0.5$.

First step: $p_3 > p_1 > p_2 > p_4 > p_5$. The processing sequence of jobs: $J_3 \to J_1 \to J_2 \to J_4 \to J_5$.

Second step:

(1) When $h = 0, d = 0, Z = 10$;
(2) When $h = 1, d = 5, Z = 13$;
(3) When $h = 2, d = 15.3, Z = 22.3$;
(4) When $h = 3, d = 25.76, Z = 31.76$;
(5) When $h = 4, d = 33.929, Z = 38.929$;
(6) When $h = 5, d = 38.52, Z = 42.52$.

Third step: The optimal due date was 0.

Table 17. Actual processing time.

$p^A_{[j]}$	$p^A_{[1]}$	$p^A_{[2]}$	$p^A_{[3]}$	$p^A_{[4]}$	$p^A_{[5]}$
Value	5	9.8	9.49	7.21	3.87

Table 18. Waiting time.

$w_{[j]}$	$w_{[1]}$	$w_{[2]}$	$w_{[3]}$	$w_{[4]}$	$w_{[5]}$
Value	0	5	14.8	24.29	31.5

Table 19. Delivery time.

$q_{[j]}$	$q_{[1]}$	$q_{[2]}$	$q_{[3]}$	$q_{[4]}$	$q_{[5]}$
Value	0	0.5	1.48	2.429	3.15

Table 20. Completion time.

$C_{[j]}$	$C_{[1]}$	$C_{[2]}$	$C_{[3]}$	$C_{[4]}$	$C_{[5]}$
Value	5	15.3	25.76	33.929	38.52

6. Conclusions

Under the common due date, slack due date and different due date, a single-machine scheduling problem with delivery times and the truncated sum-of-processing-times-based learning effect was studied in this paper. The goal was to minimize the total costs that comprised the number of early jobs, the number of tardy jobs and the due date. Under different due dates, three polynomial time algorithms were proposed to obtain the optimal sequence and due dates, whose complexity was $O(nlogn)$. The optimal sequence was arranged in an ascending order of processing time. We gave three examples to show the calculation process of the algorithms. In the future, the multi-machine environment could be considered to expand the research, i.e., a flow-shop scheduling problem with a delivery time, truncated sum-of-processing-times-based learning effect and due dates could be considered whether there were polynomial time algorithms. The truncated sum-of-processing-times-based forgetting effect was also studied in the single-machine scheduling environment.

Author Contributions: The work presented here was performed in collaboration among all authors. J.Q. designed, analyzed and wrote the paper. Y.Z. analyzed and reviewed the paper. All authors have read and agreed to the published version of the manuscript.

Funding: This study was supported by the Natural Science Foundation of Liaoning Province Project (grant no. 2021-MS-102) and the Fundamental Research Funds for the Central Universities (grant no. N2105021 and N2105020).

Data Availability Statement: Not applicable.

Acknowledgments: We thank the anonymous reviewers for their comments and insights that significantly improved our paper.

Conflicts of Interest: The authors declare no conflict of interest.

References

1. Cheng, T.C.E.; Cheng, S.R.; Wu, W.H.; Hsu, P.H.; Wu, C.C. A two-agent single-machine scheduling problem with truncated sum-of-processing-times-based learning considerations. *Comput. Ind. Eng.* **2011**, *60*, 534–541. [CrossRef]
2. Li, L.; Yang, S.W.; Wu, Y.B.; Huo, Y.Z.; Ji, P. Single machine scheduling jobs with a truncated sum-of-processing-times-based learning effect. *Int. J. Adv. Manuf. Technol.* **2013**, *67*, 261–267. [CrossRef]

3. Cheng, T.C.E.; Wu, C.C.; Chen, J.C.; Wu, W.H.; Cheng, S.R. Two-machine flowshop scheduling with a truncated learning function to minimize the makespan. *Int. J. Prod. Econ.* **2013**, *141*, 79–86. [CrossRef]
4. Wu, Y.B.; Wang, J.J. Single-machine scheduling with truncated sum-of-processing-times-based learning effect including proportional delivery times. *Neural Comput. Appl.* **2016**, *27*, 937–943. [CrossRef]
5. Wang, J.B.; Liu, M.; Yin, N. Scheduling jobs with controllable processing time, truncated job-dependent learning and deterioration effects. *J. Ind. Manag. Optim.* **2017**, *13*, 1025. [CrossRef]
6. Wu, C.C.; Wang, D.J.; Cheng, S.R.; Chung, I.H.; Lin, W.C. A two-stage three-machine assembly scheduling problem with a position-based learning effect. *Int. J. Prod. Res.* **2018**, *56*, 3064–3079. [CrossRef]
7. Yin, N. Single machine due window assignment resource allocation scheduling with job-dependent learning effect. *J. Appl. Math. Comput.* **2018**, *56*, 715–725. [CrossRef]
8. Zhang, X. Single machine and flowshop scheduling problems with sum-of-processing time based learning phenomenon. *J. Ind. Manag. Optim.* **2020**, *16*, 231. [CrossRef]
9. Qian, J.; Lin, H.; Kong, Y.; Wang, Y. Tri-criteria single machine scheduling model with release times and learning factor. *Appl. Math. Comput.* **2020**, *387*, 124543. [CrossRef]
10. Zou, Y.; Wang, D.; Lin, W.C.; Chen, J.Y.; Yu, P.W.; Wu, W.H.; Chao, Y.P.; Wu, C.C. Two-stage three-machine assembly scheduling problem with sum-of-processing-times-based learning effect. *Soft Comput.* **2020**, *24*, 5445–5462. [CrossRef]
11. Wu, C.C.; Zhang, X.; Azzouz, A.; Shen, W.L.; Cheng, S.R.; Hsu, P.H.; Lin, W.C. Metaheuristics for two-stage flow-shop assembly problem with a truncation learning function. *Eng. Optim.* **2021**, *53*, 843–866. [CrossRef]
12. Yang, S.J.; Hsu, C.J.; Chang, T.R.; Yang, D.L. Single-machine scheduling with past-sequence-dependent delivery times and learning effect. *J. Chin. Inst. Ind. Eng.* **2011**, *28*, 247–255. [CrossRef]
13. Yang, S.J.; Yang, D.L. Single-machine scheduling problems with past-sequence-dependent delivery times and position-dependent processing times. *J. Oper. Res. Soc.* **2012**, *63*, 1508–1515. [CrossRef]
14. Liu, M.; Wang, S.; Chu, C. Scheduling deteriorating jobs with past-sequence-dependent delivery times. *Int. J. Prod. Econ.* **2013**, *144*, 418–421. [CrossRef]
15. Zhao, C.; Tang, H. Single machine scheduling problems with general position-dependent processing times and past-sequence-dependent delivery times. *J. Appl. Math. Comput.* **2014**, *45*, 259–274. [CrossRef]
16. Qian, J.; Han, H. The due date assignment scheduling problem with the deteriorating jobs and delivery time. *J. Appl. Math. Comput.* **2021**, 1–14. in press. [CrossRef]
17. Yin, Y.; Liu, M.; Cheng, T.C.E.; Wu, C.C.; Cheng, S.R. Four single-machine scheduling problems involving due date determination decisions. *Inf. Sci.* **2013**, *251*, 164–181. [CrossRef]
18. Lu, Y.Y.; Li, G.; Wang, Y.B.; Ji, P. Optimal due-date assignment problem with learning effect and resource-dependent processing times. *Optim. Lett.* **2014**, *8*, 113–127. [CrossRef]
19. Li, G.; Luo, M.L.; Zhang, W.J.; Wang, X.Y. Single-machine due-window assignment scheduling based on common flow allowance, learning effect and resource allocation. *Int. J. Prod. Res.* **2015**, *53*, 1228–1241. [CrossRef]
20. Sun, L.H.; Cui, K.; Chen, J.H.; Wang, J. Due date assignment and convex resource allocation scheduling with variable job processing times. *Int. J. Prod. Res.* **2016**, *54*, 3551–3560. [CrossRef]
21. Geng, X.N.; Wang, J.B.; Bai, D. Common due date assignment scheduling for a no-wait flowshop with convex resource allocation and learning effect. *Eng. Optim.* **2019**, *51*, 1301–1323. [CrossRef]
22. Liu, W.; Jiang, C. Due-date assignment scheduling involving job-dependent learning effects and convex resource allocation. *Eng. Optim.* **2020**, *52*, 74–89. [CrossRef]
23. Tian, Y. Single–Machine Due-Window Assignment Scheduling with Resource Allocation and Generalized Earliness/Tardiness Penalties. *Asia-Pac. J. Oper. Res.* **2021**, in press. [CrossRef]
24. Wang, W. Single-machine due-date assignment scheduling with generalized earliness-tardiness penalties including proportional setup times. *J. Appl. Math. Comput.* **2021**, in press. [CrossRef]
25. Lann, A.; Mosheiov, G. Single machine scheduling to minimize the number of early and tardy jobs. *Comput. Oper. Res.* **1996**, *23*, 769–781. [CrossRef]
26. Yuan, J. Unary NP-hardness of minimizing the number of tardy jobs with deadlines. *J. Sched.* **2017**, *20*, 211–218. [CrossRef]
27. Hermelin, D.; Karhi, S.; Pinedo, M.; Shabtay, D. New algorithms for minimizing the weighted number of tardy jobs on a single machine. *Ann. Oper. Res.* **2021**, *298*, 271–287. [CrossRef]
28. Graham, R.L.; Lawler, E.L.; Lenstra, J.K.; Kan, A.H.G.R. Optimization and approximation in deterministic sequencing and scheduling: A survey. *Ann. Discret. Math.* **1979**, *5*, 287–326.

 *mathematics*

Article

Similitude for the Dynamic Characteristics of Dual-Rotor System with Bolted Joints

Lei Li [1,2], Zhong Luo [1,2,3,*], Fengxia He [1,2], Zhaoye Qin [4], Yuqi Li [5] and Xiaolu Yan [1,2]

[1] School of Mechanical Engineering and Automation, Northeastern University, Shenyang 110819, China; 1810098@stu.neu.edu.cn (L.L.); 1810099@stu.neu.edu.cn (F.H.); 1970217@stu.neu.edu.cn (X.Y.)

[2] Key Laboratory of Vibration and Control of Aero-Propulsion Systems Ministry of Education of China, School of Mechanical Engineering and Automation, Northeastern University, Shenyang 110819, China

[3] Foshan Graduate School, Northeastern University, Foshan 528312, China

[4] State Key Laboratory of Tribology, Department of Mechanical Engineering, Tsinghua University, Beijing 100086, China; qinzy@tsinghua.edu.cn

[5] School of Mechanical and Automotive Engineering, Guangxi University of Science and Technology, Liuzhou 545006, China; 100002437@gxust.edu.cn

* Correspondence: zhluo@mail.neu.edu.cn

Abstract: The dual-rotor system has been widely used in aero-engines and has the characteristics of large axial size, the interaction between the high-pressure rotor and low-pressure rotor, and stiffness nonlinearity of bolted joints. However, the testing of a full-scale dual-rotor system is expensive and time-consuming. In this paper, the scaling relationships for the dual-rotor system with bolted joints are proposed for predicting the responses of full-scale structure, which are developed by generalized and fundamental equations of substructures (shaft, disk, and bolted joints). Different materials between prototype and model are considered in the derived scaling relationships. Moreover, the effects of bolted joints on the dual-rotor system are analyzed to demonstrate the necessity for considering bolted joints in the similitude procedure. Furthermore, the dynamic characteristics for different working conditions (low-pressure rotor excitation, high-pressure rotor excitation, two frequency excitations, and counter-rotation) are predicted by the scaled model made of a relatively cheap material. The results show that the critical speeds, vibration responses, and frequency components can be predicted with good accuracy, even though the scaled model is made of different materials.

Keywords: similitude; scaling relationships; dual-rotor system; bolted joint; dynamic characteristics

Citation: Li, L.; Luo, Z.; He, F.; Qin, Z.; Li, Y.; Yan, X. Similitude for the Dynamic Characteristics of Dual-Rotor System with Bolted Joints. *Mathematics* **2022**, *10*, 3. https://doi.org/10.3390/math10010003

Academic Editors: Xiang Li, Shuo Zhang and Wei Zhang

Received: 16 November 2021
Accepted: 17 December 2021
Published: 21 December 2021

Publisher's Note: MDPI stays neutral with regard to jurisdictional claims in published maps and institutional affiliations.

1. Introduction

Dual-rotor systems are widely used in large rotating machines, such as aero-engines [1,2] and gas turbines [3,4]. The dual-rotor system of an aero-engine is composed of several components with different materials to reduce its weight. These components are usually connected by bolted joints, which change the local stiffness and affect the dynamics of the rotor system [5,6]. However, prototype testing is usually expensive and time-consuming. Thus, similitude design can be used to overcome this issue and reduce costs and difficulties.

Many scholars have studied the application of beams, plates, and cylindrical shells. For beams, Asl et al. studied the scaling laws for fundamental frequency [7] and transverse deflection [8] of I-beams. Kasivitamnuay and Singhatanadgid [9] predicted the displacement of a static-loaded beam by using the scaled model. Subsequently, they [10] investigated the similitude problem related to the static displacement of a cracked beam. As for the similitude of plates, Coutinho et al. [11] developed the scaling laws for beam-plates and predicted the transverse displacement of full-size structures. Yazdi studied the scaling laws for free vibration [12] and flutter speed [13] of plates. Frostig and Simitses [14] investigated the similitude of sandwich panels and predicted the wrinkling and global buckling through scaled models. Singhatanadgid and Songkhla [15] derived the scaling laws for natural frequencies of rectangular plates with various boundary conditions, then the effectiveness is demonstrated by experimental test. Franco et al. predicted the vibration velocity [16] of a flexural plate with a high modal overlap factor, and then the vibration responses under a turbulent boundary layer excitation [17] were put into similitude. Mazzariol and Alves [18] established the scaling laws of plates under impact load. In addition, Petrone et al. [19] conducted a similitude investigation of stiffened cylinders, and the natural frequency and forced response were considered in the prediction procedure. Rezaeepazhand et al. designed the scaled models for predicting the free vibration [20] and buckling under compressive loads [21] of cylinders. Ungbhakorn and Wattanasakulpong [22] proposed a similitude procedure for buckling and free vibration of cylindrical shells. Aiming at coupled structures, De Rosa and Franco predicted the vibration responses of assemblies of plates [23], coupling beams and plates [24], and long and short wavelength coupling structures [25]. You et al. [26] presented a scaling procedure for wing boxes and put the deflection and modal behavior into similitude. Song et al. [27] investigated the similitude of machine tools, and then the modal shape was predicted by the scaled model. However, the similitude studies of rotor systems are relatively rare. The complete scaling laws for dynamic characteristics of rotor systems were presented by Wu [28]. Li et al. [29] developed the scaling laws for critical speeds of rotor systems. Furthermore, similitude studies of dual-rotor systems considering the nonlinearity of bolted joints are not found.

During the past decades, many studies have been conducted on similitude methods. Dimensional analysis (DA) and Similitude Theory Applied to Governing Equations (STAGE) are widely used [27]. DA is simple to use and useful for those systems without a set of governing equations, such as complex or new systems [30]. The drawbacks of DA are that (1) great effort and experience are required for obtaining scaling laws and (2) this method is not suitable for partial similitude since the geometric parameters can not be scaled in different scales. STAGE obtains scaling laws directly through the governing equations or its analytical solutions and has been adopted by many scholars. For instance, Rezaeepazhand et al. investigated the similitude of laminated plates [31] and composite beam-plates [32] based on STAGE. Singhatanadgid et al. [15] developed the scaling laws for plates through the governing equations. However, STAGE needs the governing equation and a lot of work of derivation. Then energy method (EM) was presented by Ungbhakorn and Singhatanadgid [33], which considered the scaling laws of boundary conditions, but the work of derivation was also required. De Rosa et al. [34] proposed a similitude method named SAMSARA, which was applied to the similitude issue of acoustic structures, such as flexural plates [35]. In recent years, sensitivity analysis (SA) [36] was used to obtain scaling laws. However, the scaling laws established by SA lack physical meaning and may ignore important phenomena [30].

Although many meaningful works on similitude have been completed, the following issues still exist: (i) most similitude studies focused on the linear systems or simple structures, but similitude studies of dual-rotor systems considering the nonlinearity of bolted joints are not found; (ii) STAGE and EM need the governing equation and a lot of work of derivation. In addition, SA lacks physical meaning and may overlook important phenomena.

In the paper, the dynamic model of a dual-rotor system with bolted joints is developed and the effects of bolted joints on the dual-rotor system are investigated in Section 2. The scaling laws considering different materials are derived by the generalized and fundamental equations of shaft, disk, and bolted joints in Section 3. In Section 4, aiming at the working conditions and structural characteristics of dual-rotor systems, the similitude for dynamic characteristics in the cases of low-pressure (LP) rotor excitation, high-pressure (HP) rotor excitation, two frequency excitations, and counter-rotation are discussed. The conclusions are listed in Section 5.

2. Dynamic Model of the Dual-Rotor System with Bolted Joints

As shown in Figure 1, a dual-rotor system consisting of a high-pressure (HP) rotor, a low-pressure (LP) rotor, bolted joint structures and elastic supports is developed. The dual-rotor system includes five supports and is modeled by the finite element method. Support 5 denotes the intershaft bearing, which couples the vibration responses of the HP rotor and LP rotor. The parameters of the dual-rotor system are listed in Appendix A. There are two bolted joints in the model, which are used to connect the LP rotor and the HP rotor, respectively.

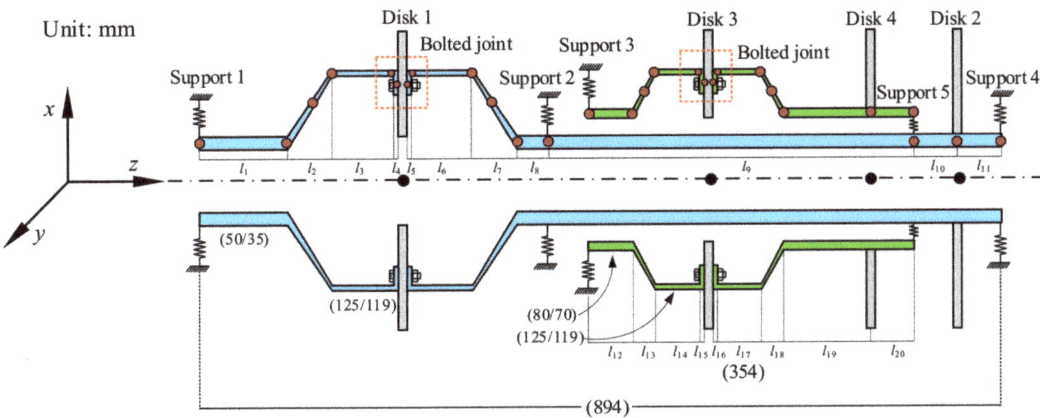

Note: taking (50/35) as an example, 50 and 35 represent the outer and inner radii, respectively.

Figure 1. Finite element model of a dual-rotor system with bolted joints.

2.1. Dual-Rotor System Model

The dual-rotor system is modeled by Timoshenko beam elements. The finite element model includes 24 beam elements. The disks and bearings are simplified as lumped mass elements and spring-damping elements, respectively. The bolted joint is a noncontinuous structure; thus, the beam elements near the bolted joint structures are connected by the joint elements.

The generalized displacement vectors of the LP rotor can be expressed as follows:

$$u_L = \left[x_1, y_1, \theta_{x1}, \theta_{y1}, \cdots, x_{15}, y_{15}, \theta_{x15}, \theta_{y15} \right]^T \tag{1}$$

where $x_1, y_1, \cdots, x_{15}, y_{15}$ are translations of nodes $1-15$, and $\theta_{x1}, \theta_{y1}, \cdots, \theta_{x15}, \theta_{y15}$ are rotations of nodes $1-15$.

The LP rotor can be described in matrix form as follows:

$$M_L \ddot{u}_L + (C_L - \Omega_L G_L)\dot{u}_L + K_L u_L = Q_L \tag{2}$$

where Ω is the rotating speed. M, C, G, and K are the mass, damping, gyroscopic, and stiffness matrices. The subscript L represents the index of the LP rotor. Rayleigh damping is applied, and the damping matrix is given as $C_L = \alpha M_L + \beta K_L$.

The generalized force vectors of the LP rotor can be described as

$$Q_L = \begin{bmatrix} 0, 0, 0, 0, \cdots, m_1 e_1 \Omega_L^2 \cos(\Omega_L t), m_1 e_1 \Omega_L^2 \sin(\Omega_L t), 0, 0, \cdots, \\ m_2 e_2 \Omega_L^2 \cos(\Omega_L t), m_2 e_2 \Omega_L^2 \sin(\Omega_L t), 0, 0, \cdots, 0, 0, 0, 0 \end{bmatrix}^T \tag{3}$$

where m and e denote the mass and eccentricity, and the subscript represents the number of disks.

The generalized displacement vectors of the HP rotor are described as follows:

$$u_{\mathrm{H}} = \left[x_{16}, y_{16}, \theta_{x16}, \theta_{y16}, \cdots, x_{28}, y_{28}, \theta_{x28}, \theta_{y28} \right]^{\mathrm{T}} \tag{4}$$

Accordingly, the motion equation of the HP rotor can be obtained:

$$M_{\mathrm{H}} \ddot{u}_{\mathrm{H}} + (C_{\mathrm{H}} - \Omega_{\mathrm{H}} G_{\mathrm{H}}) \dot{u}_{\mathrm{H}} + K_{\mathrm{H}} u_{\mathrm{H}} = Q_{\mathrm{H}} \tag{5}$$

where the subscript H denotes the index of the HP rotor.

The force of the HP rotor is expressed as follows:

$$Q_{\mathrm{H}} = \left[\begin{array}{l} 0,0,0,0,\cdots, m_3 e_3 \Omega_{\mathrm{H}}^2 \cos(\Omega_{\mathrm{H}} t), m_3 e_3 \Omega_{\mathrm{H}}^2 \sin(\Omega_{\mathrm{H}} t), 0, 0, \cdots, \\ m_4 e_4 \Omega_{\mathrm{H}}^2 \cos(\Omega_{\mathrm{H}} t), m_4 e_4 \Omega_{\mathrm{H}}^2 \sin(\Omega_{\mathrm{H}} t), 0, 0, \cdots, 0, 0, 0, 0 \end{array} \right]^{\mathrm{T}} \tag{6}$$

Consider the eccentricity of all disks, and the eccentricity is 0.5 mm. Then, the motion equation of the dual-rotor system is further written as follows:

$$\begin{bmatrix} M_{\mathrm{L}} & \\ & M_{\mathrm{H}} \end{bmatrix} \begin{bmatrix} \ddot{u}_{\mathrm{L}} \\ \ddot{u}_{\mathrm{H}} \end{bmatrix} + \begin{bmatrix} C_{\mathrm{L}} - \Omega_{\mathrm{L}} G_{\mathrm{L}} & \\ & C_{\mathrm{H}} - \Omega_{\mathrm{H}} G_{\mathrm{H}} \end{bmatrix} \begin{bmatrix} \dot{u}_{\mathrm{L}} \\ \dot{u}_{\mathrm{H}} \end{bmatrix} + \begin{bmatrix} K_{\mathrm{L}} & \\ & K_{\mathrm{H}} \end{bmatrix} \begin{bmatrix} u_{\mathrm{L}} \\ u_{\mathrm{H}} \end{bmatrix} = \begin{bmatrix} Q_{\mathrm{L}} \\ Q_{\mathrm{H}} \end{bmatrix} \tag{7}$$

Next, the stiffness of supports needs to be added to the stiffness matric of dual-rotor system, where the positions are $K(1,1)$, $K(2,2)$, $K(45,45)$, $K(46,46)$, $K(57,57)$, $K(58,58)$, $K(61,61)$, and $K(62,62)$. Damping is added in the same way. The stiffness of the intershaft bearing is added as follows:

$$K_{\mathrm{in}} = \begin{array}{c} \begin{array}{cccc} 4k-3 & 4k-2 & 4l-3 & 4l-2 \end{array} \\ \begin{bmatrix} k_{\mathrm{in},xx} & k_{\mathrm{in},xy} & -k_{\mathrm{in},xx} & -k_{\mathrm{in},xy} \\ k_{\mathrm{in},yx} & k_{\mathrm{in},yy} & -k_{\mathrm{in},yx} & -k_{\mathrm{in},yy} \\ -k_{\mathrm{in},xx} & -k_{\mathrm{in},xy} & k_{\mathrm{in},xx} & k_{\mathrm{in},xy} \\ -k_{\mathrm{in},yx} & -k_{\mathrm{in},yy} & k_{\mathrm{in},yx} & k_{\mathrm{in},yy} \end{bmatrix} \begin{array}{c} 4k-3 \\ 4k-2 \\ 4l-3 \\ 4l-2 \end{array} \end{array} \tag{8}$$

where $k = 13$ and $l = 28$.

2.2. Bolted Joint Model

The bolted joint is considered as a joint element with two nodes. One of the nodes is located at the end of the flange near the disk, and the other node is located at the position of the disk, as shown in Figure 2. The generalized displacement vectors and stiffness matrix are expressed as follows:

$$q_{\mathrm{J}} = \left[x_{\mathrm{J}}, y_{\mathrm{J}}, \theta_{x\mathrm{J}}, \theta_{y\mathrm{J}}, x_{\mathrm{J}+1}, y_{\mathrm{J}+1}, \theta_{x(\mathrm{J}+1)}, \theta_{y(\mathrm{J}+1)} \right]^{\mathrm{T}} \tag{9}$$

$$K_{\mathrm{J}} = \begin{bmatrix} k & & & & & & & \\ 0 & k & & & & \text{sym} & & \\ 0 & 0 & k_{\theta} & & & & & \\ 0 & 0 & 0 & k_{\theta} & & & & \\ -k & 0 & 0 & 0 & k & & & \\ 0 & -k & 0 & 0 & 0 & k & & \\ 0 & 0 & -k_{\theta} & 0 & 0 & 0 & k_{\theta} & \\ 0 & 0 & 0 & -k_{\theta} & 0 & 0 & 0 & k_{\theta} \end{bmatrix} \tag{10}$$

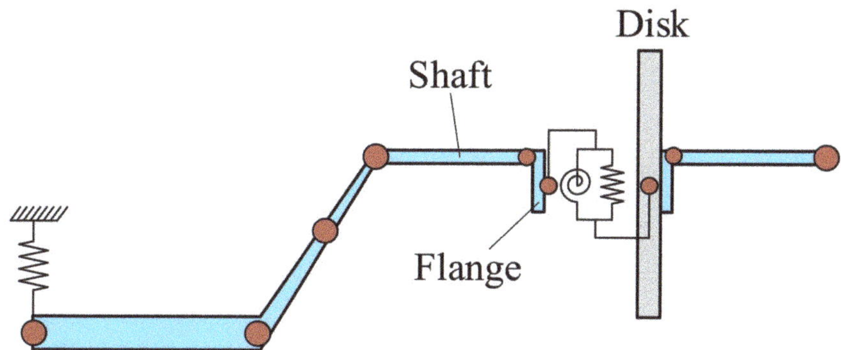

Figure 2. Schematic diagram of the bolted joint model.

In terms of [6,37,38], the stiffness of the bolted joint has piecewise linear characteristics, and the critical point occurs when the external force is equal to the effect of preload applied on the bolts. The first and second stages of piecewise linear characteristics are depicted in Figure 3a,b, respectively.

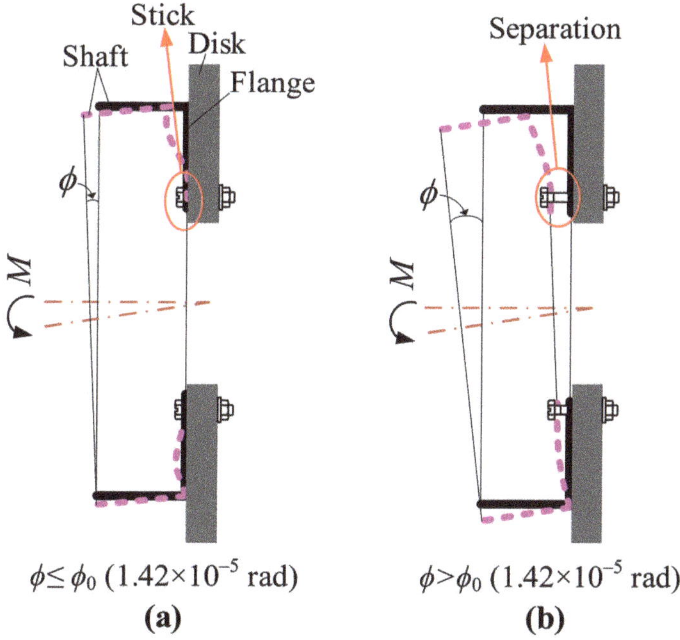

Figure 3. Schematic diagram for the deformation of the bolted joint under a bending moment: (**a**) stick state; (**b**) separation state.

The stiffness characteristics of bolted joint in [37] are expressed as

$$k_\theta = \begin{cases} k_{\theta 1}, & |\phi| \leq \phi_0 \\ k_{\theta 2}, & |\phi| > \phi_0 \end{cases} \tag{11}$$

where ϕ is the relative rotation angle between the flange and disk and is shown in Figure 3. ϕ_0 is the critical rotation angle when the external force is equal to the effect of preload applied on the bolts. $k_{\theta 1}$ and $k_{\theta 2}$ are the stiffness at the first and second stages, respectively. ϕ can be obtained as follows:

$$\phi = \sqrt{\left(\theta_{xJ} - \theta_{x(J+1)}\right)^2 + \left(\theta_{yJ} - \theta_{y(J+1)}\right)^2} \tag{12}$$

where the subscripts J and J + 1 represent the left and right nodes of the joint element, respectively. The stiffness and critical rotation angle can be calculated according to [37] and are listed in Table 1. More detailed formulas can be found in [37].

Table 1. Stiffness and critical rotation angle of bolted joints.

Parameter	Value
$k_{\theta 1}$ (N·m/rad)	3.16×10^7
$k_{\theta 2}$ (N·m/rad)	2.70×10^6
ϕ_0 (rad)	1.42×10^{-5}

2.3. Convergence Analysis

In this section, the influence of node number on the vibration responses is assessed. The element number is chosen as 24, 36, and 48. The amplitude frequency responses for 24, 36, and 48 elements are shown in Figure 4, and the spectrum cascades under different rotating speeds are illustrated in Figure 5. It is found that the amplitude frequency responses and spectrum cascades for the cases of 24, 36, and 48 elements are almost identical. The vibration responses have already converged. Therefore, the case of 24 elements is used in the following analysis.

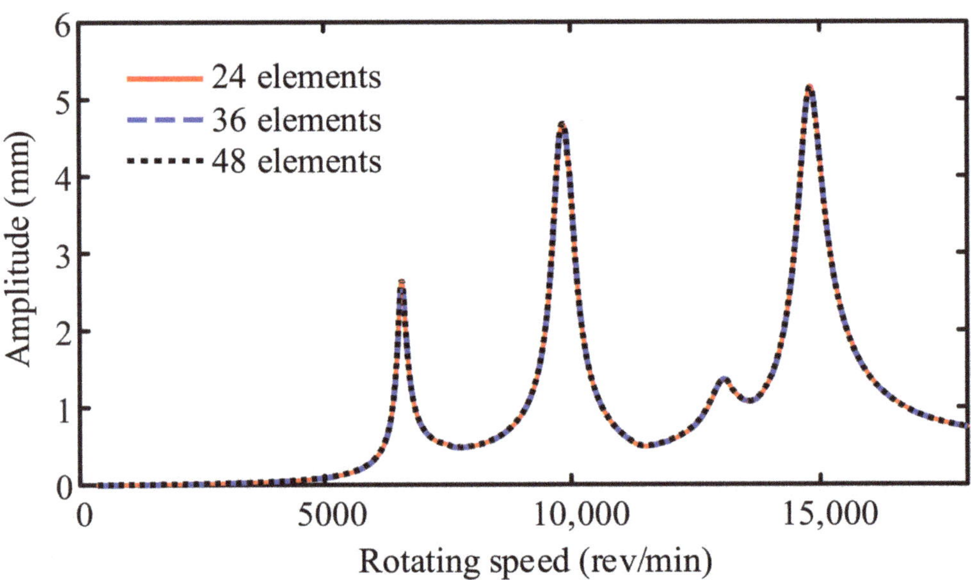

Figure 4. Amplitude frequency responses for 24, 36, and 48 elements.

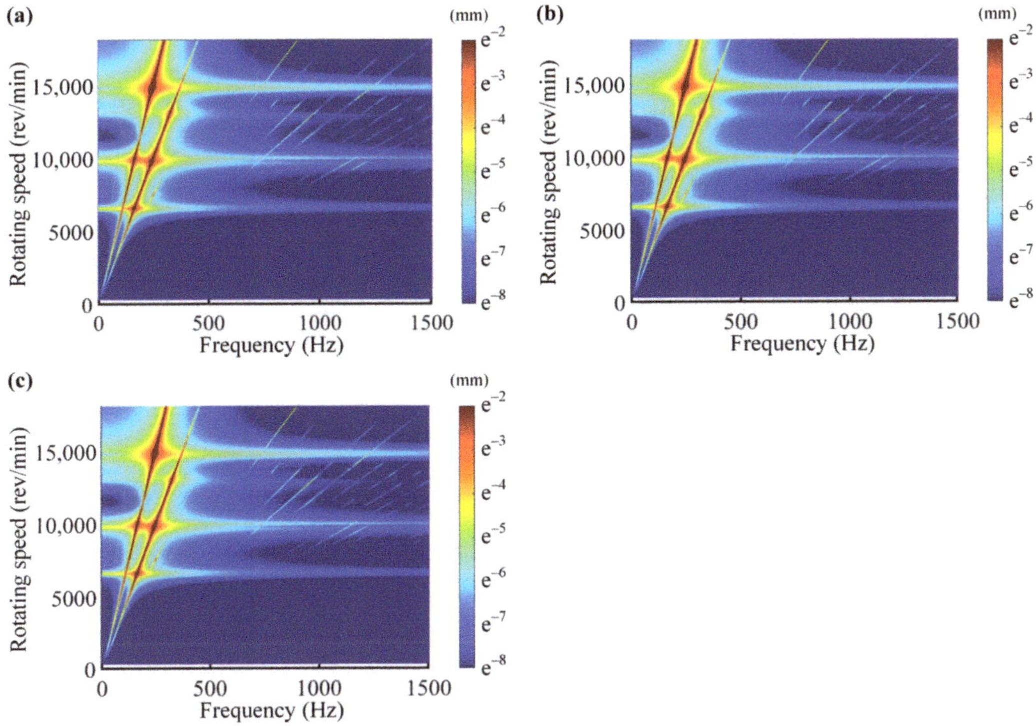

Figure 5. Spectrum cascades: (**a**) 24 elements; (**b**) 36 elements; (**c**) 48 elements.

2.4. Comparison of the Dual-Rotor System with and without Bolted Joints

The bolted joint changes the local stiffness of the rotor system subjected to a heavy load, which further influences the vibration behaviors of the rotor system [5,6]. Thus, the section aims at investigating the effect of bolted joints and further verifying the bolted joint model.

The dual-rotor system models with and without bolted joints are established to compare the vibration characteristics of these two models. The configurations of the models with and without bolted joints are the same except for the parameters of the bolted joints. Note that the positions of bolted joints are continuous structures in the model without bolted joints. The dynamic equations of these two models are obtained by the Newmark method. The ratio of rotational speed ($R = \Omega_H/\Omega_L$) is 1.5 [39] in this paper. The amplitude frequency responses of disk 1 of the two models are presented in Figure 6. The time responses at resonance of these two models are shown in Figure 7. It can be seen that the critical speeds of the model with bolted joints are less than those of the model without bolted joints. Thus, the bolted joints reduce the critical speed of the rotor system since they change the local stiffness, which is consistent with the laws in [37]. In addition, the spectrum cascades under different rotating speeds of these two models are shown in Figure 8. Only the fundamental frequencies of LP and HP rotors are prominent in the spectrum cascades of the model without bolted joints (see Figure 8b). As a contrast, for the model with bolted joints, the frequency multiplication of LP and HP rotors ($2f_L$, $3f_L$, $4f_L$, $2f_H$, $3f_H$, and $4f_H$) has occurred, which is consistent with the results of [40]. Thus, the bolted joint model is considered verified, and the bolted joints must be considered in developing scaling relationships due to the significant influence on the rotor system.

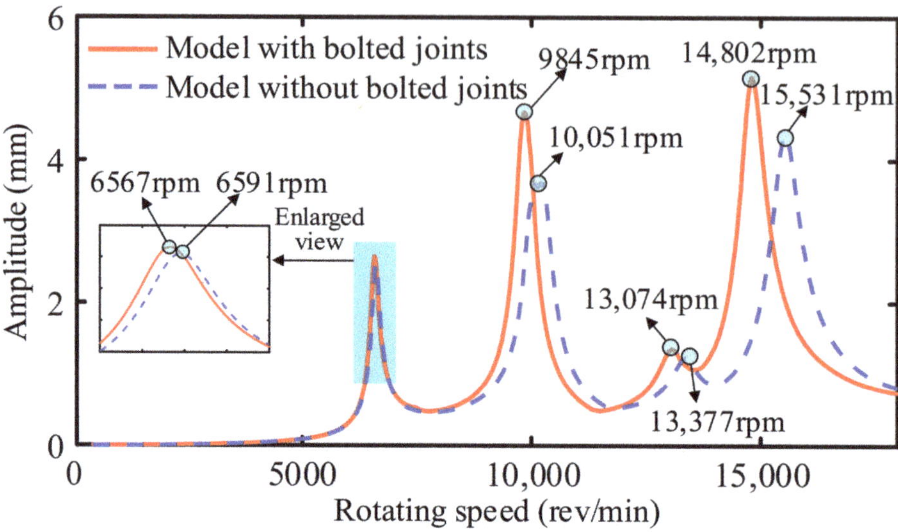

Figure 6. Comparison of the amplitude frequency responses between the models with and without bolted joints.

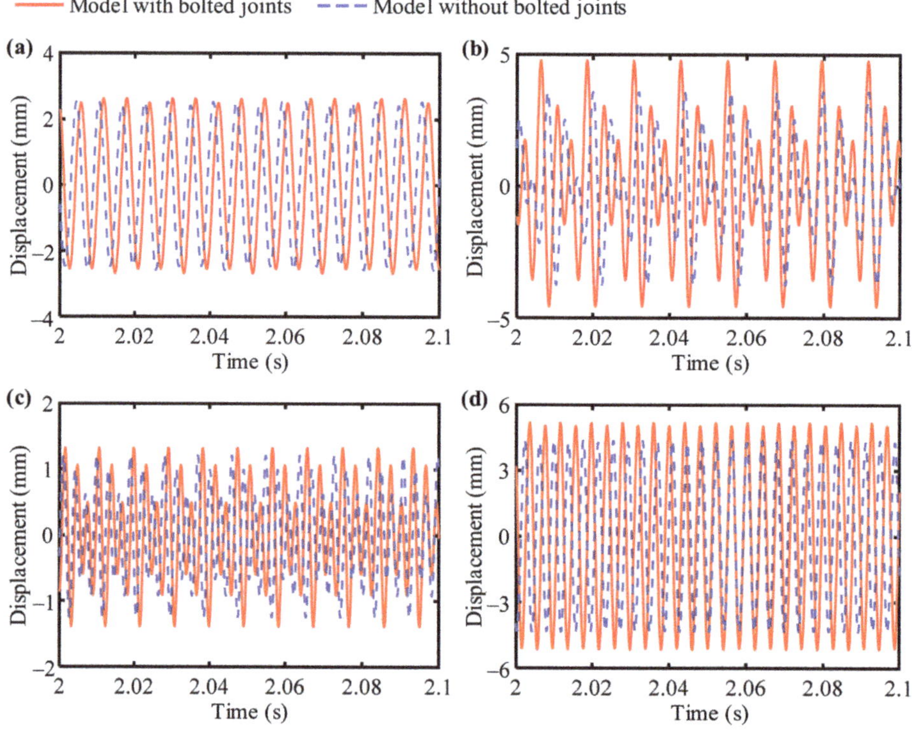

Figure 7. Time responses between the models with and without bolted joints: (**a**) 6567 and 6591 rpm; (**b**) 9845 and 10,051 rpm; (**c**) 13,074 and 13,377 rpm; (**d**) 14,802 and 15,531 rpm.

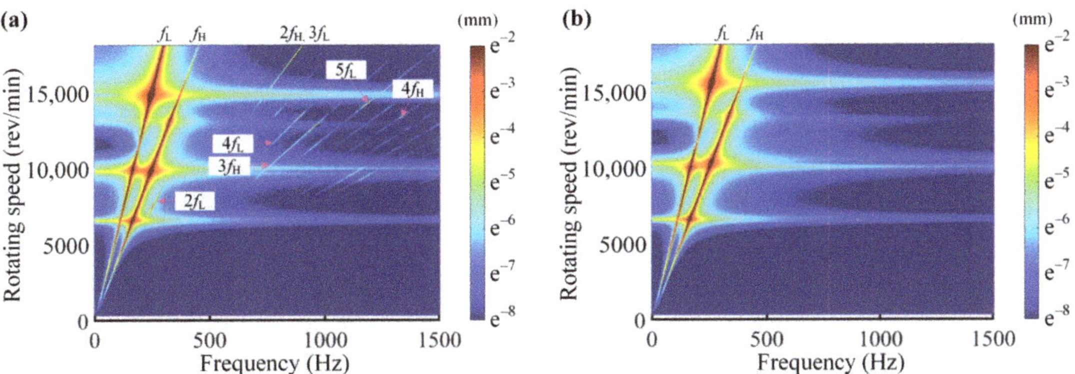

Figure 8. Spectrum cascades: (**a**) model with bolted joints; (**b**) model without bolted joints.

3. Scaling Relationships for the Dual-Rotor System with Bolted Joints

In terms of STAGE and EM, the governing equation or a certain work of derivation is required, which is not available for the complex structure. Aiming at these issues, the scaling relationships are obtained by generalized and fundamental equations, rather than the governing equation of the whole structure. The schematic diagram is shown in Figure 9. Furthermore, developing scaling relationships from generalized and fundamental equations reduces the calculation effort. As for the dual-rotor system, nonlinearity is introduced by bolted joints. The parameters of the bolt joints need to be put into similitude appropriately to obtain exact results.

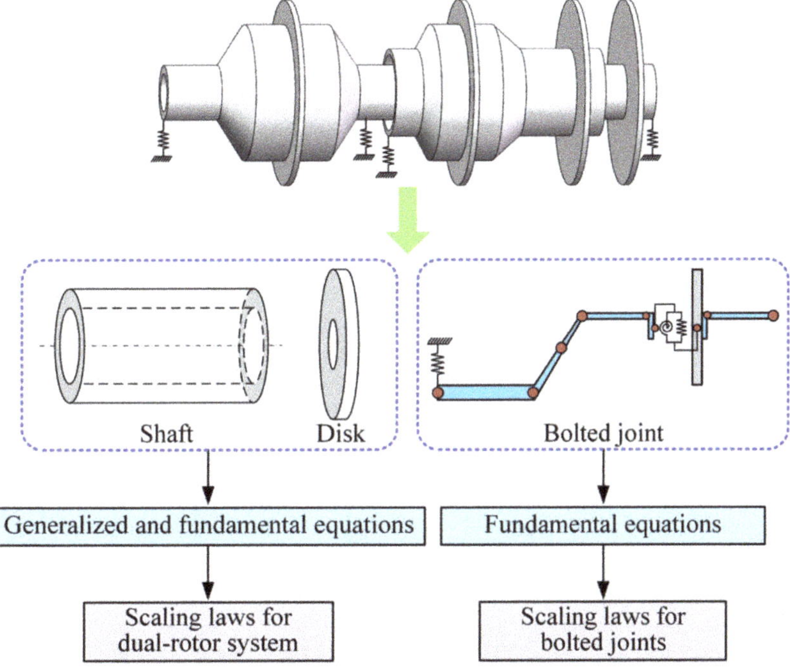

Figure 9. Schematic diagram of deriving scaling relationships.

3.1. Scaling Relationships for Dual-Rotor System

The generalized translational equation of rigid disks is expressed as

$$\rho_d \pi l_d r_d^2 \frac{d^2 x_d}{dt^2} = \rho_d \pi l_d r_d^2 e \Omega^2 \tag{13}$$

where ρ_d, l_d, and r_d are the density, thickness, and radius of the disks.

The generalized translational equation of a shaft element can be written as

$$\rho_s \pi l_s r_s^2 \frac{d^2 x_s}{dt^2} + c_s \frac{dx_s}{dt} + k_s x_s = \rho_s \pi l_s r_s^2 g \tag{14}$$

Where ρ_s, l_s, r_s, c_s, k_s, and x_s are the density, length, radius, damping, stiffness, and displacement in the x-direction of a shaft element.

The internal bending moment of the shaft can be written as

$$M = EI \frac{d^2 x_s}{dz^2} \tag{15}$$

where E and I are Young's modulus and area moment of inertia, respectively.

The internal bending moment M can be also expressed as

$$M = k_s x_s l_s \tag{16}$$

Substituting Equations (15) and (16) into Equation (14) yields

$$\rho_s \pi l_s r_s^2 \frac{d^2 x_s}{dt^2} + c_s \frac{dx_s}{dt} + \frac{EI}{l_s} \frac{d^2 x}{dz^2} = \rho_s \pi r_s^2 \tag{17}$$

According to the continuity of displacements,

$$x_d = x_s \tag{18}$$

Herein, the scaling factor λ is the prototype parameter divided by the model parameter. A parameter is written in the subscript of scaling factor λ, which indicates the scaling factor of the parameter. Then, applying similitude theory to Equations (13) and (17) yields

$$\lambda_\rho \lambda_l \lambda_r^2 \frac{\lambda_x}{\lambda_t^2} = \lambda_\rho \lambda_l \lambda_r^2 \lambda_e \lambda_\Omega^2 = \lambda_c \frac{\lambda_x}{\lambda_t} = \frac{\lambda_E \lambda_r^4 \lambda_x}{\lambda_l^3} = \lambda_\rho \lambda_r^2 \tag{19}$$

Here, the geometric parameters of the dual-rotor system are scaled by the same ratio; i.e., $\lambda_r = \lambda_l$. The following scaling relationships are obtained by Equation (19) and $\lambda_\Omega = 1/\lambda_t$:

$$\lambda_k = \lambda_E \lambda_l \tag{20}$$

$$\lambda_c = \lambda_l^2 \sqrt{\lambda_E \lambda_\rho} \tag{21}$$

$$\lambda_\omega = \lambda_\Omega = \frac{1}{\lambda_t} = \frac{1}{\lambda_l} \sqrt{\frac{\lambda_E}{\lambda_\rho}} \tag{22}$$

$$\lambda_x = \lambda_e = \frac{\lambda_l \lambda_\rho}{\lambda_E} \tag{23}$$

According to dimensional analysis [30], the parameters with the same unit can be scaled by the same scaling factor. Thus, the scaling factors of supports' stiffness and damping are equal to those of shaft; i.e., λ_k and λ_c represent the scaling factors for the stiffness and damping of both shaft and supports.

The forces on the intershaft support can be expressed as follows:

$$\begin{cases} k_{\text{in}}(x_{\text{L}} - x_{\text{H}}) = Q \\ Q = EI\frac{\partial^3 x_{\text{L}}}{\partial z^3} \end{cases} \tag{24}$$

where k_{in} is the stiffness of the intershaft support, and x_{L} and x_{H} are the displacements of LP and HP rotors, respectively. Q is the shear force.

Applying similitude theory to Equation (24) yields

$$\lambda_{k_{\text{in}}}\lambda_{x_{\text{L}}} = \lambda_E \lambda_{x_{\text{L}}} \frac{\lambda_r^4}{\lambda_l^3} \tag{25}$$

$$\lambda_{k_{\text{in}}}\lambda_{x_{\text{L}}} = \lambda_{k_{\text{in}}}\lambda_{x_{\text{H}}} \tag{26}$$

In terms of Equations (25) and (26), the following scaling relationships can be obtained:

$$\lambda_{k_{\text{in}}} = \lambda_E \frac{\lambda_r^4}{\lambda_l^3} \tag{27}$$

$$\lambda_{x_{\text{L}}} = \lambda_{x_{\text{H}}} \tag{28}$$

It is found from Equation (27) that the scaling factor of intershaft support stiffness λ_{kin} is equal to that of the shaft stiffness λ_k. According to Equation (28), the scaling factors of displacements can be represented by scaling factor λ_x.

3.2. Scaling Relationships for Bolted Joints

In this section, the scaling relationships related to the bolt joint parameters and rotor system parameters are developed. Nonlinearity is introduced by the piecewise linear stiffness of bolted joints. Therefore, the stiffness of bolted joints needs to be put into similitude first.

The piecewise linear stiffness is the angular stiffness; thus, the angular stiffness can be expressed as

$$k_\theta = \frac{M}{\phi} \tag{29}$$

where k_θ is the piecewise linear stiffness, which includes $k_{\theta 1}$ and $k_{\theta 2}$. ϕ is the deflection angle of the bolted joints, which is dimensionless.

According to Equations (15), (23), and (29), the scaling factor for the piecewise linear stiffness can be obtained:

$$\lambda_{k_\theta} = \lambda_l^3 \lambda_\rho \tag{30}$$

4. Verification of the Scaling Relationships

Two scaled models are studied and are named M1 and M2. The scaling factors of the models are listed in Table 2. Columns 2–4 of Table 2 are artificially determined scaling factors. The other scaling factors in Table 2 are obtained according to Equations (20)–(23) and (30). The parameters of the prototype are listed in tables A1 and A2, and the prototype is made of titanium alloy. The model M1 is a complete similitude model and the material is consistent with the prototype (titanium alloy). Furthermore, the material of M2 is carbon steel (density: 7850 kg/m^3, Young's modulus: 210 GPa, Poisson ratio: 0.26), which is different from M1. The purpose of M2 is to demonstrate the effectiveness of the proposed scaling relationships for the problem of different materials (between prototype and model). Note that M2 further reduces the costs of model testing since it allows for replacing the prototype with a model made of cheaper material. The sketches of the models and the prototype are presented in Figure 10.

Table 2. The scaling factors of the models M1 and M2.

Model	$\lambda_l\ (\lambda_r)$	λ_ρ	λ_E	λ_c	λ_k	$\lambda_\omega\ (\lambda_\Omega)$	λ_t	$\lambda_x\ (\lambda_e)$	$\lambda_{k\theta}$
M1	0.5	1	1	0.25	0.5	2	0.5	0.5	0.125
M2	0.5	1.8	2	0.47	1	2.11	0.47	0.45	0.23

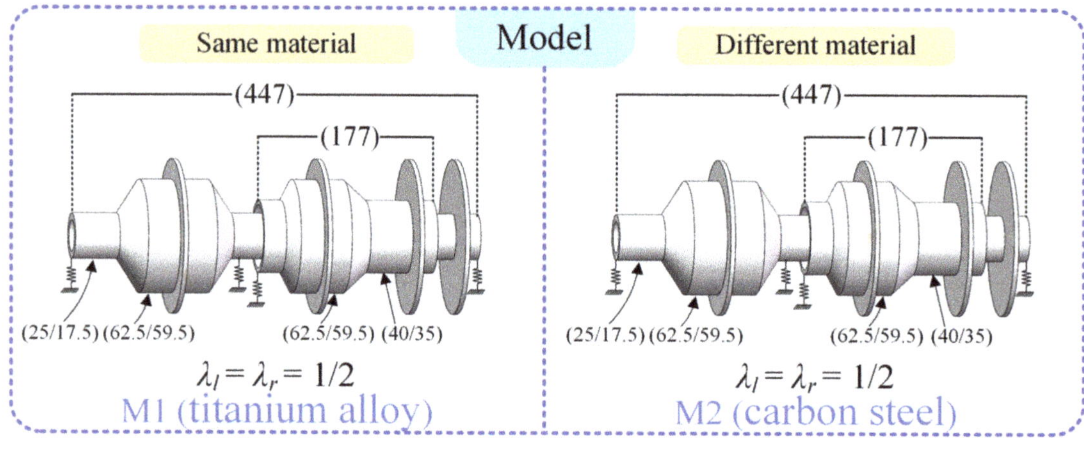

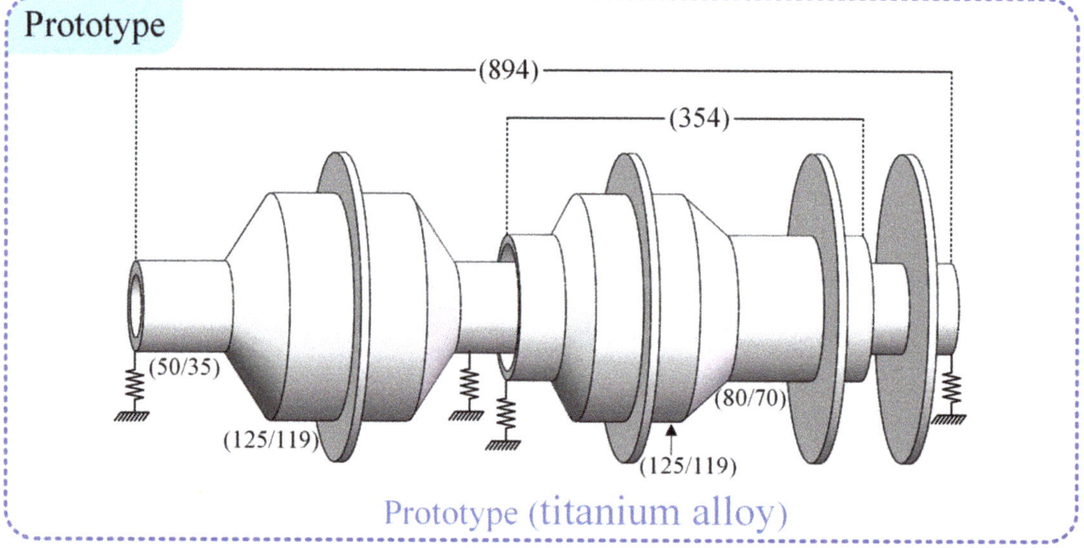

Figure 10. Scheme of models and prototype.

Aiming at the working condition and structural characteristics of dual-rotor systems, LP rotor excitation (Section 4.1), HP rotor excitation (Section 4.2), two frequency excitations

(Section 4.3), and counter-rotation (Section 4.4) are considered in predicting the vibration characteristics.

4.1. Case 1: LP Rotor Excitation

LP rotor excitation represents that disk 1 and disk 2 have mass eccentricities. Figure 8 presents the vibration responses of disk 1 of the prototype, the prediction as well as unscaled results. The aim is to predict the responses of the prototype (red line in Figure 11) by using the responses of models (dotted line in Figure 8). The dotted lines labeled as "unscaled" are the responses of models M1 and M2. The abscissa of the model's response is multiplied by λ_ω (see Table 2), and the ordinate is multiplied by λ_x. Then, the prediction results (circles and points in Figure 11) can be obtained and are compared with the results of the prototype. It can be seen from Figure 11 that the unscaled results differ greatly from the results of the prototype. After prediction, the amplitude frequency responses (AFRs) of the prototype and predicted results overlap perfectly. It is worth noting that M2 is beneficial to further reduce the test cost since it is not only reduced in size but also relatively cheap in material (compared to the prototype).

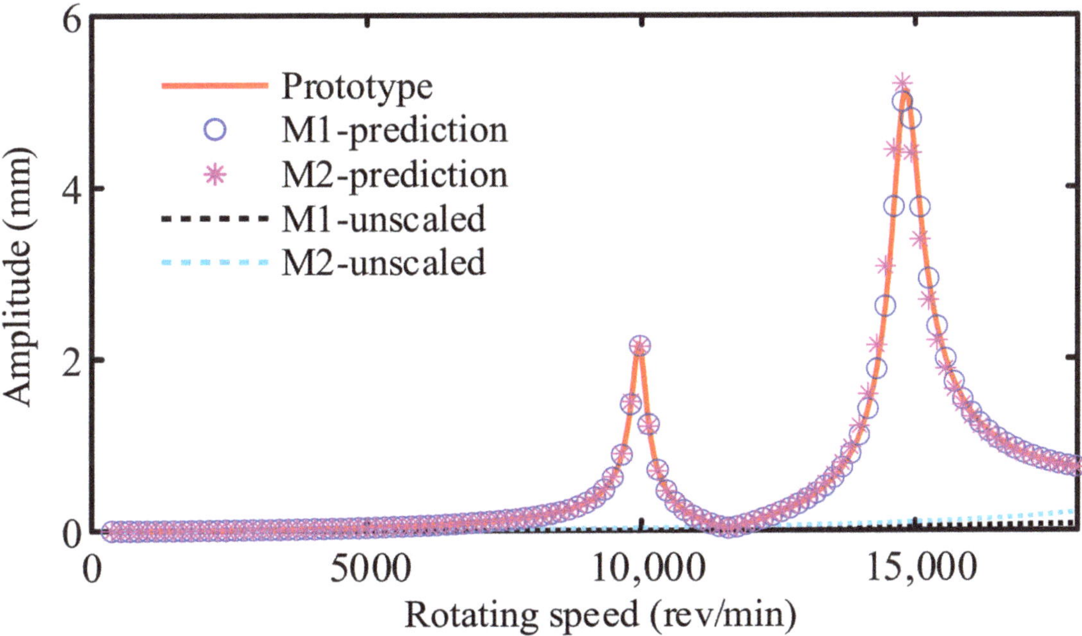

Figure 11. Prediction of AFR from M1 and M2 under LP rotor excitation.

Figure 12 presents the spectrum cascades under different rotating speeds of the prototype and corresponding predicted results for models M1 and M2. The frequency components of the prototype are made up of the frequency multiplication, such as $2f_L$, $3f_L$, $4f_L$, and $5f_L$, which is consistent with the laws in [40]. The results of models M1 and M2 are consistent with those of the prototype. This indicates that both the models M1 and M2 can accurately reproduce the frequency components of the prototype, even though M2 is made of relatively cheap material.

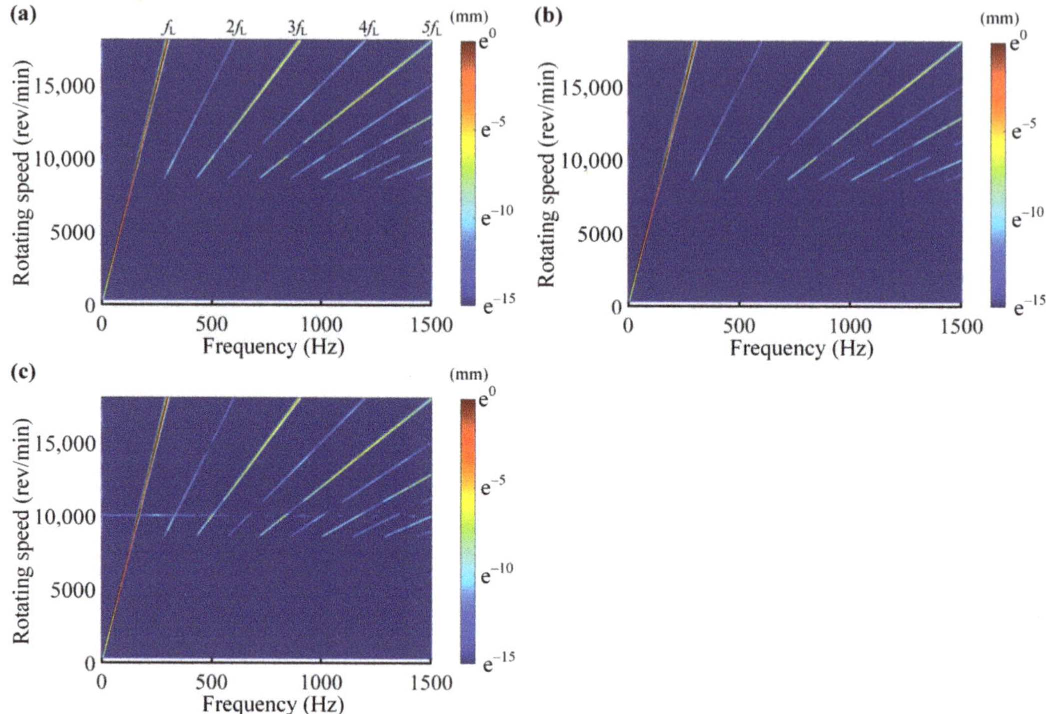

Figure 12. Spectrum cascades of (**a**) prototype and the prediction results from the models (**b**) M1 and (**c**) M2 under LP rotor excitation.

4.2. Case 2: HP Rotor Excitation

HP rotor excitation means that disk 3 and disk 4 have mass eccentricities. Figures 13 and 14 show the predicted results for the amplitude frequency responses and spectrum cascades, respectively. It is found that the vibration responses of the prototype can also be predicted accurately by the models M1 and M2, where different materials between the prototype and models are considered in the similitude procedure. In addition, the frequency components ($2f_L$, $3f_L$, $4f_L$, and $5f_L$) of the prototype can also be predicted by the two models under HP rotor excitation.

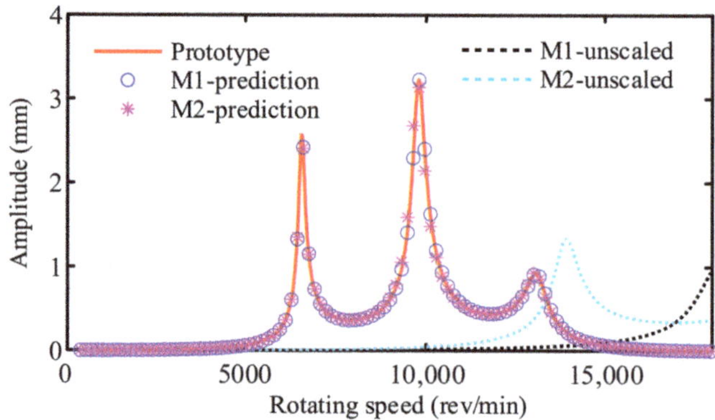

Figure 13. Prediction of AFR from M1 and M2 under HP rotor excitation.

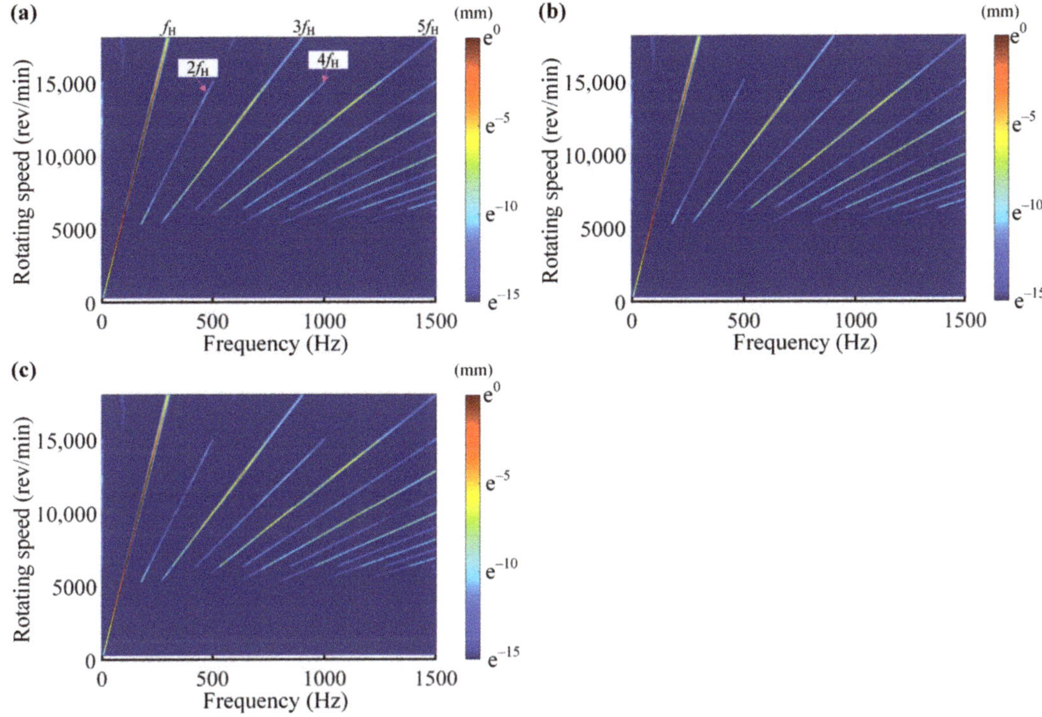

Figure 14. Spectrum cascades of (**a**) prototype and the prediction results from the models (**b**) M1 and (**c**) M2 under HP rotor excitation.

4.3. Case 3: Two Frequency Excitations

Two frequency excitations mean that all disks of LP and HP rotors have mass eccentricities. Figures 15 and 16 describe the predicted results of the amplitude frequency responses and frequency components in the case of two frequency excitations. The vibration responses of M1 and M2 agree well with those of the prototype. Besides, the frequency components of the two models match perfectly those of the prototype.

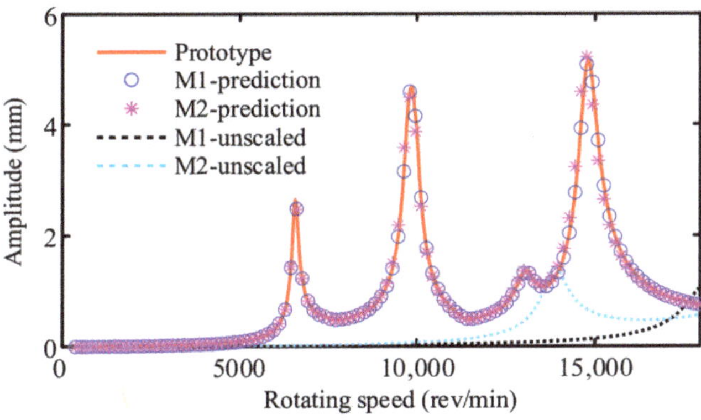

Figure 15. Prediction of AFR from M1 and M2 under two frequency excitations.

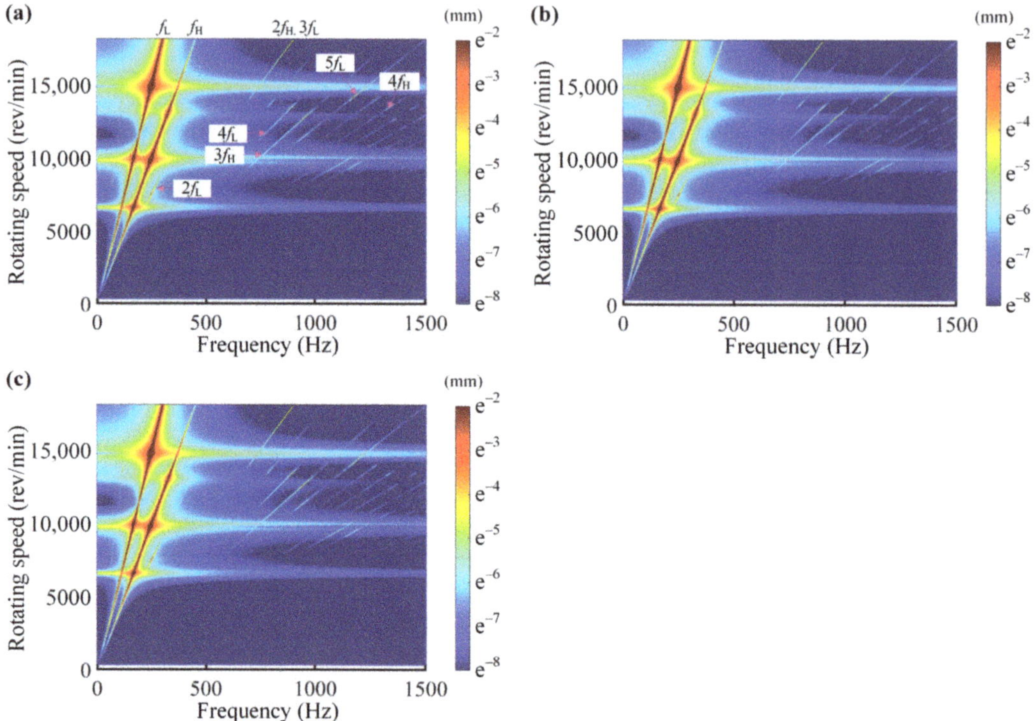

Figure 16. Spectrum cascades of (**a**) prototype and the prediction results from the models (**b**) M1 and (**c**) M2 under two frequency excitations.

4.4. Case 4: Counter-Rotation

Co- and counter-rotation indicate that the LP rotor and HP rotor rotate in the same and opposite directions, respectively. Cases 1–3 are investigated in the case of corotation; thus, counter-rotation is considered. The case of two frequency excitations is taken as an example in this section. The predictions for amplitude frequency responses and spectrum cascades are shown in Figures 17 and 18. The predicted results show exact agreement between the models M1 and M2 and the prototype. Thus, the accuracy and effectiveness of proposed scaling relationships are considered verified.

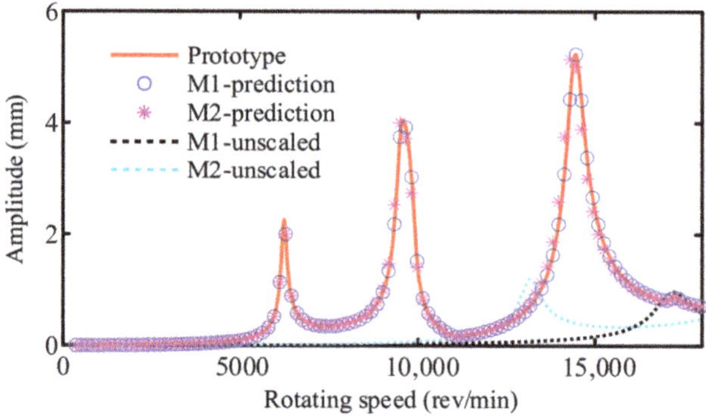

Figure 17. Prediction of AFR from M1 and M2 under counter-rotation.

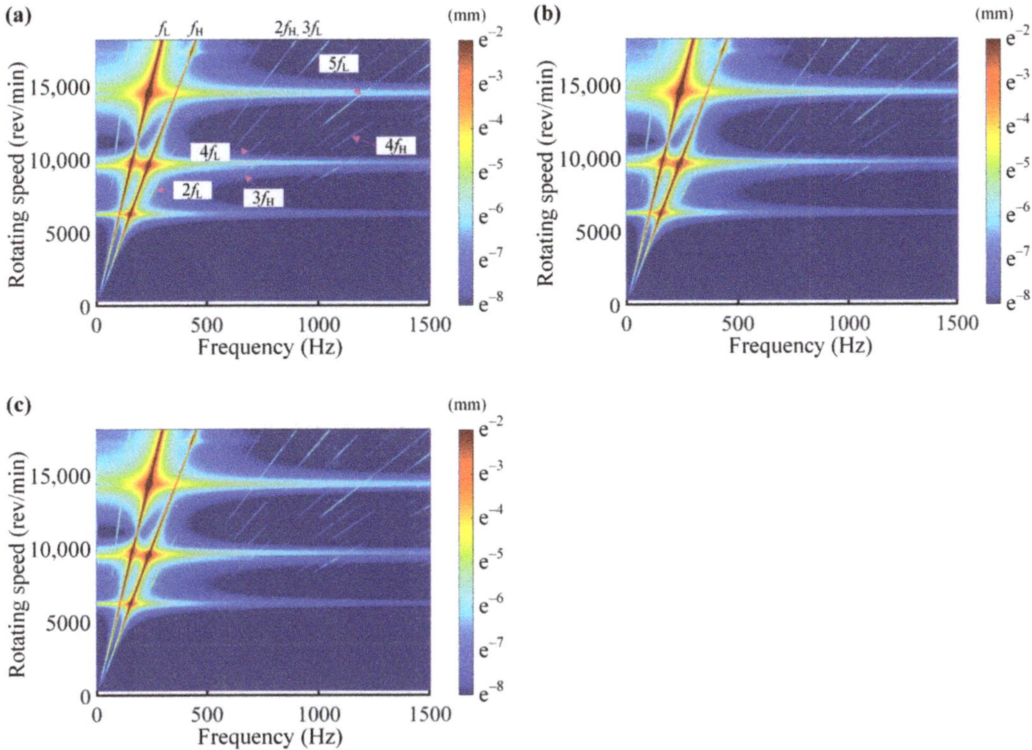

Figure 18. Spectrum cascades of (**a**) prototype and the prediction results from the models (**b**) M1 and (**c**) M2 under counter-rotation.

5. Conclusions

This paper presents the scaling relationships for predicting the dynamic characteristics of a dual-rotor system with bolted joints, where different materials between the prototype and models are taken into account. The effects of bolted joints on the dual-rotor system are investigated, and the results indicate that bolted joints should be considered in the similitude procedure. The scaling relationships are obtained by generalized and fundamental equations and are used to predict the critical speeds, vibration responses, and frequency components under different working conditions. The main findings are summarized as follows:

1. The scaling relationships are developed by generalized and fundamental equations of substructures (shaft, disk, and bolted joint). The scaling factors of geometric dimensions, support parameters, critical speed, and vibration displacement are derived and can be used to design scaled models. However, as for STAGE and EM, the governing equations of the whole structure are required when deriving scaling relationships. Thus, the scaling relationships developed in this paper can reduce the calculation effort and provide the possibility for the application of complex structures.

2. The effect of bolted joints on the dual-rotor system is considered. It is found that the bolted joints reduce the critical speed and lead to the emergence of frequency multiplication. Thus, the bolted joints need to be considered in similitude analysis. Aiming at this issue, the scaling relationships derived in this paper take the nonlinear stiffness of bolted joint into account for the first time.

3. For the case of LP rotor excitation or HP rotor excitation, only the resonance and frequency components of the LP rotor or HP rotor can be found. As for two frequency

excitations, both the resonance and frequency components of LP and HP rotors can be observed. Besides, the critical speeds decrease slightly under the case of counter-rotation. The predicted results of scaled models are compared with the results of the prototype in these cases. The results for all working conditions show that the derived scaling relationships can accurately predict the critical speeds, vibration responses, and frequency components of the prototype, even though different materials and the nonlinearity introduced by bolted joints are considered.

In our future work, the case of the shaft, disk, and bearings being made of different materials will be investigated and more emphasis will be placed on the experimental verification.

Author Contributions: Conceptualization, L.L. and Z.L.; methodology, L.L.; software, L.L. and F.H.; validation, L.L. and Z.Q.; formal analysis, Y.L.; investigation, L.L.; data curation, F.H.; writing—original draft preparation, L.L.; writing—review and editing, Z.L.; visualization, Z.Q. and X.Y.; supervision, Z.L.; project administration, Z.L.; funding acquisition, Z.L. All authors have read and agreed to the published version of the manuscript.

Funding: This research was funded by the National Science Foundation of China, grant numbers 11872148 and U1908217; the Fundamental Research Funds for the Central Universities of China, grant numbers N180703018, N2003012, and N2003013; and the Joint Foundation of Basic and Applied Basic Research of Guangdong Province, grant number 2020B1515120015.

Institutional Review Board Statement: Not applicable.

Informed Consent Statement: Not applicable.

Data Availability Statement: The data in the paper can be requested by email to the corresponding author.

Conflicts of Interest: The authors declare no conflict of interest.

Nomenclature

Roman symbols

C_H, C_L	damping matrices of HP and LP rotors
c_s, k_s	damping and stiffness of shaft
E	Young's modulus of shaft
$e_{1\text{-}4}$	eccentricities of disks 1–4
f_H, f_L	rotating frequencies of HP and LP rotors
G_H, G_L	gyroscopic matrices of HP and LP rotors
g	gravitational acceleration
I	area moment of inertia of shaft
k, l	node numbers of the intershaft support
$k_{\theta 1}, k_{\theta 2}$	stiffness of bolted joint at the first and second stages
k_{in}	stiffness matrix of the intershaft support
K_H, K_L	stiffness matrices of HP and LP rotors
K_J	stiffness matrix of joint element
l_d, l_s	thickness of disk and length of shaft
M	internal bending moment of shaft
M_H, M_L	mass matrices of HP and LP rotors
$m_{1\text{-}4}$	mass of disks 1–4
Q	shear force
Q_H, Q_L	force vectors of high- and low-pressure rotors
q_J	generalized displacement vector of joint element
R	ratio of rotational speed between HP and LP rotors
r_d, r_s	radii of disk and shaft
r_{Li}, r_{Lo}	inner and outer radii of left end of shaft element
r_{Ri}, r_{Ro}	inner and outer radii of right end of shaft element

t	time
$u_{\text{H}}, u_{\text{L}}$	displacement vectors of HP and LP rotors
$x_{1\text{-}28}, y_{1\text{-}28}$	displacements of nodes 1–28 in x and y directions
$x_{\text{J}}, y_{\text{J}}$	displacements of joint element in x and y directions
$x_{\text{d}}, y_{\text{s}}$	displacements of disk and shaft
Greek symbols	
$\theta_{x1\text{-}28}, \theta_{y1\text{-}28}$	rotations of nodes 1–28 in x and y directions
$\theta_{x\text{J}}, \theta_{y\text{J}}$	rotations of joint element in x and y directions
λ_ρ, λ_E	scaling factors of density and Young's modulus
$\lambda_l, \lambda_r, \lambda_e$	scaling factors of length, radius, and eccentricity
$\lambda_\omega, \lambda_\Omega, \lambda_t, \lambda_x$	scaling factors of critical speed, rotating speed, time, and displacement
$\lambda_{xH}, \lambda_{xL}$	scaling factors of displacement of HP and LP rotors
$\lambda_k, \lambda_c, \lambda_{k\theta}$	scaling factors of support stiffness, damping, and bolted joint stiffness
λ_{kin}	scaling factor of stiffness of intershaft support
$\rho_{\text{d}}, \rho_{\text{s}}$	densities of disk and shaft
ϕ_0, ϕ	critical rotation angle and relative rotation angle between the flange and disk
$\Omega_{\text{H}}, \Omega_{\text{L}}$	rotating speeds of HP and LP rotors

Appendix A

The configurations of the dual-rotor system are given in Tables A1 and A2.

Table A1. Dimensions of the dual-rotor system.

Parameter (m)	Value	Parameter (m)	Value			
			r_{Li}	r_{Lo}	r_{Ri}	r_{Ro}
Length of shaft element l_1	0.100	Radii of shaft element l_1	0.035	0.050	0.035	0.050
Length of shaft element l_2	0.050	Radii of shaft element l_2	0.035	0.050	0.119	0.125
Length of shaft element l_3, l_6	0.070	Radii of shaft element l_3, l_6	0.119	0.125	0.119	0.125
Length of shaft element l_4, l_5	0.002	Radii of shaft element l_4, l_5	0.105	0.125	0.105	0.125
Length of shaft element l_7	0.050	Radii of shaft element l_7	0.119	0.125	0.035	0.050
Length of shaft element l_8, l_{10}, l_{11}	0.050	Radii of shaft element l_8, l_{10}, l_{11}	0.035	0.050	0.035	0.050
Length of shaft element l_9	0.400	Radii of shaft element l_9	0.035	0.050	0.035	0.050
Length of shaft element l_{12}, l_{20}	0.050	Radii of shaft element l_{12}, l_{20}	0.070	0.080	0.070	0.080
Length of shaft element l_{13}	0.025	Radii of shaft element l_{13}	0.070	0.080	0.119	0.125
Length of shaft element l_{14}, l_{17}	0.050	Radii of shaft element l_{14}, l_{17}	0.119	0.125	0.119	0.125
Length of shaft element l_{15}, l_{16}	0.002	Radii of shaft element l_{15}, l_{16}	0.105	0.125	0.105	0.125
Length of shaft element l_{18}	0.025	Radii of shaft element l_{18}	0.119	0.125	0.070	0.080
Length of shaft element l_{19}	0.100	Radii of shaft element l_{19}	0.070	0.080	0.070	0.080

Table A2. Physical parameters of the dual-rotor system.

Parameter (m)	Value	Parameter (m)	Value
Mass of disks 1 and 2 (kg)	7.22	Moment of inertia of disks 1 and 2 (kg.m^2)	0.11
Mass of disk 3 (kg)	6.56	Moment of inertia of disk 3 (kg.m^2)	0.11
Mass of disk 4 (kg)	6.15	Moment of inertia of disk 4 (kg.m^2)	0.11
Support stiffness k_1, k_2, k_3, k_4 (N/m)	2×10^7	Support damping c_1, c_2, c_3, c_4, c_5 (N/m)	500
Support stiffness k_{in} (N/m)	4×10^7	Density (kg/m^3)	4350
Elastic modulus (GPa)	105	Poisson ratio	0.26

References

1. Yu, P.C.; Zhang, D.Y.; Ma, Y.H.; Hong, J. Dynamic modeling and vibration characteristics analysis of the aero-engine dual-rotor system with Fan blade out. *Mech. Syst. Sig. Process.* **2018**, *106*, 158–175. [CrossRef]
2. Wang, N.F.; Jiang, D.X. Vibration response characteristics of a dual-rotor with unbalance-misalignment coupling faults: Theoretical analysis and experimental study. *Mech. Mach. Theory* **2018**, *125*, 207–219. [CrossRef]
3. Sun, G.; Palazzolo, A.; Provenza, A.; Lawrence, C.; Carney, K. Long duration blade loss simulations including thermal growths for dual-rotor gas turbine engine. *J. Sound Vib.* **2008**, *316*, 147–163. [CrossRef]

4. Bab, S.; Najafi, M.; Fathi Sola, J.; Abbasi, A. Annihilation of non-stationary vibration of a gas turbine rotor system under rub-impact effect using a nonlinear absorber. *Mech. Mach. Theory* **2019**, *139*, 379–406. [CrossRef]

5. Hong, J.; Chen, X.Q.; Wang, Y.F.; Ma, Y.H. Optimization of dynamics of non-continuous rotor based on model of rotor stiffness. *Mech. Syst. Sig. Process.* **2019**, *131*, 166–182. [CrossRef]

6. Liu, S.G.; Ma, Y.H.; Zhang, D.Y.; Hong, J. Studies on dynamic characteristics of the joint in the aero-engine rotor system. *Mech. Syst. Sig. Process.* **2012**, *29*, 120–136. [CrossRef]

7. Asl, M.E.; Niezrecki, C.; Sherwood, J.; Avitabile, P. Vibration prediction of thin-walled composite I-beams using scaled models. *Thin Walled Struct.* **2017**, *113*, 151–161. [CrossRef]

8. Asl, M.E.; Niezrecki, C.; Sherwood, J.; Avitabile, P. Experimental and theoretical similitude analysis for flexural bending of scaled-down laminated I-beams. *Compos. Struct.* **2017**, *176*, 812–822. [CrossRef]

9. Kasivitamnuay, J.; Singhatanadgid, P. Scaling laws for displacement of elastic beam by energy method. *Int. J. Mech. Sci.* **2017**, *128*, 361–367. [CrossRef]

10. Kasivitamnuay, J.; Singhatanadgid, P. Scaling laws for static displacement of linearly elastic cracked beam by energy method. *Theor. Appl. Fract. Mech.* **2018**, *98*, 157–166. [CrossRef]

11. Coutinho, C.P.; Baptista, A.J.; Rodriges, J.D. Modular approach to structural similitude. *Int. J. Mech. Sci.* **2018**, *135*, 294–312. [CrossRef]

12. Yazdi, A.A. Study nonlinear vibration of cross-ply laminated plates using scale models. *Polym. Composite.* **2014**, *35*, 752–758. [CrossRef]

13. Rezaeepazhand, J.; Yazdi, A.A. Similitude requirements and scaling laws for flutter prediction of angle-ply composite plates. *Compos. Part B: Eng.* **2011**, *42*, 51–56. [CrossRef]

14. Frostig, Y.; Simitses, G.J. Similitude of sandwich panels with a soft core in buckling. *Compos. Part B: Eng.* **2004**, *35*, 599–608. [CrossRef]

15. Singhatanadgid, P.; Songkhla, A.N. An experimental investigation into the use of scaling laws for predicting vibration responses of rectangular thin plates. *J. Sound Vib.* **2008**, *311*, 314–327. [CrossRef]

16. De Rosa, S.; Franco, F. A scaling procedure for the response of an isolated system with high modal overlap factor. *Mech. Syst. Sig. Process.* **2008**, *22*, 1549–1565. [CrossRef]

17. Franco, F.; Robin, O.; Ciappi, E.; De Rosa, S.; Berry, A.; Petrone, G. Similitude laws for the structural response of flat plates under a turbulent boundary layer excitation. *Mech. Syst. Sig. Process.* **2019**, *129*, 590–613. [CrossRef]

18. Mazzariol, L.M.; Alves, M. Similarity laws of structures under impact load: Geometric and material distortion. *Int. J. Mech. Sci.* **2019**, *157*, 633–647. [CrossRef]

19. Petrone, G.; Manfredonia, M.; De Rosa, S.; Franco, F. Structural similitudes of stiffened cylinders. *Math. Mech. Solids* **2019**, *24*, 527–541. [CrossRef]

20. Rezaeepazhand, J.; Simitses, G.J.; Starnes, J.H. Design of scaled down models for predicting shell vibration response. *J. Sound Vib.* **1996**, *195*, 301–311. [CrossRef]

21. Rezaeepazhand, J.; Simitses, G.J.; Starnes, J.H. Scale models for laminated cylindrical shells subjected to axial compression. *Compos. Struct.* **1996**, *34*, 371–379. [CrossRef]

22. Ungbhakorn, V.; Wattanasakulpong, N. Structural similitude and scaling laws of anti-symmetric cross-ply laminated cylindrical shells for buckling and vibration experiments. *Int. J. Struct. Stab. Dyn.* **2007**, *7*, 609–627. [CrossRef]

23. De Rosa, S.; Franco, F.; Polito, T. Structural similitudes for the dynamic response of plates and assemblies of plates. *Mech. Syst. Sig. Process.* **2011**, *25*, 969–980. [CrossRef]

24. De Rosa, S.; Franco, F. On the use of the asymptotic scaled modal analysis for time-harmonic structural analysis and for the prediction of coupling loss factors for similar systems. *Mech. Syst. Sig. Process.* **2010**, *24*, 455–480. [CrossRef]

25. De Rosa, S.; Franco, F.; Polito, T. Partial scaling of finite element models for the analysis of the coupling between short and long structural wavelengths. *Mech. Syst. Sig. Process.* **2015**, *52–53*, 722–740. [CrossRef]

26. You, C.; Yasaee, M.; Dayyani, I. Structural similitude design for a scaled composite wing box based on optimised stacking sequence. *Compos. Struct.* **2019**, *226*, 111255. [CrossRef]

27. Song, Y.Y.; Wu, J.; Yu, G.; Huang, T. Dynamic characteristic prediction of a 5-DOF hybrid machine tool by using scale model considering the geometric distortion of bearings. *Mech. Mach. Theory* **2020**, *145*, 103679. [CrossRef]

28. Wu, J.J. Prediction of lateral vibration characteristics of a full-size rotor-bearing system by using those of its scale models. *Finite Elem. Anal. Des.* **2007**, *43*, 803–816. [CrossRef]

29. Li, L.; Luo, Z.; He, F.X.; Sun, K.; Yan, X.L. An improved partial similitude method for dynamic characteristic of rotor systems based on Levenberg–Marquardt method. *Mech. Syst. Sig. Process.* **2022**, *165*, 108405. [CrossRef]

30. Casaburo, A.; Petrone, G.; Franco, F.; De Rosa, S. A review of similitude methods for structural engineering. *Appl. Mech. Rev.* **2019**, *71*, 30802. [CrossRef]

31. Rezaeepazhand, J.; Simitses, G.J.; Starnes, J.H. Use of scaled-down models for predicting vibration response of laminated plates. *Compos. Struct.* **1995**, *30*, 419–426. [CrossRef]

32. Yazdi, A.A.; Rezaeepazhand, J. Structural similitude for flutter of delaminated composite beam-plates. *Compos. Struct.* **2011**, *93*, 1918–1922. [CrossRef]

33. Ungbhakorn, V.; Singhatanadgid, P. A scaling law for vibration response of laminated doubly curved shallow shells by energy approach. *Mech. Adv. Mater. Struc.* **2009**, *16*, 333–344. [CrossRef]

34. De Rosa, S.; Franco, F.; Li, X.; Polito, T. A similitude for structural acoustic enclosures. *Mech. Syst. Sig. Process.* **2012**, *30*, 330–342. [CrossRef]

35. De Rosa, S.; Franco, F.; Meruane, V. Similitudes for the structural response of flexural plates. *Proc. IMechE Part C J. Mech. Eng. Sci.* **2016**, *230*, 174–188. [CrossRef]

36. Adams, C.; Bos, J.; Slomski, E.M.; Melz, T. Scaling laws obtained from a sensitivity analysis and applied to thin vibrating structures. *Mech. Syst. Sig. Process.* **2018**, *110*, 590–610. [CrossRef]

37. Qin, Z.Y.; Han, Q.K.; Chu, F.L. Analytical model of bolted disk–drum joints and its application to dynamic analysis of jointed rotor. *Proc. IMechE Part C J. Mech. Eng. Sci.* **2014**, *228*, 646–663. [CrossRef]

38. Li, Y.Q.; Luo, Z.; Liu, J.X.; Ma, H.; Yang, D.S. Dynamic modeling and stability analysis of a rotor-bearing system with bolted-disk joint. *Mech. Syst. Sig. Process.* **2021**, *158*, 107778. [CrossRef]

39. Shanmugam, A.; Padmanabhan, C. A fixed–free interface component mode synthesis method for rotordynamic analysis. *J. Sound Vib.* **2006**, *297*, 664–679. [CrossRef]

40. Li, C.F.; Qiao, R.H.; Tang, Q.S.; Miao, X.Y. Investigation on the vibration and interface state of a thin-walled cylindrical shell with bolted joints considering its bilinear stiffness. *Appl. Acoust.* **2021**, *172*, 107580. [CrossRef]

 *mathematics*

Article

Parameter Identification of Photovoltaic Models by Hybrid Adaptive JAYA Algorithm

Xiaobing Yu *, Xuejing Wu and Wenguan Luo

School of Management Science and Engineering, Nanjing University of Information Science & Technology, Nanjing 210044, China; 20201224031@nuist.edu.cn (X.W.); 20211224005@nuist.edu.cn (W.L.)
* Correspondence: 002257@nuist.edu.cn

Abstract: As one of the most promising forms of renewable energy, solar energy is increasingly deployed. The simulation and control of photovoltaic (PV) systems requires identification of their parameters. A Hybrid Adaptive algorithm based on JAYA and Differential Evolution (HAJAYADE) is developed to identify these parameters accurately and reliably. The HAJAYADE algorithm consists of adaptive JAYA, adaptive DE, and the chaotic perturbation method. Two adaptive coefficients are introduced in adaptive JAYA to balance the local and global search. In adaptive DE, the Rank/Best/1 mutation operator is put forward to boost the exploration and maintain the exploitation. The chaotic perturbation method is applied to reinforce the local search further. The HAJAYADE algorithm is employed to address the parameter identification of PV systems through five test cases, and the eight latest meta-heuristic algorithms are its opponents. The mean RMSE values of the HAJAYADE algorithm from five test cases are 9.8602×10^{-4}, 9.8294×10^{-4}, 2.4251×10^{-3}, 1.7298×10^{-3}, and 1.6601×10^{-2}. Consequently, HAJAYADE is proven to be an efficient and reliable algorithm and could be an alternative algorithm to identify the parameters of PV systems.

Keywords: parameter identification; optimization; hybrid algorithm; JAYA; differential evolution

Citation: Yu, X.; Wu, X.; Luo, W. Parameter Identification of Photovoltaic Models by Hybrid Adaptive JAYA Algorithm. *Mathematics* **2022**, *10*, 183. https://doi.org/10.3390/math10020183

Academic Editors: Xiang Li, Shuo Zhang and Wei Zhang

Received: 10 December 2021
Accepted: 1 January 2022
Published: 7 January 2022

Publisher's Note: MDPI stays neutral with regard to jurisdictional claims in published maps and institutional affiliations.

1. Introduction

Nowadays, governments and the public are more concerned about environmental protection and the energy crisis, meaning that the unsustainable energy structure dominated by fossil energy urgently needs to be adjusted. They have turned to renewable energy, which may be the main alternative to fossil fuels. Among various renewable energies, solar energy is one of the most promising energies as it is clean, renewable, green, etc. [1]. For solar energy, photovoltaic (PV) systems are commonly used because they can transform solar energy into electrical energy. It is reported that the market for PV systems has increased by as much as 50%, with more than 700,000 solar panels installed every day [2]. However, PV systems are often deployed in harsh environments, so that the utilization efficiency is greatly influenced. It is indispensable to assess the performance behavior of PV systems using models on the basis of observation data. Commonly used models are the single-diode model (SDM) and double-diode model (DDM). The performance of these models relies on the involved parameters. However, they are not available directly as they vary due to the harsh environments. Therefore, it is necessary to estimate the parameters of these models.

Identifying the parameters of these models can be defined as an optimized problem. There are two main approaches to solve the problem, i.e., the mathematical method and meta-heuristic algorithms. The former often tries to minimize a suitable function by imposing restrictions such as convexity and differentiability [3]. However, the problem is often nonlinear and multimodal, making the mathematical method ineffective and causing it to quickly fall into the local optimum [4]. Hence, various approaches are based on meta-heuristic algorithms.

Meta-heuristic algorithms are widely used to estimate the parameters of PV systems as they are simple, flexible, and derivation-free. These algorithms are developed based on the evolutionary concept, biological behavior, and physical phenomena. A teaching–learning optimization algorithm that simulates the learning and teaching process was combined with the artificial bee colony algorithm that forges the behavior of honey bees [2]. An oppositional teaching–learning algorithm was put forward to solve the problem. The opposition–learning technique was used to help the algorithm escape from the local optimum [5]. The multiple learning backtracking search optimization algorithm was realized for estimating the parameters, in which multi-updating strategies were developed to boost the diversity of the population [6]. An adaptive and chaotic grey wolf optimizer was designed to deal with the issue [7]. A multi-swarm spiral leader particle swarm optimization (PSO) algorithm was implemented to identify parameters. Several search mechanisms were used in the algorithm to achieve good performance [8]. The improved slime mould algorithm introduced Lévy flight (LF) and adaptive factors to attain the same aim [8]. In other work, an advanced slime mould algorithm was developed to solve three commercial PV models [9]. The Whippy Harris Hawks algorithm, as an extended version of Harris Hawks optimization, was designed to estimate the parameters of PV systems, and superior search capability was attained [10]. A robust and reliable approach on the basis of a stochastic fractal search algorithm was used to address the problem, in which three PV models were involved [11]. A hybrid algorithm based on the Rao algorithm and the chaotic map was developed and exhibited minor deviation when addressing the problem [12]. An improved marine predators algorithm using two different mutation strategies was proposed for the issue, and serial experiments achieved better results [13]. An extended gaining–sharing knowledge algorithm was applied to extract the parameters of PV systems, in which an adaptive mechanism was incorporated into the algorithm [14]. An adaptive differential evolution (DE) algorithm was developed to address the problem, and the experimental results from three PV models proved the efficiency of the algorithm [15]. An enhanced metaphor-free Gradient-based Optimizer Algorithm (GOA) was developed to cope with the issue [16]. An opposition-based GOA was also realized to identify the parameters of PV systems [17]. An effective and efficient solver called SFLBS was employed to tackle the problem [18]. Based on GOA, chaotic GOA was realized to derive PV systems' parameters [19]. An ensemble multi-strategy-driven shuffled frog leading algorithm was developed to optimize the PV's parameters to guarantee the optimal energy conversion [20].

These algorithms have attained remarkably good results when estimating the parameters of PV systems. However, it has to be pointed out that most of the above algorithms have to use additional parameters, except for the population size. The parameter settings greatly influence the performance of these algorithms. Setting the proper parameter values for a specific problem is still challenging. The parameter tuning is also a tedious task. Therefore, developing a competitive and advanced algorithm to extract the parameters of these models is still demanding work.

JAYA, developed by Rao [21], is a novel meta-heuristic algorithm. Its parameter-free nature makes the algorithm different from the conventional meta-heuristic algorithms. For instance, the genetic algorithm employs the crossover and mutation probabilities, PSO uses the inertia weight, etc. The algorithm attains the optimal solution by approaching the best solution and avoiding the worst solution. The algorithm's structure is simple, and the algorithm is easy to implement. Therefore, the algorithm has also been used to solve problems in industrial applications [3,22–30]. For example, JAYA has been applied to solve the standard hybrid energy system [29]. It has been integrated with a branch and bound algorithm (BBA) to optimize the scheduling problem [30]. Various variants based on the JAYA algorithm have been proposed, and several variants based on JAYA have been employed to estimate the parameters of PV models. A comprehensive learning JAYA algorithm was developed by introducing the comprehensive learning mechanism to solve the parameters of three PV models [31]. An enhanced JAYA was developed to accurately and efficiently address the problem, in which three extensions were incorporated [32]. Performance-guided JAYA was offered, in which the promising search direction was controlled [4]. A logistic chaotic JAYA algorithm was realized and the algorithm used logistic chaotic map and mutation strategies to boost the population diversity [33]. An Improved JAYA (IJAYA) was realized by randomly selecting two mutation strategies. The proposed JAYA algorithm was used to address the problem [3]. Although these works have boosted the performance of JAYA, they also may demonstrate some deficiencies. For example, the two mutation strategies are randomly used in the IJAYA algorithm, without considering the quality of the solution. The search capability is limited when extracting the parameters of PV models [4] and these improvements are only based on JAYA, without considering the hybrid idea.

As demonstrated above, the aforementioned meta-heuristic algorithms have been successfully applied to solve the parameter identification of PV models [3,4,32,34,35]. However, these algorithms show different performances when attaining or approaching an optimal solution. Some have defects, such as lower robustness, premature convergence, and not exploiting the local information. It is necessary to design a competitive algorithm to address the problem. Meanwhile, these efforts seldom use the hybrid idea to create updating mechanisms, leading to limited improvements. Hybridization integrates the advantages of different algorithms to establish a hybrid algorithm while minimizing the substantial disadvantage. It is a common approach to boost the performance of evolutionary algorithms. An effective hybrid algorithm named whale optimization/DE algorithm was developed to estimate the parameters of PV models [36]. A hybrid GA-PSO algorithm was proposed to optimize the size of a house with PV panels, batteries, and wind turbines [37]. A hybrid algorithm using multiverse optimizer, equilibrium optimization, and moth flame optimization methods was implemented to tackle the optimal designs for wave energy converters [38]. A hybrid cooperative co-evolution algorithm was also developed [39]. In general, there are still shortcomings in the research on JAYA, which need to be improved by promoting the identification parameters of PV systems based on the hybrid idea.

In light of these observations, a Hybrid Adaptive JAYA and Differential Evolution (HA-JAYADE) algorithm is developed. This is proposed based on the strengths and weaknesses of JAYA and DE. For JAYA, it is simple, while the search capacity is limited. Meanwhile, the adaptive JAYA position updating mechanism introduces two adaptive coefficients to boost the local and global search balance. The DE algorithm is flexible, and the search capacity depends on mutation strategies [40,41]. Among these mutation strategies of DE, Best/1 is commonly used with powerful exploitation and weak exploitation [42]. The Rank/Best/1 is put forward to enhance the exploration of the algorithm and maintain the exploitation by introducing the ranking information of individuals into the mutation strategy. To enhance the search capacity, the solutions obtained from the proposed HAJAYADE algorithm have been updated through three mutation strategies, the adaptive JAYA position updating mechanism, the Rank/Best/1 mutation strategy of DE algorithm, and the chaotic perturbation. The chaotic perturbation is widely used in JAYA variants and is adopted here to search around the best solution so that the exploitation can be further advanced [3,4]. The search capacity of the proposed HAJAYADE algorithm is greatly enhanced and used to solve the identification of PV parameters. The HAJAYADE algorithm is compared with eight meta-heuristic algorithms, the conventional JAYA and DE algorithms. A statistical test is performed to validate the performance of the proposed HAJAYADE algorithm. Therefore, the paper narrows the knowledge gap by the following contributions:

(1) Two adaptive coefficients are introduced into JAYA to balance the local and global search so that an adaptive JAYA (AJAYA) is developed.
(2) An adaptive DE algorithm is put forward by the novel Rank/Best/1 mutation operator, which considers the quality of the solution in the mutation stage.
(3) A Hybrid Adaptive algorithm based on JAYA and Differential Evolution (HAJAYADE) is developed to identify the parameters of PV systems.
(4) The HAJAYADE is proven to be an efficient and reliable algorithm compared with eight opponents.

The PV models are introduced and the objective functions are defined in Section 2. The JAYA and DE algorithms are introduced and the proposed HAJAYADE algorithm is elaborated in Section 3. The experiments and the analysis of the results are described in Section 4. The conclusions are made in Section 5.

2. PV Modeling Formation

There are several models to describe PV systems. Among these models, SDM and DDM are widely used in electrical engineering. In this section, SDM, DDM, and PV module models, based on SDM and DDM, are briefly introduced, and the objective function of the PV model is formatted.

2.1. Mathematical Model

(1) Single-diode model (SDM)

SDM can precisely depict the static features of the solar cell. The model consists of a resistor to show the leakage current, and a serial resistor to describe the losses of the current. The model is demonstrated in [4].

The current I_L can be computed as follows:

$$I_L = I_{ph} - I_d - I_{sh} \tag{1}$$

$$I_d = I_{sd} \times \left[\exp\left(\frac{q \times (V_L + R_s \times I_L)}{n \times k \times T} \right) - 1 \right] \tag{2}$$

$$I_{sh} = \frac{V_L + R_s \times I_L}{R_{sh}} \tag{3}$$

where I_L is the current of the output, I_{ph} is the current from the solar cell, I_d is the current from the diode, which can be computed by Equation (2), R_s and R_{sh} are two resistors, V_L is the output of the cell voltage, I_{sd} is from the reverse saturation of the diode, n is the feature factor of the diode, both $k = 1.3806503 \times 10^{-23}$ J/K and $q = 1.60217646 \times 10^{-19}$ C are constants. The parameter T is the absolute temperature of the cell. Equations (1)–(3) can be combined, and the output cell can be depicted as follows:

$$I_L = I_{ph} - I_{sd} \times \left[\exp\left(\frac{q \times (V_L + R_s \times I_L)}{n \times k \times T} \right) - 1 \right] - \frac{V_L + R_s \times I_L}{R_{sh}} \tag{4}$$

where five parameters $\left(I_{ph}, I_{sd}, R_s, R_{sh}, n \right)$ are unknown and need to be estimated. These parameters have to be identified so that the performance of the solar cells can be fully measured. The problem can be addressed by optimization algorithms.

(2) Double-diode model (DDM)

Different from the SDM, the DDM has double diodes. The DDM considers the influence of recombination current loss. Ref. [4] shows the circuit, and the output can be computed as follows:

$$\begin{aligned}
I_L = I_{ph} - I_{d1} - I_{d2} - I_{sh} \\
= I_{ph} - I_{sd1} \times \left[\exp\left(\frac{q \times (V_L + R_s \times I_L)}{n_1 \times k \times T} \right) - 1 \right] \\
- I_{sd2} \times \left[\exp\left(\frac{q \times (V_L + R_s \times I_L)}{n_2 \times k \times T} \right) - 1 \right] - \frac{V_L + R_s \times I_L}{R_{sh}}
\end{aligned} \tag{5}$$

where I_{sd1} and I_{sd2} are the diffusion and saturation current, n_1 and n_2 are the diffusion diode and recombination diode ideal factor. There are seven parameters $\left(I_{ph}, I_{sd1}, I_{sd2}, R_s, R_{sh}, n_1, n_2 \right)$ that need to be estimated.

(3) PV module model

According to [4], the PV module model is built on a number of PV cells in parallel or/and in series. The module is based on the single-diode module model (SMM) and double-diode module model (DMM). The output current of the SMM is computed as follows:

$$I_L = \left(I_{ph} - I_{sd} \times \left[\exp\left(\frac{q \times (V_L \times I_L/N_s + R_s \times I_L/N_p)}{n \times k \times T} \right) - 1 \right] - \frac{V_L/N_s + R_s \times I_L/N_p}{R_{sh}} \right) \times N_p \tag{6}$$

where N_p is the number of solar cells in parallel, and N_s is the number of solar cells in series. Hence, five parameters $\left(I_{ph}, I_{sd}, R_s, R_{sh}, n \right)$ need to be estimated.

2.2. Problem Formation

The parameters of the above models need to be estimated so that the performance of PV can be measured. Generally, the issue can be transformed into an optimization problem by minimizing the calculated and experimental data difference. The error can be defined by the following equations, in which Equations (7)–(9) are for SDM, DDM, and SMM, and x is the set of unknown parameters to be evaluated.

$$\begin{cases} F(V_L, I_L, x) = I_{ph} - I_{sd} \times \left[\exp\left(\frac{q \times (V_L + R_s \times I_L)}{n \times k \times T} \right) - 1 \right] - \frac{V_L + R_s \times I_L}{R_{sh}} - I_L \\ x = \left\{ I_{ph}, I_{sd}, R_s, R_{sh}, n \right\} \end{cases} \tag{7}$$

$$\begin{cases} F(V_L, I_L, x) = I_{ph} - I_{sd1} \times \left[\exp\left(\frac{q \times (V_L + R_s \times I_L)}{n_1 \times k \times T} \right) - 1 \right] - \\ I_{sd2} \times \left[\exp\left(\frac{q \times (V_L + R_s \times I_L)}{n_2 \times k \times T} \right) - 1 \right] - \frac{V_L + R_s \times I_L}{R_{sh}} - I_L \\ x = \left\{ I_{ph}, I_{sd1}, I_{sd2}, R_s, R_{sh}, n_1, n_2 \right\} \end{cases} \tag{8}$$

$$\begin{cases} F(V_L, I_L, x) = (I_{ph} - I_{sd} \times \left[\exp\left(\frac{q \times \left(\frac{V_L \times I_L}{N_s} + R_s \times \frac{I_L}{N_p} \right)}{n \times k \times T} \right) - 1 \right] \\ - \frac{V_L/N_s + R_s \times I_L/N_p}{R_{sh}}) \times N_p - I_L \\ x = \left\{ I_{ph}, I_{sd}, R_s, R_{sh}, n \right\} \end{cases} \tag{9}$$

In previous studies, the root mean square error (RMSE) is employed as the objective function to measure the difference between simulated and experimental data [4]. If there are measurement errors, we can perform multiple measurements, and the mean result can be obtained and used as the experimental data. The measurement errors can be reduced. Minimizing the objective function is to search for the optimal solution x in the specific range.

$$\text{RMSE}(x) = \sqrt{\frac{1}{N} \sum_{k=1}^{N} f_k(V_L, I_L, x)^2} \tag{10}$$

where N is the number of experimental data, and x is the solution needed to be optimized.

3. Proposed HAYAJADE Algorithm Based on JAYA Algorithm and DE Algorithm

Both JAYA and DE are population-based evolutionary algorithms. In this section, two algorithms are briefly presented. Initialization is the first step for both algorithms. For a minimization problem, let $f(x)$ be the objective function with D-dimension $(j = 1, 2, \ldots, D)$, $x_{i,j}$ is the value of jth dimension for ith candidate solution and $x_i = \left(x_{i,1}, x_{i,2}, \ldots, x_{i,j}, \ldots, x_{i,D} \right)$ is the ith candidate solution's position. The range of $x_{i,j}$ is between L_j and U_j. The initial solution $x_{i,j}$ can be generated as follows:

$$x_{i,j} = L_j + (U_j - L_j) \times rand_{i,j}, j = 1, 2, \ldots, D \tag{11}$$

where $rand_{i,j}$ is a random number between 0 and 1, U_j and L_j are upper and lower boundaries of the jth dimension.

3.1. JAYA Algorithm

JAYA is a novel evolutionary algorithm compared with the DE algorithm. It was developed by Rao [21]. The algorithm can be employed to solve constrained and unconstrained problems. It is based on the idea that the solution should approach the best solution and avoid the worst solution when optimizing a specific problem. Unlike the conventional population-based evolutionary algorithms, JAYA is parameter-free, as it only has a common parameter, i.e., population size.

The best solution $x_{best} = \{x_{best,1}, x_{best,2}, \ldots, x_{best,D}\}$ has the minimization fitness value, while $x_{worst} = \{x_{worst,1}, x_{worst,2}, \ldots, x_{worst,D}\}$ has the maximization fitness value among the current solutions. Then, $x_{i,j}$ is updated by the following equation:

$$x'_{i,j} = x_{i,j} + rand_1 \times \left(x_{best,j} - \left|x_{i,j}\right|\right) - rand_2 \times \left(x_{worst,j} - \left|x_{i,j}\right|\right) \tag{12}$$

where $rand_1$ and $rand_2$ are two random numbers between 0 and 1, $x_{worst,j}$ and $x_{best,j}$ are values of the jth dimension for the worst and best solutions, $\left|x_{i,j}\right|$ is the absolute value of the jth dimension for the ith solution, $x'_{i,j}$ and $x_{i,j}$ are the updated and the original values of the jth dimension for the ith solution. The term $x_{best,j} - \left|x_{i,j}\right|$ is used to denote the tendency towards the optimal solution, while the term $x_{worst,j} - \left|x_{i,j}\right|$ is applied to represent the tendency to avoid the worst solution.

If the generated individual x'_i is superior to the original individual x_i, the new individual x'_i will take the place of the original one. Otherwise, the original one is kept. The process can be mathematically presented as follows:

$$x_i = \begin{cases} x'_i, \ if \ f\left(x'_i\right) < f(x_i) \\ x_i, \ otherwise \end{cases} \tag{13}$$

3.2. DE Algorithm

The DE algorithm is also a very simple and efficient population-based evolutionary algorithm that is older than the JAYA algorithm [40]. However, it is one of the most popular evolutionary algorithms due to its structure, real number encoding, and effectiveness [43]. The steps in the DE algorithm involve mutation, crossover, and selection.

There are many mutation operators in the DE algorithm. The mutation operator Best/1 is commonly used as follows:

$$v_i = x_{best} + F \times (x_{r_1} - x_{r_2}) \tag{14}$$

where r_1 and r_2 are randomly generated between 1 and the value of population size ($r_1 \neq r_2 \neq i$), x_{best} is the optimal solution found so far, v_i is the mutant vector, and F is the scalar factor in the range of 0 and 1. The term $x_{r_1} - x_{r_2}$ is the difference vector.

The following step is crossover. It is used to exchange the information between the individual $x_i = \{x_{i,1}, x_{i,2}, \ldots, x_{i,j}, \ldots, x_{i,D}\}$ and the mutant vector $v_i = \{v_{i,1}, v_{i,2}, \ldots, v_{i,j}, \ldots, v_{i,D}\}$. The most commonly used crossover operator is defined as follows:

$$u_{i,j} = \begin{cases} v_{i,j} \ if \ rand \leq CR \ or \ j = J_{rand} \\ x_{i,j} \ otherwise \end{cases} \tag{15}$$

where $rand$ is a random number between 0 and 1, CR is the crossover constant, which can be defined by the user, J_{rand} is the integer in the range of 1 and D to make use of the fact that u_i at least has a component from v_i.

The last step is the same as the JAYA algorithm, which is the greedy selection. If the u_i is superior to the x_i, the x_i is replaced by u_i. Otherwise, u_i is abandoned and x_i is kept.

$$x_i = \begin{cases} u_i, \ if \ f(u_i) < f(x_i) \\ \quad x_i, \ otherwise \end{cases} \tag{16}$$

3.3. Hybrid Adaptive JAYA and DE (HAJAYADE)

For population-based meta-heuristic algorithms, it is necessary to realize a balance between exploitation and exploration. The exploration is to search as broadly as possible to identify the potential region, while the exploitation is to search around the potential region. In the early stage of evolution, the exploration is encouraged to scatter throughout the whole search space. At the later stage of evolution, exploitation is more necessary to approach the optimal solution.

For the JAYA algorithm, the main feature is its parameter-free nature, which makes it attractive [21]. The algorithm uses information from the best and worst solutions to search around the space. The single search strategy used in JAYA is to approach the best solution and avoid the worst solution. However, the single strategy may deteriorate the exploitation and exploration capabilities of the algorithm, which may lead to the local optimum.

In recent years, many improvements have been implemented to improve the performance of JAYA [3,4,32,34,35]. However, these efforts seldom use the hybrid idea to design updating mechanisms, leading to limited improvements as the hybrid is a common approach to boost the performance for most evolutionary algorithms [44]. If the feature of DE is reasonably integrated into the framework of JAYA, the exploitation can be significantly boosted as the capacity is superior for the Best/1 mutation strategy. Meanwhile, an adaptive approach is used to enhance the exploration, and balance the exploitation and exploration in the proposed algorithm. Lastly, a chaotic method is applied to boost the exploitation further [18]. Based on the observations, we developed a Hybrid Adaptive JAYA and DE algorithm (HAJAYADE). The algorithm consists of adaptive JAYA (AJAYA), adaptive DE, and adaptive chaotic perturbation.

3.3.1. Adaptive JAYA (AJAJA)

The conventional JAYA assigns the same priority to the best and the worst solutions. The best solution can be given more priority, while the worse solution can be assigned less priority so that the search direction can approach the potential region more quickly. Hence, two adaptive coefficients are introduced as follows:

$$w_1 = \begin{cases} 1 \ f(x_{best}) = 0 \\ \dfrac{Mean(f(x))}{f(x_{best})} \ f(x_{best}) \neq 0 \end{cases} \tag{17}$$

$$w_2 = \begin{cases} 1 \ f(x_{worst}) = 0 \\ \dfrac{Mean(f(x))}{f(x_{worst})} \ f(x_{worst}) \neq 0 \end{cases} \tag{18}$$

where x_{best} and x_{worst} are the best and worst solutions found so far, $f(x_{best})$ and $f(x_{worst})$ are their fitness values, and $Mean(f(x))$ is the mean value of these fitness values. For a minimization problem, w_1 is greater than 1 while w_2 is less than 1. As the iteration increases, they approach 1, as shown in Figure 1.

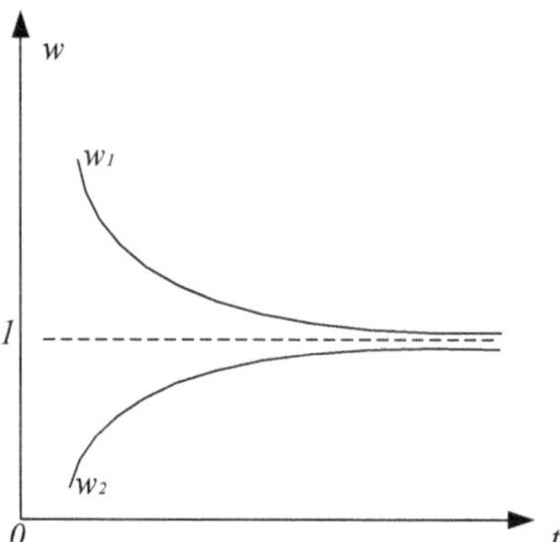

Figure 1. Trend of the two coefficients w_1 and w_2.

Then, the two adaptive coefficients are introduced into Equation (19) as follows:

$$x'_{i,j} = x_{i,j} + w_1 \times rand_1 \times \left(x_{best,j} - |x_{i,j}|\right) - w_2 \times rand_2 \times \left(x_{worst,j} - |x_{i,j}|\right) \tag{19}$$

At the beginning of the iteration, the differences among $f(x_{best})$, $f(x_{worst})$, and $Mean(f(x))$ are significant. w_1 is larger while w_2 is smaller. The search direction is directly towards the potential region. At the later stage of the iteration, the difference among the three values is slight. w_1 and w_2 are very close to 1. The x_{best} and x_{worst} are also close to each other. The local search can be implemented. Therefore, we introduce two coefficients w_1 and w_2 to balance exploration and exploitation. Their values depend on the fitness values of solutions and do not need to introduce any extra parameters.

3.3.2. Adaptive DE Algorithm

The performance of the DE algorithm mainly relies on the mutation operator. For Best/1, the exploitation is powerful while the exploration is weak. Searching around the best solution may deteriorate the exploration. To maintain the exploitation and improve the exploration, we propose the Rank/Best/1 mutation operator in Equation (20).

$$v_i = x_{best} + rand \times \left(x_{rankr_1} - x_{r_2}\right) \tag{20}$$

where $rankr_1$ is the integer in the range of 1 and population size, $rand$ is a random number in the range of 0 and 1 to take the place of the scalar factor F so that the lesser parameter is introduced. We select $rankr_1$ depending on the fitness value of $f(x_{rankr_1})$. Firstly, we sort solutions based on their fitness values in ascending order. Then, we assign the ranking values $rank_i$ to each solution. The better the solution, the smaller the $rank_i$ [45]. The selection probability p_i can be computed as follows:

$$rank_i = NP - i \tag{21}$$

$$p_i = \frac{rank_i}{NP} \tag{22}$$

where i is the rank index, $rank_i$ is the rank value, and p_i is the selection probability. The better the solution, the more the p_i.

For the conventional Best/1, r_1 and r_2 are randomly generated. The difference vector $x_{r_1} - x_{r_2}$ does not change significantly, especially at the early stage. The search range and exploration are limited. Different from Best/1, the $rankr_1$ is generated and selected depending on its corresponding p_{rankr_1}. We randomly generate a random number $rand$ in the range of 0 and 1. If $p_{rankr_1} > rand$, we accept the $rankr_1$. Otherwise, we have to regenerate the $rankr_1$. As the unique generated mechanism is used, the difference vector

$x_{rankr_1} - x_{r_2}$ changes significantly, especially at the early stage. The search range is fully extended, and the exploration is boosted. At the latter stage, the difference in the population is much smaller, so the difference vector $x_{rankr_1} - x_{r_2}$ changes slightly. The exploitation is realized. To avoid the local optimum, r_2 is randomly generated in the range of 1 and NP without using the unique approach.

3.3.3. Adaptive Chaotic Method

Lastly, the adaptive chaotic method is applied to improve the exploitation of the algorithm further. The chaotic approach has been proven valuable and successful in many evolutionary algorithms [3,4]. The method is used to explore the best solution, and a logistic map is a useful approach in many experiments of JAYA. Therefore, it is also adopted as follows:

$$z_k = \begin{cases} rand & k = 1 \\ 4 \times z_{k-1} \times (2 \times z_{k-1} - 1) & k > 1 \end{cases} \tag{23}$$

where k is the index of iteration. When $k = 1$, z_k is randomly generated between 0 and 1. z_k is used as a perturbation to the best solution.

$$x_j^* = \begin{cases} x_{best,j} & otherwise \\ x_{best,j} + rand \times (2 \times z_k - 1) & if\ rand < 1 - FES/FES_{max} \end{cases} \tag{24}$$

where $x_{best,j}$ is the value of the jth dimension for x_{best}, z_k is the value of kth chaotic, FES is the number of function evaluation, FES_{max} is the maximal function evaluation. At the early stage, the FES is small and the condition $rand < 1 - FES/FES_{max}$ is met more frequently; more chaotic perturbation is used to generate solutions around the x_{best}. At the later stage, with the increasing of FES, it is difficult to satisfy the condition $rand < 1 - FES/FES_{max}$. x_{best} is very close to the optimal solution, and more perturbation is unnecessary. If the solution x^* is superior to the worst solution, x^* will take the place of the solution. Otherwise, the solution x^* is discarded.

3.3.4. Framework of HAJAYADE

The proposed HAJAYADE algorithm is mainly based on JAYA and DE. Therefore, we use two populations for the two algorithms. By the greedy selection, the two populations form a single population. The flowchart of HAJAYADE is presented in Figure 2, and the pseudo-code of HAJAYADE is shown as follows (Algorithm 1).

3.3.5. Complexity of the Proposed HAJAYADE Algorithm

The complexity of the HAYAYADE is discussed as follows. Let the population size be NP and the dimension of the problem be D. Identifying the best and worst solutions, computing the mean fitness value demands $O(NP)$. Updating the position of population needs $O(NP \times D)$. Ranking solutions in the population requires $O(N \times Plog(NP))$. The mutant process requires $O(NP)$. The crossover operator demands $O(NP \times D)$. The greedy selection for the hybrid algorithm requires $O(NP)$. The chaotic operator requires $O(D)$. Therefore, the total complexity of the proposed HAJAYADE algorithm needs $O(NP + NP \times D + NP \times log(NP) + NP + NP \times D + D)$. As the $log(NP)$ is often smaller than D, the complexity of the proposed HAJAYADE algorithm is $O(NP \times D)$.

Algorithm 1: HAJAYADE

Input:	The population size : NP; the maximal function evaluation (FES_{max}); crossover constant CR
Output:	The optimal solution

1   Generate initial population p by Equation (11)
2   Evaluate the fitness value of population p
3   $FES = NP$;
4   While ($FES < FES_{max}$)
5   Identify the best solution x_{best} and its corresponding fitness value $f(x_{best})$
6   Identify the worst solution x_{worst} and its corresponding fitness value $f(x_{worst})$
7   Calculate the adaptive parameters w_1 and w_2 by Equations (17) and (18)
8   for $i = 1 : NP$
9   Update the population p by Equation (19) and generate the trial vector x'_i
10   end
11   Compute the selection probability p_i according to Equation (22)
12   for $i = 1 : NP$
13   Generate a *rand* in the range of 0 and 1
14   Randomly select an integer $rankr_1$ in the range of 1 and NP
15   While ($rand > p(rankr_1)||i == rankr_1$)
16   Randomly select an integer rankr1 in the range of 1 and NP
17   end
18   Randomly select an integer r_2 in the range of 1 and NP
19   While ($i == r_2||rankr_1 == r_2$)
20   Randomly select an integer r_2 in the range of 1 and NP
21   end
22   Generate the mutant vector u_i by Equation (20)
23   end
24   for $i = 1 : NP$
25   Generate the trial vector v_i by Equation (15)
26   end
27   for $i = 1 : NP$
28   Evaluate the fitness value of x'_i and v_i respectively
29   if $\left(f\left(x'_i\right) < f(x_i)\right)$
30      $x_i = x'_i;\ f(x_i) = f\left(x'_i\right)$;
31   end
32   if $(f(v_i) < f(x_i))$

---

33      $x_i = v_i;\ f(x_i) = f(v_i)$;
34   end
35     $FES = FES + 2$;
36   end
37   Identify the best solution x_{best} and the worst solution x_{worst}
38   Use the chaotic perturbation to generate the solution x^* by Equation (24)
39   if $(f(x^*) < f(x_{worst}))$
40     $x_{worst} = x^*;\ f(x^*) = f(x_{worst})$;
41   end
42    $FES = FES + 1$;
43   end
44   Output the optimal solution x_{best} and its corresponding fitness $f(x_{best})$.

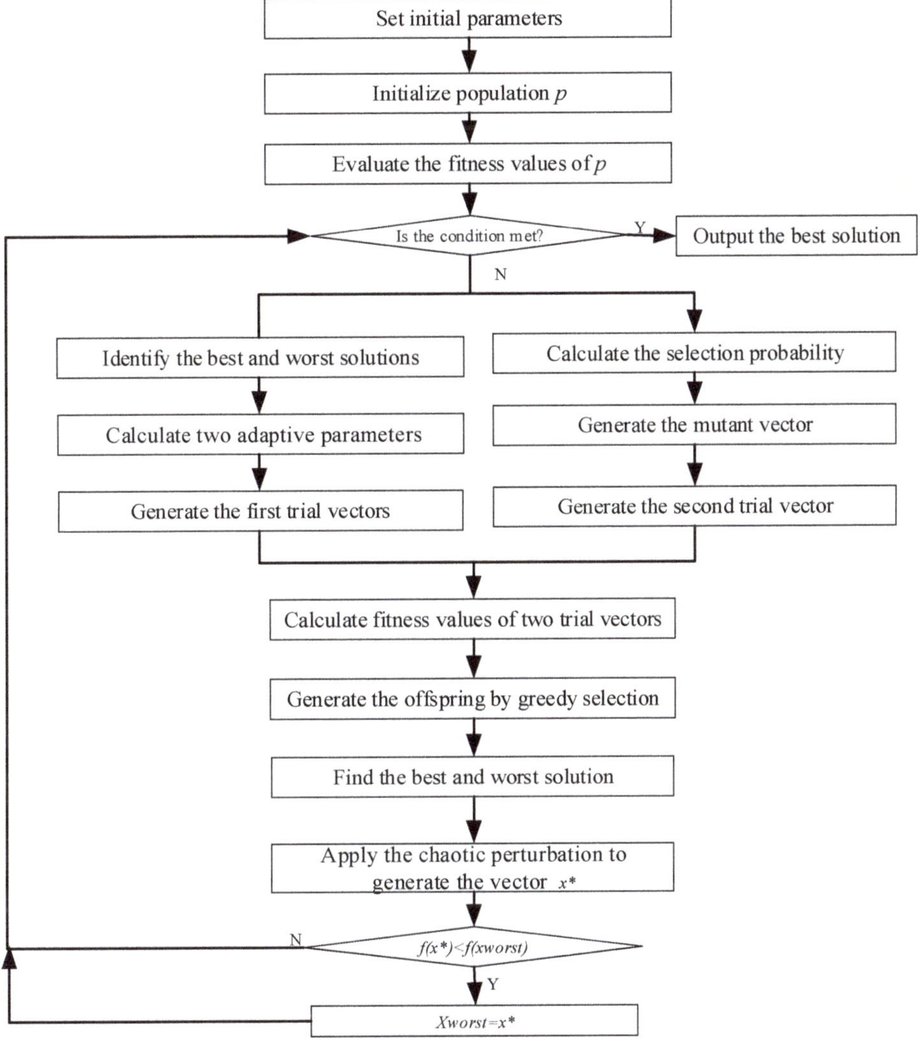

Figure 2. Flowchart of HAJAYADE.

4. Experimental Results and Analysis

The performance of the proposed HAJAYADE algorithm is used to estimate the parameters of PV models, including the SDM, DDM, and SMM. The current–voltage data are from reference [46]. They are widely employed to test diverse techniques developed to estimate the parameters of PV models. The data of SDM contain 26 groups of current and voltage under 1000 W/m² at 33 °C, which is the RTC France Si cell. The DDM is measured by 57 silicon. The SMM includes the Photowatt-PWP201 PV model, STM6-40/36 PV model, STP6-120/36 PV model. The temperatures at the three PV models are 4 °C, 51 °C, and 55 °C [32]. For the five problems, the range of parameters is listed in Table 1.

Table 1. Ranges of parameters.

Parameter	SDM/DDM		Photowatt-PWP201		STM6-40/36		STP6-120/36	
	Upper	Lower	Upper	Lower	Upper	Lower	Upper	Lower
$I_{ph}(A)$	1	0	2	0	2	0	8	0
$I_{sd}, I_{sd1}, I_{sd2}(\mu A)$	1	0	50	0	50	0	50	0
n, n_1, n_2	2	1	50	1	60	1	50	1
$R_s(\Omega)$	0.5	0	2	0	0.36	0	0.36	0
$R_p(\Omega)$	100	0	2000	0	1000	0	1500	0

To test the performance of the proposed HAJAYADE algorithm, some of the latest algorithms and their variants are used as its opponents, including GWO [47], CMAES [48], TLABC [2], TAPSO [49], MLBSA [6], GOTLBO [5], PGJAYA [4], and IJAYA [3]. GWO is a novel swarm intelligent algorithm proposed by Mirjalili et al. [47]. The self-adaptation of the mutation distribution is adopted in the CMAES algorithm to boost the local and global search [48]. TLABC is a hybrid algorithm based on TLBO and ABC, with the purpose of enhancing the reliability and accuracy of meta-heuristic algorithms [2]. In TAPSO, three archives are used to design an efficient learning model and select proper exemplars [49]. In MLBSA, a fraction of individuals learn from the elite solution, while the remaining individuals learn from the historical population and current population to balance the exploration and exploitation [6]. In GOTLBO, a generalized opposition-based learning technique is integrated into basic TLBO to enhance the convergence [5]. In the PGJAYA algorithm, each individual can adaptively select mutation strategies depending on its selection probability [4]. In IJAYA, an adaptive coefficient and an experience-based mutation operator are introduced to boost the diversity of the population and enhance the exploration [3].

The main parameters of the above nine algorithms are listed in Table 2. These parameters are mainly based on their original references so that the best performances of these algorithms can be guaranteed. The maximal function evaluations are set to 50,000. Each algorithm runs thirty times independently, and the statistical results are obtained. These algorithms run on a PC with a memory of 8 GB, primary frequency of 3.4 GHz, Win 10 OS, and Matlab R2020a.

Table 2. Parameter values of ten algorithms.

Algorithm	Parameters
GWO	$\vec{a}$ linearly decreases from 2 to 0; $NP = 20$
CMAES	$\sigma = 0.25, NP = 20$
TLABC	$limit = 200, F = rand(0,1); NP = 50$
TAPSO	$w = 0.7298, p_c = 0.5, p_m = 0.02, NP = 20$
MLBSA	$NP = 50$
GOTLBO	$NP = 50, J_r = 0.3$
PGJAYA	$NP = 20$
IJAYA	$NP = 20$
HAJAYADE	$NP = 20; C_r = 0.5$

4.1. Results and Analysis

(1)　Results of SDM

For the SDM, i.e., the RTC France Si cell, the statistical results involving the maximal, mean, minimal, and the standard deviation values of RMSE from the above nine algorithms, i.e., GWO, CMAES, TLABC, TAPSO, MLBSA, GOTLBO, PGJAYA, IJAYA, and HAJAYADE, are listed in Table 3. In terms of the minimal value, most algorithms except GWO, CMAES, and IJAYA are the best. Only three algorithms, i.e., MLBSA, PGJAYA, and HAJAYADE, can obtain the best value in terms of the mean value. However, only the proposed HAJAYADE algorithm has the lowest maximal value. Therefore, the proposed HAYAJADE algorithm is the best one for the SDM. The convergence curves of the nine algorithms are plotted in Figure 3. It can be noticed that the convergence speed of GWO and CMAES is lower compared with the remaining algorithms. When the convergence curves are magnified, it can be observed that the convergence speed of these algorithms is also different, in which the proposed HAJAYADE algorithm is the fastest. The best solutions obtained from 30 runs for each algorithm are listed in Table 4. To validate the quality of the results obtained from the proposed HAJAYADE algorithm, the best-estimated values are employed to establish the relationship between the current and voltage in Figure 4. The experimental data are highly consistent with the calculated data. The figure further validates the effectiveness of the proposed HAJAYADE algorithm.

Table 3. Statistical results from nine algorithms for the SDM problem.

Algorithm	Min	Mean	Max	Std
CMAES	2.4203×10^{-3}	4.501×10^{-3}	9.7738×10^{-3}	2.0983×10^{-3}
GWO	1.0023×10^{-3}	8.1335×10^{-3}	4.4315×10^{-2}	1.3204×10^{-2}
TLABC	$\mathbf{9.8602 \times 10^{-4}}$	9.9218×10^{-4}	1.0317×10^{-3}	1.1679×10^{-5}
TAPSO	$\mathbf{9.8602 \times 10^{-4}}$	1.0267×10^{-3}	2.2063×10^{-3}	2.228×10^{-4}
MLBSA	$\mathbf{9.8602 \times 10^{-4}}$	$\mathbf{9.8602 \times 10^{-4}}$	9.8604×10^{-4}	2.7152×10^{-9}
GOTLBO	$\mathbf{9.8602 \times 10^{-4}}$	1.01×10^{-3}	1.3865×10^{-3}	9.01×10^{-5}
PGJAYA	$\mathbf{9.8602 \times 10^{-4}}$	$\mathbf{9.8602 \times 10^{-4}}$	9.8607×10^{-4}	7.8692×10^{-9}
IJAYA	9.8625×10^{-4}	$\mathbf{9.8924 \times 10^{-4}}$	9.9869×10^{-4}	2.8943×10^{-6}
HAJAYADE	$\mathbf{9.8602 \times 10^{-4}}$	$\mathbf{9.8602 \times 10^{-4}}$	$\mathbf{9.8602 \times 10^{-4}}$	0

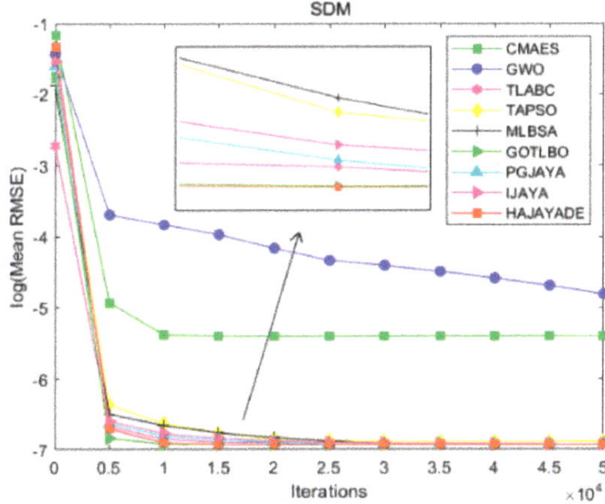

Figure 3. Convergence curve of nine algorithms for the SDM.

Table 4. Optimal solutions obtained from nine algorithms for SDM.

Algorithm	I_{ph}	I_{sd}	R_s	R_{sh}	n	RMSE
CMAES	0.76076	0.9522	0.031301	95.9066	1.5988	2.4203×10^{-3}
GWO	0.76093	0.32791	0.03631	51.4854	1.4828	1.0023×10^{-3}
TLABC	0.76078	0.32302	0.036377	53.7185	1.4812	$\mathbf{9.8602 \times 10^{-4}}$
TAPSO	0.76078	0.32302	0.036377	53.7185	1.4812	$\mathbf{9.8602 \times 10^{-4}}$
MLBSA	0.76078	0.32302	0.036377	53.7185	1.4812	$\mathbf{9.8602 \times 10^{-4}}$
GOTLBO	0.76078	0.32302	0.036377	53.7185	1.4812	$\mathbf{9.8602 \times 10^{-4}}$
PGJAYA	0.76078	0.32302	0.036377	53.7186	1.4812	$\mathbf{9.8602 \times 10^{-4}}$
IJAYA	0.76074	0.32302	0.036382	54.0089	1.4811	9.8625×10^{-4}
HAJAYADE	0.76078	0.32302	0.036377	53.7185	1.4812	$\mathbf{9.8602 \times 10^{-4}}$

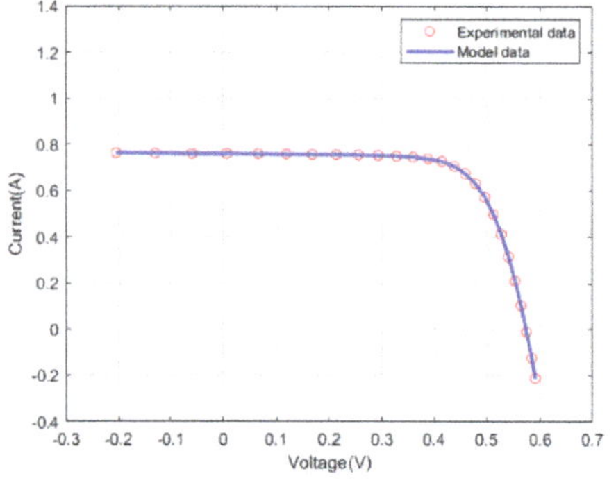
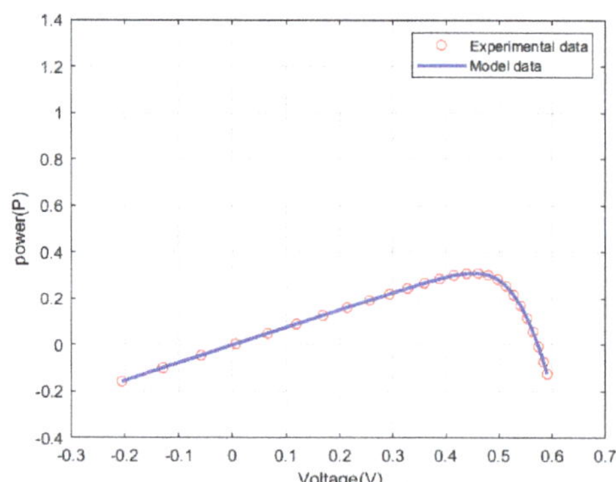

Figure 4. I-V and P-V characteristic curves of SDM.

(2)   Results on the DDM

For the DDM, seven parameters need to be optimized, and the dimension is more than the SDM. The results from the above nine algorithms are revealed in Table 5, in which HAJAYADE has attained the best results in terms of the minimal (9.8294×10^{-4}), mean (9.8641×10^{-4}), and maximal value (9.96×10^{-4}). The difference among these statistical results of the proposed HAJAYADE algorithm is tiny, indicating that the proposed HAYA-JADE algorithm is robust. The result of PGJAYA is second only to the proposed HAJAYADE algorithm, ranking second. GWO has obtained the worst result as the algorithm only uses the top three wolves to guide the search direction. The exploration is limited, and the algorithm is easily trapped into the local optimum. The standard deviation of the algorithm is the largest, which indicates that GWO is less robust. The reason behind the superior performance is that the proposed HAJAYADE algorithm uses the hybrid mechanism, which boosts exploration and exploitation. The excellent performance can also be measured by convergence curves, in which the log (mean RMSE) is used as the value of the y-axis so that the difference among the nine algorithms is apparent. The convergence speed of the proposed HAJAYADE algorithm is much faster according to Figure 5. The best results attained from these algorithms are listed in Table 6, and the result of the proposed HAJAYADE algorithm is used to construct the model. The experimental and calculated data from the proposed HAJAYADE algorithm are plotted in Figure 6. It is evident that the two groups' data are in superior accordance.

Table 5. Statistical results from nine algorithms for the DDM.

Algorithm	Min	Mean	Max	Std
CMAES	9.9015×10^{-4}	3.2883×10^{-3}	6.9683×10^{-3}	1.8499×10^{-3}
GWO	1.1429×10^{-3}	9.6965×10^{-3}	3.8045×10^{-2}	1.2305×10^{-2}
TLABC	9.8407×10^{-4}	1.0616×10^{-3}	1.4496×10^{-3}	1.2359×10^{-4}
TAPSO	9.8269×10^{-4}	1.2853×10^{-3}	2.3508×10^{-3}	4.1093×10^{-4}
MLBSA	$\mathbf{9.8285 \times 10^{-4}}$	$\mathbf{9.856 \times 10^{-4}}$	$\mathbf{9.8778 \times 10^{-4}}$	$\mathbf{9.3682 \times 10^{-7}}$
GOTLBO	9.8299×10^{-4}	1.0303×10^{-3}	1.4242×10^{-3}	1.0111×10^{-4}
PGJAYA	9.8298×10^{-4}	9.8624×10^{-4}	9.9773×10^{-4}	2.9021×10^{-6}
IJAYA	9.8631×10^{-4}	1.0107×10^{-3}	1.182×10^{-3}	4.704×10^{-5}
HAJAYADE	9.8294×10^{-4}	9.8641×10^{-4}	9.96×10^{-4}	2.8534×10^{-6}

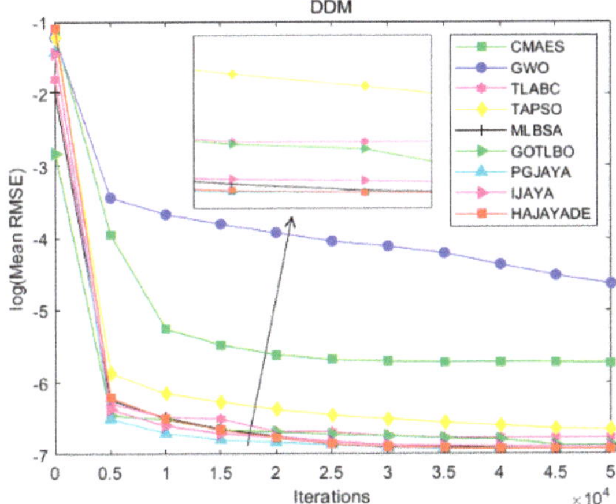

Figure 5. Convergence curve of nine algorithms for the DDM.

Table 6. Optimal solutions obtained from nine algorithms for DDM.

Algorithm	I_{ph}	I_{sd1}	R_s	R_{sh}	n_1	I_{sd2}	n_2	RMSE
CMAES	0.76062	0.26941	0.036502	56.3321	1.4674	0.1659	1.7803	9.9015×10^{-4}
GWO	0.76106	0.89499	0.036962	48.1939	1.3866	0.6471	1.729	1.1429×10^{-3}
TLABC	0.76079	0.38772	0.036647	54.6552	1.8584	0.232	1.4546	9.8407×10^{-4}
TAPSO	0.76079	0.67827	0.036741	54.9983	1.9987	0.23154	1.4529	9.8269×10^{-4}
MLBSA	0.76078	0.5284	0.036623	54.9649	1.9978	0.25212	1.4602	$\mathbf{9.8285 \times 10^{-4}}$
GOTLBO	0.76078	0.25815	0.036604	54.8163	1.4622	0.48047	1.9987	9.8299×10^{-4}
PGJAYA	0.76078	0.25828	0.036598	54.8875	1.4622	0.48583	1.461	9.8298×10^{-4}
IJAYA	0.76082	0.29722	0.036558	54.0126	1.8502	0.25073	1.461	9.8631×10^{-4}
HAJAYADE	0.76078	0.49872	0.036602	54.9059	1.9992	0.25657	1.4617	9.8294×10^{-4}

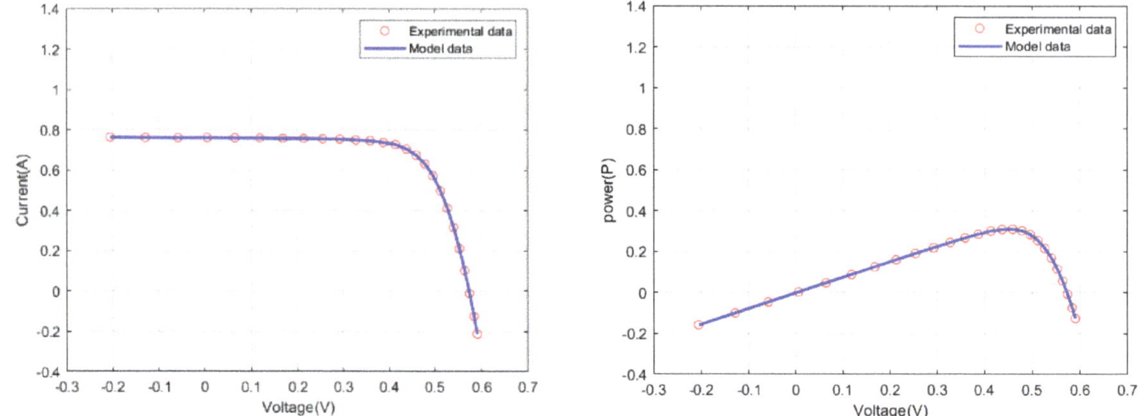

Figure 6. I-V and P-V characteristic curves of DDM.

(3)   Results on PV models

There are three PV models, the Photowatt-PWP201, the STM6-40/36, and the STP6-120/36. It is necessary to optimize five parameters. The above nine algorithms are used to identify these five parameters. The statistical results of the three groups are listed in Table 7. GWO and CMAES have attained inferior results for the three groups. Except for the two algorithms, TAPSO has obtained worse results for both Photowatt-PWP201 (2.5928×10^{-3}) and STP6-120/36 (6.2436×10^{-1}), and GOTLBO is inferior for STM6-40/36 in terms of the mean value (3.4321×10^{-3}). On the contrary, regarding the three JAYA variants, the performances of PGJAYA, IJAYA, and HAJAYADE are better. In more detail, PGJAYA and HAJAYADE have attained the best results for Photowatt-PWP201. The performances of HAJAYADE are more robust compared with PGJAYA and IJAYA. Thus, it is the best one among the nine algorithms.

The solutions attained from these algorithms are presented in Table 8. The calculated data and experimental data are visually illustrated in Figure 7. It can be further observed that the difference between the two serial data is tiny, indicating that the solutions obtained from the proposed HAJAYADE algorithm are accurate. In addition, the convergence curves of the nine algorithms for the three PV models are presented in Figure 8. It can be observed that the remaining algorithms are similar in terms of convergence speed for Photowatt-PWP201, except for GWO and CMAES. The convergence rate of the nine algorithms is significantly different for STM6-40/36 and STP6-120/36, in which the proposed HAJAYADE algorithm is the fastest.

Table 7. Statistical results from nine algorithms for three PV models.

Model	Algorithm	Min	Mean	Max	Std
Photowatt-PWP201	CMAES	4.9842×10^{-3}	5.957×10^{-2}	2.5934×10^{-1}	7.5656×10^{-2}
	GWO	2.6039×10^{-3}	3.9456×10^{-2}	2.7431×10^{-1}	9.368×10^{-2}
	TLABC	$\mathbf{2.4251 \times 10^{-3}}$	2.4266×10^{-3}	2.4496×10^{-3}	5.7303×10^{-6}
	TAPSO	$\mathbf{2.4251 \times 10^{-3}}$	2.5928×10^{-3}	4.1483×10^{-3}	3.8109×10^{-4}
	MLBSA	$\mathbf{2.4251 \times 10^{-3}}$	$\mathbf{2.4251 \times 10^{-3}}$	$\mathbf{2.4251 \times 10^{-3}}$	4.9687×10^{-10}
	GOTLBO	$\mathbf{2.4251 \times 10^{-3}}$	2.427×10^{-3}	2.4621×10^{-3}	7.5384×10^{-6}
	PGJAYA	$\mathbf{2.4251 \times 10^{-3}}$	$\mathbf{2.4251 \times 10^{-3}}$	2.426×10^{-3}	1.7877×10^{-7}
	IJAYA	$\mathbf{2.4251 \times 10^{-3}}$	2.427×10^{-3}	2.4385×10^{-3}	2.8147×10^{-6}
	HAJAYADE	$\mathbf{2.4251 \times 10^{-3}}$	$\mathbf{2.4251 \times 10^{-3}}$	$\mathbf{2.4251 \times 10^{-3}}$	$\mathbf{3.2215 \times 10^{-15}}$
STM6-40/36	CMAES	1.9343×10^{-3}	8.8897×10^{-2}	1.613×10^{-1}	5.1349×10^{-2}
	GWO	4.8387×10^{-3}	8.6059×10^{-3}	1.7596×10^{-2}	3.3055×10^{-3}
	TLABC	$\mathbf{1.7298 \times 10^{-3}}$	1.9398×10^{-3}	2.6262×10^{-3}	2.2746×10^{-4}
	TAPSO	$\mathbf{1.7298 \times 10^{-3}}$	2.3263×10^{-3}	1.0566×10^{-2}	1.5873×10^{-3}
	MLBSA	$\mathbf{1.7298 \times 10^{-3}}$	1.8×10^{-3}	3.7038×10^{-3}	3.5966×10^{-4}
	GOTLBO	$\mathbf{1.7298 \times 10^{-3}}$	3.4321×10^{-3}	2.1722×10^{-2}	3.5876×10^{-3}
	PGJAYA	$\mathbf{1.7298 \times 10^{-3}}$	1.7302×10^{-3}	1.7376×10^{-3}	1.4416×10^{-6}
	IJAYA	1.7345×10^{-3}	1.8305×10^{-3}	2.221×10^{-3}	1.2044×10^{-4}
	HAJAYADE	$\mathbf{1.7298 \times 10^{-3}}$	$\mathbf{1.7298 \times 10^{-3}}$	$\mathbf{1.7298 \times 10^{-3}}$	$\mathbf{3.6569 \times 10^{-16}}$
STP6-120/36	CMAES	1.6612×10^{-2}	5.2725×10^{-1}	1.4131	6.0591×10^{-1}
	GWO	1.733×10^{-2}	2.2768×10^{-1}	1.4131	4.1976×10^{-1}
	TLABC	1.6601×10^{-2}	1.6775×10^{-2}	1.8269×10^{-2}	3.3454×10^{-4}
	TAPSO	5.7763×10^{-2}	6.2436×10^{-1}	1.299	3.7049×10^{-1}
	MLBSA	1.6601×10^{-2}	1.6627×10^{-2}	1.6786×10^{-2}	4.1209×10^{-5}
	GOTLBO	1.6605×10^{-2}	2.2226×10^{-2}	5.9712×10^{-2}	9.5158×10^{-3}
	PGJAYA	1.6601×10^{-2}	1.6609×10^{-2}	1.6722×10^{-2}	2.7355×10^{-5}
	IJAYA	1.6733×10^{-2}	1.6813×10^{-2}	1.691×10^{-2}	4.1722×10^{-5}
	HAJAYADE	$\mathbf{1.6601 \times 10^{-2}}$	$\mathbf{1.6601 \times 10^{-2}}$	$\mathbf{1.6606 \times 10^{-2}}$	$\mathbf{9.2421 \times 10^{-7}}$

Table 8. Optimal solutions attained from nine algorithms for three PV models.

Model	Algorithm	I_{ph}	I_{sd}	R_s	R_{sh}	n	RMSE
Photowatt-PWP201	CMAES	1.0467	0.19815	1.2319	316.3977	46.6264	4.9842×10^{-3}
	GWO	1.0287	0.48801	1.1664	1544.616	49.969	2.6039×10^{-3}
	TLABC	1.0305	0.34823	1.2013	981.9822	48.6428	$\mathbf{2.4251 \times 10^{-3}}$
	TAPSO	1.0305	0.34823	1.2013	981.9824	48.6428	$\mathbf{2.4251 \times 10^{-3}}$
	MLBSA	1.0305	0.34823	1.2013	981.9823	48.6428	$\mathbf{2.4251 \times 10^{-3}}$
	GOTLBO	1.0305	0.34823	1.2013	981.9823	48.6428	$\mathbf{2.4251 \times 10^{-3}}$
	PGJAYA	1.0305	0.34823	1.2013	981.992	48.6429	$\mathbf{2.4251 \times 10^{-3}}$
	IJAYA	1.0305	0.34864	1.2011	982.0576	48.6474	$\mathbf{2.4251 \times 10^{-3}}$
	HAJAYADE	1.0305	0.34823	1.2013	981.9824	48.6428	$\mathbf{2.4251 \times 10^{-3}}$
STM6-40/36	CMAES	7.4755	2.2665	0.0046056	17.8598	1.2576	1.6612×10^{-2}
	GWO	7.4664	3.389	0.0044212	1052.2704	1.292	1.733×10^{-2}
	TLABC	7.4725	2.335	0.0045946	22.2199	1.2601	$\mathbf{1.6601 \times 10^{-2}}$
	TAPSO	7.4811	27.857	0.0028127	809.038	1.5075	5.7763×10^{-2}
	MLBSA	7.4725	2.335	0.0045946	22.2202	1.2601	$\mathbf{1.6601 \times 10^{-2}}$
	GOTLBO	7.4741	2.2787	0.0046047	19.572	1.2581	1.6605×10^{-2}
	PGJAYA	7.4725	2.3351	0.0045946	22.2253	1.2601	$\mathbf{1.6601 \times 10^{-2}}$
	IJAYA	7.4697	2.5505	0.0045678	40.1402	1.2675	1.6733×10^{-2}
	HAJAYADE	7.4725	2.3351	0.0045946	22.2199	1.2601	$\mathbf{1.6601 \times 10^{-2}}$
STP6-120/36	CMAES	7.4755	2.2665	0.0046056	17.8598	1.2576	1.6612×10^{-2}
	GWO	7.4664	3.389	0.0044212	1052.2704	1.292	1.733×10^{-2}
	TLABC	7.4725	2.335	0.0045946	22.2199	1.2601	$\mathbf{1.6601 \times 10^{-2}}$
	TAPSO	7.4811	27.857	0.0028127	809.038	1.5075	5.7763×10^{-2}
	MLBSA	7.4725	2.335	0.0045946	22.2202	1.2601	$\mathbf{1.6601 \times 10^{-2}}$
	GOTLBO	7.4741	2.2787	0.0046047	19.572	1.2581	1.6605×10^{-2}
	PGJAYA	7.4725	2.3351	0.0045946	22.2253	1.2601	$\mathbf{1.6601 \times 10^{-2}}$
	IJAYA	7.4697	2.5505	0.0045678	40.1402	1.2675	1.6733×10^{-2}
	HAJAYADE	7.4725	2.3351	0.0045946	22.2199	1.2601	$\mathbf{1.6601 \times 10^{-2}}$

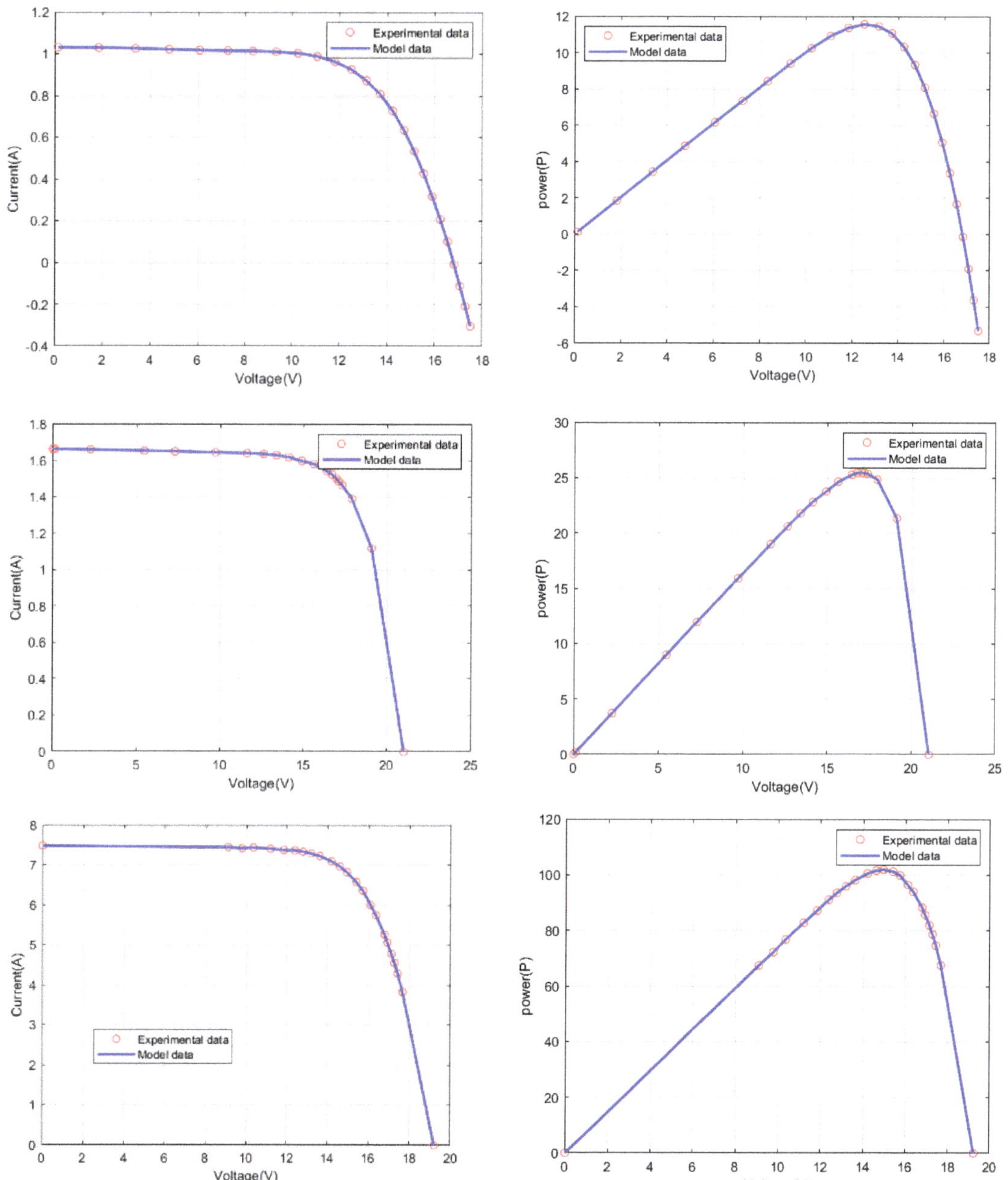

Figure 7. I-V and P-V characteristic curves of three PV models.

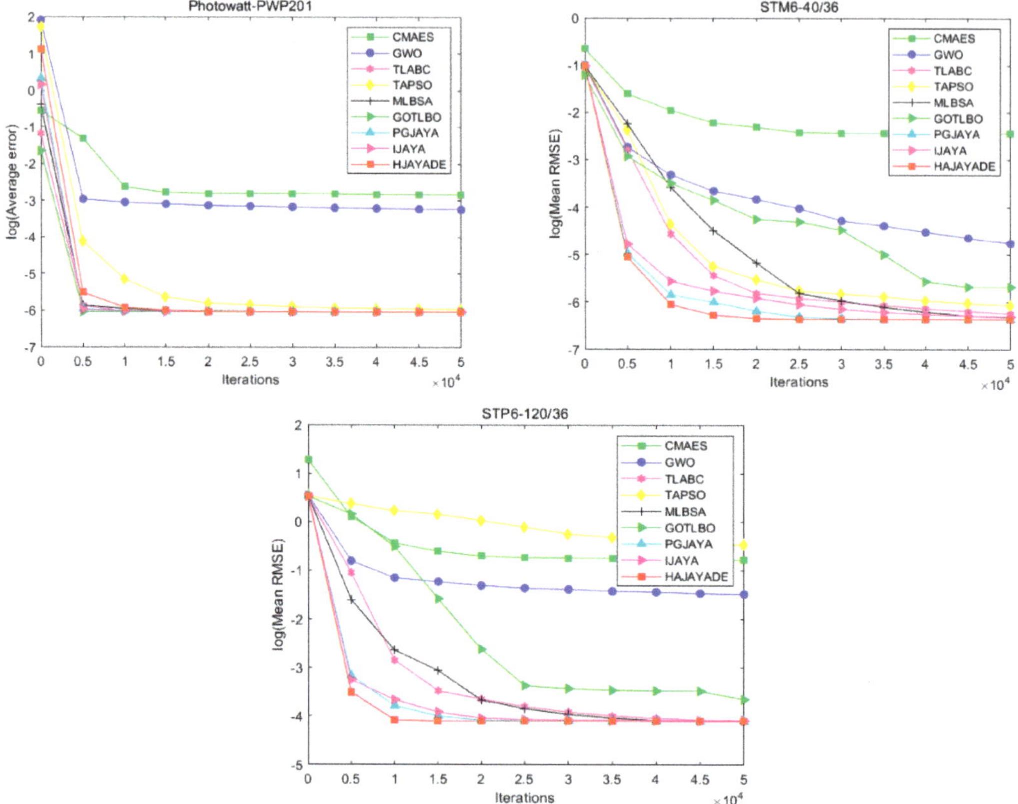

Figure 8. Convergence curves of nine algorithms for three PV models.

4.2. Statistical Results

The boxplot visually demonstrates the distribution of results from the nine meta-heuristic algorithms during 30 runs. They are plotted in Figure 9. It can be seen that the results from the CMAES and GWO are very scattered, which indicates that the two algorithms are not robust. On the contrary, the TLABC, MLBSA, IJAYA, PGJAYA, and HAJAYADE show superior performances compared with the remaining algorithms in terms of robustness.

To further compare the performance of the nine algorithms, the Wilcoxon Signed Rank test on the basis of the results from 30 independent runs is performed. The comparison results demonstrate the significant difference between the proposed HAJAYADE algorithm and its opponents. The results are listed in Table 9, in which the p-value is used to determine whether the hypothesis ($\alpha = 0.05$) should be rejected. The flags + and = indicate that the proposed HAJAYADE algorithm is superior, similar to its opponents. If the p-value is smaller than 0.05, the null hypothesis is rejected, and the performances of the two corresponding algorithms have a significant difference. Otherwise, there are no significant differences.

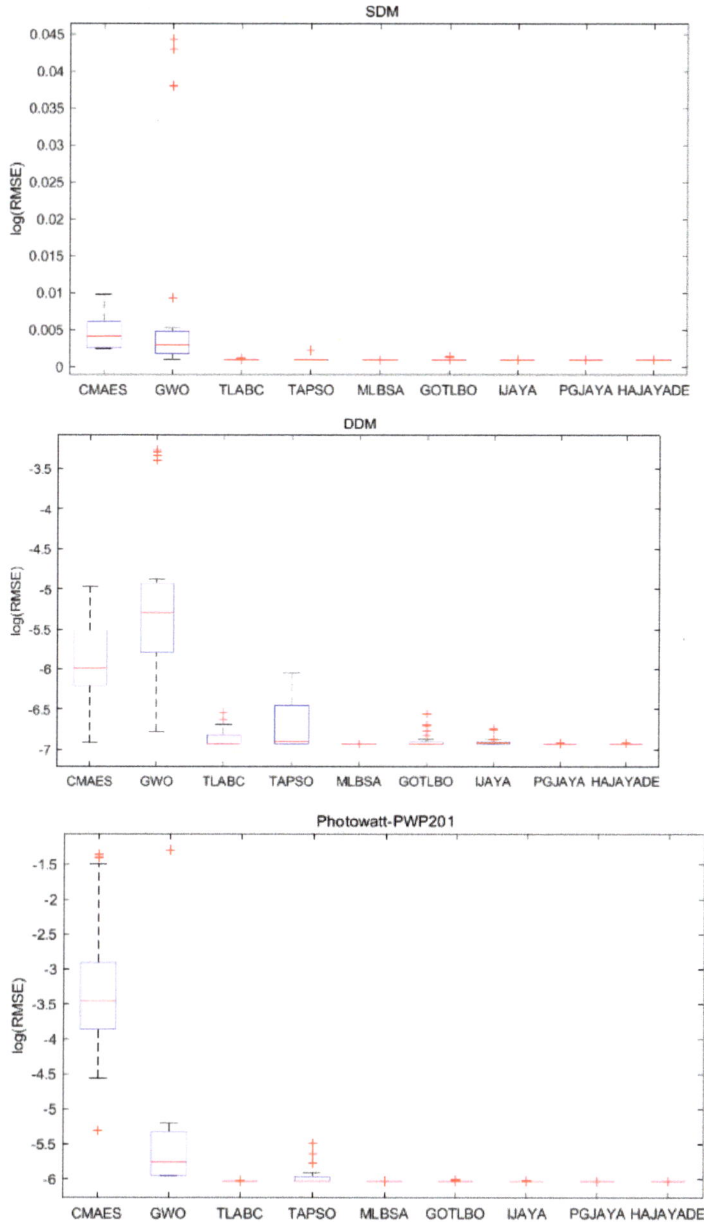

Figure 9. *Cont.*

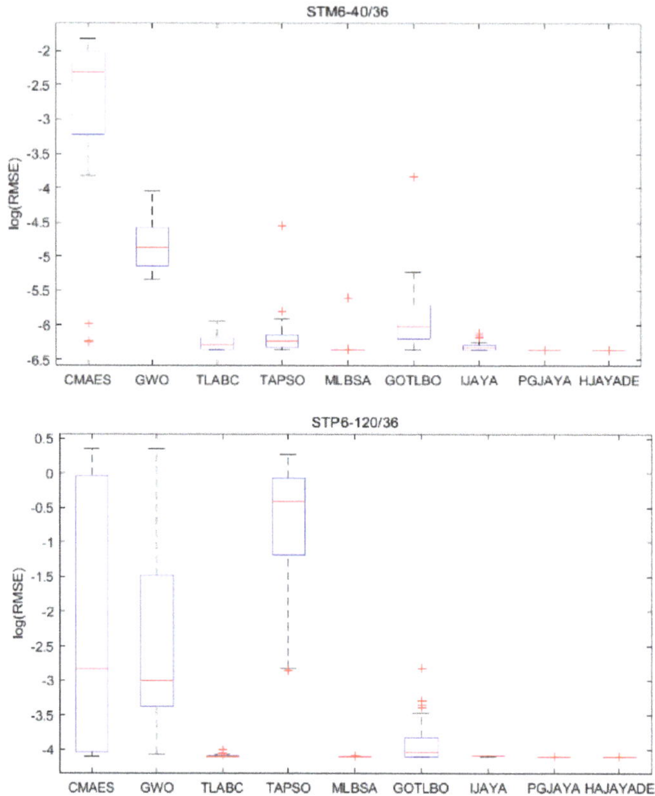

Figure 9. RMSE boxplot of nine algorithms over 30 runs.(the signs such as + and ‡ refer to abnormal points).

From Table 9, it can be seen that HAJAYADE is superior to its opponents in two models, i.e., STM6-40/36 and STP6-120/36. For SDM, the test result of the GOTLBO algorithm is similar to that of the HAYAJADE algorithm. For DDM, the PGJAYA almost achieves similar performance to HAJAYADE. For Photowatt-PWP201, TLABC and GOTLBO are equivalent to HAJAYADE in terms of the statistical test. Therefore, according to the Wilcoxon Signed Rank test, the proposed HAJAYADE algorithm is significantly superior to the remaining algorithms.

Table 9. Wilcoxon Signed Rank test results.

Model	Algorithm	p	Sig.
	CMAES	$1.7344 \times 10^{-6} < 0.05$	+
	GWO	$1.7344 \times 10^{-6} < 0.05$	+
	TLABC	$6.3198 \times 10^{-5} < 0.05$	+
SDM	TAPSO	$6.8862 \times 10^{-5} < 0.05$	+
	MLBSA	$0.0252 < 0.05$	+
	GOTLBO	$0.4653 > 0.05$	=
	IJAYA	$1.7344 \times 10^{-6} < 0.05$	+
	PGJAYA	$1.7344 \times 10^{-6} < 0.05$	+

Table 9. *Cont.*

Model	Algorithm	p	Sig.
	CMAES	$1.7344 \times 10^{-6} < 0.05$	+
	GWO	$1.7344 \times 10^{-6} < 0.05$	+
	TLABC	$4.5336 \times 10^{-4} < 0.05$	+
DDM	TAPSO	$0.0015 < 0.05$	+
	MLBSA	$0.2452 > 0.05$	=
	GOTLBO	$0.0047 < 0.05$	+
	IJAYA	$1.6394 \times 10^{-5} < 0.05$	+
	PGJAYA	$0.5440 > 0.05$	=
	CMAES	$1.7344 \times 10^{-6} < 0.05$	+
	GWO	$1.7344 \times 10^{-6} < 0.05$	+
	TLABC	$0.3388 > 0.05$	=
Photowatt-PWP201	TAPSO	$3.5152 \times 10^{-6} < 0.05$	+
	MLBSA	$0.0077 < 0.05$	+
	GOTLBO	$0.0598 > 0.05$	=
	IJAYA	$1.7344 \times 10^{-6} < 0.05$	+
	PGJAYA	$1.7344 \times 10^{-6} < 0.05$	+
	CMAES	$1.7344 \times 10^{-6} < 0.05$	+
	GWO	$1.7344 \times 10^{-6} < 0.05$	+
	TLABC	$1.7344 \times 10^{-6} < 0.05$	+
STM6-40/36	TAPSO	$1.9209 \times 10^{-6} < 0.05$	+
	MLBSA	$2.3534 \times 10^{-6} < 0.05$	+
	GOTLBO	$1.7344 \times 10^{-6} < 0.05$	+
	IJAYA	$1.7344 \times 10^{-6} < 0.05$	+
	PGJAYA	$1.7344 \times 10^{-6} < 0.05$	+
	CMAES	$1.7344 \times 10^{-6} < 0.05$	+
	GWO	$1.7344 \times 10^{-6} < 0.05$	+
	TLABC	$2.1266 \times 10^{-6} < 0.05$	+
STP6-120/36	TAPSO	$1.7344 \times 10^{-6} < 0.05$	+
	MLBSA	$4.7292 \times 10^{-6} < 0.05$	+
	GOTLBO	$1.7344 \times 10^{-6} < 0.05$	+
	IJAYA	$1.7344 \times 10^{-6} < 0.05$	+
	PGJAYA	$2.3704 \times 10^{-6} < 0.05$	+

4.3. Discussion

The proposed HAJAYADE algorithm has three components: adaptive JAYA, adaptive DE, and the chaotic perturbation method. Next, we conduct additional experiments to test the effectiveness of the hybrid mechanism. As the chaotic perturbation method is only performed on a single solution, it cannot be considered an algorithm. We combine the adaptive JAYA and chaotic perturbation method as the AJAYA algorithm. Adaptive DE and the chaotic perturbation method are regarded as ADE. In addition, the conventional DE and JAYA algorithms are used to make comparisons. For the traditional DE, $CR = 0.5$. The experimental settings are similar to all six algorithms, i.e., population size = 20 and the maximal function evaluations = 50,000. The results of the five algorithms are listed in Table 10, in which the minimum, mean, maximal, and Wilcoxon Signed Rank test results are presented.

Table 10. Results from HAJAYADE, DE, ADE, JAYA, and AJAYA.

Model	Algorithm	Min	Mean	Max	Std	p-Value	Sig.
SDM	HAJAYADE	$\mathbf{9.8602 \times 10^{-4}}$	$\mathbf{9.8602 \times 10^{-4}}$	$\mathbf{9.8602 \times 10^{-4}}$	**0**		
	DE	$\mathbf{9.8602 \times 10^{-4}}$	1.0419×10^{-3}	1.2856×10^{-3}	6.9221×10^{-5}	2.1×10^{-6}	+
	ADE	$\mathbf{9.8602 \times 10^{-4}}$	1.0051×10^{-3}	9.8602×10^{-4}	3.719×10^{-16}	0.18	=
	JAYA	$\mathbf{9.8602 \times 10^{-4}}$	1.2757×10^{-3}	2.7168×10^{-3}	3.8514×10^{-4}	1.7×10^{-6}	+
	AJAYA	$\mathbf{9.8602 \times 10^{-4}}$	1.0051×10^{-3}	1.52×10^{-3}	9.7296×10^{-5}	1.7×10^{-6}	+
DDM	HAJAYADE	$\mathbf{9.8294 \times 10^{-4}}$	$\mathbf{9.8641 \times 10^{-4}}$	$\mathbf{9.96 \times 10^{-4}}$	$\mathbf{2.8534 \times 10^{-6}}$		
	DE	9.8387×10^{-4}	1.1227×10^{-3}	1.7544×10^{-3}	1.7327×10^{-4}	7.7×10^{-6}	+
	ADE	9.8389×10^{-4}	1.0093×10^{-3}	1.2502×10^{-3}	6.5712×10^{-5}	0.0230	+
	JAYA	9.8412×10^{-4}	1.3229×10^{-3}	3.8766×10^{-3}	6.4739×10^{-4}	2.6×10^{-6}	+
	AJAYA	9.8471×10^{-4}	1.2189×10^{-3}	3.0356×10^{-3}	4.2576×10^{-4}	1.5E-5	+
Photowatt-PWP201	HAJAYADE	$\mathbf{2.4251 \times 10^{-3}}$	$\mathbf{2.4251 \times 10^{-3}}$	$\mathbf{2.4251 \times 10^{-3}}$	$\mathbf{3.22 \times 10^{-15}}$		
	DE	$\mathbf{2.4251 \times 10^{-3}}$	2.4277×10^{-3}	2.4596×10^{-3}	7.5232×10^{-6}	7.7×10^{-6}	+
	ADE	$\mathbf{2.4251 \times 10^{-3}}$	$\mathbf{2.4251 \times 10^{-3}}$	$\mathbf{2.4251 \times 10^{-3}}$	1.9962×10^{-9}	0.3933	=
	JAYA	$\mathbf{2.4251 \times 10^{-3}}$	2.4694×10^{-3}	2.7907×10^{-3}	7.9988×10^{-5}	2.4×10^{-6}	+
	AJAYA	$\mathbf{2.4251 \times 10^{-3}}$	6.2249×10^{-3}	1.1869×10^{-2}	3.1602×10^{-3}	1.7×10^{-6}	+
STM6-40/36	HAJAYADE	$\mathbf{1.7298 \times 10^{-3}}$	$\mathbf{1.7298 \times 10^{-3}}$	$\mathbf{1.7298 \times 10^{-3}}$	$\mathbf{3.656 \times 10^{-16}}$		
	DE	1.7301×10^{-3}	4.4017×10^{-3}	2.8936×10^{-2}	6.0003×10^{-3}	1.7×10^{-6}	+
	ADE	$\mathbf{1.7298 \times 10^{-3}}$	$\mathbf{1.7298 \times 10^{-3}}$	1.7299×10^{-3}	1.332×10^{-8}	0.6215	=
	JAYA	$\mathbf{1.7298 \times 10^{-3}}$	4.246×10^{-3}	1.1996×10^{-2}	3.2538×10^{-3}	1.7×10^{-6}	+
	AJAYA	$\mathbf{1.7298 \times 10^{-3}}$	1.7418×10^{-3}	1.8392×10^{-3}	2.568×10^{-5}	1.7×10^{-6}	+
STP6-120/36	HAJAYADE	$\mathbf{1.6601 \times 10^{-2}}$	$\mathbf{1.6601 \times 10^{-2}}$	$\mathbf{1.6606 \times 10^{-2}}$	$\mathbf{9.2421 \times 10^{-7}}$		
	DE	$\mathbf{1.6601 \times 10^{-2}}$	2.3981×10^{-2}	4.9865×10^{-2}	8.1081×10^{-3}	1.7×10^{-6}	+
	ADE	$\mathbf{1.6601 \times 10^{-2}}$	1.6607×10^{-2}	1.6731×10^{-2}	2.445×10^{-5}	0.2289	=
	JAYA	$\mathbf{1.6601 \times 10^{-2}}$	4.4317×10^{-2}	1.7681×10^{-1}	3.646×10^{-2}	1.9×10^{-6}	+
	AJAYA	$\mathbf{1.6601 \times 10^{-2}}$	1.6608×10^{-2}	1.6666×10^{-2}	$,1.673 \times 10^{-5}$	1.8×10^{-5}	+

From the results listed in Table 10, the following observations can be attained as follows:

(1) The min RMSE can be used to test whether the algorithm has the capacity to find a good solution. Most algorithms can find min RMSE on SDM, STM6-40/36, Photowatt-PWP201, and STP6-120/36. However, four algorithms, DE, ADE, JAYA, and AJAYA, fail to find a better RMSE compared with HAJAYADE for DDM.

(2) In terms of the mean values, the proposed HAJAYADE algorithm has attained the best mean results on the five models. In addition, ADE has achieved the same performance for two models, i.e., Photowatt-PWP201 and STM6-40/36. Hence, the average accuracy of the proposed HAJAYADE algorithm can be revealed by the mean RMSE values obtained by the algorithm.

(3) Concerning the maximal values, they demonstrate the maximum discreteness of RMSE. The proposed HAJAYADE algorithm can offer the best maximal values for SDM, Photowatt-PWP201, STM6-40/36, and STP6-120/36, which are almost the same as the mean values. For SDM and Photowatt-PWP201, ADE has attained the best maximal values.

(4) Concerning the standard deviation of the results, AJAYA, ADE, and HAJAYADE have provided superior performance as the standard deviation values are very small. The observations indicate that the three algorithms are very robust. The parameters attained by the three algorithms can be considered reliable.

(5) From the non-parametric test, it can be noticed that the proposed HAJAYADE algorithm is significantly superior to JAYA, AJAYA, and DE. Meanwhile, it is also superior

to ADE for DDM. Therefore, HAJAYADE can be ranked the highest. Meanwhile, ADE and AJAYA are better than the conventional DE and JAYA. It is demonstrated that the adaptive mechanism is effective.

From the convergence curves shown in Figure 10, we can see that the speed of the HAJAYADE is faster than that of the remaining algorithms, especially for the STM6-40/36 and the STP6-120/36. The hybrid mechanism can contribute to the superior performance. For the conventional JAYA, the single mutation strategy is too simple to exhibit better performance. Two adaptive parameters are introduced into the algorithm to boost the exploration and exploitation. For the DE, the search direction depends on the best solution when the Best/1 strategy is adopted. The rank mutation mechanism based on the Best/1 can improve the exploration ability while retaining the exploitation. Lastly, we adopt the chaotic perturbation method to boost the exploitation further. Hence, we can conclude that the HAJAYADE can offer superior and reliable performance when solving the parameter identification for various models compared with the remaining algorithms.

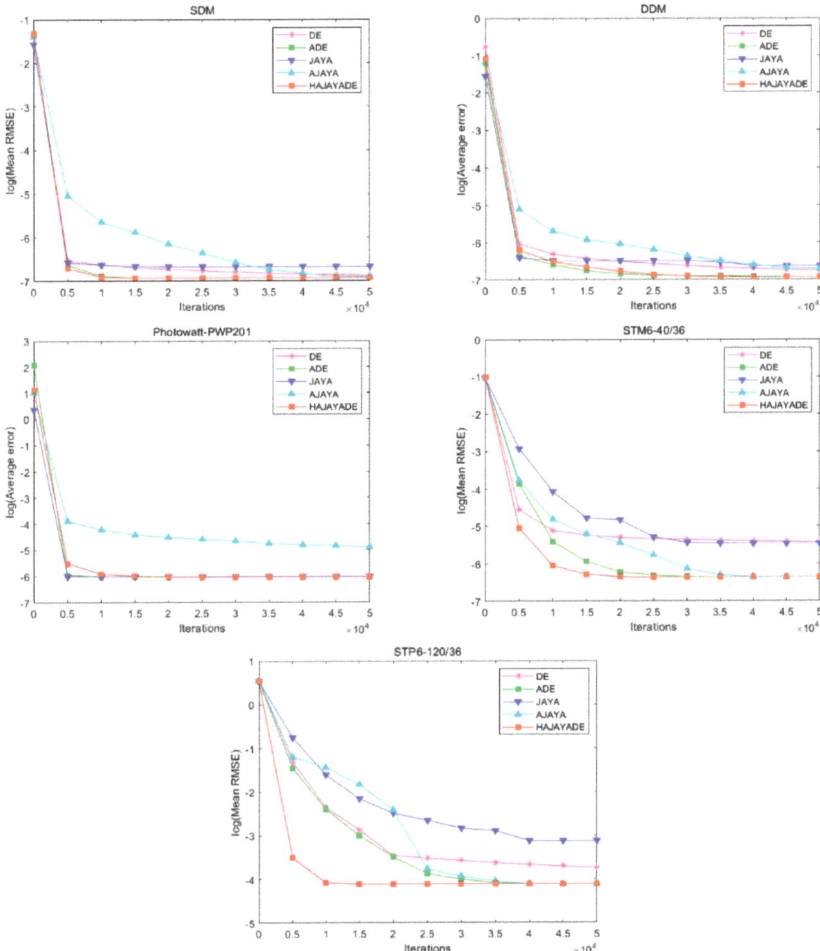

Figure 10. Convergence curves of five algorithms.

5. Conclusions

A novel hybrid algorithm, named HAJAYADE, based on JAYA and DE, is developed to estimate the parameters of PV models as the hybrid is a valuable and effective method compared with the singular ones. The novel HAJAYADE algorithm mainly consists of three components. Firstly, two adaptive coefficients are introduced to the conventional JAYA. The two coefficients can coordinate the tendency to approach the best solution and avoid the worst solutions, which can help the algorithm to move towards the potential region more quickly and strengthen the local search. Secondly, the Rank/Best/1 mutation strategy is proposed in DE. To enhance the exploration, an individual is selected depending on the ranking of the fitness value, while the other individual is randomly chosen. Thirdly, an adaptive chaotic perturbation is performed on the best solution. The solution can replace the worst solution if the worst solution is inferior to the solution.

Three typical PV models are used as benchmarks. Five test cases are implemented. Nine meta-heuristic algorithms, CMAES, GWO, TLABC, TAPSO, MLBSA, GOTLBO, IJAYA, PGJAYA, and DE, are employed to make comparisons. The experimental results reveal that the HAJAYADE is superior in terms of the minimal, mean, maximal values, robustness, and convergence speed compared with its opponents. According to the presented results, the effectiveness of the adaptive coefficients and Rank/Best/1 mutation mechanism is also validated.

In future research, the proposed HAYAJYADE algorithm will be employed to solve more complicated problems, such as economic dispatch, resource scheduling, and feature selection. Furthermore, it also can be used to optimize combinatorial issues by making some modifications, such as in the permutation flow shop scheduling problem [50] and traveling salesman problem [51].

Author Contributions: X.Y.: Conceptualization, Methodology, Writing—Original Draft Preparation. X.W.: Data Curation, Investigation. W.L.: Reviewing and Editing. All authors have read and agreed to the published version of the manuscript.

Funding: This research was funded by the China Natural Science Foundation (No.71974100), Natural Science Foundation in Jiangsu Province (No. BK20191402), Major Project of Philosophy and Social Science Research in Colleges and Universities in Jiangsu Province (2019SJZDA039), Qing Lan Project (R2019Q05), Social Science Research in Colleges and Universities in Jiangsu Province (2019SJZDA039), and Project of Meteorological Industry Research Center (sk20210032).

Institutional Review Board Statement: Not applicable.

Informed Consent Statement: Not applicable.

Data Availability Statement: Not applicable.

Conflicts of Interest: The authors declare no conflict of interest.

References

1. Humada, A.M.; Darweesh, S.Y.; Mohammed, K.G.; Kamil, M.; Mohammed, S.F.; Kasim, N.K.; Tahseen, T.A.; Awad, O.I.; Mekhilef, S. Modeling of PV system and parameter extraction based on experimental data: Review and investigation. *Sol. Energy* **2020**, *199*, 742–760. [CrossRef]
2. Chen, X.; Xu, B.; Mei, C.; Ding, Y.; Li, K. Teaching–learning–based artificial bee colony for solar photovoltaic parameter estimation. *Appl. Energy* **2018**, *212*, 1578–1588. [CrossRef]
3. Yu, K.; Liang, J.J.; Qu, B.Y.; Chen, X.; Wang, H. Parameters identification of photovoltaic models using an improved JAYA optimization algorithm. *Energy Convers. Manag.* **2017**, *150*, 742–753. [CrossRef]
4. Yu, K.; Qu, B.; Yue, C.; Ge, S.; Chen, X.; Liang, J. A performance-guided JAYA algorithm for parameters identification of photovoltaic cell and module. *Appl. Energy* **2019**, *237*, 241–257. [CrossRef]
5. Chen, X.; Yu, K.; Du, W.; Zhao, W.; Liu, G. Parameters identification of solar cell models using generalized oppositional teaching learning based optimization. *Energy* **2016**, *99*, 170–180. [CrossRef]
6. Yu, K.; Liang, J.J.; Qu, B.Y.; Cheng, Z.; Wang, H. Multiple learning backtracking search algorithm for estimating parameters of photovoltaic models. *Appl. Energy* **2018**, *226*, 408–422. [CrossRef]
7. Hao, P.; Sobhani, B. Application of the improved chaotic grey wolf optimization algorithm as a novel and efficient method for parameter estimation of solid oxide fuel cells model. *Int. J. Hydrogen Energy* **2021**, *46*, 36454–36465. [CrossRef]

8. Nunes, H.G.G.; Silva, P.N.C.; Pombo, J.A.N.; Mariano, S.J.P.S.; Calado, M.R.A. Multiswarm spiral leader particle swarm optimisation algorithm for PV parameter identification. *Energy Convers. Manag.* **2020**, *225*, 113388. [CrossRef]

9. Liu, Y.; Heidari, A.A.; Ye, X.; Liang, G.; Chen, H.; He, C. Boosting slime mould algorithm for parameter identification of photovoltaic models. *Energy* **2021**, *234*, 121164. [CrossRef]

10. Naeijian, M.; Rahimnejad, A.; Ebrahimi, S.M.; Pourmousa, N.; Gadsden, S.A. Parameter estimation of PV solar cells and modules using Whippy Harris Hawks Optimization Algorithm. *Energy Rep.* **2021**, *7*, 4047–4063. [CrossRef]

11. Rezk, H.; Babu, T.S.; Al-Dhaifallah, M.; Ziedan, H.A. A robust parameter estimation approach based on stochastic fractal search optimization algorithm applied to solar PV parameters. *Energy Rep.* **2021**, *7*, 620–640. [CrossRef]

12. Wang, S.; Yu, Y.; Hu, W. Static and dynamic solar photovoltaic models' parameters estimation using hybrid Rao optimization algorithm. *J. Clean. Prod.* **2021**, *315*, 128080. [CrossRef]

13. Abdel-Basset, M.; El-Shahat, D.; Chakrabortty, R.K.; Ryan, M. Parameter estimation of photovoltaic models using an improved marine predators algorithm. *Energy Convers. Manag.* **2021**, *227*, 113491. [CrossRef]

14. Sallam, K.M.; Hossain, A.; Chakrabortty, R.K.; Ryan, M.J. An improved gaining-sharing knowledge algorithm for parameter extraction of photovoltaic models. *Energy Convers. Manag.* **2021**, *237*, 114030. [CrossRef]

15. Li, S.; Gu, Q.; Gong, W.; Ning, B. An enhanced adaptive differential evolution algorithm for parameter extraction of photovoltaic models. *Energy Convers. Manag.* **2020**, *205*, 205. [CrossRef]

16. Ahmadianfar, I.; Gong, W.; Heidari, A.A.; Golilarz, N.A.; Samadi-Koucheksaraee, A.; Chen, H. Gradient-based optimization with ranking mechanisms for parameter identification of photovoltaic systems. *Energy Rep.* **2021**, *7*, 3979–3997. [CrossRef]

17. Premkumar, M.; Jangir, P.; Elavarasan, R.M.; Sowmya, R. Opposition decided gradient-based optimizer with balance analysis and diversity maintenance for parameter identification of solar photovoltaic models. *J. Ambient. Intell. Humaniz. Comput.* **2021**, 1–23. [CrossRef]

18. Liu, Y.; Heidari, A.A.; Ye, X.; Chi, C.; Zhao, X.; Ma, C.; Turabieh, H.; Chen, H.; Le, R. Evolutionary shuffled frog leaping with memory pool for parameter optimization. *Energy Rep.* **2021**, *7*, 584–606. [CrossRef]

19. PPremkumar, M.; Jangir, P.; Ramakrishnan, C.; Nalinipriya, G.; Alhelou, H.H.; Kumar, B.S. Identification of Solar Photovoltaic Model Parameters Using an Improved Gradient-Based Optimization Algorithm With Chaotic Drifts. *IEEE Access* **2021**, *9*, 62347–62379. [CrossRef]

20. Wang, M.; Zhang, Q.; Chen, H.; Heidari, A.A.; Mafarja, M.; Turabieh, H. Evaluation of constraint in photovoltaic cells using ensemble multi-strategy shuffled frog leading algorithms. *Energy Convers. Manag.* **2021**, *244*, 114484. [CrossRef]

21. Rao, R.V. Jaya: A simple and new optimization algorithm for solving constrained and unconstrained optimization problems. *Int. J. Ind. Eng. Comput.* **2016**, 19–34. [CrossRef]

22. Rao, R.V.; Saroj, A. Multi-objective design optimization of heat exchangers using elitist-Jaya algorithm. *Energy Syst.* **2018**, *9*, 305–341. [CrossRef]

23. Rao, R.; More, K. Optimal design and analysis of mechanical draft cooling tower using improved Jaya algorithm. *Int. J. Refrig.* **2017**, *82*, 312–324. [CrossRef]

24. Rao, R.V.; Saroj, A. Constrained economic optimization of shell-and-tube heat exchangers using elitist-Jaya algorithm. *Energy* **2017**, *128*, 785–800. [CrossRef]

25. Ravipudi, J.L.; Neebha, M. Synthesis of linear antenna arrays using Jaya, self-adaptive Jaya and chaotic Jaya algorithms. *AEU Int. J. Electron. Commun.* **2018**, *92*, 54–63. [CrossRef]

26. Rao, R.V.; Keesari, H.S. Multi-team perturbation guiding Jaya algorithm for optimization of wind farm layout. *Appl. Soft Comput.* **2018**, *71*, 800–815. [CrossRef]

27. Huang, C.; Wang, L.; Yeung, R.S.-C.; Zhang, Z.; Chung, H.; Bensoussan, A. A Prediction Model-Guided Jaya Algorithm for the PV System Maximum Power Point Tracking. *IEEE Trans. Sustain. Energy* **2017**, *9*, 45–55. [CrossRef]

28. Yu, J.; Kim, C.-H.; Wadood, A.; Khurshiad, T.; Rhee, S.-B. A Novel Multi-Population Based Chaotic JAYA Algorithm with Application in Solving Economic Load Dispatch Problems. *Energies* **2018**, *11*, 1946. [CrossRef]

29. Fares, D.; Fathi, M.; Mekhilef, S. Performance evaluation of metaheuristic techniques for optimal sizing of a stand-alone hybrid PV/wind/battery system. *Appl. Energy* **2022**, *305*, 117823. [CrossRef]

30. Li, Y.; Yang, Z.; Li, G.; Mu, Y.; Zhao, D.; Chen, C.; Shen, B. Optimal scheduling of isolated microgrid with an electric vehicle battery swapping station in multi-stakeholder scenarios: A bi-level programming approach via real-time pricing. *Appl. Energy* **2018**, *232*, 54–68. [CrossRef]

31. Zhang, Y.; Ma, M.; Jin, Z. Comprehensive learning Jaya algorithm for parameter extraction of photovoltaic models. *Energy* **2020**, *211*, 118644. [CrossRef]

32. Yang, X.; Gong, W. Opposition-based JAYA with population reduction for parameter estimation of photovoltaic solar cells and modules. *Appl. Soft Comput.* **2021**, *104*, 107218. [CrossRef]

33. Jian, X.; Weng, Z. A logistic chaotic JAYA algorithm for parameters identification of photovoltaic cell and module models. *Optik* **2020**, *203*, 164041. [CrossRef]

34. Raut, U.; Mishra, S. An improved Elitist–Jaya algorithm for simultaneous network reconfiguration and DG allocation in power distribution systems. *Renew. Energy Focus* **2019**, *30*, 92–106. [CrossRef]

35. Premkumar, M.; Jangir, P.; Sowmya, R.; Elavarasan, R.M.; Kumar, B.S. Enhanced chaotic JAYA algorithm for parameter estimation of photovoltaic cell/modules. *ISA Trans.* **2021**, *116*, 139–166. [CrossRef] [PubMed]

36. Xiong, G.; Zhang, J.; Yuan, X.; Shi, D.; He, Y.; Yao, G. Parameter extraction of solar photovoltaic models by means of a hybrid differential evolution with whale optimization algorithm. *Sol. Energy* **2018**, *176*, 742–761. [CrossRef]

37. Ghorbani, N.; Kasaeian, A.; Toopshekan, A.; Bahrami, L.; Maghami, A. Optimizing a hybrid wind-PV-battery system using GA-PSO and MOPSO for reducing cost and increasing reliability. *Energy* **2018**, *154*, 581–591. [CrossRef]

38. Neshat, M.; Mirjalili, S.; Sergiienko, N.Y.; Esmaeilzadeh, S.; Amini, E.; Heydari, A.; Garcia, D.A. Layout optimisation of offshore wave energy converters using a novel multi-swarm cooperative algorithm with backtracking strategy: A case study from coasts of Australia. *Energy* **2022**, *239*, 122463. [CrossRef]

39. Neshat, M.; Alexander, B.; Wagner, M. A hybrid cooperative co-evolution algorithm framework for optimising power take off and placements of wave energy converters. *Inf. Sci.* **2020**, *534*, 218–244. [CrossRef]

40. Storn, R.; Price, K. Differential Evolution—A Simple and Efficient Heuristic for global Optimization over Continuous Spaces. *J. Glob. Optim.* **1997**, *11*, 341–359. [CrossRef]

41. Zou, D.; Li, S.; Wang, G.-G.; Li, Z.; Ouyang, H. An improved differential evolution algorithm for the economic load dispatch problems with or without valve-point effects. *Appl. Energy* **2016**, *181*, 375–390. [CrossRef]

42. Ishaque, K.; Salam, Z.; Mekhilef, S.; Shamsudin, A. Parameter extraction of solar photovoltaic modules using penalty-based differential evolution. *Appl. Energy* **2012**, *99*, 297–308. [CrossRef]

43. Pant, M.; Zaheer, H.; Garcia-Hernandez, L.; Abraham, A. Differential Evolution: A review of more than two decades of research. *Eng. Appl. Artif. Intell.* **2020**, *90*, 103479.

44. Patwal, R.S.; Narang, N.; Garg, H. A novel TVAC-PSO based mutation strategies algorithm for generation scheduling of pumped storage hydrothermal system incorporating solar units. *Energy* **2018**, *142*, 822–837. [CrossRef]

45. Gong, W.; Cai, Z. Differential Evolution With Ranking-Based Mutation Operators. *IEEE Trans. Cybern.* **2013**, *43*, 2066–2081. [CrossRef] [PubMed]

46. Easwarakhanthan, T.; Bottin, J.; Bouhouch, I.B.; Boutrit, C. Nonlinear Minimization Algorithm for Determining the Solar Cell Parameters with Microcomputers. *Int. J. Sol. Energy* **1986**, *4*, 1–12. [CrossRef]

47. Mirjalili, S.; Mirjalili, S.M.; Lewis, A. Grey Wolf Optimizer. *Adv. Eng. Softw.* **2014**, *69*, 46–61. [CrossRef]

48. Hansen, N.; Ostermeier, A. Completely Derandomized Self-Adaptation in Evolution Strategies. *Evol. Comput.* **2001**, *9*, 159–195. [CrossRef]

49. Xia, X.; Gui, L.; Yu, F.; Wu, H.; Wei, B.; Zhang, Y.-L.; Zhan, Z.-H. Triple Archives Particle Swarm Optimization. *IEEE Trans. Cybern.* **2020**, *50*, 4862–4875. [CrossRef]

50. Santucci, V.; Baioletti, M.; Milani, A. An algebraic framework for swarm and evolutionary algorithms in combinatorial optimization. *Swarm Evol. Comput.* **2020**, *55*, 100673. [CrossRef]

51. Moraglio, A.; Togelius, J.; Silva, S. Geometric Differential Evolution for Combinatorial and Programs Spaces. *Evol. Comput.* **2013**, *21*, 591–624. [CrossRef] [PubMed]

 *mathematics*

MDPI

Article

Design on Intelligent Feature Graphics Based on Convolution Operation

Ying Li [1] and Ye Tang [2,3,*]

[1] School of Arts, Anhui Polytechnic University, Wuhu 241000, China; ly408493042@163.com
[2] School of Mechanical Engineering, Anhui Polytechnic University, Wuhu 241000, China
[3] Department of Mechanics, Tianjin University, Tianjin 300350, China
* Correspondence: tangye2010_hit@163.com; Tel.: +86-188-9531-6533

Abstract: With the development and application of artificial intelligence, the technical methods of intelligent image processing and graphic design need to be explored to realize the intelligent graphic design based on traditional graphics such as pottery engraving graphics. An optimized method is aimed to be explored to extract the image features from traditional engraving graphics on historical relics and apply them into intelligent graphic design. For this purpose, an image feature extracted model based on convolution operation is proposed. Parametric test and effectiveness research are conducted to evaluate the performance of the proposed model. Theoretical and practical research shows that the image-extracted model has a significant effect on the extraction of image features from traditional engraving graphics because the image brightness processing greatly simplifies the process of image feature extraction, and the convolution operation improves the accuracy. Based on the brightness feature map output from the proposed model, the design algorithm of intelligent feature graphic is presented to create the feature graphics, which can be directly applied to design the intelligent graphical interface. Taking some pottery engraving graphics from the Neolithic Age as an example, we conduct the practice on image feature extraction and feature graphic design, the results of which further verify the effectiveness of the proposed method. This paper provides a theoretical basis for the application of traditional engraving graphics in intelligent graphical interface design for AI products such as smart tourism products, smart museums, and so on.

Keywords: convolution operation; intelligent graphic design; brightness feature; traditional engraving graphics

Citation: Li, Y.; Tang, Y. Design on Intelligent Feature Graphics Based on Convolution Operation. *Mathematics* **2022**, *10*, 384. https://doi.org/ 10.3390/math10030384

Academic Editors: Xiang Li, Shuo Zhang and Wei Zhang

Received: 1 December 2021
Accepted: 24 January 2022
Published: 26 January 2022

Publisher's Note: MDPI stays neutral with regard to jurisdictional claims in published maps and institutional affiliations.

1. Introduction

In recent years, with the development of artificial intelligence (AI), the application of intelligent image processing has been found in many fields such as handwriting recognition, image caption, automatic vehicle navigation, and so on [1–4]. As a deep learning network in the field of artificial intelligence, the convolutional neural network (CNN) has been maturely used in image processing field, especially for the image recognition [5,6] or image feature extraction. For example, Ding et al. studied the intelligent image identification method to roughly handle the express packages by using the intelligent recognition method of the gated recursive unit in the convolutional neural network, which can be used as an intelligent fusional model [7]. Li et al. investigated the extracted method of global features from images of typical infrared targets such as people and vehicles by designing semantic segmentation algorithms, and achieved good results [8]. As the core computing module is acted in convolutional neural network, the convolution operation plays an important role in intelligent image processing [9] and image feature extraction. For example, Zhan studied the method of extracting image features of tea materials by convolution operation [10]. Chen studied the method and effect that extracted brightness features in the interest regions from the images by the improved Itti–Koch model based on the convolution operation [11].

By the other side, there is a rapid, essential, and global change in the graphic design due to the effect of artificial intelligence [12]. AI has been widely used by designers, which is considered to be an important assistant for them [13]. Intelligent algorithms play an increasingly important role in graphic design field such as real-time graphics generation, virtual scene visualization [14], 3D Graphics Engines [15], and so on. In Ref. [16], Li and Xv studied the generation and conversion method of the woodcut print style by applying a deep learning algorithm, which can be used to generate a wood engraving texture effect. In Ref. [17], Tian et al. discussed the generation method of multi-style ancient book textures via the layout analysis and style transfer techniques based on the deep learning. In Ref. [18], Liu studied the method of generating image features such as specific color, shape, and texture by using the synthetic method of artificial intelligence and data mining. On the basis of the previous studies, we use the technical method of intelligent image processing and intelligent graphic design to realize the intelligent graphic design based on traditional graphics such as pottery engraving graphics. For this purpose, the image feature extracted model is constructed to extract the image features from and apply them to intelligent graphic design with the algorithms for intelligent graphic design. This research will promote the spreading of traditional culture and artistic features in the field of intelligent application.

2. Method of Image Feature Extraction Based on Convolution Operation

2.1. Principle of Image Feature Extraction

During the 1950s and 1960s, Professor Frank Rosenblatt of Cornell University, invented the perceptron by imitating the visual system architecture of automatic pattern recognition of human body [19]. The perceptron is a simple learning algorithm, which plays an important role in the AI field. As the early prototype of deep learning network mentioned in [20], the perceptron consists of an input layer, an output layer, and a set of structures connecting with them, which is called a hidden layer in a deep neural network [21]. It can recognize, extract, and classify the images input into the perceptron through the judgment of input information. The process of machine recognition is to divide a complete picture into many small parts, extract and summarize the features in each small part, which is realized based on the perceptron. Image features such as brightness, pixel strength, and contour are extracted from the original input image and weighted, which are used as the basis of image feature recognition and classification.

2.2. Image Feature Extraction Method Based on Convolution Operation

Based on the principle of perceptron, convolutional neural network is developed. Image features can be extracted based on the structure of convolutional neural network, in which the central role is existed in convolution operation. When it is applied in the image feature extraction, the basic structure consists of the feature extraction and mapping layers [22]. It is advantaged that images can be directly input with the form of three-dimensional data [23], resulting in reducing the preprocessing process of the input original signal, and weakening the complicated extent of the recognition model by sharing the weight and worth. According to the structure of convolutional neural network, the method of image feature extraction can be described as follows.

Convolutional layer is used to extract preliminary image features. The image feature extraction is obtained via the convolution operation, of which the process contains as: inputting the original images as pixel matrices, and then setting the convolutional kernel to move on and cover the pixel matrix of original image sequentially, in which the moving interval unit in each time is called step. It realizes the extraction of the image feature such as the brightness, pixel intensity, and outline etc., by the judgment of weighted sums of convolutional kernel and the covered image pixel matrix in each movement of convolutional kernel.

Pool layer is used to enhance and extract the main features of the image. The working principle of the pooling layer is to multiply the original data output from the convolutional layer with the corresponding convolutional kernel to obtain a new matrix, which is used to strengthen and extract the main features of the image.

The full connection layer is used to summarize and output the features of each part of the image. The working principle of the full connection layer is to convert the vector matrix output by the pooling layer into some vectors, multiply it by the weight matrix, add the offset value, and then use the ReLU (rectified linear units) activation function to optimize its parameters.

3. Image Feature Extracted Model

Based on the principle of perceptron, convolutional neural network is developed, which plays an important role in the image feature extraction. Then, we use the structure of convolutional neural network to propose the new method of image feature extraction, and construct the image feature extracted model based on convolution operation. Then, the image brightness processing is adopted to further optimize this extracted model.

3.1. Image Brightness Feature Processing

Because the shapes of traditional engraving graphics on historical relics mostly take the form of lines and gullies, formed by pressing and engraving, there is a significant brightness difference between the carved lines and the surrounding of the images. Therefore, the brightness features can reflect the features of the lines in the image well. According to the image features of the traditional engraving graphics on historical relics, an algorithm for extracting brightness feature from images is designed. The image feature extracted model is constructed based on convolution operation for the batch extraction of sample image features. To highlight the brightness features of the image, simplify the process of feature extraction, and improve the accuracy, the image brightness feature processing is performed before using the convolution operation to extract the image feature of traditional engraving graphics. Taking the pottery engraving graphics from the Neolithic Age as an example, the image brightness processing and image feature extraction are carried out. The image brightness processing comprises a series of brightness feature operations, such as conversion and enhancement of image brightness value as well as the image threshold processing.

1. Conversion of image brightness value is taken to convert the storage mode of image information. It is known that the images are stored by the form of color value matrix in the computer. In addition, it is more convenient for the image feature extraction by converting the image storage mode from the color value matrix to the brightness value matrix, as showed in Figure 1.

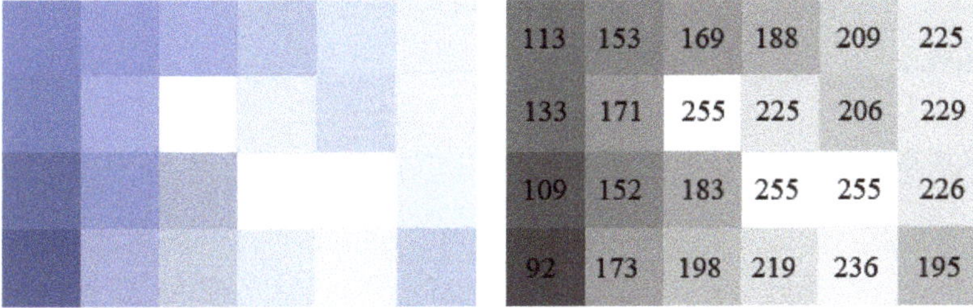

113	153	169	188	209	225
133	171	255	225	206	229
109	152	183	255	255	226
92	173	198	219	236	195

Figure 1. The conversion from color value mode to brightness value mode for image.

2. Enhancement and inverse operation of the image brightness value are exerted on the image to further emphasize the brightness feature of engraving lines, which is more convenient for extracting the image feature of line part according to the high value.

We use Equation (1) to realize the conversion of and enhancement of image brightness value, which yields

$$L = 255 - k\frac{r+g+b}{3} \tag{1}$$

where r, g, and b represent the color value matrices of red, green, and blue, respectively, and L is the brightness value matrix. Taking the 112×112-px image of pottery engraving graphic in Figure 2a as an example, the RGB color value of the pixel at coordinates (69, 69) is (4, 14, 151) and the brightness value is considered to be 56. By using this method, the image storage mode of the input image is converted to a brightness value matrix. k is the brightness enhancement coefficient, which represents the multiple of brightness enhancement compared with the original image. It is demonstrated that with the increase of the whole image brightness, the engraving lines can be displayed better. For example, most of the pottery engraving lines can be revealed better as the whole image brightness is increased to 2.5 times.

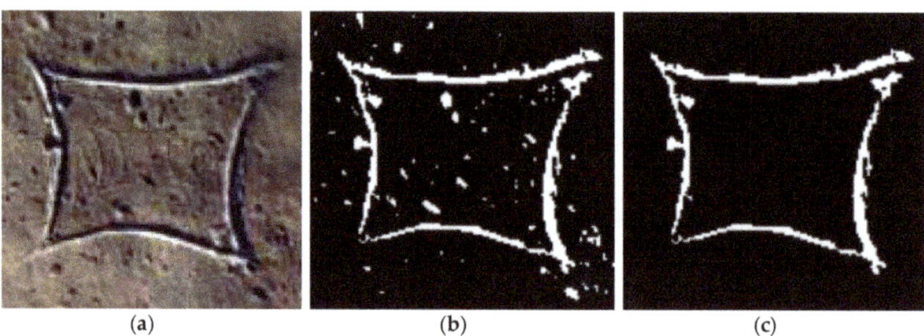

(a)   (b)   (c)

Figure 2. The image brightness processing of the pottery engraving graphic. (**a**) Input image. (**b**) Image threshold processing. (**c**) Removing discrete points.

3. Threshold operation is exerted on the image to further magnify the brightness features. We use Equation (2) to realize the image threshold processing, which yields

$$L(x,y) = \left\{ \begin{array}{l} maxval\ if\ L(x,y) > \theta_T \\ 0\ \ \ otherwise \end{array} \right\} \tag{2}$$

when the brightness value of the pixel $L(x, y)$ is greater than the threshold θ_T, it is set to the maximum value *maxval*, but is set to 0 in other cases. If *maxval* and θ_T are set as 255 and 128, respectively, the resulting image is as shown in Figure 2b, it is concluded that the binary conversion of image information is realized in the method and the brightness feature is highlighted to the utmost extent. To further enhance the image feature of lines, we use the method of remove_small_objects (T_A) to remove scattered small areas of an image, and the size of removed area can be controlled by setting the connected area threshold T_A. After these operations, the brightness value map is obtained when the connected area threshold value $T_A = 25$, as shown in Figure 2c.

After a series of image brightness processing including the conversion and enhancement of the image brightness value as well as the image threshold processing, the image brightness feature is more obvious, because the binary conversion of image brightness value is achieved and the engraving line parts is highlighted with the higher brightness values. It greatly simplifies the extraction process of image features and improves the accuracy.

3.2. Image Brightness Feature Extraction Based on Convolution Operation

The image brightness feature is extracted based on the brightness value map output from the image feature extracted model, which can greatly simplify the extracted process of image brightness feature and improve the accuracy. Convolution operation is applied to extract image features from the image matrix input with the defined convolution kernel. The method can be expressed as

$$conv = \sigma(imgMat \otimes K_i + b) \tag{3}$$

in which σ represents the active function, $imgMat$ is the image brightness value matrix, K_i is the defined convolution kernel with the size i, $\otimes$ means the convolution operation, b is the offset value. The convolution kernel is applied to extract the image feature and obtain an initialized set of feature vectors. Here, we use the Sobel convolution kernel. Because the image features have been highlighted greatly after the processing of image brightness feature, more accurate feature vectors can be obtained by a simple convolution operation. Only two convolution kernels are applied to extract the brightness feature of the image, and they can also obtain an obvious result.

Sobel—G(x) and Sobel—G(y) convolution kernels are used to carry out convolution operation with the input images, which respectively represent the kernels of horizontal and vertical directions. Substituting Sobel—G(x) and Sobel—G(y) into Equation (3) respectively, and then adding each element of this matrix with the offset value b, and inputting the results into the activation function yields

$$\sigma(x) = \frac{1}{1 + e^{-x}} \tag{4}$$

Combining the results in the convolution operation derived by G(x) and G(y) convolution kernels, we get the best feature vector matrix, which can be manifested as a feature map in python environment. After the brightness value processing, the image feature extraction has been greatly simplified because the input image is displayed with the binary mode of black and white. Therefore, we can get good extraction results for image features with only twice convolution operations derived by G(x) and G(y) convolution kernels.

3.3. Image Feature Extracted Model

The image feature extracted model based on the above research is shown in Figure 3. Sample images are put into this model, and the brightness feature matrix is obtained by convolution operation after a series of image feature processing including the conversion and enhancement of the image brightness value as well as the image threshold, which can be displayed as the brightness feature map used for the intelligent graphic design in python environment.

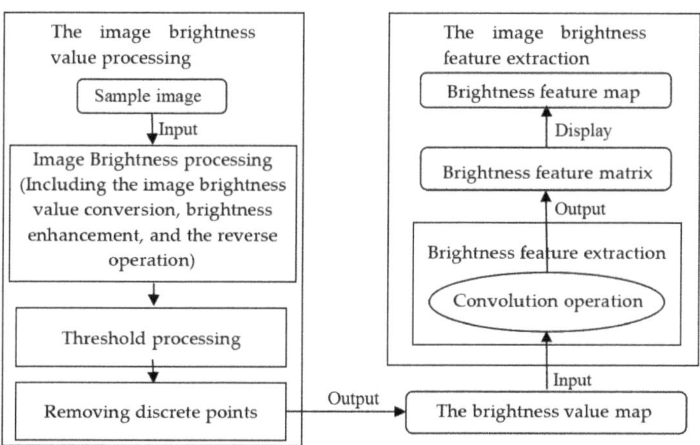

Figure 3. The image feature extracted model.

3.4. Model Parametric Test and Effect Evaluation

3.4.1. Model Parametric Test

Model performance based on the parametric test is carried out by using simple variable method, adjusting one parameter while other parameters are fixed and comparing with the results, we get the optimal parameters. The specific process involves collecting the original images and inputting them into the extracted model to test its extracted effect and find the optimal parameters. Taking the pottery engraving graphics from the Neolithic Age for example, selecting 50 sample images of representative pottery engraving graphics from Shuangdun Site in Bengbu City of Anhui province as the test samples, we input them into the model after preprocessing the images, and conducted brightness feature processing and extraction. We compared the effects of brightness feature maps, as obtained by different parameters to find that when the brightness enhancement coefficient k increases the other parameters remain fixed; the image feature extraction effects are shown in Figure 4a. Figure 4b exhibits the influence of the threshold θ_T on the image feature extraction. It is concluded from Figures 4 and 5 that the extracted effect of image brightness feature is closely related to the model parameters, which directly affects the results of intelligent graphic design.

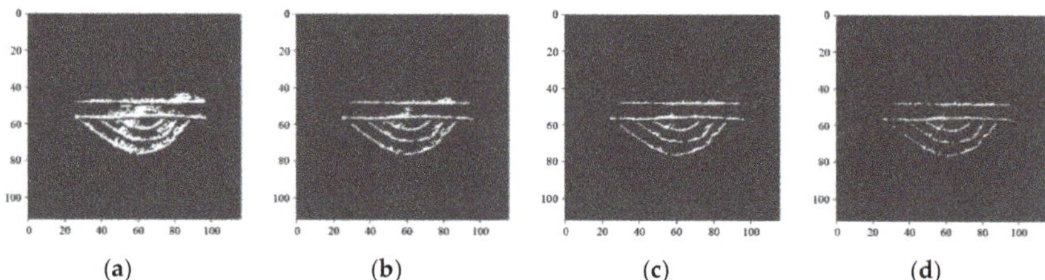

Figure 4. Influence of brightness enhancement coefficient k on image feature extraction. (**a**) $k = 1.5$, $\theta_T = 128$. (**b**) $k = 2.0$, $\theta_T = 128$. (**c**) $k = 2.5$, $\theta_T = 128$. (**d**) $k = 3.0$, $\theta_T = 128$.

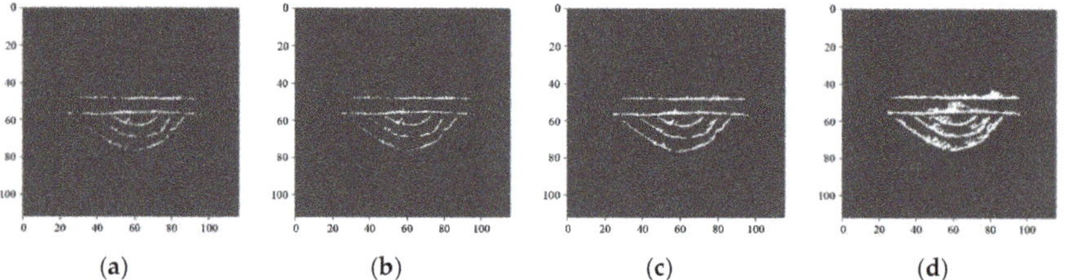

Figure 5. Influence of threshold θ_T on image feature extraction. (**a**) $k = 2.5$, $\theta_T = 96$. (**b**) $k = 2.5$, $\theta_T = 112$. (**c**) $k = 2.5$, $\theta_T = 128$. (**d**) $k = 2.5$, $\theta_T = 140$.

In the image brightness value processing, we adjust the connected area threshold T_A of the remove_small_objects() method to remove the most discrete points, and adjust the brightness enhancement coefficient k and the brightness threshold θ_T to enhance the image brightness features. From the sample testing, we conclude that, when the connected area threshold $T_A = 25$, independent discrete points can be removed well, preserving the effective parts of the engraving lines. When the brightness enhancement coefficient $k = 2.5$ and the image brightness threshold $\theta_T = 128$, the good displayed effects are obtained and the feature maps are more true, accurate, and distinctive, compared with the original image. In the image brightness feature extraction, we define the horizontal convolution kernel $G(x) = [-1, 0, 1; -2, 0, 2; -1, 0, 1]$, and the vertical convolution kernel $G(y) = [1, 2, 1; 0, 0, 0; -1, -2, -1]$. We found that the better results are achieved under these convolution kernels. When the offset value $b = 2$, the locations of the feature maps are more accurate for most of the 112×112 images of the pottery engraving graphics. The parameters are adjusted to tailor an accurate effect of the feature map for a few images when the extracted effect is not ideal.

3.4.2. Model Effectiveness Research

In order to evaluate its stability and availability, model test is conducted. Total of 50 sample images of traditional engraving graphics are inputted into the model to extract their image features. Test results are shown in Table 1, and it illustrates that image feature extraction of 45 traditional engraving graphics achieves a good result under standard parameters condition. But the defect results are obtained for the few sample images, and the extracted feature can be tuned/tailored well by adjusting the modal parameters slightly. Therefore, the application of the proposed model to the image feature extraction of traditional engraving graphics results in very good efficiency. We can conclude that the results of the image feature extraction based on the proposed model are accurate and clear for most traditional engraving graphics.

Table 1. Model test results statistics.

Number of Pottery Engraving Graphics	45	2	1	1	1
Sets of parameters in image brightness processing	$k = 2.5$; $\theta_T = 128$; $T_A = 25$	$k = 2.5$; $\theta_T = 150$; $T_A = 25$	$k = 2.0$; $\theta_T = 128$; $T_A = 25$	$k = 2.0$; $\theta_T = 150$; $T_A = 25$	$k = 3.0$; $\theta_T = 128$; $T_A = 25$
Sets of parameters in convolution operation	$G(x) = [-1, 0, 1; -2, 0, 2; -1, 0, 1]$; $G(y) = [1, 2, 1; 0, 0, 0; -1, -2, -1]$; $b = 2$				

We also compare the extracted image features, as obtained by the proposed method and complex convolutional neural networks and algorithms mentioned in literatures [8,10,11], as shown in Figure 6. It is shown that this proposed method is more simple and effective, the reason being that the binary conversion of image brightness value is achieved via conducting the image brightness processing, which consequently simplifies the process of extracting image features by virtue of the convolution operation. Furthermore, we find that image features extracted by using complex convolutional neural networks and algorithms have more detailed information, but the image features are not prominent. Image features extracted by the proposed model reflects the image features more clearly and accurately, which is more suitable for designing the feature graphic in the intelligent user interface and conveying the line features well. It is of superiority that this proposed method is used in the field of intelligent graphic design for traditional engraving graphics.

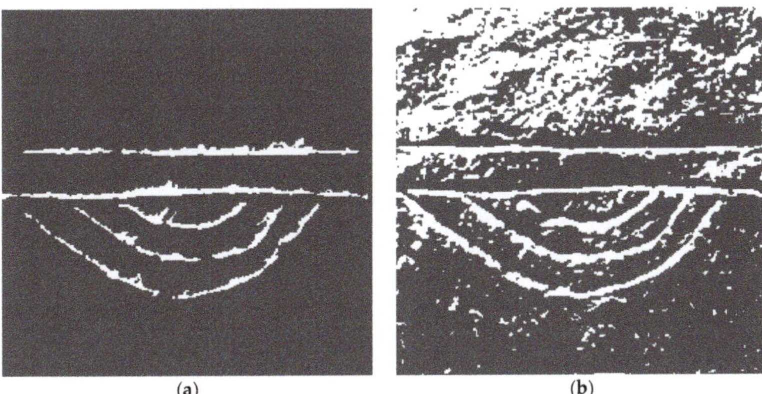

(**a**)   (**b**)

Figure 6. Comparison of image feature extraction with and without image brightness processing. (**a**) The proposed results. (**b**) The results obtained by the complex algorithms.

Based on the parametric test and effectiveness evaluation of the proposed model, we establish its execution metrics as: this extracted feature model is suitable for traditional engraving graphics on historical relics in intelligent graphic design. Through the parametric test, it can achieve an ideal effects with the optimal parameters, which are derived as the brightness enhancement coefficient $k = 2.5$, the image brightness threshold $\theta_T = 128$, the connected area threshold $T_A = 25$, the horizontal convolution kernel G(x) = $[-1, 0, 1; -2, 0, 2; -1, 0, 1]$, and the vertical convolution kernel G(y) = $[1, 2, 1; 0, 0, 0; -1, -2, -1]$, $b = 2$. However, we should adjust the parameters to obtain the appropriate effect for the non-ideal sample images.

4. Intelligent Graphic Design Based on the Brightness Feature Map

According to the brightness feature maps output from the extracted model based on convolution operation, intelligent feature graphics are generated by using the python graphic tools, and then it is applied to design the intelligent graphical interface.

4.1. Created Method of Intelligent Graphics

Many traditional engraving graphics are composed of basic lines and graphics. Their basic graphic units are defined as dots, straight lines, oblique lines, curves, arcs, circles, and so on, which can be created by python graphic tools. Python environment provides powerful graphic tools for drawing regular geometry graphics. Taking the python graphic tool of turtle for example, the general graphic drawing method is listed in Table 2.

Table 2. Drawing method of common geometric lines with python-turtle tools.

Graphics	Drawing Method	Describing
Round dot	dot (*r*)	Draw a round dot of specified radius (*r*).
Straight line	forward (*distance*) backward (*distance*)	Move a distance (*distance*) forward or backward to draw a straight line.
Oblique line	Straight line + right (*degree*) Straight line + left (*degree*)	Draw oblique lines with a clockwise or anti-clockwise angle (*degree*) based on the straight line method.
Circle	circle (*r*)	Draw circles with a radius (*r*).
Arcs	circle() + up() + down() + left() + right()	Draw arcs with different curvature by changing in different direction of up, down, left and right based on the circle method.
Curve	circle() + up() + up() + left() + right() + seth()	Draw curves with different curvature and shape by changing of angle and directions based on the circle method.

Based on the brightness feature map, more accurate graphics can be generated by Python graphic drawing tools and displayed on the user interface of intelligent products. We can also use a lots of mathematical functions provided for array operation such as sine and cosine functions, tangent and cotangent functions, linear function, quadratic function, and so on to generate geometric lines under some geometric laws. Figure 7 shows some geometric lines created by python graphic tools.

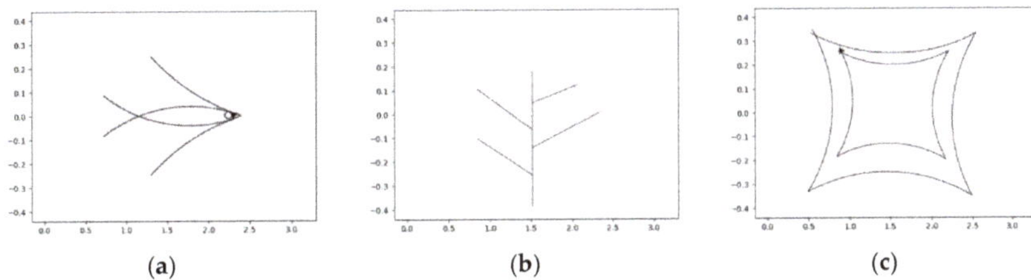

Figure 7. Geometric lines generated by python graphic tools. (**a**) Fish-shape graphic. (**b**) Tree-shape graphic. (**c**) Double-box-shape graphic.

Based on the created graphics, dynamic graphics can also be created, which are commonly applied in intelligent graphical interfaces. Recent research show that dynamic graphic system shows superiority in data exchange and information understanding [24,25], especially on intelligent user interface. In their study, the visual performance of dynamic graphics system in information dissemination is analyzed and evaluated. For intelligent user interface, Chen and Jiu studied a rapidly convert system of 3D dynamic graphics, which is suitable for the Android platform, and evaluated the stability and effectiveness of the algorithm for generating 3D dynamic graphics [26]. Technical method and model for generating dynamic graphics have also been paid attention to. For example, Ding studied the technical method of dynamic graphics with Visual C++ 2005 in the frame of Net framework to realize the dynamic change of points, lines, rectangles, and other shapes [27]. Castillo etc., proposed a dynamic graphic model associated with the graphic structure and studied the transition-probabilities of the proposed model by the method of unobservable variables via estimating the model parameters [28]. Based on the existing studies, an effective method for generating dynamic graphics is necessary to be applied for designing intelligent graphical interface. In this study, we explore an accurate and effective generated method of dynamic graphics in python environment. The specific method used to generate dynamic graphics includes: the basic animation environment is built, the graphic change method is defined and the graphic animation is generated, as shown in Figure 8.

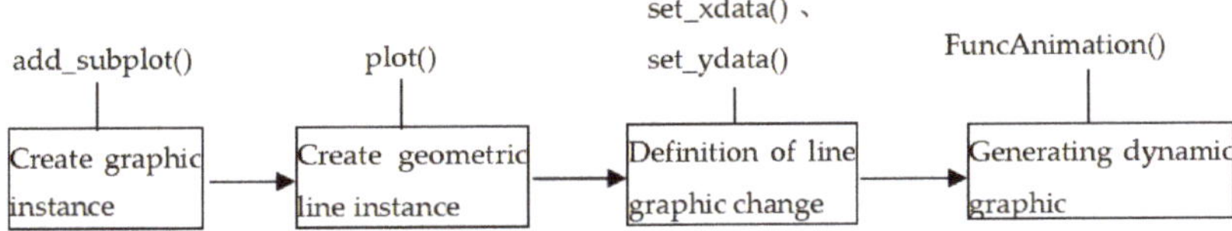

Figure 8. Flow chart of generated method of dynamic graphic.

The animation environment is created by using the matplotlib tools, in which graphic instances are then created by using the plot() method. The change method of line graphic from these graphic instances is defended with the data change in x or y directions, which is set with the methods of set_xdata() and set_ydata(). Then the graphic animation is generated by calling the animation class of FuncAnimation with the graphic change method defined in advance. Figure 9 shows the dynamic graphic of double box line generated by the above method.

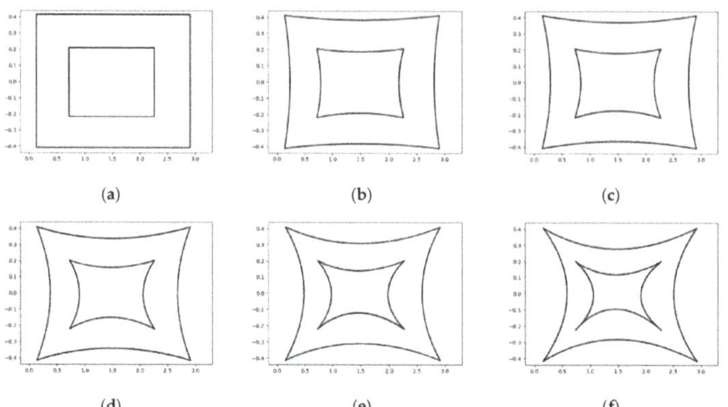

Figure 9. Dynamic graphic of double box line created by generated method of dynamic graphics. (**a**) Dynamic graphic at frame 1. (**b**) Dynamic graphic at frame 3. (**c**) Dynamic graphic at frame 4. (**d**) Dynamic graphic at frame 6. (**e**) Dynamic graphic at frame 8. (**f**) Dynamic graphic at frame 10.

4.2. Created Method of Intelligent Feature Graphics Based on Brightness Feature Map

Traditional culture and artistic features can be conveyed in the field of intelligent applications by applying the feature graphics of traditional engraving graphics into the intelligent graphical interface design. So, the created method of feature graphics including dynamic feature graphics based on the brightness feature map output from the extracted model is researched.

4.2.1. Created Method of Feature Graphics Based on Brightness Feature Map

Intelligent feature graphics are created based on the image brightness feature map output from the proposed model. Specifically, the process includes feature point sampling, optimization, and connection, as shown in Figure 10.

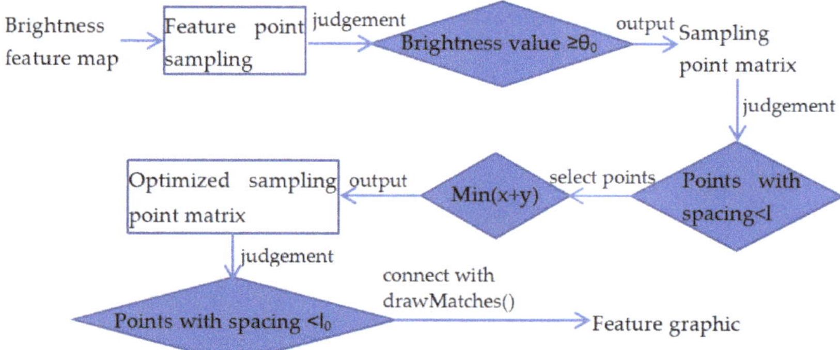

Figure 10. Flow chart of intelligent graphic created algorithm.

Step 1. Feature point sampling. The output brightness feature map is sampled, and the appropriate step size is set as the sampling interval in X and Y directions. In the array of img_array[n × s, n × s] (where s is the sampling interval, n is the number of samples, and $0 \leq n \times s \leq 112$), the pixels whose brightness value is greater than the preset brightness threshold θ_0 are sampled and output, forming the sampling matrix of feature points. This is the initial pix point sampling process of the image brightness feature map.

Step 2. Optimizing the sampling point matrix. To facilitate the connection of feature points, the sampling point matrix is further optimized, and the optimized spacing l is set. During the sampling point the spacing is less than l, the point with min x + y is output, forming the optimized sampling point matrix, where x and y respectively are the horizontal longitudinal coordinates of the sampling point. We obtain key effective points of the sampling matrix of the image brightness feature.

Step 3. Connecting the optimized sampling points to form the feature graphics. The optimized sampling points are connected to form the feature graphics, and we set the connection space as l_0 (usually $l_0 > l$). If the space is less than the set value l_0, the optimized sampling points are connected by the drawing method of drawMatches() for feature point matrix to form the feature graphics, and some smoothing calculations are performed.

4.2.2. Generated Method of Dynamic Feature Graphics

Dynamic feature graphics is generated to realize the dynamic displayed effect of feature graphics on the user interface of AI products. We use the generated method of dynamic graphic mentioned above to generate dynamic feature graphics. The specific implementation method is described as follows.

We select some points such as the middle point of a line, an intersection point, or the highest (or lowest) point of an arc of feature matrix points as the key frame feature points on the line. By setting the data change in the X or Y direction, the key frame feature points drive other feature points to form dynamic feature graphics. Specifically, the implementation method is divided into the following key steps. 1. The basic animation environment is built, and a graphic instance is created to load the feature graphics. 2. The change of the graphics is defined, with the key frame feature points as the reference, we set the date change of graphic data in the X or Y direction through the methods pf set_xdata() and set_ydata(), to define the animation method. 3. The animation method defined in the previous step is used and the animation class FuncAnimation is called to realize the dynamic effect of feature graphics. Taking the dynamic graphic of a line graphic for example, the pseudo code for algorithm implementation can be described as follows briefly:

```
# import graphic and animation tools:
import matplotlib.pyplot as plt from matplotlib;
import FuncAnimation as animation class;
# create graphic instance:
fig = plt.figure();
ax1=fig.add_subplot(num, num, num);
line1= ax1.plot(num, curve, color, linewidth);
# set keyframe feature points:
point_ani=plt.plot(x1, y1, 'point1', x2, y2, 'point2', ... );
# def updata(num):
point_ani.set_data(x[num], y[num]);
return [point_ani];
# generate dynamic graphic:
ani = animation.FuncAnimation(fig=fig,func=updata,frames=np.arange(num,num), interval=num).
```

5. Practice on the Brightness Feature Extraction and Feature Graphic Design

Taking a square engraving graphic from the Shuangdun Site as an example, the practice is conducted on the image feature extraction and intelligent feature graphic design. Specifically, the process is given as follows.

1. Image brightness feature extraction;

The 112×112 image after preprocessing is input into the image feature extracted model. With the optimal parameters are set as the brightness enhancement coefficient $k = 2.5$, brightness threshold $\theta_T = 128$ and connected region threshold $T_A = 25$, the brightness feature map output from the extracted model is shown in Figure 11a.

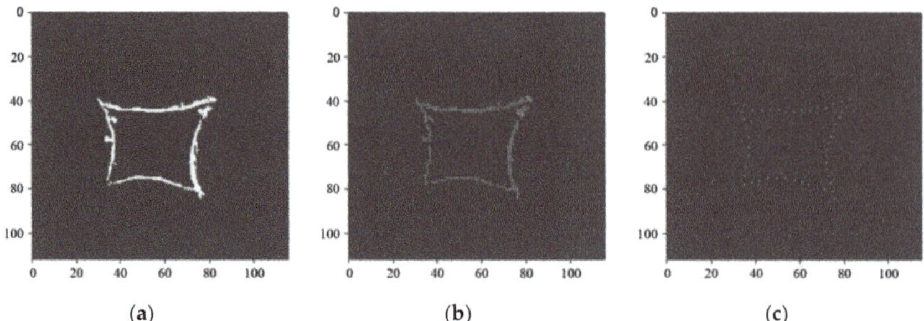

Figure 11. Feature pixel point sampling and optimization based on image brightness feature map. (**a**) Brightness feature map. (**b**) Initial sampling. (**c**) Sampling optimization.

2.   Creating feature graphics;

The brightness feature map is sampled and optimized, where the sampling interval $s = 2$, the number of samples $n = 56$, and the optimal spacing $l = 4$ pixel units. The preliminary sampling result is shown in Figure 11b and the optimized sampling result is shown in Figure 11c. The specific process is that we take the progressive scanning and interval sampling to the image brightness feature map output from the proposed model with the sampling number $n = 56$ and the sampling interval $s = 2$. Then, we select the pixel points if their brightness value is higher than the preset brightness threshold $\theta_0 = 150$ and output them to form the brightness feature sampling matrix. Further optimization is conducted with the optimized spacing $l = 4$. If the space between the sampling points is less than $l = 4$ pixel units, we reserve the pixel point with min x + y to form the key feature point matrix. At last, the drawMatches() method is used to connect the optimized sampling points whose spacing is less than the set value $l_0 = 6$, and the feature graphics is formed, which consequently shows that the lines are partially smoothed.

3.   Generation of dynamic feature graphic.

Dynamic feature graphic is generated by the generated method of dynamic graphic mentioned above, as shown in Figure 12. In the process of generating dynamic graphic, the key frame feature points are the middle points in each line. By using this method, dynamic feature graphic is generated, which can be applied to design the intelligent graphical interface. The displayed effect of this dynamic graphic shows that the better dynamic line graphics are obtained after some smoothing, which can accurately convey the image features of traditional engraving graphics and bring users to be a good visual experience.

The practical results show that the image feature extracted method proposed in this paper can effectively extract the image features of traditional engraving graphics. The feature or dynamic feature graphics created by the proposed method about the intelligent graphical design can be applied to the intelligent application interface, which can convey the image features of traditional engraving graphics well.

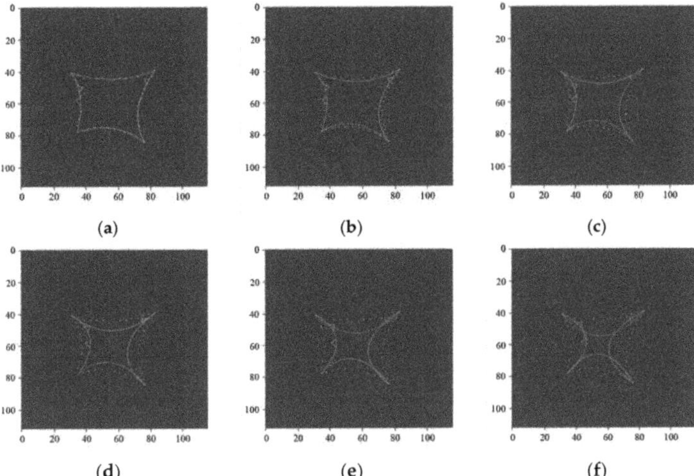

Figure 12. Dynamic graphic of square shape lines after smoothing. (**a**) Dynamic graphic at frame 1. (**b**) Dynamic graphic at frame 4. (**c**) Dynamic graphic at frame 7. (**d**) Dynamic graphic at frame 10. (**e**) Dynamic graphic at frame 13. (**f**) Dynamic graphic at frame 15.

6. Conclusions

In this study, we present the image feature extracted method, in which the image features are extracted by convolution operation after a series of image brightness feature processing. On the basis of the brightness feature map output from the proposed model, feature graphics are designed and applied on the intelligent graphical interface. Theoretical and practical research shows that the extracted model has a significant effect on the performance of the image features extracted from traditional engraving graphics. Moreover, the effect of image feature extraction is related to model parameters, which further affect the feature graphic design. The advantage of this method is that the brightness feature processing greatly simplifies the process of image feature extraction, and the extracted accuracy is improved by convolution operation. Take the pottery engraving graphics from the Neolithic Age as an example, the practice of the image feature extraction and intelligent dynamic graphic design is carried out, which further verify the effectiveness of the proposed method, especially in the field of intelligent feature graphic design and application. However, due to the limit of the sample amount and experiment condition, the image feature extracted model needs to further improve the extracted accuracy. The design efficiency of intelligent graphics needs to be further enhanced by undergoing more practice. More in-depth and extensive research needs to be taken in the next work.

Author Contributions: Conceptualization, Y.L.; methodology, Y.L.; software, Y.L. and Y.T.; validation, Y.L. and Y.T.; data curation, Y.L.; writing—original draft preparation, Y.L.; writing—review and editing, Y.T. All authors have read and agreed to the published version of the manuscript.

Funding: This research received no external funding.

Institutional Review Board Statement: Not applicable.

Informed Consent Statement: Not applicable.

Data Availability Statement: The datasets supporting the conclusion of this article are included within the article.

Acknowledgments: This work is supported by the Key Research Project of Humanities and Social Sciences in Colleges and Universities of Anhui Province (no.SK2019A0121); Support Program for Outstanding Young Talents in Colleges and Universities in Anhui Province (no. gxyq2020166); Scientific Research Project of Anhui Polytechnic University (no.Xjky2020115); Natural Science Research Project of Institutions of Higher Education in Anhui Province of China (no. KJ2017A114); National Natural Science Foundation of China (no. 11902001); Middle-aged Top-notch Talent Support Programs of Anhui Polytechnic University.

Conflicts of Interest: The authors declare no conflict of interest.

References

1. Navaei, J.; Babakmehr, M.; Kalamdani, R.; Liu, Y.N.; Qiu, S.; Farhan, J.; Blackful, J. An intelligent image processing-based approach to optimize vehicle headlamp aiming. In Proceedings of the 18th International Multi-Conference on Systems, Signals & Devices (SSD), Monastir, Tunisia, 22–25 March 2021.
2. Chen, M.Y.; Wu, H.T. Real-time intelligent image processing for the internet of things. *J. Real-Time Image Process.* **2021**, *18*, 997–998. [CrossRef]
3. Singh, A.; Li, P.; Singh, K.K.; Saravana, V. Real-time intelligent image processing for security applications. *J. Real-Time Image Process.* **2021**, *18*, 1787–1788. [CrossRef]
4. LeCun, Y.; Boser, B.; Denker, J.; Henderson, D.; Howard, R.; Hubbard, W.; Jackel, L. Handwritten digit recognition with a back-propagation network. *Adv. Neural Inf. Process. Syst.* **1990**, *2*, 396–404.
5. Duan, M.; Wang, G.P.; Niu, C.Y. Sample image recognition method on convolutional neural network. *Comput. Eng. Des.* **2018**, *39*, 224–229.
6. Liu, J.Z. Sample bark image recognition method on convolutional neural network. *J. Northwest For. Univ.* **2019**, *34*, 230–235.
7. Ding, A.; Zhang, Y.; Zhu, L.; Li, H.; Huang, L. Intelligent recognition of rough handling of express parcels based on CNN-GRU with the channel attention mechanism. *J. Ambient. Intell. Humaniz. Comput.* **2021**, 1–18. [CrossRef]
8. Li, H.C.; Cai, Y.; Wang, L.X. Semantic segmentation of full convolutional network image based on global feature extraction. *Infrared Technol.* **2019**, *41*, 595–615.
9. Domínguez, A. A history of the convolution operation. *IEEE Pulse* **2015**, *6*, 38–49. [CrossRef] [PubMed]
10. Zhan, J. Technical analysis of intelligent image processing of tea. In Proceedings of the 2021 IEEE International Conference on Power Electronics, Computer Applications (ICPECA), Shenyang, China, 22–24 January 2021.
11. Chen, Z.L.; Zou, B.J.; Huang, M.Z.; Shen, H.L.; Xin, G.J. The influence of image brightness characteristics on ROI extraction. *J. Cent. South Univ. Sci. Technol.* **2012**, *43*, 208–214.
12. Maeda, J. *Design in Tech Report 2019*; MIT Press: Cambridge, MA, USA, 2019; pp. 10–21.
13. Xue, Z.R. *AI Changes the Design: Designer's Survival Manual in the Age of Artificial Intelligence*; Tsinghua University Press: Beijing, China, 2019; pp. 62–68.
14. Noguchi, K.; Okada, Y. IntelligentBox for web: A constructive visual development system for interactive web 3D graphics applications. In *Complex, Intelligent, and Software Intensive Systems*; Springer: Berlin, Germany, 2020; pp. 757–767.
15. Bao, W. The application of intelligent algorithms in the animation design of 3D graphics engines. *Int. J. Gaming Comput. Mediat. Simul.* **2021**, *13*, 26–37. [CrossRef]
16. Li, Y.T.; Xv, D. Deep learning algorithm of woodcut style conversion. *J. Comput. Aided Des. Graph.* **2020**, *32*, 1804–1812.
17. Tian, Y.L.; Chen, S.X.; Zhao, F.J.; Lin, X.Y.; Xiong, H.L. Handwritten layout analysis and multi style background fusion of ancient books. *J. Comput. Aided Des. Graph.* **2020**, *25*, 1115–1220.
18. Chen, L.Q.; Wang, P.; Dong, H.; Shi, F.; Han, J.; Guo, Y.; Childs, P.R.N.; Xiao, J.; Wu, C. An artificial intelligence based data-driven approach for design ideation. *J. Vis. Commun. Image* **2019**, *61*, 10–22. [CrossRef]
19. Sejnowski, T. *Deep Learning: The Core Driving Force in the Era of Intelligence*; Citic Press: Beijing, China, 2019; pp. 50–57.
20. Sejnowski, T. *The Deep Learning Revolution*; MIT Press: Cambridge, MA, USA, 2018; pp. 50–57.
21. Chen, D.X.; Zhan, Y.Y.; Yang, B. Application and analysis of deep learning technology in the field of educational big data mining. In Proceedings of the International Conference on Big Data and Social Sciences (ICBDSS), Xi'an, China, 14–16 August 2019; pp. 68–76.
22. Lecun, Y.; Bottou, L.; Bengio, Y.; Haffner, P. Gradient-based learning applied to document recognition. *Proc. IEEE* **1998**, *86*, 2278–2324. [CrossRef]
23. Saito, K. *Introduction to Deep Learning: Theory and Implementation Based on Python*; Posts & Telecom Press: Beijing, China, 2018; pp. 201–203.
24. Morota, G.; Cheng, H.; Cook, D.; Tanaka, E. ASAS-NANP SYMPOSIUM: Prospects for interactive and dynamic graphics in the era of data-rich animal science 1. *J. Anim. Sci.* **2021**, *99*, skaa402. [CrossRef] [PubMed]

25. Zhou, N.G. Analysis on the design and information communication of motion graphic. *Packag. Eng.* **2017**, *38*, 147–151.
26. Chen, S.H.; Jiu, Z. A method of stereoscopic display for dynamic 3D graphics on android platform. *J. Web Eng.* **2020**, *19*, 849–864. [CrossRef]
27. Ding, Y.H. Methods for dynamic drawing based on .NET Framework. *J. Eng. Graph.* **2009**, *30*, 71–75.
28. Castillo, E.; Lacruz, B.; Lasala, P.; Lekuona, A. Estimating transition-probabilities in a dynamic graphic model with unobservable variables. *IEEE Trans. Reliab.* **2001**, *50*, 135–144. [CrossRef]

Article

Intelligent Robust Cross-Domain Fault Diagnostic Method for Rotating Machines Using Noisy Condition Labels

Abhijeet Ainapure [1], Shahin Siahpour [1], Xiang Li [2,*], Faray Majid [1] and Jay Lee [1]

[1] Department of Mechanical Engineering, University of Cincinnati, Cincinnati, OH 45221, USA; ainapuar@mail.uc.edu (A.A.); siahposn@mail.uc.edu (S.S.); majidfy@mail.uc.edu (F.M.); lj2@ucmail.uc.edu (J.L.)

[2] Key Laboratory of Education Ministry for Modern Design and Rotor-Bearing System, Xi'an Jiaotong University, Xi'an 710049, China

* Correspondence: lixiang@xjtu.edu.cn

Abstract: Cross-domain fault diagnosis methods have been successfully and widely developed in the past years, which focus on practical industrial scenarios with training and testing data from numerous machinery working regimes. Due to the remarkable effectiveness in such problems, deep learning-based domain adaptation approaches have been attracting increasing attention. However, the existing methods in the literature are generally lower compared to environmental noise and data availability, and it is difficult to achieve promising performance under harsh practical conditions. This paper proposes a new cross-domain fault diagnosis method with enhanced robustness. Noisy labels are introduced to significantly increase the generalization ability of the data-driven model. Promising diagnosis performance can be obtained with strong noise interference in testing, as well as in practical cases with low-quality data. Experiments on two rotating machinery datasets are carried out for validation. The results indicate that the proposed algorithm is well suited to be applied in real industrial environments to achieve promising performance with variations of working conditions.

Keywords: fault diagnosis; domain adaptation; noisy label; deep learning; convolutional neural network; rotating machine

Citation: Ainapure, A.; Siahpour, S.; Li, X.; Majid, F.; Lee, J. Intelligent Robust Cross-Domain Fault Diagnostic Method for Rotating Machines Using Noisy Condition Labels. *Mathematics* **2022**, *10*, 455. https://doi.org/10.3390/math10030455

Academic Editor: Yolanda Vidal

Received: 12 December 2021
Accepted: 27 January 2022
Published: 30 January 2022

Publisher's Note: MDPI stays neutral with regard to jurisdictional claims in published maps and institutional affiliations.

1. Introduction

Being the most essential part of any rotating machinery, the rolling element bearing has a wide range of applications in the manufacturing industry. Unexpected failures of mechanical components can result in heavy operational losses and serious safety concerns. Rotating elements are usually at a higher risk of mechanical failure due to the fatigue stresses experienced during their operation. Efficient and accurate fault detection and diagnosis is of vital significance, which not only helps to enhance production but also ensures improvement in reliability and operational safety of a machine. Over these years, different signal processing techniques have been utilized for analyzing vibration signals from mechanical systems and components to monitor their health condition. These traditional techniques, however, require expert knowledge about failure mechanics.

In recent times, there have been successful implementations of machine learning and deep learning-based methods for machinery condition monitoring. In deep learning models that are purely data driven, different layers are stacked together to form a deep network architecture. A complex network and deeper network generally results in more efficient feature extraction compared to shallower networks, which makes deep learning a very useful tool in machine health monitoring and fault diagnosis purposes [1–3].

To develop a deep learning-based fault diagnosis model, data are collected from the labeled healthy condition of the system [4–6]. The labeled data are then exploited for training model and subsequently predict the underlying machine health condition of the unlabeled testing data. However, this process is normally performed under the assumption that the data are obtained from a single distribution. In practical scenarios, the systems are operated under variable operating conditions in terms of speed and load. Therefore, there exists a discrepancy between the distributions of the training and testing data provided by the model [7]. This issue undermines the generalization ability of the model to obtain accurate results over different distributions. This problem is referred to as the domain shift phenomenon.

To address this issue, many deep learning-based approaches have been proposed to transfer the knowledge that is obtained from the source domain to the target domain while the target domain is collected under different operating conditions [8,9]. Hasan et al. [10] proposed a deep learning-based transfer learning approach to improve the feature extraction capability of bearing fault diagnosis systems. On the other hand, domain adaptation (DA) approaches are widely used to reduce the discrepancy between source and target domain data distributions [11–14]. As demonstrated in Figure 1, the distribution discrepancy between the source and target domains results in the ineffective performance of source domain classifier when applied in the target domain. Fundamentally, in most of DA approaches, the classifier built using source domain data is adapted for its use in the target domain by aligning the source and target domain distribution in a latent feature space.

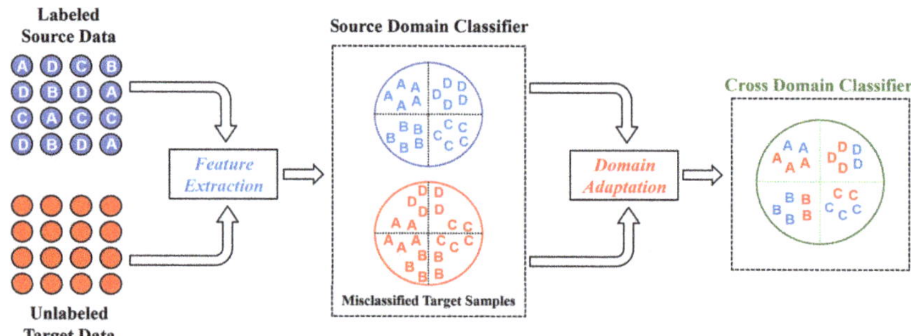

Figure 1. The schematic representation of domain adaptation methodology.

In some situations, even with the application of cross-domain adaptation, there is still a significant distribution discrepancy between the source and target data that reduces the accuracy of the fault diagnosis models. Although data can be acquired easily using state-of-the-art sensors, it usually has a fixed representation and is mostly unlabeled. Moreover, most parts of the collected raw data comes from the healthy working condition of the machine with limited data from different faulty conditions [15]. This makes it difficult to develop a robust model that can be generalized over a wider range of machine health conditions. Li et al. [16] proposed a domain augmentation approach to improve the generalization of the deep learning-based fault diagnosis model. Hu et al. [17] suggests a data augmentation technique that uses a resampling technique to simulate data through partial overlap for different operating conditions. Gao et al. [18] used a Generative Adversarial Network (GAN) to artificially produce fake samples from the limited amount of training data for effective training of a robust cross domain classifier. Wang et al. [19] proposed a novel domain adaptation method based on adversarial networks for improving the waveform recognition performance in the target domain. In [20], the authors have exploited the idea of parameter freezing to ameliorate the performance in the target domain by freezing part of the model parameters and fine-tuning the rest for preventing overfitting issues.

To further enhance the effectiveness of the model, a novel algorithm is proposed in this paper for improving model performances in cross-domain adaptation scenarios. The key novelty and contributions of the paper is as follows:

- The health state labels in the form of one hot encoded vectors are induced with a random noise in the training stage.

- This increases the variability of the source dataset, making the training more robust and achieving better optimization of the model.
- This algorithm has been implemented on two different bearing datasets to validate the performance of the proposed approach.

The remainder of this paper begins with the theoretical background in Section 2. The proposed method is presented in Section 3. The experimental study and conclusion are covered in Sections 4 and 5.

2. Conceptual Background

2.1. Problem Formulation

A transfer learning problem for rotating machinery fault diagnosis is investigated in this paper. The knowledge is learned from the labeled source domain and unlabeled target domain samples using the distribution discrepancy metric. Let $\mathcal{D}_s = \{(\mathbf{x}_i^s, y_i^s)\}_{i=1}^{n_s}$ be the source domain, where $\mathbf{x}_i^s \in R^{M_s}$ shows the M_s-dimensional source data, y_i^s is the system health condition label and n_s is the number of source samples. Likewise, the target domain is also denoted as $\mathcal{D}_t = \{(\mathbf{x}_i^t, y_i^t)\}_{i=1}^{n_t}$, where $\mathbf{x}_i^t \in R^{M_t}$ represents the M_t-dimensional target data, y_i^t denotes the system health condition label and n_t is the target sample. The source and target domain have identical label spaces in this study.

2.2. Convolutional Neural Networks

In this study, a convolutional neural network (CNN) architecture, including convolutional, pooling and fully connected (FC) layers, is utilized to establish a deep learning model for fault diagnosis purposes. The main function of a convolutional layer is to generate meaningful features by convolving raw input data with predefined filters. Subsequently, the most significant feature information is recognized by the pooling layer and is further propagated through the network. The convolution operation can be expressed as follows:

$$z_j^l = \mathcal{F}\left(\sum_i z_i^{l-1} * k_{ij}^l + b_j^l\right) \tag{1}$$

where z_j^l and z_i^{l-1} denote the j-th feature map at l-th layer. The convolutional kernel that connects the i-th feature map with j-th feature map of the l-th layer is denoted as k_{ij}^l. The term b_j^l represents the bias, and operation $*$ is the convolution operation. The function $\mathcal{F}$ is the activation function.

The length of the feature maps can be reduced within the pooling layers without losing key spatial information. Among the important operations, the max pooling operation extracts the maximum out of the set of values, predefined by the pooling size. After multiple alternating convolutional and pooling layers, abstract features are passed through the fully connected layer to perform the desired fault diagnosis task.

2.3. Maximum Mean Discrepancy

Maximum Mean Discrepancy (MMD) has been utilized as a discrepancy measurement between the considered distributions in this article [21]. For domain adaptation application, the MMD, as a non-parametric criterion, is used to compare the source and target distributions by measuring the squared distance between the kernel embeddings of marginal distributions mapped in the Reproducing Kernel Hilbert Space (RKHS). The following is the mathematical formulation:

$$MMD_k(S, T) \triangleq \left\| \mathbf{E}_S[\phi(\mathbf{x}^s)] - \mathbf{E}_T[\phi(\mathbf{x}^t)] \right\|_{\mathcal{H}_k}^2 \tag{2}$$

where S and T are the data distribution corresponding to the source and target domains, respectively. The RKHS endowed with a characteristic kernel k is represented by $\mathcal{H}_k$. The operation $\phi(\cdot)$ is the mapping function, and $\mathbf{E}_S$ denotes the expectation with regards to the distribution S.

As it is stated in [22], the process of calculating the MMD is highly influenced by the choice of kernels. Therefore, a combination of five radial basis function (RBF) kernels is used to exploit the power of multiple kernels (MK).

2.4. Concept of Noisy Health Labels

A novel technique is introduced in this study for enhancing the deep learning-based domain adaptation performance of the model in the fault diagnosis framework. For improving the model's generalization ability, a random noise is injected into the health state labels of the data, for strong regularization purposes. With the help of this technique, data diversity can be elevated, and model randomness can be improved for better optimization.

For the supervised classification tasks, the softmax layer in the deep learning model requires health condition labels in the form of one-hot encoded vectors. During the network's training process, a random noise value N_y is homogeneously selected from the interval $[0, N_{range}]$, with reference to each labeled training data sample in the mini batch [23]. An optimal noise level N_{range} is finalized for this study after running multiple experiments on the data. The results of these experiments are summarized in Section 4.3.2. The randomly selected noise value N_y is then injected into the one-hot encoded health label of each training sample in the mini batch. As per the requirement of the softmax function, N_y is subtracted from the true class element, and the corresponding increments are made in the remaining label elements to ensure the sum remains equal to unity.

For instance, consider $[0, 0, 0, 1, 0, \cdots, 0]$ as the one-hot encoded health label of a sample, where N_{class} denotes the number of classes in the problem. After injecting a random noise value N_y, the noisy health label thus becomes $[N_y/(N_{class} - 1), N_y/(N_{class} - 1), N_y/(N_{class} - 1), 1 - N_y, N_y/(N_{class} - 1), \cdots, N_y/(N_{class} - 1)]$. In this manner, the noisy health label still maintains its compatibility with the softmax function such as the typical one-hot vector labels. For a better understanding of this concept, a schematic representation of this proposed technique is presented in Figure 2.

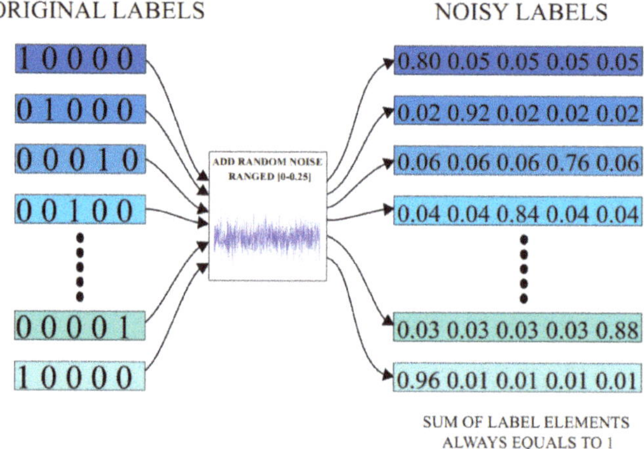

Figure 2. Illustrative explanation of the noisy label algorithm.

3. Proposed Method

An illustrative explanation of the proposed CNN architecture has been presented in Figure 3. In this study, data are organized in two different groups, viz., source-domain data $\mathbf{x}^s$, and target-domain data $\mathbf{x}^t$. Raw vibration data have been directly used as input for the network. Without any specialized pre-processing, a windowing approach is used for preparing raw data samples for training. To extract high-level features from the raw data, three stacks of two consecutive 1D convolutional layers followed by a max-pooling operation have been designed. At the network's final step, the learned features are used as the input of the fully connected layer for obtaining high-level representation. Commonly, the rectified linear units (ReLU) activation function is utilized all over the the network while the softmax activation function is exploited to obtain the desired classification output. The dropout technique has been employed to reduce the chance of overfitting phenomenon. Generally, the network optimization objective has two factors, which are detailed below.

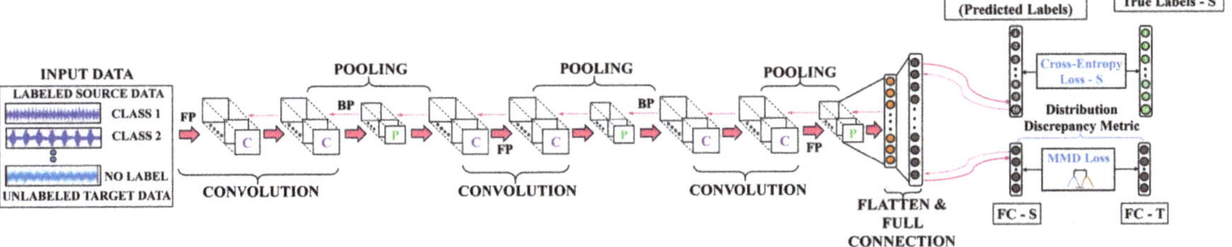

Figure 3. The proposed deep learning architecture for cross-domain fault diagnosis.

(1) Categorical cross-entropy loss: The suggested CNN architecture employs an objective function to reduce training sample classification errors. The usual cross-entropy loss function is used in this work, which is defined as follows:

$$L_s = \frac{1}{n_s} \sum_{i=1}^{n_s} \sum_{j=1}^{N_c} 1\{y_i^s = j\} \log\left(y_{ij}^s\right) \tag{3}$$

where N_c is the number of system health conditions, y_{ij}^s is the i-th sample's predicted probability corresponding to the j-th class, while y_i^s is the corresponding system condition label.

(2) Distribution discrepancy loss: The MMD metric is utilized in the optimization function to calculate and minimize the distribution discrepancy between source and target. The loss function l_d can be formulated as follows:

$$L_d = MMD_k(F_s, F_t) \tag{4}$$

where F_s and F_t denote high-level feature representations of the source and target domain in FC layer, respectively.

By integrating the two objective functions, the final objective function is derived as follows:

$$min L_{opt} = \alpha_s L_s + \alpha_d L_d \tag{5}$$

where α_s and α_d are the penalty coefficients for losses L_s, and L_d, respectively. The network's parameters can be adjusted as follows during each training epoch:

$$\theta \leftarrow \theta - \delta\left(\alpha_s \frac{\partial L_s}{\partial \theta} + \alpha_d \frac{\partial L_d}{\partial \theta}\right) \tag{6}$$

where θ and δ are the model parameters and learning rate, respectively. The flowchart of the proposed cross-domain fault diagnosis method is demonstrated in Figure 4.

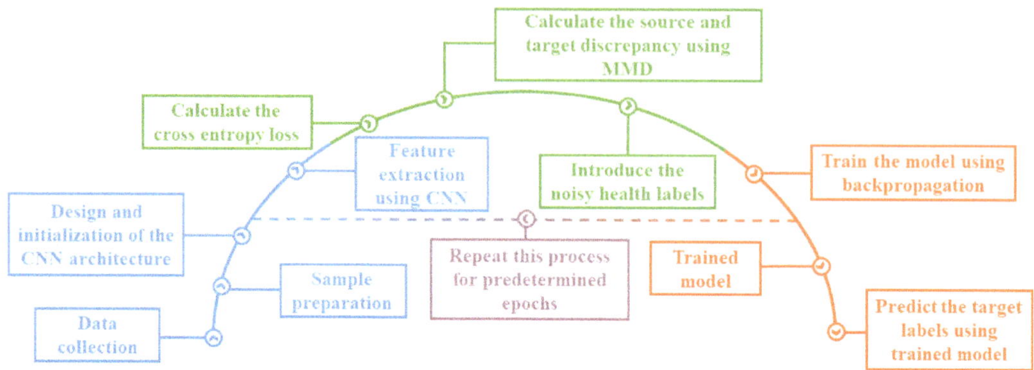

Figure 4. The flowchart of the proposed deep learning model.

4. Result Analysis

4.1. Data Description

To validate the methodology proposed in this paper, two vibration datasets collected from the Bearing Data Centre of Case Western Reserve University (CWRU) and the Chair of Design and Drive Technology, Paderborn University, have been studied. The description of these datasets has been provided below.

4.1.1. CWRU Data Description

Vibration data acquired from four motor loads of 0, 1, 2 and 3 hp, corresponding to the motor speeds of 1797, 1772, 1750 and 1730 rpm, are utilized in this study. In this dataset, three types of bearing defects are implemented, i.e., inner race defect (IRD), outer race defect (ORD) and ball fault (BD). The faults having diameters in the range of 0.007, 0.014 and 0.021 inches were artificially induced in the drive-end (DE) bearings (SKF deep-groove ball bearings: 6205-2RS JEM) of the test rig motor at various locations. Hence, there are totally ten health classes considered in this study. For classification purpose, these ten health conditions with different fault locations (IRD, ORD and BD) and fault levels (0.007″, 0.014″ and 0.021″) are indicated using class labels 1 to 10 respectively. While acquiring data, a sampling frequency of 12 kHz was used.

4.1.2. Paderborn Data Description

In this dataset, the vibration data used for developing condition monitoring methods, which has been generated using a modular test rig, were devised and operated at the Paderborn University. Being a modular system, different defects are flexibly produced in the drive train for generating failure data using the experimental test rig. The test rig consists of the following modules: (a) an electric motor to drive the system, (b) a shaft for torque measurement, (c) the rolling bearing test module, (d) a flywheel module and (e) a load motor. A detailed description of the experimental setup is provided in [24].

The vibration signals collected in this dataset are sampled at a rate of 64 kHz. For ball bearings of type 6203 used in the experiments, artificial faults are generated by using different methods such as electrical discharge machining (EDM), drilling and manual electric engraving, etc. From the complete dataset comprising artificially induced faults and naturally occurring accelerated failure, the data corresponding to artificial damage are used in this study. Depending on the type of defect and the extent of damage produced, five health conditions are implemented in this study. To make the classification easier, these five conditions are denoted using labels 1 to 5, respectively. The details of each health class along with its corresponding test bearing description have been summarized in Table 1.

Table 1. Description of health classes for Paderborn dataset.

Bearing Code	Health Condition Label	Type of Bearing Health Condition	Extent of Damage	Damage Method
K001	1	Healthy (undamaged)	-	-
KI05	2	Inner race defect	1	Electric engraver
KI07	3	Inner race defect	2	Electric engraver
KA05	4	Outer race defect	1	Electric engraver

From the entire dataset, the selection of the above-mentioned bearings helps to cover different artificial faults along with different levels of these faults. The healthy bearing in the above table was operated for a longer duration in more complex conditions and, hence, has been selected in this study. In this dataset, the bearing in the test rig is operated at four different operating conditions, as listed in Table 2. Each operating condition provides 80 s of vibration data (20 measurements of 4 s each) with a sampling frequency of 64 kHz. In this study, multiple transfer tasks covering speed transfer, load torque transfer and radial force transfer are performed to evaluate the influence of change in operating conditions on the fault diagnosis performance. The experiments are targeted to evaluate the model's performance when there is a distribution discrepancy between the training (source) and testing (target) data in terms of operating conditions.

Table 2. Operating Conditions corresponding to the Paderborn Dataset.

Operating Condition	Rotational Speed (rpm)	Load Torque (N·m)	Radial Force (N)
A	1500	0.7	1000
B	900	0.7	1000
C	1500	0.1	1000
D	1500	0.7	400

4.2. Transfer Tasks

4.2.1. Transfer Tasks for CWRU Dataset

The specific details of each transfer task performed in this study are presented in Table 3. N_S and N_T indicate the number of the the samples for each health class under certain speed condition in source and target domains, respectively. In order to avoid additional complexity, the value of N_S is kept equal to that of N_T during the experiments. The dimensionality of each sample obtained from sequential acceleration data is indicated using N_{dim}. All transfer tasks consist of ten health classes (one healthy and nine faulty conditions). Since this dataset is comparably clean in terms of noise level, performing fault diagnosis on these data is straightforward. To make diagnosis more challenging, additional white Gaussian noise with signal-to-noise ratio (SNR) equal to 2 is added in the target domain data. The training of the model using clean source domain data and its testing on noisy target domain data helps in simulating industrial data environment to evaluate the model's robustness. The standard network parameters used in this study are presented in Table 4. Multiple experiments were performed on a sample transfer task for determining the optimal values of certain parameters such as filter number, filter size, etc., while finalizing the network's architecture.

Table 3. Details of each transfer task for CWRU dataset.

Transfer Task	Source Domain	Target Domain	No of Source Samples	No of Target Samples
T_1	0 hp	3 hp	$10 \times N_S$	$10 \times N_T$
T_1	3 hp	0 hp	$10 \times N_S$	$10 \times N_T$
T_1	0 hp	2 hp	$10 \times N_S$	$10 \times N_T$
T_1	2 hp	0 hp	$10 \times N_S$	$10 \times N_T$
T_1	1 hp	3 hp	$10 \times N_S$	$10 \times N_T$
T_1	3 hp	1 hp	$10 \times N_S$	$10 \times N_T$

Table 4. Parameter specification in the proposed methodology.

CWRU Parameter	Value	Paderborn Parameter	Value
Number of epochs	500	Number of epochs	800
δ	1.8×10^{-2}	δ	1.8×10^{-2}
F_N	40	F_N	40
F_S	25	F_S	25
N_S	100	N_S	400
N_T	100	N_T	400
N_{dim}	1000	N_{dim}	600
Batch size for cross entropy	32	Batch size for cross entropy	32
Batch size for MMD	100	Batch size for MMD	100

4.2.2. Transfer Tasks for Paderborn Dataset

A detailed description of each transfer task performed on the Paderborn dataset is presented in Table 5. The information of standard network parameters for Paderborn dataset is also presented in Table 4. For simplicity, N_S is again kept equal to that of N_T during the experiments. Each task consists of five health classes (one healthy and four faulty conditions). Similarly to the experiments with the CWRU dataset, additional white Gaussian noise with SNR equal to 2 is added in the target domain data to make the task more challenging and evaluate the model's performance in noisy environments. The network architecture is finalized using a sample task from the CWRU dataset and is directly used for performing experiments on the Paderborn dataset. All experimental results for both datasets are obtained using a PC with 16-GB RAM, Core i5 CPU and NVIDIA GeForce TX 2080 Ti. The experiments were executed in Python using Tensorflow on a GPU-based device.

Table 5. Details of each transfer task for Paderborn dataset.

Transfer Task	Source Domain	Target Domain	No of Source Samples	No of Target Samples
T_1	A	B	$5 \times N_S$	$5 \times N_T$
T_2	A	C	$5 \times N_S$	$5 \times N_T$
T_3	A	D	$5 \times N_S$	$5 \times N_T$
T_4	B	A	$5 \times N_S$	$5 \times N_T$
T_5	C	A	$5 \times N_S$	$5 \times N_T$
T_6	D	A	$5 \times N_S$	$5 \times N_T$

4.3. Experimental Results

4.3.1. Determination of Architectural Parameters

In this section, a sample task from the CWRU dataset is analyzed for finalizing the network architecture parameters used for performing the experiments. Four main hyperparameters, viz., the number of filters (F_N), filter size (F_S), number of convolutional layers and the number of neurons in the fully connected layer are mainly focused on, as they significantly affect the network optimization process in the fault diagnosis framework.

These experimental tests for parameter finalization were performed using a 5-fold cross-validation approach. In the CWRU dataset, the transfer task from 0 hp to 3 hp, having the maximum domain discrepancy, is selected for running the tests in this section. The experimental results for the above-mentioned parameters are presented in Figure 5.

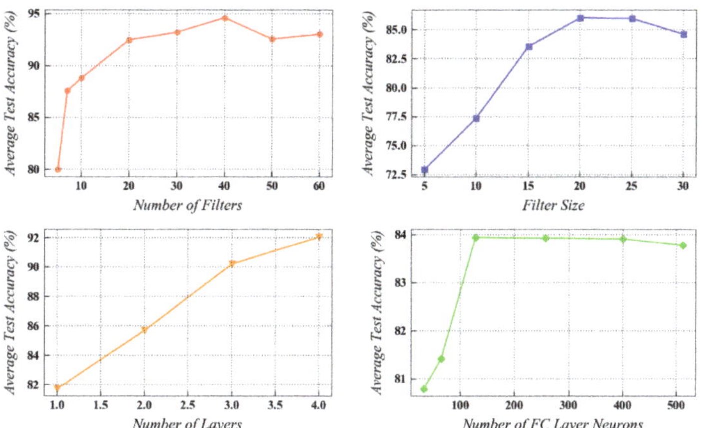

Figure 5. The effect of four hyperparameters on the performance of the network in task T_1 of CWRU dataset.

As indicated in the Figure 5, a larger number of convolutional filters generally improves the model's performance, resulting in higher test accuracies. A similar trend is observed while evaluating the effect of filter size on the model's effectiveness. It was observed that the four double-convolutional layers provided higher accuracy compared to the three double-convolutional layers, but at the same time, significantly increased the computational load. Moreover, an increase in the number of fully connected neurons in the last layer of the network sharply improved the testing accuracy initially. After a certain point, the model's performance started to deteriorate with an increase in the number of fully connected neurons due to possible overfitting. From the point of view of the network's training efficiency and testing accuracy, a well-balanced trade-off needs to be achieved while selecting these parameters during actual implementation. In this study, a filter number of 40, filter size of 25, fully connected neurons equal to 128, and three double-convolutional layers were finalized for experimentation. This selection resulted in high testing accuracy along with acceptable computational time for network's training.

4.3.2. Selection of Optimal Noise Range for the Health Labels

For a deeper assessment of the proposed noisy label methodology, multiple experiments were performed by changing the extent of induced noise in small increments (0.05 increase) and then monitoring its effect on the test accuracy. A sample transfer task of 3 HP to 0 HP from the CWRU dataset, with a higher noise (SNR = −2) in the target data, was focused on. Higher noise level in the target domain data ensured a better evaluation of the method's robustness and noise level selection. The test results are presented in Figure 6. It is clearly indicated in the figure that the addition of a smaller noise level in the health labels results in a significant increase in the model's diagnostic performance. However, it should be noted that the introduction of a larger noise level above a certain threshold will reduce the testing accuracy of the model. For instance, when a higher noise level above 0.25 is injected into the health labels, a significant drop of almost 3% is observed in the testing accuracy. According to these experiments, an optimum level of noise, $N_{range} = 0.25$, was chosen, and a random noise value in the interval of [0, 0.25] was created for every epoch to obtain the needed noisy health labels for the experiments.

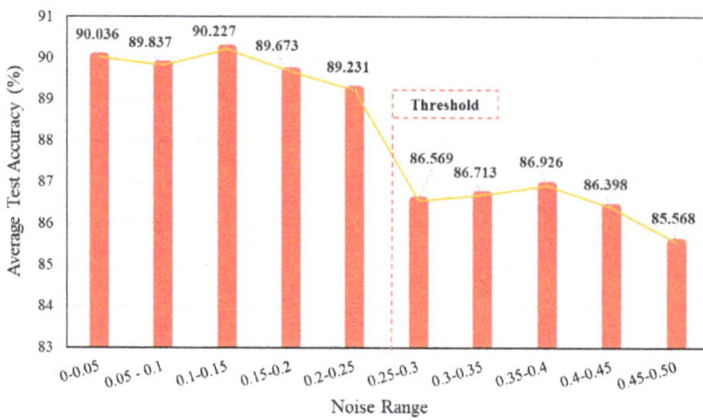

Figure 6. Evaluating results for selecting the optimal noise range.

4.3.3. Compared Methods

In this section, a benchmarking study is performed for validating the effectiveness and reliability of the proposed noisy label-based domain adaptation method. The performance of the proposed method is compared with the following fault diagnosis tools:

1. Deep Neural Network (DNN) [25] is a conventional deep learning method which consists of multiple FC layers stacked together for supervised learning. A network having four FC layers with 128 neurons in each layer is used for feature extraction. Finally, a softmax output layer with number of neurons equal to the number of health classes is adopted for classification.
2. Support Vector Machine (SVM) [26] is a popular supervised machine learning algorithm traditionally used for classification as well as regression tasks. For establishing the SVM model, a structural risk minimization criterion adopted from the statistical learning theory is used for performing the desired task. Manually extracted features are provided as inputs to the model, along with the selection of an appropriate kernel.
3. Transfer Component Analysis (TCA) [27] is a popular domain adaptation technique that tries to learn certain transfer components across the source and target domains and, hence, find a feature subspace in which similar data properties are encountered for the two domains with closer data distributions. On creating the new subspace, a standard SVM classifier is trained using the transformed source domain data for testing in the target domain.
4. Joint Distribution Adaptation (JDA) [28] is a transfer learning approach that is useful when there exists a discrepancy between the marginal as well as the conditional distributions of the labeled source domain and unlabeled target domain data. JDA tries to formulate new feature representations for the domains by jointly adapting their marginal as well as conditional distributions during the dimensionality reduction process. These transformed representations are highly robust and effective for domain generalization.
5. Balanced Distribution Adaptation (BDA) [29] is a transfer learning technique that targets the distribution adaptation problem by leveraging the importance of the marginal and conditional distribution discrepancies in an adaptive manner. It can also be effectively used in transfer learning problems having class imbalance scenarios.
6. Geodesic Flow Kernel (GFK) [30] is a kernel-based unsupervised domain adaptation approach. It tackles the domain shift problem by integrating infinite subspaces that are used for mapping the geometric and statistical changes from the source domain data to the target domain data.
7. Traditional Convolutional Neural Network (CNN) without any cross-domain adaptation, but having a similar architecture as the proposed method, is considered in this comparison study. The stacked convolutional and pooling layers are used for extracting meaningful features from the raw data signals. At the end, a fully con-

nected layer is placed, which is followed by the softmax layer for classification. After training the model using only source domain data, the model is directly tested on target domain data.

8. Convolutional Neural Network with MK-MMD [31]: The proposed method implements the CNN with cross-domain adaptation features. The maximum mean discrepancy metric is used for the alignment of source and target domain distributions.

4.3.4. Benchmarking Results and Performance Analysis

In this section, the experimental results for both datasets are explained in detail. Figures 7 and 8 represent the benchmarking results for all six transfer tasks of CWRU and Paderborn dataset, respectively. For the tests on CWRU dataset, $N_S = N_T = 100$ was used and for the Paderborn dataset, and $N_S = N_T = 400$ was implemented. As depicted in both figures, the proposed methodology that uses noisy health labels in CNN-based cross-domain adaptation framework, achieves the best test accuracy for all transfer tasks. A similar trend in the results is observed for both datasets, which further strengthens the reliability and validates the effectiveness of the proposed method. Being a conventional machine learning method, SVM is not able to generalize well when it is trained on source domain data and directly tested on target domain data. In comparison to traditional methods, domain adaptation approaches such as TCA, JDA, BDA and GFK demonstrate a competitive performance for all tasks. However, the proposed method still outperforms these techniques.

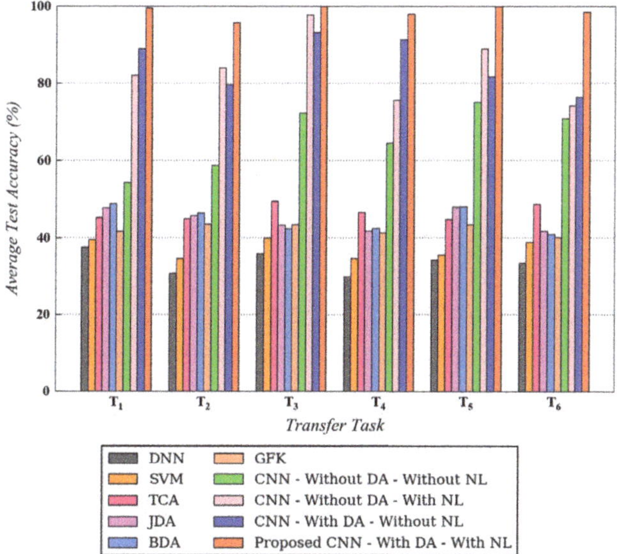

Figure 7. Testing diagnosis performances on target domain for different transfer tasks using different algorithms on CWRU dataset. $N_S = 100$ is used.

Moreover, for the CWRU dataset, the results for CNN with domain adaptation and without noisy health labels and CNN without domain adaptation and with noisy health labels are always in proximity with the former surpassing the latter in certain tasks. However, for the Paderborn dataset, CNN with domain adaptation and without noisy health labels always produces a better diagnosis compared with CNN without domain adaptation (with or without noisy labels). For both the datasets, however, the introduction of noisy labels noticeably enhanced the performance of CNN-based domain adaptation model. The explanation for the performance enhancement after incorporating noisy labels is mainly originated from the regularization effect introduced by this technique during the model's training process. Data augmentation is realized due to the availability of more valid training data samples with discrete health labels, resulting in stronger generalization ability. Correspondingly, a model augmentation effect is also generated, similar to other regularization techniques such as dropout.

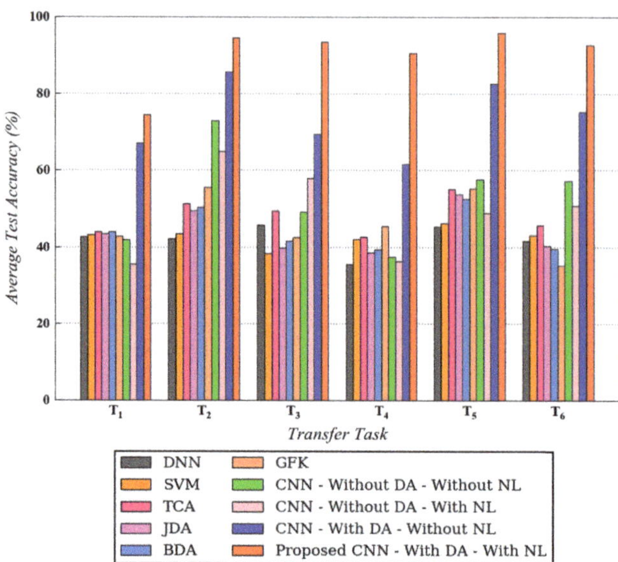

Figure 8. Testing diagnosis performances on target domain for different transfer tasks using different algorithms on Paderborn dataset. $N_S = 400$ is used.

For quantitatively investigating the effect of training data size on the diagnostic performance of the proposed method, a performance analysis was also conducted in this study for both the datasets. The experimental results for this analysis are presented in Figures 9 and 10 for the CWRU and Paderborn dataset, respectively. As observed in both figures, for each transfer task, the availability of a larger number of training data samples generally resulted in higher test accuracy. As stated in the literature, the performance of data-driven models usually improves when more data are available for training. The test results from this analysis are in accordance with the above statement; hence, they further validate our proposed approach.

The performance analysis results also depict the difficulty in minimizing the domain discrepancy for different transfer scenarios. For instance, in Figure 10, it can be observed that the testing accuracy, using the proposed method, is considerably less for task T_1 as compared to tasks T_2 and T_3 in different scenarios. The possible explanation for this result can be that domain discrepancy is usually higher in tasks involving transfer across different speed conditions (task T_1). Since the tasks T_2 and T_3 involve the difference in load and force conditions, respectively, the transfer of learned knowledge across the domains is comparatively easier for these tasks. Hence, the model's performance under various transfer scenarios is well evaluated in this section.

It should be highlighted that a novel technique that integrates the noisy label algorithm into the domain adaptation framework is proposed in this paper for enhancing the cross-domain diagnosis performance. The use of noisy label algorithm, without any domain adaptation features, will unnecessarily reduce the model's diagnostic performance due to additional noise in most of the cases. The simultaneous execution of domain adaptation and noisy label approach will ensure the extraction of domain-invariant features along with improved model generalization, ultimately resulting in performance enhancement. Hence, the effectiveness of the proposed methodology has been strongly validated in this section using different tests and comparisons with popular transfer learning methods in the literature.

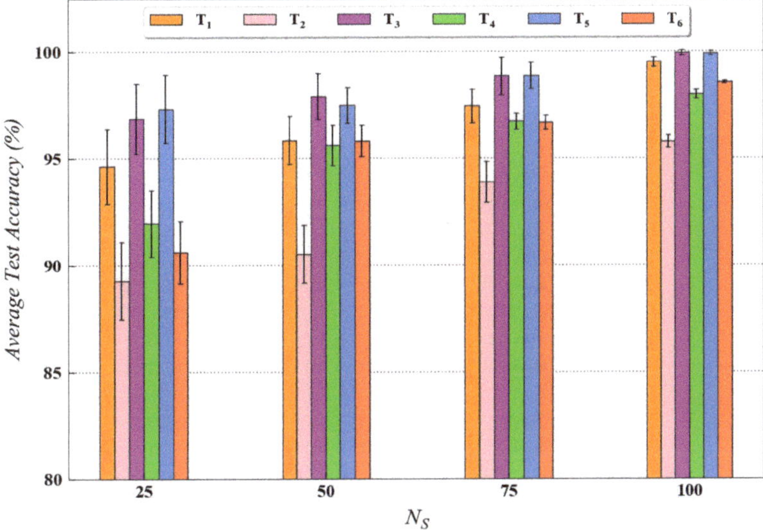

Figure 9. Performance analysis results for various transfer tasks of CWRU dataset with different training data size using the proposed method.

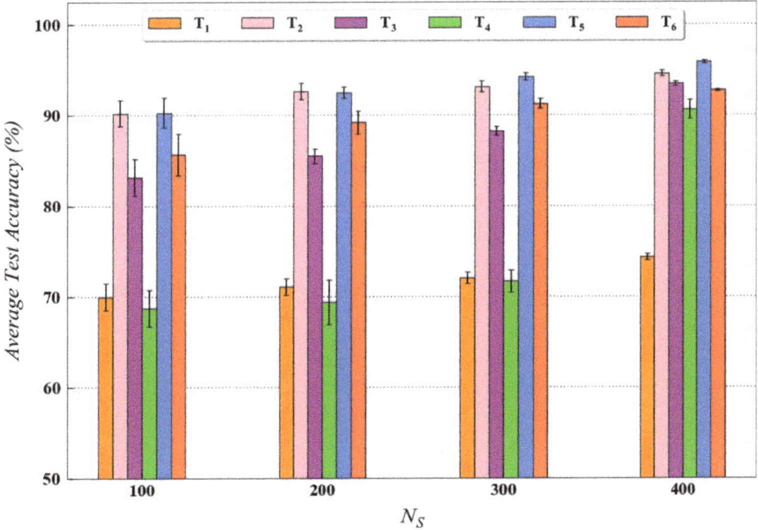

Figure 10. Performance analysis results for various transfer tasks of Paderborn dataset with different training data size using the proposed method.

4.4. Visualization of High-Level Features

In this section, the high-level feature representations, captured by the fully connected layer in the network, are visualized for better interpretation and understanding of the cross-domain fault diagnosis results. The popular t-distributed stochastic neighbor embedding (t-SNE) technique was utilized for visualizing the high-level fault features. Compared to other multi-dimensional scaling methods or techniques such as PCA, t-SNE provides additional flexibility while capturing the local data characteristics, improved ability to handle outliers and better illustration of minor changes in the data structure [32,33].

Figures 11 and 12 present the two-dimensional plots of the learned high-level features obtained using four different methods for the transfer task: T_1 and T_5 from the CWRU and Paderborn dataset, respectively. As depicted, similar representations were obtained for both the studied datasets. When domain adaptation is not implemented, the learned features with the same health labels are clustered together as well, but there exist notable gaps between the data from the source and target domains. Furthermore, due to such domain discrepancies, the respective health condition labels of the source and target domains are mapped into far-off regions. This negatively impacts the generalization of learned feature knowledge from the source domain data to target domain data. After using the proposed idea of domain adaptation, the high-level feature representations with the same health labels from the source and target are well aligned to each other in the feature space. This demonstrates that the domain-invariant features are well extracted during network optimization. Correspondingly, the influence of the proposed noisy label algorithm on the domain adaptation performance is also depicted in Figures 11 and 12 . For the ten health classes in the CWRU dataset, a clear clustering effect was observed in Figure 11 using the proposed methodology. Similarly, five distinct clusters are also obtained for the Paderborn dataset, as seen in Figure 12. Hence, the effectiveness of the proposed noisy label-based domain adaptation method has been quantitatively validated in this section.

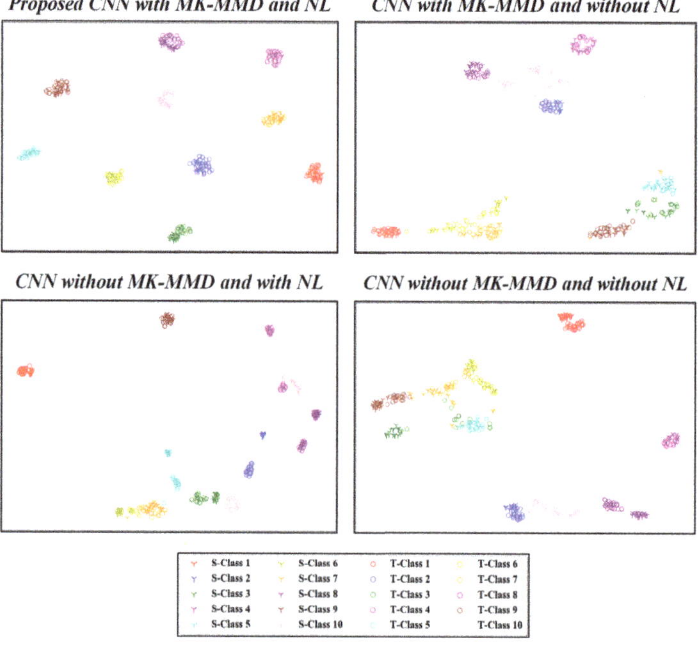

Figure 11. Visualization results of high-level features in the fully connected layer by different methods. *S-* and *T-*denotes source and target domains, respectively. Task T_1 of the CWRU dataset is focused on.

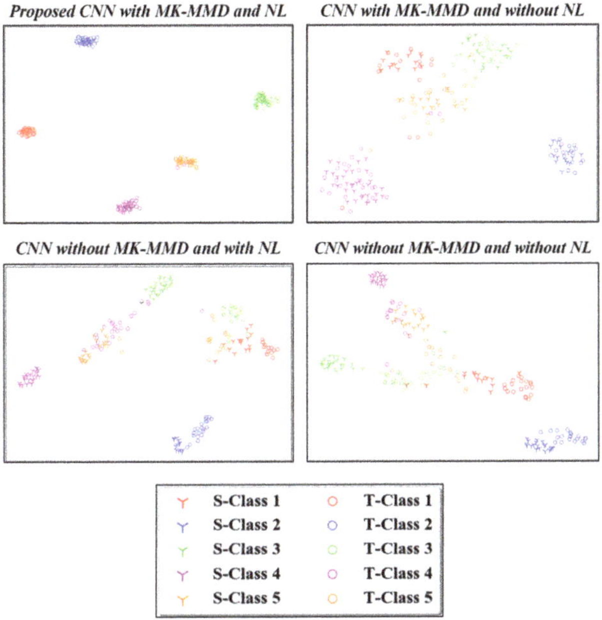

Figure 12. Visualization results of high-level features in the fully connected layer by different methods. *S*- and *T*-denotes source and target domains, respectively. Task T_5 of the Paderborn dataset is focused on.

5. Conclusions

In this paper, a novel methodology for enhancing the performance of deep learning-based cross-domain fault diagnosis using noisy label algorithm is proposed. By injecting additional noise in the health condition labels of source data, the model's generalization ability can be substantially enhanced as compared to its optimization using the conventional one-hot vector labels. Experiments on two popular rotating machinery datasets have been performed in this study to demonstrate the method's usefulness. The presented findings indicate that the proposed technique can effectively extract domain-invariant features and generalize well on the target domain for better addressing the challenging cross-domain diagnosis problem. Although, promising results have been achieved in this paper, the proposed approach still relies on the availability of sufficient target domain data during the network's training process. To address this limitation, future research work will be mainly concentrated on the development of efficient fault diagnosis models that require a limited amount of target domain data.

Author Contributions: Data curation, A.A.; Methodology, F.M.; Project administration, X.L. and J.L.; Writing — original draft, S.S. All authors have read and agreed to the published version of the manuscript.

Funding: This research received no external funding.

Institutional Review Board Statement: Not applicable.

Informed Consent Statement: Not applicable.

Data Availability Statement: Not applicable.

Conflicts of Interest: The authors declare no conflict of interest.

References

1. Jia, F.; Lei, Y.; Guo, L.; Lin, J.; Xing, S. A neural network constructed by deep learning technique and its application to intelligent fault diagnosis of machines. *Neurocomputing* **2018**, *272*, 619–628. [CrossRef]
2. Xiao, D.; Qin, C.; Yu, H.; Huang, Y.; Liu, C. Unsupervised deep representation learning for motor fault diagnosis by mutual information maximization. *J. Intell. Manuf.* **2020**, *32*, 377–391. [CrossRef]
3. Li, X.; Jia, X.D.; Zhang, W.; Ma, H.; Luo, Z.; Li, X. Intelligent cross-machine fault diagnosis approach with deep auto-encoder and domain adaptation. *Neurocomputing* **2020**, *383*, 235–247. [CrossRef]
4. Li, X.; Siahpour, S.; Lee, J.; Wang, Y.; Shi, J. Deep learning-based intelligent process monitoring of directed energy deposition in additive manufacturing with thermal images. *Procedia Manuf.* **2020**, *48*, 643–649. [CrossRef]
5. Joshi, G.P.; Alenezi, F.; Thirumoorthy, G.; Dutta, A.K.; You, J. Ensemble of Deep Learning-Based Multimodal Remote Sensing Image Classification Model on Unmanned Aerial Vehicle Networks. *Mathematics* **2021**, *9*, 2984. [CrossRef]
6. Shi, S.; Li, J.; Li, G.; Pan, P.; Liu, K. XPM: An Explainable Deep Reinforcement Learning Framework for Portfolio Management. In Proceedings of the 30th ACM International Conference on Information & Knowledge Management, Gold Coast, Australia, 1–5 November 2021; pp. 1661–1670.
7. Siahpour, S.; Li, X.; Lee, J. Deep learning-based cross-sensor domain adaptation for fault diagnosis of electro-mechanical actuators. *Int. J. Dyn. Control* **2020**, *8*, 1054–1062. [CrossRef]
8. Li, X.; Zhang, W.; Ma, H.; Luo, Z.; Li, X. Degradation Alignment in Remaining Useful Life Prediction Using Deep Cycle-Consistent Learning. *IEEE Trans. Neural Netw. Learn. Syst.* **2021**, 1–12. [CrossRef]
9. Zhang, W.; Li, X.; Ma, H.; Luo, Z.; Li, X. Federated learning for machinery fault diagnosis with dynamic validation and self-supervision. *Knowl.-Based Syst.* **2021**, *213*, 106679. [CrossRef]
10. Hasan, M.J.; Kim, J.M. Bearing fault diagnosis under variable rotational speeds using stockwell transform-based vibration imaging and transfer learning. *Appl. Sci.* **2018**, *8*, 2357. [CrossRef]
11. Ainapure, A.; Li, X.; Singh, J.; Yang, Q.; Lee, J. Deep learning-based cross-machine health identification method for vacuum pumps with domain adaptation. *Procedia Manuf.* **2020**, *48*, 1088–1093. [CrossRef]
12. Zhang, Z.; Chen, H.; Li, S.; An, Z. Sparse filtering based domain adaptation for mechanical fault diagnosis. *Neurocomputing* **2020**, *393*, 101–111. [CrossRef]
13. Li, S.; Liu, C.H.; Lin, Q.; Wen, Q.; Su, L.; Huang, G.; Ding, Z. Deep residual correction network for partial domain adaptation. *IEEE Trans. Pattern Anal. Mach. Intell.* **2020**, *43*, 2329–2344. [CrossRef] [PubMed]
14. Zhang, W.; Li, X.; Ma, H.; Luo, Z.; Li, X. Open set domain adaptation in machinery fault diagnostics using instance-level weighted adversarial learning. *IEEE Trans. Ind. Informatics* **2021**, *17*, 7445–7455. [CrossRef]
15. Wang, Q.; Michau, G.; Fink, O. Missing-class-robust domain adaptation by unilateral alignment. *IEEE Trans. Ind. Electron.* **2020**, *68*, 663–671. [CrossRef]
16. Li, X.; Zhang, W.; Ma, H.; Luo, Z.; Li, X. Domain generalization in rotating machinery fault diagnostics using deep neural networks. *Neurocomputing* **2020**, *403*, 409–420. [CrossRef]
17. Hu, T.; Tang, T.; Lin, R.; Chen, M.; Han, S.; Wu, J. A simple data augmentation algorithm and a self-adaptive convolutional architecture for few-shot fault diagnosis under different working conditions. *Measurement* **2020**, *156*, 107539. [CrossRef]
18. Gao, X.; Deng, F.; Yue, X. Data augmentation in fault diagnosis based on the Wasserstein generative adversarial network with gradient penalty. *Neurocomputing* **2020**, *396*, 487–494. [CrossRef]
19. Wang, Q.; Du, P.; Liu, X.; Yang, J.; Wang, G. Adversarial unsupervised domain adaptation for cross scenario waveform recognition. *Signal Process.* **2020**, *171*, 107526. [CrossRef]
20. Kim, H.; Youn, B.D. A new parameter repurposing method for parameter transfer with small dataset and its application in fault diagnosis of rolling element bearings. *IEEE Access* **2019**, *7*, 46917–46930. [CrossRef]
21. Gretton, A.; Borgwardt, K.M.; Rasch, M.J.; Schölkopf, B.; Smola, A. A kernel two-sample test. *J. Mach. Learn. Res.* **2012**, *13*, 723–773.
22. Gretton, A.; Sejdinovic, D.; Strathmann, H.; Balakrishnan, S.; Pontil, M.; Fukumizu, K.; Sriperumbudur, B.K. Optimal kernel choice for large-scale two-sample tests. *Adv. Neural Inf. Process. Syst.* **2012**, *25*, 1205–1213.
23. Ainapure, A.; Li, X.; Singh, J.; Yang, Q.; Lee, J. Enhancing intelligent cross-domain fault diagnosis performance on rotating machines with noisy health labels. *Procedia Manuf.* **2020**, *48*, 940–946. [CrossRef]
24. Lessmeier, C.; Kimotho, J.K.; Zimmer, D.; Sextro, W. Condition monitoring of bearing damage in electromechanical drive systems by using motor current signals of electric motors: A benchmark data set for data-driven classification. In Proceedings of the European Conference of the Prognostics and Health Management Society, Bilbao, Spain, 5–8 July 2016; pp. 05–08.
25. Chen, Z.; Deng, S.; Chen, X.; Li, C.; Sanchez, R.V.; Qin, H. Deep neural networks-based rolling bearing fault diagnosis. *Microelectron. Reliab.* **2017**, *75*, 327–333. [CrossRef]
26. Yang, Y.; Yu, D.; Cheng, J. A fault diagnosis approach for roller bearing based on IMF envelope spectrum and SVM. *Measurement* **2007**, *40*, 943–950. [CrossRef]
27. Pan, S.J.; Tsang, I.W.; Kwok, J.T.; Yang, Q. Domain adaptation via transfer component analysis. *IEEE Trans. Neural Netw.* **2010**, *22*, 199–210. [CrossRef]
28. Long, M.; Wang, J.; Ding, G.; Sun, J.; Yu, P.S. Transfer feature learning with joint distribution adaptation. In Proceedings of the IEEE International Conference on Computer Vision, Sydney, NSW, Australia, 1–8 December 2013; pp. 2200–2207.

29. Wang, J.; Chen, Y.; Hao, S.; Feng, W.; Shen, Z. Balanced distribution adaptation for transfer learning. In Proceedings of the 2017 IEEE International Conference on Data Mining (ICDM), New Orleans, LA, USA, 18–21 November 2017; pp. 1129–1134.
30. Gong, B.; Shi, Y.; Sha, F.; Grauman, K. Geodesic flow kernel for unsupervised domain adaptation. In Proceedings of the 2012 IEEE Conference on Computer Vision and Pattern Recognition, Providence, RI, USA, 16–21 June 2012; pp. 2066–2073.
31. Li, X.; Zhang, W.; Ding, Q.; Sun, J.Q. Multi-layer domain adaptation method for rolling bearing fault diagnosis. *Signal Process.* **2019**, *157*, 180–197. [CrossRef]
32. Li, W.; Cerise, J.E.; Yang, Y.; Han, H. Application of t-SNE to human genetic data. *J. Bioinform. Comput. Biol.* **2017**, *15*, 1750017. [CrossRef]
33. Maaten, L.V.d.; Hinton, G. Visualizing data using t-SNE. *J. Mach. Learn. Res.* **2008**, *9*, 2579–2605.

 *mathematics*

Article

Adaptive Guided Spatial Compressive Cuckoo Search for Optimization Problems

Wangying Xu [1] and Xiaobing Yu [1,2,*]

[1] School of Management Science and Engineering, Nanjing University of Information Science & Technology, Nanjing 211544, China; 20201224033@nuist.edu.cn
[2] Ministry of Education & Collaborative Innovation Center on Forecast and Evaluation of Meteorological Disasters (CIC-FEMD), Nanjing University of Information Science & Technology, Nanjing 211544, China
* Correspondence: 002257@nuist.edu.cn

Abstract: Cuckoo Search (CS) is one of the heuristic algorithms that has gradually drawn public attention because of its simple parameters and easily understood principle. However, it still has some disadvantages, such as its insufficient accuracy and slow convergence speed. In this paper, an Adaptive Guided Spatial Compressive CS (AGSCCS) has been proposed to handle the weaknesses of CS. Firstly, we adopt a chaotic mapping method to generate the initial population in order to make it more uniform. Secondly, a scheme for updating the personalized adaptive guided local location areas has been proposed to enhance the local search exploitation and convergence speed. It uses the parent's optimal and worst group solutions to guide the next iteration. Finally, a novel spatial compression (SC) method is applied to the algorithm to accelerate the speed of iteration. It compresses the convergence space at an appropriate time, which is aimed at improving the shrinkage speed of the algorithm. AGSCCS has been examined on a suite from CEC2014 and compared with the traditional CS, as well as its four latest variants. Then the parameter identification and optimization of the photovoltaic (PV) model are applied to examine the capacity of AGSCCS. This is conducted to verify the effectiveness of AGSCCS for industrial problem application.

Keywords: cuckoo search; adaptive method; spatial compression; photovoltaic model

Citation: Xu, W.; Yu, X. Adaptive Guided Spatial Compressive Cuckoo Search for Optimization Problems. *Mathematics* **2022**, *10*, 495. https://doi.org/10.3390/math10030495

Academic Editors: Xiang Li, Shuo Zhang and Wei Zhang

Received: 30 December 2021
Accepted: 26 January 2022
Published: 3 February 2022

Publisher's Note: MDPI stays neutral with regard to jurisdictional claims in published maps and institutional affiliations.

1. Introduction

The optimization problems cover a wide range, including economic dispatch [1], data clustering [2], structure design [3], image processing [4], and so on. The aim of optimization is to find the optimal solution only when the constraint conditions are satisfied. If the optimization has no constraint conditions, it is named an unconstrained optimization. Otherwise, it is called a constraint optimization problem [5]. A mathematical model is derived below, which can be concluded in most of the above cases:

$$\begin{cases} minimize: \ f(x) \\ subject\ to: \ g(x) \leq 0, \ h(x) = 0 \\ g(x) = \{g_1(x), g_2(x), \ldots, g_m(x) \\ h(x) = \{h_1(x), h_2(x), \ldots, h_n(x)\} \end{cases} \tag{1}$$

where $f(x)$ is the objective function, i exhibits the number of objective functions, $g(x)$ and $h(x)$ are constraint functions, $g(x)$ is an inequality constraint and $h(x)$ is an equality constraint. When the problem is unconstrained, $g(x)$ and $h(x)$ are equal to 0 and m and n represent the number of constraints, respectively.

To solve the optimization problem, various solutions have been proposed. In the beginning, some accurate numerical algorithms were developed, such as gradient descent technology [6,7], linear programming [8], nonlinear programming [9], quadratic programming [10,11], Lagrange multiplier method [12,13] and λ-iteration method [14,15].

However, these numerical methods do not show absolute computational advantages in high-dimensional problems. Contrarily, it loses time because of its accurate search methods [16]. Later on, some heuristic algorithms are gradually invented. The earliest and most famous one is the genetic algorithm (GA), first proposed in the 1970s by John Holland [17]. It draws lessons from the process of chromosome gene crossover and mutation in biological evolution to transform the accurate solution of the problem into an optimization. Since heuristic algorithms often lack global guidance rules, they are easy to fall into local stagnation. In the past two decades, some intelligent algorithms imitating the biological behavior of nature have begun to appear, which are called metaheuristics. Particle Swarm Optimization (PSO) can be regarded as one of the earliest swarm intelligence algorithms [18]. PSO is a random search algorithm based on group cooperation, which simulates the foraging behavior of birds. A bat-inspired algorithm (BA) was proposed by X.S. Yang et al. [19]. The BA makes use of the process of a bat population moving and searching prey. The Artificial Bee Colony Algorithm (ABC) was invented by Karaboga et al. [20]. It is a metaheuristic algorithm that imitates bee foraging behavior. It regards the population as bees and divides bees into several species. Different bees exchange information in a specific way, thereby guiding the bee colony to a better solution. The Grey Wolf Optimizer (GWO) is another metaheuristic algorithm and was proposed by Mirjalili [21]. It has three intelligent behaviors containing encircling prey, hunting, and attacking. In addition, the Cuckoo Search (CS) algorithm was proposed by Xin-She Yang [22]. CS is a nature-inspired algorithm that imitates the brood reproductive strategy of cuckoo birds to increase the survival probability of their offspring. Different from other metaheuristic algorithms, CS adapts its parameters by relying on the random walk possibility P_a, which is easy to control for the iterations of the simple parameters. What is more, CS adopts two searching methods including *Levy* Flight and random walk flight. This combination of large and small step size makes the global searchability stronger when compared with other algorithms.

Although CS has been easily accepted, there are still some weaknesses, such as insensitive parameters and easy convergence to the local optimal [23,24]. Commonly, conventional improvements for CS mainly aim at the following steps:

(1) Improve *Levy* Flight. *Levy* Flight is proposed to enhance the disorder and randomness in the search process to increase the diversity of solutions. It combines considerable step length with a small step length to strengthen global searchability. Researchers modified *Levy* Flight to achieve a faster convergence. Naik cancelled the step of *Levy* flight and made the adaptive step according to the fitness function value and its current position in the search space [25]. In reference [26], Ammar Mansoor Kamoona improved CS by replacing the Gaussian random walk with a virus diffusion instead of the Lévy flights for a more stable process of nest updating in traditional optimization problems. Hu Peng et al. [27] used the combination of Gaussian distribution and *Levy* distribution to control the global search by means of random numbers. S. Walton et al. [28] changed the step size generation method in *Levy* flight and obtained a better performance. A new nearest neighbor strategy was adopted to replace the function of *Levy* flight [29]. Moreover, he changed the strategy for crossover in global search. Jiatang Cheng et al. [30] drew lessons from ABC and employed two different one-dimensional update rules to balance the global and local search performance.

However, the above work is always aimed at global search. Too much attention is paid to global search and ignores local search. *Levy* flight provides a rough position for the optimization process, while local walking deteriorates the mining ability of CS. Therefore, the improvement of local walking is also important.

(2) Secondly, the parameter and strategy adjustment have always been a significant concern for improving the metaheuristic algorithm. The accuracy and convergence speed of CS are increased through the adaptive adjustment of parameters or the innovation of strategies in the algorithm. For example, Pauline adopted a new adaptive step size adjustment strategy for the *Levy* Flight weight factor, which can converge to the global optimal solution faster [31]. Tong et al. [32] proposed an improved CS; ImCS

drew on the opposite learning strategy and combined it with the dynamic adjustment of the score probability. It was used for the identification of the photovoltaic model. Wang et al. [33] used chaotic mapping to adjust the step size of cuckoo in the original CS method and applied an elite strategy to retain the best population information. Hojjat Rakhshani et al. [34] proposed two population models and a new learning strategy. The strategy provided an online trade-off between the two models, including local and global searches via two snap and drift modes.

These approaches in this area have indeed improved the diversity of the population. However, in adaptive and multi-strategy methods, the direction of the optimal solution is often used as the reference direction for the generation of children. If the population searches along the direction of the optimal solution, the population may be trapped into a local optimization. In addition, the elite strategy based on a single optimal solution rather than a group solution is not stable enough. Once the elite solution does not take effect, it will affect the iterative process of the whole solution group.

(3)　Thirdly, the combination of optimization and other algorithms is another improvement focus. For example, M. Shehab et al. [35] innovatively adopted the hill-climbing method into CS. The algorithm used CS to obtain the best solution and passed the solution to the hill-climbing algorithm. This intensification process accelerated the search and overcame the slow convergence of the standard CS algorithm. Jinjin Ding et al. [23] combined PSO with CS. The selection scheme of PSO and the elimination mechanism of CS gave the new algorithm a better performance. DE and CS also could be combined. In ref [36], Z. Zhang et al. made use of the characteristics of the two algorithms dividing the population into two subgroups independently.

This kind of improvement method generally uses one algorithm to optimize the parameters of another algorithm. Later, global optimization would be carried out. This method has strong operability, but there are two or more cycles, which increases the complexity of the algorithm.

Based on the above discussion, we proposed three strategies to solve the above problems of CS. Firstly, a scheme of initializing the population by chaotic mapping has been proposed to solve the problem of uneven distribution in high-dimensional cases. Experiments show that the iterative operation using the chaotic sequence as the initial population will influence the whole process of the algorithm [33]. Furthermore, this often achieves better results than a pseudo-random number [37]. Secondly, aiming at enhancing the process of random walk, we put forward an adaptive guided local search method, which reduces the instability of randomness by the original local search. This search method ranks all of the species according to their adaptability. In this segment, we believe that the information for optimal solutions and poor solutions are both important to the iterative process. Thus, the position of the best of the first $p\%$ and the worst of the last $p\%$ calculates the difference and gets the direction of the next generation's solution. This measure reasonably takes advantage of the best and worst solutions because they are considered to have potential information related to the ideal solution [38]. The solution group ensures the universality of the optimization process and avoids the occurrence of individual abnormal solutions affecting the optimization direction. Thirdly, as discussed before, to increase the optimization ability some researchers like to use different algorithms combined with CS. However, compared with the original CS, this measure increases many additional segments. Moreover, there is added algorithm complexity, which wastes computational time. Therefore, we propose a spatial compression (SC) technique that positively impacts the algorithm from the outside. The SC technique was firstly proposed by A. Hirrsh and can help the algorithm converge by artificial extrusion [39]. This method that adjusts the optimization space with the help of external pressure has been proved to be effective [40].

We incorporated these three improvements into CS and propose an Adaptive Guided Spatial Compressive CS (AGSCCS). It has the following merits compared with CS and other improved algorithms: (1) An even and effective initial population. This population generation method is applicable when solving high-dimensional problems. (2) Reasonable and efficient information from each generation of optimal solutions while avoiding the population search bias caused by random sequences. (3) Increasing the precision of the population iteration while maintaining the convergence rate. The imposed spatial compression also boosts the exploration power of the algorithm to some extent, as it could identify potentially viable regions, judge the next direction of spatial reduction, and avoid getting trapped in local optimal. The AGSCCS algorithm will be simulated and compared on 30 reference functions with single, multi-peak, rotation, and displacement characteristics. Moreover, we also applied the proposed algorithm to the photovoltaic (PV) model problem to verify its feasibility for practical issues. Research on PV systems is vital for the efficient use of renewable energy. Its purpose is to accurately, stably, and quickly identify the important parameters in the PV model. The results show that both the effectiveness and efficiency of the proposed algorithm are proven. Compared with other algorithms, the new algorithm is competitive in dealing with various optimization problems, which is mainly reflected in:

(1) An initialization method of a logistic chaotic map is used to replace the random number generation method regardless of the dimension.
(2) A guiding method that includes the information of optimal solutions and worst solutions is used to facilitate the generation of offspring.
(3) An adaptive update step size replaces the random step size to make the search radius more reasonable.
(4) In the iterative process, the SC technique is added to compress the space to help rapid convergence artificially.

The rest of the thesis is divided into the following six parts. The introduction of the original CS is briefly exhibited in Section 2. Section 3 concisely introduces the main idea of AGSCS. In Section 4, the experimental simulation results and their interpretations are presented. Furthermore, a sensitive discussion is performed to compare the enhancement of the improved strategies. In Section 5, AGSCCS is applied to the parameter identification and optimization of the PV model. The work is summarized in Section 6.

2. Cuckoo Search (CS)

2.1. Cuckoo Breeding Behavior

CS is a heuristic algorithm proposed by Yang [22]. It is an intelligent algorithm that imitates the feeding method of cuckoos. As shown in Figure 1, cuckoo mothers choose other birds' nests to lay eggs. In nature, cuckoo mothers prefer to choose the best nest among a plenty of nests [41]. In addition, baby cuckoos have some methods to ensure their safety. For one thing, some cuckoo eggs are pretty similar to those of hosts. Another thing is that the hatching time of the cuckoo is often earlier than those of the host birds. Therefore, once the little cuckoo breaks its shell, they have a chance to throw some eggs out of the nest to enhance their possibility of survival. Moreover, the little cuckoo can imitate the cry of the child of the host bird to get more food. However, the survival of a baby cuckoo is not easy. If the host recognizes the egg, it will be discarded. In that case, host mothers only choose to get rid of their eggs or abandon the nests altogether. Later, cuckoo mothers will move to build a new nest somewhere else. If the eggs are lucky enough not to be recognized, they will survive. Therefore, for the safety of the children, cuckoo mothers always choose some birds similar to their living habits [42].

Figure 1. Feeding habits of cuckoos in nature. ①: Mother cuckoos find the best nest within plenty of nests and lay their babies. ②: Baby cuckoos are raised by the hosts. ③: If the hosts find that the cuckoos are not their babies, they will discard them. If the babies are lucky enough not to be found, they will survive ④: If the baby cuckoos are abandoned, mother cuckoos will continue to find the best nest to lay their eggs.

2.2. Lévy Flights Random Walk (LFRW)

There are some different methods to find the best solution for a local search in the conventional evolutionary algorithms. For example, Evolutionary Strategy (ES) [40] follows a Gaussian distribution. GA and evolutionary programming (EP) choose the random selection mode to find the best solution. A random searching measure is always a better choice in most heuristic algorithms. However, blindly random selection will only reduce the efficiency of the algorithm. Therefore, CS applies a new searching method to enhance itself. In a global search, CS adopts a new searching space technique, which is called *Levy Flight Random Walk (LFRW)*. A quantity of evidence has confirmed that some birds and fish in nature use a mixture of *Levy* flight and Brownian motion to capture prey [43]. In a nutshell, *Levy* flight is the approach that combines long and short steps. The step length of *Levy* flight obeys *Levy* distribution. Sometimes, the direction of *Levy* flight will suddenly turn 90 degrees. Its 2D plane flight trajectory is simulated in Figure 2. In local search, CS adopts a novel measure called random walk [44]. As we all know, it is challenging to balance the breadth and depth when the population is in convergence. *Levy* flight has a promising performance in a searching space as it mixes long and short steps, which benefits global search. Random walk describes the behavior of random diffusion. Combining the two methods is beneficial to improve the depth and breadth of the algorithm, which is conducive to improving the accuracy of the algorithm.

In a word, *Levy* flight is a random walk that is used in the second stage of CS. The offspring is generated by *Levy* flight as follows:

$$X_i^{g+1} = X_i^g + \alpha \otimes Levy(\beta)\alpha = \alpha_0 \otimes \left(X_i^g - X_k^g \right) \tag{2}$$

where X_i^{t+1} is the next generation, X_i^t is the current generation, and X_k^t is a randomly generated solution; α ($\alpha > 0$) is the step size of *Levy* flight; $Levy(s, \lambda)$ is a random search path following *Levy* distribution; $\otimes$ is a special multiplication indicating the entry-wise multiplication; and α_0 is a step control parameter. Yang simplified the *Levy* distribution function and Fourier transform to obtain the probability density function in power form, which is given by:

$$Levy(\beta) \sim \mu = t^{-1-\beta}, 0 < \beta < 2 \tag{3}$$

Actually, the integral expression of *Levy* distribution is quite complex, and it has not been analyzed. However, Mantegna proposed a method to solve for random numbers with a positive distribution in 1994 [45], which is similar to the distribution law of *Levy* distribution. Thus, this method is used in Yang's approach as follows:

$$Levy(\beta) \sim \frac{u}{|v|^{\frac{1}{\beta}}} \tag{4}$$

where both u, v follow the Gaussian normal distribution. The specific expressions are given by:

$$u \sim Norm\left(0, \sigma^2\right), v \sim Norm(0, 1)\sigma = \left\{ \frac{\Gamma(1 + \beta)\sin\left(\frac{\pi\beta}{2}\right)}{\beta\Gamma\left(\frac{1+\beta}{2}\right)2^{\frac{\beta-1}{2}}} \right\}^{\frac{1}{\beta}} \tag{5}$$

Usually, $1 < \beta \leq 3$. In original CS, β is set to $3/2$ and Γ is a gamma function, which is formulated as:

$$\Gamma(z) = \int_0^{+\infty} \frac{t^{z-1}}{e^t} dt \tag{6}$$

Therefore, the calculated formula of the offspring is as follows:

$$X_i^{t+1} = X_i^t + \alpha_0 \frac{u}{|v|^{\frac{1}{\beta}}} \left(X_i^t - X_k^t\right) \tag{7}$$

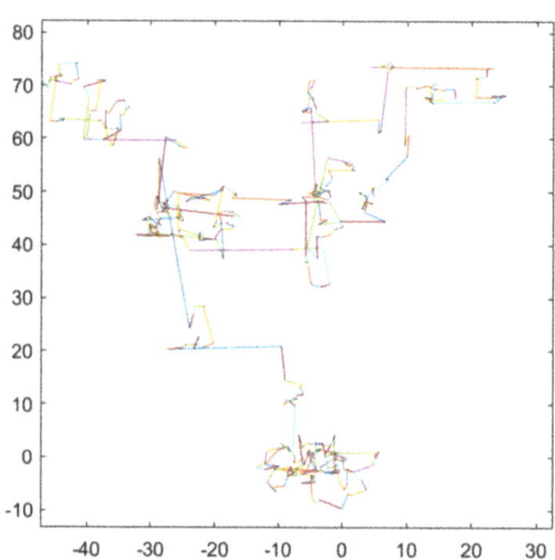

Figure 2. 2D plane *Levy* flight simulation diagram.

2.3. Local Random Walk

As is mentioned above, CS has two location updating methods for global and local searches. In global search, it adopts *Levy* flights to evolve the population. In local search, it adopts random walk to excavate potential information for solutions, which enhances the exploitation of CS. In this section, CS proposed a threshold that is called P_a. The application law of P_a is:

$$u_i = \left\{ \begin{array}{ll} v_i, & rand > P_a \\ x_i, & otherwise \end{array} \right. \tag{8}$$

where x_i is the population generated by *Levy* Flight, i is the position of the solution vectors in the population, and v_i is a trial vector, which is obtained by the random walk of x_i. In general, CS enforces random walk only when the generated value satisfies the threshold P_a. Random walk of CS shall be carried out according to the following rules:

$$v_i = x_i + \alpha \otimes H(P_a - r) \otimes (x_m - x_n) \tag{9}$$

where i means the index of the current solution in the population, α is the coefficient of the step size, H is a Heaviside function, r is a random number following a normal distribution, and x_m and x_n are both the two random solution vectors in the current population. In this way, the local optimization is more stable. Moreover, it is easy to obtain excellent solution information. Algorithm 1 shows the pseudo-code of CS.

Algorithm 1 The pseudo-code of CS

Input: N: the population size
        D: the dimension of the population
        G: the maximum iteration numbers
        g: the current iteration
        P_a: the possibility of being discovered
        X_i: a single solution in the population
        X_{best}: the best solution of all solution vectors in the current iteration
1: **For** $i = 1 : N$
2:     Initialize the X_i
3: **End**
4: Calculate $f\ (X_i)$, find the best nest X_{best} and record its fitness $f(X_{best})$
5: **While** $g < G$ **do**
6:     Randomly choose ith solution to make a LFRW and calculate fitness $f(U_i)$
7:    **If** $f(U_i) \leq f(X_i)$
8:      Replace $f(X_i)$ by $f(U_i)$ and update the location of the nest by Equation (2)
9:    **End If**
10:   **For** $i = 1{:}N$
11:    **If** the egg is discovered by the host
12:      Random walk on current generation and generate a new solution V_i by Equation (9)
13:      **If** $f(V_i) \leq f(X_i)$
14:        Replace $f(X_i)$ by $V(X_i)$ and update the location of the nest
15:      **End If**
16:    **End If**
17:   **End for**
18:   Replace X_{best} with the best solution obtained so far
19:   $g = g + 1$
20: **End while**
Output: The best solution

---

3. Main Ideas of Improved AGSCCS

Although many attempts have been made to improve the performance of CS, there are still some disadvantages of CS because of its simple structure [23]. Firstly, the local search follows the pseudo-random number distribution in the original CS. In this case, the population cannot balance the global search and local search in the later stage due to the nonuniformity of the distribution in high-dimensional space, which will fall into a local optimization [46,47]. In other words, the exploration and exploitation ability of the algorithm will be limited due to the pseudo-random distribution. Secondly, the original CS uses a static method to calculate the step size, leading to slow convergence [48]. Thirdly, the global search capacity has been improved by *Levy* Flight. It uses the combination of long and short distances for spatial search and quickly determines the feasible region. However, the local search needs to be enhanced because of the uncertainty of random search, which may also cause the local optimal [24].

Based on the above problems, AGSCCS has been proposed. AGSCCS retains the core idea of the original CS algorithm and makes some adjustments to the drawback of CS. Firstly, it uses the chaotic mapping to generate the initial population instead of the pseudo-random distribution. This measure solves the problem of the nonuniformity of the distribution in high-dimensional space. Secondly, the generation step size is modified. An adaptive coefficient is added to control the change in the step size. A guided sorting method is added to make full use of the optimum group and worst group. This measure solves the defect of the imbalance between exploration and exploitation in the later period, giving an excellent promotion for the exploitation. Thirdly, a SC technique is also proposed. It mainly aims at quickly determining the vicinity of the ideal solution and prevents the population from falling into the local optimal. The following sections introduce the three above strategies.

3.1. Initialization

The standard evolutionary algorithms will tend to appear premature because of the decline in population diversity and the setting of control parameters in the later stage [49]. The randomly generated initial population can easily cause population convergence and aggregation. The chaotic mapping method is used to initialize the population to improve the effectiveness and universality of the CS algorithm. Chaos is a common nonlinear phenomenon, which can traverse all states and generate chaotic sequences without repetition in a specific range [50]. Compared with the traditional initialization, the chaotic mapping method preferentially selects the position and velocity of particles in the initialization population. It can also use the algorithm to randomly generate the initial value of the population, which maintains the diversity of the population and makes full use of the space and regularity of the initial ergodic of chaotic dynamics.

As can be seen from Figure 3, the initial population generated by using Logistic chaotic initialization mapping is more uniform. Assuming that the (0,0) point is the segmentation point, the whole search domain is divided into four spaces. Points 13, 9, 12, 16 are randomly generated in the four quadrants by common initialization, and the initial populations for 11, 13, 12, 14 are generated by the chaotic mapping method. From the distribution's point of view, the initial population generated by the chaotic mapping method is more uniform.

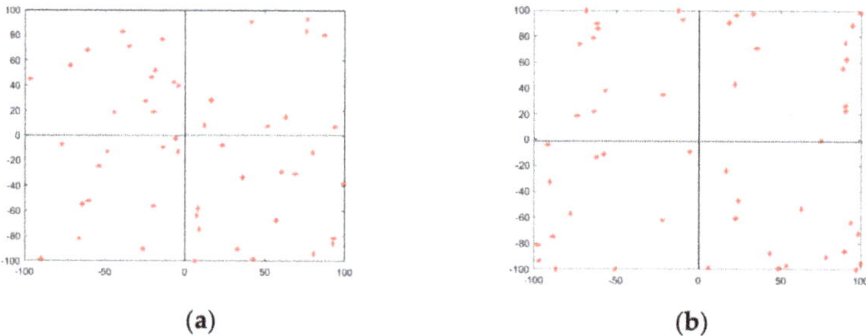

(a)   (b)

Figure 3. Comparison between common initialization and chaotic initialization. (**a**) Common initialization; (**b**) Chaotic initialization.

Common chaotic mapping models include piecewise linear tent mapping, chaotic characteristics of a one-dimensional Iterative Map with Infinite Collapses (ICMIC), sinusoidal chaotic mapping (sine mapping), etc. [50,51]. However, the tent chaotic map has unstable periodic points, which easily affects the generation of chaotic sequences. The pseudo-random number generated by the ICMIC model is between $[-1,1]$, which does not meet the initialization value required in this paper. The scope of the application of the sine mapping function also has significant limitations. Its independent variables and value range are often controlled between $[-1,1]$. To simplify the model and improve the efficiency of the algorithm, we will adopt a logistic nonlinear mapping after considering the above factors. The logical mapping can be described as:

$$y_i^{g+1} = \mu y_i^g \left(1 - y_i^g\right) \tag{10}$$

where y_i is a random value that follows a uniform distribution, i means the current position of the current solution vector in the population, g is the current iteration, and μ is the control coefficient of the expression, and it is a positive constant. The value of g is a positive integer, which indicates the current number of iterations. When $3.5699 \leq \mu \leq 4$, the system is in full chaos and has no stable solution [2]. Therefore, the population initiation is given as:

$$X_i^0 = (X_{max} - X_{min}) * y_i^1 + X_{min} \tag{11}$$

where y_i^1 is an initial value generated by the chaotic map according to Equation (10), and X_{max} and X_{min} are the upper and lower limits of the search space, respectively.

3.2. A Scheme of Updating Personalized Adaptive Guided Local Location Areas

In nature, if the host does not find the cuckoo's eggs, the eggs can continue to survive. Once the cuckoo's eggs are found, they will be abandoned by the host and the cuckoo's mother can only find another nest to lay eggs. In the CS algorithm, the author proposed a 'random walk' method. P_a is the probability of the eggs being discovered. Once found, these solutions need to be transferred randomly and immediately to improve their survival rate. The total number of solutions in each iteration remains unchanged [52]. The above process is the random walk. However, any random behavior can affect the accuracy of the algorithm. The global optimal may be missed if the step size is too long. Meanwhile, if the step size is too short, the population will always search around the local optimal. Thus, an adaptive differential guided location updating strategy is proposed to avoid this situation.

Intuitively, a completely random step size is risky for the iteration because it may run counter to the direction of the solution. The common method is to use the information of excellent solutions to pass on to the next generation to generate children [53,54]. Literature [38] adopts a new variation rule. It uses two randomly selected vectors coming from the top and bottom $100p\%$ individuals in the current size population, and the third vector is randomly selected from the middle $[NP - 2\,(100p\%)]$ individuals (NP is the population size). The three groups set the balance between the global search ability and local development tendency and improve the convergence speed of the algorithm. In this study, we combine this improvement concept with CS.

The original CS always uses the pseudo-random number method to generate a new step size in the local search phase. However, pseudo-random numbers are easy for showing the nonuniformity, especially in high-dimensional space. In some literature [55,56], researchers often used the information of the optimal solution and the worst solution in the previous generation solution set to replace the random step-size, which can make full use of the information of the solution. However, suppose we only use the single optimal solution and the worst solution in each generation of the population. In that case, the population may fall into local stagnation because of following the direction of the optimal solution. Therefore, the definitions of 'optimal solution group' and 'worst solution group' are proposed. The optimal solution group is the top $100p\%$ individuals, while the worst solution group is the bottom $100p\%$ individuals in the current NP size population. The advantage of using a solution group instead of an optimal solution is to avoid always following the same iterative direction of the optimal solution. This specific idea can refer to Figure 3 (②). Furthermore, this measure contributes to the diversity of the population, which is beneficial to the iteration in the latter stage. The formula is described as follows:

$$nest_i^{g+1} = nest_i^g + K \cdot \left(nest_{pbest}^g - nest_{pworst}^g \right) \tag{12}$$

where nest is the iterative population, g is the current iteration, i means the position of the decision vector in population, *pbest* and *pworst* are the top and bottom $p\%$ solutions in population, and K is a coefficient of controlling step size. The core idea of this method is: (1) for each population, we can learn the information of the best solution group and the worst solution group from the current generation. (2) The effect of difference is understood as the positive effect of the best solution group and the negative effect of the worst solution group. In the iterative process, the variation direction of the offspring follows the same direction as the best solution group vector while maintaining the opposite direction to the worst solution group of the random vector. The specific optimization direction of the offspring will be determined by the parent and the variation direction. This specific idea will be visualized in Figure 3.

Figure 4 shows the specific ideas for population evolution—where a is the current optimal solution, b is current worst solution, and c is the parent solution. In some improvements of CS, researchers utilize a and c to generate the offspring. However, they do not notice that the worst group affects the iteration at the same time. It will make the population evolve along the direction of the optimal solution and lead to falling into local optimization. In our method, a and b will firstly generate the direction of the next generation variation direction. Then, the parent will combine with the variation direction to produce a new searching direction.

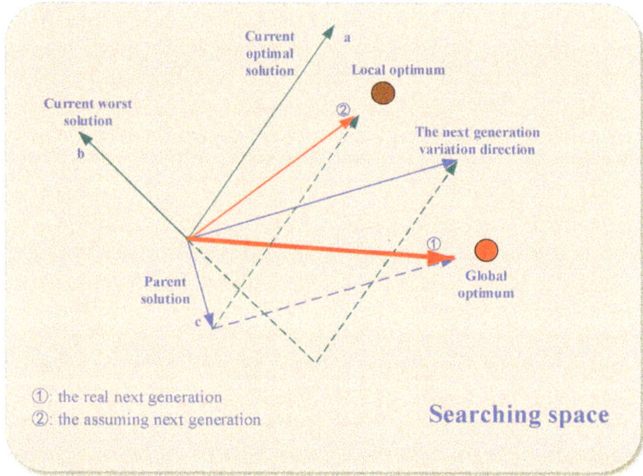

Figure 4. Population evolution diagram.

Moreover, the adjustment for the operator K is also essential. The best solution group and the worst solution group previously proposed are used to control the direction of the iteration step, and K is the coefficient controlling this iteration step. Its randomness will also affect the efficiency of the algorithm. Our idea is to control the size of K so that the algorithm maintains a relatively large step size at the beginning of the iteration, and it could quickly converge near the ideal solution. In the later stage, we will gradually reduce the step size to converge to the position of the ideal solution accurately. In this study, we proposed an adaptive method to control K. The pseudo-code can be shown in Algorithm 2.

Algorithm 2 The pseudo-code of K

Input: g: the current iteration
       G: the maximum number of iterations
1: $K_{max} = 1, K_{min} = 0.1$
2: Initialize $K, K_0 = 0.4$
3: $\lambda = e^{1 - \frac{g}{G+1-g}}$
4: **Update** $K', K' = K_0 * 2^\lambda$
5: **Judge** whether the current K is within the threshold
6: **If** rand < threshold do
7:     $K = K_{min} + \text{rand} * K_{max}$
8: **Else**
9:     $K = K'$
10: **End if**
11: Calculate new step size by Equation (12)
Output: The value of *stepsize*

K is a parameter for the step size. It can be seen from Algorithm 2 that the value of K increases during iteration. In the beginning, the value of the vector K is close to $2K_0$, which is convenient for the population, thereby accelerating the convergence of the optimal solution. In the later stage, K gradually decreases into K_0, which prevents excessive convergence. The above measure can ensure the algorithm is searching around the feasible areas all along. The threshold is set to appropriately increase the diversity of the algorithms and reduce the possibility of searching for the local optimal. It allows random change for the step size, which increases the diversity of the algorithm. Thus, the population variety remains in the later stage.

3.3. Spatial Compressions Technique

Original CS uses simple boundary constraints, which have no benefits for spatial convergence. In this section, a SC technique is proposed to actively adjust the optimization space. Briefly, its primary function is to properly change the optimization space of the algorithm in the iterative process. In the evolutionary early stage, the algorithm space is compressed to converge near the ideal solution quickly. In the late stage of evolution, the behavior of the compressing space will be slowed down appropriately to prevent a fall into the local optimal [40].

SC should cooperate with the optimization population convergence. The shrinkage operator is set larger than the one in the later stage. Therefore, the population can quickly eliminate the infeasible area in the beginning. In the later stage, the shrinkage operator should be set smaller to improve the convergence accuracy of the algorithm. Based on the above methods, we propose two different shrinkage operators for the different stages according to the current population. The first operator accelerates the population searching around the space used in the beginning stage. The second one is used to improve the accuracy of the algorithm and find more potential solutions.

$$\Delta 1 = 0.5 * X_{max} - X_{min} \tag{13}$$

$$\Delta 2 = \frac{\beta * u_i^t - l_i^t - (X_{max} - X_{min})}{2} \tag{14}$$

where X_{max} and X_{min} represent the upper and lower bounds of the ith decision variable in the population, u_i^t and l_i^t, respectively, represent the actual limit of the decision variable in the current generation, β is a zoom parameter, and D is the dimension of the population. According to the above operators, Equation (13) is used in the beginning stage and Equation (14) is used later. In this article, the first third of the iteration is the beginning stage and the last two-thirds are the later stage. Based on the above analysis and some improvements, the new boundary calculation formula is as follows:

$$u_i^{t+1} = X_{max} + \Delta; l_i^{t+1} = X_{min} - \Delta \tag{15}$$

where Δ is a shrink operator. It has different values depending on the current iteration. The pseudo-code of the section of the SC technique is shown in Algorithm 3.

Algorithm 3 The pseudo-code of shrink space technique

Input: g: the current iteration
   G: the maximum number of iterations
   N: the population size
1: Initialize Δ, $T = 20$
2: **If** mod $(g, T) = 0$
3: **For** $g = 1$ to G do
4:   Calculating $\Delta 1$ and $\Delta 2$ for different individuals in the population by Equations (13) and (14)
5:   **If** $g < G/3$ do
6:    choose $\Delta 1$ as shrinking operator
7:   **Else**
8:    choose $\Delta 2$ as shrinking operator
9:   **End if**
10: **End for**
11: Update the new upper and lower bounds by Equation (15)
12: **End if**
Output: new upper and lower bounds

There is no need to shrink the space frequently, which is likely to cause over-convergence. Given this, we choose to perform a spatial convergence every 20 generations. It will not only ensure the efficiency of the algorithm, but also effectively save computing resources. The pseudo-code and flow diagrams of AGSCCS are presented in Algorithm 4 and Figure 5.

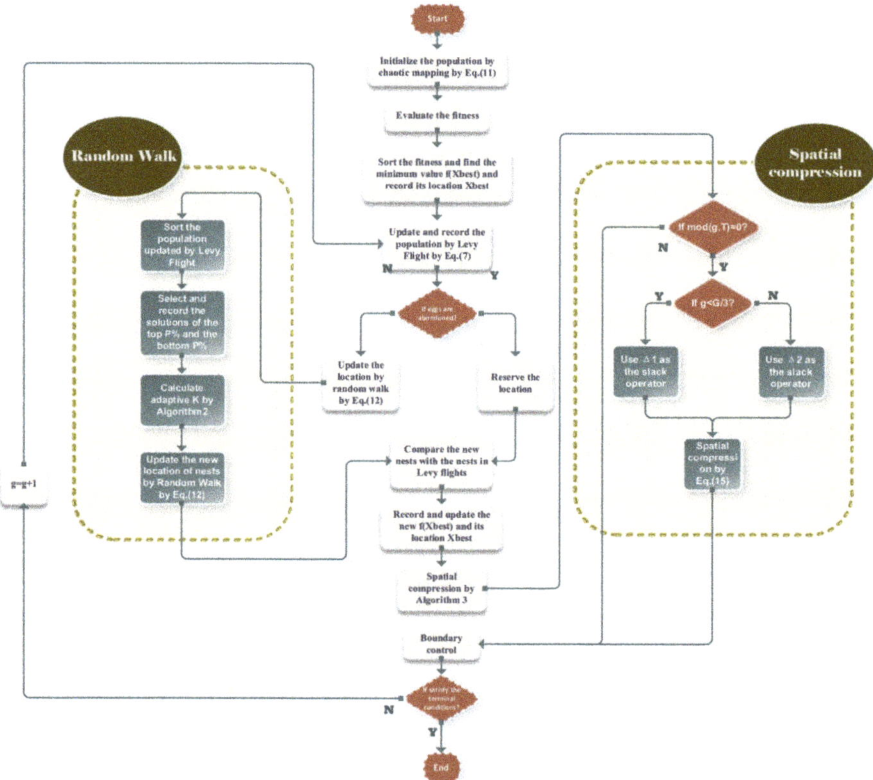

Figure 5. Flow chart of AGSCCS.

Algorithm 4 The pseudo-code of AGSCCS

Input: N: the population size
      D: the dimension of decision variables
      G: the maximum iteration number
      P_a: the possibility of being discovered
      X_i: a single solution in the population
      X_{best}: the best solution of the all solutions in the current iteration
1: **For** $i = 1 : N$
2:     Initialize the population X_i^0 by Equation (11)
3: **End**
4: Calculate $f\left(X_i^0\right)$, find the best nest X_{best} and record its fitness $f(X_{best})$
5: **While** $g < G$ **do**
6:     Make a LFRW for X_i and calculate fitness $f(X_i)$
7:     **If** $f(U_i) \leq f(X_i)$
8:       Replace $f(X_i)$ with $f(U_i)$ and update the location of the nest
9:     **End If**
10:   Sort the population and find the top and bottom $p\%$
11:   **If** the egg is discovered by the host
12:      Calculate the adaptive step size by Algorithm 2 and Equation (12)
13:      Random walk on current generation and generate a new solution V_i
14:   **End If**
15:   **If** $f(V_i) \leq f(X_i)$
16:      Replace X_i with V_i and update the location of the nest
17:   **End If**
18:   Replace X_{best} with the best solution obtained so far
19:   **If** $mod\,(t,\,T) = 0$
20:      Conduct the shrink space technique as shown in Algorithm 3
21:      **If** the new boundary value is not within limits
22:       Conduct boundary condition control
23:      **End if**
24:     **End if**
25: $g = g + 1$
26: **End while**
Output: The best solution after iteration

3.4. Computational Complexity

If N is the wolf pack size, then D is the dimension of the optimization problem and M is the maximum iteration number. The computational complexity of each operator of AGSCCS is given below:

(1)   The chaotic mapping of AGSCCS initialization in $O(N)$ time.
(2)   Adaptive guided local location areas require $O(2)$ time.
(3)   Adaptive operator F requires $O(N)$ time.
(4)   The shrinking space technique demands $O(\frac{M}{T} \times D)$, where T is the threshold controlling spatial compress technique.

In conclusion, the time complexity of each iteration is $O(2N+2 + \frac{M}{T} \times D)$. As $2N$ is more than two, the overall time complexity of the proposed AGSCCS algorithm can be expressed as $O(2N + \frac{MD}{T})$. Therefore, the total computational complexity of AGSCCS is equal to $O\left(\left(2N + \frac{MD}{T}\right) \times M\right)$ for the maximum iteration number M.

4. Experiment and Analysis

In this section, some experiments will be performed to examine the performance of AGSCCS. To make a comparison, the test will be done on the other algorithms, including CS [22], ACS, ImCS, GBCS, and ACSA at the same time. All of them improve the original CS algorithm from different angles. For example, ACS changes the parameters in the random walk method to increase the diversity of the mutation [25]. GBCS combines the process of a random walk with PSO, which realizes adaptive controlling and updating of parameters through external archiving events [27]. ImCS draws on the opposite learning strategy and combines it with the dynamic adjustment of score probability [32]. ACSA is another improved CS algorithm that adjusts the generating step size [31]. It uses the average value, maximum, and minimum to calculate the next generation's step size.

4.1. Benchmark Test

The benchmark test is a necessary part of the algorithm. It can verify both the performance and characteristics of the algorithm. During these years, lots of benchmark tests have been proposed. In this paper, CEC2014 will be adopted to examine the algorithm. It is a classic collection of the test function, including Ackley, Schwefel's, Rosenbrock's, Rastrigin's, etc. [57]. It covers 30 benchmark functions. In general, these 30 test functions can be summarized as four parts:

(1) Unimodal Functions ($F_1 - F_3$)
(2) Simple multimodal Functions ($F_4 - F_{16}$)
(3) Hybrid functions ($F_{17} - F_{22}$)
(4) Composition functions ($F_{22} - F_{30}$)

The specific content of each function has been listed in a lot of research [58].

4.2. Comparison between AGSCCS and Other Algorithms

CS is a heuristic algorithm that was proposed in recent years. Given this, in order to test its performance comprehensively, we chose four differently related CS algorithms to make the comparison.

The population size is set to $N = 50$, and the dimension of the problems is set to $D = 30$. The function evaluation times are set to FES = 100,000. Each experiment is run 30 times and six algorithms are completed to get the mean and standard values.

To comprehensively analyze the performance of AGSCCS, five relevant algorithms were chosen: CS, ACS, ImCS, GBCS, and ACSA. In this study, the population size of each algorithm is set to 30. Thirty turns tests would be run to avoid any randomness caused by one turn. The experimental results show both the mean and standard values of all the experiments in Table 1. The mean values show the precision performance, while the standard value shows the stability. According to the instruction of the CEC2014 benchmark tests, different kinds of functions are exhibited to verify the performance of the algorithms. For example, the unimodal function can reflect the exploitation capacity while the multimodal function shows the exploration capacity.

(1) Unimodal functions ($F_1 - F_3$). In Table 1, AGSCCS shows better performances in two functions in a group of three algorithms compared with CS, ACS, ImCS, GBCS, and ACSA when D = 30. Actually, except for function F_2, it may be because the CS algorithm cannot find the best value for the function, whereas AGSCCS always gets the best results in F_1 and F_3 compared to the other four algorithms. Given that the whole domain of the unimodal function is smooth, it is easy for the algorithm to find the minimum on the unimodal function. In this situation, AGSCCS can also score the best grades that prove the pretty exploitation capacity compared to other algorithms. This may owe to the SC technique. It quickly distinguishes the current environment to the extreme value of the region. Additionally, it benefits the capacity for algorithm convergence.

(2) Simple multimodal functions ($F_4 - F_{16}$). These functions are comparatively difficult for iterations compared to unimodal functions, given that they have more local extremums. In a total of 13 functions, AGSCCS performs better compared to eight functions, while CS, ACS, ImCS, GBCS, and ACSA have outstanding performances in functions 2, 1, 1, 3, 2, respectively; especially F_{15} shown in Figure 6, given that it is a shifted and rotated expanded function with multiple extreme points. Moreover, it adds some characteristics of the Rosenbrock function into the search space, which strengthens the difficulty for finding the solution. AGSCCS achieves good iterative

results on this function, which shows an excellent exploration capacity. This good exploration capacity is from the adaptive guided updating location method. The guided differential step size method can help the algorithm search for the direction of good solutions while avoiding bad solutions.

(3)   Hybrid functions ($F_{17} - F_{22}$). In these functions, AGSCCS still achieves the best compared to the other four algorithms. It has better performances on F_{17}, F_{19}, F_{20}, and F_{21}. In the total of six functions, CS, ACS, ImCS, GBCS, and ACSA lead in only functions 0, 1, 1, 2, 0. In F_{20}, the six algorithms almost converge to smaller values while AGSCCS can converge to a better value, which exhibits the excellent capacity of exploration of AGSCCS. Although GBCS has better results in F_{22}, AGSCCS is extremely close to its results. These experimental results can prove the leading position of AGSCCS in hybrid functions.

(4)   Composition functions ($F_{22} - F_{30}$). In $F_{22} - F_{30}$, AGSCCS shows better performances in four functions in total. Intuitively, AGSCCS has the best results in $F_{23} - F_{26}$. In these four functions, it always gets full marks. Although ACS performs unsatisfactorily on $F_{27} - F_{30}$, it cannot deny its excellent exploration and exploration ability. On the previous unimodal and multimodal functions, the comprehensive performances of ACS have been certified. The poor performances of ACS may be due to the instability of its state under multi-dimensional and multimodal problems. Therefore, AGSCCS does not show any disadvantages compared with the other four algorithms in hybrid composition functions.

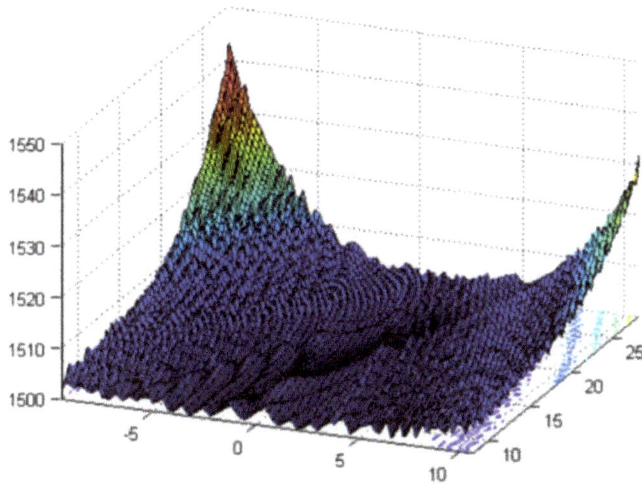

Figure 6. 3D graph of Shifted and Rotated Expanded Griewank's plus Rosenbrock's Function.

Table 1. Experimental results of CS, ACS, ImCS, GBCS, ACSA, and AGSCCS at $D = 30$. (Bold is the optimal algorithm results of each test function.)

	CS		ACS		ImCS		GBCS		ACSA		AGSCCS	
	Mean	Std	Mean	Std	Mean	Std	Mean	Std	Mean	Std	Mean	Std
f1	9.76×10^6	2.42×10^6	1.19×10^7	3.35×10^6	1.60×10^7	2.34×10^5	1.99×10^7	5.97×10^6	3.21×10^7	1.05×10^7	$\mathbf{4.23 \times 10^6}$	1.40×10^6
f2	$\mathbf{1.00 \times 10^{10}}$	0.00	$\mathbf{1.00 \times 10^{10}}$	0.00	1.00×10^{10}	0.00	$\mathbf{1.00 \times 10^{10}}$	0.00	$\mathbf{1.00 \times 10^{10}}$	0.00	$\mathbf{1.00 \times 10^{10}}$	0.00
f3	2.31×10^2	8.32×10^1	4.98×10^2	1.34×10^2	4.49×10^1	1.98×10^1	3.99×10^2	9.55×10^1	4.76×10^2	2.10×10^2	$\mathbf{2.80 \times 10^1}$	7.34
f4	1.02×10^2	1.87×10^1	9.24×10^1	2.54×10^1	7.94×10^1	2.29×10^1	9.79×10^1	1.80×10^1	1.18×10^2	2.12×10^1	$\mathbf{7.08 \times 10^1}$	2.28×10^1
f5	2.09×10^1	8.99×10^{-2}	$\mathbf{2.06 \times 10^1}$	5.57×10^{-2}	$\mathbf{2.06 \times 10^1}$	4.87×10^{-2}	2.09×10^1	5.06×10^{-2}	2.09×10^1	5.56×10^{-2}	2.09×10^1	7.94×10^{-2}
f6	2.77×10^1	9.62×10^{-1}	2.84×10^1	2.29	2.80×10^1	2.39	$\mathbf{2.42 \times 10^1}$	3.36	3.16×10^1	1.69	2.78×10^1	1.32
f7	2.03×10^{-1}	5.60×10^{-2}	2.35×10^{-1}	7.40×10^{-2}	1.20×10^{-1}	5.70×10^{-2}	$\mathbf{2.12 \times 10^{-2}}$	1.30×10^{-2}	3.70×10^{-1}	9.40×10^{-2}	7.51×10^{-2}	5.61×10^{-2}
f8	1.04×10^2	1.44×10^1	8.24×10^1	1.41×10^1	8.39×10^1	1.30×10^1	1.05×10^2	1.54×10^1	1.49×10^2	1.69×10^1	$\mathbf{5.53 \times 10^1}$	8.21
f9	1.67×10^2	2.16×10^1	1.10×10^2	1.55×10^1	1.21×10^2	1.42×10^1	1.53×10^2	1.46×10^1	2.18×10^2	1.80×10^1	$\mathbf{1.05 \times 10^2}$	1.48×10^1
f10	2.65×10^3	1.81×10^2	3.45×10^3	4.12×10^2	3.61×10^3	4.40×10^2	3.83×10^3	5.35×10^2	3.68×10^3	4.45×10^2	$\mathbf{2.12 \times 10^3}$	1.96×10^2
f11	3.87×10^3	1.91×10^2	4.23×10^3	5.23×10^2	4.28×10^3	3.90×10^2	5.70×10^3	4.25×10^2	5.16×10^3	2.14×10^2	$\mathbf{3.85 \times 10^3}$	2.67×10^2
f12	1.05	1.23×10^{-1}	1.36	2.29×10^{-1}	1.36	2.34×10^{-1}	2.10	3.45×10^{-1}	1.61	2.18×10^{-1}	$\mathbf{9.89 \times 10^{-1}}$	1.43×10^{-1}
f13	$\mathbf{3.37 \times 10^{-1}}$	4.61×10^{-2}	3.64×10^{-1}	3.85×10^{-2}	3.66×10^{-1}	4.43×10^{-2}	4.40×10^{-1}	5.97×10^{-2}	3.81×10^{-1}	5.12×10^{-2}	4.97×10^{-1}	5.75×10^{-2}
f14	2.70×10^{-1}	2.67×10^{-2}	2.68×10^{-1}	2.83×10^{-2}	2.79×10^{-1}	2.97×10^{-2}	3.00×10^{-1}	3.44×10^{-2}	$\mathbf{2.62 \times 10^{-1}}$	2.14×10^{-2}	4.31×10^{-1}	2.80×10^{-1}
f15	1.47×10^1	1.38	1.78×10^1	1.81	1.66×10^1	1.52	1.61×10^1	1.41	1.82×10^1	1.36	$\mathbf{1.07 \times 10^1}$	1.01
f16	$\mathbf{1.27 \times 10^1}$	1.72×10^{-1}	1.28×10^1	1.89×10^{-1}	1.28×10^1	2.09×10^{-1}	$\mathbf{1.27 \times 10^1}$	1.97×10^{-1}	$\mathbf{1.27 \times 10^1}$	3.91×10^{-1}	$\mathbf{1.27 \times 10^1}$	2.34×10^{-1}
f17	9.32×10^4	3.24×10^4	1.11×10^5	4.40×10^4	2.87×10^4	3.86×10^2	1.99×10^5	6.36×10^4	2.44×10^5	1.02×10^5	$\mathbf{2.72 \times 10^4}$	7.89×10^3
f18	3.69×10^3	4.06×10^3	3.12×10^4	1.55×10^4	$\mathbf{3.60 \times 10^2}$	1.42×10^2	2.17×10^3	1.25×10^3	3.11×10^3	3.66×10^3	3.33×10^8	1.83×10^9
f19	1.10×10^1	6.24×10^{-1}	$\mathbf{9.83}$	6.15×10^{-1}	9.91	5.67×10^{-1}	9.88	8.77×10^{-1}	1.16×10^1	2.13	$\mathbf{9.83}$	1.58
f20	3.21×10^2	5.94×10^1	3.86×10^2	9.66×10^1	3.76×10^2	1.75×10^1	3.69×10^2	1.13×10^2	7.06×10^2	1.72×10^3	$\mathbf{1.65 \times 10^2}$	3.27×10^1
f21	5.08×10^3	1.08×10^3	8.29×10^3	1.67×10^3	3.53×10^3	1.80×10^2	1.41×10^4	5.17×10^3	1.29×10^4	4.31×10^3	$\mathbf{2.54 \times 10^3}$	4.35×10^2
f22	3.45×10^2	9.51×10^1	2.87×10^2	1.12×10^2	3.08×10^2	7.07×10^1	$\mathbf{2.31 \times 10^2}$	9.23×10^1	4.45×10^2	1.79×10^2	2.64×10^2	1.15×10^2
f23	$\mathbf{3.15 \times 10^2}$	2.59×10^{-3}	$\mathbf{3.15 \times 10^2}$	1.10×10^{-2}	$\mathbf{3.15 \times 10^2}$	4.61×10^{-3}	$\mathbf{3.15 \times 10^2}$	3.54×10^{-4}	$\mathbf{3.15 \times 10^2}$	4.27×10^{-5}	$\mathbf{3.15 \times 10^2}$	1.49×10^{-1}
f24	2.34×10^2	4.11	2.34×10^2	3.50	2.33×10^2	3.34	2.29×10^2	5.04	2.31×10^2	2.09	$\mathbf{2.28 \times 10^2}$	2.09
f25	2.12×10^2	1.23	2.11×10^2	2.18	2.07×10^2	1.26	2.12×10^2	1.61	2.14×10^2	1.83	$\mathbf{2.06 \times 10^2}$	1.23
f26	$\mathbf{1.00 \times 10^2}$	4.02×10^{-2}	$\mathbf{1.00 \times 10^2}$	4.05×10^{-2}	$\mathbf{1.00 \times 10^2}$	3.44×10^{-2}	$\mathbf{1.00 \times 10^2}$	6.63×10^{-2}	$\mathbf{1.00 \times 10^2}$	7.58×10^{-2}	$\mathbf{1.00 \times 10^2}$	8.99×10^{-2}
f27	4.34×10^2	1.07×10^1	4.24×10^2	6.68	$\mathbf{4.19 \times 10^2}$	1.22×10^1	6.43×10^2	1.93×10^2	6.45×10^2	2.02×10^2	8.25×10^2	2.12×10^2
f28	1.06×10^3	4.33×10^1	1.03×10^3	4.44×10^1	1.03×10^3	5.14×10^1	9.41×10^2	3.91×10^1	$\mathbf{8.68 \times 10^2}$	2.68×10^2	1.03×10^3	1.19×10^2
f29	4.31×10^3	1.99×10^3	7.85×10^3	3.10×10^3	2.05×10^3	5.96×10^2	2.83×10^5	1.53×10^6	$\mathbf{3.46 \times 10^2}$	9.98×10^1	5.85×10^6	4.59×10^6
f30	4.93×10^3	9.64×10^2	5.96×10^3	2.56×10^3	3.16×10^3	7.30×10^2	3.81×10^3	8.84×10^2	$\mathbf{1.68 \times 10^3}$	2.09×10^2	3.62×10^3	1.32×10^3
$+/-/\approx$	$22/3/5$		$22/4/4$		$18/8/4$		$17/8/5$		$19/6/5$		$-$	

To further analyze the searching process of AGSCCS, the iterative graphs for the CEC2014 benchmark are as follows.

Given that there is a considerable statistical difference between each function, we take the logarithm of the obtained function values to get the iterative graph. As can be seen from Figure 7, in 19 of the 30 test functions AGSCCS performs better than CS, ACS, ImCS, GBCS, and ACSA in terms of accuracy and stability. On the one hand, 19 functions of AGSCCS reach the minimum fitness value in the mean of iteration results, which is the algorithm with the largest number of minimum values among the six algorithms. This is due to the chaotic initialization and adaptive guided population iteration. The method of chaotic initialization improves the diversity of the population. The best and worst solution group of the previous generation are retained to provide references for the next generation and improve the exploration ability of the population, thus obtaining a smaller adaptation value. However, on the other hand, the AGSCCS algorithm performs equally well with the mean error. Compared with the second ImCS algorithm, AGSCCS achieves a minimum error on 20 test functions, while the second ImCS algorithm only shows better results on 5 test functions. This is due to the method of shrinking space. This method actively compresses the space in proper time, reduces the optimization range, improves the convergence speed, and enhances the stability of the algorithm. Similarly, in terms of convergence speed, AGSCCS's convergence is faster than CS, ACS, ImCS, GBCS, and ACSA. In the same iteration, AGSCCS always tends to achieve a smaller value. There is no doubt that the SC technique contributes to the fast speed of convergence. In F_6, even if GBCS achieves the best solution compared with other algorithms within a relatively short time, it still F_{10}, F_{11}, and F_{12}, which belong to the multimodal functions. Hence, it is not hard to conclude that GBCS has a worse iteration capacity than AGSCCS. Due to the SC technique, AGSCCS can easily and quickly find the optimal value in the searching space. The adaptive random replacement nest step ensures that the searching direction is not easy to fall into the local optimal. Therefore, in terms of comprehensive strength, the AGSCCS algorithm performs better.

In summary, it isn't easy to find the best solution to perfectly solve all kinds of problems, whether it is through the original CS or some improved method. Therefore, the proposed AGSCCS is hard to find at all of the optimal solutions simultaneously. However, according to the above analysis, it can be seen that AGSCCS is a noteworthy method for optimization problems. It vastly improves the performance of the conventional CS on various issues, no matter if the problems are unimodal or multimodal. Furthermore, it shows better results than CS, ACS, ImCS, GBCS, and ACSA. AGSCCS adopts chaotic mapping generation and adaptive guided step size to avoid local stagnation. SC accelerates the speed of convergence. Three methods contribute to a stable balance between the exploitation and exploration capacity for AGSCCS.

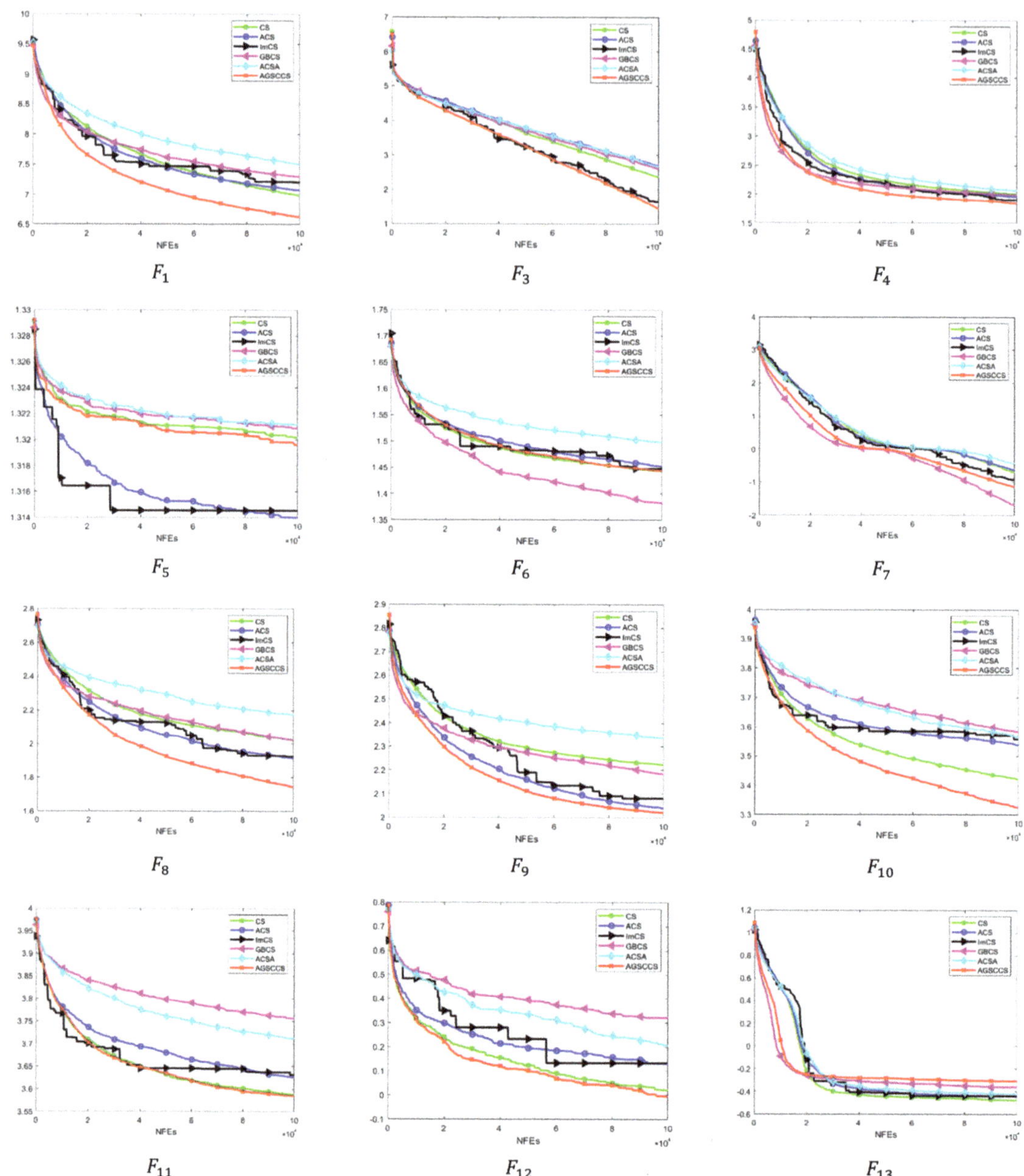

Figure 7. *Cont.*

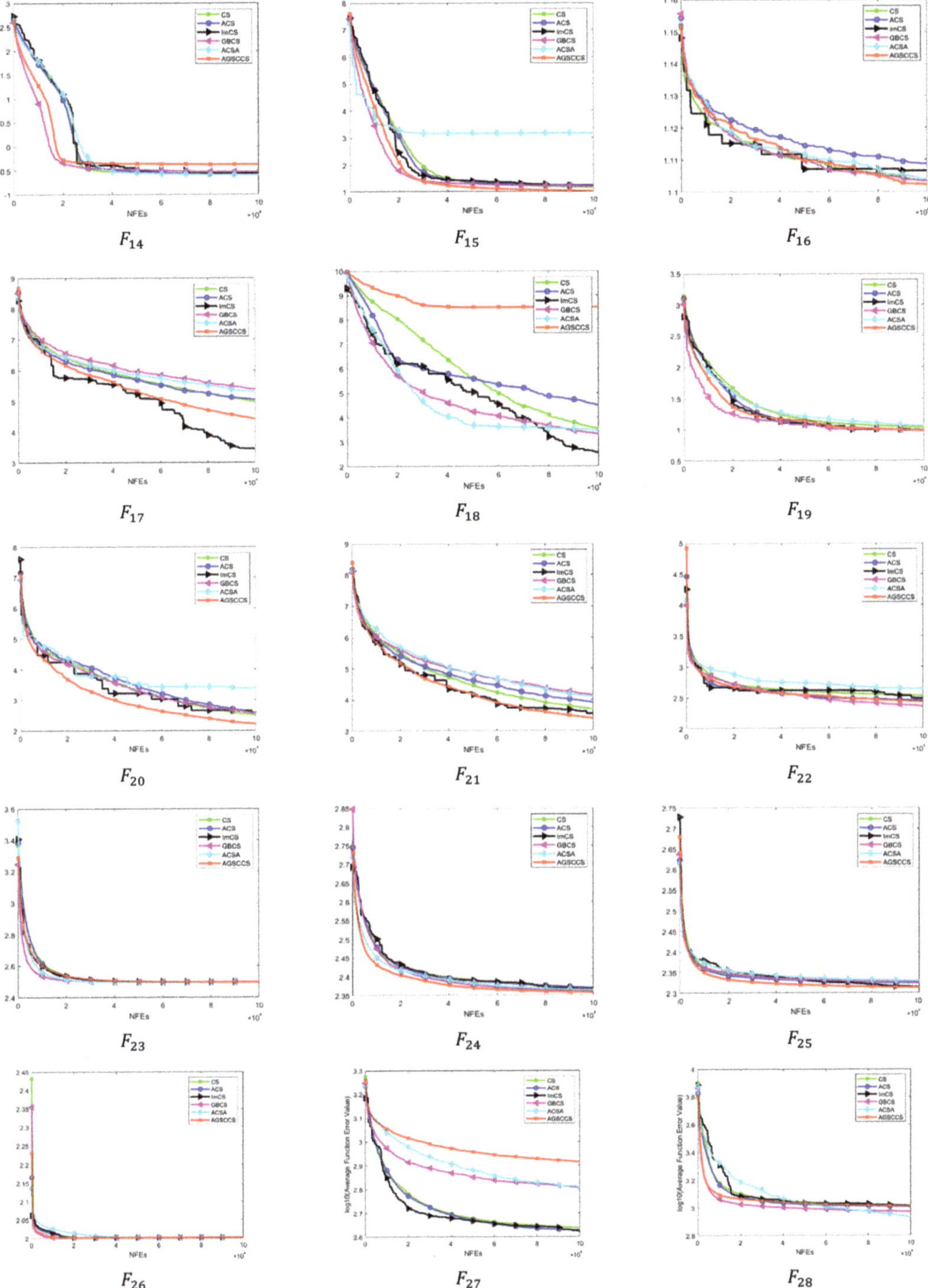

F_{14}

F_{15}

F_{16}

F_{17}

F_{18}

F_{19}

F_{20}

F_{21}

F_{22}

F_{23}

F_{24}

F_{25}

F_{26}

F_{27}

F_{28}

Figure 7. *Cont.*

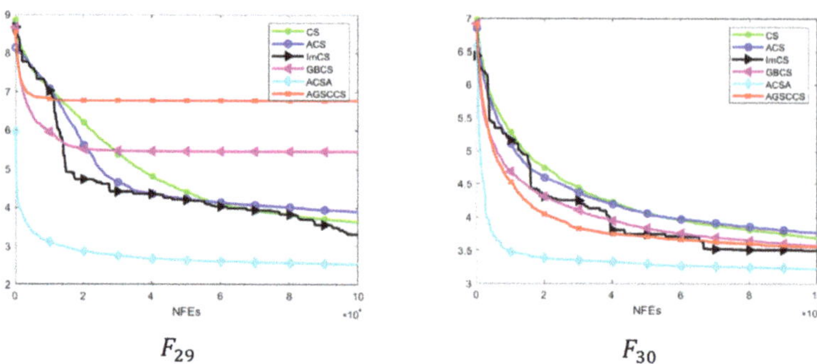

Figure 7. Convergence curve of AGSCCS in CEC2014.

4.3. Discussion

A sensitivity test will be done to verify the validity of the three improved strategies. It covers four experimental subjects called AGSCCS-1, AGSCCS-2, AGSCCS-3, and AGSCCS itself. During this process, we take the control variable method to examine the influence of each strategy. For convenience, the three improved strategies are recorded as the improvement I (IM I), improvement II (IM II), and improvement III (IM III), which represent the chaotic mapping initialization, adaptive guided updating local areas, and SC technique, respectively. The matching package of each subject is shown in Table 2.

Table 2. Matching package of each subject.

	AGSCCS-1	AGSCCS-2	AGSCCS-3	AGSCCS
IM 1 (Logistic chaotic mapping)	×	√	√	√
IM 2 (Adaptive guided updating local areas)	√	×	√	√
IM 3 (SC technique)	√	√	×	√

As can be seen from Table 2, each algorithm reduces one strategy compared with AGSCCS. These reduced strategies will be filled with some parts of the original CS. For example, AGSCCS-1 has no SC technique. From here, we will choose the common boundary condition treatment method, which comes from the original CS. The whole sensitivity test will be done at $D = 30$. Each benchmark test will be run for 30 turns and the average value will be taken. The population size is set as 50 and FES = 100,000. The specific experimental results are shown in Table 3.

Obviously, the three strategies all play a necessary part in the algorithms. AGSCCS acquires 21 champions in the total of 30 benchmark tests, while AGSCCS-1, AGSCCS-2, and ACS-CS-3 score 7, 5, and 6 points in total. Among IM1, IM2, and IM3, IM3 has the most important effects on AGSCCS. Without IM3, it will be inferior in 22 functions. In other words, without the assistant of SC, AGSCCS-3 shows mediocre performance. IM1 and IM2 seem to have almost the same effect on AGSCCS. AGSCCS-1 is inferior in 19 functions and AGSCCS-2 is inferior in 20 functions. Although there is no significant difference in the data performance among the 30 test functions, it is obvious that any of the three improvements have improved the algorithm's performance. As mentioned earlier, the SC technique is the most critical part of the improvement measures because it compresses the searching space and improves the algorithm's efficiency. Moreover, the adaptive measures that adjust the updating methods are both verified to be valid. Although the results brought by the adaptive measures have a little enhancement, it can be inferred that the two measures bring a positive affection for the AGSCCS algorithm. Thus, it is certain that these three strategies are indispensable, given that they jointly promote the performance of AGSCCS.

Table 3. Sensitive test of AGSCCS. (Bold is the optimal algorithm results of each test function.)

	AGSCCS-1		AGSCCS-2		AGSCCS-3		AGSCCS	
	Mean	Std	Mean	Std	Mean	Std	Mean	Std
f1	5.24×10^6	2.01×10^6	9.60×10^6	2.74×10^6	5.38×10^6	1.82×10^6	$\mathbf{4.23 \times 10^6}$	1.40×10^6
f2	$\mathbf{1.00 \times 10^{10}}$	0.00	$\mathbf{1.00 \times 10^{10}}$	0.00	$\mathbf{1.00 \times 10^{10}}$	0.00	$\mathbf{1.00 \times 10^{10}}$	0.00
f3	2.90×10^1	7.75	2.10×10^2	5.89×10^1	2.96×10^1	1.09×10^1	$\mathbf{2.80 \times 10^1}$	7.34
f4	8.02×10^1	2.56×10^1	9.86×10^1	1.35×10^1	$\mathbf{6.95 \times 10^1}$	3.26×10^1	7.08×10^1	2.28×10^1
f5	$\mathbf{2.09 \times 10^1}$	7.14×10^{-2}	$\mathbf{2.09 \times 10^1}$	5.53×10^{-2}	$\mathbf{2.09 \times 10^1}$	6.35×10^{-2}	2.09×10^1	7.94×10^{-2}
f6	2.69×10^1	1.21	2.79×10^1	1.29	$\mathbf{2.68 \times 10^1}$	1.18	2.78×10^1	1.32
f7	8.43×10^{-2}	5.51×10^{-2}	2.23×10^{-1}	7.58×10^{-2}	8.09×10^{-2}	6.20×10^{-2}	$\mathbf{7.51 \times 10^{-2}}$	5.61×10^{-2}
f8	5.96×10^1	8.44	1.04×10^2	1.43×10^1	5.68×10^1	8.98	$\mathbf{5.53 \times 10^1}$	8.21
f9	$\mathbf{1.05 \times 10^2}$	1.66×10^1	1.63×10^2	1.82×10^1	1.08×10^2	1.46×10^1	$\mathbf{1.05 \times 10^2}$	1.48×10^1
f10	2.33×10^3	2.56×10^2	2.63×10^3	1.83×10^2	2.25×10^3	2.53×10^2	$\mathbf{2.12 \times 10^3}$	1.96×10^2
f11	3.89×10^3	2.09×10^2	3.91×10^3	2.10×10^2	$\mathbf{3.78 \times 10^3}$	2.09×10^2	3.85×10^3	2.67×10^2
f12	1.10	1.61×10^{-1}	1.04	1.73×10^{-1}	1.10	1.36×10^{-1}	$\mathbf{9.89 \times 10^{-1}}$	1.43×10^{-1}
f13	4.61×10^{-1}	8.30×10^{-2}	$\mathbf{3.36 \times 10^{-1}}$	4.15×10^{-2}	4.66×10^{-1}	8.13×10^{-2}	4.97×10^{-1}	5.75×10^{-2}
f14	4.33×10^{-1}	2.71×10^{-1}	$\mathbf{2.61 \times 10^{-1}}$	2.46×10^{-2}	4.01×10^{-1}	2.37×10^{-1}	4.31×10^{-1}	2.80×10^{-1}
f15	1.08×10^1	1.57	1.45×10^1	1.85	1.08×10^1	1.08	$\mathbf{1.07 \times 10^1}$	1.01
f16	$\mathbf{1.27 \times 10^1}$	2.52×10^{-1}	1.28×10^1	2.22×10^{-1}	1.28×10^1	2.52×10^{-1}	$\mathbf{1.27 \times 10^1}$	2.34×10^{-1}
f17	3.13×10^4	1.30×10^4	8.39×10^4	3.65×10^4	3.29×10^4	1.42×10^4	$\mathbf{2.72 \times 10^4}$	7.89×10^3
f18	5.03×10^2	1.13×10^2	2.86×10^3	1.91×10^3	$\mathbf{4.75 \times 10^2}$	1.05×10^2	3.33×10^8	1.83×10^9
f19	9.86	1.45	1.09×10^1	5.97×10^{-1}	$\mathbf{9.37}$	1.12	9.83	1.58
f20	1.70×10^2	3.37×10^1	3.15×10^2	8.00×10^1	1.67×10^2	2.56×10^1	$\mathbf{1.65 \times 10^2}$	3.27×10^1
f21	2.65×10^3	4.75×10^2	4.90×10^3	8.26×10^2	2.60×10^3	3.03×10^2	$\mathbf{2.54 \times 10^3}$	4.35×10^2
f22	3.44×10^2	9.97×10^1	3.91×10^2	8.90×10^1	3.09×10^2	1.09×10^2	$\mathbf{2.74 \times 10^2}$	1.15×10^2
f23	$\mathbf{3.15 \times 10^2}$	7.55×10^{-5}	$\mathbf{3.15 \times 10^2}$	3.32×10^{-3}	$\mathbf{3.15 \times 10^2}$	3.76×10^{-5}	$\mathbf{3.15 \times 10^2}$	1.49×10^{-1}
f24	2.29×10^2	3.86	2.35×10^2	3.72	2.28×10^2	2.98	$\mathbf{2.28 \times 10^2}$	2.09
f25	2.06×10^2	1.05	2.11×10^2	1.51	2.07×10^2	1.16	$\mathbf{2.06 \times 10^2}$	1.23
f26	$\mathbf{1.00 \times 10^2}$	9.09×10^{-2}	$\mathbf{1.00 \times 10^2}$	4.51×10^{-2}	1.09×10^2	4.83×10^1	$\mathbf{1.00 \times 10^2}$	8.99×10^{-2}
f27	7.94×10^2	2.44×10^2	$\mathbf{4.30 \times 10^2}$	9.86	8.42×10^2	1.99×10^2	8.25×10^2	2.12×10^2
f28	1.06×10^3	2.10×10^2	1.05×10^3	4.76×10^1	1.06×10^3	1.49×10^2	$\mathbf{1.03 \times 10^3}$	1.19×10^2
f29	6.41×10^5	2.44×10^6	$\mathbf{4.53 \times 10^3}$	2.07×10^3	6.19×10^6	2.08×10^6	5.85×10^6	4.59×10^6
f30	3.64×10^3	1.69×10^3	4.23×10^3	8.66×10^2	3.80×10^3	2.41×10^3	$\mathbf{3.62 \times 10^3}$	1.32×10^3
$+/-/\approx$	19/5/6		20/6/4		22/7/1		-	

4.4. Statistical Analysis

In this paper, a Wilcoxon signed rank test and Friedman test are used to verify the significant difference between AGSCCS and its competitors. The signs '+', '−', and '≈' indicate that our methods perform better, lower, and the same as their competitors. The results are shown in the last rows in Tables 1 and 3. The Wilcoxon test was performed at $\alpha = 0.05$ as the significance level. The final average ranking of all 30 functions by the above six algorithms is shown in Table 4 through the Friedman test. Obviously, from the results in the last row of Tables 1 and 3 and the average ranking in Table 3, AGSCCS achieved the best overall performance among the six algorithms, which statistically verified the excellent search efficiency and accuracy of AGSCCS over traditional CS and its three modern variants.

Table 4. Average rankings of CS, ACS, ImCS, GBCS, ACSA, and AGSCCS according to Friedman test for 30 functions.

Algorithm	Ranking ($D = 30$)
CS	3.4000
ACS	3.6833
ImCS	3.0000
GBCS	3.8333
ACSA	4.5667
AGSCCS	2.5167

5. Engineering Applications of AGSCCS

As mentioned in Section 1, CS has been widely used in various engineering problems. To verify the validity of AGSCCS, some issues covering the current–voltage characteristics of the solar cells and PV module will be solved by the proposed algorithm [59]. The other five algorithms (CS, ACS, ImCS, GBCS, and ACSA) will also be applied to settle the problems.

5.1. Problem Formulation

Obviously, since the output characteristics of the PV modules change with the external environment, it is essential to use an accurate model to describe the PV cells' characteristics closely. Especially in the PV model, it is crucial to calculate the current voltage curve correctly. Generally, the accuracy and reliability of the current–voltage (I–V) characteristic curve, especially on the diode model parameters, is crucial to accurately identify its internal parameters. In this section, several equivalent PV models are proposed.

5.1.1. Single Diode Model (SDM)

In this situation, there is only one diode in the circuit diagram. The model has the following part: a current source, a parallel resistor considering leakage current, and a series resistor that represents the loss associated with the load current. The formula of the output current I of SDM is shown in Equation (16).

$$I = I_{pv} - I_{sd} * \left[e^{\frac{q(V+R_s*I)}{a \cdot k \cdot T}} - 1 \right] - \frac{V + R_s * I}{R_{sh}} \tag{16}$$

where I_{pv} means the photo-generated current and I_{sd} is the reverse saturation current of the diode, R_s and R_{sh} are the series and shunt resistances, V is the cell output voltage, n is the ideal diode factor, T indicates the junction temperature in Kelvin, k is the Boltzmann constant ($1.3806503 \times 10^{-23}$ J/K), and q is the electron charge ($1.60217646 \times 10^{-19}$ C). There are five unknown parameters in DDM, including I_{pv}, I_{sd}, a, R_s and R_{sh}.

5.1.2. Double Diode Model

Due to the influence of compound current loss in the depletion region, researchers have developed a more accurate DDM model than SDM. Its equivalent circuit has two diodes in parallel. The formula of the output current I of SDM is shown in Equation (17).

$$I = I_{pv} - I_{sd1} * \left[e^{\frac{q(V+R_s*I)}{a1 \cdot k \cdot T}} - 1 \right] - I_{sd2} * \left[e^{\frac{q(V+R_s*I)}{a2 \cdot k \cdot T}} - 1 \right] - \frac{V + R_s * I}{R_{sh}} \tag{17}$$

where $a1$ and $a2$ are the ideal factors in the situation of the two diodes. There are seven unknown parameters in DDM, including $I_{pv}, I_{sd1}, I_{sd2}, a1, a2, R_s$ and R_{sh}.

5.1.3. PV Module Model

The PV module model relies on SDM and DDM as the core architecture, which is usually composed of several series or parallel PV cells and other modules. The models, in this case, are called the single diode module model (SMM) and double diode module model (DMM).

The output current I of the SMM formula is written in Equation (18).

$$I = I_{pv}N_p - I_{sd}N_p * \left[e^{\frac{q(V/N_p + R_s * I/N_p)}{a \cdot k \cdot T}} - 1 \right] - \frac{N_p * V/N_s + R_s * I}{R_{sh}} \tag{18}$$

The formula of the output current I of SMM is written in Equation (19).

$$I = I_{pv}N_p - I_{sd1}N_p * \left[e^{\frac{q(\frac{V}{N_p} + R_s * \frac{I}{N_p})}{a1 \cdot k \cdot T}} - 1 \right] - I_{sd2}N_p * \left[e^{\frac{q(\frac{V}{N_p} + R_s * \frac{I}{N_p})}{a2 \cdot k \cdot T}} - 1 \right] - \frac{N_p * V/N_s + R_s * I}{R_{sh}} \tag{19}$$

where N_s represents the number of series solar cells and N_p denotes the number of solar cells in parallel.

5.2. Results and Analysis

Now, we apply AGSCCS to the PV module parameter optimization problems. To test the performance, it will be compared with ACS, ImCS, GBCS, ACSA, and CS. The specific parameter of the algorithms is set the same. The population size is set to 30 and the function evaluations are set to 50,000. The typical experimental results are stated in Table 5. Tables 6–8 exhibit the particular value on the SDM PV cells.

Table 5 describes the results of the PV model parameter optimization. Due to the complex nonlinear relationship between the external output characteristics and the internal parameters of the PV modules with the external environment changes, parameter identification of the PV model is a highly complex optimization problem. AGSCCS has the best performance of the six tests. It acquires all the champions in question for the PV model identification compared with the other five algorithms. Especially in SDM, the RMSE of AGSCCS reaches 9.89×10^{-4}, which is much smaller than the rest of the algorithms. It also shows strong competitiveness in other models. It can be said that the comprehensive performance of AGSCCS has been dramatically improved compared with CS. Tables 6–8 explicitly exhibit the specific parameter values on the PV model.

Tables 6–8 show the parameters associated with identifying the PV model using the AGSCCS algorithm and other five algorithms. As seen from the above table, the optimization results before the algorithm are pretty close. This can be understood as several local optimal near the optimal solution, which will increase the difficulty of convergence of the algorithm. Therefore, CS, ACS, ImCS, GBCS, and ACSA converge only at the local optimal solution. However, AGSCCS can recognize these local optimum solutions and converge to smaller ones, which is sufficient to prove that its exploration ability and exploitation ability have significant advantages over other algorithms.

Table 5. Experimental results in PV module.

	CS		ACS		ImCS		GBCS		ACSA		AGSCCS	
	Mean	Std	Mean	Std	Mean	Std	Mean	Std	Mean	Std	Mean	Std
SDM	1.08×10^{-3}	6.73×10^{-5}	1.16×10^{-3}	9.57×10^{-5}	1.01×10^{-3}	4.84×10^{-5}	1.04×10^{-3}	4.84×10^{-5}	1.05×10^{-3}	5.92×10^{-5}	9.89×10^{-4}	1.26×10^{-5}
DDM	1.49×10^{-3}	2.18×10^{-4}	1.80×10^{-3}	3.32×10^{-4}	1.80×10^{-3}	3.09×10^{-4}	1.35×10^{-3}	2.36×10^{-4}	1.69×10^{-3}	2.89×10^{-4}	1.33×10^{-3}	3.28×10^{-4}
Photowatt-PWP-201	2.44×10^{-3}	7.93×10^{-6}	3.00×10^{-3}	1.58×10^{-3}	2.88×10^{-3}	1.12×10^{-3}	2.43×10^{-3}	1.17×10^{-6}	2.45×10^{-3}	3.61×10^{-5}	2.43×10^{-3}	5.32×10^{-6}
STM6-40/36	4.66×10^{-3}	5.42×10^{-4}	4.97×10^{-3}	6.27×10^{-4}	4.17×10^{-3}	5.90×10^{-4}	3.35×10^{-3}	2.95×10^{-4}	5.51×10^{-2}	1.03×10^{-1}	3.14×10^{-3}	5.76×10^{-3}
STP6-120/36	3.68×10^{-2}	4.91×10^{-3}	4.17×10^{-2}	6.37×10^{-3}	3.74×10^{-2}	3.40×10^{-3}	2.95×10^{-2}	5.19×10^{-3}	1.38×10^{-1}	3.23×10^{-1}	2.02×10^{-2}	5.85×10^{-3}

Table 6. Comparison among different algorithms on SDM PV cell.

Algorithm	$I_{pv}(A)$	$I_{sd}(A)$	$R_s(\Omega)$	$R_p(\Omega)$	α	RMSE
CS	0.7607	3.70×10^{-7}	0.0358	57.3751	1.4943	1.08×10^{-3}
ACS	0.7606	4.36×10^{-7}	0.0352	64.9443	1.5110	1.16×10^{-3}
ImCS	0.7607	3.54×10^{-7}	0.0360	56.7892	1.4905	1.01×10^{-3}
GBCS	0.7607	3.64×10^{-7}	0.0359	58.2349	1.4928	1.04×10^{-3}
ACSA	0.7607	3.57×10^{-7}	0.0360	57.2252	1.4910	1.05×10^{-3}
AGSCCS	0.7608	3.47×10^{-7}	0.0362	54.9470	1.4860	9.89×10^{-4}

Table 7. Comparison among different algorithms on DDM PV cell.

Algorithm	$I_{pv}(A)$	$I_{sd1}(A)$	$R_s(\Omega)$	$R_p(\Omega)$	$\alpha1$	$I_{sd2}(\mu A)$	$\alpha2$	RMSE
CS	0.7606	4.15×10^{-7}	0.0350	69.7383	1.6110	2.67×10^{-7}	1.6206	1.49×10^{-3}
ACS	0.7607	4.88×10^{-7}	0.0343	79.6598	1.7060	4.13×10^{-7}	1.6896	1.80×10^{-3}
ImCS	0.7606	3.65×10^{-7}	0.0340	83.2859	1.5794	3.40×10^{-7}	1.5826	1.80×10^{-3}
GBCS	0.7607	2.77×10^{-7}	0.0355	66.2202	1.7133	3.38×10^{-7}	1.6354	1.35×10^{-3}
ACSA	0.7608	4.24×10^{-7}	0.0350	65.8916	1.6702	2.98×10^{-7}	1.6187	1.69×10^{-3}
AGSCCS	0.7594	2.69×10^{-7}	0.0400	79.9490	1.3166	6.61×10^{-8}	1.6569	1.33×10^{-3}

Table 8. Comparison among different algorithms on SMM PV modules.

	Algorithm	$I_{pv}(A)$	$I_{sd}(A)$	$R_s(\Omega)$	$R_p(\Omega)$	α	RMSE
Photowatt-PWP-201	CS	1.0302	3.67×10^{-6}	1.1959	1048.6362	48.8467	2.44×10^{-3}
	ACS	1.0316	3.09×10^{-6}	1.2298	928.8406	47.6362	3.00×10^{-3}
	ImCS	1.0466	2.68×10^{-6}	1.2030	802.3769	46.7762	2.88×10^{-3}
	GBCS	1.0304	3.55×10^{-6}	1.1992	1007.7580	48.7176	2.43×10^{-3}
	ACSA	1.0304	3.53×10^{-6}	1.2003	1005.9862	48.6883	2.45×10^{-3}
	AGSCCS	1.0305	3.48×10^{-6}	1.2013	982.0053	48.6428	2.43×10^{-3}
STM6-40/36	CS	1.6552	6.95×10^{-6}	0.0002	88.9366	1.6890	4.66×10^{-3}
	ACS	1.6556	7.41×10^{-6}	0.0002	157.7937	1.6976	4.97×10^{-3}
	ImCS	1.6603	5.57×10^{-6}	0.0004	30.7576	1.6591	4.17×10^{-3}
	GBCS	1.6603	5.43×10^{-6}	0.0004	28.2830	1.6562	3.35×10^{-3}
	ACSA	1.6468	2.27×10^{-5}	0.0060	167.4477	1.8746	5.51×10^{-2}
	AGSCCS	1.6633	4.69×10^{-6}	0.0034	161.7657	1.7099	3.14×10^{-3}
STP6-120/36	CS	7.4960	1.57×10^{-5}	0.0036	596.5901	1.4274	3.68×10^{-2}
	ACS	7.5113	2.30×10^{-5}	0.0032	558.4491	1.4857	4.17×10^{-2}
	ImCS	7.5110	2.14×10^{-5}	0.0034	1034.5552	1.4677	3.74×10^{-2}
	GBCS	7.4909	1.03×10^{-5}	0.0038	826.8380	1.3977	2.95×10^{-2}
	ACSA	7.4705	4.37×10^{-1}	0.0028	349.0301	4.6720	1.38×10^{-1}
	AGSCCS	7.4708	3.57×10^{-6}	0.0044	418.9095	1.2865	2.02×10^{-2}

From Figure 8, AGSCCS shows excellent performance in the PV module parameter setting problems. It always achieves the best results compared with the other five algorithms corresponding with CS. The five problems are nonlinear optimization problems, which are more complex than linear problems. The reason why AGSCCS has the best convergence capacity may owe to the adaptive random step size in the local searching process. It helps search different directions, rather than always search through the best solution's directions. This measure reduces the risk of falling into the local optimum. Indeed, the increase of accuracy may also give credit to the help of chaotic map initialization, which promotes population diversity in the beginning stage. Moreover, AGSCCS has the fastest convergence speed compared with the other four algorithms. For example, in Figure 8c,d, AGSCCS is close to convergence when the number of function evaluations reaches 30,000, while other algorithms have not reached the convergence value at this time. This is because the SC technique helps accelerate the convergence speed. Compressing the upper and lower bounds reduces the search space without interfering with the direction selection of the algorithm to speed up the convergence speed of the algorithm.

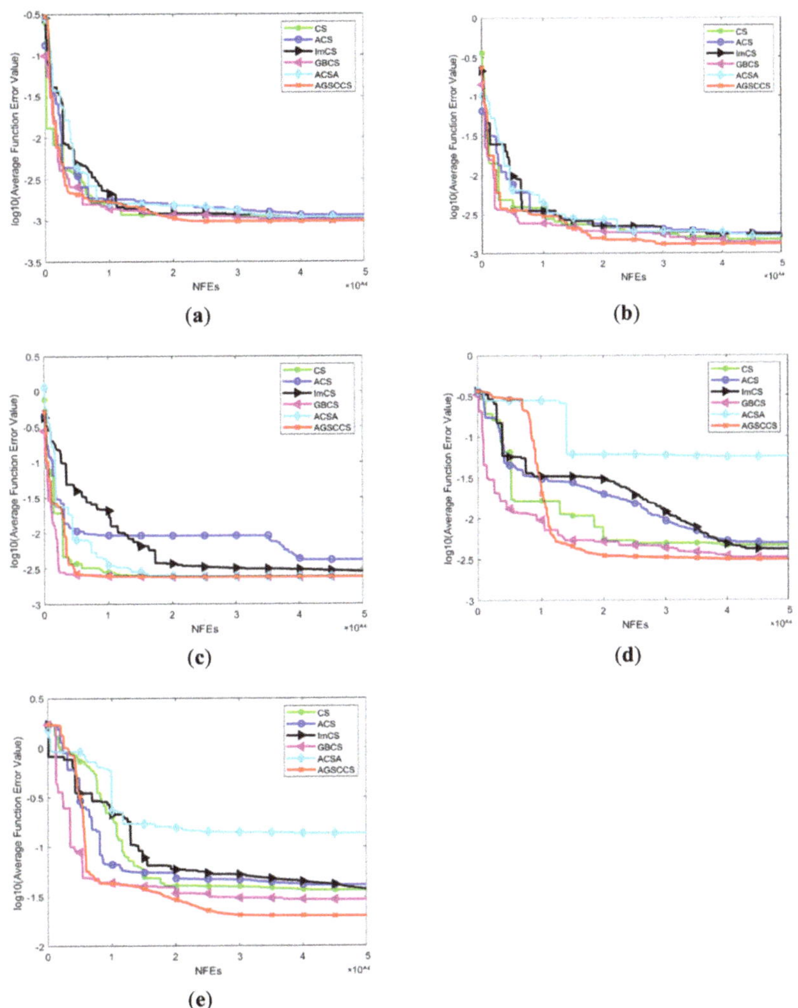

Figure 8. Convergence curve of AGSCCS in PV module. (**a**) SDM; (**b**) DDM; (**c**) Photowatt-PWP-201; (**d**) STM6-40/36; (**e**) STP6-120/36.

6. Conclusions

In this paper, an Adaptive Guided Spatial Compressive CS (AGSCCS) has been proposed. It mainly aims at improving the section of the local search, which helped enhance the exploitation of AGSCCS. The improvements have been implemented through three steps. The first one was the adjustment of the method of population generation. Due to the heterogeneity of the random number generation method, we adopted a chaotic mapping instead. In this method, chaotic system mapping is used to form the initial solution, which increases the irregularity of the solution arrangement and makes it more like a uniform random distribution. The second one was an adaptive guided scheme of updating location areas. It retained information about the best and worst solution sets in the population and transmitted these to the next generation as clues for finding the ideal solution. The last improvement was a SC technique. It was a novel technique that aimed at quick convergence and better algorithm precision. When taking the SC technique, the population was gathered around the optimal solution, whether the current generation was in local search or global search. Next, it would collect the information of some excellent solutions and transmit the information to the offspring. The three measures above sufficiently considered the balance between exploration and exploitation, giving an outstanding performance. To test the performance of AGSCCS, we tested the algorithm with the other five algorithms (CS, ACS, ImCS, GBCS, and ACSA) on the 2014 CEC benchmark. The experimental results were compared with CS, ACS, ImCS, GBCS, and ACSA. In total, AGSCCS got the best grade. A sensitive examination has been completed to compare the three promotion strategies, which were the most significant contributions. We adopted the controlling variables and compared them. The results revealed that the SC technique has the most significant impact on AGSCCS. In other words, the SC technique made the most contributions to the algorithm. The remaining two strategies were almost equal. However, according to the experimental sensitive test, both of them also contributed to the improvement of the algorithm. At last, we applied AGSCCS into the PV model to verify the feasibility of a practical application. The experiments showed that AGSCCS acquired the best results, which further exemplifies the outstanding performance of the proposed algorithm.

As a metaheuristic algorithm, CS has not been valued for practical applications. As a metaheuristic with few parameters, CS will achieve development in practical applications without question. Next, we will strive to find a competitive CS and apply it into more practical applications in the future. In fact, in Section 5, the photovoltaic model has a deeper level of research value due to its different weather, climate, etc. Using the CS algorithm to study these deeper and more complex models will be a potential direction.

Author Contributions: W.X.: Writing—Original draft preparation, Data curation, Investigation. X.Y.: Conceptualization, Methodology. All authors have read and agreed to the published version of the manuscript.

Funding: This research was funded by the China Natural Science Foundation (No. 71974100, 71871121), Natural Science Foundation in Jiangsu Province (No. BK20191402), Major Project of Philosophy and Social Science Research in Colleges and Universities in Jiangsu Province (2019SJZDA039), Qing Lan Project (R2019Q05), Social Science Research in Colleges and Universities in Jiangsu Province (2019SJZDA039), and Project of Meteorological Industry Research Center (sk20210032).

Institutional Review Board Statement: Not applicable.

Informed Consent Statement: Not applicable.

Data Availability Statement: Not applicable.

Conflicts of Interest: The authors declare no conflict of interest.

References

1. Sinha, N.; Chakrabarti, R.; Chattopadhyay, P.K. Evolutionary programming techniques for economic load dispatch. *IEEE Trans. Evol. Comput.* **2003**, *7*, 83–94. [CrossRef]
2. Boushaki, S.I.; Kamel, N.; Bendjeghaba, O. A new quantum chaotic cuckoo search algorithm for data clustering. *Expert Syst. Appl.* **2018**, *96*, 358–372. [CrossRef]
3. Tejani, G.G.; Pholdee, N.; Bureerat, S.; Prayogo, D.; Gandomi, A.H. Structural optimization using multi-objective modified adaptive symbiotic organisms search. *Expert Syst. Appl.* **2019**, *125*, 425–441. [CrossRef]
4. Kamoona, A.M.; Patra, J.C. A novel enhanced cuckoo search algorithm for contrast enhancement of gray scale images. *Appl. Soft Comput.* **2019**, *85*, 105749. [CrossRef]
5. Bérubé, J.-F.; Gendreau, M.; Potvin, J.-Y. An exact-constraint method for biobjective combinatorial optimization problems: Application to the Traveling Salesman Problem with Profits. *Eur. J. Oper. Res.* **2009**, *194*, 39–50. [CrossRef]
6. Dodu, J.C.; Martin, P.; Merlin, A.; Pouget, J. An optimal formulation and solution of short-range operating problems for a power system with flow constraints. *Proc. IEEE* **1972**, *60*, 54–63. [CrossRef]
7. Vorontsov, M.A.; Carhart, G.W.; Ricklin, J.C. Adaptive phase-distortion correction based on parallel gradient-descent optimization. *Opt. Lett.* **1997**, *22*, 907–909. [CrossRef]
8. Parikh, J.; Chattopadhyay, D. A multi-area linear programming approach for analysis of economic operation of the Indian power system. *IEEE Trans. Power Syst.* **1996**, *11*, 52–58. [CrossRef]

9. Kim, J.S.; Ed Gar, T.F. Optimal scheduling of combined heat and power plants using mixed-integer nonlinear programming. *Energy* **2014**, *77*, 675–690. [CrossRef]
10. Fan, J.Y.; Zhang, L. Real-time economic dispatch with line flow and emission constraints using quadratic programming. *IEEE Trans. Power Syst.* **1998**, *13*, 320–325. [CrossRef]
11. Reid, G.F.; Hasdorff, L. Economic Dispatch Using Quadratic Programming. *IEEE Trans. Power Appar. Syst.* **1973**, *6*, 2015–2023. [CrossRef]
12. Oliveira, P.; Mckee, S.; Coles, C. Lagrangian relaxation and its application to the unit-commitment-economic-dispatch problem. *Ima J. Manag. Math.* **1992**, *4*, 261–272. [CrossRef]
13. El-Keib, A.A.; Ma, H. Environmentally constrained economic dispatch using the LaGrangian relaxation method. *Power Syst. IEEE Trans.* **1994**, *9*, 1723–1729. [CrossRef]
14. Aravindhababu, P.; Nayar, K.R. Economic dispatch based on optimal lambda using radial basis function network. *Int. J. Electr. Power Energy Syst.* **2002**, *24*, 551–556. [CrossRef]
15. Obioma, D.D.; Izuchukwu, A.M. Comparative analysis of techniques for economic dispatch of generated power with modified Lambda-iteration method. In Proceedings of the IEEE International Conference on Emerging & Sustainable Technologies for Power & Ict in A Developing Society, Owerri, Nigeria, 14–16 November 2013; pp. 231–237.
16. Mohammadian, M.; Lorestani, A.; Ardehali, M.M. Optimization of Single and Multi-areas Economic Dispatch Problems Based on Evolutionary Particle Swarm Optimization Algorithm. *Energy* **2018**, *161*, 710–724. [CrossRef]
17. Goldberg, D.E.; Deb, K. A Comparative Analysis of Selection Schemes Used in Genetic Algorithms. *Found. Genet. Algorithm.* **1991**, *1*, 69–93.
18. Kennedy, J.; Eberhart, R. Particle Swarm Optimization. In Proceedings of the Icnn95-International Conference on Neural Networks, Perth, WA, Australia, 27 November–1 December 1995.
19. Yang, X. A new metaheuristic bat-inspired algorithm. In *Nature Inspired Cooperative Strategies for Optimization (NICSO)*; Springer: Berlin/Heidelberg, Germany, 2010.
20. Karaboga, D.; Basturk, B. A powerful and efficient algorithm for numerical function optimization: Artificial bee colony (ABC) algorithm. *J. Glob. Optim.* **2007**, *39*, 459–471. [CrossRef]
21. Sm, A.; Smm, B.; Al, A. Grey Wolf Optimizer. *Adv. Eng. Softw.* **2014**, *69*, 46–61.
22. Yang, X.S.; Deb, S. Engineering Optimisation by Cuckoo Search. *Int. J. Math. Model. Numer. Optim.* **2010**, *1*, 330–343. [CrossRef]
23. Ding, J.; Wang, Q.; Zhang, Q.; Ye, Q.; Ma, Y. A Hybrid Particle Swarm Optimization-Cuckoo Search Algorithm and Its Engineering Applications. *Math. Probl. Eng.* **2019**, *2019*, 5213759. [CrossRef]
24. Mareli, M.; Twala, B. An adaptive Cuckoo search algorithm for optimisation. *Appl. Comput. Inform.* **2018**, *14*, 107–115. [CrossRef]
25. Naik, M.K.; Panda, R. A novel adaptive cuckoo search algorithm for intrinsic discriminant analysis based face recognition. *Appl. Soft Comput.* **2016**, *38*, 661–675. [CrossRef]
26. Selvakumar, A.I.; Thanushkodi, K. Optimization using civilized swarm: Solution to economic dispatch with multiple minima. *Electr. Power Syst. Res.* **2009**, *79*, 8–16. [CrossRef]
27. Hu, P.; Deng, C.; Hui, W.; Wang, W.; Wu, Z. Gaussian bare-bones cuckoo search algorithm. In Proceedings of the the Genetic and Evolutionary Computation Conference Companion, Kyoto, Japan, 15–19 July 2018.
28. Walton, S.; Hassan, O.; Morgan, K.; Brown, M.R. Modified cuckoo search: A new gradient free optimisation algorithm. *Chaos Solitons Fractals* **2011**, *44*, 710–718. [CrossRef]
29. Wang, L.; Zhong, Y.; Yin, Y. Nearest neighbour cuckoo search algorithm with probabilistic mutation. *Appl. Soft Comput.* **2016**, *49*, 498–509. [CrossRef]
30. Cheng, J.; Wang, L.; Jiang, Q.; Xiong, Y. A novel cuckoo search algorithm with multiple update rules. *Appl. Intell.* **2018**, *48*, 4192–4211. [CrossRef]
31. Ong, P. Adaptive cuckoo search algorithm for unconstrained optimization. *Sci. World J.* **2014**, *2014*, 943403. [CrossRef] [PubMed]
32. Kang, T.; Yao, J.; Jin, M.; Yang, S.; Duong, T. A Novel Improved Cuckoo Search Algorithm for Parameter Estimation of Photovoltaic (PV) Models. *Energies* **2018**, *11*, 1060. [CrossRef]
33. Wang, G.G.; Deb, S.; Gandomi, A.H.; Zhang, Z.; Alavi, A.H. Chaotic cuckoo search. *Soft Comput.* **2016**, *20*, 3349–3362. [CrossRef]
34. Rakhshani, H.; Rahati, A. Snap-drift cuckoo search: A novel cuckoo search optimization algorithm. *Appl. Soft Comput.* **2017**, *52*, 771–794. [CrossRef]
35. Shehab, M.; Khader, A.T.; Al-Betar, M.A.; Abualigah, L.M. Hybridizing cuckoo search algorithm with hill climbing for numerical optimization problems. In Proceedings of the 2017 8th International Conference on Information Technology (ICIT), Amman, Jordan, 17–18 May 2017.
36. Zhang, Z.; Ding, S.; Jia, W. A hybrid optimization algorithm based on cuckoo search and differential evolution for solving constrained engineering problems. *Eng. Appl. Artif. Intell.* **2019**, *85*, 254–268. [CrossRef]
37. Pareek, N.K.; Patidar, V.; Sud, K.K. Image encryption using chaotic logistic map. *Image Vis. Comput.* **2006**, *24*, 926–934. [CrossRef]
38. Mohamed, A.W.; Mohamed, A.K. Adaptive guided differential evolution algorithm with novel mutation for numerical optimization. *Int. J. Mach. Learn. Cybern.* **2017**, *10*, 253–277. [CrossRef]
39. Aguirre, A.H.; Rionda, S.B.; Coello Coello, C.A.; Lizárraga, G.L.; Montes, E.M. Handling constraints using multiobjective optimization concepts. *Int. J. Numer. Methods Eng.* **2004**, *59*, 1989–2017. [CrossRef]

40. Wang, Y.; Cai, Z.; Zhou, Y. Accelerating adaptive trade-off model using shrinking space technique for constrained evolutionary optimization. *Int. J. Numer. Methods Eng.* **2009**, *77*, 1501–1534. [CrossRef]
41. Kaveh, A. *Cuckoo Search Optimization*; Springer: Cham, Switzerland, 2014; pp. 317–347. [CrossRef]
42. Ley, A. The Habits of the Cuckoo. *Nature* **1896**, *53*, 223. [CrossRef]
43. Humphries, N.E.; Queiroz, N.; Dyer, J.; Pade, N.G.; Musyl, M.K.; Schaefer, K.M.; Fuller, D.W.; Brunnsc Hw Eiler, J.M.; Doyle, T.K.; Houghton, J. Environmental context explains Lévy and Brownian movement patterns of marine predators. *Nature* **2010**, *465*, 1066–1069. [CrossRef]
44. Wang, R.; Cui, X.; Li, Y. Self-Adaptive adjustment of cuckoo search K-means clustering algorithm. *Appl. Res. Comput.* **2018**, *35*, 3593–3597.
45. Wilk, G.; Wlodarczyk, Z. Interpretation of the Nonextensivity Parameter q in Some Applications of Tsallis Statistics and Lévy Distributions. *Phys. Rev. Lett.* **1999**, *84*, 2770–2773. [CrossRef]
46. Nguyen, T.T.; Phung, T.A.; Truong, A.V. A novel method based on adaptive cuckoo search for optimal network reconfiguration and distributed generation allocation in distribution network. *Int. J. Electr. Power Energy Syst.* **2016**, *78*, 801–815. [CrossRef]
47. Li, X.; Yin, M. Modified cuckoo search algorithm with self adaptive parameter method. *Inf. Sci.* **2015**, *298*, 80–97. [CrossRef]
48. Naik, M.; Nath, M.R.; Wunnava, A.; Sahany, S.; Panda, R. A new adaptive Cuckoo search algorithm. In Proceedings of the IEEE International Conference on Recent Trends in Information Systems, Kolkata, India, 9–11 July 2015.
49. Farswan, P.; Bansal, J.C. Fireworks-inspired biogeography-based optimization. *Soft Comput.* **2018**, *23*, 7091–7115. [CrossRef]
50. Birx, D.L.; Pipenberg, S.J. Chaotic oscillators and complex mapping feed forward networks (CMFFNs) for signal detection in noisy environments. In Proceedings of the International Joint Conference on Neural Networks, Baltimore, MD, USA, 7–11 June 2002.
51. Qi, W. A self-adaptive embedded chaotic particle swarm optimization for parameters selection of Wv-SVM. *Expert Syst. Appl.* **2011**, *38*, 184–192.
52. Wang, L.; Yin, Y.; Zhong, Y. Cuckoo search with varied scaling factor. *Front. Comput. Sci.* **2015**, *9*, 623–635. [CrossRef]
53. Das, S.; Mallipeddi, R.; Maity, D. Adaptive evolutionary programming with p-best mutation strategy. *Swarm Evol. Comput.* **2013**, *9*, 58–68. [CrossRef]
54. Zhang, J.; Sanderson, A.S. JADE: Adaptive Differential Evolution With Optional External Archive. *IEEE Trans. Evol. Comput.* **2009**, *13*, 945–958. [CrossRef]
55. Deb, K. An efficient constraint handling method for genetic algorithms. *Comput. Methods Appl. Mech. Eng.* **2000**, *186*, 311–338. [CrossRef]
56. Armani, R.F.; Wright, J.A.; Savic, D.A.; Walters, G.A. Self-Adaptive Fitness Formulation for Evolutionary Constrained Optimization of Water Systems. *J. Comput. Civ. Eng.* **2005**, *19*, 212–216. [CrossRef]
57. Bo, Y.; Gallagher, M. Experimental results for the special session on real-parameter optimization at CEC 2005: A simple, continuous EDA. In Proceedings of the 2005 IEEE Congress on Evolutionary Computation, Edinburgh, UK, 2–5 September 2005.
58. Liang, J.J.; Qu, B.Y.; Suganthan, P.N. *Problem Definitions and Evaluation Criteria for the CEC 2014 Special Session and Competition on Single Objective Real-Parameter Numerical Optimization*; Technical Report 201311; Computational Intelligence Laboratory, Zhengzhou University: Zhengzhou, China; Nanyang Technological University: Singapore, December 2013.
59. Yang, X.; Gong, W. Opposition-based JAYA with population reduction for parameter estimation of photovoltaic solar cells and modules. *Appl. Soft Comput.* **2021**, *104*, 107218. [CrossRef]

mathematics

Article

An Adaptive Neuro-Fuzzy Model for Attitude Estimation and Control of a 3 DOF System

Xin Wang [1,*]**, Seyed Mehdi Abtahi** [2]**, Mahmood Chahari** [3] **and Tianyu Zhao** [4,*]

[1] Department of Kinesiology, Shenyang Sport University, Shenyang 110102, China
[2] Department of Mechanical Engineering, University of Illinois at Chicago, Chicago, IL 60607, USA; sabtah2@uic.edu
[3] Department of Mechanical Engineering, State University of New York at Binghamton, 4400 Vestal Parkway, Binghamton, NY 13902, USA; mchahar1@binghamton.edu
[4] Key Laboratory of Structural Dynamics of Liaoning Province, College of Sciences, Northeastern University, Shenyang 110819, China
* Correspondence: wangxin@syty.edu.cn (X.W.); zhaotianyu@mail.neu.edu.cn (T.Z.)

Abstract: In recent decades, one of the scientists' main concerns has been to improve the accuracy of satellite attitude, regardless of the expense. The obvious result is that a large number of control strategies have been used to address this problem. In this study, an adaptive neuro-fuzzy integrated system (ANFIS) for satellite attitude estimation and control was developed. The controller was trained with the data provided by an optimal controller. Furthermore, a pulse modulator was used to generate the right ON/OFF commands of the thruster actuator. To evaluate the performance of the proposed controller in closed-loop simulation, an ANFIS observer was also used to estimate the attitude and angular velocities of the satellite using magnetometer, sun sensor, and data gyro data. However, a new ANFIS system was proposed that can jointly control and estimate the system attitude. The performance of the proposed controller was compared to the optimal PID controller in a Monte Carlo simulation with different initial conditions, disturbance, and noise. The results show that the proposed controller can surpass the optimal PID controller in several aspects including time and smoothness. In addition, the ANFIS estimator was examined and the results demonstrate the high ability of this designated observer. Consequently, evaluating the performance of PID and the proposed controller revealed that the proposed controller consumed less control effort for satellite attitude estimation under noise and uncertainty.

Keywords: integrated control and estimation; adaptive neuro fuzzy; noise; uncertainty

MSC: 93C42

Citation: Wang, X.; Abtahi, S.M.; Chahari, M.; Zhao, T. An Adaptive Neuro-Fuzzy Model for Attitude Estimation and Control of a 3 DOF System. *Mathematics* **2022**, *10*, 976. https://doi.org/10.3390/math10060976

Academic Editors: Xiang Li, Shuo Zhang and Wei Zhang

Received: 18 February 2022
Accepted: 16 March 2022
Published: 18 March 2022

Publisher's Note: MDPI stays neutral with regard to jurisdictional claims in published maps and institutional affiliations.

1. Introduction

Satellite attitude control plays a significant role in most space missions. Therefore, the development of an accurate and stable controller is an essential part of conducting a space mission [1–8]. The most advanced satellite attitude control techniques use the concept of quaternion feedback [9–12]. However, various linear and nonlinear attitude control strategies based on quaternion feedback have been investigated [13,14]. The quaternion feedback approach is also used to stabilize the attitude of microsatellites [15].

In recent years, many control techniques have been proposed for satellite attitude control in the presence of uncertainty and disturbance [16,17]. Li et al. [18] proposed a robust finite time control algorithm for controlling satellite attitude in the presence of uncertainty; and Xiao et al. [19] developed a control approach with a simple structure to perform an attitude tracking maneuver for rigid satellites in the case of disturbances and uncertain inertia parameters. In another study, Vatankhahghadim and Damaren [20] proposed a linear passivity-based controller design for hybrid attitude control of spacecraft using magnetic torques and thrusters.

Several different types of optimal controllers have been used to enhance the performance of the satellite attitude control system. In order to enhance the pointing accuracy of a small satellite, an attempt was made to optimize the attitude control model based on the optimal control algorithm [21]. In another study, the optimal magnetic attitude control for small satellites was studied [22]. Moreover, Arantes et al. [23] tried to analyze and design a reaction thruster attitude controller and then improve the performance of the control subsystem. All these optimal control design algorithms inevitably led to a specific mathematical model, leading to inappropriate behavior compared to external pulses in the comparison simulation state. It is noteworthy to mention that an optimal controller may not guarantee the stability of the closed-loop system in the presence of uncertainties.

The adaptive control method is one of the most powerful approaches that can deal with the problem of system uncertainty. In this regard, Wen et al. [24] proposed a novel adaptive control method for the spacecraft's attitude tracking control problem with inertia uncertainties. Moreover, Lee and Singh [25] proposed an adaptive controller in order to control the satellite attitude by solar radiation pressure. In another research, they presented a novel adaptive controller for attitude control of satellites with large uncertainties in the system parameters utilizing solar radiation pressure [26]. All of these adaptive control algorithms are model-based, and although they are able to deal accurately with uncertainties, they are incapable of dealing with different dynamic models. The problem of satellite attitude determination has been extensively studied, and has been the main concern of many studies in recent decades [27–29]. In a study by Kouyama et al. [30], they proposed an automated and robust scheme to determine the satellite attitude, which of course follows an exact map projection. They employed this method in combination with the classic onboard sensors. In another study, Wu et al. [13] proposed a method by which the problem of orientation based on a single sensor observation could be solved.

The enormous ability of fuzzy logic to solve various mathematical problems of modeling, control, and estimation is undeniable. Daley et al. [31] utilized the self-organizer fuzzy logic controller (SOC) for attitude control of a flexible satellite with significant dynamic coupling of the axes that cannot be modeled easily. In another paper, Mukherjee et al. [32] employed fuzzy logic to control the attitude of Earth-pointing satellites, in which they used the genetic algorithm to optimize the performance of their proposed nonlinear fuzzy PID controller. In other research, Huo et al. [33] proposed an adaptive fuzzy fault tolerance attitude control for a rigid spacecraft. In recent years, fuzzy logic has been used for a variety of satellite attitude estimation purposes [34]. However, Ran et al. [35] studied an adaptive fuzzy fault tolerance control for rigid spacecraft attitude maneuvers. Furthermore, Sun et al. [36] utilized an adaptive fuzzy estimator for spacecraft attitude determination.

In this paper, an ANFIS (adapted neuro-fuzzy inference system) [37] controller was introduced to control and estimate the satellite attitude. However, to the best of the authors' knowledge, no study in the literature has been conducted on the integrated control and estimation of satellite attitude using ANFIS, which is a kind of artificial neural network and is based on the Takagi–Sugeno fuzzy inference system. The most significant advantage of the proposed model is the elimination of interphase (sensor equations and equations used to calculate quaternion errors). This, in turn, eliminates systematic errors and noise that are unavoidable in classical approaches. Consequently, the ANFIS control method is mostly applicable in terms of measurement noise, model uncertainty, and external disturbance [38].

The rest of this paper is organized as follows. First, a summary of the satellite attitude dynamics is given. A brief overview of the optimal PID controller design for control systems is then given. Next, the general ANFIS structure and the learning algorithms are discussed. Subsequently, structures of ANFIS controller and satellite attitude estimator are given. Finally, an ANFIS integrated control and estimation subsystem are introduced to reduce the complexity of the control system. The usefulness of this model is then examined by comparing the proposed model results with those of the classical controller.

2. Modeling of System

2.1. Satellite Dynamics Model

In this section, we introduce equations of motion of a satellite with the Euler equation and quaternion kinematics. The Euler equation of the rigid body satellite attitude around its principal axes coordinates is [39]:

$$
\begin{aligned}
I_1\dot{\omega}_1 &= M_{c1} + M_{d1} - (I_3-I_2)\omega_2\omega_3 \\
I_2\dot{\omega}_2 &= M_{c2} + M_{d2} - (I_1-I_3)\omega_1\omega_3 \\
I_3\dot{\omega}_3 &= M_{c3} + M_{d3} - (I_2-I_1)\omega_2\omega_1
\end{aligned}
\tag{1}
$$

where ω_1, ω_2, and ω_3 are the elements of the angular velocity vector of the satellite. In addition, I_1, I_2, and I_3 are the moments of inertia about the principal axes. M_c and M_d are the control and disturbance moments, respectively, which are expressed in the body frame.

For kinematic representation, the quaternion vector $\bar{q} = (q_1, q_2, q_3, q_4)^T$ is utilized, which is defined as follows:

$$
\begin{bmatrix} q_1 \\ q_2 \\ q_3 \end{bmatrix} = \sin\frac{\theta}{2} \begin{bmatrix} e_1 \\ e_2 \\ e_3 \end{bmatrix} , \quad q_4 = \cos\frac{\theta}{2}
\tag{2}
$$

where θ is the rotation angle about the Euler axis $\bar{e} = (e_1, e_2, e_3)$. The kinematic differential equations for quaternions are as follows:

$$
\begin{bmatrix} \dot{q}_1 \\ \dot{q}_2 \\ \dot{q}_3 \\ \dot{q}_4 \end{bmatrix} = \frac{1}{2} \begin{bmatrix} 0 & \omega_3 & -\omega_2 & \omega_1 \\ -\omega_3 & 0 & \omega_1 & \omega_2 \\ \omega_2 & -\omega_1 & 0 & \omega_3 \\ -\omega_1 & -\omega_2 & -\omega_3 & 0 \end{bmatrix} \begin{bmatrix} q_1 \\ q_2 \\ q_3 \\ q_4 \end{bmatrix}
\tag{3}
$$

2.2. Measurements

The sun sensor and the magnetometer were used as reference sensors in this study to estimate the setting. In order to simulate the magnetometer sensor (magnetic field), height, latitude, longitude date, were considered as inputs and the magnetic field vector can be calculated as inertia frame $\bar{B}^I$ using the IGRF11 model [40]. Therefore, the magnetic field is transformed into the body frame $\bar{B}^B$ including a random white noise $\bar{n}_B$:

$$
\bar{B}^B = C_I^B \bar{B}^I + \bar{n}_B
\tag{4}
$$

The rotation matrix C_I^B can be calculated using the quaternion vector as follows:

$$
C_I^B = \begin{bmatrix} 1 - 2(q_2^2 + q_3^2) & 2(q_1q_2 + q_3q_4) & 2(q_1q_3 + q_2q_4) \\ 2(q_2q_1 + q_3q_4) & 1 - 2(q_1^2 + q_3^2) & 2(q_2q_3 + q_1q_4) \\ 2(q_3q_1 + q_2q_4) & 2(q_3q_2 + q_1q_4) & 1 - 2(q_1^2 + q_2^2) \end{bmatrix}
\tag{5}
$$

The attitude measurement only needs the direction of the magnetic field, which can be calculated as follows:

$$
\bar{u}_B^B = \bar{B}^B / \left|\bar{B}^B\right|
\tag{6}
$$

The sun vector direction in inertial frame $\bar{u}_s^I$ can be found by the following formulation [41]:

$$
\bar{u}_S^I = \left(\cos\left(\lambda_{ecliptic}\right) \cos(\varepsilon) \sin\left(\lambda_{ecliptic}\right) \sin(\varepsilon) \sin\left(\lambda_{ecliptic}\right) \right)^T
\tag{7}
$$

where

$$JD = 367\text{year} - INT\left[\frac{7\left(\text{year}+INT\left(\frac{\text{month}+9}{12}\right)\right)}{4}\right] + INT\left(\frac{275\text{month}}{9}\right) + \text{day} + 1721013.5$$
$$+ \frac{\frac{\left(\frac{\text{second}}{60}+\text{minute}\right)}{60}+\text{hour}}{24}$$

$$T = (JD - 2451545.0)/36525,$$

$$\lambda_M = 280.4606184° + 36000.77005361T,$$

$$M = 357.5277233° + 35999.05034T,$$

$$\lambda_{ecliptic} = \lambda_M + 1.914666471° \sin(M) + 0.019994643\sin(2M),$$

$$\varepsilon = 23.439291° - 0.0130042T,$$

In the above equations, JD is Julian Day based on the date and time (year, month, day, hour, minute, and second); T is the Julian centuries; λ_M is mean longitude of the sun; M is the mean anomaly of the sun; $\lambda_{ecliptic}$ is the ecliptic longitude of the sun; and ε is the tilt angle of the Earth rotation axis.

Similar to the magnetometer, the output of the sun sensor as the direction of the sun vector in body frame $\overline{u}_S^B$ can be estimated as follows:

$$\overline{u}_S^B = C_I^B \overline{u}_S^I + \overline{n}_S \tag{8}$$

Furthermore, to provide the angular velocity measurements, a three-axis rate-gyro with random white noise was used.

3. Adaptive Neural Fuzzy Inference System

3.1. Fuzzy Logic

Most traditional tools for modeling, thinking, and arithmetic are crisp, deterministic, and precise in character, so yes or no types instead of more or less types. In conventional dual logic, for example, a statement may be true or false and nothing in between. For the first time, L.A. Zadeh [42] proposed a fuzzy logic that contained "true", "false", and "partially true". He emphasized that real situations are often not clear and deterministic and cannot be described accurately.

A fuzzy control system is based on fuzzy logic, which analyzes input values in the form of logical variables that assume continuous values between 0 and 1. Rather than designing algorithms that explicitly define the control action as a function of the control input variables, the developer of a fuzzy controller writes rules that associate the input variables with the control variables through expressions of linguistic variables [43,44]. After all rules have been defined, the control process begins with the calculation of all rule consequences. Then, the consequences are summarized into a fuzzy set that describes the possible control actions.

3.2. ANFIS

In general, the fuzzy control logic has two main approaches: (1) Mamdani [45] and (2) Takagi–Sugeno [46]. The basis of ANFIS as an adaptive network-based fuzzy system is the Takagi–Sugeno fuzzy system method [37,47]. Its inference system corresponds to a set of fuzzy IF–THEN rules that have a learning ability to approximate non-linear functions. ANFIS is a combination of neural networks and fuzzy systems. However, ANFIS has become a very powerful simulation method that uses both fuzzy and neural network methods [48]. Recently, ANFIS modeling has become widespread in various space missions [49–51].

The main characteristic of the ANFIS controller is the ability to handle inaccuracy and uncertainty, which allows the use of real data and, more importantly, the design of a controller based on the provided real data [14,52]. The other considerable superiority of the ANFIS system is the required number of input variables for control and estimation. Simplicity of modeling compared to classical modeling, along with the superiority of this method in the presence of noise and uncertainty compared to PID controllers, which makes our proposed model more accurate.

ANFIS has five layers (as shown in Figure 1) as follows:

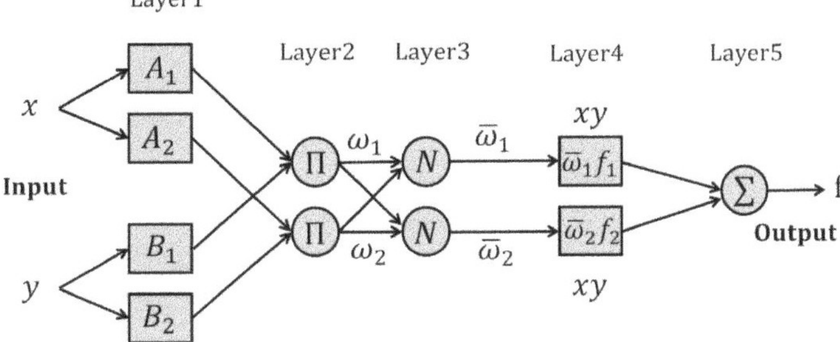

Figure 1. ANFIS structure.

Layer 1: Define membership function of input variables.

$$O_{1,i} = \mu_{A_i}(x) \ for \ i = 1,2$$

$$O_{1,i} = \mu_{B_{i-2}}(x) \ for \ i = 3,4$$

Layer 2: Product of the membership function for each input.

$$O_{2,i} = \omega_i = \mu_{A_i}(x) \, \mu_{B_i}(x) \ i = 1,2$$

Layer 3: Normalize the output of layer 2.

$$O_{3,i} = \overline{\omega}_i = \frac{\omega_i}{\omega_1 + \omega_2} \ i = 1,2$$

Layer 4: The output of this layer is:

$$O_{4,i} = \overline{\omega}_i f_i = \overline{\omega}_i (p_i x + q_i y + r_i)$$

Layer 5: The output of this layer is the summation of all outputs in layer 4.

$$O_{5,i} = \sum \overline{\omega}_i f_i = \frac{\sum \omega_i f_i}{\sum \omega_i}$$

3.3. Hybrid Learning Algorithm

Least square gradient reduction was used to train the ANFIS system (locating the membership function parameters) and the pattern between the input and the output data provided by an optimal PID controller.

Each learning level can be divided into two parts. In the forward stage, the inputs and outputs of each layer are calculated and the optimal coefficients are provided. Then, in the reverse stage, the parameters of the ANFIS system are updated.

3.4. Optimal PID Controller

The control moment vector by using the PID controller can be calculated as follows:

$$M_c = K_p q_e + K_d \omega + K_q \int q_e dt + K_\omega \int \omega dt \tag{9}$$

where q_e is the quaternion error and can be obtained from the following equation [39]:

$$\begin{bmatrix} \bar{q}_e \\ q_4 \end{bmatrix} = \begin{bmatrix} q_{1e} \\ q_{2e} \\ q_{3e} \\ q_{4e} \end{bmatrix} = \begin{bmatrix} q_{4c} & q_{3c} & -q_{2c} & -q_{1c} \\ -q_{3c} & q_{4c} & q_{1c} & -q_{2c} \\ q_{2c} & -q_{1c} & q_{4c} & -q_{3c} \\ q_{1c} & q_{2c} & q_{3c} & q_{4c} \end{bmatrix} \begin{bmatrix} q_1 \\ q_2 \\ q_3 \\ q_4 \end{bmatrix} \tag{10}$$

where q_cs are the quaternions of the command attitude.

The control gains $\left(K_p, K_d, K_q\right)$ in Equation (9) are optimized in order to minimize the following cost function:

$$J = \int \left(\sum_{i=1}^{3} |\omega_i| + \sum_{i=1}^{3} |q_{e_i}| \right) dt \tag{11}$$

By considering the following constraint as:

$$|M_c| \leq M_{c_{max}} \tag{12}$$

Consequently, this constraint guarantees the appropriate signal command to input the modulator for ON–OFF command of the thrusters with torque $M_{c_{max}}$.

4. ANFIS Controller and Estimator

4.1. ANFIS Controller

The aim of this training is to model an optimal PID controller as close as possible. The control input variables are angular velocity and quaternion errors, and the control output variable is the control torque M_C (as shown in Figure 2).

Figure 2. Block diagram of the ANFIS controller.

After the input and output variables are supplied by a system with PID controller, the collection of these data is repeated several times, taking into account 15 different initial conditions (each simulation for 20 s with 0.01 s sampling time). This means that the initial quaternions and initial angular velocities are changed to provide a wide range of data for ANFIS learning. Thereafter, the ANFIS controller training process begins and the ANFIS system learns the path from the inputs to the outputs. Now, the ANFIS controller can work with all initial conditions.

4.2. ANFIS Estimator

In this study, we utilized sun sensor and magnetometer outputs to estimate attitude. Therefore, data for ANFIS estimation learning from these two sensors were provided both in the body (sensor) and in the inertia frame (calculation) (as shown in Figure 3). However, several different scenarios were considered to provide a large database for learning the ANFIS estimator.

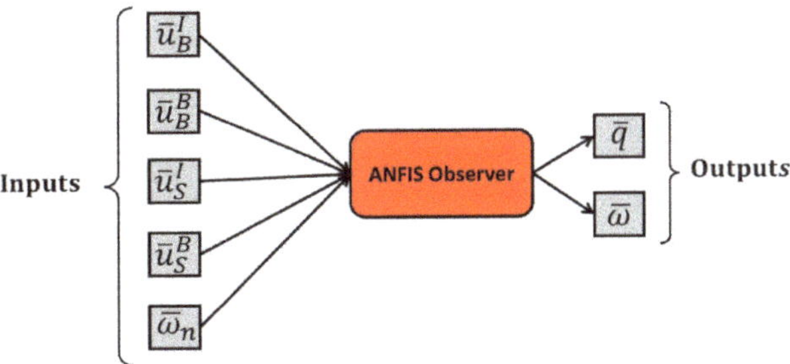

Figure 3. Block diagram of the ANFIS observer.

4.3. Combined Control and Estimation Using ANFIS

In this study, both the ANFIS estimator and ANFIS controller were used in a closed loop simulation. The nesting simulations show the performance of these two ANFIS subsystems working simultaneously (as shown in Figure 4).

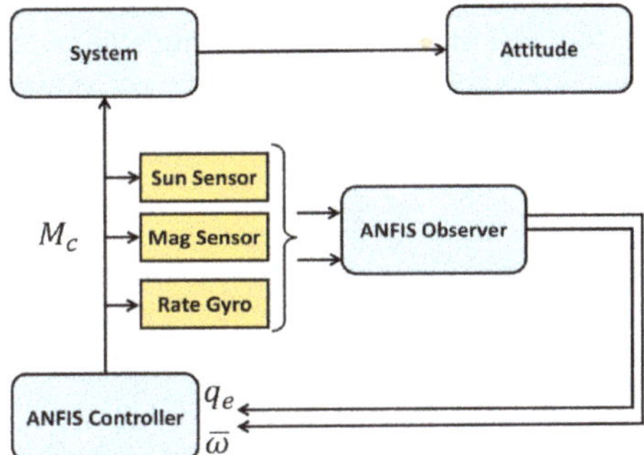

Figure 4. Block diagram of the combined ANFIS observer and controller.

4.4. Integrated Control and Estimation Using ANFIS

As mentioned in the introduction, the main purpose of this study was to evaluate the performance of an ANFIS system as a combination of estimator and controller instead of two separate subsystems (ANFIS estimator and ANFIS controller). As shown in Figure 5, for the proposed ANFIS subsystem, input variables are the inputs of the estimator (sensor data), and output variables are the outputs of the controller (control torque). In fact, the ANFIS integrated control and estimation subsystem receives data read by the sun sensor and the magnetic sensor as input variables and then passes the control torque directly to the system dynamics, as shown in Figure 6).

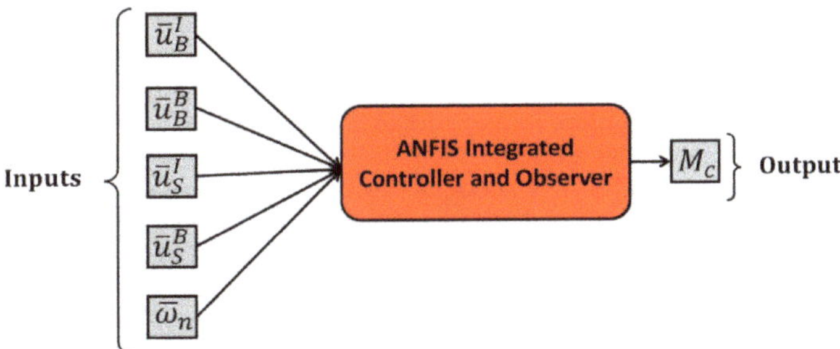

Figure 5. Block diagram of the integrated ANFIS controller and observer.

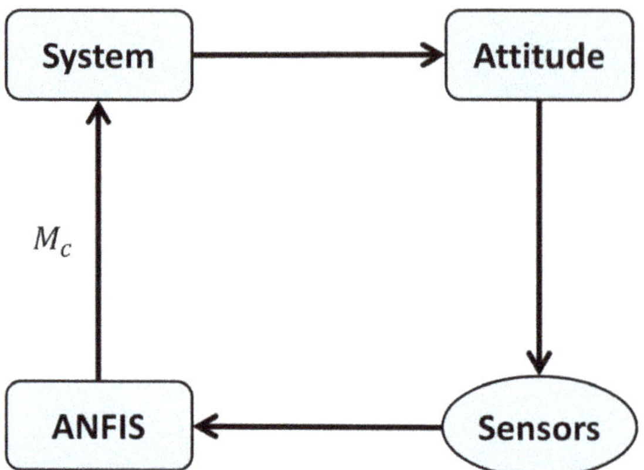

Figure 6. Block diagram of the control system using the ANFIS integrated controller and observer.

5. Evaluation of ANFIS Control and Estimation

To study the performance of attitude estimation and the control of satellites using ANFIS, a satellite with the moments of inertia that presented in Table 1 was considered. For all simulations, the final simulation duration time was selected to be 20 s, and the sampling time for estimation was 0.01 s. The system initial conditions and the desire attitude are provided in Table 2.

Table 1. Nominal and indeterminate moments of inertia (in Kg·m^2).

	I_x	I_y	I_z
Moment of Inertia	1.5	2.6	3
Moments of Inertia in case of uncertainty	2.5	4	3.3

Table 2. Sample initial condition (this initial condition is not in the training set).

	ω_x(Rad/s)	ω_y(Rad/s)	ω_z(Rad/s)	ϕ (deg)	θ (deg)	φ (deg)
Initial condition	0.0125	0.05	0.075	10	5	10
Desired condition	0	0	0	5	0	0

5.1. ANFIS Performance Comparison

As the simulations are presented for the stabilization of satellite attitude on zero condition, the most important characteristics of the results are the settling time of control, the control effort (fuel consumption), and the steady state error. Therefore, these characteristics are considered as the criteria for a comparison of the results.

The comparison of time histories of control moments for PID and ANFIS in the presence of noise and uncertainty are shown in Figures 7 and 8, respectively. The trajectory of the Euler angles are also presented in Figures 9 and 10. As shown in Figure 7, it can be seen that the PID controller is noisy and the ANFIS controller design method produces smoother control actions. Moreover, the trajectory of the attitude angles using PID controller has larger over-shoot values. As a result, the attitude angles are smoother and they can quickly reach the desired values.

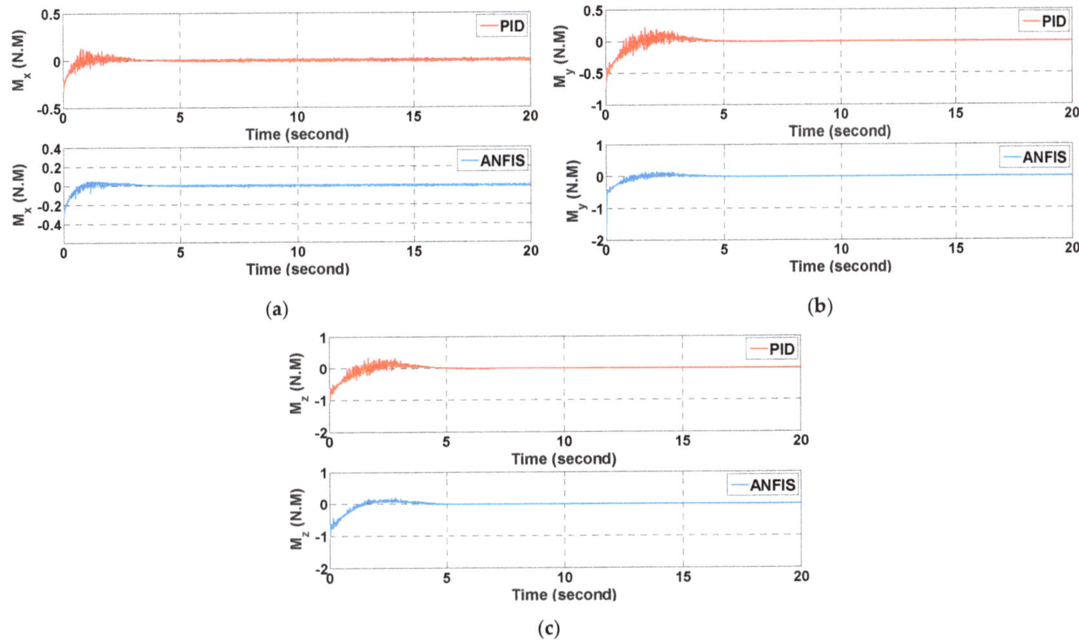

Figure 7. Comparison of control moments in (**a**) X, (**b**) Y, and (**c**) Z directions using ANFIS and PID in the presence of noise.

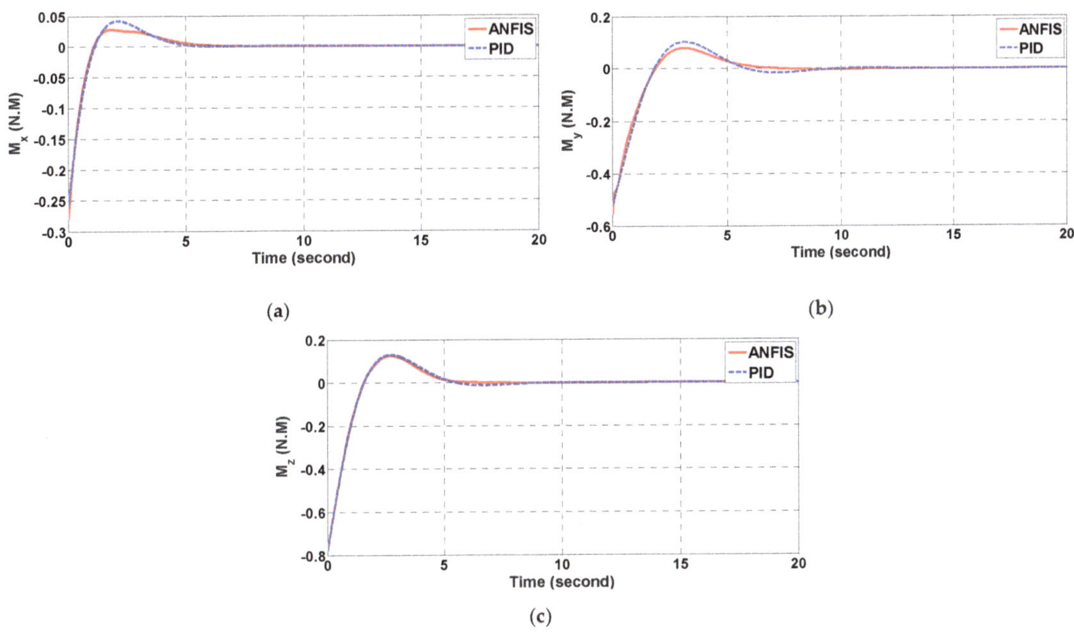

Figure 8. Comparison of control moment in (**a**) X, (**b**) Y, and (**c**) Z directions using ANFIS and PID in the presence of uncertainty.

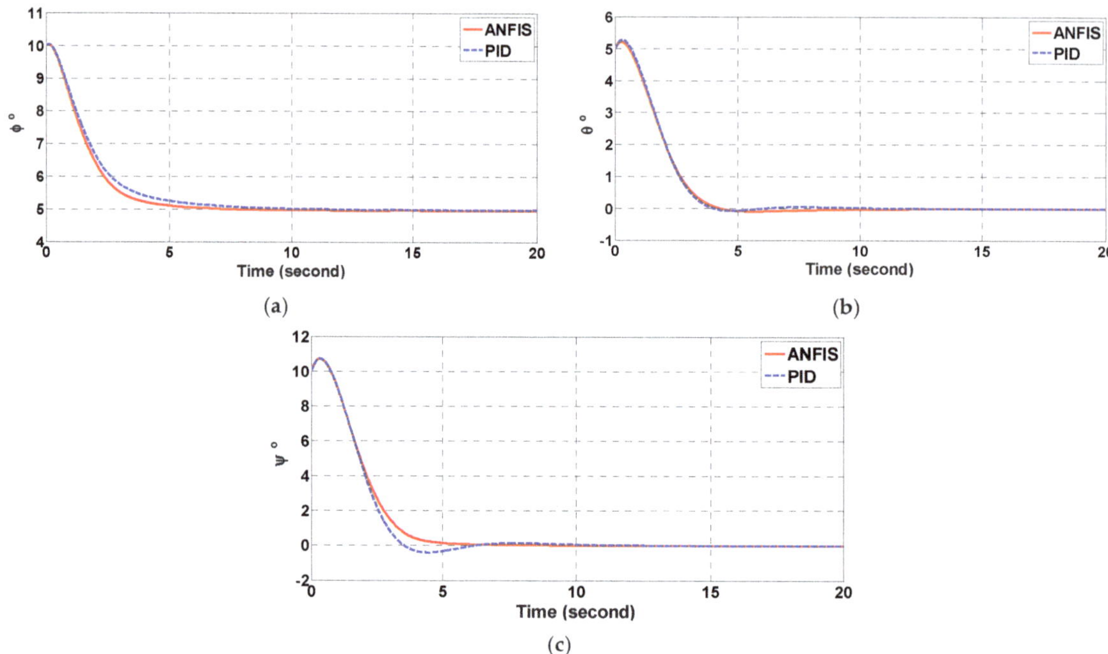

Figure 9. Comparison of Euler angles (**a**) φ, (**b**) θ, and (**c**) ψ using ANFIS and PID controllers in the presence of noise.

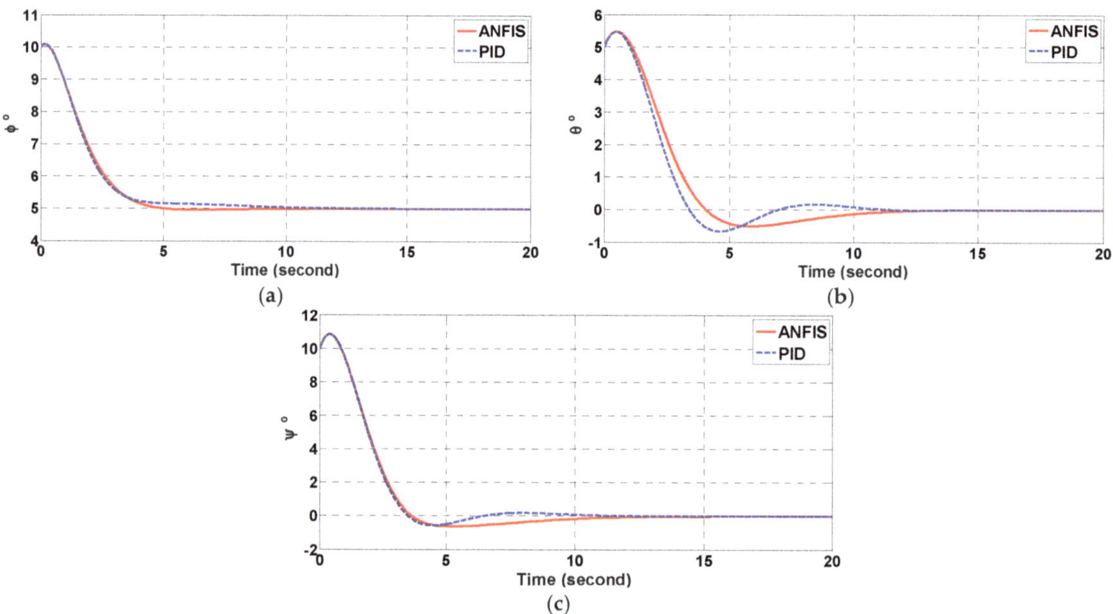

Figure 10. Comparison of Euler angles (**a**) φ, (**b**) θ, and (**c**) ψ using ANFIS and PID controllers in the presence of uncertainty.

The numerical results of the comparison of the ANFIS controller and PID controller are provided in Table 3 with/without noise and uncertainty. It is clear from this table that the fuel consumption of the ANFIS controller was 5% lower than PID, even if there is no uncertainty and/or measurement noise. The presence of noise and uncertainty induced more fuel consumption (14% and 9%, respectively). Accordingly, the ANFIS controller used less control effort (fuel) in all situations (noise and uncertainty).

Table 3. Fuel consumption of the PID and ANFIS controllers (in N.M.S).

	X Axis	**Y Axis**	**Z Axis**	**Total**
	Without noise and uncertainty			
ANFIS	0.1311	0.3956	0.7208	1.2475
PID	0.1287	0.4282	0.7485	1.3054
	Considering noise			
ANFIS	0.1732	0.4117	0.6925	1.2774
PID	0.1983	0.4719	0.8126	1.4830
	Considering uncertainty			
ANFIS	0.1910	0.6030	0.7891	1.5831
PID	0.1992	0.7048	0.8343	1.7383

The settling time with 1% error is listed in Table 4 for both controllers. The improvement in settling time using ANFIS over the PID was more obvious. In some cases, the settling time of ANFIS was almost half the PID, which is very important in space systems.

Table 4. Settling time for 1% error for satellite Euler angles using PID and ANFIS controllers (in seconds).

	X Axis	**Y Axis**	**Z Axis**
	Without noise and uncertainty		
ANFIS	7.23	4.87	8.88
PID	9.62	8.82	9.51
	Considering noise		
ANFIS	6.4	6.62	4.94
PID	9.34	8.68	9.46
	Considering uncertainty		
ANFIS	4.59	11.38	10.9
PID	9.84	10.65	10

5.2. Command Modulation

To evaluate the ANFIS controller results for the real thruster actuator, the control moments should be converted to ON–OFF commands. However, a PWPF (pulse-width pulse-frequency) modulator is used to transform the continuous control moment command to the ON–OFF commands. The trajectory of the attitude angles and the thruster commands are shown in Figures 11 and 12, respectively. It is clear that the limit of thrust results in a slower approach to the final attitudes. However, the results are acceptable considering the model uncertainty and measurement noise.

5.3. Monte Carlo Simulation

To analyze the robustness of the proposed integrated ANFIS estimator and controller, a Monte-Carlo simulation was conducted. A random initial condition (between -15 and $+15$ degrees) was considered in addition to the random noise and random uncertainty (I 1 Kg·m^2). The attitude control error of Euler angles of time = 20 s are shown for each Monte-Carlo simulation and the average and 3σ (standard deviation) until each iteration are shown in Figure 13 for 200 iterations. The maximum control error was less than 0.02 degrees, which is considerably low.

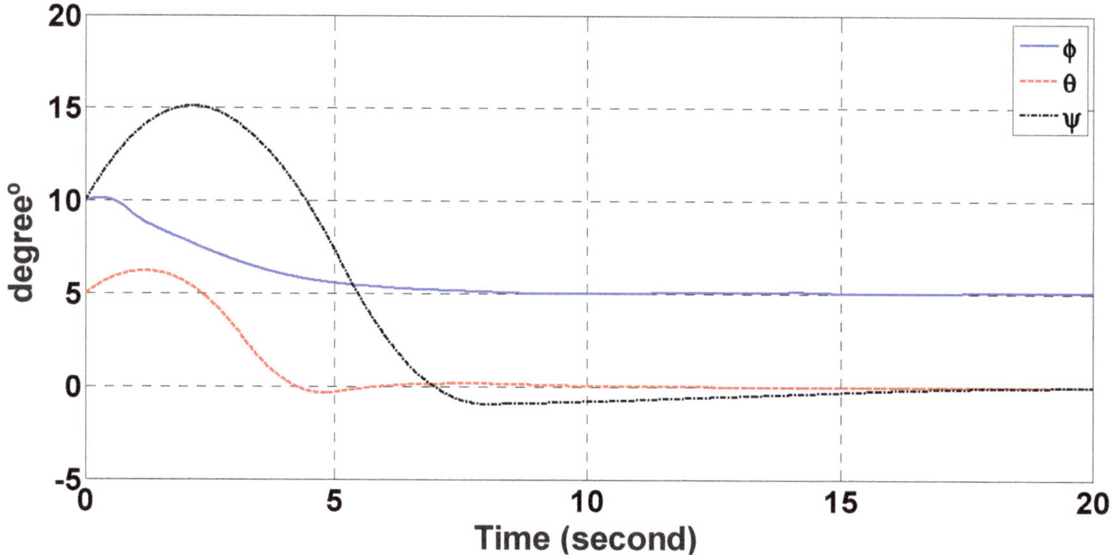

Figure 11. Euler angles time history using a PWPF modulator.

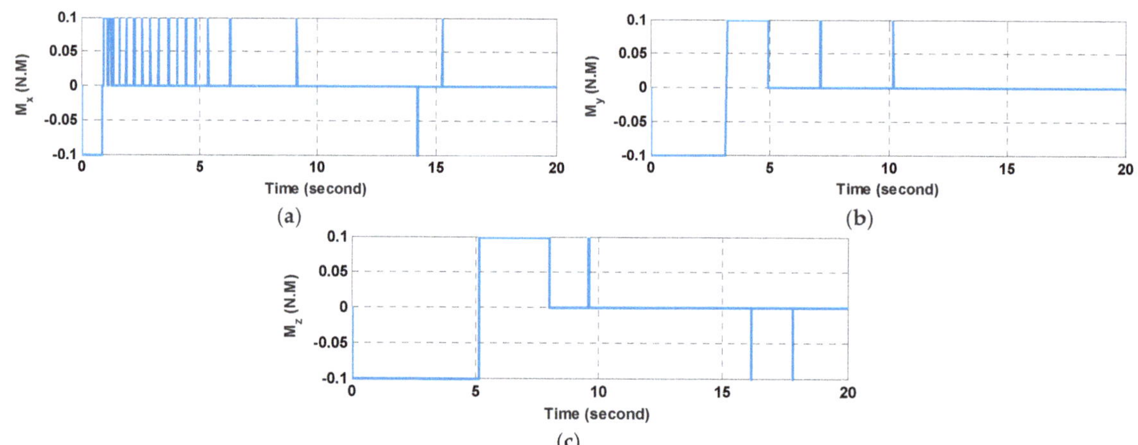

Figure 12. The control moment of the thruster in the (**a**) X, (**b**) Y, and (**c**) Z axis.

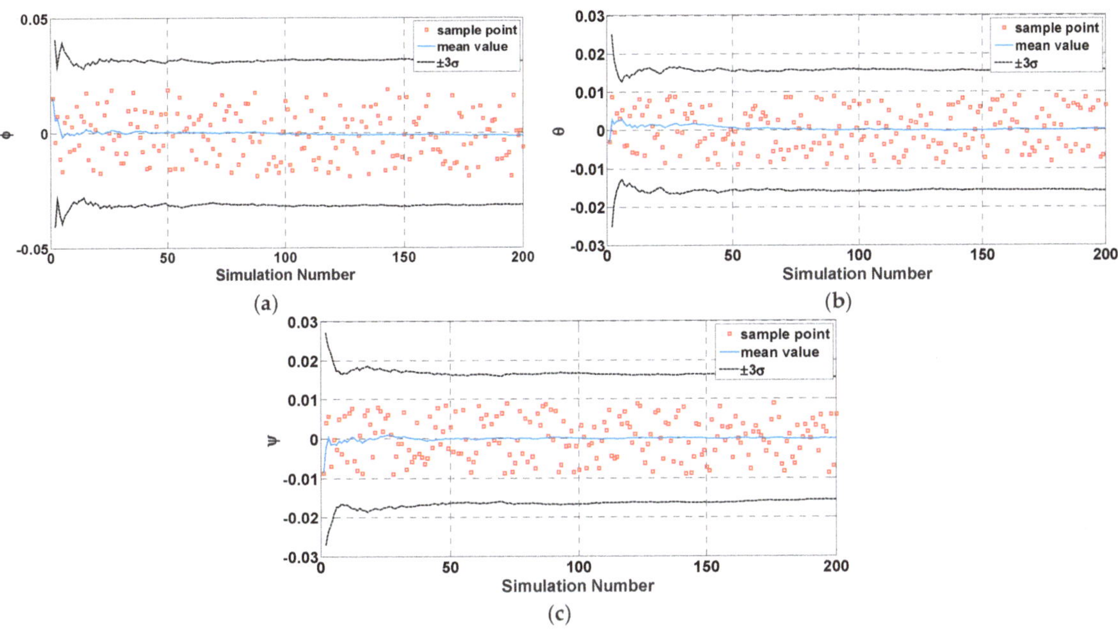

Figure 13. Monte-Carlo simulation error for (**a**) φ, (**b**) θ, and (**c**) ψ.

6. Conclusions

In this study, an ANFIS (adaptive neuro-fuzzy inference system) controller and estimator was proposed in order to estimate and control the attitude of a satellite. However, the ANFIS controller was trained using an optimal PID. The other significant ability of the proposed system is in estimating the necessary states accurately via an ANFIS observer. To train the observer, a satellite in several different conditions (noise and uncertainty) was considered. The performance of the ANFIS controller and estimator was also compared with the PID controller in the presence of uncertainties and noises.

A comparison oof the performance of the PID and ANFIS controllers showed that the proposed ANFIS controller consumed less control effort (fuel) in all situations (noise and uncertainty). In addition, the proposed controller outputs behaved smoother and reached stability in a shorter time interval than the PID controller. Likewise, system outputs (control angles) were smoother and reached the desired angles faster. Furthermore, using an ANFIS estimator in the system showed that despite its simple design, it can estimate the states, even in the presence of uncertainty. Results of using the synchronous control and estimation ANFIS simulator showed that although both stages (control and estimation) were conducted in one-step, the performance of the integrated system was similar to the combined controller and estimator. Due to the proven abilities of the ANFIS controller and observer, it can be concluded that it is able to work with black box systems. It means that the determined dynamic is not essential, which makes it possible to be used for unknown space bodies (e.g., space debris) as well as fast parameter varying space objects (e.g., space robots and manipulators). In this study, we aimed to utilize as less feedback parameters as possible while the simplicity and practicability of determining those parameters were considered. Future work will focus on the attitude control of flexible satellites with multi-section appendages as well as considering fluid fuel sloshing using the ANFIS controller.

Author Contributions: Conceptualization, M.C. and S.M.A.; methodology, T.Z. and X.W.; software, S.M.A. and M.C.; validation, X.W., T.Z. and M.C.; formal analysis, S.M.A.; investigation, S.M.A. and M.C.; resources, T.Z.; data curation, X.W.; writing—original draft preparation, S.M.A. and M.C.; writing—review and editing, M.C. and S.M.A.; visualization, S.M.A.; supervision, T.Z.; project administration, X.W.; funding acquisition, T.Z. All authors have read and agreed to the published version of the manuscript.

Funding: This study is funded by the key R&D plan of China for Winter Olympics (No. 2021YFF0306401), and the Key Special Project of the National Key Research and Development Program "Technical Winter Olympics" (2018YFF0300502 and 2021YFF0306400).

Institutional Review Board Statement: Not applicable.

Informed Consent Statement: Not applicable.

Data Availability Statement: Not applicable.

Conflicts of Interest: The authors declare no conflict of interest.

References

1. Ismail, Z.; Varatharajoo, R. A study of reaction wheel configurations for a 3-axis satellite attitude control. *Adv. Sp. Res.* **2010**, *45*, 750–759. [CrossRef]
2. Inamori, T.; Sako, N.; Nakasuka, S. Compensation of time-variable magnetic moments for a precise attitude control in nano- and micro-satellite missions. *Adv. Sp. Res.* **2011**, *48*, 432–440. [CrossRef]
3. Siahpour, S.; Zand, M.M.; Mousavi, M. Dynamics and vibrations of particle-sensing MEMS considering thermal and electrostatic actuation. *Microsyst. Technol.* **2018**, *24*, 1545–1552. [CrossRef]
4. Mousavi, M.; Rahnavard, M.; Haddad, S. Observer based fault reconstruction schemes using terminal sliding modes. *Int. J. Control* **2020**, *93*, 881–888. [CrossRef]
5. Mousavi, M.; Rahnavard, M.; Yazdi, M.R.H.; Ayati, M. On the Development of Terminal Sliding Mode Observers. In Proceedings of the 26th Iranian Conference on Electrical Engineering (ICEE), Mashhad, Iran, 8–10 May 2018; pp. 951–956. [CrossRef]
6. Mousavi, M.; Rahnavard, M.; Ayati, M.; Hairi Yazdi, M.R. Terminal sliding mode observers for uncertain linear systems with matched disturbance. *Asian J. Control* **2019**, *21*, 377–386. [CrossRef]
7. Sajjadi, M.; Chahari, M.; Pishkenari, H.N. Imaging performance of trolling mode atomic force microscopy: Investigation of effective parameters. *Arch. Appl. Mech.* **2022**, *2022*, 1–20. [CrossRef]
8. Rahnavard, M.; Ayati, M.; Hairi Yazdi, M.R.; Mousavi, M. Finite time estimation of actuator faults, states, and aerodynamic load of a realistic wind turbine. *Renew. Energy* **2019**, *130*, 256–267. [CrossRef]
9. Sajjadi, M.; Pishkenari, H.N.; Vossoughi, G. Dynamic modeling of trolling-mode AFM: Considering effects of cantilever torsion, nanoneedle flexibility and liquid-nanoneedle interactions. *Ultramicroscopy* **2017**, *182*, 99–111. [CrossRef]
10. Fossen, T.I. Marine Control Systems. *J. Guid. Control Dyn.* **2002**, *28*, 1689–1699.
11. Sajjadi, M.; Chahari, M.; Pishkenari, H.N.; Vossoughi, G. Designing nonlinear observer for topography estimation in trolling mode atomic force microscopy. *J. Vib. Control* **2021**. [CrossRef]
12. Chahari, M.; Sajjadi, M. Modeling of eccentric nanoneedle in trolling-mode atomic force microscope. *Microsc. Res. Tech.* **2020**, *84*, 639–655. [CrossRef] [PubMed]
13. Wu, J.; Zhou, Z.; Li, R.; Yang, L.; Fourati, H. Attitude determination using a single sensor observation: Analytic quaternion solutions and property discussion. *IET Sci. Meas. Technol.* **2017**, *11*, 731–739. [CrossRef]
14. Abtahi, S.; Sharifi, M. Machine learning method to control and observe for treatment and monitoring of hepatitis b virus. *arXiv* **2020**, arXiv:2004.09751.
15. Kristiansen, R.; Nicklasson, P.J. Satellite attitude control by quaternion-based backstepping. In Proceedings of the 2005, American Control Conference, Portland, OR, USA, 8–10 June 2005; pp. 907–912.
16. Kang, J.; Zhu, Z.H.; Wang, W.; Li, A.; Wang, C. Fractional order sliding mode control for tethered satellite deployment with disturbances. *Adv. Sp. Res.* **2017**, *59*, 263–273. [CrossRef]
17. Aleksandrov, A.Y.; Aleksandrova, E.B.; Tikhonov, A.A. Stabilization of a programmed rotation mode for a satellite with electrodynamic attitude control system. *Adv. Sp. Res.* **2018**, *62*, 142–151. [CrossRef]
18. Li, Y.; Ye, D.; Sun, Z. Robust finite time control algorithm for satellite attitude control. *Aerosp. Sci. Technol.* **2017**, *68*, 46–57. [CrossRef]
19. Xiao, B.; Yin, S.; Wu, L. A structure simple controller for satellite attitude tracking maneuver. *IEEE Trans. Ind. Electron.* **2016**, *64*, 1436–1446. [CrossRef]
20. Vatankhahghadim, B.; Damaren, C.J. Magnetic attitude control with impulsive thrusting using the hybrid passivity theorem. *J. Guid. Control Dyn.* **2017**, *40*, 1860–1876. [CrossRef]

21. Fan, Z.; Hua, S.; Chundi, M.; Yuchang, L. An optimal attitude control of small satellite with momentum wheel and magnetic torquerods. In Proceedings of the 4th World Congress on Intelligent Control and Automation (Cat. No. 02EX527), Shanghai, China, 10–14 June 2002; Volume 2, pp. 1395–1398.
22. Wisniewski, R.; Markley, F.L. Optimal magnetic attitude control. *IFAC Proc. Vol.* **1999**, *32*, 7991–7996. [CrossRef]
23. Arantes, G.; Martins-Filho, L.S.; Santana, A.C. Optimal on-off attitude control for the Brazilian multimission platform satellite. *Math. Probl. Eng.* **2009**, *2009*, 750945. [CrossRef]
24. Wen, H.; Yue, X.; Li, P.; Yuan, J. Fast spacecraft adaptive attitude tracking control through immersion and invariance design. *Acta Astronaut.* **2017**, *139*, 77–84. [CrossRef]
25. Lee, K.W.; Singh, S.N. $\mathcal{L}1$ adaptive attitude control of satellites in elliptic orbits using solar radiation pressure. *Proc. Inst. Mech. Eng. Part G J. Aerosp. Eng.* **2014**, *228*, 611–626. [CrossRef]
26. Lee, K.W.; Singh, S.N. Non-certainty-equivalent adaptive satellite attitude control using solar radiation pressure. *Proc. Inst. Mech. Eng. Part G J. Aerosp. Eng.* **2009**, *223*, 977–988. [CrossRef]
27. Zhang, J.; Swain, A.K.; Nguang, S.K. Robust sensor fault estimation scheme for satellite attitude control systems. *J. Franklin Inst.* **2013**, *350*, 2581–2604. [CrossRef]
28. Cao, L.; Li, H. Unscented predictive variable structure filter for satellite attitude estimation with model errors when using low precision sensors. *Acta Astronaut.* **2016**, *127*, 505–513. [CrossRef]
29. Zeng, Z.; Zhang, S.; Xing, Y.; Cao, X. Robust adaptive filter for small satellite attitude estimation based on magnetometer and gyro. *Abstr. Appl. Anal.* **2014**, *2014*, 159149. [CrossRef]
30. Kouyama, T.; Kanemura, A.; Kato, S.; Imamoglu, N.; Fukuhara, T.; Nakamura, R. Satellite attitude determination and map projection based on robust image matching. *Remote Sens.* **2017**, *9*, 90. [CrossRef]
31. Daley, S.; Gill, K.F. A design study of a self-organizing fuzzy logic controller. *Proc. Inst. Mech. Eng. Part C J. Mech. Eng. Sci.* **1986**, *200*, 59–69. [CrossRef]
32. Mukherjee, B.K.; Giri, D.K.; Sinha, M. Lorentz-force-based fuzzy proportional–integral–derivative attitude control for earth-pointing satellites. *J. Spacecr. Rockets* **2017**, *54*, 1153–1160. [CrossRef]
33. Huo, B.; Xia, Y.; Yin, L.; Fu, M. Fuzzy adaptive fault-tolerant output feedback attitude-tracking control of rigid spacecraft. *IEEE Trans. Syst. Man Cybern. Syst.* **2016**, *47*, 1898–1908. [CrossRef]
34. Zhong, C.; Guo, Y.; Wang, L. Fuzzy active disturbance rejection attitude control of spacecraft with unknown disturbance and parametric uncertainty. *Int. J. Control Autom.* **2015**, *8*, 233–242. [CrossRef]
35. Ran, D.; Chen, X.; Sheng, T. Adaptive fuzzy fault-tolerant control for rigid spacecraft attitude maneuver with finite-time convergence. *Proc. Inst. Mech. Eng. Part G J. Aerosp. Eng.* **2016**, *230*, 779–792. [CrossRef]
36. Sun, G.; Chen, J.; Zhu, B. Generalized predictive control for spacecraft attitude based on adaptive fuzzy estimator. *J. Aerosp. Eng.* **2017**, *30*, 4017024. [CrossRef]
37. Jang, J.-S. ANFIS: Adaptive-network-based fuzzy inference system. *IEEE Trans. Syst. Man. Cybern.* **1993**, *23*, 665–685. [CrossRef]
38. Jenkins, B.M.; Annaswamy, A.M.; Lavretsky, E.; Gibson, T.E. Convergence Properties of Adaptive Systems and the Definition of Exponential Stability. *SIAM J. Control Optim.* **2018**, *56*, 2463–2484. [CrossRef]
39. Wie, B. *Space Vehicle Dynamics and Control*; Aiaa: Reston, VA, USA, 1998; ISBN 1563472619.
40. Finlay, C.C.; Maus, S.; Beggan, C.D.; Bondar, T.N.; Chambodut, A.; Chernova, T.A.; Chulliat, A.; Golovkov, V.P.; Hamilton, B.; Hamoudi, M. International geomagnetic reference field: The eleventh generation. *Geophys. J. Int.* **2010**, *183*, 1216–1230.
41. Vallado, D.A. *Fundamentals of Astrodynamics and Applications*; Springer Science & Business Media: Berlin/Heidelberg, Germany, 2001; Volume 12, ISBN 0792369033.
42. Zadeh, L.A. Fuzzy sets. *Inf. Control* **1965**, *8*, 338–353. [CrossRef]
43. Li, X.; Zhang, W.; Ma, H.; Luo, Z.; Li, X. Degradation Alignment in Remaining Useful Life Prediction Using Deep Cycle-Consistent Learning. *IEEE Trans. Neural Netw. Learn. Syst.* **2021**, 1–12. [CrossRef] [PubMed]
44. Zhang, W.; Li, X.; Ma, H.; Luo, Z.; Li, X. Open-Set Domain Adaptation in Machinery Fault Diagnostics Using Instance-Level Weighted Adversarial Learning. *IEEE Trans. Ind. Inform.* **2021**, *17*, 7445–7455. [CrossRef]
45. Mamdani, E.H.; Assilian, S. An experiment in linguistic synthesis with a fuzzy logic controller. *Int. J. Man. Mach. Stud.* **1975**, *7*, 1–13. [CrossRef]
46. Takagi, T.; Sugeno, M. Fuzzy identification of systems and its applications to modeling and control. *IEEE Trans. Syst. Man. Cybern.* **1985**, *SMC-15*, 116–132. [CrossRef]
47. Ramos-Fernández, J.C.; López-Morales, V.; Márquez-Vera, M.A.; Pérez, J.M.X.; Suarez-Cansino, J. Neuro-Fuzzy Modelling and Stable PD Controller for Angular Position in Steering Systems. *Int. J. Automot. Technol.* **2021**, *22*, 1495–1503. [CrossRef]
48. Zhang, W.; Li, X.; Ma, H.; Luo, Z.; Li, X. Transfer learning using deep representation regularization in remaining useful life prediction across operating conditions. *Reliab. Eng. Syst. Saf.* **2021**, *211*, 107556. [CrossRef]
49. Hanafy, T.O.S. Modeling and Identification of Spacecraft Systems Using Adaptive Neuro Fuzzy Inference Systems (ANFIS). *IOSR J. Eng.* **2014**, *4*, 47–59. [CrossRef]
50. Gupta, A.K.; Kumar, P.; Sahoo, R.K.; Sahu, A.K.; Sarangi, S.K. Performance measurement of plate fin heat exchanger by exploration: ANN, ANFIS, GA, and SA. *J. Comput. Des. Eng.* **2017**, *4*, 60–68. [CrossRef]

51. Ting, W.; Bo, X. ANFIS Controller for Spacecraft Formation Flying. In Proceedings of the International Conference on Computer Science Education Innovation & Technology (CSEIT), Phuket, Thailand, 28–29 October 2013; Global Science and Technology Forum: Singapore, 2013; p. 45.

52. Abtahi, S.; Sharifi, M. Machine Learning Method Used to find Discrete and Predictive Treatment of Cancer. *arXiv* **2020**, arXiv:2004.09753.

 *mathematics*

MDPI

Article

Unsupervised Fault Diagnosis of Sucker Rod Pump Using Domain Adaptation with Generated Motor Power Curves

Dezhi Hao and Xianwen Gao *

College of Information Science and Engineering, Northeastern University, Shenyang 110819, China; 1510327@stu.neu.edu.cn
* Correspondence: gaoxianwen@mail.neu.edu.cn

Abstract: The poor real-time performance and high maintenance costs of the dynamometer card (DC) sensors have been significant obstacles to the timely fault diagnosis in the sucker rod pumping system (SRPS). In contrast to the DCs, the motor power curves (MPCs), which are accessible easily and highly associated with the entire system, have been attempted to predict the working conditions of the SRPS in recent years. However, the lack of labeled MPCs limits the successful applications in the industrial scenario. Thereby, this paper presents an unsupervised fault diagnosis methodology to leverage the generated MPCs of different working conditions to diagnose the actual unlabeled MPCs. Firstly, the MPCs of six working conditions are generated with an integrated dynamics mathematical model. Secondly, a framework named mechanism-assisted domain adaptation network (MADAN) is proposed to minimize the distribution discrepancy between the generated and actual MPCs. Specifically, benefiting from introducing the mechanism analysis to label the collected MPCs preliminarily, a conditional distribution discrepancy metric is defined to guarantee a more accurate distribution matching with respect to different working conditions. Eventually, validation experiments are performed to evaluate the mathematical model and the diagnosis method with a set of actual MPCs collected by a self-developed device. The experimental result demonstrates that the proposed method offers a promising approach for the unsupervised diagnosis of the SRPS.

Keywords: domain adaptation; fault diagnosis; mathematical model; motor power curve; sucker rod pump

MSC: 68T07

Citation: Hao, D.; Gao, X. Unsupervised Fault Diagnosis of Sucker Rod Pump Using Domain Adaptation with Generated Motor Power Curves. *Mathematics* **2022**, *10*, 1224. https://doi.org/10.3390/math10081224

Academic Editors: Xiang Li, Shuo Zhang and Wei Zhang

Received: 15 March 2022
Accepted: 3 April 2022
Published: 8 April 2022

1. Introduction

The sucker rod pump system (SRPS) plays an indispensable role in the field of oil exploitation [1]. Due to the long-time operations and harsh working environment, some faults will inevitably occur, resulting in economic loss and energy consumption [2]. With the rapid development of machine learning, many data-driven fault diagnosis methods have been utilized to guarantee manufacturing security and improve production efficiency in the SRPS [3,4]. However, the most traditional and commonly used diagnostic methods universally depend on the dynamometer card (DC), which is measured by the load sensor installed on the "horse head". These DC-based methods inevitably suffer from the high maintenance cost and low detection frequency, resulting in poor ability in the real-time diagnosis of the SRPS.

Owing to power's advantages of accessibility and high correlation with the SRPS, the motor power-based diagnosis methods have received ever-increasing attention [5]. Ref. [6] distilled seven features from the motor power curves (MPCs) and utilized improved hidden conditional random fields to diagnose different working conditions. An MPC-based broad learning method was proposed in [7].

Even though conspicuous achievements have been achieved, these methodologies lack applicability due to their reliance on the massive labeled data, which is invalid in the real industrial scenarios [8]. Some researchers tried to tackle this problem by implementing a transformation between the MPC and the DC to facilitate the diagnosis based on the MPCs. In [9], the MPCs were labeled by transforming into DCs with a mechanism model considering many crucial factors. However, the inversed DCs were not closed because the torque factor was zero at the dead points, resulting in huge discrepancies between the actual and inversed DCs. Nowadays, new research transformed the DC to MPC to alleviate the discrepancies at the dead points in [10]. However, the complete DC dataset is still a problematic prerequisite for some wells with incomplete data.

In order to reduce the dependence on the labeled dataset, this paper tries to propose a model-based method to generate the MPCs. Although many scholars have been committed to the process modeling of the SRPS, their purpose is to obtain the polished load without correlating the uphole portion to simulate the MPC [11–13]. In this respect, this paper is dedicated to establishing an integrated dynamics mathematical model involving the motor, the four-bar linkage, the sucker rod, and the pump to generate the MPCs at normal and five kinds of faulty scenarios.

Even though the labeled MPCs can be obtained from the model-based method, the traditional intelligent diagnosis strategies trained with such samples possibly fail in classifying actual MPCs. The distribution discrepancy that arises from unavoidable assumptions and simplifications in the model limits the successful applications of these strategies. Domain adaptation (DA), which is a popular branch of transfer learning, has advantages in solving the problem of inconsistent feature distribution [14–17]. Traditional DA employs the Maximum Mean Discrepancy (MMD) term as the discrepancy penalty to extract the domain-invariant features [18–20]. Inspired by the idea of the generative adversarial network, the domain discriminator was explored to align the distributions in an adversarial manner [21]. Ref. [22] leveraged a one-dimensional convolutional neural network (1-D CNN) to bridge the distribution discrepancy by maximizing the discriminator loss and minimizing the classifier loss. In [23], Wasserstein distance replaced the traditional discriminator to minimize the distribution discrepancy. A strong–weak learning framework was proposed to solve the imbalanced data and mismatched domain simultaneously based on the domain adversarial training in [24]. In [25], discriminator and MMD were exploited together to enhance feature representation. The discriminator network was extended to partial domain adaptation in [26,27].

The aforementioned discriminator and MMD are dedicated to aligning the marginal probability distribution. Specifically, inspired by [28], the conditional probability distribution is also increasingly integrated into the domain adversarial training in recent years. In [29], the adversarial training was utilized to realize marginal fusion, and a variance matrix was defined to achieve conditional alignments. The joint distribution supplanted the marginal distribution for conditional distribution alignments in [30]. In [31], a pre-training network was designed for pseudo-label learning and MMD was applied to align the conditional distribution. Ref. [32] utilized the adversarial network and the joint adaptation network to alleviate the distribution discrepancy of the label and feature spaces.

Although conditional distribution alignment has made some progress to the DA, little attention has been paid to the pseudo-label learning of the target domain. The common pseudo-label methodologies rely on the traditional clustering algorithm, source domain classifier, and the pre-trained network with source domain data. Limited by the inaccuracy of the initial phase of the neural network and the huge distribution gap between the target and source domains, these algorithms will assign extensive inaccurate pseudo-labels to interfere with the domain alignment. Therefore, in order to achieve more accurate pseudo-labels to narrow down the distribution discrepancy, a novel method named mechanism-assisted domain adaptation network (MADAN) is proposed. In the MADAN, the mechanical properties of the MPCs under different working conditions are adopted for pseudo-label learning along with the label classifier. Particularly, the classifier iterates continuously with training to alleviate conditional distribution discrepancy through a well-defined MMD term. The marginal distribution alignment is implemented with the help of the adversarial domain adaptation, and 1-D CNN constructs the feature generator network to extract the features of the time-series signal.

The main contributions of this paper can be summarized as follows:

1. An integrated dynamics mathematical model is established to generate the MPCs at normal and five kinds of faulty scenarios. The model calculates "four-bar" linkage movement, sucker rod vibration, the pump chamber pressure, and the liquid flow rate. The adjustment strategies of the model and relevant parameters under different working conditions are also presented.

2. A novel DA method named MADAN is proposed to exploit the knowledge learned from the generated MPCs to facilitate diagnosing the MPCs collected in practical scenarios. The mechanism-assisted pseudo-label learning is constructed to realize better conditional distribution alignment of the collected and generated MPCs under different working conditions. Furthermore, the domain classifier is designed for the marginal distribution alignment of the collected and generated MPCs.

3. Experiments demonstrate the superiority of the proposed fault diagnosis methodology with the MPCs collected by self-developed portable devices in the practical application scenario. The model's validity is verified by analyzing crucial downhole parameters and comparing the generated and actual MPCs. Furthermore, we experimentally show that MADAN outperforms five other state-of-the-art methods in terms of diagnostic accuracy and distribution alignment.

The rest of this article is organized as follows. The integrated dynamics mathematical model to generate the MPCs under various working conditions is surveyed in Section 2. Section 3 describes the proposed MADAN method. Section 4 shows the effectiveness of the proposed method through experimental verification. Finally, Section 5 concludes this article.

2. Generation of the Motor Power Curves

Driven by the motor, the pump connected with a series of transmissions is in a reciprocating up-and-down motion to pull the oil from the down-hole to the ground in the SRPS. As the energy for the whole system, the MPCs involve information about the SRPS working properties. Homoplastically, the MPCs of the well can be obtained by the inversion of the individual components simulation. To generate supplementary power waveforms of different working states for fault diagnosis, a detailed and integrated discussion of the mathematical model for the SRPS is presented in this section.

2.1. Mathematical Model of the Sucker Rod Pumping System

Figure 1 indicates a typical structure of the SRPS.

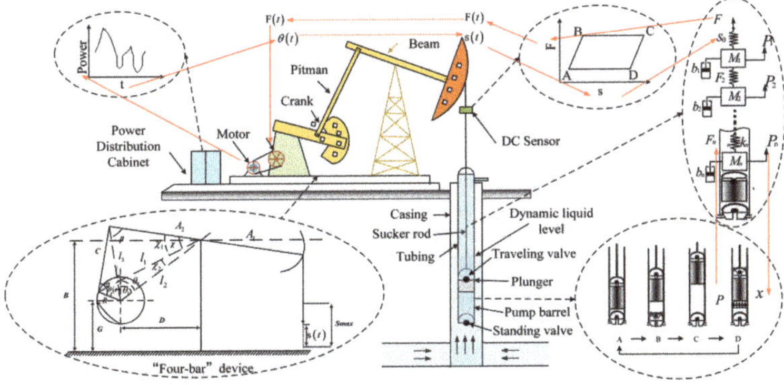

Figure 1. Sucker rod pump system.

Aiming at the MPCs composed by the power vs. time, the mathematical model follows the order as the red arrows in Figure 1 as time $\rightarrow$ crank angle $\rightarrow$ polished rod motion $\leftrightarrows$ plunger motion $\rightleftarrows$ pump pressure $\leftrightarrows$ polished rod load $\rightarrow$ crank torque $\rightarrow$ power. The prediction of SRPS behavior involves calculating "four-bar" linkage movement, sucker rod vibration, down-hole pump simulation of the pump, etc. Of these items, the operation of the down-hole pump, the polished rod motion, and the vibrations of the rod string are of the most difficulty but primary importance. In this subsection, the establishment of the mathematical model centers on the difficulties mentioned.

2.1.1. Polished Rod Motion Simulation

As the crank angular velocity approaches constant speed in practice, the crank angle θ vs. time is given by

$$\theta(t) = \omega t = \frac{2\pi n t}{60}. \tag{1}$$

From trigonometrical considerations, the calculation for the displacement of the polished rod $s(t)$ is listed as follows:

$$\begin{cases}
s(t) = s_{max}\dfrac{X_{max} - X}{X_{max} - X_{min}}, \\[4pt]
X_1 = \arcsin\dfrac{C\sin\beta}{l_1}, \\[4pt]
X_2 = \arcsin\dfrac{R\sin(\theta_1 + \theta(t))}{l_1}, \\[4pt]
\beta = \arccos\dfrac{A_2^2 + C^2 - l_2^2 - R^2 + 2l_2 R\cos(\theta_1 + \theta(t))}{2A_2 C}, \\[4pt]
l_1 = \sqrt{l_2^2 + R^2 - 2l_2 R\cos(\theta_1 + \theta(t))}, \\[4pt]
\theta_1 = \arctan\dfrac{D}{B - G}, \\[4pt]
X_{max} = \arccos\dfrac{l_2^2 + A_2^2 - (C + R)^2}{2l_2 A_2}, \\[4pt]
X_{min} = \arccos\dfrac{l_2^2 + A_2^2 - (C - R)^2}{2l_2 A_2}.
\end{cases} \tag{2}$$

The polished rod load is obtained as the summation torque acting on the polished rod of the crank torque, the counterbalance torque arising from the balanced weight and the net weight of the crankshaft, and counterbalance torque. The crank torque is derived backward by the relation

$$F_c = \overline{TF}(F - W_{ub})\eta_b^{\mu} - (W_{ck}R_{ck} + W_{cb}R)\sin\theta(t), \tag{3}$$

where $\mu = 1$ when $\overline{TF} < 0$, and $\mu = -1$ when $\overline{TF} \geqq 0$. The torque factor as obtained from mechanics is given by

$$\overline{TF} = \frac{A_1 R}{A_2}\frac{\sin\beta}{\sin\varphi}. \tag{4}$$

2.1.2. Rod String Simulation

Considering the rod string is up to thousands of meters long, the elastic deformation and vibration should not be neglected during the reciprocating up-and-down motion. Simulation of the rod string involves the calculation of a boundary problem. The boundary upon the ground is regarded as a compulsive movement, which is determined by the motion of the polish rod. The boundary of the down-hole is decided by the pump pressure acting at the plunger and the elastic force of the rod string. Benefiting from the rod string acting as a spring-mass-damping system with multiple degrees of freedom, the rod string is divided into individual parts connected by an equivalent spring, as illustrated in Figure 1.

Combined with buoyancy, gravity, frictional damping of the rod, and tubing, the dynamic analysis of the rod string can be deduced as

$$
\left\{
\begin{aligned}
&F = k_1(P_0 - P_1 - l_1), \\
&M_1\ddot{P}_1 + b_1\dot{P}_1 + k_2(P_1 - P_2 - l_2) + M_1 g - \rho_0 g(P_0 - P_1)S_r \\
&\quad + f_r(P_0 - P_1)C_l\sigma_v = k_1(P_0 - P_1 - l_1), \\
&M_2\ddot{P}_2 + b_2\dot{P}_2 + k_3(P_2 - P_3 - l_3) + M_2 g - \rho_0 g(P_1 - P_2)S_r \\
&\quad + f_r(P_1 - P_2)C_l\sigma_v = k_2(P_1 - P_2 - l_2), \\
&\qquad\qquad\qquad\qquad \vdots \\
&M_{n-1}\ddot{P}_{n-1} + b_{n-1}\dot{P}_{n-1} + k_n(P_{n-1} - P_n - l_n) + M_{n-1}g - \rho_0 g(P_{n-2} \\
&\quad - P_{n-1})S_r + f_r(P_{n-2} - P_{n-1})C_l\sigma_v = k_{n-1}(P_{n-2} - P_{n-1} - l_{n-1}), \\
&M_n\ddot{P}_n + b_n\dot{P}_n - k_n(P_{n-1} - P_n - l_n) + M_n g - \rho_0 g(P_{n-1} - P_n)S_r \\
&\quad + f_r(P_{n-1} - P_{n-2})C_l t\sigma_v = -F_n,
\end{aligned}
\right.
\tag{5}
$$

where $\dot{P}_i$ and $\ddot{P}_i$ denote the first and second derivatives of P_i regarding time, respectively. C_l can be caculated as $C_l = \pi(d_p + d_r)$.

2.1.3. Down-Hole Pump Simulation

Equal to the force on the bottom of the rod string F_n, the force on the plunge can also be deduced from the down-hole pump simulation as follows:

$$
F_n(t) = S_p(P_d - P_p(t)) - S_r P_d + f_p \dot{P}_n.
\tag{6}
$$

It is mainly related to the pressure of the pump. Suffering from various coupled variables and sophisticated processes existing in the down-hole, the simulation of pressure remains a severe issue but is the core of the whole model. In order to get around this impasse, the basic concepts of iterative algorithms are applied in this subsection. The pressure proportional to the mass per unit volume of free gas can be deduced as follows:

$$
P_p(t) = \frac{M_{fg}(t)\xi}{V_p(t) - V_w(t) - V_o(t)}.
\tag{7}
$$

The variation of gas, liquid, and oil in the pump can be calculated by flow rate. When the standing valve is closed, the flow rate is zero. When the standing valve is open, the flow rate can be calculated as

$$
Q(t) = \frac{C_1 S_s \rho_l}{\sqrt{\sigma_s}}\sqrt{\frac{P_p(t) - P_s}{\rho_l}}.
\tag{8}
$$

Considering a bit of gas dissolved in the oil, the solubility of the gas is calculated based on Henry's Law. On the assumption that the water–oil–gas mass ratio of flows is constant in one stroke, the specific calculation is organized as follows:

$$
\left\{
\begin{aligned}
&M_{fg}(t) = M_g(t)\frac{\rho_g(t-1)V_{fg}(t-1)}{\rho_g(t-1)V_{fg}(t-1) + \delta_g(t-1)M_o(t-1)}, \\
&M_g(t) = M_g(t-1) + \gamma_g Q(t-1)\,\triangle t, \\
&M_o(t) = V_o(t)\rho_o = M_o(t-1) + \gamma_o Q(t-1)\,\triangle t, \\
&M_w(t) = V_w(t)\rho_w = M_w(t-1) + \gamma_w Q(t-1)\,\triangle t, \\
&\rho_g(t-1) = \frac{P_p(t-1)M_{mol}}{C_2 T_d}, \\
&\delta_g(t-1) = C_h P_p(t-1).
\end{aligned}
\right.
\tag{9}
$$

An iterative equation for estimating the pump pressure P_p is given as

$$\frac{P_p(t)}{P_p(t-1)} = \frac{M_{fg}(t)}{M_{fg}(t-1)} \frac{V_p(t-1) - V_w(t-1) - V_o(t-1)}{V_p(t) - V_w(t) - V_o(t)}. \tag{10}$$

2.1.4. Moter and Gearbox Simulation

Considering the energy loss in the gearbox and the motor, the crank toque vs. the motor power is simplified as

$$P_m = \frac{F_c n_m \eta_m^\sigma}{9540}, \ when \ P > 0, \sigma = 1, else \ \sigma = -1. \tag{11}$$

2.1.5. Dynamic Implementation of the Overall Model

As the order of the red arrows in Figure 1, Algorithm 1 outlines the procedure of the whole generating power method mentioned above combining the standing and traveling valve switch situations. By the proposed mathematical model, the theoretical MPC can be obtained based on the mechanical parameters of the specific oil well.

Algorithm 1: Generation of motor power waveforms.

Input: Times of stroke: n, a series of mechanical parameters of the system
Output: $P_m(t)$
for $t = 1$ *to* $60/n$ **do**
    $S(t) \leftarrow t$ refer to Equations (1) and (2);
    $P_n(t), \dot{P}_n(t) \leftarrow S(t)$ refer to Equation (5);
    if $P_p(t-1) \leqq P_s$ **then**
        $Q(t) \leftarrow P_p(t-1)$ refer to Equation (8);
    else
        $Q(t) = 0$;
    end
    if $P_p(t-1) \leqq P_d$ **then**
        $M_{fg}(t), V_g(t), V_o(t), V_w(t), V_p(t) \leftarrow Q(t-1), P_n(t)$ refer to Equation (9);
        $P_p(t) \leftarrow P_p(t-1), M_{fg}(t), V_g(t), V_o(t), V_w(t), V_p(t)$ refer to Equation (10);
    else
        $P_p(t) = P_d$;
    end
    $F_n(t) \leftarrow P_p(t)$ refer to Equation (6);
    $F(t) \leftarrow F_n(t)$ refer to Equation (5);
    $F_c(t) \leftarrow F(t)$ refer to Equations (3) and (4);
    $P_m(t) \leftarrow F_c(t)$ refer to Equation (11);
end

2.2. Generation for Faulty Working States

Based on the mathematical model of the SRPS, the MPCs of five faulty working states are analyzed in this subsection. The characteristics forming reasons and representation in the model will be discussed emphatically.

2.2.1. Traveling Valve Leakage

After repeating the switch operation numerous times, the traveling valve will wear out so that the oil in the sucker rod leaks into the chamber with the rate concerned to the $P_p(t)$. In order to simulate this state, the leaked oil is divided into static and dynamic parts. The pressure and the flow rate are the same as the normal state when the traveling valve is open. When the traveling valve is closed, the static part that is caused by the pressure discrepancy between the top and bottom of the plunger can be deduced as

$$\triangle Q_s(t) = \frac{\rho_l C_3 S_{lt}}{\sqrt{\sigma_t}} \sqrt{\frac{P_d - P_p(t)}{\rho_l}}. \tag{12}$$

The dynamic part that is caused by the motion of the plunger can be calculated as

$$\triangle Q_d(t) = \pi S_{lt} \dot{P}_n. \tag{13}$$

The leaked oil can be obtained from the sum of the static part and the dynamic part.

2.2.2. Insufficient Liquid Supply

After a long extraction period, the reservoir formation pressure usually decreases, resulting in insufficient fluid supply capacity. In this working state, the submergence pressure P_s is less than the pressure under the normal working state. There will be less oil flowing into the pump, and the traveling valve will open in a shorter time. To simulate this working state, only the submergence pressure P_s needs to be set as a smaller value.

2.2.3. Gas Affected

During the oil production process, the remaining free gas accumulates due to the sealing performance of the pump. In the upstroke, the remaining free gas will slow down the reduction of pressure in the pump, which in turn delays the opening of the standing valve, resulting in a low fluid intake. Analogously, in the downstroke, the remaining free gas will also delay the opening of the traveling valve because of the deferred increase of pressure in the pump. In the simulation, the initial mass of the free gas in the pump and the gas mass ratio of flows are set as higher proportions than the normal working state.

2.2.4. Gas Locking

This working state is the special case of gas affected. When the remaining free gas is accumulating to a threshold, the pressure $P_p(t)$ is greater than the submergence pressure P_s so that the valves remain closed without any inflow or outflow all the time. In order to simulate this state, the pressure is set as $P_s \leq P_p(t) \leq P_d$.

2.2.5. Parting Rod

The rod string may crack suffering from corrosion, mechanical vibration, and friction in the down-hole after a long period of continuous work. In this working state, the polished rod load is only related to the rod weight, vibration, and friction above the breakpoint because the pump departs from the rod string. So, the $P_p(t)$ is equal to 0, and only the department above the breakpoint needs to be calculated in Equation (5) during the simulation.

3. Domain Adaptation Based on Generated Motor Power Curves

Although the labeled MPCs are supplemented with the mechanism model, the distribution discrepancies between generated and collected MPCs limit the diagnosis accuracy. A novel domain adaptation diagnostic network combining the mechanism analysis is proposed in this section to tackle this issue. Considering the load characteristics of the SRPS in one period, the pseudo-labels are assigned for the collected MPCs preliminarily. Then, the conditional and marginal probability distribution of the generated and collected MPCs are well aligned by distilling the domain-invariant features. That implements to acquire knowledge from the generated MPCs to facilitate the diagnosis of collected MPCs. The method's detailed architecture and training process are discussed in the subsequent section.

3.1. Problem Setting

Benefiting from the dynamic mechanism analysis, the MPCs of different working conditions are generated. However, the data-driven diagnosis methods trained with such generated curves possibly fail in diagnosing actual curves even though the waves have the same varying tendency under different conditions. The simplification and idealization in the mechanism simulation should be the main reason for the misdiagnosis. Take the vibration simulation of the sucker rod as an example. The rod is divided into several individually connected segments to simulate elastic deformation and vibration. The simulated MPCs with different quantities of segments and a similar actual MPC are illustrated in Figure 2.

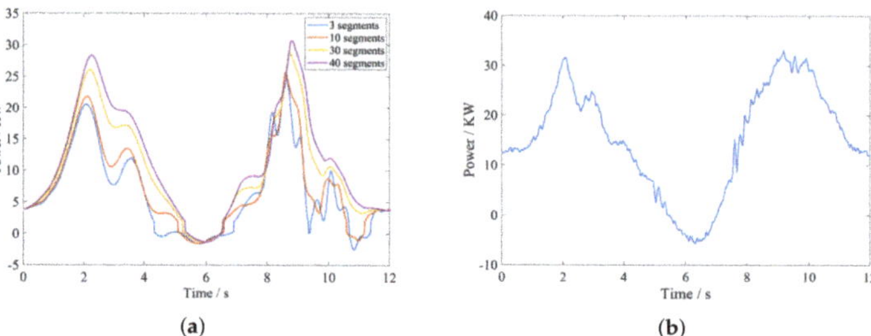

Figure 2. The comparison between the actual and generated MPCs with different segments of the rod. (**a**) Generated power curves. (**b**) Actual power curve.

Dividing the rod into different segments changes the vibration analysis of the rod, which in turn affects the transformation of the DCs to the MPCs. Similar simplified features, e.g., gearbox vibrations, liquid flow rate, and crankshaft speed, lead to the difference between the generated and actual curves collectively.

Inspired by the idea of domain adaptation, which can project the data from various domains into a shared subspace, this section proposes an innovative fault diagnosis approach. It can leverage the knowledge learned from the generated MPCs with labels to facilitate diagnosing actual unlabeled MPCs. In order to promote the features between the generated and actual MPCs to be aligned, a domain classifier is built for marginal distribution adaptation. What is more, a conditional distribution discrepancy metric is employed for conditional distribution adaptation. Therefore, the proposed domain adaptive method not only considers all in-domain features as a whole for feature alignment but also ensures category features of different domains to be aligned.

3.2. Network Architecture

According to the above-mentioned description, the generated MPCs with labels are denoted as the source domain $\mathbb{D}_s = \{(\chi_i^s, y_i^s)\}_{i=1}^{n_s}$ of six categories of working conditions, and the actual MPCs are denoted as the target domain $\mathbb{D}_t = \{(\chi_j^t)\}_{j=1}^{n_t}$ without labels. Leveraging the knowledge learned from $\mathbb{D}_s$ to facilitate diagnosing for $\mathbb{D}_t$, the proposed framework is illustrated in Figure 3. Overall, the methodology contains a feature generator network f_g with parameters θ_g, a domain classifier f_d with parameters θ_d, a label classifier f_c with parameters θ_c, a conditional distribution discrepancy metrics M, and a pseudo-label learning layer f_P. The detailed description of the methodology is discussed as follows:

3.2.1. Pseudo-Label Learning Layer

Different from the marginal distribution, which does not require the category label, conditional distribution needs the labels to adapt the category-level discrepancy. Unfortunately, the samples in the target domain are unlabeled. Many existing approaches assign pseudo-labels to these samples based on maximum predictive probability, clustering algorithms, or pre-trained models trained with source domain samples. However, since the initial pseudo-labels learned by these methods are inaccurate, some errors will be caused by incorrect labels and accumulate with the strategy training, resulting in negative effects on fault diagnosis. In this respect, a novel pseudo-label learning method combining the mechanism analysis in the SRPS and the source domain samples is proposed to tackle this problem.

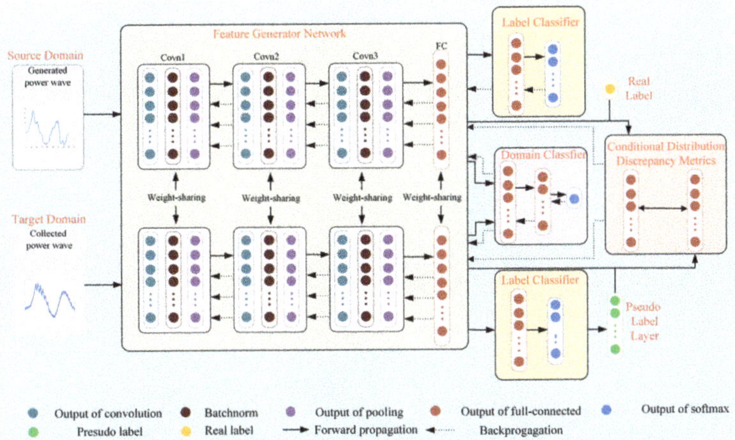

Figure 3. The framework of the proposed approach.

The mechanism analysis of the MPCs under different working conditions is summarized as follows:

1. Normal working condition Y_0: The MPCs of the upstroke and the downstroke are relatively full with similar peaks. 2. Traveling valve leakage Y_1: The leakage will delay the increase of the pressure during the upstroke, resulting in the delayed opening of the standing valve. Therefore, the power of the upstroke will be less than the normal working condition. 3. Insufficient liquid supply Y_2: The pump chamber can not be fulled in the upstroke. During the downstroke, the load reduces in the initial stage of the opening of the traveling valve. The load increases rapidly when the plunger hits the oil interface, resulting in double peaks in the power curve. The average value of the MPC is also lower than the normal power. 4. Gas affected Y_3: Similar to the condition of insufficient liquid supply, the pump chamber also can not be filled because of the superabundant gas dissolved in oil, resulting in the lower average power in the downstroke. The difference is that more gas is present to act as a buffer to the plunger, so there is no second peak in the downstroke. 5. Gas locking Y_4: The gas in the chamber makes the pressure insufficient to open the standing and traveling valve, so the oil cannot be adequately discharged. During the downstroke, the motor power curve will have negative values due to the gravity of the oil in the sucker rod. 6. Parting rod Y_5: The motor load is mainly caused by the crank and the weight of the rod above the breakpoint. During the upstroke, the energy stored in the crank is more than the requirement to uplift the remaining rod, resulting in the apparent negative power in the MPC.

On the basis of the above analysis, the mechanistic pseudo-labels of the source domain $\{\bar{y}_i^s\}_{i=1}^{n_s}$ and the target domain $\{\bar{y}_j^t\}_{j=1}^{n_t}$ are obtained as shown in Figure 4, where P_u and P_d denote the power points of the upstroke and the downstroke in one stroke, respectively. N_u and N_d denote the numbers of the points in the upstroke and the downstroke. a_1 and a_2 are set as 0.9 and 1.1.

With the help of mechanism analysis, the accuracy of the initial pseudo-labels is improved. However, as the training continues, the accuracy of the classifier gradually outperforms the mechanical analysis. Therefore, we design the pseudo-label learning layer based on the comparison between the accuracy of the mechanical analysis P_m and the accuracy of the classifier in the current epoch P_c with the date of the source domain. The P_m and P_c can be calculated as follows:

$$P_m = \frac{1}{N_s} \sum_{n=1}^{N} \mathcal{L}(\bar{y}_i^s, y_i^s), \tag{14}$$

$$P_c = \frac{1}{N_s} \sum_{n=1}^{N} \mathcal{L}(f_c(f_g(\chi_i^s, \theta_g), \theta_c), y_i^s), \tag{15}$$

where $\mathcal{L}(,)$ denotes the cross-entropy loss function.

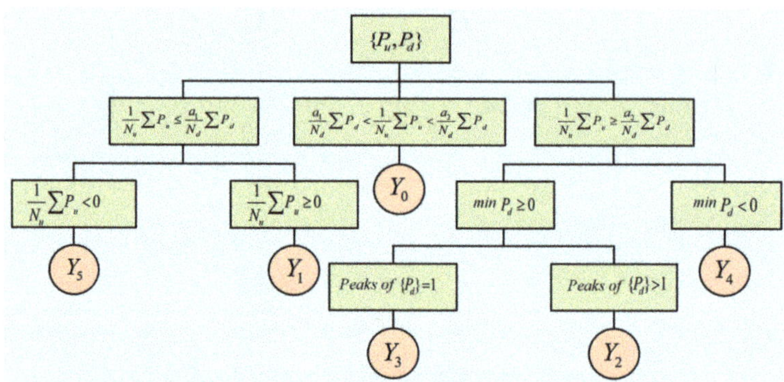

Figure 4. Pseudo-label learning based on the mechanism analysis.

The final pseudo-labels in the target domain $\hat{y}_t^j$ can be obtained as follows:

$$\hat{y}_j^t = \begin{cases} \overline{y}_j^t, & P_m \geq P_c. \\ f_c(f_g(\chi_j^t, \theta_g), \theta_c), & P_m < P_c. \end{cases} \tag{16}$$

The target domain with the pseudo-labels are defined as $\hat{\mathbb{D}}_t = \{(\chi_j^t, \hat{y}_j^t)\}_{j=1}^{n_t}$.

3.2.2. Feature Generator Network

Inspired by the great nonlinear characterization capabilities of convolutional neural network (CNN), 1-D CNN specializing in the time-series signal is selected to extract features from the generated and actual power curves. The feature generator is implemented based on a 3-layer 1-D CNN associated with a fully connected layer (FC), whose structure is detailed in Table 1.

Table 1. The structure of the feature generator network.

Layer Type	Activation Function	Kernel Number	Kernel Size × Stride	Output Size
Input	/	/	/	$(1024, 1)$
Conv1	Relu	16	64×1	$(16, 1024, 1)$
MaxPooling1	/	16	2×2	$(16, 512, 1)$
Conv2	Relu	32	5×1	$(32, 512, 1)$
MaxPooling2	/	32	2×2	$(32, 256, 1)$
Conv3	Relu	64	5×1	$(64, 256, 1)$
MaxPooling3	/	64	2×2	$(64, 128, 1)$
Flatten	/	/	/	$(8192, 1)$
FC	Relu	1024	/	$(1024, 1)$

3.2.3. Label Classifier

The label classifiers aim to recognize the working condition and direct the feature generator to retain the information of each working condition. As illustrated in Figure 3, the label classifier consists of one hidden layer with the neurons of 256 and one output layer with the Softmax as the activation function. The dropout ratio is set as 0.5. For the classifier of the source domain $\mathbb{D}_s = \{(\chi_i^s, y_i^s)\}_{i=1}^{n_s}$, the desired objective function can be defined as

$$L_c = \frac{1}{N_s} \sum_{\chi_i, y_i \in \mathbb{D}_s} \mathcal{L}(f_c(f_g(\chi_i, \theta_g), \theta_c), y_i). \tag{17}$$

It is noteworthy that the classifier of the target domain is not involved in the back-propagation. It is only used for pseudo-label learning, and its parameters are kept the same as the parameters of the source domain label classifier.

3.2.4. Domain Classifier

In order to direct the feature generator to extract the domain-invariant features, a domain classifier f_d is designed by following the idea of DANN [21]. The f_d consists of three FCs with neurons as 1024-256-1. The output is a binary classifier that outputs 0 for all target samples and 1 for all source samples. The desired objective function can be defined as

$$L_d = \frac{1}{N_s + N_t} \sum_{\chi_i, \dot{y}_i \in \mathbb{D}_s \cup \mathbb{D}_t} \mathcal{L}(f_d(f_g(\chi_i, \theta_g), \theta_d), \dot{y}_i), \tag{18}$$

where $\dot{y}_i$ denotes the domain label.

3.2.5. Conditional Distribution Discrepancy Metrics

Regarding all the samples in one domain as one class, the marginal distributions can be well aligned by the domain classifier. However, only adapting the marginal distributions is insufficient, since the discriminative hyperplane may differ for diverse domain tasks. The conditional distribution adaptation, which aims to match the discriminative structures between source and target data, is also indispensable and highly effective. With the aid of the pseudo-label learning layer, pseudo-labels for target data can be preliminarily supplied. Defining C as the total number of categories and the category $c \in \{Y_0, Y_1 \cdots, Y_5\}$, the distance index, MMD, can be designed to measure the discrepancy of conditional distributions $\mathbb{D}_s$ and $\hat{\mathbb{D}}_t$ as

$$D_M = \sum_{c=1}^{C} \| \frac{1}{n_s^c} \sum_{\chi_i \in \mathbb{D}_s} f_g(\chi_i | y_i = c, \theta_g) - \frac{1}{n_t^c} \sum_{\chi_j \in \hat{\mathbb{D}}_t} f_g(\chi_j | \hat{y}_j = c, \theta_g) \|_{\mathbb{H}}^2, \tag{19}$$

where $\| \cdot \|_{\mathbb{H}}$ represents the Reproducing Kernel Hilbert Space.

3.3. Optimization

According to the network losses discussed above, the optimization objective of the proposed MADAN is summarized as

$$L = L_c - \lambda_1 L_d + \lambda_2 D_M, \tag{20}$$

where the hyperparameters λ_1 and λ_2 indicate the penalty coefficient for different loss functions. A gradient reversal layer (GRL) [33] is placed before the domain classifier to receive the gradient of L_d by multiplying a negative factor. The network is updated employing the adaptive moment estimation optimizer (Adam) with the learning rate τ, which is set to 0.001. The parameters θ_g, θ_c, and θ_d are updated simultaneously at each step as

$$\begin{cases} \theta_g \leftarrow \theta_g - \tau(\frac{\partial L_c}{\partial \theta_g} - \lambda_1 \frac{\partial L_d}{\partial \theta_g} + \lambda_2 \frac{\partial D_M}{\partial \theta_g}), \\[2mm] \theta_c \leftarrow \theta_c - \tau \frac{\partial L_c}{\partial \theta_c}, \\[2mm] \theta_d \leftarrow \theta_d - \tau \lambda_1 \frac{\partial L_d}{\partial \theta_d}. \end{cases} \tag{21}$$

With the updates of the parameters, the extracted features are domain-invariant and discriminative simultaneously. The label classifier not only can predict labels for generated MPCs but also is available for the collected MPCs.

4. Industrial Experiments

A series of industrial experiments are conducted in this section with the MPCs collected in SRPS with self-developed equipment to verify the feasibility of the proposed mathematic model and the diagnosis method in practical application scenarios. The generated MPCs with the mathematic model are discussed with the mechanical characteristics and compared with the collected MPCs under different working conditions. Moreover, we compare the MADAN with some baseline methods in the field of DA to demonstrate the effectiveness of the improvement in practical applications.

4.1. Data Collection

As illustrated in Figure 5, the portable device developed by the authors' team in Northeastern University implements the MPCs acquisition by collecting the three-phase current and voltage of the motor. The device consists of five core units as follows:

1. Power acquisition unit: realize the motor power calculation with the help of the ATT7022B.
2. Transmission unit: realize remote query and parameter adjustment on mobiles and computers.
3. Human–machine interaction unit: a touch screen is equipped to facilitate parameter entry, data query, and data display.
4. Data storage unit: it is used to store the collected and calculated data and parameters.
5. Data processing unit: with the help of the XC7Z020CLG400 chip, it implements the core calculation, including the trained diagnostic model, device operation, etc.

Figure 5. A self-developed data acquisition and analysis equipment employed in the SRPS.

After long-term practice, 300 groups of MPCs are collected from seven oil wells with the same mechanical parameters as shown in Table 2. All simulations are implemented in the MATLAB and Pytorch framework and conducted on a workstation with a Core i7-9700K CPU@3.60 GHz and a GTX2080TI GPU with 11-GB memory.

Table 2. The main parameters of the test well.

Parameters	Value	Parameters	Value
Well	CYJ14-5-73HB	Moter	Y250M-6
A_1/mm	7000	n/min^{-1}	4
A_2/mm	3110	P_s/atm	120
C/mm	5790	P_d/atm	180
B/mm	7210	$\gamma_g{:}\gamma_w{:}\gamma_o$	0.1:0.2:0.2
G/mm	1460	d_p/mm	44
D/mm	3110	d_r/mm	22
R/mm	1270	S_p/mm^2	1520
W_{ck}/kg	5374	$\int l_i/\text{m}$	1600
W_{cb}/kg	5378	$\int M_i/\text{kg}$	5139.2
W_{ub}/kg	1229	$M_{mol}/\text{g·mol}^{-1}$	16

4.2. Validation of the Generated Motor Power Curves

According to the working and mechanical parameters listed in Table 2, the analysis results of six working conditions generated with the model in Section 2 are illustrated in Figures 6–11. Each working state contains four sub-figures. The first sub-figures express the variation curves of the crucial variables in the pump containing the chamber volume, oil and water volume, the pressure, and the flow rate through the standing valve. The second and third sub-figures illustrate the generated DCs and MPCs under different working conditions. The fourth sub-figures are typical MPCs selected from the collected samples in practical scenarios.

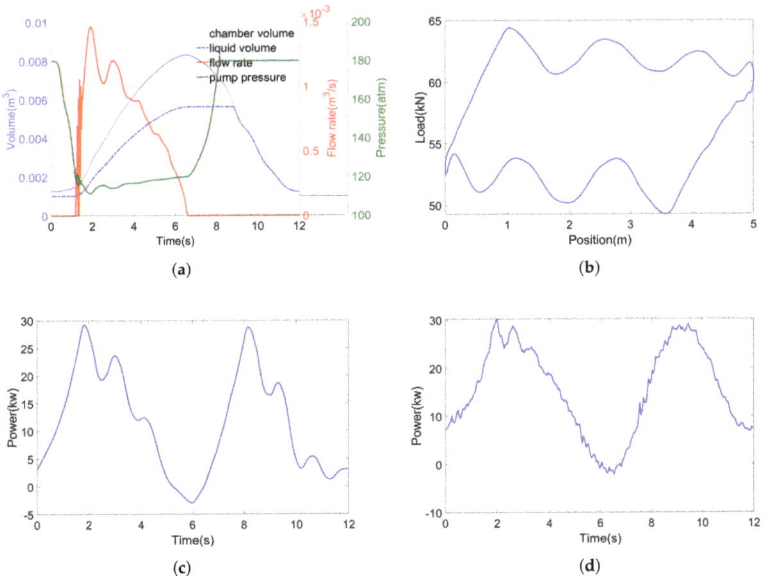

Figure 6. Normal working state. (**a**) Pump simulation. (**b**) Generated DC. (**c**) Generated MPC. (**d**) Actual MPC.

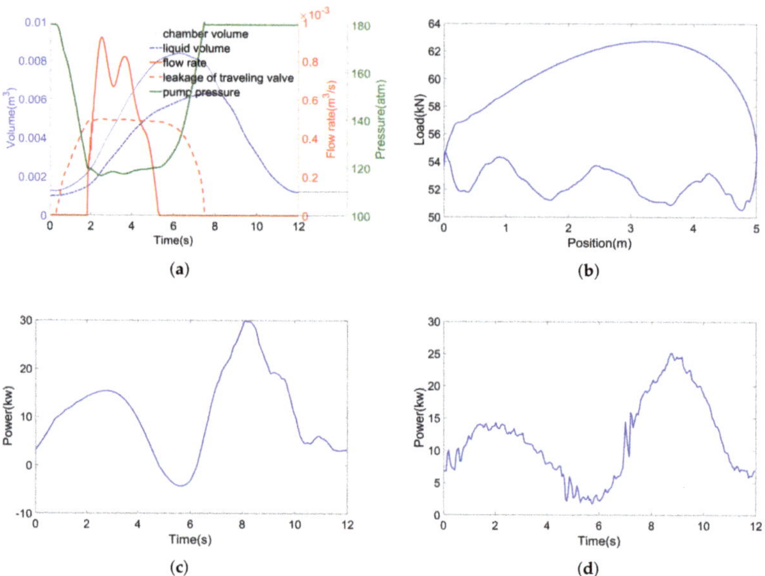

Figure 7. Traveling valve leakage working state. (**a**) Pump simulation. (**b**) Generated DC. (**c**) Generated MPC. (**d**) Actual MPC.

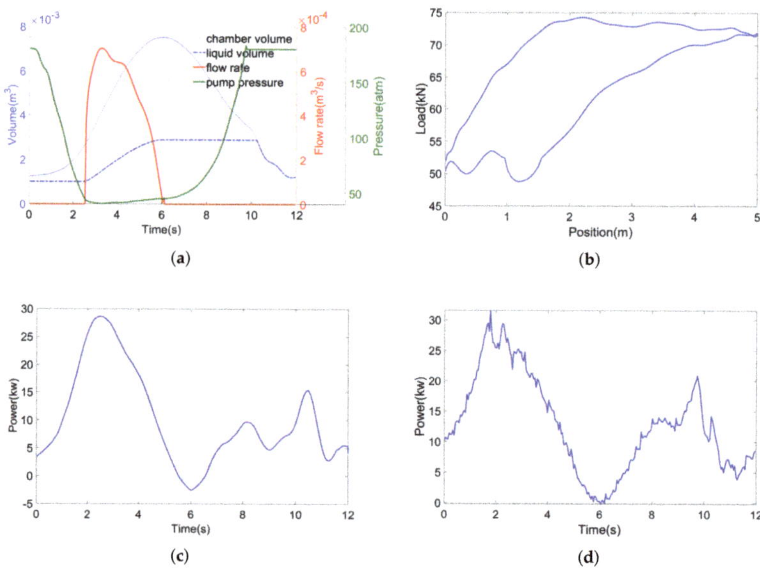

Figure 8. Insufficient liquid supply working state. (**a**) Pump simulation. (**b**) Generated DC. (**c**) Generated MPC. (**d**) Actual MPC.

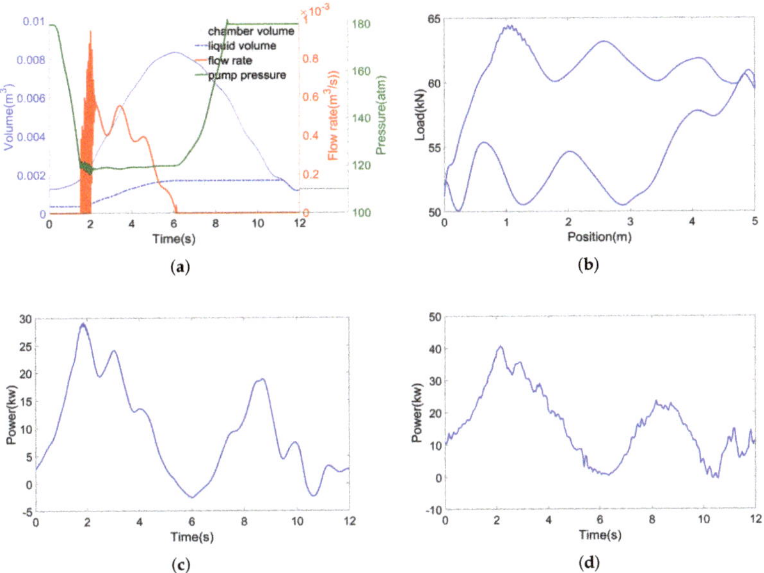

Figure 9. Gas affected working state. (**a**) Pump simulation. (**b**) Generated DC. (**c**) Generated MPC. (**d**) Actual MPC.

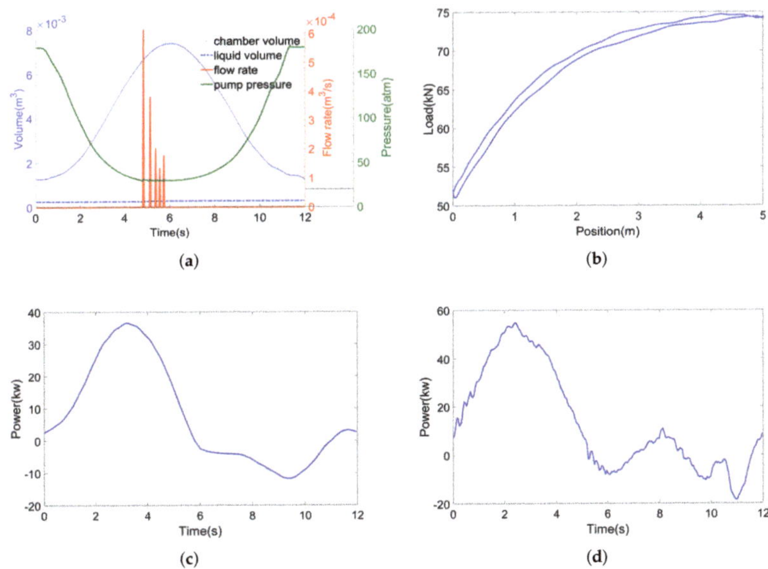

Figure 10. Gas locking working state. (**a**) Pump simulation. (**b**) Generated DC. (**c**) Generated MPC. (**d**) Actual MPC.

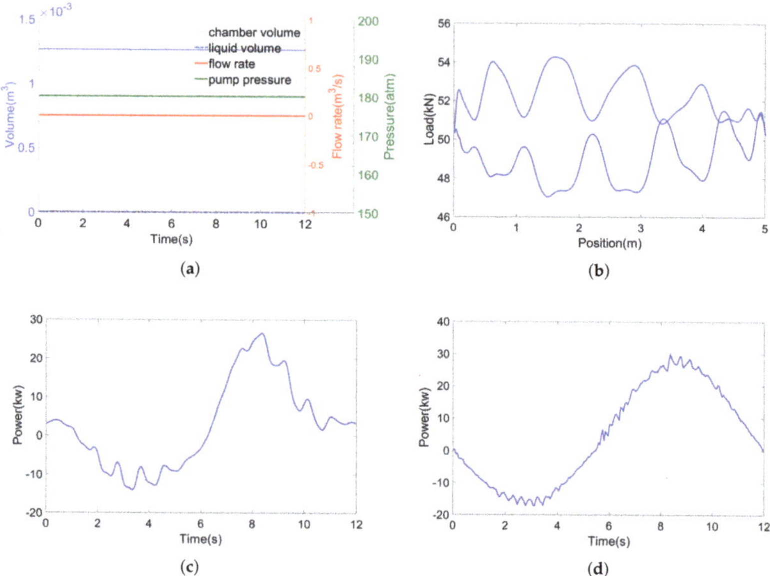

Figure 11. Parting rod working state. (**a**) Pump simulation. (**b**) Generated DC. (**c**) Generated MPC. (**d**) Actual MPC.

As illustrated in the figures, the variation of essential parameters is consistent with the settings in Section 2.2. The characteristics embodied in the generated DCs under the different working conditions conform to the historical experience learned from the extensive data collected in different practical application scenarios. The generated and measured power curves have similar trends, and their characteristics are consistent with the previous mechanical analysis in Section 3.2.1. These results verify the rationality of the model on the mechanism analysis.

In order to take a more in-depth validity on the quantitative analysis, 50 samples of the MPCs under each working condition are generated as the training data by adjusting the downhole parameters to diagnose 300 groups of collected samples, which are testing data. The diagnostic method employs the mechanical feature extraction combined with the conditional random field (MCRF), which is mentioned in [6]. The experimental result is presented in Figure 12, where the diagnostic accuracy achieves 73% without the help of collected samples at all. This demonstrates the effectiveness of the generated data. However, the diagnostic accuracy does not meet the industrial requirement. The main reason mainly includes two aspects. On the one hand, limited by the insufficiency of the mechanism feature extraction method, some MPCs of critical working conditions are difficult to identify. On the other hand, the generated samples deviate from the actual samples' distribution because of the model's simplifications and interference in the data acquisition.

Moreover, the collected data are divided into two parts, where 240 groups are randomly selected as the training set, and the remaining 60 groups are the testing set. To comprehensively investigate the generated data, we set various scenarios with different amounts of generated samples adding to the training set of the collected data to monitor the working conditions in the SRPS. Three methods named 1-D CNN, CNN, and MCRF are selected from three perspectives of time-series, image, and mechanism to conduct experiments. The diagnostic results are shown in Table 3.

As illustrated in Table 3, the diagnosis accuracy presents an upward trend as the generated samples are added to the original training set. Machine learning is more capable of extracting features than mechanistic feature analysis, and the time-series-based approach is more applicable to the MPCs than the curves acting as pictures.

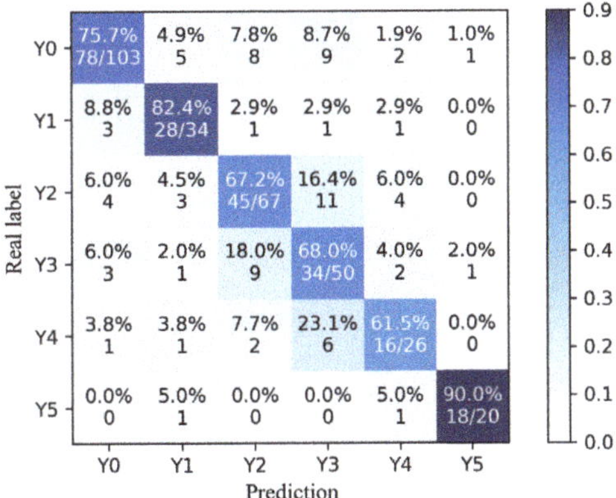

Figure 12. The confusion matrices of diagnosis result.

Table 3. Diagnostic results with different amount of generated samples.

Method	A	B	C	D	E
Collected samples	0	240	240	240	240
Generated samples	300	0	150	300	450
1-D CNN	0.747	0.863	0.907	0.933	0.94
CNN	0.713	0.843	0.883	0.90	0.9133
MCRF	0.733	0.837	0.883	0.893	0.9067

4.3. Diagnosis Based on Domain Adaptation

In this section, the proposed MADAN is employed to minimize the distribution discrepancy across domains in practical application scenarios. Since the new conditional metrics and pseudo-label learning strategy are appended to the objective function for the distribution alignment, the convergence analysis is imperative to illustrate the stability and transfer ability. As shown in Figure 13a, the discrepancy in diagnostic accuracy between the source and target domain gradually decreases with the iteration of optimization, which illustrates the effectiveness of the feature generator network in bridging the distribution discrepancy. In addition, the accuracy curves converge rapidly and finally approach 1, which demonstrates the superiority of this method in industrial diagnosis.

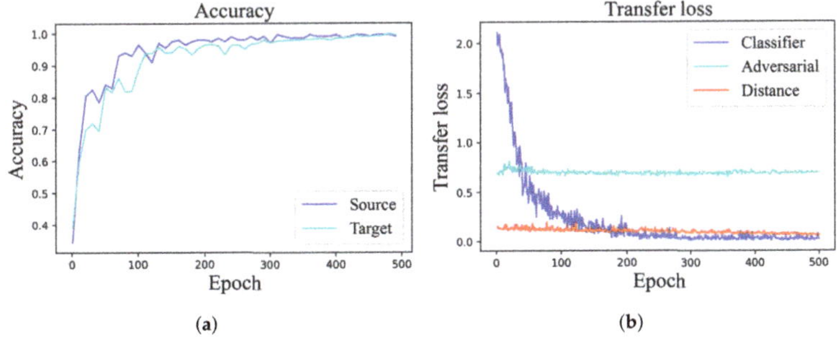

Figure 13. The trend of training accuracy and loss on the MADAN. (**a**) Accuracy. (**b**) Loss.

Furthermore, the training loss including classification loss (classifier_loss), domain classifier error (adversarial_loss), and conditional distribution loss (distance_loss) are plotted in Figure 13b, respectively. It can be found that the classification loss is gradually decreasing with the increasing of training epoch and finally approaches 0. The reciprocal oscillation of the adversarial loss illustrates that the domain classifier efficiently guides the feature generator network to explore domain-invariant features. This is because the feature extraction network keeps improving the information extraction capability under the requirement of the classifier error reduction, which makes the domain classifier keep improving the ability to discriminate domain features to inhibit the feature extraction network from retaining domain-related information. The conditional distribution loss presents a gradual declining trend. This demonstrates that the conditional distribution discrepancy is gradually disappearing.

For comparison purposes, several state-of-the-art methods are considered for comparisons with the MADAN, including 1-D CNN, DANN [21], DATLN [22], DTN [30], and MiDAN [24]. In order to make a fair comparison, all the compared methods adopt the same 1-D CNN architectures to explore features. The details of the compared methods are presented in Table 4, where MDA denotes the marginal distributions alignment and CDA denotes the conditional distributions alignment.

Table 4. Detailed description of the compared methods.

Method	MDA	CDA	Pseudo-Labels
1-D CNN	/	/	/
DANN	MMD	/	/
DATLN	MMD + Adversail	/	/
DTN	MMD	MMD	Pre-train network
MiDAN	Adversail	MMD	Pre-train network
MADAN (ours)	Adversail	MMD	Mechanism + Classifier

The diagnostic result is an average of five random tests, where the testing set is 60 groups randomly split from the 300 groups of collected MPCs. To comprehensively show the capabilities of the proposed method, three evaluation indicators including Accuracy, F1-score, and MCC are selected to assess the performance of each method. The expressions of the MCC are defined as follows:

$$MCC = \frac{TN \times TP - FN \times FP}{\sqrt{(TF + TP)(FN + TN)(TP + FN)(FP + TN)}}. \tag{22}$$

The results are listed in Table 5.

Table 5. Comparison research under various methodologies.

Method	Accuracy (%)	F1 (%)	MCC (%)
1-D CNN	83.33	83.25	79.9
DANN	91.67	91.38	89.69
DATLN	92.33	92.17	90.58
DTN	95.33	95.34	94.39
MiDAN	97	97.03	96.42
MADAN (ours)	98.33	98.51	98.17

As the results show, the MADAN performs better than other diagnostic methodologies in all evaluation indicators. Concretely, t-distributed stochastic neighbor embedding (t-SNE) is employed to demonstrate visual insights into the distribution discrepancy of features distilled by different methods from the generated and collected MPC. The t-SNE visualization for the original data and the features after the alignment by the methods mentioned above are illustrated in Figure 14.

From Table 5 and Figure 14, some results can be clearly obtained. Firstly, in terms of classification performance, the outlier source samples are much less with the help of transfer learning. In addition, the MADAN can better cluster the same categories and separate different categories than the other methods. Secondly, in terms of the marginal distributions alignment, the adversarial training is superior to the MMD, where Figure 14c,e correspond to Figure 14b,d, respectively. Thirdly, in terms of the conditional distributions alignment, the data in different domains within each category are more evenly distributed, where Figure 14d–f correspond to Figure 14a–c. Fourthly, in terms of pseudo-label learning, despite MiDAN having achieved good results, our MADAN performs better in the same number of iterations due to the higher pseudo-label accuracy resulting from assisted mechanisms during the initial training. From the analysis and discussion above, it can be seen that the proposed MADAN can effectively bridge the distribution discrepancy, resulting in better diagnosis performance in practical application scenarios.

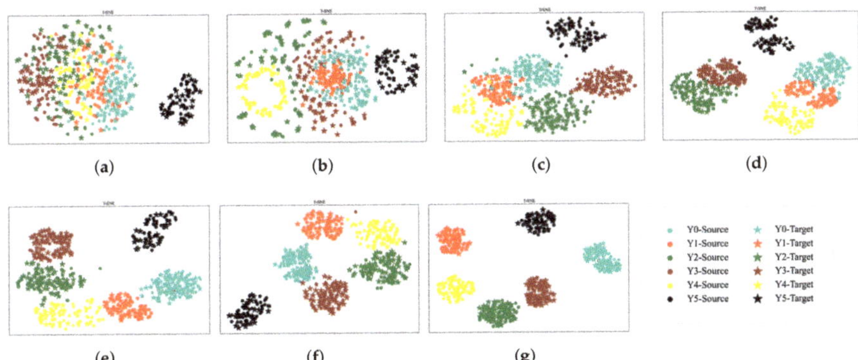

Figure 14. T-SNE feature visualization. (**a**) Source sample. (**b**) 1-D CNN. (**c**) DANN. (**d**) DATLN. (**e**) DTN. (**f**) MiDAN. (**g**) MADAN (ours).

5. Conclusions

The motor power as an easily collected signal contains information about the working status of the SRPS. In order to tackle the issue of an insufficiently labeled MPC database due to the early stage of the electrical parameters research on the SRPS, this paper has proposed an unsupervised fault diagnosis methodology named MADAN to leverage the generated MPCs of different working conditions to diagnose the actual MPCs. Firstly, an integrated dynamics mathematical model has been established to generate the MPCs under different working conditions. Secondly, a mechanism-assisted pseudo-label learning strategy and a conditional distribution discrepancy metric have been added to the adversarial domain adaptation model to bridge the marginal and conditional distribution discrepancy of the generated and collected MPCs. Finally, a set of actual MPCs collected by self-developed portable devices has been utilized to verify the feasibility of the proposed methodology. The experimental results indicated that the generated and the actual MPCs had similar trends, and the MADAN can effectively utilize the generated and actual unlabeled MPCs to realize the power fault diagnosis of oil wells.

Author Contributions: Conceptualization, D.H.; methodology, D.H. and X.G.; software, D.H.; validation, D.H. and X.G.; formal analysis, D.H.; investigation, D.H.; resources, X.G.; data curation, D.H.; writing—original draft preparation, D.H.; writing—review and editing, D.H.; visualization, D.H.; supervision, D.H.; project administration, X.G.; funding acquisition, X.G. All authors have read and agreed to the published version of the manuscript.

Funding: This work was supported by the National Natural Science Foundation of China (62173073).

Institutional Review Board Statement: Not applicable.

Informed Consent Statement: Not applicable.

Data Availability Statement: Not applicable.

Conflicts of Interest: The authors declare no conflict of interest.

Abbreviations

The following abbreviations are used in this manuscript:

b_i	Damping coefficient of ith rod string
$C_0 C_1 C_2 C_3$	Constant
C_h	Henry's law constant
C_l	Perimeter of the rod string and pump
d_p	Diameter of pump
d_r	Diameter of sucker rod
F	Polished rod load
F_c	Crank torque
f_i	Friction coefficient of ith rod string
f_d	Friction coefficient of plunger
k_i	ith rod modulus of elasticity
l_i	Length of ith rod string
M_i	Mass of ith rod string
M_{fg}	Mass of free gas in pump
M_g	Mass of whole gas in pump
M_o	Mass of oil in pump
M_{mol}	Molar mass of methane
M_w	Mass of water in pump
n	Times of stroke
n_m	Motor speed
P_m	Motor power
P_d	Discharge pressure of the pump
P_p	Load on the plunger
P_s	Submergence pressure (Mpa)
Q	Flow rate though standing valve
R_{ck}	Weight radius of crankshaft
S	Displacement of sucker rod node
S_r	Are of sucker rod
S_{lt}	Leaked area of traveling valve
S_s	Passage area of standing valve
S_t	Passage area of traveling valve
S_p	Passage area of plunger
T_d	Absolute temperature
$\overline{TF}$	Torque factor
V_o	Volume of oil in the pump
V_p	Volume of the pump
V_w	Volume of water in the pump
W_{cb}	Balanced weight of crankshaft
W_{ck}	Weight of crankshaft
W_{ub}	Counterbalance weight
γ_g	Gas mass ratio of produced fluid
γ_o	Oil mass ratio of produced fluid
γ_w	Water mass ratio of produced fluid
δ_g	Gas solubility
η_b	Efficiency of four-bar linkage
η_m	Efficiency of motor and reduction gearbox
ξ	Gas related constant
ρ_l	Density of produced fluid
ρ_o	Density of oil
ρ_w	Density of water
σ_v	Damping coefficient of standing valve
ω	Angular velocity of crankshaft

References

1. Lv, X.; Wang, H.; Zhang, X.; Liu, Y.; Jiang, D.; Wei, B. An evolutional SVM method based on incremental algorithm and simulated indicator diagrams for fault diagnosis in sucker rod pumping systems. *J. Pet. Sci. Eng.* **2021**, *203*, 108806. [CrossRef]
2. Han, Y.; Song, X.; Li, K.; Yan, X. Hybrid modeling for submergence depth of the pumping well using stochastic configuration networks with random sampling. *J. Pet. Sci. Eng.* **2022**, *208*, 109423. [CrossRef]
3. Li, K.; Han, Y.; Wang, T. A novel prediction method for down-hole working conditions of the beam pumping unit based on 8-directions chain codes and online sequential extreme learning machine. *J. Pet. Sci. Eng.* **2018**, *160*, 285–301. [CrossRef]
4. Han, Y.; Li, K.; Ge, F.; Wang, Y.; Xu, W. Online fault diagnosis for sucker rod pumping well by optimized density peak clustering. *ISA Trans.* **2021**, *120*, 222–234. doi: 10.1016/j.isatra.2021.03.022. [CrossRef] [PubMed]
5. Takacs, G.; Kis, L. A new model to find optimum counterbalancing of sucker-rod pumping units including a rigorous procedure for gearbox torque calculations. *J. Pet. Sci. Eng.* **2021**, *205*, 108792. [CrossRef]
6. Zheng, B.; Gao, X.; Pan, R. Sucker rod pump working state diagnosis using motor data and hidden conditional random fields. *IEEE Trans. Ind. Electron.* **2019**, *67*, 7919–7928. [CrossRef]
7. Wei, J.; Gao, X. Fault Diagnosis of Sucker Rod Pump Based on Deep-Broad Learning Using Motor Data. *IEEE Access* **2020**, *8*, 222562–222571. [CrossRef]
8. Zhang, B.; Gao, X.; Li, X. Complete Simulation and Fault Diagnosis of Sucker-Rod Pumping. *SPE Prod. Oper.* **2021**, *36*, 277–290.
9. Zheng, B.; Gao, X.; Li, X. Fault detection for sucker rod pump based on motor power. *Control Eng. Pract.* **2019**, *86*, 37–47. [CrossRef]
10. Chen, L.; Gao, X.; Li, X. Using the motor power and XGBoost to diagnose working states of a sucker rod pump. *J. Pet. Sci. Eng.* **2021**, *199*, 108329. [CrossRef]
11. Gibbs, S. Predicting the behavior of sucker-rod pumping systems. *J. Pet. Technol.* **1963**, *15*, 769–778. [CrossRef]
12. Zheng, B.; Gao, X.; Li, X. Diagnosis of sucker rod pump based on generating dynamometer cards. *J. Process Control* **2019**, *77*, 76–88. [CrossRef]
13. Lv, X.; Wang, H.; Liu, Y.; Chen, S.; Lan, W.; Sun, B. A novel method of output metering with dynamometer card for SRPS under fault conditions. *J. Pet. Sci. Eng.* **2020**, *192*, 107098. [CrossRef]
14. Zhao, Z.; Zhang, Q.; Yu, X.; Sun, C.; Wang, S.; Yan, R.; Chen, X. Applications of Unsupervised Deep Transfer Learning to Intelligent Fault Diagnosis: A Survey and Comparative Study. *IEEE Trans. Instrum. Meas.* **2021**, *70*, 1–28. [CrossRef]
15. Zhang, W.; Li, X.; Ma, H.; Luo, Z.; Li, X. Open-Set Domain Adaptation in Machinery Fault Diagnostics Using Instance-Level Weighted Adversarial Learning. *IEEE Trans. Ind. Inf.* **2021**, *17*, 7445–7455. [CrossRef]
16. Ainapure, A.; Siahpour, S.; Li, X.; Majid, F.; Lee, J. Intelligent Robust Cross-Domain Fault Diagnostic Method for Rotating Machines Using Noisy Condition Labels. *Mathematics* **2022**, *10*, 455. [CrossRef]
17. Zhang, H.; Ren, H.; Mu, Y.; Han, J. Optimal Consensus Control Design for Multiagent Systems with Multiple Time Delay Using Adaptive Dynamic Programming. *IEEE Trans. Cybern.* **2021**. [CrossRef]
18. Wen, L.; Gao, L.; Li, X. A new deep transfer learning based on sparse auto-encoder for fault diagnosis. *IEEE Trans. Syst. Man Cybern. Syst.* **2017**, *49*, 136–144. [CrossRef]
19. Ye, Z.; Yu, J.; Mao, L. Multisource Domain Adaption for Health Degradation Monitoring of Lithium-Ion Batteries. *IEEE Trans. Transp. Electrif.* **2021**, *7*, 2279–2292. [CrossRef]
20. Zhao, B.; Zhang, X.; Zhan, Z.; Wu, Q. Deep multi-scale separable convolutional network with triple attention mechanism: A novel multi-task domain adaptation method for intelligent fault diagnosis. *Expert Syst. Appl.* **2021**, *182*, 115087. [CrossRef]
21. Ganin, Y.; Ustinova, E.; Ajakan, H.; Germain, P.; Larochelle, H.; Laviolette, F.; Marchand, M.; Lempitsky, V. Domain-adversarial training of neural networks. *J. Mach. Learn. Res.* **2016**, *17*, 2030–2096.
22. Guo, L.; Lei, Y.; Xing, S.; Yan, T.; Li, N. Deep convolutional transfer learning network: A new method for intelligent fault diagnosis of machines with unlabeled data. *IEEE Trans. Ind. Electron.* **2018**, *66*, 7316–7325. [CrossRef]
23. Cheng, C.; Zhou, B.; Ma, G.; Wu, D.; Yuan, Y. Wasserstein distance based deep adversarial transfer learning for intelligent fault diagnosis with unlabeled or insufficient labeled data. *Neurocomputing* **2020**, *409*, 35–45. [CrossRef]
24. Tan, Y.; Guo, L.; Gao, H.; Lin, Z.; Liu, Y. MiDAN: A framework for cross-domain intelligent fault diagnosis with imbalanced datasets. *Measurement* **2021**, *183*, 109834. [CrossRef]
25. Li, Y.; Song, Y.; Jia, L.; Gao, S.; Li, Q.; Qiu, M. Intelligent fault diagnosis by fusing domain adversarial training and maximum mean discrepancy via ensemble learning. *IEEE Trans. Ind. Inf.* **2020**, *17*, 2833–2841. [CrossRef]
26. Li, X.; Zhang, W. Deep Learning-Based Partial Domain Adaptation Method on Intelligent Machinery Fault Diagnostics. *IEEE Trans. Ind. Electron.* **2021**, *68*, 4351–4361. [CrossRef]
27. Zhang, W.; Li, X.; Ma, H.; Luo, Z.; Li, X. Universal domain adaptation in fault diagnostics with hybrid weighted deep adversarial learning. *IEEE Trans. Ind. Inf.* **2021**, *17*, 7957–7967. [CrossRef]
28. Long, M.; Wang, J.; Ding, G.; Sun, J.; Yu, P.S. Transfer feature learning with joint distribution adaptation. In Proceedings of the IEEE International Conference on Computer Vision, Sydney, Australia, 2–8 December 2013; pp. 2200–2207.
29. Li, X.; Zhang, W.; Xu, N.X.; Ding, Q. Deep learning-based machinery fault diagnostics with domain adaptation across sensors at different places. *IEEE Trans. Ind. Electron.* **2019**, *67*, 6785–6794. [CrossRef]
30. Han, T.; Liu, C.; Yang, W.; Jiang, D. Deep transfer network with joint distribution adaptation: A new intelligent fault diagnosis framework for industry application. *ISA Trans.* **2020**, *97*, 269–281. [CrossRef]

31. Lu, N.; Xiao, H.; Sun, Y.; Han, M.; Wang, Y. A new method for intelligent fault diagnosis of machines based on unsupervised domain adaptation. *Neurocomputing* **2021**, *427*, 96–109. [CrossRef]
32. Liu, Y.; Zhong, L.; Qiu, J.; Lu, J.; Wang, W. Unsupervised Domain Adaptation for Nonintrusive Load Monitoring Via Adversarial and Joint Adaptation Network. *IEEE Trans. Ind. Inf.* **2022**, *18*, 266–277. [CrossRef]
33. Ganin, Y.; Lempitsky, V. Unsupervised domain adaptation by backpropagation. In Proceedings of the International Conference on Machine Learning, PMLR, Lille, France, 6–11 July 2015; pp. 1180–1189.

Article

The Due Window Assignment Problems with Deteriorating Job and Delivery Time

Jin Qian and Yu Zhan *

College of Science, Northeastern University, Shenyang 110819, China; qianjin@mail.neu.edu.cn
* Correspondence: zhanyu@mail.neu.edu.cn

Abstract: This paper considers the single machine scheduling problem with due window, delivery time and deteriorating job, whose goal is to minimize the window location, window size, earliness and tardiness. Common due window and slack due window are considered. The delivery time depends on the actual processing time of past sequences. The actual processing time of the job is an increasing function of the start time. Based on the small perturbations technique and adjacent exchange technique, we obtain the propositions of the problems. For common and slack due window assignment, we prove that the two objective functions are polynomial time solvable in $O(nlogn)$ time. We propose the corresponding algorithms to obtain the optimal sequence, window location and window size.

Keywords: scheduling; due window; deteriorating job; delivery time; earliness; tardiness

MSC: 90B35

Citation: Qian, J.; Zhan, Y. The Due Window Assignment Problems with Deteriorating Job and Delivery Time. *Mathematics* **2022**, *10*, 1672. https://doi.org/10.3390/math10101672

Academic Editors: Xiang Li, Shuo Zhang and Wei Zhang

Received: 8 April 2022
Accepted: 11 May 2022
Published: 13 May 2022

Publisher's Note: MDPI stays neutral with regard to jurisdictional claims in published maps and institutional affiliations.

1. Introduction

In order to gain the competitive advantage, modern operations management advocates that companies improve customer service. Operationally, good customer service means fulfilling orders within a specified time period. The research on due window usually assumes three situations. First, the jobs that are completed before the start time of the due window have earliness costs. Second, the jobs that are completed after the end of the due window have tardiness costs. Third, the jobs that are completed within the due window do not incur any costs. For cost considerations, we need to take into account the comprehensive factors, which contain earliness costs, tardiness costs, starting time of the window and window size.

Based on the research gap found in the literature review, this paper studies scheduling problems involving both simple linear degradation and past sequence dependent delivery time under the common and slack due window assignment. To the best of our knowledge, such articles are rare for the common or slack due window assignment. In this paper, the single machine scheduling problem with delivery time and deteriorating job is considered. The actual processing time of job is an increasing function of the start time. The delivery time depends on the actual processing time of past sequence. The goal is to minimize the window location, window size, earliness and tardiness. Small perturbation technique and adjacent switching technique are effective methods to deal with scheduling problems. Based on the small perturbations technique and adjacent exchange technique, we obtain the propositions of the method. By the propositions, we propose the polynomial time solvable algorithms to obtain the optimal sequence, window location and window size. The complexity of the algorithms is $O(nlogn)$.

2. Literature Review

In the field of production sequencing and scheduling, the scheduling problem with due window has received a lot of attention. In 1955, Jackson first proposed the concept of due date [1]. The scheduling problem of the optimal due date was considered by

Seidmann [2] and Panwalkar [3]. In 2015, Li et al. studied the scheduling problem with the slack due window, resource allocation and learning effect [4]. In 2015, Yang et al. studied the scheduling problem with deteriorating jobs, learning effect and due window [5]. In 2016, Yin et al. studied the scheduling problem with resource allocation and slack due window [6]. In 2017, Wang et al. studied the scheduling problem with the slack due window and controllable processing times [7]. In 2020, Wang et al. considered the scheduling problem with due window and position-dependent weights [8]. In 2020, Sun et al. considered the proportional flow shop scheduling problem with due window and position-dependent weights [9]. In 2021, Yue et al. studied a scheduling model with due window and the processing time as a special function [10].

The processing time of deteriorating job is variable. As the jobs are processed, and the processing times of jobs increase. The concept of deteriorating jobs was proposed by Gupta [11]. Under the common due window assignment, Yue et al. considered the scheduling problem with deteriorating jobs [12]. In 2018, Wang et al. studied the unrelated parallel processors scheduling problem with a maintenance activity and deterioration effect [13]. In 2019, Sun et al. considered the single machine scheduling problem with machine maintenance and deteriorating jobs [14]. In 2020, Cheng et al. studied the single machine scheduling problem whose processing time was a stage function of the start time [15]. In 2020, Liang et al. studied the scheduling problem with resource allocation and deteriorating jobs [16].

After a job is processed, the job should be delivered to the customer, which is called the past sequence dependent (psd) delivery time. Koulamas and Kyparisis first proposed the past sequence dependent delivery time [17]. In 2012, Liu et al. studied some new results on single machine scheduling with past sequence dependent delivery times [18]. In 2014, Zhao et al. studied single machine scheduling problems with general position-dependent processing times and past sequence dependent delivery times [19]. In 2020, Mir et al. studied parallel machine problem with delivery time and deterioration effect [20]. In 2021, Toksari et al. studied some scheduling problems with learning effect and past sequence dependent delivery times [21]. In 2021, Wang et al. studied single machine scheduling with position-dependent weights and delivery times [22].

The problem is described in the third Section 3. The research method is given in the forth Section 4. The summary is given in the last Section 5.

3. Notation and Problem Statement

There are n independent jobs $S = \{J_1, \ldots, J_n\}$ processed at time t_0 ($t_0 > 0$) on a machine. The actual processing time p_i of J_i is

$$p_i = b_i t_i, \tag{1}$$

where b_i is the deterioration rate, t_i is the start time. The delivery time $q_{[i]}$ of $J_{[i]}$ is

$$q_{[i]} = r w_{[i]} = r \sum_{j=0}^{i-1} p_{[j]}, \tag{2}$$

where r is the delivery rate, $p_{[i]}$ is the actual possessing time of $J_{[i]}$ and $w_{[i]} = \sum_{j=0}^{i-1} p_{[j]} = t_0 \prod_{j=1}^{i-1}(1 + b_{[j]})$, $p_{[0]} = t_0$. The subscript $[i]$ indicates that the job is arranged at the ith position. The completion time $C_{[i]}$ of $J_{[i]}$ is

$$C_{[i]} = w_{[i]} + p_{[i]} + q_{[i]} = t_0(1 + b_{[i]} + r) \prod_{j=1}^{i-1}(1 + b_{[j]}). \tag{3}$$

The common due window (CONW) and slack due window (SLKW) are considered. Let $[d_i', d_i'']$ be the due window of J_i, where d_i' and d_i'' are the start time and end time of due window, respectively. For the common due window, all jobs have the same start time d' and end time d'' of due window. For the slack due window, $d_i' = p_i + q_1$ and $d_i'' = p_i + q_2$. $D = d_i'' - d_i'$ is the size of due window, $D = q_2 - q_1$, q_1 and q_2 are the decision variables. C_i represents the completion time of J_i. E_i is the earliness of J_i, $E_i = \max\{0, d_i' - C_i\}$; T_i is the tardiness of J_i, $T_i = \max\{0, C_i - d_i''\}$.

The goal is to minimize the earliness, tardiness, start time of window and window size. The objective functions are

$$M = \sum_{i=1}^{n} [aE_{[i]} + cT_{[i]} + ed' + fD], \tag{4}$$

$$M = \sum_{i=1}^{n} [aE_{[i]} + cT_{[i]} + eq_1 + fD], \tag{5}$$

where a, c, e, f represent the unit cost of earliness, the unit cost of tardiness, and the unit cost of the start time and window size. If $C_{[h]} < d' < C_{[h+1]}$ and $C_{[l]} < d'' < C_{[l+1]}$ (CONW), the objective function is

$$M = \sum_{i=1}^{h} a(d' - C_{[i]}) + \sum_{i=l+1}^{n} c(C_{[i]} - d'') + ned' + nf(d'' - d')$$
$$= -a \sum_{i=1}^{h} C_{[i]} + c \sum_{i=l+1}^{n} C_{[i]} + [ha + n(e - f)]d' + [nf - (n-1)c]d''. \tag{6}$$

If $d' = C_{[h+1]}$ and $d'' = C_{[l]}$ (CONW), the objective function is

$$M = \sum_{i=1}^{h} a(C_{[h+1]} - C_{[i]}) + \sum_{i=l+1}^{n} c(C_{[i]} - C_{[l]}) + neC_{[h+1]} + nf(C_{[l]} - C_{[h+1]})$$
$$= -a \sum_{i=1}^{h} C_{[i]} + c \sum_{i=l+1}^{n} C_{[i]} + [ha + n(e - f)]C_{[h+1]} + [nf - (n-1)c]C_{[l]}. \tag{7}$$

The objective function of SLKW model is similar to that of CONW model. By the three-region notation, the models can be defined as

$$1|\text{CONW}, p_i = b_i t_i, q_{psd}| \sum_{i=1}^{n} [aE_{[i]} + cT_{[i]} + ed' + fD],$$

$$1|\text{SLKW}, p_i = b_i t_i, q_{psd}| \sum_{i=1}^{n} [aE_{[i]} + cT_{[i]} + eq_1 + fD],$$

where q_{psd} represents the past sequence dependent delivery time.

4. Research Method

In this section, we present several properties for an optimal schedule. First, we show the optimal common and slack due window positions by using the technique of small perturbations. Then, the sequence of jobs within different sets is determined by the adjacent exchange technique. Finally, we propose the polynomial time algorithms to obtain the optimal sequence.

4.1. The Problem $1|CONW, p_i = b_i t_i, q_{psd}| \sum_{i=1}^{n}[aE_{[i]} + cT_{[i]} + ed' + fD]$

4.1.1. Optimal Properties of the Problem

Lemma 1. *For any job sequence, d' of the optimal schedule is the start time of some job.*

Proof. (a) When $C_{[h]} < d' < C_{[h+1]}$ and $d'' = C_{[l]}, 0 \le h < l \le n, C_{[0]} = t_0$. The objective function is

$$M = -a \sum_{i=1}^{h} C_{[i]} + c \sum_{i=l+1}^{n} C_{[i]} + [ha + n(e - f)]d' + [nf - (n - l)c]C_{[l]}. \tag{8}$$

when $d' = C_{[h]}$, the objective function is

$$M_1 = -a \sum_{i=1}^{h-1} C_{[i]} + c \sum_{i=l+1}^{n} C_{[i]} + [(h - 1)a + n(e - f)]C_{[h]} + [nf - (n - l)c]C_{[l]}. \tag{9}$$

$$M - M_1 = [ha + n(e - f)][d' - C_{[h]}]. \tag{10}$$

when $d' = C_{[h+1]}$, the objective function is

$$M_2 = -a \sum_{i=1}^{h} C_{[i]} + c \sum_{i=l+1}^{n} C_{[i]} + [ha + n(e - f)]C_{[h+1]} + [nf - (n - l)c]C_{[l]}. \tag{11}$$

$$M - M_2 = [ha + n(e - f)][d' - C_{[h+1]}]. \tag{12}$$

when $ha + n(e - f) < 0, M > M_2$; otherwise, $M \ge M_1$.

(b) When $C_{[h]} < d' < C_{[h+1]}$ and $C_{[l]} < d'' < C_{[l+1]}, 0 \le h \le l < n$. The objective function is

$$M = -a \sum_{i=1}^{h} C_{[i]} + c \sum_{i=l+1}^{n} C_{[i]} + [ha + n(e - f)]d' + [nf - (n - l)c]d''. \tag{13}$$

when $d' = C_{[h]}$, the objective function is

$$M_3 = -a \sum_{i=1}^{h-1} C_{[i]} + c \sum_{i=l+1}^{n} C_{[i]} + [(h - 1)a + n(e - f)]C_{[h]} + [nf - (n - l)c]d''. \tag{14}$$

$$M - M_3 = [ha + n(e - f)][d' - C_{[h]}]. \tag{15}$$

when $d' = C_{[h+1]}$, the objective function is

$$M_4 = -a \sum_{i=1}^{h} C_{[i]} + c \sum_{i=l+1}^{n} C_{[i]} + [ha + n(e - f)]C_{[h+1]} + [nf - (n - l)c]d''. \tag{16}$$

$$M - M_4 = [ha + n(e - f)][d' - C_{[h+1]}]. \tag{17}$$

when $ha + n(e - f) < 0, M > M_4$; otherwise, $M \ge M_3$. $\square$

Lemma 2. *For any job sequence, d'' of the optimal schedule is the completion time of some job.*

Proof. (a) When $d' = C_{[h]}$ and $C_{[l]} < d'' < C_{[l+1]}, 0 \le h \le l < n$. The objective function is

$$M = -a \sum_{i=1}^{h-1} C_{[i]} + c \sum_{i=l+1}^{n} C_{[i]} + [(h - 1)a + n(e - f)]C_{[h]} + [nf - (n - l)c]d''. \tag{18}$$

when $d'' = C_{[l]}$, the objective function is

$$M_1 = -a \sum_{i=1}^{h-1} C_{[i]} + c \sum_{i=l+1}^{n} C_{[i]} + [(h-1)a + n(e-f)]C_{[h]} + [nf - (n-l)c]C_{[l]}. \tag{19}$$

$$M - M_1 = [nf - (n-l)c][d'' - C_{[l]}]. \tag{20}$$

when $d'' = C_{[l+1]}$, the objective function is

$$M_2 = -a \sum_{i=1}^{h-1} C_{[i]} + c \sum_{i=l+2}^{n} C_{[i]} + [(h-1)a + n(e-f)]C_{[h]} + [nf - (n-l-1)c]C_{[l+1]}. \tag{21}$$

$$M - M_2 = [nf - (n-l)c][d'' - C_{[l+1]}]. \tag{22}$$

when $nf - (n-l)c < 0$, $M > M_2$; otherwise, $M \geq M_1$.

(b) When $C_{[h]} < d' < C_{[h+1]}$ and $C_{[l]} < d'' < C_{[l+1]}$, $0 \leq h \leq l < n$. The objective function is

$$M = -a \sum_{i=1}^{h} C_{[i]} + c \sum_{i=l+1}^{n} C_{[i]} + [ha + n(e-f)]d' + [nf - (n-l)c]d''. \tag{23}$$

when $d'' = C_{[l]}$, the objective function is

$$M_3 = -a \sum_{i=1}^{h} C_{[i]} + c \sum_{i=l+1}^{n} C_{[i]} + [ha + n(e-f)]d' + [nf - (n-l)c]C_{[l]}. \tag{24}$$

$$M - M_3 = [nf - (n-l)c][d'' - C_{[l]}]. \tag{25}$$

When $d'' = C_{[l+1]}$, the objective function is

$$M_4 = -a \sum_{i=1}^{h} C_{[i]} + c \sum_{i=l+2}^{n} C_{[i]} + [ha + n(e-f)]d' + [nf - (n-l-1)c]C_{[l+1]}. \tag{26}$$

$$M - M_4 = [nf - (n-l)c][d'' - C_{[l+1]}]. \tag{27}$$

when $nf - (n-l)c < 0$, $M > M_4$; otherwise, $M \geq M_3$. $\square$

Lemma 3. *For the optimal schedule, d' is the completion time $C_{[h]}$, d'' is the completion time $C_{[l]}$, $h = \lceil \frac{n(f-e)}{a} \rceil$, $l = \lceil \frac{n(c-f)}{c} \rceil$.*

Proof. when $d' = C_{[h]}$ and $d'' = C_{[l]}$ for the optimal schedule, the objective function is

$$M = -a \sum_{i=1}^{h-1} C_{[i]} + c \sum_{i=l+1}^{n} C_{[i]} + [(h-1)a + n(e-f)]C_{[h]} + [nf - (n-l)c]C_{[l]}. \tag{28}$$

(a) When $d' = C_{[h-1]}$ and $d'' = C_{[l]}$, the objective function is

$$M_1 = -a \sum_{i=1}^{h-2} C_{[i]} + c \sum_{i=l+1}^{n} C_{[i]} + [(h-2)a + n(e-f)]C_{[h-1]} + [nf - (n-l)c]C_{[l]}. \tag{29}$$

$$M - M_1 = [(h-1)a + n(e-f)][C_{[h]} - C_{[h-1]}] \leq 0. \tag{30}$$

So, $h \leq 1 + \frac{n(f-e)}{a}$.

When $d' = C_{[h+1]}$ and $d'' = C_{[l]}$, the objective function is

$$M_2 = -a \sum_{i=1}^{h} C_{[i]} + c \sum_{i=l+1}^{n} C_{[i]} + [ha + n(e-f)]C_{[h+1]} + [nf - (n-l)c]C_{[l]}. \tag{31}$$

$$M - M_2 = [ha + n(e-f)][C_{[h]} - C_{[h+1]}] \le 0. \tag{32}$$

So $\frac{n(f-e)}{a} \le h \le 1 + \frac{n(f-e)}{a}$, $h = \lceil \frac{n(f-e)}{a} \rceil$.

(b) When $d'' = C_{[l-1]}$ and $d' = C_{[h]}$, the objective function is

$$M_3 = -a \sum_{i=1}^{h-1} C_{[i]} + c \sum_{i=l}^{n} C_{[i]} + [(h-1)a + n(e-f)]C_{[h]} + [nf - (n-l+1)c]C_{[l-1]}. \tag{33}$$

$$M - M_3 = [nf - (n-l+1)c][C_{[l]} - C_{[l-1]}] \le 0. \tag{34}$$

So, $l \le 1 + \frac{n(c-f)}{c}$.

when $d'' = C_{[l+1]}$ and $d' = C_{[h]}$, the objective function is

$$M_4 = -a \sum_{i=1}^{h-1} C_{[i]} + c \sum_{i=l+2}^{n} C_{[i]} + [(h-1)a + n(e-f)]C_{[h]} + [nf - (n-l-1)c]C_{[l+1]}. \tag{35}$$

$$M - M_4 = [nf - (n-l)c][C_{[l]} - C_{[l+1]}] \le 0. \tag{36}$$

So $\frac{n(c-f)}{c} \le l \le 1 + \frac{n(c-f)}{c}$, $l = \lceil \frac{n(c-f)}{c} \rceil$. $\square$

Suppose $d' = C_{[h]}$ and $d'' = C_{[l]}$ for the optimal schedule. Three sets $\Omega_1 = \{J_i \in \Omega | i \le h-1\}$, $\Omega_2 = \{J_i \in \Omega | i = h\}$, $\Omega_3 = \{J_i \in \Omega | h+1 \le i \le l-1\}$, $\Omega_4 = \{J_i \in \Omega | i = l\}$, $\Omega_5 = \{J_i \in \Omega | l+1 \le i \le n\}$, Ω is the job sequence.

Lemma 4. *In the optimal schedule, the jobs in Ω_1 can be processed in descending order of b_j.*

Proof. J_g is at the uth position and J_k is at the $(u+1)$th position in Ω_1. $\pi_1 = \{J_1, \ldots, J_g, J_k, \ldots, J_n\}$, $1 \le u < u+1 \le h-1$. The objective function of π_1 is M_1. Swap J_g and J_k to get sequence $\pi_2 = \{J_1, \ldots, J_k, J_g, \ldots, J_n\}$. The objective function of π_2 is M_2.

$$M_1 - M_2 = at_0(b_k - b_g)(1+r) \prod_{i=1}^{u-1} (1 + b_{[i]}). \tag{37}$$

If $b_g > b_k$, $M_1 < M_2$. $\square$

Lemma 5. *The deterioration rate of the job in Ω_2 is less than the deterioration rate of any job in Ω_1.*

Proof. J_g is at the $(h-1)$th position, and J_k is at the hth position. $\pi_1 = \{J_1, \ldots, J_g, J_k, \ldots, J_n\}$. The objective function of π_1 is M_1. Swap J_g and J_k to get sequence $\pi_2 = \{J_1, \ldots, J_k, J_g, \ldots, J_n\}$. The objective function of π_2 is M_2.

$$M_1 - M_2 = \{[(h-1)a + n(e-f)]r - a\}t_0(b_g - b_k) \prod_{i=1}^{h-2} (1 + b_{[i]}). \tag{38}$$

If $b_k < b_g$, $M_1 < M_2$. $\square$

Lemma 6. *In the optimal schedule, the jobs in Ω_3 can be processed in any order of b_j.*

Proof. J_g is at the uth position and J_k which is at the $(u+1)$th position in Ω_3, $\pi_1 = \{J_1, \ldots, J_g, J_k, \ldots, J_n\}$, $h + 1 \leq u < u + 1 \leq l - 1$. The objective function of π_1 is M_1. Swap J_g and J_k to get sequence $\pi_2 = \{J_1, \ldots, J_k, J_g, \ldots, J_n\}$. The objective function of π_2 is M_2.

$$M_1 = M_2. \tag{39}$$

$\square$

Lemma 7. *The deterioration rate of any job in Ω_3 is less than the deterioration rate of the job in Ω_4.*

Proof. J_g is at the uth position, $h + 1 \leq u \leq l - 1$. J_k is at the lth position. $\pi_1 = \{J_1, \ldots, J_g, \ldots, J_k, \ldots, J_n\}$. The objective function of π_1 is M_1. Swap J_g and J_k to get sequence $\pi_2 = \{J_1, \ldots, J_k, \ldots, J_g, \ldots, J_n\}$. The objective function of π_2 is M_2.

$$M_1 - M_2 = [nf - (n-l)c]t_0 r(b_g - b_k) \prod_{i=1, i \neq u}^{l-1} (1 + b_{[i]}). \tag{40}$$

If $b_g < b_k$, $M_1 < M_2$. $\square$

Lemma 8. *In the optimal schedule, the jobs in Ω_5 can be processed in ascending order of b_j.*

Proof. J_g is at the uth position and J_k is at the $(u+1)$th position in Ω_5, $\pi_1 = \{J_1, \ldots, J_g, J_k, \ldots, J_n\}$, $l + 1 \leq u < u + 1 \leq n$. The objective function of π_1 is M_1. Swap J_g and J_k to get sequence $\pi_2 = \{J_1, \ldots, J_k, J_g, \ldots, J_n\}$. The objective function of π_2 is M_2.

$$M_1 - M_2 = ct_0(1 + r)(b_g - b_k) \prod_{i=1}^{u-1} (1 + b_{[i]}). \tag{41}$$

If $b_g < b_k$, $M_1 < M_2$. $\square$

Lemma 9. *The deterioration rate of the job in Ω_4 is less than the deterioration rate of any job in Ω_5.*

Proof. J_g is at the lth position, and J_k is at the $(l+1)$th position. $\pi_1 = \{J_1, \ldots, J_g, J_k, \ldots, J_n\}$. The objective function of π_1 is M_1. Swap J_g and J_k to get sequence $\pi_2 = \{J_1, \ldots, J_k, J_g, \ldots, J_n\}$. The objective function of π_2 is M_2.

$$M_1 - M_2 = \{cr + [nf - (n-l)c]\}t_0(b_g - b_k) \prod_{i=1}^{l-1} (1 + b_{[i]}). \tag{42}$$

If $b_g < b_k$, $M_1 < M_2$. $\square$

Suppose J_g is at the uth position and J_k is at the vth position in the sequence $\pi_1 = \{J_1, \ldots, J_g, \ldots, J_k, \ldots, J_n\}$, $1 \leq u \leq h, l \leq v \leq n$. The objective function of π_1 is M_1. Swap J_g and J_k to get sequence $\pi_2 = \{J_1, \ldots, J_k, \ldots, J_g, \ldots, J_n\}$. The objective function of π_2 is M_2.

$$
\begin{aligned}
M_1 - M_2 = {}& t_0(b_g - b_k) \prod_{i=1}^{u-1} (1 + b_{[i]}) \Big\{ -a - a \sum_{i=u+1}^{h} (1 + r + b_{[i]}) \prod_{m=u+1}^{i-1} (1 + b_{[m]}) \\
& + c \sum_{i=l}^{v-1} (1 + r + b_{[i]}) \prod_{m=u+1}^{i-1} (1 + b_{[m]}) + cr \prod_{i=u+1}^{v-1} (1 + b_{[i]}) \\
& + [ha + n(e - f)](1 + r + b_{[h]}) \prod_{i=u+1}^{h-1} (1 + b_{[i]}) \\
& + [nf - (n - l + 1)c](1 + r + b_{[l]}) \prod_{i=u+1}^{l-1} (1 + b_{[i]}) \Big\}.
\end{aligned}
\tag{43}
$$

Define

$$\pi_{uv} = -a - a\sum_{i=u+1}^{h}(1+r+b_{[i]})\prod_{m=u+1}^{i-1}(1+b_{[m]}) + c\sum_{i=l}^{v-1}(1+r+b_{[i]})\prod_{m=u+1}^{i-1}(1+b_{[m]})$$

$$+ cr\prod_{i=u+1}^{v-1}(1+b_{[i]}) + [ha + n(e-f)](1+r+b_{[h]})\prod_{i=u+1}^{h-1}(1+b_{[i]})$$

$$+ [nf - (n-l+1)c](1+r+b_{[l]})\prod_{i=u+1}^{l-1}(1+b_{[i]}).$$

$$(44)$$

If $\pi_{uv} > 0$, J_g should be at the uth position; otherwise, J_g should be at the vth position.

4.1.2. Optimal Algorithm

The Algorithm 1 is summarized as follows:

Algorithm 1 $1|CONW, p_j = b_j t_j, q_{psd}| \sum_{i=1}^{n}[aE_{[i]} + cT_{[i]} + ed' + fD]$

Input: t_0, a, c, e, f, b_j, r
Output: The optimal sequence, d', d''
  1: **First step :** Sorted by $b_{[1]} \leq \cdots \leq b_{[n]}$.
  2: **Second step:** Determine $h = \lceil \frac{n(f-e)}{a} \rceil, l = \lceil \frac{n(c-f)}{c} \rceil, d' = C_{[h]}, d'' = C_{[l]}$.
  3: **Third step:** Determine set Ω_3 that contains $l - h - 1$ jobs, i.e., $b_{[1]}, \ldots, b_{[l-h-1]}$.
  4: **Last step:** Determine the jobs of sets $\Omega_1 \cup \Omega_2$ and $\Omega_4 \cup \Omega_5$ by π_{uv}.

Theorem 1. *For the problem* $1|CONW, p_i = b_i t_i, q_{psd}| \sum_{i=1}^{n}[aE_{[i]} + cT_{[i]} + ed' + fD]$, *the complexity of the algorithm is* $O(nlogn)$.

Proof. The first step requires $O(nlogn)$ time. The second and third steps are completed in constant time. The last step requires $O(n)$ time. So the complexity of the algorithm is $O(nlogn)$. $\square$

Example 1. *There are 4 jobs processed in sequence on a single machine.* $t_0 = 1, r = 0.1, b_1 = 2, b_2 = 0.3, b_3 = 1, b_4 = 0.7, a = 4, c = 5, e = 1, f = 2$.
Step 1. *Because* $b_2 \leq b_4 \leq b_3 \leq b_1$, $J_2 \to J_4 \to J_3 \to J_1$.
Step 2. *Calculate the values* $h = \lceil \frac{n(f-e)}{a} \rceil = 1, l = \lceil \frac{n(c-f)}{c} \rceil = 3, d' = C_{[1]}, d'' = C_{[3]}$.
Step 3. J_2 *is contained in set* Ω_3 *which is at the second position.*
Step 4. *(a) When* $u = 1$ *and* $v = 3$, $\pi_{[1][3]} = -3.61 < 0$, J_4 *is determined at the third position;*
(b) When $u = 1$ *and* $v = 4$, $\pi_{[1][4]} = 4.125 > 0$, J_3 *is determined at the first position.*
    Therefore, the optimal sequence is $J_3 \to J_2 \to J_4 \to J_1$.

4.2. The Problem $1|SLKW, p_i = b_i t_i, q_{psd}| \sum_{i=1}^{n}[aE_{[i]} + cT_{[i]} + eq_1 + fD]$

4.2.1. Optimal Properties of the Problem

Lemma 10. *For any job sequence,* q_1 *of the optimal schedule is the* $(1 + r)$ *times the sum of actual processing time for some jobs or* t_0.

Proof. (a) When $(1+r)\sum_{i=0}^{h-1} p_{[i]} < q_1 < (1+r)\sum_{i=0}^{h} p_{[i]}$ and $q_2 = (1+r)\sum_{i=0}^{l-1} p_{[i]}, 1 \leq h < l \leq n$. The objective function is

$$M = -a(1+r)\sum_{i=1}^{h} w_{[i]} + c(1+r)\sum_{i=l+1}^{n} w_{[i]} + [ha + n(e-f)]q_1 + [nf - (n-l)c](1+r)\sum_{i=0}^{l-1} p_{[i]}. \quad (45)$$

when $q_1 = (1+r) \sum\limits_{i=0}^{h-1} p_{[i]}$, the objective function is

$$M_1 = -a(1+r)\sum_{i=1}^{h-1} w_{[i]} + c(1+r)\sum_{i=l+1}^{n} w_{[i]} + [(h-1)a + n(e-f)](1+r)\sum_{i=0}^{h-1} p_{[i]} \\ + [nf - (n-l)c](1+r)\sum_{i=0}^{l-1} p_{[i]}. \tag{46}$$

$$M - M_1 = [ha + n(e-f)][q_1 - (1+r)\sum_{i=0}^{h-1} p_{[i]}]. \tag{47}$$

when $q_1 = (1+r) \sum\limits_{i=0}^{h} p_{[i]}$, the objective function is

$$M_2 = -a(1+r)\sum_{i=1}^{h+1} w_{[i]} + c(1+r)\sum_{i=l+1}^{n} w_{[i]} + [(h+1)a + n(e-f)](1+r)\sum_{i=0}^{h} p_{[i]} \\ + [nf - (n-l)c](1+r)\sum_{i=0}^{l-1} p_{[i]}. \tag{48}$$

$$M - M_2 = [ha + n(e-f)][q_1 - (1+r)\sum_{i=0}^{h} p_{[i]}]. \tag{49}$$

when $ha + n(e-f) < 0$, $M > M_2$; otherwise, $M \geq M_1$.

(b) When $(1+r) \sum\limits_{i=0}^{h-1} p_{[i]} < q_1 < (1+r) \sum\limits_{i=0}^{h} p_{[i]}$ and $(1+r) \sum\limits_{i=0}^{l-1} p_{[i]} < q_2 < (1+r) \sum\limits_{i=0}^{l} p_{[i]}$, $1 \leq h \leq l \leq n$. The objective function is

$$M = -a(1+r)\sum_{i=1}^{h} w_{[i]} + c(1+r)\sum_{i=l+1}^{n} w_{[i]} + [ha + n(e-f)]q_1 + [nf - (n-l)c]q_2. \tag{50}$$

when $q_1 = (1+r) \sum\limits_{i=0}^{h-1} p_{[i]}$, the objective function is

$$M_3 = -a(1+r)\sum_{i=1}^{h-1} w_{[i]} + c(1+r)\sum_{i=l+1}^{n} w_{[i]} + [(h-1)a + n(e-f)](1+r)\sum_{i=0}^{h-1} p_{[i]} \\ + [nf - (n-l)c]q_2. \tag{51}$$

$$M - M_3 = [ha + n(e-f)][q_1 - (1+r)\sum_{i=0}^{h-1} p_{[i]}]. \tag{52}$$

when $q_1 = (1+r) \sum\limits_{i=0}^{h} p_{[i]}$, the objective function is

$$M_4 = -a(1+r)\sum_{i=1}^{h} w_{[i]} + c(1+r)\sum_{i=l+1}^{n} w_{[i]} + [ha + n(e-f)](1+r)\sum_{i=0}^{h} p_{[i]} \\ + [nf - (n-l)c]q_2. \tag{53}$$

$$M - M_4 = [ha + n(e-f)][q_1 - (1+r)\sum_{i=0}^{h} p_{[i]}]. \tag{54}$$

when $ha + n(e-f) < 0$, $M > M_4$; otherwise, $M \geq M_3$. $\quad\square$

Lemma 11. *For any job sequence, q_2 of the optimal schedule is $(1 + r)$ times sum of actual processing time for some jobs or t_0.*

Proof. (a) When $q_1 = (1 + r) \sum\limits_{i=0}^{h-1} p_{[i]}$ and $(1 + r) \sum\limits_{i=0}^{l-1} p_{[i]} < q_2 < (1 + r) \sum\limits_{i=0}^{l} p_{[i]}$, $1 \leq h \leq l \leq n$. The objective function is

$$M = -a(1 + r) \sum_{i=1}^{h-1} w_{[i]} + c(1 + r) \sum_{i=l+1}^{n} w_{[i]} + [(h - 1)a + n(e - f)](1 + r) \sum_{i=0}^{h-1} p_{[i]} \tag{55}$$
$$+ [nf - (n - l)c]q_2.$$

when $q_2 = (1 + r) \sum\limits_{i=0}^{l-1} p_{[i]}$, the objective function is

$$M_1 = -a(1 + r) \sum_{i=1}^{h-1} w_{[i]} + c(1 + r) \sum_{i=l+1}^{n} w_{[i]} + [(h - 1)a + n(e - f)](1 + r) \sum_{i=0}^{h-1} p_{[i]}$$
$$+ [nf - (n - l)c](1 + r) \sum_{i=0}^{l-1} p_{[i]}. \tag{56}$$

$$M - M_1 = [nf - (n - l)c][q_2 - (1 + r) \sum_{i=0}^{l-1} p_{[i]}]. \tag{57}$$

when $q_2 = (1 + r) \sum\limits_{i=0}^{l} p_{[i]}$, the objective function is

$$M_2 = -a(1 + r) \sum_{i=1}^{h-1} w_{[i]} + c(1 + r) \sum_{i=l+2}^{n} w_{[i]} + [(h - 1)a + n(e - f)](1 + r) \sum_{i=0}^{h-1} p_{[i]}$$
$$+ [nf - (n - l - 1)c](1 + r) \sum_{i=0}^{l} p_{[i]}. \tag{58}$$

$$M - M_2 = [nf - (n - l)c][q_2 - (1 + r) \sum_{i=0}^{l} p_{[i]}]. \tag{59}$$

when $nf - (n - l)c < 0$, $M > M_2$; otherwise, $M \geq M_1$.

(b) When $(1 + r) \sum\limits_{i=0}^{h-1} p_{[i]} < q_1 < (1 + r) \sum\limits_{i=0}^{h} p_{[i]}$ and $(1 + r) \sum\limits_{i=0}^{l-1} p_{[i]} < q_2 < (1 + r) \sum\limits_{i=0}^{l} p_{[i]}$, $1 \leq h \leq l \leq n$. The objective function is

$$M = -a(1 + r) \sum_{i=1}^{h} w_{[i]} + c(1 + r) \sum_{i=l+1}^{n} w_{[i]} + [ha + n(e - f)]q_1 + [nf - (n - l)c]q_2. \tag{60}$$

when $q_2 = (1 + r) \sum\limits_{i=0}^{l-1} p_{[i]}$, the objective function is

$$M_3 = -a(1 + r) \sum_{i=1}^{h} w_{[i]} + c(1 + r) \sum_{i=l+1}^{n} w_{[i]} + [ha + n(e - f)]q_1$$
$$+ [nf - (n - l)c](1 + r) \sum_{i=0}^{l-1} p_{[i]}. \tag{61}$$

$$M - M_3 = [nf - (n - l)c][q_2 - (1 + r) \sum_{i=0}^{l-1} p_{[i]}]. \tag{62}$$

when $q_2 = (1+r)\sum_{i=0}^{l} p_{[i]}$, the objective function is

$$M_4 = -a(1+r)\sum_{i=1}^{h} w_{[i]} + c(1+r)\sum_{i=l+2}^{n} w_{[i]} + [ha + n(e-f)]q_1 \\ + [nf - (n-l-1)c](1+r)\sum_{i=0}^{l} p_{[i]}. \tag{63}$$

$$M - M_4 = [nf - (n-l)c][q_2 - (1+r)\sum_{i=0}^{l} p_{[i]}]. \tag{64}$$

when $nf - (n-l)c < 0$, $M > M_4$; otherwise, $M \geq M_3$. $\square$

Lemma 12. *For the optimal schedule, q_1 is $(1+r)\sum_{i=0}^{h-1} p_{[i]}$, q_2 is $(1+r)\sum_{i=0}^{l-1} p_{[i]}$, $h = \lceil \frac{n(f-e)}{a} \rceil$, $l = \lceil \frac{n(c-f)}{c} \rceil$.*

Proof. When $q_1 = (1+r)\sum_{i=0}^{h-1} p_{[i]}$ and $q_2 = (1+r)\sum_{i=0}^{l-1} p_{[i]}$ for the optimal schedule, the objective function is

$$M = -a(1+r)\sum_{i=1}^{h-1} w_{[i]} + c(1+r)\sum_{i=l+1}^{n} w_{[i]} + [(h-1)a + n(e-f)](1+r)\sum_{i=0}^{h-1} p_{[i]} \\ + [nf - (n-l)c](1+r)\sum_{i=0}^{l-1} p_{[i]}. \tag{65}$$

(a) When $q_1 = (1+r)\sum_{i=0}^{h-2} p_{[i]}$ and $q_2 = (1+r)\sum_{i=0}^{l-1} p_{[i]}$, the objective function is

$$M_1 = -a(1+r)\sum_{i=1}^{h-2} w_{[i]} + c(1+r)\sum_{i=l+1}^{n} w_{[i]} + [(h-2)a + n(e-f)](1+r)\sum_{i=0}^{h-2} p_{[i]} \\ + [nf - (n-l)c](1+r)\sum_{i=0}^{l-1} p_{[i]}. \tag{66}$$

$$M - M_1 = [(h-1)a + n(e-f)](1+r)p_{[h-1]} \leq 0. \tag{67}$$

So $h \leq 1 + \frac{n(f-e)}{a}$.

when $q_1 = (1+r)\sum_{i=0}^{h} p_{[i]}$ and $q_2 = (1+r)\sum_{i=0}^{l-1} p_{[i]}$, the objective function is

$$M_2 = -a(1+r)\sum_{i=1}^{h} w_{[i]} + c(1+r)\sum_{i=l+1}^{n} w_{[i]} + [ha + n(e-f)](1+r)\sum_{i=0}^{h} p_{[i]} \\ + [nf - (n-l)c](1+r)\sum_{i=0}^{l-1} p_{[i]}. \tag{68}$$

$$M - M_2 = -[ha + n(e-f)](1+r)p_{[h]} \leq 0. \tag{69}$$

So, $\frac{n(f-e)}{a} \leq h \leq 1 + \frac{n(f-e)}{a}$, $h = \lceil \frac{n(f-e)}{a} \rceil$.

(b) When $q_2 = (1+r) \sum\limits_{i=0}^{l-2} p_{[i]}$ and $q_1 = (1+r) \sum\limits_{i=0}^{h-1} p_{[i]}$, the objective function is

$$M_3 = -a(1+r) \sum_{i=1}^{h-1} w_{[i]} + c(1+r) \sum_{i=l}^{n} w_{[i]} + [(h-1)a + n(e-f)](1+r) \sum_{i=0}^{h-1} p_{[i]} \tag{70}$$
$$+ [nf - (n-l+1)c](1+r) \sum_{i=0}^{l-2} p_{[i]}.$$

$$M - M_3 = [nf - (n-l+1)c](1+r)p_{[l-1]} \le 0. \tag{71}$$

So, $l \le 1 + \frac{n(c-f)}{c}$.

When $q_2 = (1+r) \sum\limits_{i=0}^{l} p_{[i]}$ and $q_1 = (1+r) \sum\limits_{i=0}^{h-1} p_{[i]}$, the objective function is

$$M_4 = -a(1+r) \sum_{i=1}^{h-1} w_{[i]} + c(1+r) \sum_{i=l+2}^{n} w_{[i]} + [(h-1)a + n(e-f)](1+r) \sum_{i=0}^{h-1} p_{[i]} \tag{72}$$
$$+ [nf - (n-l-1)c](1+r) \sum_{i=0}^{l} p_{[i]}.$$

$$M - M_4 = -[nf - (n-l)c](1+r)p_{[l]} \le 0. \tag{73}$$

So $\frac{n(c-f)}{c} \le l \le 1 + \frac{n(c-f)}{c}, l = \lceil \frac{n(c-f)}{c} \rceil.$ $\square$

Suppose $q_1 = (1+r) \sum\limits_{i=0}^{h-1} p_{[i]}$ and $q_2 = (1+r) \sum\limits_{i=0}^{l-1} p_{[j]}$ for the optimal schedule. Three sets $\Omega_1 = \{J_i \in \Omega | i \le h-1\}, \Omega_2 = \{J_i \in \Omega | h \le i \le l-1\}, \Omega_3 = \{J_i \in \Omega | l \le i \le n\}, \Omega$ is the job sequence.

Lemma 13. *In the optimal schedule, the jobs in Ω_1 can be processed in descending order of b_j.*

Proof. J_g is at the uth position and J_k is at the $(u+1)$th position in Ω_1, $\pi_1 = \{J_1, \ldots, J_g, J_k, \ldots, J_n\}, 1 \le u < u+1 \le h-1$. The objective function of π_1 is M_1. Swap J_g and J_k to get sequence $\pi_2 = \{J_1, \ldots, J_k, J_g, \ldots, J_n\}$. The objective function of π_2 is M_2.

$$M_1 - M_2 = -a(1+r)t_0(b_g - b_k) \prod_{i=1}^{u-1}(1 + b_{[i]}). \tag{74}$$

If $b_g > b_k$, $M_1 < M_2$. $\square$

Lemma 14. *In the optimal schedule, the jobs in Ω_2 can be processed in any order of b_j.*

Proof. J_g is at the uth position and J_k is at the $(u+1)$th position in Ω_2, $\pi_1 = \{J_1, \ldots, J_g, J_k, \ldots, J_n\}, h \le u < u+1 \le l-1$. The objective function of π_1 is M_1. Swap J_g and J_k to get sequence $\pi_2 = \{J_1, \ldots, J_k, J_g, \ldots, J_n\}$. The objective function of π_2 is M_2.

$$M_1 = M_2. \tag{75}$$

$\square$

Lemma 15. *In the optimal schedule, the jobs in Ω_3 can be processed in ascending order of b_j.*

Proof. J_g is at the uth position and J_k is at the $(u+1)$th position in Ω_3, $\pi_1 = \{J_1, \ldots, J_g,$ $J_k, \ldots, J_n\}$, $l \le v < v+1 \le n$. The objective function of π_1 is M_1. Swap J_g and J_k to get sequence $\pi_2 = \{J_1, \ldots, J_k, J_g, \ldots, J_n\}$. The objective function of π_2 is M_2.

$$M_1 - M_2 = c(1+r)t_0(b_g - b_k)\prod_{i=1}^{u-1}(1 + b_{[i]}). \tag{76}$$

If $b_g < b_k$, $M_1 < M_2$. $\quad\square$

Lemma 16. *The deterioration rate of any job in Ω_2 is less than the deterioration rate of any job in Ω_1.*

Proof. J_g is at the $(h-1)$th position, and J_k is at the hth position. $\pi_1 = \{J_1, \ldots, J_g, J_k, \ldots,$ $J_n\}$. The objective function of π_1 is M_1. Swap J_g and J_k to get sequence $\pi_2 = \{J_1, \ldots, J_k,$ $J_g, \ldots, J_n\}$. The objective function of π_2 is M_2.

$$M_1 - M_2 = [(h-1)a + n(e-f)](1+r)t_0(b_g - b_k)\prod_{i=1}^{h-2}(1 + b_{[i]}). \tag{77}$$

If $b_k < b_g$, $M_1 < M_2$. $\quad\square$

Lemma 17. *The deterioration rate of any job in Ω_2 is less than the deterioration rate of any job in Ω_3.*

Proof. J_g is at the $(l-1)$th position and J_k is at the lth position. $\pi_1 = \{J_1, \ldots, J_g, J_k, \ldots,$ $J_n\}$. The objective function of π_1 is M_1. Swap J_g and J_k to get sequence $\pi_2 = \{J_1, \ldots, J_k,$ $J_g, \ldots, J_n\}$. The objective function of π_2 is M_2.

$$M_1 - M_2 = [nf - (n-l)c](1+r)t_0(b_g - b_k)\prod_{i=1}^{l-2}(1 + b_{[i]}). \tag{78}$$

If $b_g < b_k$, $M_1 < M_2$. $\quad\square$

Suppose J_g is at the uth position and J_k is at the vth position in the sequence $\pi_1 = \{J_1, \ldots, J_g, \ldots, J_k, \ldots, J_n\}$, $1 \le u \le h-1$, $l \le v \le n$. The objective function of π_1 is M_1. Swap J_g and J_k to get sequence $\pi_2 = \{J_1, \ldots, J_k, \ldots, J_g, \ldots, J_n\}$. The objective function of π_2 is M_2.

$$\begin{aligned}
M_1 - M_2 =\ & t_0(1+r)(b_g - b_k)\prod_{i=1}^{u-1}(1 + b_{[i]})\Big\{-a - a\sum_{i=u+1}^{h-2}\prod_{m=u+1}^{i}(1 + b_{[m]}) \\
& + c\sum_{i=l}^{v-1}\prod_{m=u+1}^{i}(1 + b_{[m]}) + [nf - (n-l)c]\prod_{i=u+1}^{l-1}(1 + b_{[i]}) \\
& + [(h-1)a + n(e-f)]\prod_{i=u+1}^{h-1}(1 + b_{[i]})\Big\}.
\end{aligned} \tag{79}$$

Define

$$\begin{aligned}
\pi_{uv} =\ & -a - a\sum_{i=u+1}^{h-2}\prod_{m=u+1}^{i}(1 + b_{[m]}) + [(h-1)a + n(e-f)]\prod_{i=u+1}^{h-1}(1 + b_{[i]}) \\
& + c\sum_{i=l}^{v-1}\prod_{m=u+1}^{i}(1 + b_{[m]}) + [nf - (n-l)c]\prod_{i=u+1}^{l-1}(1 + b_{[i]}).
\end{aligned} \tag{80}$$

If $\pi_{uv} > 0$, J_g should be at the uth position; otherwise, J_g should be at the vth position.

4.2.2. Optimal Algorithm

The Algorithm 2 is summarized as follows:

Algorithm 2 $1|SLKW, p_i = b_i t_i, q_{psd}| \sum_{i=1}^{n}[aE_{[i]} + cT_{[i]} + eq_1 + fD]$

Input: t_0, a, c, e, f, b_j, r
Output: The optimal sequence, q_1, q_2
  1: **First step :** Sorted by $b_{[1]} \leq \cdots \leq b_{[n]}$.
  2: **Second step:** When $c \leq f \leq e, q_1 = q_2 = t_0, \Omega_1 \cup \Omega_2 = \phi, \Omega_3 = \{J_{[1]}, \ldots, J_{[n]}\}$.
  3: **Third step:** When $c > f$ and $f \leq e, q_1 = t_0, q_2 = (1+r)\sum_{i=0}^{l-1} p_{[i]}, l = \lceil \frac{n(c-f)}{c} \rceil$. $\Omega_1 = \phi$,
    $\Omega_2 = \{J_{[1]}, \ldots, J_{[l]}\}, \Omega_3 = \{J_{[l+1]}, \ldots, J_{[n]}\}$.
  4: **Forth step:** Determine $h = \lceil \frac{n(f-e)}{a} \rceil, l = \lceil \frac{n(c-f)}{c} \rceil, q_1 = (1+r)\sum_{i=0}^{h-1} p_{[i]}, q_2 = (1+$
    $r)\sum_{i=0}^{l-1} p_{[i]}$.
  5: **Last step:** $\Omega_2 = \{J_{[1]}, \ldots, J_{[l-h]}\}$. Determine the jobs of sets Ω_1 and Ω_3 by π_{uv}.

Theorem 2. *For the problem* $1|SLKW, p_i = b_i t_i, q_{psd}| \sum_{i=1}^{n}[aE_{[i]} + cT_{[i]} + eq_1 + fD]$, *the complexity of the algorithm is* $O(nlogn)$.

Proof. The first step requires $O(nlogn)$ time. The second, third and forth steps are completed in constant time. The last step requires $O(n)$ time. So the complexity of the algorithm is $O(nlogn)$. $\square$

Example 2. *There are 4 jobs processed in sequence on a single machine.* $t_0 = 1, r = 0.1, b_1 = 2,$
$b_2 = 0.3, b_3 = 1, b_4 = 0.7, a = 4, c = 5, e = 1, f = 2.$
Step 1. Because $b_2 \leq b_4 \leq b_3 \leq b_1, J_2 \rightarrow J_4 \rightarrow J_3 \rightarrow J_1$.
Step 2. Calculate the values $h = \lceil \frac{n(f-e)}{a} \rceil = 1, l = \lceil \frac{n(c-f)}{c} \rceil = 3, q_1 = (1+r)t_0, q_2 = (1+r)w_{[3]}$.
Step 3. J_2 *and* J_4 *are contained in set* Ω_2 *which are at the first and second position.*
Step 4. J_3 *and* J_1 *are contained in set* Ω_3, *which are at the third and forth positions,* $\Omega_1 = \phi$.
    Therefore, the optimal sequence is $J_2 \rightarrow J_4 \rightarrow J_3 \rightarrow J_1$.

4.3. Discussion

This paper studies scheduling problems involving both simple linear degradation and past sequence dependent delivery time under the common and slack due window assignment. To the best of our knowledge, such articles are rare for the common or slack due window assignment. Small perturbation technique and adjacent switching technique are effective methods to deal with scheduling problems. Based on the small perturbations technique and adjacent exchange technique, we obtain the propositions of the method. By the propositions, the polynomial time algorithms are proposed to obtain the optimal sequence. However, not all scheduling problems can be solved by these techniques. Specific problems need to be analyzed in detail. In the future research, it is worth investigating multi-machine scheduling problems.

5. Conclusions

The single machine scheduling problem with deteriorating jobs and delivery time is considered under due window assignment. The goal is to minimize the window location, window size, earliness and tardiness. Based on the small perturbations technique and adjacent exchange technique, we obtain the propositions of the problems. However, not all scheduling problems can be solved by these techniques. Specific problems need to be analyzed in detail. For common and slack due window assignment, we prove that the two objective functions are polynomial time solvable in $O(nlogn)$ time. We propose the corresponding algorithms to obtain the optimal sequence, window location and window size. In the future, the multi-machine environment can be considered to expand the research, i.e., parallel machines and flow shop setting. The more general deterioration processing time is also considered for a single machine scheduling or the multi-machine scheduling.

Author Contributions: Conceptualization, J.Q. ; methodology, J.Q.; validation, Y.Z.; investigation, Y.Z.; writing—original draft preparation, J.Q.; writing—review and editing, Y.Z.; supervision, Y.Z. All authors have read and agreed to the published version of the manuscript.

Funding: This research was funded by J.Q. of the Fundamental Research Funds for the Central Universities grant number N2105020. and Y.Z. of the Fundamental Research Funds for the Central Universities grant number N2105021. and Y.Z. of the Natural Science Foundation of Liaoning Province Project grant number 2021-MS-102.

Data Availability Statement: Not applicable.

Acknowledgments: We thank the anonymous for their helpful comments and insights that significantly improved our paper.

Conflicts of Interest: The authors declare no conflict of interest.

References

1. Jackson, J.R. Scheduling a production line to minimize maximum tardiness. In *Management Science Research Project*; University of California: Los Angeles, CA, USA, 1955.
2. Seidmann, A.; Panwalkar, S.S.; Smith, M.L. Optimal assignment of due-dates for a single processor scheduling problem. *Int. J. Prod. Res.* **1981**, *19*, 393–399. [CrossRef]
3. Panwalkar, S.S.; Smith, M.L.; Seidmann, A. Common due date assignment to minimize total penalty for the one machine scheduling problem. *Oper. Res.* **1982**, *30*, 391–399. [CrossRef]
4. Li, G.; Luo, M.L.; Zhang, W.J.; Wang, X.Y. Single-machine due-window assignment scheduling based on common flow allowance, learning effect and resource allocation. *Int. J. Prod. Res.* **2015**, *53*, 1228–1241. [CrossRef]
5. Yang, S.W.; Wan, L.; Yin, N. Research on single machine SLK/DIF due window assignment problem with learning effect and deteriorating jobs. *Appl. Math. Model.* **2015**, *39*, 4593–4598. [CrossRef]
6. Yin, Y.; Wang, D.; Cheng, T.C.E.; Wu, C.C. Bi-criterion single machine scheduling and due wWindow assignment with common flow allowances and resource allocation. *J. Oper. Res. Soc.* **2016**, *67*, 1169–1183. [CrossRef]
7. Wang, D.; Yin, Y.; Cheng, T.C.E. A bicriterion approach to common flow allowances due window assignment and scheduling with controllable processing times. *Nav. Res. Log.* **2017**, *64*, 41–63. [CrossRef]
8. Wang, J.B.; Zhang, B.; Li, L.; Bai, D.; Feng, Y.B. Due-window assignment scheduling problems with position-dependent weights on a single machine. *Eng. Optimiz.* **2020**, *52*, 185–193. [CrossRef]
9. Sun, X.Y.; Geng, X.N.; Liu, T. Due-window assignment scheduling in the proportionate flow shop setting. *Ann. Oper. Res.* **2020**, *292*, 113–131. [CrossRef]
10. Yue, Q.; Zhou, S. Due-window assignment scheduling problem with stochastic processing times. *Eur. J. Oper. Res.* **2021**, *290*, 453–468. [CrossRef]
11. Gupta, J.N.D.; Gupta, S.K. Single facility scheduling with nonlinear processing times. *Comput. Ind. Eng.* **1998**, *14*, 387–393. [CrossRef]
12. Yue, Q.; Wang, G. Scheduling deteriorating jobs with common due window assignment. *Ind. Eng. Manag.* **2015**, *20*, 42–47.
13. Wang, J.B.; Li, L. Machine scheduling with deteriorating jobs and modifying maintenance activities. *Comput. J.* **2018**, *61*, 47–53. [CrossRef]
14. Sun, X.; Geng, X.N. Single-machine scheduling with deteriorating effects and machine maintenance. *Int. J. Prod. Res.* **2019**, *57*, 3186–3199. [CrossRef]
15. Cheng, T.C.E.; Kravchenko, S.A.; Lin, B.M.T. Scheduling step-deteriorating jobs to minimize the total completion time. *Comput. Ind. Eng.* **2020**, *144*, 106329. [CrossRef]
16. Liang, X.X.; Liu, M.Q.; Feng, Y.B.; Wang, J.B.; Wen, L.S. Solution algorithms for single machine resource allocation scheduling with deteriorating jobs and group technology. *Eng. Optimiz.* **2020**, *52*, 1184–1197. [CrossRef]
17. Koulamas, C.; Kyparisis, G.J. Single-machine scheduling problems with past-sequence-dependent setup times. *Eur. J. Oper. Res.* **2008**, *187*, 1045–1049. [CrossRef]
18. Liu, M.; Zheng, F.; Chu, C.; Xu, Y. New results on singlemachine scheduling with past-sequence-dependent delivery times. *Teor. Comput. Sci.* **2012**, *438*, 55–61. [CrossRef]
19. Zhao, C.; Tang, H. Single machine scheduling problems with general position-dependent processing times and past sequence dependent delivery times. *J. Appl. Math. Comput.* **2014**, *45*, 259–274. [CrossRef]
20. Mir, S.S.M.; Javad, R.; Hossein, M. Scheduling parallel machine problem under general effects of deterioration and learning with past-sequence-dependent setup time: Heuristic and meta-heuristic approaches. *Soft Comput.* **2020**, *24*, 1335–1355.

21. Toksari, M.D.; Aydogan, E.K.; Atalay, B.; Sari, S. Some scheduling problems with sum of logarithm processing times based learning effect and exponential past sequence dependent delivery times. *J. Ind. Manag. Optim.* **2021**, *ahead of print.*
22. Wang, J.B.; Cui, B.; Ji, P.; Liu, W.W. Research on single-machine scheduling with position-dependent weights and past-sequence-dependent delivery times. *J. Comb. Optim.* **2021**, *41*, 290–303. [CrossRef]

 *mathematics*

Article

Analyzing the Collatz Conjecture Using the Mathematical Complete Induction Method

Mercedes Orús-Lacort [1,2] **and Christophe Jouis** [3,4,*]

1   College Mathematics, Universitat Oberta de Catalunya, Rambla del Poblenou 156, 08018 Barcelona, Spain;
    mercedes.orus@gmail.com
2   College Mathematics, Universidad Nacional de Educación a Distancia, Calle Pintor Sorolla 21,
    46002 Valencia, Spain
3   Département Langues Etrangères Appliquées (LEA), Université de la Sorbonne Nouvelle Paris 3,
    75005 Paris, France
4   Centre d'Analyse et de Mathématique Sociales—CAMS, 75006 Paris, France
*   Correspondence: christophe.jouis@sorbonne-nouvelle.fr

Abstract: In this paper, we demonstrate the Collatz conjecture using the mathematical complete induction method. We show that this conjecture is satisfied for the first values of natural numbers, and in analyzing the sequence generated by odd numbers, we can deduce a formula for the general term of the Collatz sequence for any odd natural number n after several iterations. This formula is used in one case that we analyze using the mathematical complete induction method in the process of demonstrating the conjecture.

Keywords: number theory; Collatz conjecture

MSC: 11-02

Citation: Orús-Lacort, M.; Jouis, C. Analyzing the Collatz Conjecture Using the Mathematical Complete Induction Method. *Mathematics* **2022**, *10*, 1972. https://doi.org/10.3390/math10121972

Academic Editors: Xiang Li, Shuo Zhang and Wei Zhang

Received: 10 May 2022
Accepted: 5 June 2022
Published: 8 June 2022

Publisher's Note: MDPI stays neutral with regard to jurisdictional claims in published maps and institutional affiliations.

1. Introduction

The Collatz conjecture is one of the best-known unsolved problems in sequences and series of number theory. It states:

"For any positive integer n, if a sequence is defined by recurrence, so that, if the previous term is even then the next term is obtained by dividing by 2 the previous term, and if it is odd it is obtained by multiplying by 3 the previous term and adding 1, this sequence always reaches the number 1, and therefore, its last terms will always be the cycle 4, 2, 1.".

This conjecture is called the Collatz Conjecture because it was stated by Lothar Collatz in 1937 [1]. However, it is also known by other names such as the $3n + 1$ conjecture, the Ulam conjecture, Kakutani's problem, the Thwaites conjecture, Hasse's algorithm, the Syracuse problem [2], the hailstone sequence or hailstone numbers, because the values ascend or descend multiple times [3], or the wondrous numbers [4].

This conjecture has not been proven; however, many mathematicians have studied it and achieved important results, see [5–18]. Most of them have argued that the conjecture is true, as a result of the experimental evidence and heuristic arguments [12].

In this paper, we demonstrate the Collatz conjecture using the mathematical complete induction method. We show that this conjecture is satisfied for the first values of natural numbers. From this analysis, we can deduce a formula for the general term of Collatz sequence for any odd natural number n after several iterations, and this formula is used in one case that we analyze using the mathematical complete induction method in the process of demonstrating the conjecture.

The paper is organized as follows: In Section 2, we show that the conjecture is satisfied for the first values of natural numbers, and we deduce a formula for the general term of the Collatz sequence for any odd natural number n after several iterations. In Section 3, we demonstrate the Collatz conjecture using the mathematical complete induction method. Finally, we discuss our conclusions in Section 4.

2. Sequences for the First Natural Numbers and Formula for the General Term of Collatz Sequence for Any Odd Natural Number n

Formally, each term of the sequence of numbers is equivalent to applying the following function to n, and each term of the sequence:

$$f(n) = \begin{cases} \frac{n}{2}, & \text{if } n \text{ is even} \\ 3n+1, & \text{if } n \text{ is odd} \end{cases}$$

Therefore, given any natural number, we can consider its orbit; that is, the successive images when iterating the function, in the following way.

For example, if $n = 13$:

$$\begin{aligned} x_1 &= f(13) = 3 \times 13 + 1 = 40 \\ x_2 &= f(40) = \frac{40}{2} = 20 \\ x_3 &= f(20) = \frac{20}{2} = 10; \text{ etc} \end{aligned} \tag{1}$$

The conjecture says that we will always reach 1 (and therefore cycle 4, 2, 1) when starting with any natural number.

We will now present what happens with the first natural numbers.

For $n = 1$:

$$\begin{aligned} x_1 &= f(1) = 3 \times 1 + 1 = 4 \\ x_2 &= f(4) = \frac{4}{2} = 2 \\ x_3 &= f(2) = \frac{2}{2} = 1 \end{aligned} \tag{2}$$

For $n = 2$:

$$x_1 = f(2) = \frac{2}{2} = 1 \tag{3}$$

For $n = 3$:

$$\begin{aligned} x_1 &= f(3) = 3 \times 3 + 1 = 10 \\ x_2 &= f(10) = \frac{10}{2} = 5 \\ x_3 &= f(5) = 3 \times 5 + 1 = 16 \\ x_4 &= f(16) = \frac{16}{2} = 8 \\ x_5 &= f(8) = \frac{8}{2} = 4 \\ x_6 &= f(4) = \frac{4}{2} = 2 \\ x_7 &= f(2) = \frac{2}{2} = 1 \end{aligned} \tag{4}$$

Therefore, for the first value of n, we observe that the conjecture is satisfied. The conjecture is also satisfied for numerous other numbers greater than 3, and for numbers that are a power of 2, we will also always reach 1, dividing successively by 2.

Given this, at a certain point in the process of demonstration using the mathematical complete induction method, we will need a formula that could represent the general term of the Collatz sequence for any odd natural number n after several iterations, and we examine how this formula could be below.

If n is an odd natural number, then using the definition of $f(n)$, the first iteration would be:

$$x_1 = 3n + 1$$

Since $3n + 1$ is always an even number, the next iteration would be:

$$x_2 = \frac{3n + 1}{2}$$

The next iteration will depend on whether the previously obtained result is even or odd, and since it is possible to obtain an even number in the following or next iterations, let us assume that an even number is obtained in the following $r_1 - 1$ iteration until we again obtain an odd number ($r_1 \geq 1$). Therefore, the result obtained after $r_1 - 1$ iteration would be:

$$x_{r_1+1} = \frac{3n+1}{2^{r_1}}$$

Now, if $\frac{3n+1}{2^{r_1}}$ is an odd number, the next iteration would be:

$$x_{r_1+2} = 3 \cdot \frac{3n+1}{2^{r_1}} + 1$$
$$x_{r_1+2} = \frac{3^2n+3+2^{r_1}}{2^{r_1}}$$

Since $\frac{3^2n+3+2^{r_1}}{2^{r_1}}$ is an even number, the next iteration would be:

$$x_{r_1+3} = \frac{3^2n + 3 + 2^{r_1}}{2^{r_1+1}}$$

Moreover, for the same reason as before, we will assume that we obtain an even number in the next $r_2 - 1$ iteration until we obtain again an odd number ($r_2 \geq 1$). Therefore, the result would be:

$$x_{r_1+r_2+2} = \frac{3^2n + 3 + 2^{r_1}}{2^{r_1+r_2}}$$

Following the same reasoning, this process will continue, and after several iterations, for example, $r_1 + r_2 + \ldots + r_k + k$ iterations, we would find that the term $x_{r1+r2+ \ldots +rk+k}$ of the sequence would be:

$$x_{r_1+r_2+\ldots+r_k+k} = \frac{3^k n + 3^{k-1} + 3^{k-2}2^{r_1} + 3^{k-3}2^{r_1+r_2} + \ldots + 2^{r_1+r_2+\ldots+r_{k-1}}}{2^{r_1+r_2+\ldots+r_k}} \tag{5}$$

This formula will be used in the next section when we analyze a specific case using the mathematical complete induction method.

3. Proof of the Collatz Conjecture Using Mathematical Complete Induction

We need to prove that, for all $n \in N$, the obtained sequence reaches 1.

In the previous section, we saw that this holds true for values of n from 1 to 3. Moreover, it is also proven to be true for values higher than $n = 3$, and it is found to also be true, for example, for all $n = 2^s$, $s \in N$, because we always reach 1 when dividing successively by 2.

To apply the mathematical complete induction method, we will assume that, for a certain $m \in N$ that is sufficiently high in value and for any other natural number less than m, we can reach the number 1 with successive iterations. Hence, if we can prove that it is true for $m + 1$, we can conclude that it is true for all $n \in N$. Therefore, in our induction hypothesis, we assume that it is true for a sufficiently large $m \in N$ value and any other natural number less than m.

We explore below if this is true also for $m + 1$. Note that $m + 1$ can be an odd or even number, depending on whether m is even or odd, respectively. Hence, we will analyze both cases:

Case 1: $m + 1$ is an even number

If $m + 1$ is an even number, it is because m is an odd number; that is, $m = 2t + 1$ for $t \in N$. Hence, $m + 1 = 2t + 2$, and the first iteration applying the definition of $f(n)$ would be:

$$x_1 = \frac{2t+2}{2} = t+1$$

Note that $t + 1 < 2t + 1 = m$, and as we were assuming that we reach the number 1 for all natural numbers less or equal than m, then we reach the number 1 for $t + 1$.

Therefore, if $m + 1$ is an even number, the obtained sequence reaches 1.

Case 2: $m + 1$ is an odd number

If $m + 1$ is an odd number, it is because m is an even number; that is, $m = 2t$ for $t \in \mathbb{N}$, and $t > 1$. Hence, $m + 1 = 2t + 1$, and the first iteration applying the definition of $f(n)$ would be:

$$x_1 = 3(2t + 1) + 1 = 6t + 4$$

Given that $6t + 4$ is an even number, the next iteration would be:

$$x_2 = \frac{6t + 4}{2} = 3t + 2$$

At this point, note that the next iteration depends on whether t is an even or odd number; if t is an even number, then $3t + 2$ will be an even number; however, if t is an odd number, then $3t + 2$ will be an odd number.

Next, we will analyze both options:

Option 1: t is an even number:

If t is an even number, then $3t + 2$ is an even number, and the next iteration applying the definition of $f(n)$ would be:

$$x_3 = \frac{3t + 2}{2}$$

Note that $\frac{3t+2}{2} \leq 2t = m$ because $t \geq 2$, and as we were assuming that we reach the number 1 for all natural numbers less or equal than m, then we can reach number 1 for $\frac{3t+2}{2}$ and for $m + 1$. Therefore, if $m + 1$ is an odd number and t an even number, the sequence obtained reaches 1.

Option 2: t is an odd number:

If t is an odd number, then $3t + 2$ is an odd number, and now using the formula from Equation (5), which represents the general term of Collatz sequence for any odd natural number after several iterations, we have that after $r_1 + r_2 + \ldots + r_k + k$ iterations, we would obtain:

$$x_{r_1+r_2+\ldots+r_k+k} = \frac{3^k(3t + 2) + 3^{k-1} + 3^{k-2}2^{r_1} + 3^{k-3}2^{r_1+r_2} + \ldots + 2^{r_1+r_2+\ldots+r_{k-1}}}{2^{r_1+r_2+\ldots+r_k}} \tag{6}$$

Rewriting the above formula, we have:

$$\frac{3^k t + 3^{k-1} + 3^{k-2}2^{r_1} + 3^{k-3}2^{r_1+r_2} + \ldots + 2^{r_1+r_2+\ldots+r_{k-1}}}{2^{r_1+r_2+\ldots+r_k}} + \frac{3^k(2t + 2)}{2^{r_1+r_2+\ldots+r_k}} \tag{7}$$

At this point, note that for $m = 2t$, t being an odd natural number, we were assuming that the sequence reaches number 1, and calculating the first terms for the sequence of $m = 2t$, we have:

$$\begin{aligned} x_1 &= \tfrac{2t}{2} = t \\ x_2 &= 3t + 1 \\ x_3 &= \tfrac{3t+1}{2} \end{aligned} \tag{8}$$

The next iteration will depend on whether the previously obtained result is even or odd, and since we can obtain an even number in the following or next iterations, then using the formula from Equation (5) and after the next $s_1 + s_2 + \ldots + s_u + u - 3$ iterations, we would obtain:

$$x_{s_1+s_2+\ldots+s_u+u} = \frac{3^u t + 3^{u-1} + 3^{u-2}2^{s_1} + 3^{u-3}2^{s_1+s_2} + \ldots + 2^{s_1+s_2+\ldots+s_{u-1}}}{2^{s_1+s_2+\ldots+s_u}} \tag{9}$$

If we call $S = \sum_{i=1}^{u} s_i$, and since for $m = 2t$ we were assuming that the sequence reaches the number 1, it means that the limit of x_{S+u} when S and u tend to infinity is equal to 1.

Thus, if we call $R = \sum_{i=1}^{k} r_i$ in Equation (7) and we calculate the limit when R and k tend to infinity, we have:

$$\lim_{(R,k)\to(\infty,\infty)} \frac{3^k t + 3^{k-1} + 3^{k-2}2^{r_1} + 3^{k-3}2^{r_1+r_2} + \dots + 2^{r_1+r_2+\dots+r_{k-1}}}{2^{r_1+r_2+\dots+r_k}} + \frac{3^k(2t+2)}{2^{r_1+r_2+\dots+r_k}} =$$

$$= \lim_{(R,k)\to(\infty,\infty)} \frac{3^k t + 3^{k-1} + 3^{k-2}2^{r_1} + 3^{k-3}2^{r_1+r_2} + \dots + 2^{r_1+r_2+\dots+r_{k-1}}}{2^{r_1+r_2+\dots+r_k}} + \lim_{(R,k)\to(\infty,\infty)} \frac{3^k(2t+2)}{2^{r_1+r_2+\dots+r_k}} =$$

$$= \lim_{(S,u)\to(\infty,\infty)} \frac{3^u t + 3^{u-1} + 3^{u-2}2^{s_1} + 3^{u-3}2^{s_1+s_2} + \dots + 2^{s_1+s_2+\dots+s_{u-1}}}{2^{s_1+s_2+\dots+s_u}} + \lim_{(R,k)\to(\infty,\infty)} \frac{3^k(2t+2)}{2^{r_1+r_2+\dots+r_k}} =$$

$$= 1 + \lim_{(R,k)\to(\infty,\infty)} \frac{3^k(2t+2)}{2^R}$$

Note now that the value of R cannot be less than k, because in using the definition of the sequence, every time a term x_i in the sequence is odd, the next calculated term is always even.

The value of R cannot be equal to k either, because for this to happen, it would mean that all $r_i = 1$ that is, every time we divide by 2, the value obtained is an odd number. Moreover, it can be shown how this is only possible if the value of t is a value that increases as we calculate new iterations. However, we should remember that the value of t is an odd number that we take at random so that $3t + 2$ is an odd number, but without changing the t value in each iteration.

Next, it is shown how this t value should be changing, so R would be equal to k.

Recall that $3t + 2$ is odd because t is also odd, and therefore, the next term of the sequence would be:

$$x_4 = 3(3t + 2) + 1 = 9t + 7$$

Since $9t + 7$ is even, the next term in the sequence would be:

$$x_5 = \frac{9t + 7}{2}$$

For $\frac{9t+7}{2}$ to be odd, there must be an $a \in \mathbb{N}$ such that:

$$\frac{9t + 7}{2} = 2a + 1$$

Hence, the question now is: Are there natural numbers t and a that satisfy the previous equation? The answer is yes, when $t = 4w + 3$ and $a = 9w + 8$ for $w \in \mathbb{N}$.

Therefore, assuming that $\frac{9t+7}{2}$ is odd because $t = 4w + 3$ for $w \in \mathbb{N}$, the next term in the sequence would be:

$$x_6 = 3\left(\frac{9t + 7}{2}\right) + 1 = \frac{27t + 23}{2}$$

Since this value is even, the next term would be:

$$x_7 = \frac{27t + 23}{2}$$

The question now is: Can the previous value be odd? That is, are there natural numbers t and a such that $27t + 23 = 8a + 4$? The answer is yes when $t = 8w + 7$ for $w \in \mathbb{N}$.

Hence, we can observe that the value of t has increased. Previously, it was $t = 4w + 3 = 2^2 w + (2^2 - 1)$, and now it should be $t = 8w + 7 = 2^3 w + (2^3 - 1)$ for $w \in \mathbb{N}$, and so on.

Hence, for $R = k$, the t value would be increasing, increasing the exponent of the power of 2, which means that, in this case, it is not possible when setting an odd value of t; however, to make it possible, the value of t must be changing, increasing in the way we have seen. Hence, this implies that the case $R = k$ is not possible.

Therefore $R > k$, then $R = k + v$ for $v \in \mathbb{N}$, and then $v > k$ or $v < k$ (this last option could happen if many $r_i = 1$).

Analyzing both cases, we have:

- First case $v > k$: If $v > k$ then $v = k + w$ for $w \in \mathbb{N}$, $R = 2k + w$, and the above limit when R and k tend to infinity would be calculated as:

$$1 + \lim_{(R,k) \to (\infty,\infty)} \frac{3^k(2t+2)}{2^R} = 1 + \lim_{k \to \infty} \frac{3^k(2t+2)}{2^{2k+w}} = 1 + \lim_{k \to \infty} \left(\frac{3}{4}\right)^k \frac{2t+2}{2^w} = 1 + 0 = 1$$

- Second case $v < k$: If $v < k$ then $v = k - w$ for $w \in \mathbb{N}$ and $w < k$, $R = 2k - w$, and the above limit when R and k tend to infinity would be calculated as:

$$1 + \lim_{(R,k) \to (\infty,\infty)} \frac{3^k(2t+2)}{2^R} = 1 + \lim_{k \to \infty} \frac{3^k(2t+2)}{2^{2k-w}} = 1 + \lim_{k \to \infty} \left(\frac{3}{4}\right)^k \frac{2t+2}{2^{-w}} = 1 + 0 = 1$$

Thus, for an odd number $m + 1$ and an odd number t, the obtained sequence also reaches 1.

Therefore, for an $m + 1$ even or odd number, the sequence reaches 1, and this means that, for all natural numbers n, the Collatz sequence always reaches 1, as we sought to prove.

4. Conclusions

We have shown how to use the mathematical complete induction method to prove the Collatz conjecture. We show that this conjecture is satisfied for the first values of natural numbers. From this analysis, we can deduce a formula for the general term of a Collatz sequence for any odd natural number n after several iterations. This formula is used in one case that we analyzed by mathematical complete induction during the demonstration. Thus, using the mathematical complete induction method, we have demonstrated that the Collatz conjecture is true.

Author Contributions: Conceptualization, M.O.-L. and C.J.; Data curation, C.J.; Formal analysis, M.O.-L. and C.J.; Funding acquisition, C.J.; Investigation, M.O.-L.; Methodology, M.O.-L.; Software, C.J.; Writing—original draft, M.O.-L. All authors have read and agreed to the published version of the manuscript.

Funding: This research received no external funding.

Acknowledgments: We acknowledge Roman Orus for proposing the dissemination of this result.

Conflicts of Interest: The authors declare no conflict of interest.

References

1. O'Connor, J.J.; Robertson, E.F. *Lothar Collatz*; St Andrews University School of Mathematics and Statistics: St Andrews, UK, 2006.
2. Maddux, C.D.; Johnson, D.L. *Logo: A Retrospective*; The Problem Is Also Known by Several Other Names, Including: Ulam's Conjecture, the Hailstone Problem, the Syracuse Problem, Kakutani's Problem, Hasse's Algorithm, and the Collatz Problem; Haworth Press: New York, NY, USA, 1997; p. 160. ISBN 0-7890-0374-0.
3. Pickover, C.A. *Wonders of Numbers*; Oxford University Press: Oxford, UK, 2001; pp. 116–118.
4. Hofstadter, D.R. *Gödel, Escher, Bach*; Basic Books: New York, NY, USA, 1979; pp. 400–402. ISBN 0-465-02685-0.
5. Guy, R.K. E17: Permutation Sequences. In *Unsolved Problems in Number Theory*, 3rd ed.; Springer: Berlin/Heidelberg, Germany, 2004; pp. 336–337. ISBN 0-387-20860-7.
6. Guy, R.K. Don't try to solve these problems. *Am. Math. Mon.* **1983**, *90*, 35–41. [CrossRef]
7. Lagarias, J.C. (Ed.) *The Ultimate Challenge: The 3x + 1 Problem*; American Mathematical Society: Providence, RI, USA, 2010; p. 4, ISBN 0821849409.
8. Leavens, G.T.; Vermeulen, M. 3x + 1 Search Programs. *Comput. Math. Appl.* **1992**, *24*, 79–99. [CrossRef]
9. Simons, J.; de Weger, B. Theoretical and computational bounds for m–cycles of the 3n + 1 problem (PDF). *Acta Arith.* **2003**, *117*, 51–70. [CrossRef]
10. Steiner, R.P. A Theorem on the Syracuse Problem. In Proceedings of the 7th Manitoba Conference on Numerical Mathematics, 29 September–1 October 1977; Utilitas Mathematica Pub.: Winnipeg, MB, Canada, 1977; pp. 553–559.
11. Simons, J.L. On the nonexistence of 2–cycles for the 3x + 1 problem. *Math. Comput.* **2005**, *74*, 1565–1572. [CrossRef]

12. Krasikov, I.; Lagarias, J.C. Bounds for the $3x + 1$ problem using difference inequalities. *arXiv* **2003**, arXiv:math/0205002. [CrossRef]
13. Colussi, L. The convergence classes of Collatz function. *Theor. Comput. Sci.* **2011**, *412*, 5409–5419. [CrossRef]
14. Hew, P.C. Working in binary protects the repetends of 1/3 h: Comment on Colussi's The convergence classes of Collatz function. *Theor. Comput. Sci.* **2016**, *618*, 135–141. [CrossRef]
15. Terras, R. A stopping time problem on the positive integers (PDF). *Pol. Akad. Nauk.* **1976**, *30*, 241–252.
16. Chamberland, M. A continuous extension of the $3x + 1$ problem to the real line. *Dyn. Contin. Discret. Impulsive Syst.* **1996**, *2*, 495–509.
17. Letherman, S.; Schleicher, D.; Wood, R. The $(3n + 1)$-Problem and Holomorphic Dynamics. *Exp. Math.* **1999**, *8*, 241–252. [CrossRef]
18. Conway, J.H. Unpredictable Iterations. In Proceedings of the 1972 Number Theory Conference, Boulder, CO, USA, 14–18 August 1972; pp. 49–52.

Article

Landslide Displacement Prediction Based on Time-Frequency Analysis and LMD-BiLSTM Model

Zian Lin [1,2], Yuanfa Ji [2,3], Weibin Liang [2,3] and Xiyan Sun [2,3,*]

[1] School of Computer Science and Information Security, Guilin University of Electronic Technology, Guilin 541004, China; 20031102010@mails.guet.edu.cn
[2] Guangxi Key Laboratory of Precision Navigation Technology and Application, Guilin University of Electronic Technology, Guilin 541004, China; jiyuanfa@guet.edu.cn (Y.J.); weibin@guet.edu.cn (W.L.)
[3] Information and Communication School, Guilin University of Electronic Technology, Guilin 541004, China
* Correspondence: sunxiyan1@163.com

Abstract: In landslide displacement prediction, random factors that would affect the performance of prediction are usually ignored by using a time series analysis method. In order to solve this problem, in this paper, a landslide displacement prediction model, the local mean decomposition-bidirectional long short-term memory (LMD-BiLSTM), is proposed based on the time-frequency analysis method. The model uses the local mean decomposition (LMD) algorithm to decompose landslide displacement and obtains several subsequences of landslide displacement with different frequencies. This paper analyzes the internal relationship between the landslide displacement and rainfall, reservoir water level, and landslide state. The maximum information coefficient (MIC) algorithm is used to calculate the intrinsic correlation between each subsequence of landslide displacement and rainfall, reservoir water level, and landslide state. Subsequences of influential factors with high correlation are selected as input variables of the bidirectional long short-term memory (BiLSTM) model to predict each subsequence. Finally, the predicted results of each of the subsequences are added to obtain the final predicted displacement. The proposed LMD-BiLSTM model effectiveness is verified based on the Baishuihe landslide. The prediction results and evaluation indexes show that the model can accurately predict landslide displacement.

Keywords: landslide displacement prediction; local mean decomposition; bidirectional long short-term memory; maximal information coefficient

MSC: 68T07

Citation: Lin, Z.; Ji, Y.; Liang, W.; Sun, X. Landslide Displacement Prediction Based on Time-Frequency Analysis and LMD-BiLSTM Model. *Mathematics* **2022**, *10*, 2203. https://doi.org/10.3390/math10132203

Academic Editors: Xiang Li, Shuo Zhang and Wei Zhang

Received: 24 May 2022
Accepted: 22 June 2022
Published: 24 June 2022

Publisher's Note: MDPI stays neutral with regard to jurisdictional claims in published maps and institutional affiliations.

1. Introduction

Landslide geological disasters are a serious type of geological disaster that occur worldwide, inducing serious threats and losses to the development of human society. In recent years, under the influence of extreme global climate change, seismic activities, coupled with the rapid development of human engineering activities, have become more intense interferences to the natural environment, directly leading to geological disasters with greater intensity and higher frequency [1,2]. This increases the difficulty of developing landslide disaster reduction strategies [3]. Combined with land use change, population growth, uncontrolled urbanization, and so on in vulnerable areas, the landslide risk level continues to rise [4]. The Three Gorges Reservoir Area is one of the areas with a high incidence of landslide disasters in China [5,6]. Every year, landslides cause very large losses to local lives and property, so it is necessary to prevent and control such landslide disasters [7].

Landslide displacement refers to the distance that the soil or rock mass on the slope slides along the slope as a whole or separately under the influence of gravity under the influence of river erosion, groundwater activity, rain immersion, earthquakes, and artificial slope cutting [8]. The generation of landslide displacement is influenced by both the internal geological conditions (geological structure, landform, lithology, etc.) and external influencing factors (rainfall, reservoir water level, etc.) of a given landslide location [9–11]. Landslide displacement prediction is a frontier problem in the international landslide research field [12]. Landslide displacement prediction is an important part of landslide disaster loss reduction [13]. It can be used to summarize the historical displacement of landslides and environmental conditions and also to analyze the potential relationship between geological and meteorological environmental changes and disasters. The combination of an accurate landslide displacement prediction model and landslide warning model can effectively improve people's ability to determine landslides in daily life, help decision-makers make more accurate decisions [14], and take active disaster reduction actions in advance [15] to achieve adaptive risk avoidance [16] and protect people's lives and health, and to achieve the purpose of improving people's livelihood [14]. In the Three Gorges Reservoir area, affected by rainfall and reservoir water level, landslide displacement usually shows the characteristic of a "step shape" that represents accelerated activity in the rainy season and remains almost steady in the dry season [17]. Therefore, defining methods for predicting the increase in landslide displacement has become the focus of scholars. However, landslides are very complex systems, and their deformation is affected by their own engineering geological conditions and externally induced factors [14]. The displacement curve is often highly nonlinear, which makes it difficult to accurately predict the landslide displacement [8].

At present, landslide displacement prediction models are mainly divided into physics-based and data-based models [18]. Although both models can predict landslide displacement, physics-based models are complex, time-consuming, expensive [19], difficult to establish [5], and have strict application conditions [11], which can only be used in limited cases [20]. However, the data-based model has a simple process, accurate prediction, and low cost [19], and it is good at dealing with nonlinear relations [21]. Therefore, physics-based models are not as popular as data-based models [10]. Thus, most of the landslide displacement prediction models in recent years are based on data models. The key factors for the occurrence of landslides can be roughly divided into two categories: the slope, lithology, and soil type are internal factors affecting landslides, while the rainfall, reservoir water level, and snowfall are external factors affecting landslides [22].

Based on the principle of time series analysis, many studies have decomposed landslide displacement into trend displacement and periodic displacement [5,8,10,14,15,23], which has well separated the nonlinear characteristics of landslide displacement. There have also been studies on the decomposition of landslide displacement data into several subsequences of different frequencies based on the time-frequency analysis method. Guo et al. [24] combined the variational modal decomposition (VMD) method with the WA-GWA-BP model, and Liu et al. [6] combined the VMD method with the periodic neural network (PNN) model to predict landslide displacement. The empirical mode decomposition (EMD) method was combined with the LSTM model, and a linear interpolation technique was used to increase the size of the training dataset to accurately predict landslide displacement [25]. According to the wavelet transform, multiscale analysis can be carried out on landslide displacement data through the operation functions of stretching and shifting [26–28]. To solve the problems of modal aliasing in EMD, the Ensemble Empirical Mode Decomposition (EEMD) algorithm was used to decompose the landslide data series, further improving the prediction ability of the model [29–31]. Taking into consideration the fact that EMD and EEMD have randomness and uncontrollability built in the decomposition times of landslide displacement, Xing et al. [32] used VMD to decompose landslide displacement.

Taking into consideration the lag fluctuation of the groundwater level, the SVC-PSO-SVR model was proposed to predict landslide displacement by Han et al. [33]. Deng et al. [34] used acoustic emission sound generation and rainfall as data inputs, and the equivalent reservoir water level function model was combined with Lasso-ELM to improve the accuracy of landslide displacement prediction. Based on the traditional gray prediction model, L et al. improved and proposed a new gray prediction model [13]. SVR and the Hausdorff derivative operator were used to determine model parameters with the improved SALP group algorithm, further improving the prediction performance of the traditional gray model [35]. Based on the optimal weight allocation method, Li et al. [36] assigned different weights to the verhulst model and GM(1,1) model, and combined the advantages of the two models to form a new prediction model. Considering the importance of past experience, Hu et al. [37] used the verhulst inverse function to describe the motion characteristics of landslides, and constructed a displacement prediction model combined with a random forest algorithm. To predict the displacement more accurately, two new concepts, the trend sequence and sensitivity state, were proposed, and a new model was obtained by integrating the trend sequence and sensitivity state [38]. The cost function and the penalty mechanism were proposed in order to force the underestimated landslide displacement to be transferred to a higher estimate, and the ability of the model to avoid landslide risk is taken into full consideration while predicting landslide displacement [16].

Researchers considered that it is normal that the landslide displacement will fluctuate within the normal range in the future, and the prediction interval method was adopted instead of point prediction; this method can obtain clear data, and the resulting model was presented as an interval [15,29,39,40]. Interval prediction can not only predict the future variation trend of data but also obtain the variation range of landslide displacement, providing an important basis for decision-making regarding landslide disaster prevention and mitigation [21]. In recent years, with the development of technology, the local mean decomposition (LMD) algorithm has been increasingly applied, and an increasing number of studies have begun to use the LMD algorithm to address nonlinear problems in various fields [41–45]. Inspired by previous studies, this paper presents a new theory that intends to apply the LMD algorithm to process typical nonlinear landslide displacement data on the basis of previous research results and time-frequency analysis methods and to propose a new local mean decomposition-bidirectional long short-term memory (LMD-BiLSTM) model.

The LMD-BiLSTM model can decompose nonlinear and nonstationary data series well, it can solve the problem of ignoring random displacement in time series analysis, and the LMD algorithm is used to decompose the original displacement data and influencing factors into several sub-time-series data of different frequencies. Due to the complex relationship between influencing displacement factors and landslide displacement, the correlation between them cannot be well quantified. Therefore, to improve the accuracy of prediction, the maximum information coefficient (MIC) algorithm is introduced in this paper.

MIC correlation calculations are carried out between the subsequence of influencing displacement factors and each of the subsequences of landslide displacement, and the data with high correlation are selected as the input variable of each subsequence prediction, which improves the validity and reliability of the input data. Considering that the rainfall and reservoir water level of landslides have a similar change trend in each time period, the bidirectional long short-term memory (BiLSTM) model is used to predict each sub-series and the final predicted displacement of the landslide is obtained by adding the predicted results. The case of a Baishuihe landslide in the Three Gorges region of China is taken to verify the prediction performance and advantages of the model.

The main contributions of this study are as follows.

1. In order to solve the problem where the time series analysis method ignores the random factors, which would affect the accuracy of prediction, based on the time-frequency analysis method, the LMD algorithm is used for the first time to decompose landslide displacement data and factors affecting displacement into multiple instantaneous frequency subsequences with physical significance. The disadvantages of EMD or EEMD mode aliasing and endpoint effects are solved, and the integrity of the signal is better preserved.

2.   The internal relationship between landslide displacement, rainfall, and reservoir water level are analyzed after obtaining the landslide displacement and the subsequences of the influencing displacement factors through the LMD algorithm. The MIC method is used to calculate the correlation between each subsequence of landslide displacement and each of the subsequences of the influencing displacement factors. The MIC method can improve the reliability and validity of data, it discards less correlated data, and it selects more correlated data as the input variables of each subsequence.

3.   Considering that the rainfall and reservoir water level of the Baishuihe landslide have the same change trend in each time period, the BiLSTM model is used to predict each subsequence of landslide displacement. Finally, the displacement obtained by adding the subsequence data is the predicted displacement of the landslide.

2. Materials and Methods

2.1. Local Mean Decomposition

The LMD algorithm was first proposed by Jonathan S. Smith [46], and its advantages over EMD in EEG signal processing were discussed. In recent years, the LMD algorithm, a decomposition method for nonlinear nonstationary signals, has been applied to tool chatter areas [41], solar radiation prediction [42], underwater acoustic signal processing [43], daily natural gas load forecasting [44], time series compressor stall processes [45], and many other fields.

The core idea of the LMD algorithm is to adaptively decompose a complex nonstationary multicomponent signal into the sum of several product functions (PF) with the physical significance of instantaneous frequency, for which each PF component is directly calculated by an envelope signal and a pure frequency modulation (FM) signal. The envelope signal is the instantaneous amplitude of the PF component, and the instantaneous frequency of the PF component can be directly calculated from the pure frequency modulation signal. Furthermore, by combining the instantaneous amplitude and instantaneous frequency of all PF components, the complete time-frequency distribution of the original signal can be obtained. The LMD algorithm can decompose complex nonlinear landslide displacement data into several PFs with physical significance, and its decomposition steps are as follows [43,46]:

$$m_i = \frac{n_i + n_{i+1}}{2} \tag{1}$$

$$\alpha_i = \frac{|n_i - n_{i+1}|}{2} \tag{2}$$

where m_i is the i-th average value of two consecutive extreme values n_i; $n_{i+1}\alpha_i$ is the local magnitude of each halfwave oscillation; $i = 1, 2, \ldots, m - 1$ (where m is the number of extrema). The mean m_i of all continuous extreme values must form a straight line. The moving average method is used to smooth the mean m_i and α_i, and the local mean function $m_{11}(t)$ and the envelope estimation function $\alpha_{11}(t)$ are obtained. Then, $m_{11}(t)$ is separated from the original signal $X(t)$ to obtain the residual signal $h_{11}(t)$:

$$h_{11} = X(t) - m_{11}(t) \tag{3}$$

Then, $h_{11}(t)$ is divided by $\alpha_{11}(t)$ to conduct amplitude modulation and yield:

$$s_{11}(t) = \frac{h_{11}(t)}{\alpha_{11}} \tag{4}$$

where $s_{11}(t)$ is a pure frequency modulation signal, and the process is repeated q times until a pure FM signal $s_{1q}(t)$ whose envelope function meets $\alpha_{1(q+1)}(t) = 1$ is obtained. The corresponding envelope $\alpha_1(t)$ is shown in the formula:

$$\alpha_1(t) = \alpha_{11}(t)\alpha_{12}(t)\cdots\alpha_{1n}(t) = \prod_{q-1}^{n} \alpha_{1q}(t) \tag{5}$$

where q is the number of iterations and the first component $PF_1(t)$ is:

$$PF_1(t) = s_{1q}(t) \times \alpha_1(t) \tag{6}$$

The $PF_1(t)$ is subtracted from the original signal $X(t)$ to obtain the new signal. The above steps are repeated to obtain $PF_2(t)$. These steps are repeated until the last signal becomes a constant or contains no more oscillations, and then the residual signal $u_k(t)$ can be obtained. Therefore, the original signal $X(t)$ can be decomposed into the sum of the PF component and $u_k(t)$, as shown in the formula below:

$$X(t) = \sum_{p-1}^{k} PF_p(t) + u_k(t) \tag{7}$$

2.2. Maximal Information Coefficient

Reshef et al. [47] proposed the MIC concept that can be used to measure the nonlinear correlation between two variables based on mutual information theory in information theory. The main idea is as follows: if there is some correlation between the two variables, then after some sort of meshing on the scatter plot of the two variables, the mutual information of these two variables can be calculated according to the approximate probability density distribution of the variables in the grid. After regularization, this value can be used to measure the correlation between the two variables. When the MIC is 0, it indicates that the pairs of variables are completely independent; when the MIC is 1, it indicates that there is some functional relationship between the pairs of variables. The larger the MIC is, the stronger the correlation between variables is. For a set of ordered pair datasets $D = \{(x_i, y_i), i = 1, 2, \ldots, n\}$, if the X-axis is divided into X cells and the Y-axis into Y cells, the result is an $x \times y$ grid G. The points in the dataset D land on G based on the proportion of approximate $D \mid G$, representing its probability distribution. Therefore, the maximum mutual information can be defined as follows:

$$I^*(D, x, y) = \max I(D|G) \tag{8}$$

where the maximum value in the above formula is the maximum value of mutual information on G of all possible networks in which D divides the X-axis into X grids and the Y-axis into Y grids. $I(D|G)$ indicates mutual information in the case of probability distribution $D \mid G$. The elements of the x-th row and y-th column of the eigenmatrix $M(D)$ on the ordered pair dataset D are shown in the formula:

$$M(D)_{x,y} = \frac{I^*(D, x, y)}{\log(\min\{x, y\})} \tag{9}$$

Then, the ordered pair dataset D divided by data scale n and the number of grids is less than or equal to $B(n)$. Then, the MIC of dataset D is defined as follows:

$$MIC(D) = \max_{xy < B(n)} \left\{ M(D)_{x,y} \right\} \tag{10}$$

According to the actual application [47–49], $B(n) = n^{0.6}$ is recommended, so this paper also chooses this value.

2.3. Bidirectional Long Short-Term Memory Model

Landslide displacement is affected by external factors such as rainfall and reservoir level, and the collected data series have certain fluctuations and periodicities. To analyze and predict the time series data of landslide displacement, this paper uses an improved recurrent neural network (RNN) model to predict landslide displacement. A long short-term memory network (LSTM) was proposed by Hochreiter et al. [50]; it is a special RNN that, because of the added gate mechanism that is added, can solve the RNN gradient explosion and gradient disappearance problems to a certain extent.

On the basis of a traditional RNN, the LSTM model introduces c_t to store long-term memory. The model can be made to selectively update the memory unit so that the current node learns the characteristics of the input data from a long time ago. There are three control gates in each LSTM unit, namely the input gate i_t, forget gate f_t, and output gate o_t. The structure of the LSTM model is shown in Figure 1.

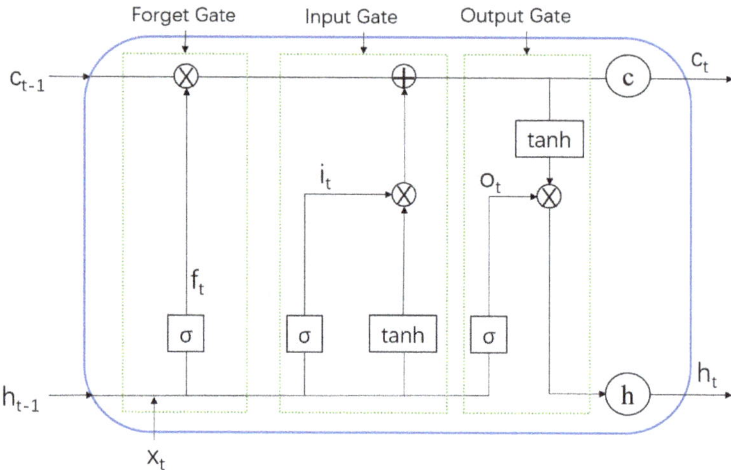

Figure 1. The LSTM model structure.

Assuming the input sequence $x = \{x_1, x_2, \ldots x_t\}$, $x_t = \{x_{t1}, x_{t2}, \ldots x_{tk}\}$ represents the real vector data of the k-dimension under time step t, the LSTM model is used to construct landslide displacement data, and the updating formula of each internal unit is as follows.

The forget gate f_t is used to forget the information of the state c_{t-1} of the upper memory unit, and its formula is

$$f_t = \sigma\left(W_f x_t + U_f h_{t-1} + b_f\right) \tag{11}$$

where W_f is the weight matrix of the forget gate, b_f is the bias of the forget gate, and σ is the sigmoid function.

The calculation of the candidate state of memory unit $\tilde{c}_t$ is shown in the formula, and the input gate i_t determines the reserved information of the candidate state in the current unit.

$$\tilde{c}_t = tanh(W_c x_t + U_c h_{t-1} + b_c) \tag{12}$$

$$i_t = \sigma(W_i x_t + U_i h_{t-1} + b_i) \tag{13}$$

where W_i and W_c represent the weight matrices of the input gate i_t and candidate state $\tilde{c}_t$, respectively; b_i and b_c represent the corresponding bias quantities of i_t and $\tilde{c}_t$. i_t and f_t combine with the previous memory state c_{t-1} and the current candidate state $\tilde{c}_t$ to update the current memory unit state c_t.

$$c_t = f_t \odot c_{t-1} + i_t \odot \tilde{c}_t \tag{14}$$

where $\odot$ indicates multiplication. The input gate o_t is mainly used to control the output of the memory unit state value.

$$o_t = \sigma(W_o x_t + U_o h_{t-1} + b_o) \tag{15}$$

The weight and bias of each unit in the above types are dynamic and can be updated through data training to predict landslide displacement in time series. In traditional LSTM models, the information is one-way, and the model can use past information but not future information. To adapt to the variation characteristics of landslide displacement, precipitation, and reservoir water level, the BiLSTM model was selected to construct the prediction model.

The BiLSTM model is formed by the combination of positive and reverse LSTM [51], and its structure is shown in Figure 2. Forward LSTM can obtain the past data information of the input sequence, and backward LSTM can obtain the future data information of the input sequence [52]. The forward and backward LSTM training processes of time series data can further improve the global integrity of feature extraction. At time t, the output value H_t of the hidden layer of BiLSTM is composed of forward $\overrightarrow{h}_t$ and backward $\overleftarrow{h}_t$:

$$\overrightarrow{h}_t = \overrightarrow{\text{LSTM}}\,(h_{t-1}, x_t, c_{t-1}), t \in [1, T] \tag{16}$$

$$\overleftarrow{h}_t = \overleftarrow{\text{LSTM}}\,(h_{t+1}, x_t, c_{t+1}), t \in [T, 1] \tag{17}$$

$$H_t = \left[\overrightarrow{h}_t, \overleftarrow{h}_t\right] \tag{18}$$

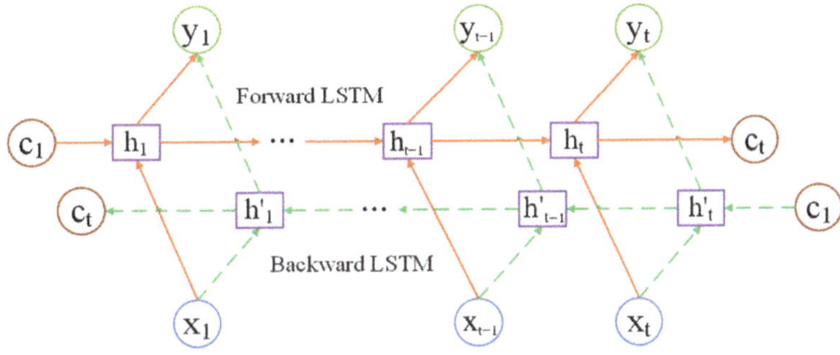

Figure 2. The BiLSTM model structure.

After obtaining H_t, the landslide displacement is obtained by a fully connected layer as the prediction output of the model.

3. Results

3.1. A Real Case

The Baishuihe landslide is located on the south bank of the main trunk road of the Yangtze River between Zigui County and Badong County, 56 km away from the three Gorges Dam sites, with a longitude of 110′32″09″ and latitude of 31′01″34″. The specific geographical location of the Baishuihe landslide is shown in Figure 3.

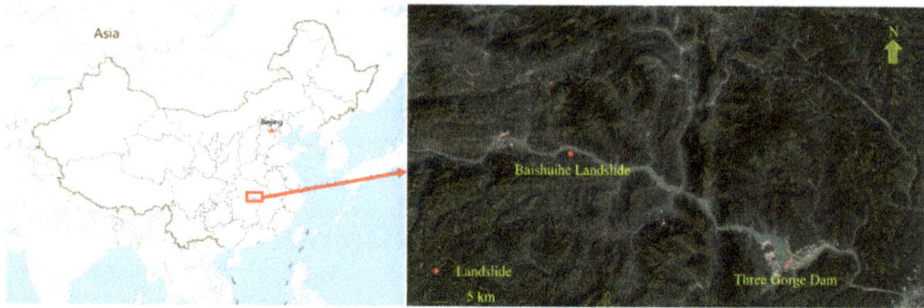

Figure 3. The geographical location of Baishuihe landslide.

The overall topography of the landslide area is high in the south and low in the north. The relative elevation difference of the terrain in the landslide area is approximately 300 m, the frontal elevation is approximately 70 m, the north–south length is 600 m, the east–west width is 700 m, and the average thickness of the slide body is approximately 30 m [6,10]. The longitudinal sliding surface of the Baishuihe landslide area is a folded line, which is steep at the back and shallow at the front, and the middle slide surface is between the two sliding surfaces. The Baishuihe landslide area has two slip zone layers, the shallow slide zone is the interface of gravel soil and cataclasite, the thickness is approximately 0.9~3.13 m, and the buried depth is 12.4~20.3 m [19,27]. The deep slide zone is the contact surface between cataclastic rock and carbonaceous silt mudstone, with a thickness of 0.6~1.5 m and burial depth of 18.9~34.1 m [31]. According to the classification of Hungr et al. [53], the Baishuihe landslide belongs to the clay/silt planar slide. Its deformation is slow. A topographical map of the Baishuihe landslide area is shown in Figure 4.

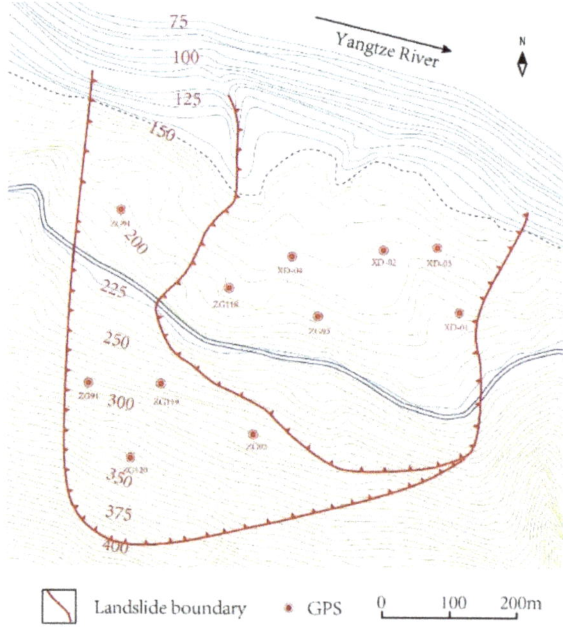

Figure 4. The GPS monitoring location of the Baishuihe landslide area.

Eleven global positioning system (GPS) monitoring sites have been installed in the Baishuihe landslide area. The GPSs are installed by the National Cryosphere Desert Data Center. The purpose is to observe the impact of the Three Gorges Dam on landslides in this area. The ZG118 monitoring station is located in the center of the landslide area, and it can well reflect the whole situation of the Baishuihe landslide. It is used by most research institutes [11,19,54], so the data from the ZG118 monitoring station are also used as representatives of Baishuihe landslide data in this study. In this study, the displacement data of the Baishuihe landslide area for 108 months are used, and the variations in rainfall and reservoir water level within the landslide range in the same period are monitored. The data-collection time period was from January 2004 to December 2012, and one data point was collected every month, as shown in Figure 5. This dataset and the topographical map are provided by the National Cryosphere Desert Data Center/National Service Center for Speciality Environmental Observation Stations.

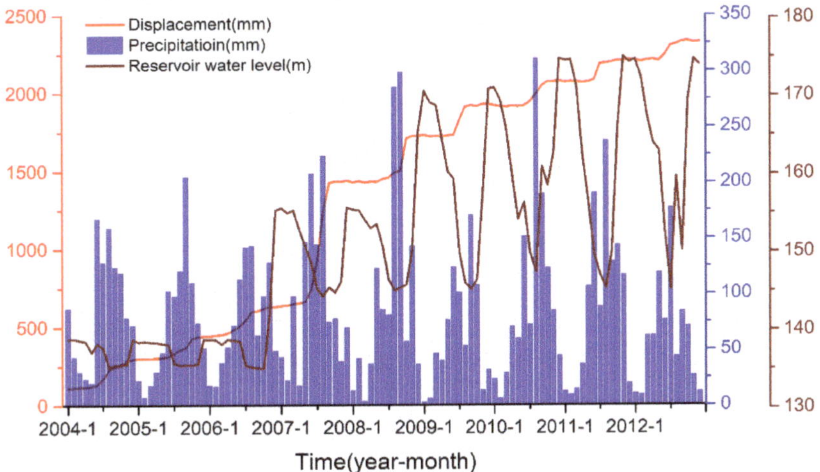

Figure 5. The variations in the displacement, rainfall, and reservoir water level of the Baishuihe landslide area.

3.2. Analysis of Influencing Factors

Figure 5 shows that from April to August every year, the rainy season of the Baishuihe landslide area occurs, and the amount of rainfall continues to rise. Every year, Baishuihe's landslide displacement increases most rapidly during the height of the rainy season, and the largest increase in landslide displacement occurred during the rainy season in 2007. The dry season in the Baishuihe landslide area is from January to March. There is less rainfall in these months, and the landslide displacement hardly increases. As rainfall increases, the amount of water entering the slope increases, making the overall weight of the slope rise, thus increasing the speed of the landslide. After rainwater enters the slope, the interior of the slope becomes wet, reducing the friction force and increasing the landslide probability. Rainfall is usually used as one of the inputs to predict landslide displacement models [55–58].

Although the largest increase in landslide displacement occurred during the rainy season of 2007, there were three years with more rainfall than that in 2007, suggesting that rainfall is not the only factor affecting landslide displacement. Because of the complexity of the internal geological structure of a landslide, landslides usually contain several different states, and landslide stability differs between such states. When a landslide is relatively stable, it is difficult to produce a large displacement when strong external factors are encountered. When a landslide is in an unstable state, a large displacement may occur even if external factors of general strength are encountered. Therefore, the maximum rainfall is not the factor that corresponds to the maximum landslide displacement; this is consistent with the actual displacement in the Baishuihe landslide area. To some extent, the displacement before the landslide can represent the state of the landslide at that time and the stability of the landslide [14,17,28,59]. Therefore, we take the displacement of the landslide in the previous month as the state of the landslide as one of the inputs of the prediction model.

Since 2003, the Three Gorges Dam has released water during the rainy season to ensure that the dam is safe; subsequently, the reservoir level of the dam has dropped significantly. It can be observed from Figure 5 that the rate of landslide displacement increases at the end of the decrease in the reservoir water level every year, indicating that the decrease in the reservoir water level has a certain lag effect on landslide displacement. When the water level of the reservoir decreases for a certain period of time, the resistance of the landslide surface will be reduced. When the reservoir releases more water, the impact force of the landslide also increases with the increase in water flow, making the structure of the landslide more easily affected such that a landslide is more likely to occur. Therefore, the reservoir water level is also considered one of the influencing factors of landslide displacement [60–63].

In this paper, it is speculated that landslide displacement is the result of the comprehensive action of rainfall, reservoir level, and landslide state. Therefore, rainfall, reservoir water level, and landslide state are selected as the input for the prediction model in this paper.

3.3. Decomposition Data Using the LMD Algorithm

In this experiment, we used 108 months of data for simulation verification. The data of the first 96 months were used as a training set for the training model, and the data from the last 12 months were used as a test set for model prediction to verify the performance of the landslide displacement prediction model. According to the time-frequency analysis method, the LMD algorithm was used to decompose the landslide displacement, precipitation, reservoir water level, and landslide state from high frequency to low frequency into six subsequences, as shown in Figure 6.

The landslide displacement, rainfall, reservoir water level, and landslide state were decomposed by the LMD algorithm, and five PF_s with different frequencies and one u_k residual component were obtained.

3.4. Calculating the Correlation between Landslide Displacement and Influencing Factors

Due to the complexity of the landslide attributes, there are many factors affecting landslides, and different landslide states cause different landslide consequences when the same influence conditions are met. After the landslide displacement and influencing factor data are decomposed into subsequence data of different frequencies by the LMD algorithm, the subsequences of landslide displacement for each frequency correspond to multiple influencing factors of different frequencies. However, any influencing factors with too little correlation reduce the prediction performance of the model; additionally, using too many irrelevant factors for prediction leads to an increasing number of deviations in the results. Therefore, the MIC algorithm is adopted in this paper to calculate the correlation degree between each of the subsequences of the landslide displacement and the different frequency subsequences of the various influencing factors. Table 1 shows the MIC correlation results for each set of landslide displacement subsequence with other subsequences.

The selection of an appropriate MIC value is particularly critical for the selection of influencing factors and the final prediction results of the model. MIC values that are too small result in factors with low correlation participating in the training and prediction of the prediction model. A large range of MIC values leads to fewer datasets for the model to use. According to the results of the study [17] and several experiments, this paper selects the influential factors with MIC > 0.3 as the input of the prediction model. The final results show that there are 16, 13, 16, 17, 14, and 17 input variables for PF_1, PF_2, PF_3, PF_4, PF_5, and u_k in the landslide displacement subsequences, respectively.

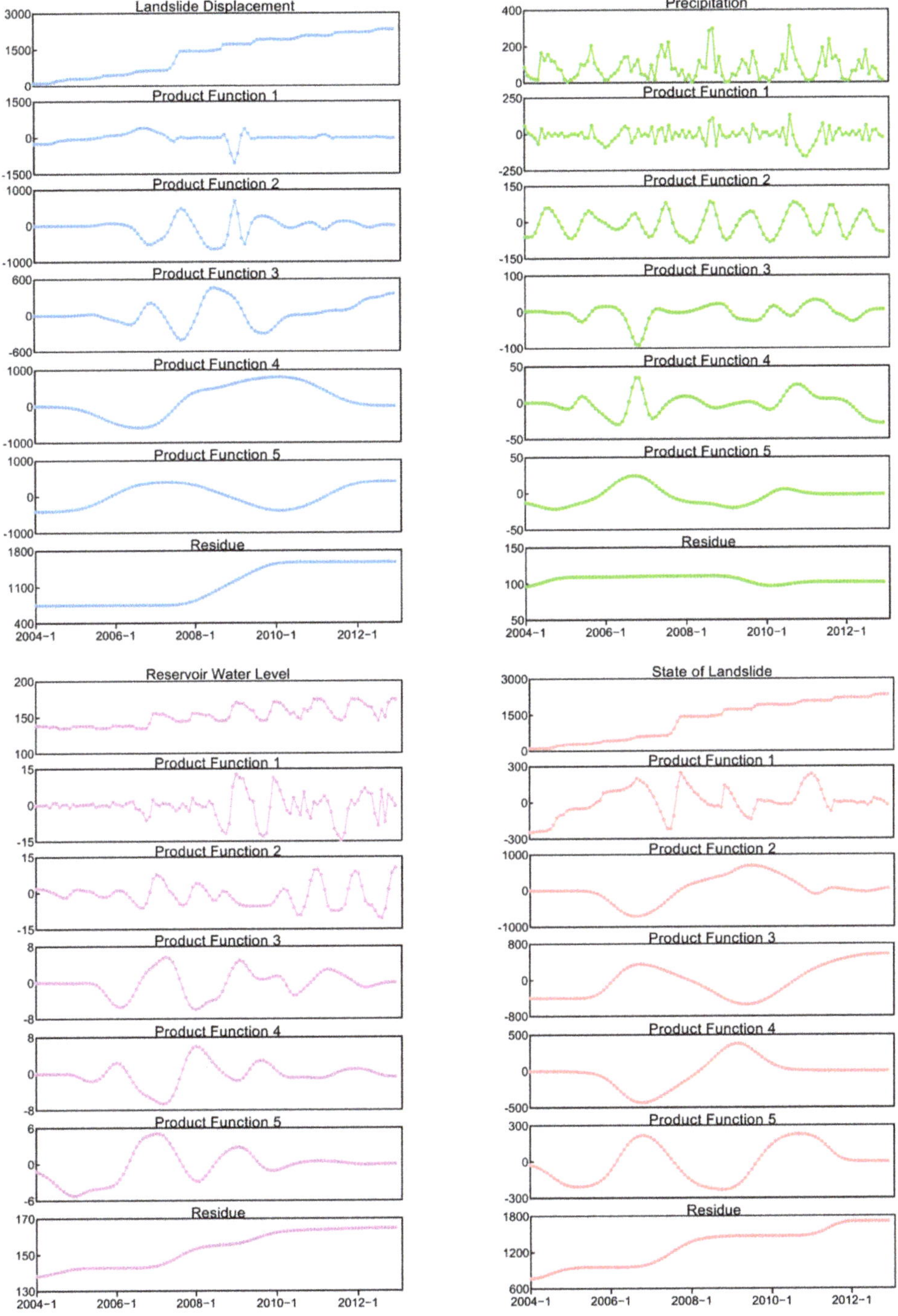

Figure 6. Subsequence decomposition of the landslide displacement, precipitation, reservoir water level, and landslide state.

Table 1. MIC results for each landslide displacement subsequence with other subsequences.

Landslide Displacement Subsequences	Influence Factor Types	Influence Factor Subsequences					
		PF_1	PF_2	PF_3	PF_4	PF_5	u_k
PF_1	Precipitation	0.317	0.375	0.418	0.331	0.479	0.404
	Reservoir water level	0.267	0.255	0.403	0.351	0.424	0.521
	State of landslide	0.477	0.526	0.521	0.422	0.386	0.521
PF_2	Precipitation	0.245	0.231	0.289	0.287	0.568	0.508
	Reservoir water level	0.241	0.364	0.396	0.419	0.383	0.678
	State of landslide	0.413	0.616	0.569	0.423	0.546	0.681
PF_3	Precipitation	0.208	0.317	0.521	0.403	0.486	0.697
	Reservoir water level	0.281	0.419	0.353	0.448	0.528	0.915
	State of landslide	0.529	0.471	0.525	0.545	0.579	0.955
PF_4	Precipitation	0.237	0.345	0.573	0.512	0.523	0.901
	Reservoir water level	0.366	0.454	0.448	0.566	0.646	0.897
	State of landslide	0.541	0.813	0.591	0.978	0.517	0.923
PF_5	Precipitation	0.228	0.246	0.697	0.524	0.591	0.891
	Reservoir water level	0.258	0.278	0.325	0.615	0.525	0.971
	State of landslide	0.448	0.652	0.679	0.601	0.379	0.982
u_k	Precipitation	0.251	0.348	0.472	0.423	0.684	0.793
	Reservoir water level	0.636	0.442	0.433	0.565	0.888	0.879
	State of landslide	0.402	0.909	0.704	0.861	0.602	0.972

3.5. Prediction Using the BiLSTM Model

After the MIC algorithm calculation, the input variables of each subsequence of landslide displacement are obtained. The forecasting process of the BiLSTM model is introduced with PF_1 as an example. PF_1 has 16 input variables, which are combined into two 16-dimensional vectors. A vector of the model's training set contains data for the first 96 months, and the other vector contains data for the next 12 months as a test set for the model. Training sets are used to train the BiLSTM model, and the model adjusts the parameters adaptively in the training process. After the training, the test set is input into the trained BiLSTM model to obtain the prediction results. The process of PF_1 prediction is similar to those of the other five subsequences, and the prediction results obtained are shown in Figure 7.

After the six components of landslide displacement are predicted, they are summed to obtain the final prediction result, as shown in Figure 8.

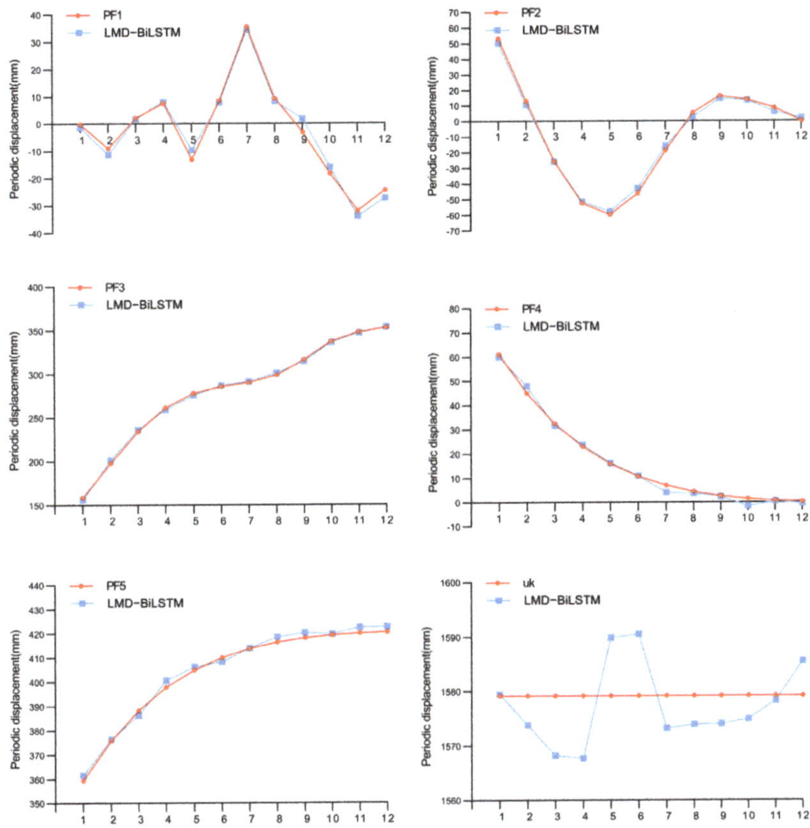

Figure 7. The components of the landslide displacement prediction results.

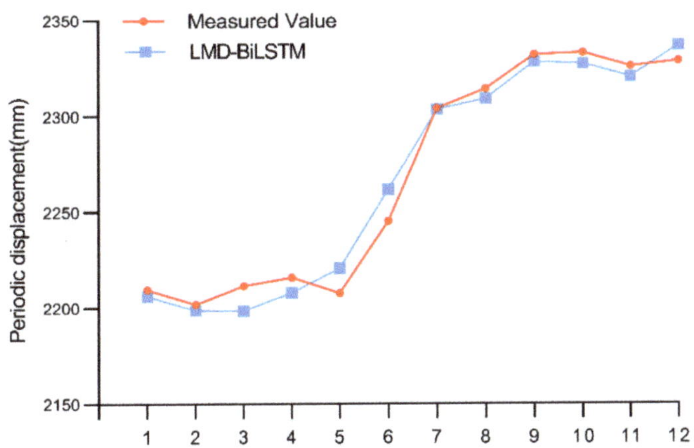

Figure 8. Final prediction results of landslide displacement.

4. Discussion

Landslide displacement prediction is a typical regression problem, so to describe the prediction performance of the LMD-BiLSTM model more accurately, this study selects four performance indicators to evaluate the prediction effects of various models. The mean absolute percentage error (MAPE), mean absolute error (MAE), root-mean-square error (RMSE), and determination coefficient R-squared (R^2) are calculated. Each evaluation index is defined as follows:

$$\text{MAE} = \frac{1}{n}\sum_{i=1}^{n}|\hat{y}_i - y_i| \tag{19}$$

$$\text{RMSE} = \sqrt{\frac{1}{n}\sum_{i=1}^{n}(\hat{y}_i - y_i)^2} \tag{20}$$

$$\text{MAPE} = \frac{100\%}{n}\sum_{i=1}^{n}\left|\frac{\hat{y}_i - y_i}{y_i}\right| \tag{21}$$

$$R^2 = 1 - \frac{\sum_{i=1}^{n}(\hat{y}_i - y_i)^2}{\sum_{i=1}^{n}(\overline{y}_i - y_i)^2} \tag{22}$$

where n indicates the number of landslide data points, $\hat{y} = \{\hat{y}_1, \hat{y}_2, \ldots, \hat{y}_n\}$ is the predicted value of the model, $y = \{y_1, y_2, \ldots y_n\}$ is the actual value of the Baishuihe landslide, and $\overline{y} = \{\overline{y}_1, \overline{y}_2, \ldots \overline{y}_n\}$ is the average value of the actual Baishuihe landslide. The three evaluation indexes MAE, RMSE, and MAPE all indicate that the smaller the value is, the better the performance and accuracy of the model. R^2 also evaluates the model according to the numerical value, and the higher the evaluation value is, the better the performance and accuracy of the model.

To further verify the effectiveness and predictive performance of the LMD-BiLSTM model, this study uses the LMD-BiLSTM without MIC and the LMD-LSTM model to simulate 108 data points of the Baishuihe landslide simultaneously. Four models are used to simultaneously predict five PF components and u_k components, and the prediction results are shown in Figure 9.

After obtaining five PF components and u_k components, the final prediction result is obtained by adding the subsequence prediction results of these models. To make a better comparison, the BiLSTM model is added to compare the final landslide displacement prediction results. The comparison of the final landslide displacement prediction results is shown in Figure 10.

We can see from Figures 9 and 10 that the BiLSTM model can also be used to predict landslide displacement without the processing of the LMD algorithm and MIC method, but it can only roughly predict the overall trend, and the predicted fluctuations are large. The prediction result of the LMD-BiLSTM model is similar to the curve of the LMD-BiLSTM without the MIC model, but it can be observed that the prediction deviation of some points is too large, which is the result of selecting too many input factors with low correlation without the MIC algorithm. The prediction results of the LMD-LSTM model are not as accurate as those of the LMD-BiLSTM model either on the whole or at a certain point, due to the lack of information about the future during model training and prediction. The experimental results also verify this idea.

To intuitively compare the performance of these prediction models, this paper uses MAE, MAPE, RMSE, and R^2 to evaluate the models. The results are shown in Table 2.

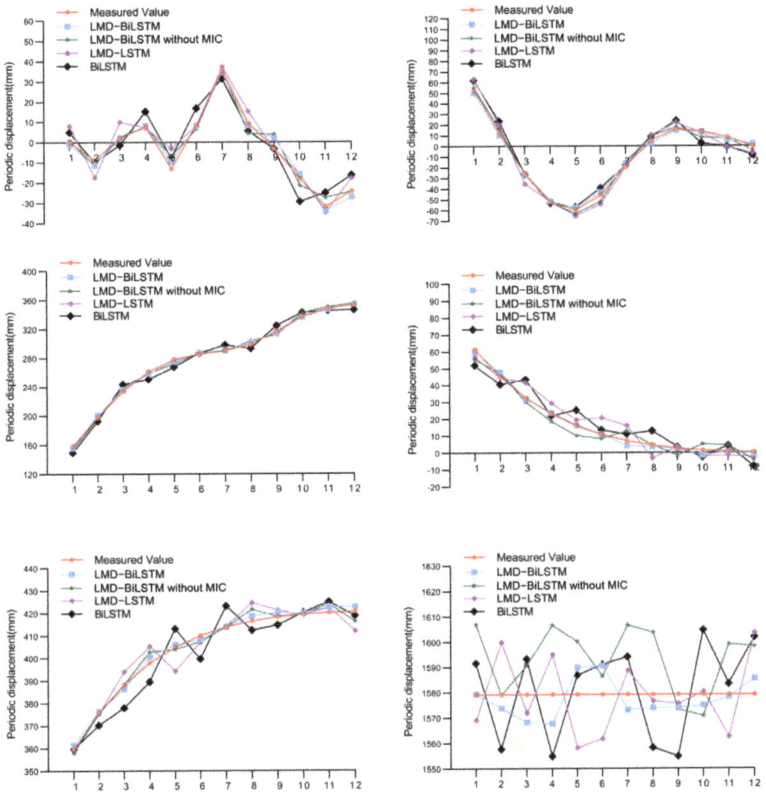

Figure 9. Comparison of the subsequence prediction results for landslide displacement based on four models.

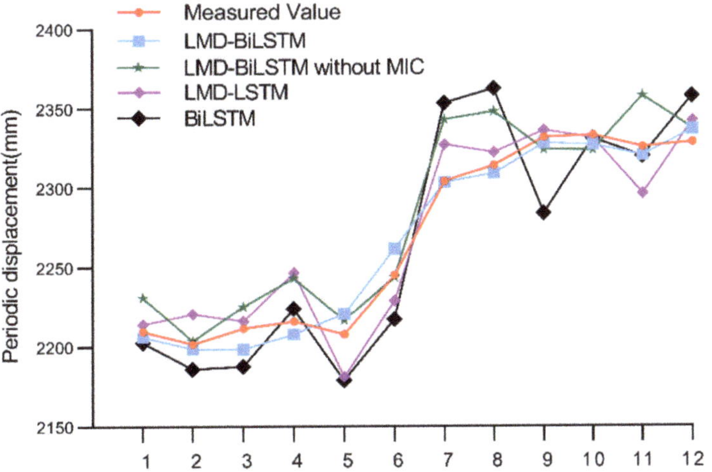

Figure 10. Final prediction results for the landslide displacement of four models.

Table 2. Comparison of four models for landslide displacement prediction.

Models	MAE	MAPE	RMSE	R^2
LMD-BiLSTM	7.276	0.322	8.511	0.976
LMD-BiLSTM without MIC	17.061	0.749	21.156	0.853
LMD-LSTM	15.147	0.670	18.215	0.891
BiLSTM	24.501	1.074	29.524	0.713

In addition to using the model prediction performance evaluation index to evaluate the prediction results of these models, this paper also uses the minimum error, maximum error, relative error, and mean absolute error to intuitively judge the prediction performance of the model, and the results are shown in Table 3.

Table 3. Accuracy of the predicted landslide displacement based on the four models.

Models	Minimum Error	Maximum Error	Relative Error	Mean Absolute Error
LMD-BiLSTM	0.518	16.544	3.784	7.109
LMD-BiLSTM without MIC	1.386	39.061	9.016	17.062
LMD-LSTM	1.680	30.583	7.983	15.168
BiLSTM	1.987	49.078	12.861	24.489

Tables 2 and 3 show that the model processed by the LMD algorithm and MIC algorithm is superior to the pure neural network BiLSTM model in terms of the comprehensive prediction level at all time points, the stability of the whole prediction, and the fluctuation change at a single time point. This superiority is because the hybrid model exploits the advantages of the LMD algorithm, which is good at analyzing the characteristics of data signals and reasonably reflecting the time and frequency distribution of data in various spaces and scales, which are advantages of the use of the MIC algorithm, which can calculate the degree of nonlinear association between two variables and also use the advantages of the BiLSTM model, which is good at processing time series data. Therefore, the hybrid model has the advantages of these algorithms and models. Because LMD-BiLSTM without the MIC model does not have the MIC algorithm to calculate the correlation of influencing factors, its prediction performance is between the LMD-BiLSTM model and BiLSTM model. Although the BiLSTM model takes the information sharing each cycle into account in the prediction, its prediction performance degrades because it does not remove redundant influencing factors, with the final prediction result being inferior to LMD-LSTM.

5. Conclusions

Landslide displacement prediction has been studied for a long time but is still a challenging research topic. In order to solve the disadvantage of ignoring random displacement in most time analysis methods, this paper proposes an LMD-BiLSTM model based on the time-frequency analysis method for landslide displacement prediction. The LMD algorithm is used for the first time to deconstruct the nonlinear and nonstationary data series of landslide displacement and influencing factors into multiple subseries. To improve the prediction accuracy, the MIC algorithm is used to quantify the correlation between the subsequences of landslide displacement and the subsequences of factors affecting the displacement; moreover, the factors with greater correlation are selected as the input variables of the model. According to the constantly changing characteristics of landslide displacement, precipitation, and reservoir water level in multiple time periods, the BiLSTM model is used to predict the subsequence components of landslide displacement, and the final landslide predicted displacement is obtained by adding the predicted results. The real landslide dataset of the Baishuihe landslide in the Three Gorges Reservoir area of China is used in the experiment, and excellent results are obtained. The final results show that the new LMD-BiLSTM model proposed in this study can predict landslide displacement smoothly and accurately. In the future, the LMD-BiLSTM model will be improved according to the different characteristics of each landslide and then popularized and applied to the displacement prediction of other landslides. In addition, the LMD-BiLSTM model could also be applied to other forecasting fields, such as rainfall prediction and power generation prediction, to assist decision-makers in continuously improving the process of making reasonable judgments. The decision makers can add the landslide displacement prediction results into the landslide warning system to make their own judgment according to the landslide displacement, and the scientific community can build on these findings and apply these methods to other areas of prediction. The results presented in this paper may not be applicable to the early warning of landslides, because prediction models require a certain amount of monitoring data, which is not suitable for early warning.

Author Contributions: Conceptualization, X.S., Y.J. and Z.L.; methodology, Z.L. and X.S.; formal analysis, Y.J. and X.S.; resources, Z.L., Y.J., W.L. and X.S.; writing—original draft preparation, Z.L., Y.J. and X.S.; writing—review and editing, Z.L., Y.J. and X.S.; funding acquisition, X.S. and W.L. All authors have read and agreed to the published version of the manuscript.

Funding: This research was funded by the National Natural Science Foundation of China (Grant No. 62161007, Grant No. 62061010, and Grant No. 61861008), Technology Major Project of Nanning Qingxiu District (Grant No. 2018001), Department of Science and Technology of Guangxi Zhuang Autonomous Region (Grant No. AB21196041, Grant No. AA20302022, Grant No. AA19182007, and Grant No. AA19254029), Natural Science Foundation of Guangxi Province of China (Grant No. 2019GXNSFBA245072 and Grant No. 2018GXNSFAA294054), and Young Teachers Promotion Project of Guangxi Universities (Grant No. 2022KY0182).

Institutional Review Board Statement: Not applicable.

Informed Consent Statement: Not applicable.

Data Availability Statement: Restrictions apply to the availability of these data. Data were obtained from the National Cryosphere Desert Data Center/National Service Center for Speciality Environmental Observation Stations and are available from the http://data.casnw.net/portal/ (accessed on 19 January 2021) with the permission of the National Cryosphere Desert Data Center/National Service Center for Speciality Environmental Observation Stations.

Conflicts of Interest: The authors declare no conflict of interest.

References

1. Du, B.; Zhao, Z.; Hu, X.; Wu, G.; Han, L.; Sun, L.; Gao, Q. Landslide susceptibility prediction based on image semantic segmentation. *Comput. Geosci.* **2021**, *155*, 104860. [CrossRef]
2. Depina, I.; Oguz, E.A.; Thakur, V. Novel Bayesian framework for calibration of spatially distributed physical-based landslide prediction models. *Comput. Geotech.* **2020**, *125*, 103660. [CrossRef]
3. Shou, K.-J.; Lin, J.-F. Evaluation of the extreme rainfall predictions and their impact on landslide susceptibility in a sub-catchment scale. *Eng. Geol.* **2019**, *265*, 105434. [CrossRef]
4. Chikalamo, E.E.; Mavrouli, O.C.; Ettema, J.; van Westen, C.J.; Muntohar, A.S.; Mustofa, A. Satellite-derived rainfall thresholds for landslide early warning in Bogowonto Catchment, Central Java, Indonesia. *Int. J. Appl. Earth Obs. Geoinf.* **2020**, *89*, 102093. [CrossRef]
5. Liu, Z.; Guo, D.; Lacasse, S.; Li, J.; Yang, B.; Choi, J. Algorithms for intelligent prediction of landslide displacements. *J. Zhejiang Univ. Sci. A* **2020**, *21*, 412–429. [CrossRef]
6. Liu, Q.; Lu, G.; Dong, J. Prediction of landslide displacement with step-like curve using variational mode decomposition and periodic neural network. *Bull. Eng. Geol. Environ.* **2021**, *80*, 3783–3799. [CrossRef]
7. Huang, F.; Ye, Z.; Jiang, S.-H.; Huang, J.; Chang, Z.; Chen, J. Uncertainty study of landslide susceptibility prediction considering the different attribute interval numbers of environmental factors and different data-based models. *CATENA* **2021**, *202*, 105250. [CrossRef]
8. Lin, Z.; Sun, X.; Ji, Y. Landslide Displacement Prediction Model Using Time Series Analysis Method and Modified LSTM Model. *Electronics* **2022**, *11*, 1519. [CrossRef]

9. Tang, M.; Xu, Q.; Yang, H.; Li, S.; Iqbal, J.; Fu, X.; Huang, X.; Cheng, W. Activity law and hydraulics mechanism of landslides with different sliding surface and permeability in the Three Gorges Reservoir Area, China. *Eng. Geol.* **2019**, *260*, 105212. [CrossRef]

10. Huang, F.; Huang, J.; Jiang, S.; Zhou, C. Landslide displacement prediction based on multivariate chaotic model and extreme learning machine. *Eng. Geol.* **2017**, *218*, 173–186. [CrossRef]

11. Miao, F.; Wu, Y.; Xie, Y.; Li, Y. Prediction of landslide displacement with step-like behavior based on multialgorithm optimization and a support vector regression model. *Landslide* **2017**, *15*, 475–488. [CrossRef]

12. Krkac, M.; Gazibara, B.S.; Arbanas, Z.; Sečanj, S.; Arbanas, S.M. A comparative study of random forests and multiple linear regression in the prediction of landslide velocity. *Landslide* **2020**, *17*, 2515–2531. [CrossRef]

13. Wu, L.Z.; Li, S.H.; Huang, R.Q.; Xu, Q. A new grey prediction model and its application to predicting landslide displacement. *Appl. Soft Comput.* **2020**, *95*, 106543. [CrossRef]

14. Lin, Z.; Sun, X.; Ji, Y. Landslide Displacement Prediction based on Time Series Analysis and Double-BiLSTM Model. *Int. J. Environ. Res. Public Health* **2022**, *19*, 2077. [CrossRef] [PubMed]

15. Wang, Y.; Tang, H.; Wen, T.; Ma, J. A hybrid intelligent approach for constructing landslide displacement prediction intervals. *Appl. Soft Comput.* **2019**, *81*, 105506. [CrossRef]

16. Xing, Y.; Yue, J.; Chen, C.; Qin, Y.; Hu, J. A hybrid prediction model of landslide displacement with risk-averse adaptation. *Comput. Geosci.* **2020**, *141*, 104527. [CrossRef]

17. Long, J.; Li, C.; Liu, Y.; Feng, P.; Zuo, Q. A multi-feature fusion transfer learning method for displacement prediction of rainfall reservoir-induced landslide with step-like deformation characteristics. *Eng. Geol.* **2022**, *297*, 106494. [CrossRef]

18. Zhang, J.; Tang, H.; Tannant, D.D.; Lin, C.; Xia, D.; Liu, X.; Zhang, Y.; Ma, J. Combined forecasting model with CEEMD-LCSS reconstruction and the ABC-SVR method for landslide displacement prediction. *J. Clean. Prod.* **2021**, *293*, 126205. [CrossRef]

19. Yang, B.; Yin, K.; Lacasse, S.; Liu, Z. Time series analysis and long short-term memory neural network to predict landslide displacement. *Landslides* **2019**, *16*, 677–694. [CrossRef]

20. Ma, J.; Tang, H.; Liu, X.; Wen, T.; Zhang, J.; Tan, Q.; Fan, Z. Probabilistic forecasting of landslide displacement accounting for epistemic uncertainty: A case study in the Three Gorges Reservoir area, China. *Landslides* **2018**, *15*, 1145–1153. [CrossRef]

21. Lian, C.; Zeng, Z.; Yao, W.; Tang, H.; Chen, C.L.P. Landslide Displacement Prediction With Uncertainty Based on Neural Networks With Random Hidden Weights. *IEEE Trans. Neural Netw. Learn. Syst.* **2016**, *27*, 2683–2695. [CrossRef] [PubMed]

22. Khan, S.; Kirschbaum, D.B.; Stanley, T. Investigating the potential of a global precipitation forecast to inform landslide prediction. *Weather. Clim. Extrem.* **2021**, *33*, 100364. [CrossRef]

23. Zhang, Y.; Tang, J.; He, Z.; Tan, J.; Li, C. A novel displacement prediction method using gated recurrent unit model with time series analysis in the Erdaohe landslide. *Nat. Hazards* **2021**, *105*, 783–813. [CrossRef]

24. Guo, Z.; Chen, L.; Gui, L.; Du, J.; Do, H.M. Landslide displacement prediction based on variational mode decomposition and WA-GWO-BP model. *Landslides* **2019**, *17*, 567–583. [CrossRef]

25. Xu, S.; Niu, R. Displacement prediction of Baijiabao landslide based on empirical modedecomposition and long short-term memory neural network in Three Gorgesarea, China. *Comput. Geosci.* **2018**, *111*, 87–96. [CrossRef]

26. Cai, Z.; Xu, W.; Meng, Y.; Chong, S.; Wang, R. Prediction of landslide displacement based on GA-LSSVM with multiple factors. *Bull. Eng. Geol. Environ.* **2015**, *75*, 637–646. [CrossRef]

27. Huang, F.; Yin, K.; Zhang, G.; Gui, L.; Yang, B.; Liu, L. Landslide displacement prediction using discrete wavelet transform and extreme learning machine based on chaos theory. *Environ. Earth Sci.* **2016**, *75*, 1376. [CrossRef]

28. Zhou, C.; Yin, K.; Ying, C.; Emanuele, I.; Bayes, A.; Filippo, C. Displacement prediction of step-likelandslide by applying a novel kernel extreme learning machine method. *Landslides* **2018**, *15*, 2211–2225. [CrossRef]

29. Lian, C.; Zeng, Z.; Wang, X.; Yao, W.; Su, Y.; Tang, H. Landslide displacement interval prediction using lower upper bound estimation method with pre-trained random vector functional link network initialization. *Neural Netw.* **2020**, *130*, 286–296. [CrossRef]

30. Du, H.; Song, D.; Chen, Z.; Shu, H.; Guo, Z. Prediction model oriented for landslide displacement with step-like curve by applying ensemble empirical mode decomposition and the PSO-ELM method. *J. Clean. Prod.* **2020**, *270*, 122248. [CrossRef]

31. Lian, C.; Zeng, Z.; Yao, W.; Tang, H. Extreme learning machine for the displacement prediction of landslide under rainfall and reservoir level. *Stoch. Environ. Res. Risk Assess.* **2014**, *28*, 1957–1972. [CrossRef]

32. Xing, Y.; Yue, J.; Chen, C.; Cong, K.; Zhu, S.; Bian, Y. Dynamic Displacement Forecasting of Dashuitian Landslide in China Using Variational Mode Decomposition and Stack Long Short-Term Memory Network. *Appl. Sci.* **2019**, *9*, 2951. [CrossRef]

33. Han, H.; Shi, B.; Zhang, L. Prediction of landslide sharp increase displacement by SVM with considering hysteresis of groundwater change. *Eng. Geol.* **2021**, *280*, 105876. [CrossRef]

34. Deng, L.; Smith, A.; Dixon, N.; Yuan, H. Machine learning prediction of landslide deformation behaviour using acoustic emission and rainfall measurements. *Eng. Geol.* **2021**, *293*, 106315. [CrossRef]

35. Li, S.; Wu, N. A new grey prediction model and its application in landslide displacement prediction. *Chaos Solitons Fractals* **2021**, *147*, 110969. [CrossRef]

36. Li, X.; Kong, J.; Wang, Z. Landslide displacement prediction based on combining method with optimal weight. *Nat. Hazards* **2012**, *61*, 635–646. [CrossRef]

37. Hu, X.; Wu, S.; Zhang, G.; Zheng, W.; Liu, C.; He, C.; Liu, Z.; Guo, X.; Zhang, H. Landslide displacement prediction using kinematics-based random forests method: A case study in Jinping Reservoir Area, China. *Eng. Geol.* **2021**, *283*, 105975. [CrossRef]

38. Liu, Y.; Xu, C.; Huang, B.; Ren, X.; Liu, C.; Hu, B.; Chen, Z. Landslide displacement prediction based on multi-source data fusion and sensitivity states. *Eng. Geol.* **2020**, *271*, 105608. [CrossRef]
39. Lian, C.; Chen, C.L.P.; Zeng, Z.; Yao, W.; Tang, H. Prediction Intervals for Landslide Displacement Based on Switched Neural Networks. *IEEE Trans. Reliab.* **2016**, *65*, 1483–1495. [CrossRef]
40. Lian, C.; Zhu, L.; Zeng, Z.; Su, Y.; Yao, W.; Tang, H. Constructing prediction intervals for landslide displacement using bootstrapping random vector functional link networks selective ensemble with neural networks switched. *Neurocomputing* **2018**, *291*, 1–10. [CrossRef]
41. Gupta, P.; Singh, B. Local mean decomposition and artificial neural network approach to mitigate tool chatter and improve material removal rate in turning operation operation. *Appl. Soft Comput.* **2020**, *96*, 106714. [CrossRef]
42. Yue, S.; Wang, Y.; Wei, L.; Zhang, Z. The joint empirical mode decomposition-local mean decomposition method and its application to time series of compressor stall process. *Aerosp. Sci. Technol.* **2020**, *105*, 105969. [CrossRef]
43. Lu, T.; Yu, F.; Wang, J.; Wang, X.; Han, B. Application of adaptive complementary ensemble local mean decomposition in underwater acoustic signal processing. *Appl. Acoust.* **2021**, *178*, 107966. [CrossRef]
44. Huynh, A.N.-L.; Deo, R.C.; Ali, M.; Abdulla, S.; Raj, N. Novel short-term solar radiation hybrid model: Long short-term memory network integrated with robust local mean decomposition. *Appl. Energy* **2021**, *298*, 117193. [CrossRef]
45. Peng, S.; Chen, R.; Yu, B.; Xiang, M.; Lin, X.; Liu, E. Daily natural gas load forecasting based on the combination of long short term memory, local mean decomposition, and wavelet threshold denoising algorithm. *J. Nat. Gas Sci. Eng.* **2021**, *95*, 104175. [CrossRef]
46. Smith, J.S. The local mean decomposition and its application to EEG perception data. *Interface* **2005**, *2*, 443–454. [CrossRef]
47. Reshef, D.N.; Reshef, Y.A.; Finucane, H.K.; Grossman, S.R.; McVean, G.; Turnbaugh, P.J.; Lander, E.S.; Mitzenmacher, M.; Sabeti, P.C. Detecting novel associations in large data sets. *Science* **2011**, *334*, 1518–1524. [CrossRef] [PubMed]
48. Guo, Z.; Yu, B.; Hao, M.; Wang, W.; Jiang, Y.; Zong, F. A novel hybrid method for flight departure delay prediction using Random Forest Regression and Maximal Information Coefficient. *Aerosp. Sci. Technol.* **2021**, *116*, 106822. [CrossRef]
49. Huang, X.; Luo, Y.-P.; Xia, L. An efficient wavelength selection method based on the maximal information coefficient for multivariate spectral calibration. *Chemom. Intell. Lab. Syst.* **2019**, *194*, 103872. [CrossRef]
50. Hochreiter, S.; Schmidhuber, J. Long short-term memory. *Neural Comput.* **1997**, *9*, 1735–1780. [CrossRef]
51. Yin, J.; Deng, Z.; Ines, A.V.M.; Wu, J.; Rasu, E. Forecast of short-term daily reference evapotranspiration under limited meteorological variables using a hybrid bi-directional long short-term memory model (Bi-LSTM). *Agric. Water Manag.* **2020**, *242*, 106386. [CrossRef]
52. Yadav, S.; Ekbal, A.; Saha, S.; Kumar, A.; Bhattacharyya, P. Feature assisted stacked attentive shortest dependency path based Bi-LSTM model for protein–protein interaction. *Knowl. Based Syst.* **2019**, *166*, 18–29. [CrossRef]
53. Hungr, O.; Leroueil, S.; Picarelli, L. The Varnes classification of landslide types, anupdate. *Landslides* **2014**, *11*, 167–194. [CrossRef]
54. Chen, J.; Zeng, Z.; Jiang, P.; Tang, H. Deformation prediction of landslide based on functional network. *Neurocomputing* **2014**, *149*, 151–157. [CrossRef]
55. Li, S.H.; Wu, L.; Chen, J.J.; Huang, R. Multiple data-driven approach for predicting landslide deformation. *Landslide* **2020**, *17*, 709–718. [CrossRef]
56. Wang, R.; Zhang, K.; Wang, W.; Meng, Y.; Yang, L.; Huan, H. Hydrodynamic landslide displacement prediction using combined extreme learning machine and random search support vector regression model. *Eur. J. Environ. Civ. Eng.* **2020**, *2020*, 1–13. [CrossRef]
57. Wen, T.; Tang, H.; Wang, Y.; Lin, C.; Xiong, C. Landslide displacement prediction using the GA-LSSVM model and time series analysis: A case study of Three Gorges Reservoir, China. *Nat. Hazards Earth Syst. Sci.* **2017**, *17*, 2181–2198. [CrossRef]
58. Li, X.; Li, S. Large-Scale Landslide Displacement Rate Prediction Based on Multi-Factor Support Vector Regression Machine. *Appl. Sci.* **2021**, *11*, 1381. [CrossRef]
59. Wang, C.; Zhao, Y.; Bai, L.; Guo, W.; Meng, Q. Landslide Displacement Prediction Method Based on GA-Elman Model. *Appl. Sci.* **2021**, *11*, 11030. [CrossRef]
60. Zhou, C.; Yin, K.; Cao, Y.; Ahmed, B. Application of time series analysis and PSO–SVM model in predicting the Bazimen landslide in the Three Gorges Reservoir, China. *Eng. Geol.* **2016**, *204*, 108–120. [CrossRef]
61. Jiang, Y.; Luo, H.; Xu, Q.; Lu, Z.; Liao, L.; Li, H.; Hao, L. A Graph Convolutional Incorporating GRU Network for Landslide Displacement Forecasting Based on Spatiotemporal Analysis of GNSS Observations. *Remote Sens.* **2022**, *14*, 1016. [CrossRef]
62. Wang, J.; Nie, G.; Gao, S.; Wu, S.; Li, H.; Ren, X. Landslide Deformation Prediction Based on a GNSS Time Series Analysis and Recurrent Neural Network Model. *Remote Sens.* **2021**, *13*, 1055. [CrossRef]
63. Wang, Y.; Tang, H.; Huang, J.; Wen, T.; Ma, J.; Zhang, J. A comparative study of different machine learning methods for reservoir landslide displacement prediction. *Eng. Geol.* **2022**, *298*, 106544. [CrossRef]

 *mathematics*

Article

Single-Machine Group Scheduling Model with Position-Dependent and Job-Dependent DeJong's Learning Effect

Jin Qian and Yu Zhan *

College of Science, Northeastern University, Shenyang 110819, China; qianjin@mail.neu.edu.cn
* Correspondence: zhanyu@mail.neu.edu.cn

Abstract: This paper considers the single-group scheduling models with Pegels' and DeJong's learning effect and the single-group scheduling models with Pegels' and DeJong's aging effect. In a classical scheduling model, Pegels' and DeJong's learning effect is a constant or position-dependent, while the learning effect and aging effect are job-dependent in this paper. Compared with the classical learning model and aging model for scheduling, the proposed models are more general and realistic. The objective functions are to minimize the total completion time and makespan. We propose polynomial time methods to solve all the studied problems.

Keywords: single-machine scheduling; aging effect; learning effect; group technology

MSC: 90B35; 90B36

Citation: Qian, J.; Zhan, Y. Single-Machine Group Scheduling Model with Position-Dependent and Job-Dependent DeJong's Learning Effect. *Mathematics* **2022**, *10*, 2454. https://doi.org/10.3390/math 10142454

Academic Editors: Xiang Li, Shuo Zhang and Wei Zhang

Received: 30 May 2022
Accepted: 12 July 2022
Published: 14 July 2022

Publisher's Note: MDPI stays neutral with regard to jurisdictional claims in published maps and institutional affiliations.

1. Introduction

In the traditional scheduling field, the processing time of a job is a constant, while in some actual situations, the processing times become shorter. A different approach to decreasing processing times is due to the concept of learning. A steady decline in processing times usually takes place by performing the same task repeatedly. This is called the learning effect. For instance, if a worker repeatedly processes the same jobs, due to the improvement of production technology and the accumulation of experience, the processing times become less. In some cases, the processing times of jobs may also become longer. As the machine ages, the processing times become longer. This is called the aging effect.

Compared with the classical learning model and aging model for scheduling, the proposed models are more general and realistic. In some classical scheduling model, Pegels' and DeJong's learning effect is a constant or position-dependent, while the learning effect and aging effect are job-dependent in this paper. This paper considers the single-group scheduling models with Pegels' and DeJong's learning effect and the single-group scheduling models with Pegels' and DeJong's aging effect. The objective functions are to minimize the total completion time and makespan. We propose polynomial time methods to solve all the studied problems.

2. Literature Review

The learning effect model was first proposed by Biskup [1]. Subsequently, many researchers have done a lot of work on the learning effect and aging effect. Mosheiov [2] explained the aging effect and deteriorating jobs. The SPT rule was no longer applicable to the optimal solution for the aging effect model. Yang [3] studied a single-machine scheduling problem with maintenance times and maintenance activities. This was an aging effect model that considered the linear deterioration and exponential deterioration of processing time. Zhang and Yan [4] considered a single-machine scheduling problem with setup time whose learning effect was based on group and position. The objective functions were to minimize the total completion time and makespan. They gave polynomial time algorithms. Li et al. [5] considered a single-machine scheduling problem with linear resource or convex resource allocation. The learning effect of the processing time was based on position. They dealt with the problem of the slack due window by an assignment method. Lu et al. [6] considered a single-machine scheduling problem with setup time and convex resource allocation whose learning effect was based on the group position and the position within the group. The optimal sequence was for the jobs in each group to be sorted according to the SPT rule. Mustu and Eren [7] considered a single-machine learning scheduling problem with setup time which was based on position. The objective function was to minimize the total tardiness and it was an NP-hard problem. They proposed some heuristic algorithms to deal with the NP-hard problem. A single-machine group scheduling problem with setup time about linear resource and convex resource allocation was considered by Yin et al. [8], Zhang et al. [9], Zhao et al. [10] and Li et al. [11].

This paper studies the Pegels' and DeJong's learning effect scheduling model and Pegels' and DeJong's aging effect scheduling model. De Jong [12] proposed a learning scheduling model. Wang et al. [13] considered a single-machine scheduling problem with setup time which was a linear function of the previous actual processing time. A learning effect that was similar to DeJong's learning effect was based on the sum of previous processing times. When the objective functions were to minimize the total completion time and makespan, they proved that the optimal schedule was sorted according to the SPT rule. Okołowski and Gawiejnowicz [14] studied a parallel-machine scheduling problem whose learning effect was DeJong's learning effect. The objective function was to minimize the makespan. Since $Pm||C_{\max}$ is a NP-hard problem, this problem was also a NP-hard problem. They proposed two branch-and-bound algorithms to solve this problem. Ji et al. [15] considered the machine scheduling problem with DeJong's learning effect. For the single-machine scheduling problem, the objective functions were to minimize the total completion time and makespan. They proved that the optimal schedule was sorted according to the SPT rule. Ji et al. [16] studied a parallel-machine deteriorating scheduling problem with DeJong's learning effect. The objective functions were to minimize the total completion time and makespan. When the objective functions were to minimize the total completion time, the jobs were sorted according to the SPT rule on each machine. Zhang et al. [17] considered both Pegels' and DeJong's learning effect scheduling model and Pegels' and DeJong's aging effect scheduling model. The objective functions were to minimize the total completion time and makespan. The optimal solution was that the jobs were sorted according to the SPT rule in each group. The group order was related to the objective functions. Sun et al. [18] considered a single-machine scheduling problem. A learning effect similar to DeJong's learning effect was based on the sum of previous processing times and positions. The objective functions were to minimize the total completion time and makespan. They proved that the jobs in each group were sorted according to the SPT rule. Under different objective functions, they also gave a conclusion on the group order.

To increase efficiency, similarly designed or processed products are processed in groups. This phenomenon is known as group technology in the literature. Ji et al. considered a single-machine group scheduling and job-dependent due-window assignment problem [19]. Sun et al. considered a single-machine group scheduling with learning effect and resource allocation [20]. There have also been many scholars who have done a lot of work on group technology [21–25].

The problem is described in the Section 3. The proof of the polynomial time algorithm for four problems are given in the Section 4. A summary is given in the Section 5.

3. Notation and Problem Statement

Some notations that are used in this paper are introduced.

Symbol	Meaning
l	the number of jobs
t	the number of groups
job_{uv}	the initial job at the uth position in the vth group
$job_{[u][v]}$	the job at the uth position in the vth group
$job_{[v]}$	the job in the vth group
l_v	the number of $job_{[v]}$
t_v	the setup time of group v
$t_{[v]}$	the setup time of $job_{[v]}$
p_{uv}	the normal processing time of job_{uv}
$p_{[u][v]}$	the normal processing time of $job_{[u][v]}$
$p_{[u][v]}^{a}$	the actual processing time of $job_{[u][v]}$
$C_{[u][v]}$	the completion time of $job_{[u][v]}$
$C_{\max}$	the makespan
α_{uv}	the DeJong's aging or learning effect of job_{uv}
$\alpha_{[u][v]}$	the DeJong's aging or learning effect of $job_{[u][v]}$
β_{uv}	the Pegels' aging or learning effect of job_{uv}
$\beta_{[u][v]}$	the Pegels' aging or learning effect of $job_{[u][v]}$

Suppose there are l independent jobs $J = \{J_1, \ldots, J_l\}$ processed on a machine. The l jobs are divided into t groups $G = \{G_1, \ldots, G_t\}$, $1 \leq t \leq l$. There is a sequence-dependent setup time before each group is processed. The jobs are processed continuously in each group. The machine can only process one job at a time. The actual processing time is

$$p_{[u][v]}^{a} = p_{[u][v]}[K + (1 - K)s^{\alpha_{[u][v]}}], u = 1, \ldots, l_v; v = 1, \ldots, t; \tag{1}$$

$$p_{[u][v]}^{a} = p_{[u][v]}[K + (1 - K)\beta_{[u][v]}^{s-1}], u = 1, \ldots, l_v; v = 1, \ldots, t, \tag{2}$$

where K is a constant, $K \geq 0$, $\alpha_{[u][v]} < 0$ and $0 < \beta_{[u][v]} < 1$. When $K = 0$, $p_{[u][v]}^{a}$ is inversely proportional to position s. When $0 < K < 1$, the actual processing time of each job is less than the normal processing time of each job. They are the learning scheduling models. When $K = 1$, the actual processing time is equal to the normal processing time. When $K > 1$, the actual processing time of each job is more than the normal processing time of each job. They are the aging scheduling models.

Our objectives are to minimize the total completion time and the makespan. By the three-region notation, DeJong's and Pegels' models can be defined as

$$1|p_{[u][v]}^{a} = p_{[u][v]}[K + (1 - K)s^{\alpha_{[u][v]}}], GT, t_v|C_{\max},$$

$$1|p_{[u][v]}^{a} = p_{[u][v]}[K + (1 - K)\beta_{[u][v]}^{s-1}], GT, t_v|C_{\max},$$

$$1|p_{[u][v]}^{a} = p_{[u][v]}[K + (1 - K)s^{\alpha_{[u][v]}}], GT, t_v|\sum_{v=1}^{t}\sum_{u=1}^{l_v} C_{[u][v]},$$

$$1|p_{[u][v]}^{a} = p_{[u][v]}[K + (1 - K)\beta_{[u][v]}^{s-1}], GT, t_v|\sum_{v=1}^{t}\sum_{u=1}^{l_v} C_{[u][v]}.$$

4. Research Method

The parameters of the traditional Pegels' and DeJong's learning effect are constants which are job-independent. This paper considers Pegels' and DeJong's models whose parameters are job-dependent. When $0 < K < 1$, they are the learning scheduling models. When $K > 1$, they are the aging scheduling models.

4.1. Makespan Minimization

Theorem 1. *For the* $1|p^a_{[u][v]} = p_{[u][v]}[K + (1 - K)s^{\alpha_{[u][v]}}], GT, t_v|C_{\max}$ *problem, the optimal solution is that the job sequence within the group is solved by the assignment method and the order of the groups is arbitrary.*

Proof. Suppose there are l_v jobs in the vth group, $l_1 + \cdots + l_t = l, 1 \le v \le t$. The completion time of each group is

$$C_{[l_1][1]} = t_{[1]} + \sum_{u=1}^{l_1} p_{[u][1]}[K + (1 - K)u^{\alpha_{[u][1]}}], \tag{3}$$

$$C_{[l_{v+1}][v+1]} = C_{[l_v][v]} + t_{[v+1]} + \sum_{u=1}^{l_{v+1}} p_{[u][v+1]}[K + (1 - K)u^{\alpha_{[u][v+1]}}], \tag{4}$$

$$C_{\max} = C_{[l_t][t]} = \sum_{v=1}^{t} t_{[v]} + \sum_{v=1}^{t} \sum_{u=1}^{l_v} p_{[u][v]}[K + (1 - K)u^{\alpha_{[u][v]}}]. \tag{5}$$

It can be seen from $C_{\max}$ that the order of the groups is arbitrary, and the job sequence within the group can be solved by the assignment method. So, the problem of sequencing jobs in each group could be solved in polynomial time.

$$\min \quad \sum_{u=1}^{l_{[v]}} \sum_{h=1}^{l_{[v]}} p_{[u][v]}[K + (1 - K)h^{\alpha_{[u][v]}}]e_{u[v]h},$$

$$\text{s.t.} \quad \sum_{h=1}^{l_{[v]}} e_{u[v]h} = 1, \quad v = 1,\ldots,t; u = 1,\ldots,l_{[v]}, \tag{6}$$

$$\sum_{u=1}^{l_{[v]}} e_{u[v]h} = 1, \quad v = 1,\ldots,t; h = 1,\ldots,l_{[v]},$$

$$e_{u[v]h} = 0, or 1, \quad v = 1,\ldots,t; u, h = 1,\ldots,l_{[v]}.$$

□

The algorithm is summarized as follows:
It is easy to show that the total time for Algorithm 1 is $O(n^3)$.

Algorithm 1 $1|p^a_{[u][v]} = p_{[u][v]}[K + (1 - K)s^{\alpha_{[u][v]}}], GT, t_v|C_{\max}$

Require: $t, K, l_v, t_v, p_{uv}, \alpha_{uv}$
Ensure: The job sequence within the group and $C_{\max}$
  1: **First step:** Using the assignment method, the job sequence within the group is solved.
  2: **Second step:** The order of the groups is arbitrary.
  3: **Last step:** Calculate $C_{\max}$.

Example 1. *If there are five jobs in total, they are divided into two groups.* $l = 5, t = 2,$ $G_1 = \{job_{11}, job_{21}, job_{31}\}, G_2 = \{job_{12}, job_{22}\}, K = 0.5, t_1 = 2, t_2 = 3, p_{11} = 7, p_{21} = 5,$ $p_{31} = 3, p_{12} = 4, p_{22} = 2, \alpha_{11} = -0.5, \alpha_{21} = -0.1, \alpha_{31} = -0.6, \alpha_{12} = -0.2, \alpha_{22} = -0.8.$

Solution:

The processing time of the jobs in G_1 and G_2 at different positions are shown in Table 1 and Table 2, respectively.

Table 1. Processing time of the group G_1 jobs in different positions.

Job \ Position	1	2	3
1	7	$7(0.5 + 0.5 \times 2^{-0.5})$	$7(0.5 + 0.5 \times 3^{-0.5})$
2	5	$5(0.5 + 0.5 \times 2^{-0.1})$	$5(0.5 + 0.5 \times 2^{-0.1})$
3	3	$3(0.5 + 0.5 \times 2^{-0.6})$	$3(0.5 + 0.5 \times 2^{-0.6})$

By the assignment method, the order of the jobs is $job_{31} \to job_{21} \to job_{11}$ in G_1.

Table 2. Processing time of the group G_2 jobs in different positions.

Job \ Position	1	2
1	4	$4(0.5 + 0.5 \times 2^{-0.2})$
2	2	$2(0.5 + 0.5 \times 2^{-0.8})$

By the assignment method, the order of the jobs is $job_{12} \to job_{22}$ in G_2.

$$
\begin{aligned}
C_{\max} &= \sum_{v=1}^{2} t_{[v]} + \sum_{v=1}^{2} \sum_{u=1}^{l_v} p_{[u][v]}[0.5 + 0.5 \times u^{\alpha_{[u][v]}}] \\
&= 2 + 3 + 5(0.5 + 0.5 \times 2^{-0.1}) + 7(0.5 + 0.5 \times 3^{-0.5}) + 3 + 4 + 2(0.5 + 0.5 \times 2^{-0.8}) \\
&= 23.924.
\end{aligned}
\tag{7}
$$

Theorem 2. *For the $1|p^a_{[u][v]} = p_{[u][v]}[K + (1 - K)\beta^{s-1}_{[u][v]}], GT, t_v|C_{\max}$ problem, the optimal solution is that the job sequence within the group is solved by the assignment method and the order of the groups is arbitrary.*

Proof. The completion time of each group is

$$
C_{[l_1][1]} = t_{[1]} + \sum_{u=1}^{l_1} p_{[u][1]}[K + (1 - K)\beta^{u-1}_{[u][1]}],
\tag{8}
$$

$$
C_{[l_{v+1}][v+1]} = C_{[l_v][v]} + t_{[v+1]} + \sum_{u=1}^{l_{v+1}} p_{[u][v+1]}[K + (1 - K)\beta^{u-1}_{[u][v+1]}],
\tag{9}
$$

$$
C_{\max} = C_{[l_t][t]} = \sum_{v=1}^{t} t_{[v]} + \sum_{v=1}^{t} \sum_{u=1}^{l_v} p_{[u][v]}[K + (1 - K)\beta^{u-1}_{[u][v]}].
\tag{10}
$$

It can be seen from $C_{\max}$ that the order of the groups is arbitrary, and the job sequence within the group can be solved by the assignment method. So, the problem of sequencing jobs in each group could be solved in polynomial time.

$$
\begin{aligned}
\min \quad & \sum_{u=1}^{l_{[v]}} \sum_{h=1}^{l_{[v]}} p_{[u][v]}[K + (1 - K)\beta^{h-1}_{[u][v]}] e_{u[v]h}, \\
s.t. \quad & \sum_{h=1}^{l_{[v]}} e_{u[v]h} = 1, \quad v = 1,\ldots,t; u = 1,\ldots,l_{[v]}, \\
& \sum_{u=1}^{l_{[v]}} e_{u[v]h} = 1, \quad v = 1,\ldots,t; h = 1,\ldots,l_{[v]}, \\
& e_{u[v]h} = 0, or 1, \quad v = 1,\ldots,t; u,h = 1,\ldots,l_{[v]}.
\end{aligned}
\tag{11}
$$

$\square$

The algorithm is summarized as follows:

It is easy to show that the total time for Algorithm 2 is $O(n^3)$.

Algorithm 2 $1|p^a_{[u][v]} = p_{[u][v]}[K + (1 - K)\beta^{s-1}_{[u][v]}], GT, t_v|C_{\max}$

Require: t, K, l_v, t_v, p_{uv}, β_{uv}
Ensure: The job sequence within the group and $C_{\max}$
  1: **First step:** Using the assignment method, the job sequence within the group is solved.
  2: **Second step:** The order of the groups is arbitrary.
  3: **Last step:** Calculate $C_{\max}$.

4.2. Total Completion Time Minimization

Theorem 3. *For the* $1|p^a_{[u][v]} = p_{[u][v]}[K + (1 - K)s^{\alpha_{[u][v]}}], GT, t_v| \sum_{v=1}^{t} \sum_{u=1}^{l_v} C_{[u][v]}$ *problem, the optimal solution is that the job sequence within the group can be solved by the assignment method and the groups are arranged in nondecreasing order of* $\dfrac{t_b + \sum_{u=1}^{l_b} p_{[u]b}[K+(1-K)u^{\alpha_{[u]b}}]}{l_b}$.

Proof. Suppose there are l_v jobs in the vth group, $l_1 + \cdots + l_t = l$, $1 \le v \le t$. The completion time of each job is

$$C_{[u][1]} = t_{[1]} + \sum_{k=1}^{u} p_{[k][1]}[K + (1 - K)k^{u_{[k][1]}}], 1 \le u \le l_1, \tag{12}$$

$$C_{[u][v+1]} = C_{[l_v][v]} + t_{[v+1]} + \sum_{k=1}^{u} p_{[k][v+1]}[K + (1 - K)k^{\alpha_{[k][v+1]}}], 1 \le u \le l_{v+1}. \tag{13}$$

Therefore, the total completion time is

$$\sum_{v=1}^{t} \sum_{u=1}^{l_v} C_{[u][v]} = \sum_{v=1}^{t} l_v t_v + \sum_{v=2}^{t} l_v C_{[l_{v-1}][v-1]} + \sum_{v=1}^{t} \sum_{u=1}^{l_v} (l_v - u + 1) p_{[u][v]}[K + (1 - K)u^{\alpha_{[u][v]}}]. \tag{14}$$

The first term is a constant in the above formula. The second term is

$$\sum_{v=2}^{t} l_v C_{[l_{v-1}][v-1]} = \sum_{v=2}^{t} l_v \sum_{k=1}^{v-1} \{t_{[k]} + \sum_{u=1}^{l_k} p_{[u][k]}[K + (1 - K)u^{\alpha_{[u][k]}}]\}. \tag{15}$$

We prove that the second term obtains the optimal solution by the adjacent exchange method. Let $S_1 = (\theta_1, G_b, G_c, \theta_2)$ and $S_2 = (\theta_1, G_c, G_b, \theta_2)$ be two job sequences with the same sequence except G_b and G_c. G_b is at the γth position in the S_1 sequence, and G_c is at the $(\gamma + 1)$th position in the S_1 sequence. There are l_b jobs in group G_b, and there are l_c jobs in group G_c.

$$\sum_{v=2}^{t} l_v C_{[l_{v-1}][v-1]}(S_1) - \sum_{v=2}^{t} l_v C_{[l_{v-1}][v-1]}(S_2)$$

$$= l_b \sum_{v=1}^{\gamma-1} \{t_{[v]} + \sum_{u=1}^{l_v} p_{[u][v]}[K + (1 - K)u^{\alpha_{[u][v]}}]\} + l_c \sum_{v=1}^{\gamma} \{t_{[v]} + \sum_{u=1}^{l_v} p_{[u][v]}[K + (1 - K)u^{\alpha_{[u][v]}}]\}$$

$$- l_c \sum_{v=1}^{\gamma-1} \{t_{[v]} + \sum_{u=1}^{l_v} p_{[u][v]}[K + (1 - K)u^{\alpha_{[u][v]}}]\} - l_b \sum_{v=1}^{\gamma} \{t_{[v]} + \sum_{u=1}^{l_v} p_{[u][v]}[K + (1 - K)u^{\alpha_{[u][v]}}]\} \tag{16}$$

$$= l_c \{t_b + \sum_{u=1}^{l_b} p_{[u]b}[K + (1 - K)u^{\alpha_{[u]b}}]\} - l_b \{t_c + \sum_{u=1}^{l_c} p_{[u]c}[K + (1 - K)u^{\alpha_{[u]c}}]\}.$$

If S_1 is better than S_2, the above formula is less than 0. Then,

$$l_c\{t_b + \sum_{u=1}^{l_b} p_{[u]b}[K + (1-K)u^{\alpha_{[u]b}}]\} < l_b\{t_c + \sum_{u=1}^{l_c} p_{[u]c}[K + (1-K)u^{\alpha_{[u]c}}]\}, \qquad (17)$$

$$\frac{t_b + \sum\limits_{u=1}^{l_b} p_{[u]b}[K + (1-K)u^{\alpha_{[u]b}}]}{l_b} < \frac{t_c + \sum\limits_{u=1}^{l_c} p_{[u]c}[K + (1-K)u^{\alpha_{[u]c}}]}{l_c}. \qquad (18)$$

The third term can be solved by the assignment method.

$$\begin{aligned}
\min \quad & \sum_{u=1}^{l_{[v]}} \sum_{h=1}^{l_{[v]}} (l_{[v]} - h + 1) p_{[u][v]}[K + (1-K)h^{\alpha_{[u][v]}}]e_{u[v]h}, \\
s.t. \quad & \textstyle\sum_{h=1}^{l_{[v]}} e_{u[v]h} = 1, \quad v = 1,\ldots,t; u = 1,\ldots,l_{[v]}, \\
& \textstyle\sum_{u=1}^{l_{[v]}} e_{u[v]h} = 1, \quad v = 1,\ldots,t; h = 1,\ldots,l_{[v]}, \\
& e_{u[v]h} = 0, or\, 1, \quad v = 1,\ldots,t; u,h = 1,\ldots,l_{[v]}.
\end{aligned} \qquad (19)$$

$\square$

The algorithm is summarized as follows:

It is easy to show that the total time for Algorithm 3 is $O(n^3)$.

Algorithm 3 $1|p^a_{[u][v]} = p_{[u][v]}[K + (1-K)s^{\alpha_{[u][v]}}], GT, t_v| \sum_{v=1}^{t} \sum_{u=1}^{l_v} C_{[u][v]}$

Require: $t, K, l_v, t_v, p_{uv}, \alpha_{uv}$

Ensure: The job sequence within the group, group sequence and $\sum_{v=1}^{t} \sum_{u=1}^{l_v} C_{[u][v]}$

1: **First step:** Using the assignment method, the job sequence within the group is solved.

2: **Second step:** Calculate the order of the groups by nondecreasing order of

$$\frac{t_b + \sum\limits_{u=1}^{l_b} p_{[u]b}[K+(1-K)u^{\alpha_{[u]b}}]}{l_b}.$$

3: **Last step:** Calculate $\sum_{v=1}^{t} \sum_{u=1}^{l_v} C_{[u][v]}$.

Example 2. *The conditions are the same as in Example 1 and the objective function is changed from $C_{\max}$ to $\sum_{v=1}^{t} \sum_{u=1}^{l_v} C_{[u][v]}$.*

Solution:

By the assignment method, the order of the jobs is $job_{31} \to job_{21} \to job_{11}$ in G_1 and the order of the jobs is $job_{12} \to job_{22}$ in G_2.

$$f(G_1) = \frac{t_1 + \sum\limits_{u=1}^{l_1} p_{[u]1}[K + (1-K)u^{\alpha_{[u]1}}]}{l_1} = \frac{2 + \sum\limits_{u=1}^{3} p_{[u]1}[0.5 + 0.5 \times u^{\alpha_{[u]1}}]}{3} = 5.12,$$

$$f(G_2) = \frac{t_2 + \sum\limits_{u=1}^{l_2} p_{[u]2}[K + (1-K)u^{\alpha_{[u]2}}]}{l_2} = \frac{3 + \sum\limits_{u=1}^{2} p_{[u]2}[0.5 + 0.5 \times u^{\alpha_{[u]2}}]}{2} = 4.29.$$

$$(20)$$

Therefore, the order of the groups is $G_2 \to G_1$.

$$\sum_{v=1}^{2} \sum_{u=1}^{l_v} C_{[u][v]} = 3 + 4 + 8.57 + 13.57 + 18.4 + 23.92 = 71.46. \qquad (21)$$

The proof of the $1|p^a_{[u][v]} = p_{[u][v]}[K + (1-K)\beta^{s-1}_{[u][v]}], GT, t_v| \sum_{v=1}^{t} \sum_{u=1}^{l_v} C_{[u][v]}$ problem is the same as that of Theorem 3.

Theorem 4. *For the* $1|p^a_{[u][v]} = p_{[u][v]}[K + (1 - K)\beta^{s-1}_{[u][v]}], GT, t_v| \sum_{v=1}^{t} \sum_{u=1}^{l_v} C_{[u][v]}$ *problem, the optimal solution is that the job sequence within the group can be solved by the assignment method and the groups are arranged in nondecreasing order of* $\dfrac{t_b + \sum_{u=1}^{l_b} p_{[u]b}[K+(1-K)\beta^{s-1}_{[u]b}]}{l_b}$.

The algorithm is summarized as follows:

It is easy to show that the total time for Algorithm 4 is $O(n^3)$.

Algorithm 4 $1|p^a_{[u][v]} = p_{[u][v]}[K + (1 - K)\beta^{s-1}_{[u][v]}], GT, t_v| \sum_{v=1}^{t} \sum_{u=1}^{l_v} C_{[u][v]}$

Require: $t, K, l_v, t_v, p_{uv}, \beta_{uv}$

Ensure: The job sequence within the group, group sequence and $\sum_{v=1}^{t} \sum_{u=1}^{l_v} C_{[u][v]}$

  1: **First step:** Using the assignment method, the job sequence within the group is solved.

  2: **Second step:** Calculate the order of the groups by nondecreasing order of $\dfrac{t_b + \sum_{u=1}^{l_b} p_{[u]b}[K+(1-K)\beta^{s-1}_{[u]b}]}{l_b}$.

  3: **Last step:** Calculate $\sum_{v=1}^{t} \sum_{u=1}^{l_v} C_{[u][v]}$.

---

5. Conclusions

This paper considered the single-group scheduling models with Pegels' and DeJong's learning effect and the single-group scheduling models with Pegels' and DeJong's aging effect. When $0 < K < 1$, they are the learning scheduling models. When $K > 1$, they are the aging scheduling models. In a classical scheduling model, Pegels' and DeJong's learning effect is a constant or position-dependent, while the learning effect and aging effect were job-dependent in this paper. Compared with the classical learning model and aging model for scheduling, the proposed models were more general and realistic. The objective functions were to minimize the total completion time and makespan. We proposed polynomial time methods to solve all the studied problems.

In the future, we can also consider the multimachine Pegels' and Dejong's learning scheduling.

6. Limitations

The problem comes from a real production scheduling problem. In some practical single-group scheduling problems, the learning effect and aging effect are job-dependent. We conducted a deep research study on this issue to prove whether it was an NP-hard problem or polynomial-time solvable problem. After a long period of exploration, the present result was achieved.

Author Contributions: The work presented here was performed in collaboration among all authors. Conceptualization, J.Q.; methodology, J.Q.; validation, Y.Z.; investigation, Y.Z.; writing—original draft preparation, J.Q.; writing—review and editing, Y.Z.; supervision, Y.Z. All authors have read and agreed to the published version of the manuscript.

Funding: This research was funded by J. Qian of the Fundamental Research Funds for the Central Universities grant number N2105020, Y. Zhan of the Fundamental Research Funds for the Central Universities grant number N2105021. and Y. Zhan of the Natural Science Foundation of Liaoning Province Project grant number 2021-MS-102.

Institutional Review Board Statement: Not applicable.

Informed Consent Statement: Not applicable.

Data Availability Statement: Not applicable.

Acknowledgments: We thank the editor and the anonymous reviewers for their helpful comments and insights that significantly improved our paper.

Conflicts of Interest: The authors declare no conflict of interest.

References

1.   Biskup, D. Single-machine scheduling with learning considerations. *Eur. J. Oper. Res.* **1985**, *115*, 173–178. [CrossRef]
2.   Mosheiov, G. Parallel machine scheduling with a learning effect. *Int. J. Prod. Res.* **2001**, *52*, 1165–1169. [CrossRef]
3.   Yang, S.; Yang, D. Minimizing the makespan on single-machine scheduling with aging effect and variable maintenance activities. *Omega* **2010**, *38*, 528–533. [CrossRef]
4.   Zhang, X.; Yan, G. Single-machine group scheduling problems with deteriorated and learning effect. *Appl. Math. Comput.* **2010**, *216*, 1259–1266. [CrossRef]
5.   Li, G.; Luo, M.; Zhang, W.; Wang, X. Single-machine due-window assignment scheduling based on common flow allowance, learning effect and resource allocation. *Int. J. Prod. Res.* **2015**, *53*, 1228–1241. [CrossRef]
6.   Lu, Y.; Wang, J.; Ji, P.; He, H. A note on resource allocation scheduling with group technology and learning effects on a single machine. *Eng. Optim.* **2017**, *49*, 1621–1632. [CrossRef]
7.   Mustu, S.; Eren, T. The single machine scheduling problem with sequence-dependent setup times and a learning effect on processing times. *Appl. Soft. Comput.* **2018**, *71*, 291–306. [CrossRef]
8.   Yin, Y.; Wu, W.; Cheng, T.C.E.; Wu, C. Due-date assignment and single-machine scheduling with generalised position-dependent deteriorating jobs and deteriorating multi-maintenance activities. *Int. J. Prod. Res.* **2014**, *52*, 2311–2326. [CrossRef]
9.   Zhang, X.; Lin, W.C.; Hsu, C.J.; Wu, C.C. Resource constrained scheduling problems with general truncated sum-of-processing time dependent effect under single machine and unrelated parallel machines. *Comput. Ind. Eng.* **2017**, *110*, 344–352. [CrossRef]
10. Zhao, C.; Hsu, C.J.; Wu, W.; Cheng, S.; Wu, C. Note on a unified approach to the single-machine scheduling problem with a deterioration effect and convex resource allocation. *J. Manuf. Syst.* **2016**, *38*, 134–140. [CrossRef]
11. Li, L.; Yan, P.; Ji, P.; Wang, J. Scheduling jobs with simultaneous considerations of controllable processing times and learning effect. *Neural Comput. Appl.* **2018**, *29*, 1155–1162. [CrossRef]
12. De Jong, J.R. The effects of increasing skill on cycle time and its consequences for time standards. *Ergonomics* **1957**, *1*, 51–60. [CrossRef]
13. Wang, J.; Wang, D.; Wang, L.; Lin, L.; Yin, N.; Wang, W. Single machine scheduling with exponential time-dependent learning effect and past-sequence-dependent setup times. *Comput. Math. Appl.* **2009**, *57*, 9–16. [CrossRef]
14. Okołowski, D.; Gawiejnowicz, S. Exact and heuristic algorithms for parallel-machine scheduling with DeJong's learning effect. *Comput. Ind. Eng.* **2010**, *59*, 272–279. [CrossRef]
15. Ji, M.; Yao, D.; Yang, Q.; Cheng, T.C.E. Machine scheduling with DeJong's learning effect. *Comput. Ind. Eng.* **2015**, *80*, 195–200. [CrossRef]
16. Ji, M.; Tang, X.; Zhang, X.; Cheng, T.C.E. Machine scheduling with deteriorating jobs and DeJong's learning effect. *Comput. Ind. Eng.* **2016**, *91*, 42–47. [CrossRef]
17. Zhang, X.; Liao, L.; Zhang, W.; Cheng, T.C.E.; Tan, Y.; Ji, M. Single-machine group scheduling with new models of position-dependent processing times. *Comput. Ind. Eng.* **2018**, *117*, 1–5. [CrossRef]
18. Sun, L.; Ning, L.; Huo, J. Group Scheduling Problems with Time-Dependent and Position-Dependent DeJong's Learning Effect. *Math. Probl. Eng.* **2020**, *2020*, 5161872. [CrossRef]
19. Ji, M.; Chen, K.; Ge, J.; Cheng, T.C.E. Group scheduling and job-dependent due window assignment based on a common flow allowance. *Comput. Ind. Eng.* **2014**, *68*, 35–41. [CrossRef]
20. Sun, L.; Yu, A.J.; Wu, B. Single machine common flow allowance group scheduling with learning effect and resource allocation. *Comput. Ind. Eng.* **2020**, *139*, 106126. [CrossRef]
21. Lee, W.C.; Lu, Z.S. Group scheduling with deteriorating jobs to minimize the total weighted number of late jobs. *Appl. Math. Comput.* **2012**, *218*, 8750–8757. [CrossRef]
22. Keshavarz, T.; Savelsbergh, M.; Salmasi, N. A branch-and-bound algorithm for the single machine sequence-dependent group scheduling problem with earliness and tardiness penalties. *Appl. Math. Model.* **2015**, *39*, 6410–6424. [CrossRef]
23. Ji, M.; Zhang, X.; Tang, X.; Cheng, T.C.E.; Wei, G.; Tan, Y. Group scheduling with group-dependent multiple due windows assignment. *Int. J. Prod. Res.* **2016**, *54*, 1244–1256. [CrossRef]
24. Wang, L.Y.; Liu, M.; Wang, J.B.; Lu, Y.Y.; Liu, W.W. Optimization for Due-Date Assignment Single–Machine Scheduling under Group Technology. *Complexity* **2021**, *2021*, 6656261. [CrossRef]
25. Ren, J.; Yang, Y. Common due-window assignment and minmax scheduling with resource allocation and group technology on a single machine. *Eng. Optim.* **2021**, 1961761. [CrossRef]

 *mathematics*

Article

An Intelligent Athlete Signal Processing Methodology for Balance Control Ability Assessment with Multi-Headed Self-Attention Mechanism

Nannan Xu [1], Xinze Cui [2], Xin Wang [2,*], Wei Zhang [3] and Tianyu Zhao [4,*]

[1] Sports Training Institute, Shenyang Sport University, Shenyang 110115, China
[2] Department of Kinesiology, Shenyang Sport University, Shenyang 110115, China
[3] School of Aerospace Engineering, Shenyang Aerospace University, Shenyang 110136, China
[4] Key Laboratory of Structural Dynamics of Liaoning Province, College of Sciences, Northeastern University, Shenyang 110819, China
* Correspondence: wangxin@syty.edu.cn (X.W.); zhaotianyu@mail.neu.edu.cn (T.Z.)

Abstract: In different kinds of sports, the balance control ability plays an important role for every athlete. Therefore, coaches and athletes need accurate and efficient assessments of the balance control ability to improve the athletes' training performance scientifically. With the fast growth of sport technology and training devices, intelligent and automatic assessment methods have been in high demand in the past years. This paper proposes a deep-learning-based method for a balance control ability assessment involving an analysis of the time-series signals from the athletes. The proposed method directly processes the raw data and provides the assessment results, with an end-to-end structure. This straight-forward structure facilitates its practical application. A deep learning model is employed to explore the target features with a multi-headed self-attention mechanism, which is a new approach to sports assessments. In the experiments, the real athletes' balance control ability assessment data are utilized for the validation of the proposed method. Through comparisons with different existing methods, the accuracy rate of the proposed method is shown to be more than 95% for all four tasks, which is higher than the other compared methods for tasks containing more than one athlete of each level. The results show that the proposed method works effectively and efficiently in real scenarios for athlete balance control ability evaluations. However, reducing the proposed method's calculation costs is an important task for future studies.

Keywords: athlete signal processing; deep learning; balance control ability; multi-headed self-attention mechanism

MSC: 68T07

Citation: Xu, N.; Cui, X.; Wang, X.; Zhang, W.; Zhao, T. An Intelligent Athlete Signal Processing Methodology for Balance Control Ability Assessment with Multi-Headed Self-Attention Mechanism. *Mathematics* **2022**, *10*, 2794. https://doi.org/10.3390/math10152794

Academic Editor: Jakub Nalepa

Received: 9 July 2022
Accepted: 3 August 2022
Published: 6 August 2022

1. Introduction

Because of its significance, almost every sport requires accurate and efficient assessments of the balance control ability of athletes [1]. Meanwhile, the scientific management of athletes depends on good assessments of their balance control ability, including for selection, training, and competition. It is very difficult to accurately assess the balance control ability, since massive and complex data are produced during training and events, and large amounts of expert knowledge and human labor are also required in order to explore the underlying ability of the athletes from the data, making it hard to carry out such assessments in practical scenarios [2,3].

In recent years, with the rapid development of measurement devices and artificial intelligence technology, data-driven methods of balance control ability assessment have demonstrated some excellent effects [4]. In this paper, all of the utilized data were collected from the athletes using a movement pressure measurement machine. When an athlete stands on the machine, the pressure signals are collected, which reflect the balance control ability of the athlete. In general, a smaller movement pressure indicates better balance control ability, while a larger movement pressure shows a lower level of balance control [5]. Therefore, we can analyze the data to assess the balance control ability of the athletes and even explore their underlying abilities.

In the traditional methods, statistical features are usually used to assess the balance control ability, such as the mean, root mean square, and so on. However, these methods are too simple to reflect the complex features in the collected data. In recent years, many signal processing methods have been used to extract better features, such as wavelet analysis [6] and stochastic resonance [7] techniques. In addition, it is very popular to use machine learning and statistical inference techniques for related problems, such as artificial neural network (ANN) [8], support vector machine (SVM), random forest, fuzzy inference, and other techniques [9–11]. Although the existing methods have achieved success, they are generally less capable of dealing with the collected movement pressure data, which contain a lot of noise. Furthermore, the distinction of the balance control ability among athletes at different levels is quite hard, especially for professional high-level freestyle skiing athletes, which makes it difficult to use the existing methods for assessments of balance control ability. This is also a great challenge for the traditional data-driven methods with related problems.

With the rapid development of computing technologies, deep neural networks have been the advanced methods of choice for artificial intelligence in recent years [12–16], which have achieved a lot of effective and fruitful results in many fields, such as image recognition [17–21] and natural language processing [22]. Deep neural networks can achieve high prediction accuracy via training with big data to automatically learn the mapping function between the input data and the output target. They can automatically analyze the input data without prior knowledge related to signal processing or domain expertise. Therefore, DNNs are quite suitable for the assessment of balance control ability with freestyle skiing athlete data.

For the analysis of time-series data, the recent studies [23–28] show many good applications of deep neural network models, and higher feature learning efficiency can be achieved using deep neural network models. Therefore, deep learning is being used on various types of time-series data, such as in financial analyses, traffic monitoring, industrial optimization, machinery fault diagnosis problems, and so on [29–33]. In a related study [34], a deep-learning-based LSTM method was used for COVID-19 pandemic spread forecasting, which achieved great success.

However, the simple structure of the basic deep neural network models cannot be applied well in real tasks with quite complicated data. Normally, adding a number of inside neurons and layers can enhance the learning ability. However, the consumption of computing power also increases in the meantime. On the other hand, the deep architecture generally causes losses of feature information.

In this paper, a novel multi-headed self-attention mechanism is proposed to address the assessment problem of balance control ability for freestyle skiing athletes. The main novelties and contributions of this paper are as follows:

1. A multi-headed self-attention mechanism is used to automatically learn features with many standalone heads and to process the information using a residual connection structure. The heads have the same structure but with different initial parameters, which can explore different information features at the same time. This structure is very advanced in the field of deep learning. Through this structure, we can efficiently explore the deep features of the data;

2. As one of the first attempts, this paper proposes a deep-learning-based method for automatic feature exploration and freestyle skiing athlete balance control ability assessment, which have been seldomly studied in the current literature;

3.   A real freestyle skiing athlete under-feet movement pressure measurement dataset is adopted to validate the adopted method, which shows high assessment accuracy and promise for applications in real scenarios.

However, we have to say that the proposed method becomes inefficient when processing high-dimension data because of the multi-headed self-attention structure, which causes excessive calculation costs.

In this paper, the preliminary aspects are described in Section 1. The proposed method is presented in Section 2. The experiments used to validate the proposed method and the results are presented in Section 3. We close the paper with our conclusions in Section 4.

2. Dataset and Methodology

2.1. Dataset

2.1.1. Introduction of the Dataset

In this paper, a dataset collected from the real freestyle skiing aerial athletes involved in the balance control ability assessment task is used to validate the proposed method. The dataset includes a number of people in different balance control levels. They are required to stand with a balance meter under their feet and try their best to keep still with their eyes closed. This is done to achieve a better balance control effect by reducing the vision disturbance and focusing on the body control. The area of the balance meter measures 65 cm × 40 cm, and the balance meter can collect the movement pressure data in the anteroposterior and mediolateral directions, which are denoted as Y and X. The scenarios for data collection are shown in Figure 1.

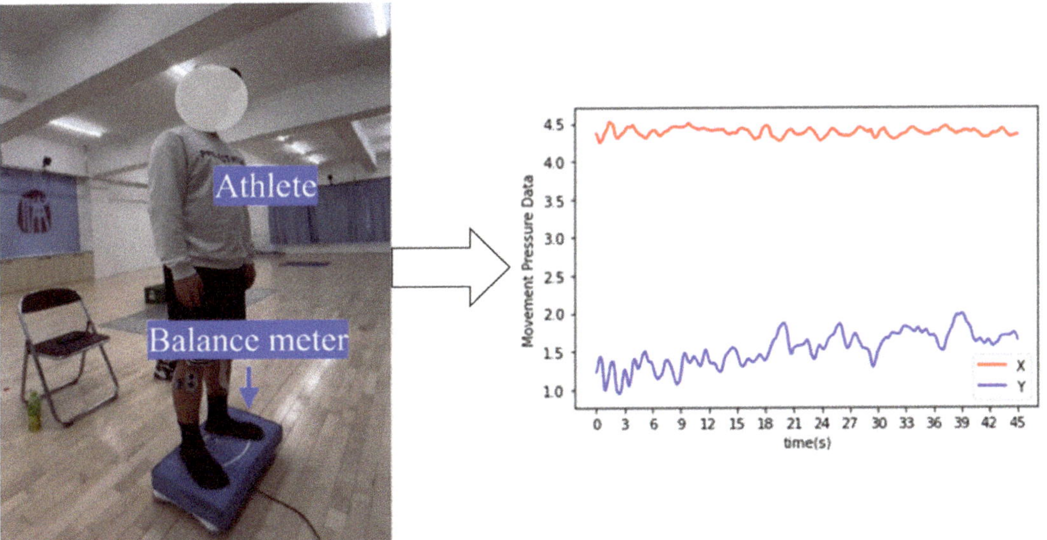

Figure 1. The scenarios of the athlete movement pressure data collection experiments.

The levels of balance control ability are divided into four classes. Specifically, they people from different groups, including top freestyle skiing athletes, professional skill athletes, normally trained students from non-skill sports, and common people. The four classes are denoted as A, B, C, and D, respectively. The balance control ability levels decrease from A to D. For instance, the A group has the best ability, and the B group has the second best ability. We select three athletes from each level, who are represented by #1, #2, and #3 respectively. The athletes are required to keep their upper bodies stationary to and use two feet while standing with their eyes closed, then to reduce their body swing.

The movement pressure data sampling frequency is 100 Hz. We show the information for the dataset used in this study in Table 1.

Table 1. Information for the athlete movement pressure measurement dataset used in this paper.

Athlete Level	Number of Athletes	Code Names	Sampling Frequency
A	3	A#1, A#2, A#3	100 Hz
B	3	B#1, B#2, B#3	100 Hz
C	3	C#1, C#2, C#3	100 Hz
D	3	D#1, D#2, D#3	100 Hz

2.1.2. Pre-Processing of the Dataset

In this study, the task involves predicting different athlete balance control ability levels through learning features from the collected data with the proposed method. In order to fully examine the performance of the proposed method, we implement 5 tasks with different training and testing datasets, which include different athletes in each level. The tasks are demonstrated in Table 2. Every sample of the tasks contains 200 continuous points. The proposed method and compared methods can be fairly evaluated through the tasks by using a wide range of experimental settings.

Table 2. Information for the different athlete balance control ability evaluation tasks used in this study.

Task Name	Concerned Athletes	Sample Number of Every Athlete	Ratio of Training to Testing
T0	A#1, B#1, C#1, D#1	200	4:1
T1	A#2, B#2, C#2, D#2	200	4:1
T2	A#1, B#1, C#1, D#1 A#2, B#2, C#2, D#2	200	4:1
T3	A#1, B#1, C#1, D#1 A#2, B#2, C#2, D#2	400	4:1
T4	A#1, B#1, C#1, D#1 A#2, B#2, C#2, D#2 A#3, B#3, C#3, D#3	200	4:1

2.2. Methods

The flow chart of our proposed method is displayed in Figure 2.

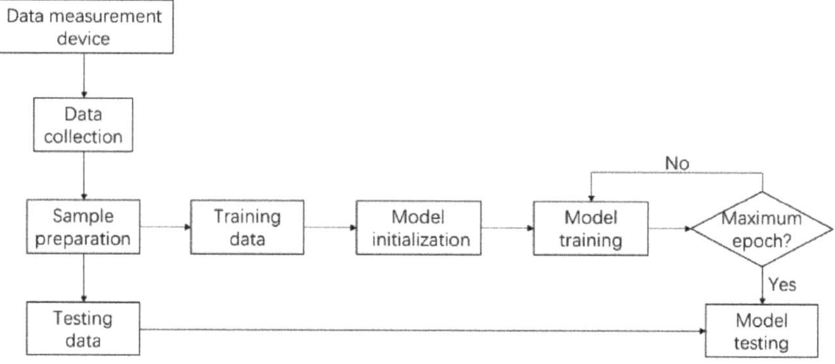

Figure 2. The general flow chart for our proposed method.

2.2.1. Proposed Method

In this paper, we propose a novel method based on the Transformer. The Transformer is one type of auto-encoder (AE). Auto-encoder are some of the most popular neural network structures in the current research, and are wildly used in many application scenarios, such as in image classification tasks, speech recognition problems, video processing problems, and so on [35–37].

In general, an auto-encoder includes an encoder and a decoder, which are symmetric. The function of the encoder is to compress the input data, while the function of the decoder is to decompress the data that the encoder outputs close to the original data. In brief, the auto-encoder is used to reproduce the input data. In this way, the auto-encoder can explore the features of the input data automatically. The process can be expressed as:

$$h(f(x)) \approx x \tag{1}$$

where x is the input data. The function f represents the encoder and the function h represents the decoder, which are inverse processes. The encoder and decoder require different building approaches. For example, the Vanilla Auto-Encoder is made of fully connected neural networks and is the most primitive auto-encoder. Convolutional neural networks (CNNs) are also used to build the auto-encoder [38].

As one of the latest and most powerful auto-encoders, the Transformer was originally used in natural language processing [39], and the encoder and decoder of the Transformer mainly rely on the self-attention mechanism. In addition to being used to solve natural language processing problems, the Transformer is also reformed to deal with the image classification tasks and video processing problems [40,41]. Its effectiveness has been well validated for analyzing time-series signals.

The basic Transformer consists of an input layer, multi-headed self-attention block, normalization layer, feedforward layer, and residual connected layer. Because the basic Transformer is used in natural language processing, the input layer includes word embedding and position embedding. The word embedding is used to transform the words of input sentences to a series of vectors, while the position embedding is used to describe the information about the corresponding positions of the words in the sentence. The multi-headed self-attention block is the most important part to explore for the features of the input data. The details of the structure of the basic Transformer are illustrated in Figure 3.

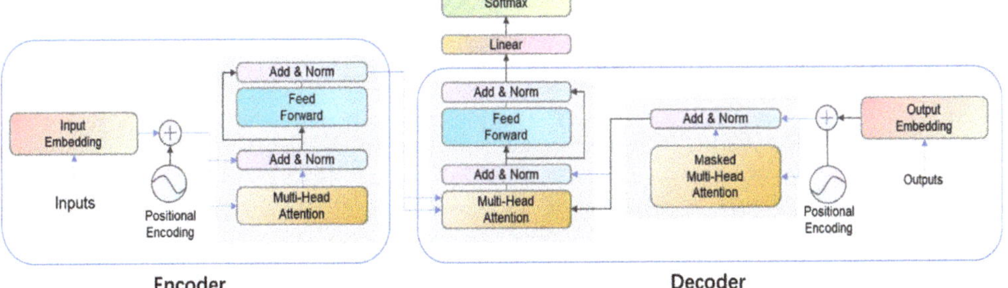

Figure 3. The architecture of the basic Transformer.

The basic Transformer consists of an encoder and decoder. It is mostly used in natural language processing tasks, the input data and target data for which are sentences that contain complex information. In such tasks, researchers use the encoder to analyze the input data and the decoder to analyze the target data. The underlying connection between the two results is also explored. In this paper, only the encoder part of the basic Transformer is adopted. This is because the target data for our task are class numbers without complex information such as sentences. This means we only need to explore the input data and predict their class. The detailed structure is illustrated in Figure 4.

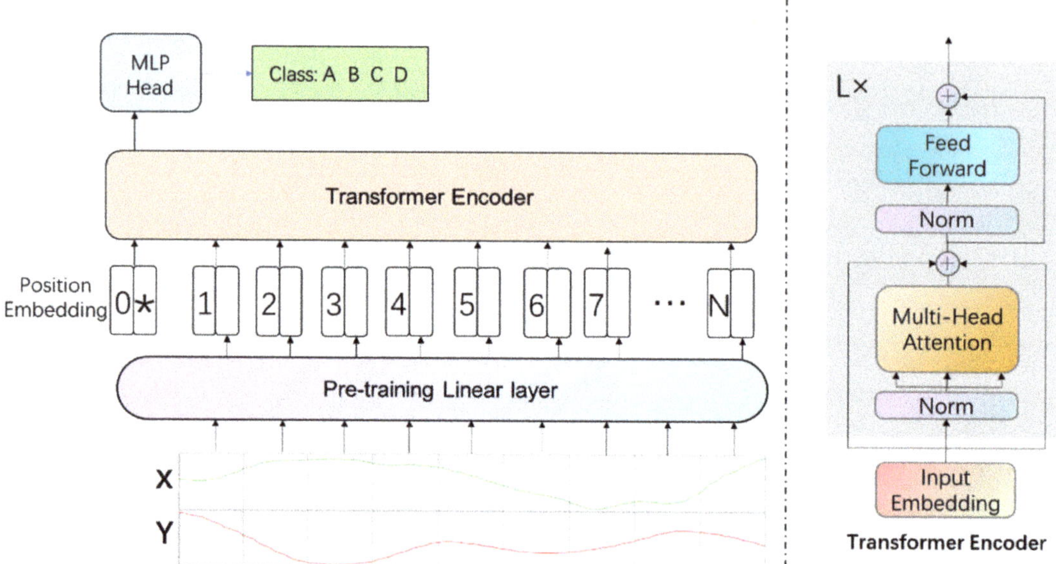

Figure 4. The detailed architecture of our proposed Transformer.

Before the Transformer encoder block, the dimensions of the input data should be extended with a trainable pre-training linear layer in order to explore the deep information. In the results of the experiments, we will show the significant effectiveness of such layers. In addition, similar to most existing methods for natural language processing [42], we propose a learnable embedding approach to the input data, whose state at the output of the Transformer encoder is as the representation of the input data.

After the aforementioned operations, the input data for the Transformer encoder are transformed into a series of vectors. Therefore, the word embedding layers are not required. Specifically, the position embedding layer is needed to describe the information about the time point order of the time series, such as the word position in the sentence.

There are two common ways to achieve the position embedding. The first one is to randomly generate a series of vectors and update them during the training, while the second one is to encode the information with sin and cos functions. We choose the first method in this paper. In both the methods, we should create a matrix whose shape is the same as the input data, and assign its parameters using one of the above methods. Afterwards, the matrix is added to the input data.

The core of the Transformer is the self-attention mechanism. Its function is calculating the relationships between all parts of the input data, which are always sequential data, and the relationships are expressed by a series of probabilities whose sum is one. According to the probabilities, the mechanism will distribute different weights to corresponding parts of the input data.

In this study, the self-attention mechanism is modified from the attention mechanism. In the attention mechanism, the input part consists of three matrices, Q, K, and V. K and V come from the input data, while Q generally comes from the output data. In the self-attention mechanism, all matrices are from the input data. In addition, the attention mechanism is usually used to connect the outputs of the encoder and decoder. However, the self-attention mechanism is the core in the structures of the encoder and decoder. The generator method of the three matrices can be expressed as:

$$X \bullet W_Q = Q$$
$$X \bullet W_K = K$$
$$X \bullet W_V = V$$

(2)

where X is the input data, whose length equals the number of the time steps; W_Q, W_K, W_V are three matrices with the same shape but different parameters, and the parameters can be changed by the training. The operation $\bullet$ is the dot product. The calculation of the self-attention mechanism can be defined as:

$$Self\text{-}Attention(Q, K, V) = softmax(\frac{Q \bullet K^T}{\sqrt{d_k}}) \bullet V$$

(3)

where d_k is the dimension of the matrix K, which can prevent the result of the dot product from flooding. The $softmax$ function can transform the results of the dot product into probabilities as the weights that describe the relationship between all parts of the data.

Based on the self-attention mechanism, the multi-headed self-attention block can explore the features of the input data effectively. The multi-headed self-attention approach involves using many self-attention blocks to explore the same data together, then integrating the results of every block. It should be noted that one block is called one head.

In general, there are two ways to achieve a multi-headed self-attention block. In the first one, we map the input data to Q, K, V without changing the shape and evenly divide them into many small matrices. Next, we calculate them with the self-attention mechanism. In another approach, we can map the input data to Q, K, V with the same shape, which equals the input data dimension multiplied by the number of heads that are needed, then we can calculate them with the self-attention mechanism and finally map the result to the matrix with the linear projection, whose shape is same as the input data. In this way, we can set the number of heads freely. However, more computing power will be consumed. In this paper, we select the later one.

In the $softmax$ function, we let $x^{(i)}$ denote the input samples and $r^{(i)}$ denote the corresponding class labels for them; $i = 1, 2, \cdots, N$, where i is the number of trained samples and N is the quantity of samples. We also have $x^{(i)} \in R^{d \times 1}$ and $r^{(i)} \in \{1, 2, \cdots, L\}$, where L is the whole number of target classes in this paper. According to the input data $x^{(i)}$, the function can give the probability $p(r^{(i)} = j | x^{(i)})$ for different class labels. The calculation is based on the below algorithm:

$$J_\lambda(x^{(i)}) = \begin{bmatrix} p(r^{(i)} = 1 | x^{(i)}; \lambda) \\ p(r^{(i)} = 2 | x^{(i)}; \lambda) \\ \vdots \\ p(r^{(i)} = L | x^{(i)}; \lambda) \end{bmatrix} = \frac{1}{\sum_{l=1}^{L} e^{\lambda_l^T \bullet x^{(i)}}} \begin{bmatrix} e^{\lambda_1^T \bullet x^{(i)}} \\ e^{\lambda_2^T \bullet x^{(i)}} \\ \vdots \\ e^{\lambda_L^T \bullet x^{(i)}} \end{bmatrix}$$

(4)

where $\lambda = [\lambda_1, \lambda_2, \cdots, \lambda_L]^T$ represents the coefficients of the $softmax$ function. The output values of the $softmax$ function are all positive and the sum of them is one. Therefore, the result of the $softmax$ function can be used to predict the probabilities of the target classes and to evaluate the relationship among the parts of the input data in the self-attention mechanism.

After the multi-headed self-attention block, there is a feedforward layer block, which is used to explore the output of the Transformer encoder block again. The core of the block is a MLP model that consists of two linear layers with a GELU non-linearity activation function. In the Transformer encoder, the normalization layer is applied before the multi-headed self-attention block and feedforward layer block, and there are residual connections after every block. The MLP head is set after the Transformer encoder, which carries the task as a classifier to predict the class of the input data. The MLP head contains two linear layers.

At last, we select the Adam optimizer for the proposed method.

2.2.2. Compared Methods

The proposed Transformer model offers a new perspective for the assessment of the athletes' balance control performance with artificial intelligence technology. In this paper, we also implement some popular methods in the current literature for comparisons in order to prove the effectiveness and superiority of the proposed method. The following methods are included.

1. NN

As a typical neural connection method, we select the basic neural network (NN) to join the comparisons, which includes one hidden layer with 1000 neurons, a leaky ReLU activation function, and other typical operations.

2. DNN

The deep neural network (DNN) is based on the basic neural network structure. The used DNN method consists of three layers with 1000, 1000, and 500 neurons. Likewise, similar techniques are also employed, such as a leaky ReLU activation function and so on.

3. DSCNN

The deep single-scale convolution neural network (DSCNN) method is a basic and popular deep learning neural network, which is widely used as a basic cell to build many complex networks, such as LeNet-5, Alex-Net, VGG-16, and so on [43–45]. In the comparison, we use a basic network with one convolutional filter size for the feature extraction.

4. RNN

The recurrent neural network (RNN) method is a typical deep learning neural network, which works well in dealing with sequential data. Therefore, we can better demonstrate the advantage of the proposed method.

5. Random Forest

The random forest is a classical machine learning approach, which is widely used for classification tasks. It consists of a lot of decision trees, and every one of them works independently. The approach performs well with noise. Therefore, it can be used as a suitable comparison method.

3. Results

3.1. Experiment Description

We organize our experiments here as follows. Experiment 1 aims to show the necessity of the pre-training linear layer before the Transformer encoder. Experiment 2 aims to find the optimal hyper-parameters for the proposed method. Experiment 3 aims to show the superiority of the proposed method by competing with the compared methods. The parameters in the experiments are listed in Table 3. The test data are involved into the parameter selection process and the accuracy score might potentially be biased. The selected parameters are popular choices for the deep learning framework, which can be generally used in different applications.

Table 3. Parameter information.

Parameter	Value	Parameter	Value
Batch size	32	Learning rate	1×10^{-4}
Epoch number	100	Sample dimension	200×2

3.2. Experiment and Results Analysis

3.2.1. Experiment 1

In experiment 1, we aim to investigate the influence of the pre-training linear layer. Therefore, we set one group with a linear layer and the control group without a linear layer. Then, we set 512 neurons for the pre-training linear layer, with a 12-layered Transformer encoder with 8 heads for the multi-headed self-attention part. There are 32 dimensions for every head, and the output layer of the feedforward part contains 64 neurons. The results of the 5 tasks are displayed in Figure 5.

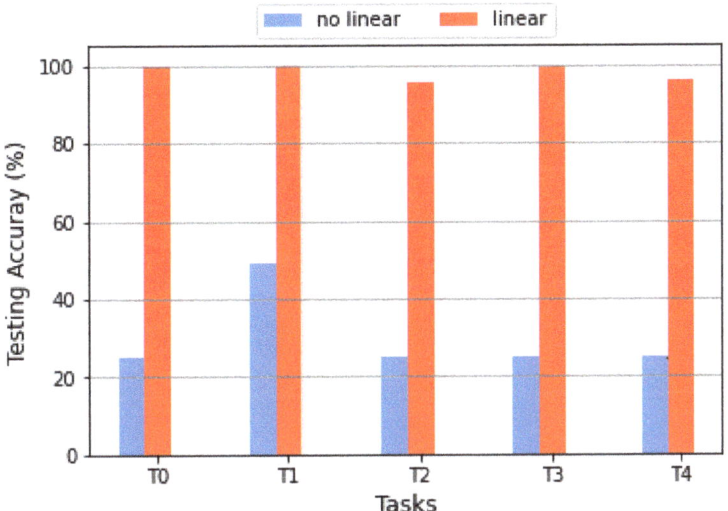

Figure 5. The experimental results of the proposed method with the pre-training linear layer and the method without the pre-training linear layer.

In the figure, the accuracy of the method with the pre-training linear layer is significantly higher than the method without the pre-training linear layer. The pre-training linear layer plays an important role in exploring features of the input data, which we will investigate in the following section.

3.2.2. Experiment 2

In experiment 2, we investigate the optimal hyper-parameters for the proposed method, which include the depth of the Transformer encoder block, the number of pre-training layer neurons, the number of multi-headed self-attention heads, the dimensions of every head, and the output dimensions of the feedforward block. We select the T2 dataset to train the proposed method.

Firstly, we investigate the influence of the Transformer encoder block. Therefore, we set the number of pre-training layer neurons, the number of multi-headed self-attention heads, the dimensions of every head, and the output dimensions of the feedforward block as (512, 8, 32, 64), the results of which are shown in Figure 6.

According to the results, the multi-layer approaches are much more effective than the mono-layer approach. However, the larger Transformer encoder's depth does not usually lead to better results. The accuracy does not significantly increase when the depth of the multi-layer approach increases.

Secondly, the number of pre-training layer neurons is an important factor for the effectiveness of the proposed method. We set the parameters of the proposed method as (6, 8, 32, 64). According to Figure 7a, the accuracy of the proposed method increases as the neuron number of the pre-training linear layer increases. In particular, the accuracy becomes significantly higher when the number of neurons increases compared with the dimensions of the input data. According to Figure 7b, the training loss function of the methods, whose neuron number is smaller than the dimensions of the input data, decreases slowly or changes a little. However, the training loss function decreases rapidly as the neuron number is bigger than the dimensions of the input data. In this study, it is found that the number of neurons has the largest influence on the training of the proposed method.

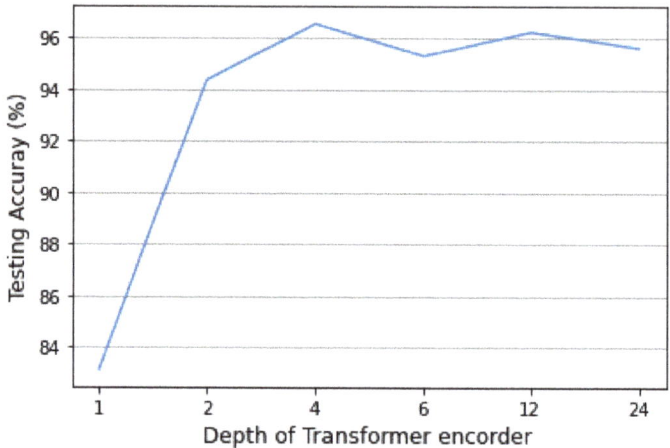

Figure 6. The influence of the depth of the Transformer encoder.

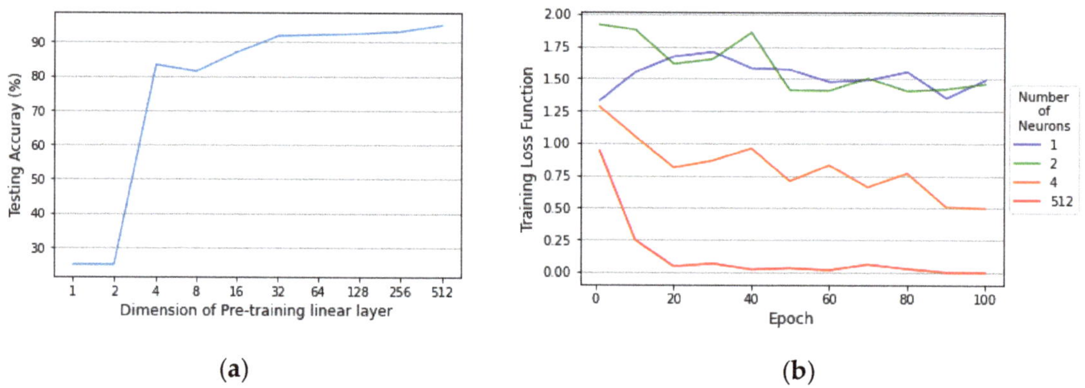

(a)

(b)

Figure 7. The influence of the dimensions of the pre-training linear layer. (**a**) influence on testing accuracy; (**b**) influence on training loss.

Thirdly, the influence of the number of multi-headed self-attention heads is shown in Figure 8. The parameters are set as (6, 512, 32, 64). It is shown that more than 2 heads is suitable, which means the multi-headed self-attention is more effective than the basic self-attention.

In addition, the dimensions of every head also play an important role in the proposed method, which are displayed in Figure 9. The parameters are set as (2, 64, 4, 64). In general, it is noted that the testing accuracy increases as the dimensions of every head increase.

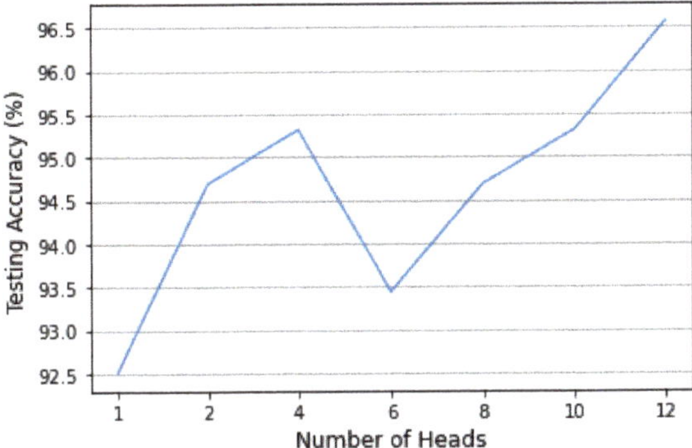

Figure 8. The influence of the number of multi-headed self-attention heads.

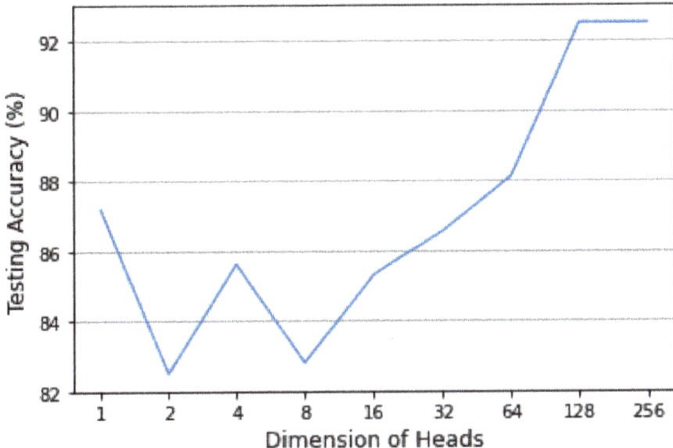

Figure 9. The influence of the dimension of the multi-headed self-attention heads.

Finally, the output dimensions of the feedforward layer are investigated with the parameters of (4, 128, 4, 64). The results are shown in Figure 10. It can be observed that the dimensions have a great influence on the testing accuracy. To be specific, the minimum accuracy is about 8 percentage points less than the maximum accuracy.

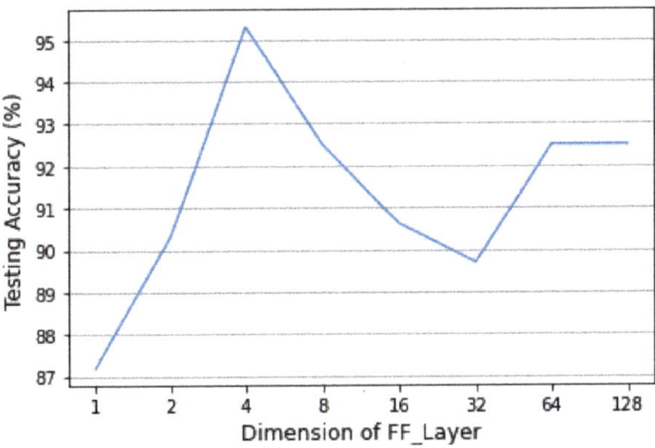

Figure 10. The influence of the dimensions of the feedforward layer.

3.2.3. Experiment 3

In the experiment, we compare the proposed method with the current methods that were mentioned before, in order to demonstrate the superiority and effectiveness of the proposed method. The results are displayed in Figure 11.

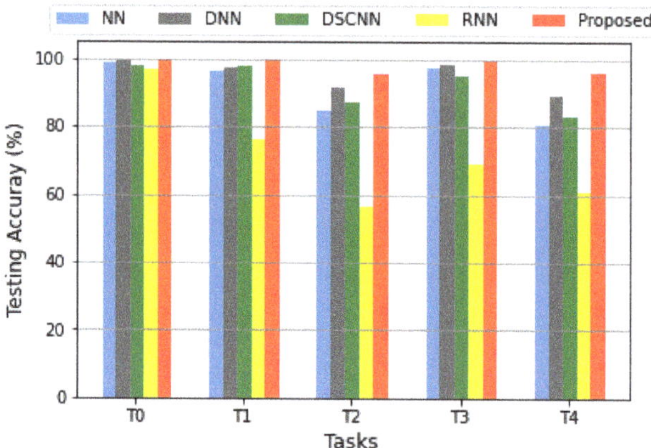

Figure 11. The results of the different compared methods for different tasks.

In Figure 11, it is obvious that the learning ability of the proposed method is much better than the others, whose testing accuracy levels for all tasks are all higher than 95%. Although every method performs well in task T0, which only contains one athlete's data of every level, it should be noted that task T1 also contains only one athlete's data for every level. However, all methods' accuracy levels are reduced to different degrees, except for the proposed method. According to the results for T2 and T4, when different athletes' data are used, every method's accuracy is reduced. The proposed method maintains the accuracy to higher than 95%, although the others all drop to lower than 90%.

In addition, in Figures 12–14, we use the T-SNE algorithm to process the features of the methods for dimension reductions and visualizations of the learned features [46]. Especially, we compare the proposed method with the DNN method. It is clear that the discrimination effect of the proposed method is better. The different clusters of the DNN method are more overlapped by comparison with the proposed method.

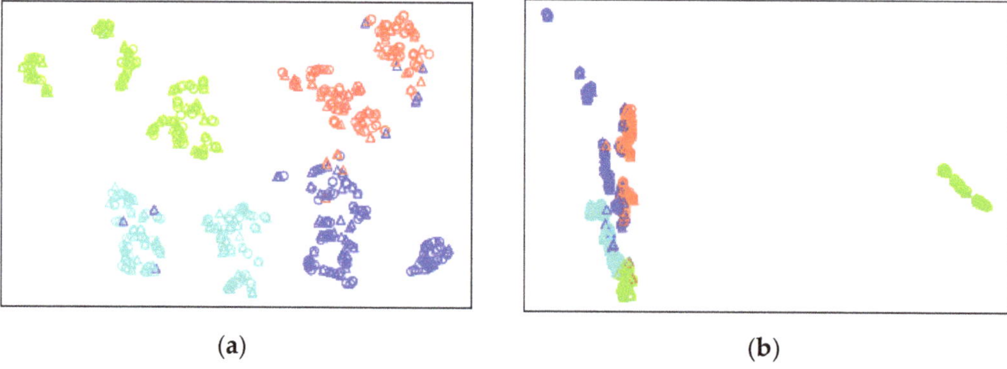

(**a**)   (**b**)

Figure 12. The visualization results of the learned features using different methods for task T2. The different colors represent different athletes; balance control ability levels: (**a**) the result of our proposed method; (**b**) the result of the DNN method.

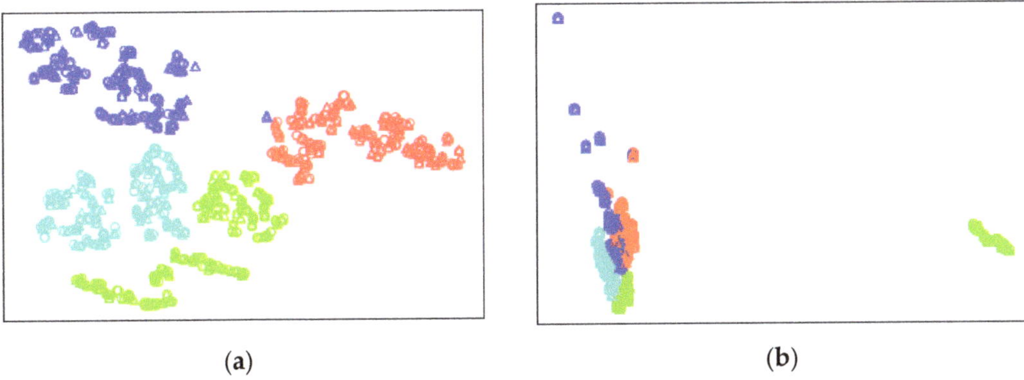

(a) (b)

Figure 13. The visualization results of the learned features using different methods for task T3. The different colors represent different athletes' balance control ability levels: (**a**) the result of our proposed method; (**b**) the result of the DNN method.

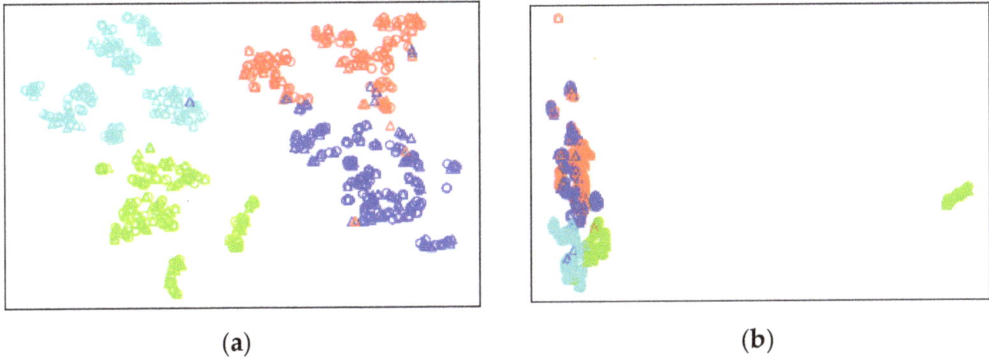

(a) (b)

Figure 14. The visualization results of the learned features using different methods for task T4. The different colors represent different athletes' balance control ability levels: (**a**) the result of our proposed method; (**b**) the result of the DNN method.

From Figure 11, we can see that the DNN is the best of the compared methods; sometimes its accuracy is close to the proposed method's, such as for task T3, but Figure 13 shows their clustering effects using scatter diagrams. It is obvious that the scatter diagram of the proposed method shows the clusters of the results with clear boundaries, but the scatter diagram of the DNN shows that the clusters are farraginous, which means there is a great difference between the features of the two methods, and the proposed method's effect is significantly better.

In addition, it shows that the proposed method maintains the excellent ability for exploring the deep features of the data in Figures 12 and 14, when the sampling frequency becomes sparse and the numbers of athletes at every level increase. In contrast, the results of the DNN method become more chaotic.

4. Conclusions and Future Works

In this paper, a simplified Transformer-based deep neural network model was proposed for the assessment of athlete balance control ability, which processes and analyzes the time-series pressure measurement data from the balance meter. The original data were directly used as the inputs to the model for an automatic assessment without any prior knowledge. Therefore, it is well suited for real applications in various industries.

The multi-headed self-attention process is the core of the proposed method, which calculates the deep connections between every point of the input time-series data and explores complex features via the calculations. In addition, the pre-training linear layer is also necessary, which is used to expand the dimensions of the raw input data to expose the deep information. The connection of two parts can enhance the model training efficiency and quality, making it well suited for many tasks with time series data. The real freestyle skiing athletes under-feet pressure measurement dataset was used in the experiments for validation. The results showed that the proposed method has many advantages in the intelligent assessment of freestyle skiing athletes' balance control abilities. It holds promise for achieving significant success in practical implementations in real scenarios.

However, it should be pointed out that the proposed method generally requires significant computing power, especially with large amounts of data for freestyle skiing athletes. In addition, in order to more efficiently and accurately assess the balance control ability and other related abilities, we could use high-dimension data for freestyle skiing athletes in the future. Therefore, a reduction in the computational burden of the proposed method will be investigated, as well as optimization of the deep neural network architecture. Better pre-processing methods will also be proposed in the next study.

Author Contributions: Conceptualization, X.W.; Formal analysis, N.X.; Investigation, X.C.; Project administration, W.Z.; Resources, T.Z. All authors have read and agreed to the published version of the manuscript.

Funding: This study was funded by the Key R&D Plan of China for the Winter Olympics (No. 2021YFF0306401), the Key Special Project of the National Key Research and Development Program "Technical Winter Olympics" (2018YFF0300502 and 2021YFF0306400), and the Key Research Program of Liaoning Province (2020JH2/10300112).

Institutional Review Board Statement: Not applicable.

Informed Consent Statement: Not applicable.

Data Availability Statement: Data is contained within the article.

Conflicts of Interest: The authors declare no conflict of interest.

References

1. Snyder, N.; Cinelli, M. Comparing balance control between soccer players and non-athletes during a dynamic lower limb reaching task. *Res. Q. Exerc. Sport* **2020**, *91*, 166–171. [CrossRef] [PubMed]
2. Nolan, L.; Grigorenko, A.; Thorstensson, A. Balance control: Sex and age differences in 9- to 16-year-olds. *Child. Neurol.* **2005**, *47*, 449–454.
3. Andreeva, A.; Melnikov, A.; Skvortsov, D.; Akhmerova, K.; Vavaev, A.; Golov, A.; Draugelite, V.; Nikolaev, R.; Chechelnickaia, S.; Zhuk, D.; et al. Postural stability in athletes: The role of age, sex, performance level, and athlete shoe features. *Sports* **2020**, *8*, 89. [CrossRef]
4. Cloak, R.; Nevill, A.; Day, S.; Wyon, M. Six-week combined vibration and wobble board training on balance and stability in footballers with functional ankle instability. *Clin. J. Sport Med.* **2013**, *23*, 384–391. [CrossRef]
5. Bruijn, S.M.; van Dieën, J.H. Control of human gait stability through foot placement. *J. R. Soc. Interface* **2018**, *15*, 20170816. [CrossRef]
6. Adewusi, S.A.; Al-Bedoor, B.O.B. Wavelet analysis of vibration signals of an overhang rotor with a propagating transverse crack. *J. Sound Vib.* **2001**, *246*, 777–793. [CrossRef]
7. Chen, X.; Cheng, G.; Shan, X.L.; Hu, X.; Guo, Q.; Liu, H.G. Research of weak fault feature information extraction of planetary gear based on ensemble empirical mode decomposition and adaptive stochastic resonance. *Measurement* **2015**, *73*, 55–67. [CrossRef]
8. Singh, A.N.R.; Peters, B.E.M. Artificial neural networks in the determination of the fluid intake needs of endurance athletes. *AASRI Procedia* **2014**, *8*, 9–14. [CrossRef]
9. Li, X.; Jia, X.; Yang, Q.; Lee, J. Quality analysis in metal additive manufacturing with deep learning. *J. Intell. Manuf.* **2020**, *31*, 2003–2017. [CrossRef]
10. Zhao, T.; Li, K.; Ma, H. Study on dynamic characteristics of a rotating cylindrical shell with uncertain parameters. *Anal. Math. Phys.* **2022**, *12*, 1–18. [CrossRef]
11. Zhao, T.Y.; Yan, K.; Li, H.W.; Wang, X. Study on theoretical modeling and vibration performance of an assembled cylindrical shell-plate structure with whirl motion. *Appl. Math. Model.* **2022**, *110*, 618–632. [CrossRef]

12. Lv, J.; Wang, C.; Gao, W.; Zhao, Q. An economic forecasting method based on the lightgbm-optimized lstm and time-series model. *Comput. Intell. Neurosci.* **2021**, *2021*, 8128879. [CrossRef] [PubMed]

13. Chen, S.; Han, X.; Shen, Y.; Ye, C. Application of improved lstm algorithm in macroeconomic forecasting. *Comput. Intell. Neurosci.* **2021**, *2021*, 4471044. [CrossRef] [PubMed]

14. He, K.; Zhang, X.; Ren, S.; Sun, J. Deep residual learning for image recognition. In Proceedings of the IEEE Conference on Computer Vision and Pattern Recognition, Las Vegas, NV, USA, 27–30 June 2016; pp. 770–778.

15. Zhang, W.; Li, X.; Ma, H.; Luo, Z.; Li, X. Transfer learning using deep representation regularization in remaining useful life prediction across operating conditions. *Reliab. Eng. Syst. Saf.* **2021**, *211*, 107556. [CrossRef]

16. Li, X.; Zhang, W.; Xu, N.X.; Ding, Q. Deep learning-based machinery fault diagnostics with domain adaptation across sensors at different places. *IEEE Trans. Ind. Electron.* **2019**, *67*, 6785–6794. [CrossRef]

17. Wang, K.; Chen, K.; Du, H.; Liu, S.; Xu, J.; Zhao, J.; Chen, H.; Liu, Y.; Liu, Y. New image dataset and new negative sample judgment method for crop pest recognition based on deep learning models. *Ecol. Inform.* **2022**, *69*, 101620. [CrossRef]

18. Fujiyosh, H.; Hirakawa, T.; Yamashita, T. Deep learning-based image recognition for autonomous driving. *IATSS Res.* **2019**, *43*, 244–252. [CrossRef]

19. Qian, C.; Xu, F.; Li, H. User Authentication by Gait Data from Smartphone Sensors Using Hybrid Deep Learning Network. *Mathematics* **2022**, *10*, 2283.

20. De-Prado-Gil, J.; Osama, Z.; Covadonga, P.; Martínez-García, R. Prediction of Splitting Tensile Strength of Self-Compacting Recycled Aggregate Concrete Using Novel Deep Learning Methods. *Mathematics* **2022**, *10*, 2245. [CrossRef]

21. Shankar, K.; Kumar, S.; Dutta, A.K.; Alkhayyat, A.; Jawad, A.J.A.M.; Abbas, A.H.; Yousif, Y.K. An Automated Hyperparameter Tuning Recurrent Neural Network Model for Fruit Classification. *Mathematics* **2022**, *10*, 2358. [CrossRef]

22. Anand, M.; Sahay, K.B.; Ahmed, M.A.; Sultan, D.; Chandan, R.R.; Singh, B. Deep learning and natural language processing in computation for offensive language detection in online social networks by feature selection and ensemble classification techniques. *Theor. Comput. Sci.* **2022**. [CrossRef]

23. Yang, G.; Li, J.; Xu, W.; Feng, H.; Zhao, F.; Long, H.; Meng, Y.; Chen, W.; Yang, H.; Yang, G. Fusion of optical and SAR images based on deep learning to reconstruct vegetation NDVI time series in cloud-prone regions. *Int. J. Appl. Earth Obs. Geoinf.* **2022**, *112*, 102818.

24. Yang, H.; Li, X.; Zhang, W. Interpretability of deep convolutional neural networks on rolling bearing fault diagnosis. *Meas. Sci. Technol.* **2022**, *33*, 055005. [CrossRef]

25. Wu, B.; Cai, W.; Cheng, F.; Chen, H. Simultaneous-fault diagnosis considering time series with a deep learning transformer architecture for air handling units. *Energy Build.* **2022**, *257*, 111608. [CrossRef]

26. Saadallah, A.; Abdulaaty, O.; Morik, K.; Büscher, J.; Panusch, T.; Deuse, J. Early quality prediction using deep learning on time series sensor data. *Procedia CIRP* **2022**, *107*, 611–616. [CrossRef]

27. Zhang, W.; Li, X.; Li, X. Deep learning-based prognostic approach for lithium-ion batteries with adaptive time-series prediction and on-line validation. *Measurement* **2020**, *164*, 108052. [CrossRef]

28. Li, X.; Li, X.; Ma, H. Deep representation clustering-based fault diagnosis method with unsupervised data applied to rotating machinery. *Mech. Syst. Signal Processing* **2020**, *143*, 106825. [CrossRef]

29. Li, X.; Zhang, W.; Ma, H.; Luo, Z.; Li, X. Degradation alignment in remaining useful life prediction using deep cycle-consistent learning. *IEEE Trans. Neural Netw. Learn. Syst.* **2021**, 1–12. [CrossRef]

30. Zhang, W.; Li, X.; Ma, H.; Luo, Z.; Li, X. Universal domain adaptation in fault diagnostics with hybrid weighted deep adversarial learning. *IEEE Trans. Ind. Inform.* **2021**, *17*, 7957–7967. [CrossRef]

31. Zhang, W.; Li, X.; Ma, H.; Luo, Z.; Li, X. Federated learning for machinery fault diagnosis with dynamic validation and self-supervision. *Knowl.-Based Syst.* **2021**, *213*, 106679. [CrossRef]

32. Zhang, W.; Li, X. Federated transfer learning for intelligent fault diagnostics using deep adversarial networks with data privacy. *IEEE/ASME Trans. Mechatron.* **2021**, *27*, 430–439. [CrossRef]

33. Zhang, W.; Li, X.; Ma, H.; Luo, Z.; Li, X. Open-set domain adaptation in machinery fault diagnostics using instance-level weighted adversarial learning. *IEEE Trans. Ind. Inform.* **2021**, *17*, 7445–7455. [CrossRef]

34. Mwata-Velu, T.Y.; Avina-Cervantes, J.G.; Ruiz-Pinales, J.; Garcia-Calva, T.A.; González-Barbosa, E.A.; Hurtado-Ramos, J.B.; González-Barbosa, J.J. Improving Motor Imagery EEG Classification Based on Channel Selection Using a Deep Learning Architecture. *Mathematics* **2022**, *10*, 2302. [CrossRef]

35. Ghasrodashti, E.K.; Sharma, N. Hyperspectral image classification using an extended Auto-Encoder method. *Signal Process. Image Commun.* **2021**, *92*, 116111. [CrossRef]

36. Sertolli, B.; Zhao, R.; Schuller, B.W.; Cummins, N. Representation transfer learning from deep end-to-end speech recognition networks for the classification of health states from speech. *Comput. Speech Lang.* **2021**, *68*, 101204. [CrossRef]

37. Ribeiro, M.; Lazzaretti, A.E.; Lopes, H.S. A study of deep convolutional auto-encoders for anomaly detection in videos. *Pattern Recognit. Lett.* **2018**, *105*, 13–22. [CrossRef]

38. Yu, F.; Liu, J.; Liu, D.; Wang, H. Supervised convolutional autoencoder-based fault-relevant feature learning for fault diagnosis in industrial processes. *J. Taiwan Inst. Chem. Eng.* **2022**, *132*, 104200. [CrossRef]

39. Vaswani, A.; Shazeer, N.; Parmar, N.; Uszkoreit, J.; Jones, L.; Gomez, A.N.; Kaiser, Ł.; Polosukhin, I. Attention is all you need. *Adv. Neural Inf. Processing Syst.* **2017**, *30*.

40. Dosovitskiy, A.; Beyer, L.; Kolesnikov, A.; Weissenborn, D.; Zhai, X.; Unterthiner, T.; Dehghani, M.; Minderer, M.; Heigold, G.; Gelly, S.; et al. An image is worth 16x16 words: Transformers for image recognition at scale. *arXiv* **2020**, arXiv:2010.11929, 2010.
41. Huang, K.; Tian, C.; Su, J.; Lin, J.C.W. Transformer-based cross reference network for video salient object detection. *Pattern Recognit. Lett.* **2022**, *160*, 122–127. [CrossRef]
42. Rai, N.; Kumar, D.; Kaushik, N.; Raj, C.; Ali, A. Fake news classification using transformer based enhanced LSTM and BERT. *Int. J. Cogn. Comput. Eng.* **2022**, *3*, 98–105. [CrossRef]
43. Islam, M.R.; Martin, A. Detection of COVID 19 from CT image by the novel LeNet-5 CNN architecture. In Proceedings of the 2020 23rd International Conference on Computer and Information Technology (ICCIT), IEEE, Dhaka, Bangladesh, 19–21 December 2020; pp. 1–5.
44. Sun, J.; Cai, X.; Sun, F.; Zhang, J. Scene image classification method based on Alex-Net model. In Proceedings of the 2016 3rd International Conference on Informative and Cybernetics for Computational Social Systems (ICCSS), IEEE, Jinzhou, China, 26–29 August 2016; pp. 363–367.
45. Rezaee, M.; Zhang, Y.; Mishra, R.; Tong, F.; Tong, H. Using a vgg-16 network for individual tree species detection with an object-based approach. In Proceedings of the 2018 10th IAPR Workshop on Pattern Recognition in Remote Sensing (PRRS), IEEE, Beijing, China, 19–20 August 2018; pp. 1–7.
46. Gisbrecht, A.; Schulz, A.; Hammer, B. Parametric nonlinear dimensionality reduction using kernel t-SNE. *Neurocomputing* **2015**, *147*, 71–82. [CrossRef]

mathematics

Article

Study on Dynamic Characteristics of a Rotating Sandwich Porous Pre-Twist Blade with a Setting Angle Reinforced by Graphene Nanoplatelets

Jiapei Peng [1], Lefa Zhao [2,*] and Tianyu Zhao [1,*]

[1] Key Laboratory of Structural Dynamics of Liaoning Province, School of Sciences, Northeastern University, Shenyang 110819, China
[2] Department of General Education, Shenyang Sport University, Shenyang 110115, China
* Correspondence: larry2012@syty.edu.cn (L.Z.); zhaotianyu@mail.neu.edu.cn (T.Z.)

Abstract: Lightweight blades with high strength are urgently needed in practical rotor engineering. Sandwich structures with porous core and reinforced surfaces are commonly applied to achieve these mechanical performances. Moreover, blades with large aspect ratios are established by the elastic plate models in theory. This paper studies the vibration of a rotating sandwich pre-twist plate with a setting angle reinforced by graphene nanoplatelets (GPLs). Its core is made of foam metal, and GPLs are added into the surface layers. Supposing that nanofillers are perfectly connected with matrix material, the effective mechanical parameters of the surface layers are calculated by the mixing law and the Halpin–Tsai model, while those of the core layers are determined by the open-cell scheme. The governing equation of the rotating plate is derived by employing the Hamilton principle. By comparing with the finite element method obtained by ANSYS, the present model and vibration analysis are verified. The material and structural parameters of the blade, including graphene nanoplatelet (GPL) weight faction, GPL distribution pattern, porosity coefficient, porosity distribution pattern, length-to-thickness ratio, length-to-width ratio, setting angle and pre-twist angle of the plate are discussed in detail. The finds provide important inspiration in the designing of a rotating sandwich blade.

Keywords: sandwich plate; graphene nanoplates; vibration; rotating; porosity

MSC: 74K20

Citation: Peng, J.; Zhao, L.; Zhao, T. Study on Dynamic Characteristics of a Rotating Sandwich Porous Pre-Twist Blade with a Setting Angle Reinforced by Graphene Nanoplatelets. *Mathematics* **2022**, *10*, 2814. https://doi.org/10.3390/math10152814

Academic Editors: Xiang Li, Shuo Zhang and Wei Zhang

Received: 26 April 2022
Accepted: 29 July 2022
Published: 8 August 2022

Publisher's Note: MDPI stays neutral with regard to jurisdictional claims in published maps and institutional affiliations.

1. Introduction

Blade structures are commonly applied in several rotating machineries, such as aero engines and wind turbines. As the mechanical performance of the rotor structure is required to improve, the blade structure is designed to be lighter and thinner. Blades are extremely susceptible to vibration damage, which accounts for a very large proportion of the failure of the blade. So, it is very meaningful to study vibration behaviors of blades. In previous studies, blades are often simplified as rotating plates or rotating beams, which have been studied comprehensively [1–10]. Based on Chebyshev polynomials, Gen et al. [11] studied the nonlinear dynamic behavior of blades with variable rotating speed. By using the Galerkin method, Avramov et al. [12] investigated the bending-torsional nonlinear vibration behavior of a rotating beam with asymmetric cross-section. By adopting the Ritz method, Mcgee [13] calculated natural frequencies of cantilever parallelepipeds that were skewed and twisted in the meantime. Yao et al. [14] studied the nonlinear dynamic behavior of high-speed rotating plates. Based on the Hamilton principle, Xu et al. [15] studied the nonlinear vibration of a rotating cantilever beam in the magnetic field. Wang et al. [16] studied the nonlinear stability of rotating blades. Hashemia et al. [17] presented the finite element formulas for vibration analysis of rotating thick plates. Li et al. [18] studied the free vibration of variable rotating cantilever rectangular functionally graded (FG) plates moving in a wide range. By using the Donner shell theory, Shakour [19] studied vibrations of a rotating FG conical shell in different thermal environment. Based on the Hamilton principle, Qin et al. [20] investigated the bent-bending coupled vibration of rotating composite thin-walled beams under aerodynamic and humid conditions. Yutaek et al. [21] proposed a dynamic model of rotating pre-torsional blades with variable cross-section. Yang et al. [22] promoted the FG plate theory proposed by Mian and Spencer from two aspects. Arumugam et al. [23] studied vibration behaviors of a planar layered laminate with rotational effects. Tuzzi et al. [24] conducted a study of coupling vibrations between shaft-bending and disk-zero nodal diameter mode vibration in a flexible shaft–disk assembly. Based on classical plate theory and Hamilton principle, Sun et al. [25] investigated the vibration characteristics of rotating blades with a staggered angle.

Due to the influence of aerodynamic loads on the blade during rotation, higher requirements are put forward for the structural strength of the blade. The traditional blade material has not met the needs. GPLs have been very popular as a reinforced material in the past few years and widely used in various engineering fields, such as physics, electrical engineering, materials science and nanoengineering applications [26–30]. Its structural stiffness and lightweight meet the requirements, which has become the focus of scholars' research. Zhao et al. [31] studied the free vibration of GPL reinforced rotating FG pre-twisted blade-shaft assembly. Li et al. [32] carried out nonlinear vibration and dynamic buckling analysis of laminated FG porous plates reinforced by GPLs. Yang et al. [33] studied the buckling and free vibration behavior of FG porous nanocomposite plates reinforced with GPLs. Based on the Timoshenko beam theory, Chen et al. [34] analyzed the elastic buckling and static bending of shear deformable FG porous beams. Wu et al. [35] studied the parameter instability of FG-GPL reinforced nanocomposite plate under the action of periodic uniaxial plane internal force in uniform temperature field. Lei et al. [36] used element-free -Ritz method to conduct free vibration analysis on single-walled carbon nanotube reinforced FG nanocomposite plate. Yang et al. [37] studied the buckling and post-buckling behavior of FG multilayer nanocomposite beams reinforced by low content GPLs on elastic foundation. Wang et al. [38] studied the eigenvalue buckling of multilayer FG cylindrical shells reinforced with GPLs by using finite element method.

To sum up, GPL reinforced porous rotor structures are suitable for high-speed rotating blades to achieve high strength or light weight. Moreover, the sandwich blade structure with GPL reinforced surfaces and porous core could be designed to avoid air turbulence. This paper investigated the theoretical modeling and free vibration of a pre-twist sandwich blade. To the authors' knowledge, almost no study focused on the vibration analysis of a rotating sandwich blade with GPL reinforced porous core. Based on the Kirchhoff plate theory, the rotating pre-twist blade with a setting angle is established in this paper. The equations of motion are derived by applying the Hamilton principle and then solved by the using the hypothetical modal method. The effects of material and structural parameters of the sandwich blade on its free vibration are examined in detail. The findings shed a bright light on the design of sandwich blades with GPL reinforced porous core to achieve better mechanical performance.

2. Theoretical Model

Figure 1 shows a rotating pre-twist blade with a setting angle, which attached to a rigid body. To describe the motion and displacements of the blade, three coordinate systems are carried out. The O-XYZ coordinate system is established on the rigid body, while the reference coordinate system o-xyz is fixed on the blade root. Moreover, another reference coordinate system o'-uvw is fixed on the blade at a distance x away from the point o. The radius of the rigid body is R_d, and it rotates around the Y axis at a constant speed Ω. The length, width and thickness of the blade are a, b and h, respectively. Moreover, h_c and h_f are the thicknesses of the porous core and the GPL reinforced face layer, respectively. It can be known that $h = h_c + 2\,h_f$. Then, define $m = h_c/h_f$, which is the ratio of the core to the surface layer. The setting angle and pre-twist angle of the blade are θ and φ, respectively. The twist angle at an arbitrary point on the blade is $\beta(x) = \theta + kx$, where $k = (\varphi - \theta)/a$.

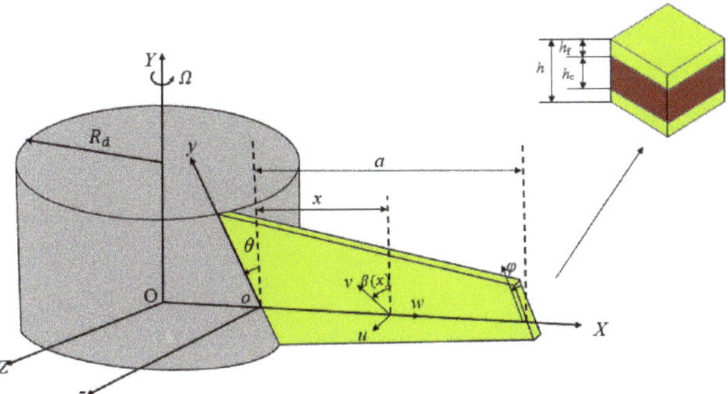

Figure 1. A rotating pre-twist blade with a setting angle attached to a rigid body.

3. Material Properties

As shown in Figure 2, three different porosity distribution patterns are considered in this paper. Plus, it can be seen clearly that the material parameters vary along the blade thickness direction. Pattern X means that more pores are distributed around the edges; Pattern O tells more pores are distributed in the middle surface; Pattern U gives the uniform porosity distribution. Based on the open-cell scheme [39], the material properties are

$$
\text{Pattern X}: \begin{cases} E(Z) = E_1[1 - e_0\cos(\pi Z/h)] \\ \nu(Z) = \nu_1[1 - e_0\cos(\pi Z/h)] \\ \rho(Z) = \rho_1[1 - e_m\cos(\pi Z/h)] \end{cases}
$$

$$
\text{Pattern U}: \begin{cases} E(Z) = E_1\alpha \\ \nu(Z) = \nu_1\alpha \\ \rho(Z) = \rho_1\alpha' \end{cases} \tag{1}
$$

$$
\text{Pattern O}: \begin{cases} E(Z) = E_1[1 - e_0^*(1 - \cos(\pi Z/h))] \\ \nu(Z) = \nu_1[1 - e_0^*(1 - \cos(\pi Z/h))] \\ \rho(Z) = \rho_1[1 - e_m^*(1 - \cos(\pi Z/h))] \end{cases}
$$

where $E(Z), \rho(Z), \nu(Z)$ are the effective elasticity modulus, mass density, Poisson's ratio of the core layer, respectively. E_1, ρ_1, ν_1 are the corresponding material parameters of core layer without pores. e_0, α, e_0^* are the porosity coefficients of the three distribution patterns. e_m, α', e_m^* are the mass density coefficients of the three distribution patterns.

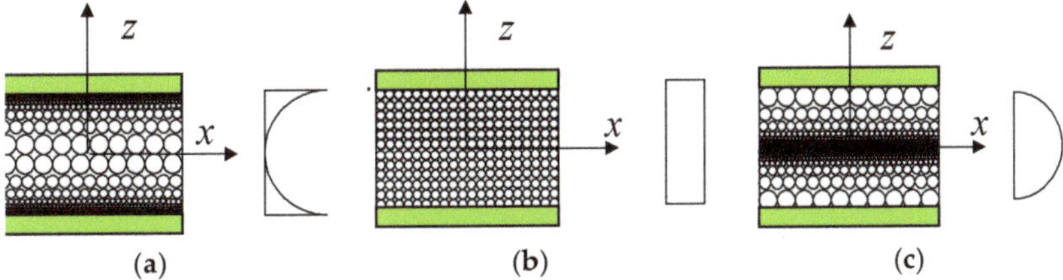

Figure 2. Porosity distribution patterns of the core layer: (**a**) Pattern X_P; (**b**) Pattern U_P; (**c**) Pattern O_P.

The relationship between porosity coefficients and mass density coefficients can be given by

$$\begin{cases} 1 - e_m \cos(\pi Z/h) = \sqrt{1 - e_0 \cos(\pi Z/h)} \\ \alpha' = \sqrt{\alpha} \\ 1 - e_m^*[1 - \cos(\pi Z/h)] = \sqrt{1 - e_0^*[1 - \cos(\pi Z/h)]} \end{cases} \quad (2)$$

Table 1 shows the relationship of porosity coefficients of the three patterns.

Table 1. Relationship of porosity coefficients.

e_0	α	e_0^*
0.1	0.9361	0.1738
0.2	0.8716	0.3442
0.3	0.8064	0.5103
0.4	0.7404	0.6708

GPLs are added to the surface layers. Due to high precision, the Halpin–Tsai model [40,41] is used to calculate the surface layers' effective elasticity modulus. The formula is shown as

$$E_S = E_M \left[\frac{3}{8} \left(\frac{1 + \xi_L \eta_L V_{GPL}}{1 - \eta_L V_{GPL}} \right) + \frac{5}{8} \left(\frac{1 + \xi_T \eta_T V_{GPL}}{1 - \eta_T V_{GPL}} \right) \right] \quad (3)$$

where η_T and η_L are given by

$$\begin{cases} \eta_L = \frac{E_{GPL} - E_M}{E_{GPL} + \xi_L E_M} \\ \eta_T = \frac{E_{GPL} - E_M}{E_{GPL} + \xi_T E_M} \end{cases} \quad (4)$$

and ξ_T and ξ_L can be expressed as

$$\begin{cases} \xi_L = 2L_{GPL}/t_{GPL} \\ \xi_T = 2w_{GPL}/t_{GPL} \end{cases} \quad (5)$$

where E_M and E_{GPL} are the elasticity modulus of the matrix and GPLs. L_{GPL}, w_{GPL} and t_{GPL} are the length, width and thickness of GPLs.

Based on the mixing rule, the mass density and Poisson's ratio are

$$\begin{cases} \rho_s = V_{GPL}\rho_{GPL} + (1 - V_{GPL})\rho_M \\ v_s = V_{GPL}v_{GPL} + (1 - V_{GPL})v_M \end{cases} \quad (6)$$

where v_{GPL} and v_m are the Poisson's ratio of matrix and GPLs, respectively. ρ_{GPL} and ρ_m are the mass density of matrix material GPLs, respectively. V_{GPL} is the volume fraction of GPLs in the plate, expressed as

$$V_{GPL} = \frac{W_{GPL}}{W_{GPL} + \rho_{GPL}(1 - W_{GPL})/\rho_M} \quad (7)$$

where, W_{GPL} is the weight fraction of GPLs, obtained as

$$W_{GPL} = \begin{cases} \frac{4Z^2}{h_f^2}\lambda_1 W_0 & \text{Pattern} X_p \\ \lambda_2 W_0 & \text{Pattern} U_p \\ \left(1 - \frac{4Z^2}{h_f^2}\right)\lambda_3 W_0 & \text{Pattern} O_p \end{cases} \quad (8)$$

where W_0 is the GPL characteristic value; $\lambda_1, \lambda_2, \lambda_3$ are the GPL weight fraction indices determined by the GPL weight distribution patterns, as listed in Table 2.

Table 2. Values of GPL weight fraction indices.

$g_{GPL}(\%)$	λ_1	λ_2	λ_3
0	0.00	0.00	0.00
0.33	1.00	0.33	0.50
0.67	2.00	0.67	1.00
1	3.00	1.00	1.50

The corresponding GPL distribution patterns are as shown in Figure 3.

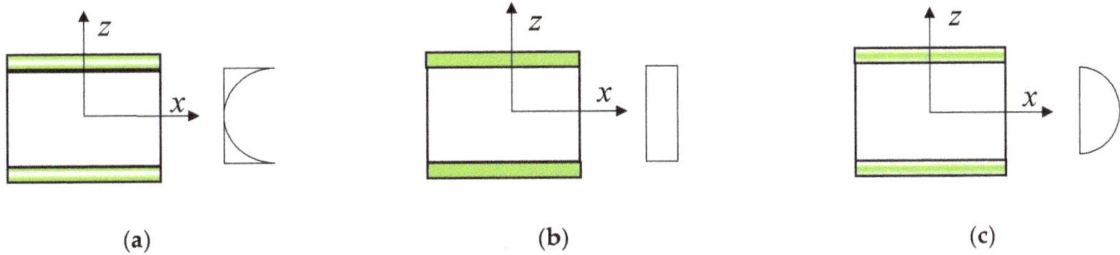

Figure 3. GPL distribution patterns in the surface layer of the plate: (**a**) Pattern X_G; (**b**) Pattern U_G; (**c**) Pattern O_G.

4. Equations of Motion

To describe the motion of the rotating plate, three coordinate systems are established. The coordinates of an arbitrary point on the plate in the local coordinate system are $R = (x + R_d)i + yj + (z + w)k$.

Then, the coordinate of the same point on the plate in the fixed coordinate system is

$$R = \begin{pmatrix} 1 & 0 & 0 \\ 0 & \cos\beta(x) & -\sin\beta(x) \\ 0 & \sin\beta(x) & \cos\beta(x) \end{pmatrix} \begin{pmatrix} x + R_d \\ y \\ z + w \end{pmatrix} \tag{9}$$

The speed of the plate is $V = \dot{R} + (\Omega i \times R)$, where Ω is the rotating speed. Then, the kinetic energy of the rotating blade can be obtained as

$$T_P = \frac{1}{2}\rho h \int_0^b \int_0^a \left[w^2\Omega^2 + \left(\frac{\partial w}{\partial t}\right)^2 + (R + x)^2 - 2w(\cos\beta(x))\frac{\partial w}{\partial t}(R + x)\Omega + y^2 \right] dxdy \tag{10}$$

Considering the gyroscopic effect, the rotating strain potential energy is

$$U_1 = \frac{Eh^3}{24(1 - v^2)} \int_0^b \int_0^a \left\{ \frac{1}{B^4}\left(\frac{\partial^2 w}{\partial x^2} + \frac{\partial^2 w}{\partial y^2}\right)^2 - \frac{2(1 - v)}{B^2}\left[\frac{\partial^2 w}{\partial x^2}\frac{\partial^2 w}{\partial y^2} - \left(\frac{\partial^2 w}{\partial x\partial y}\right)^2\right] \right\} dxdy \tag{11}$$

where f_{c1} and f_{c2} are the centrifugal forces in two directions of the blade, expressed as

$$f_{c1} = \rho h\Omega^2 \int_x^a (R + x)dx \tag{12}$$

$$f_{c2} = \rho h\Omega^2 \int_y^{\frac{b}{2}} y(\sin(\beta(x))^2)dy \tag{13}$$

The total potential energy can be given by

$$U_P = \frac{Eh^3}{24(1 - v^2)} \int_0^b \int_0^a \left\{ \frac{1}{B^4}\left(\frac{\partial^2 w}{\partial x^2} + \frac{\partial^2 w}{\partial y^2}\right)^2 - \frac{2(1-v)}{B^2}\left[\frac{\partial^2 w}{\partial x^2}\frac{\partial^2 w}{\partial y^2} - \left(\frac{\partial^2 w}{\partial x\partial y}\right)^2\right] \right\} dxdy$$
$$+ \frac{1}{2}\rho h\Omega^2 \int_0^b \int_0^a \left\{ \left[R(a - x) + \frac{1}{2}(a^2 - x^2)\right]\left(\frac{\partial w}{\partial x}\right)^2 + (b^2 - y^2)(\sin(\beta(x)))^2 \right\} dxdy \tag{14}$$

Applying the Hamiltonian variational principle $\delta \int_{t_0}^{t_1} (T_P - U_P)\mathrm{d}t = 0$, the equations of motion can be derived as

$$\int_0^b \int_0^a \left\{ \begin{array}{l} \rho h\left(\omega^2 + \Omega^2\right) W \delta W \\[2mm] -\frac{1}{2}\rho h \Omega^2 \left[\begin{array}{l} \left[R(a-x) + \frac{1}{2}\left(a^2 - x^2\right)\right]\frac{\partial W}{\partial x}\delta\left(\frac{\partial W}{\partial x}\right) \\[2mm] +\left(\frac{b^2}{4} - y^2\right)(\sin\beta(x))^2\frac{\partial W}{\partial y}\delta\left(\frac{\partial W}{\partial y}\right) \end{array} \right] \\[2mm] -\frac{D}{B^4}\left[\begin{array}{l} \left(\frac{\partial^2 W}{\partial x^2}\right)\delta\left(\frac{\partial^2 W}{\partial x^2}\right) + \left(\frac{\partial^2 W}{\partial y^2}\right)\delta\frac{\partial^2 W}{\partial y^2} \\[2mm] +\frac{\partial^2 W}{\partial x^2}\delta\left(\frac{\partial^2 W}{\partial y^2}\right) + \frac{\partial^2 W}{\partial y^2}\delta\left(\frac{\partial^2 W}{\partial x^2}\right) \end{array} \right] \\[2mm] +\frac{D(1-v)}{B^2}\left[\begin{array}{l} \frac{\partial^2 W}{\partial x^2}\delta\left(\frac{\partial^2 W}{\partial y^2}\right) + \frac{\partial^2 W}{\partial y^2}\delta\left(\frac{\partial^2 W}{\partial x^2}\right) \\[2mm] -2\frac{\partial^2 W}{\partial x \partial y}\delta\left(\frac{\partial^2 W}{\partial x \partial y}\right) \end{array} \right] \end{array} \right\} \mathrm{d}x\mathrm{d}y = 0 \tag{15}$$

According to the approximation method of combined series of beam function, the vibration mode expression, satisfying all displacement boundary conditions, is

$$W(x,y) = \sum_{m=1}^M \sum_{n=1}^N A_{mn}\phi_m(x)\varphi_n(y) \tag{16}$$

The fixed-free beam function $\phi_m(x)$ and the free-free beam function $\varphi_n(y)$ are given by

$$\begin{cases} \phi_m(x) = \cosh(\alpha_m x) - \cos(\alpha_m x) - c_m[\sinh(\alpha_m x) - \sin(\alpha_m x)] \\[1mm] \varphi_n(y) = \cosh(\beta_n y) + \cos(\beta_n y) - d_n[\sinh(\beta_n y) + \sin(\beta_n y)] \\[1mm] c_m = \frac{\cos(\alpha_m a)+\cosh(\alpha_m a)}{\sin(\alpha_m a)+\sinh(\alpha_m a)}, d_n = \frac{\cos(\beta_n b)-\cosh(\beta_n b)}{\sin(\beta_n b)-\sinh(\beta_n b)} \\[1mm] \cosh(\alpha_m a)\cos(\alpha_m a) + 1 = 0, \cosh(\beta_n b)\cos(\beta_n b) - 1 = 0 \end{cases} \tag{17}$$

By substituting the Equation (16) into Equation (15) and making the variational coefficient δA_{mn} zero, the frequency equation can be obtained as

$$\int_0^b \int_0^a \left\{ \begin{array}{l} \rho h\left(\omega^2 + \Omega^2\right) \sum_{m=1}^M \sum_{n=1}^N A_{mn}\varphi_m(x)\varphi_n(y)\phi_i(x)\varphi_j(y) \\[2mm] -\frac{D}{B^4}\left[\begin{array}{l} \sum_{m=1}^M \sum_{n=1}^N A_{mn}\varphi_m''(x)\varphi_n(y)\varphi_i''(x)\varphi_j(y) + \sum_{m=1}^M \sum_{n=1}^N A_{mn}\varphi_m(x)\varphi_n''(y)\varphi_i(x)\varphi_j''(y) \\[2mm] +\sum_{m=1}^M \sum_{n=1}^N A_{mn}\varphi_m''(x)\varphi_n(y)\varphi_i(x)\varphi_j''(y) + \sum_{m=1}^M \sum_{n=1}^N A_{mn}\varphi_m(x)\varphi_n''(y)\varphi_i''(x)\varphi_j(y) \end{array} \right] \\[2mm] +\frac{D(1-v)}{B^2}\left[\begin{array}{l} \sum_{m=1}^M \sum_{n=1}^N A_{mn}\varphi_m''(x)\varphi_n(y)\varphi_i(x)\varphi_j''(y) \\[2mm] +\sum_{m=1}^M \sum_{n=1}^N A_{mn}\varphi_m(x)\varphi_n''(y)\varphi_i''(x)\varphi_j(y) \\[2mm] -2\sum_{m=1}^M \sum_{n=1}^N A_{mn}\varphi_m'(x)\varphi_n'(y)\varphi_i'(x)\varphi_j'(y) \end{array} \right] \\[2mm] -\frac{1}{2}\rho h \Omega^2\left[R(a-x) + \frac{1}{2}\left(a^2 - x^2\right)\right]\sum_{m=1}^M \sum_{n=1}^N A_{mn}\varphi_m'(x)\varphi_n(y)\varphi_i'(x)\varphi_j(y) \\[2mm] -\frac{1}{2}\rho h \Omega^2\left[\left(\frac{b^2}{4} - y^2\right)(\sin\beta(x))^2\right]\sum_{m=1}^M \sum_{n=1}^N A_{mn}\varphi_m(x)\varphi_n'(y)\varphi_i(x)\varphi_j'(y) \end{array} \right\} \mathrm{d}x\mathrm{d}y = 0 \tag{18}$$

where, ω is the natural frequency of the plate.

5. Results and Discussions

Before discussing the parameters, we need to conduct convergence analysis to verify correctness of theoretical solution. The structural and material parameters are shown as Table 3.

Table 3. Structural and material parameters.

Parameter	Value
a	150 mm
b	100 mm
h	3 mm
φ	$\pi/18$
θ	$\pi/18$
E	214 GPa
ρ	7800 kg/m^3
v	0.3

Table 4 shows variations of the first four frequencies with different mode numbers. It is seen that the mode number tends to be convergent at $M = N = 15$, which will be adopted in the following discussion.

Table 4. Frequencies with different mode numbers.

Frequency (Hz)	$M = N = 5$	$M = N = 10$	$M = N = 15$
First	116.7	116.5	116.4
Second	725.4	724.2	723.6
Third	2709.7	2707.3	2704.7
Fourth	4036.4	4033.2	4025.1

The comparison between theoretical results and finite element results obtained from ANSYS of the first four-order frequencies and corresponding vibration modes is depicted in Figure 3 and Table 4, the Solid 186 element in ANSYS is applied. Plus, the numbers of elements and nodes are 11,616 and 23,735, respectively. The convergence analysis for the element number is conducted as given in Figure 4 and Table 5. It can be clearly seen from Figure 5 and Table 6 that the error is less than 2%, and the vibration modes are in good agreement, which indicates that the present model and analysis are correct.

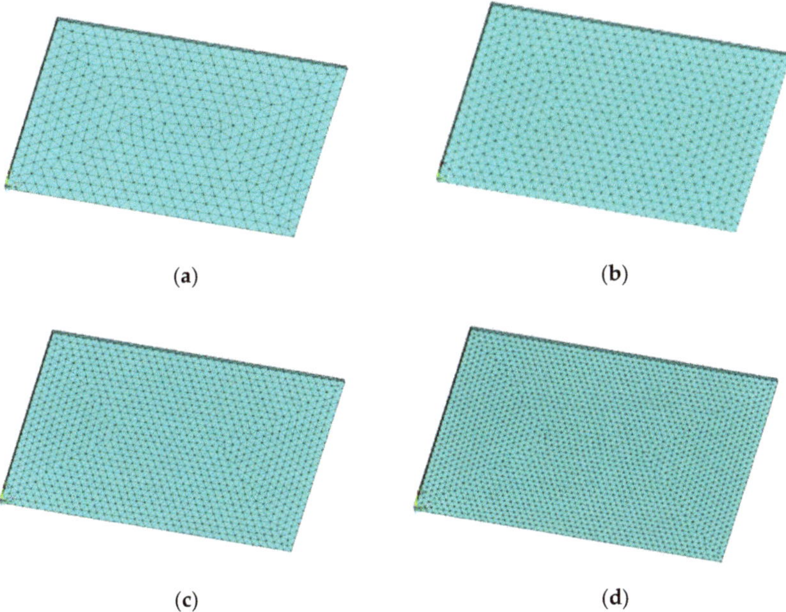

(a)   **(b)**

(c)   **(d)**

Figure 4. Finite element grid diagram. (**a**) $Ne = 2868$; (**b**) $Ne = 4092$; (**c**) $Ne = 6523$; (**d**) $Ne = 11,616$.

Table 5. Frequencies with different finite element numbers.

Frequency (Hz)	*Ne* = 2868	*Ne* = 4092	*Ne* = 6523	*Ne* = 11,616
First	116.04	116.07	116.06	116.06
Second	720.91	720.61	720.39	720.29
Third	2678.4	2674.3	2670.8	2668.8
Fourth	4001.0	3994.2	3989.3	3986.7

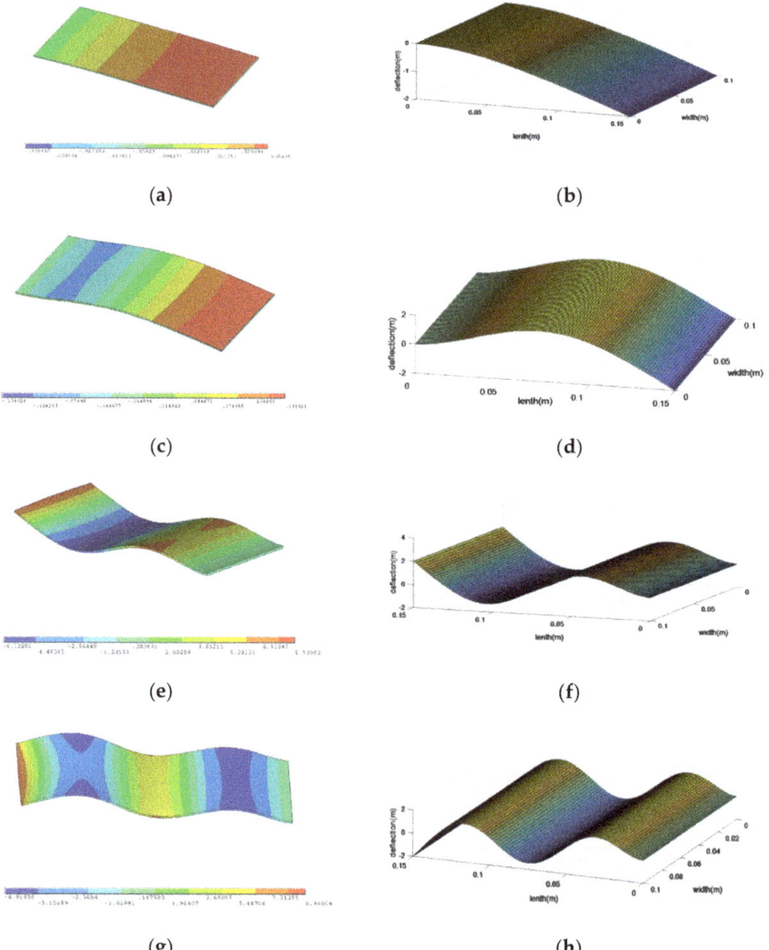

Figure 5. Comparison of the first-four vibration modes between theoretical and finite element results: (**a**,**b**) are the first vibration mode; (**c**,**d**) are the second vibration mode; (**e**,**f**) are the third vibration mode; (**g**,**h**) are the fourth vibration mode.

Table 6. Comparison between theoretical and finite element results.

Frequency (Hz)	Theoretical Result	ANSYS	Error
First	116.4	116.1	0.3%
Second	723.6	720.6	0.4%
Third	2704.7	2673.6	1.1%
Fourth	4025.1	3992.7	0.8%

The idea of controlling variable method is adopted for the argument discussion in this article. The parameters are demonstrated in the Table 7. Moreover, the GPL distribution and pore distribution are Pattern X, and the porosity coefficient $e_0 = 0.1$, if not specified.

Table 7. Values of structural and material parameters.

Parameter	Value
a	150 mm
b	20 mm
h	3 mm
φ	$\pi/18$
θ	$\pi/18$
E_{GPL}	1.01 TPa
ρ_{GPL}	1062.5 kg/m^3
v_{GPL}	0.186
l_{GPL}	2.5 μm
w_{GPL}	1.5 μm
t_{GPL}	1.5 nm
E_f	2.85 GPa
ρ_f	1200 kg/m^3
v_f	0.34
E_m	68.3 GPa
ρ_m	2688.8 kg/m^3
v_m	0.34

Figure 6 shows variations of the first four frequencies with the rotating plate in the case of different GPL weight fraction. The frequencies of the plate gradually increase as the rotating speed rises. Moreover, it can be clearly seen that adding more GPLs into the matrix leads to the higher frequencies. Therefore, we can add more GPLs in a small amounts to the surface layers of the plate to improve its mechanical performance.

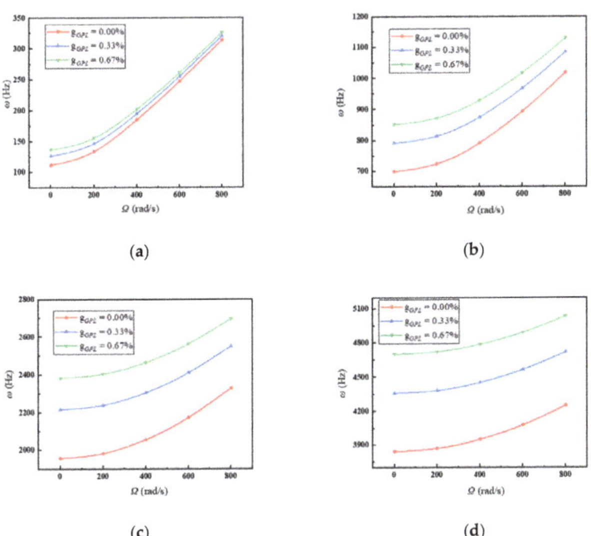

Figure 6. Variations of frequencies with rotating speed under different GPL weight fractions. (**a**) First frequency; (**b**) second frequency; (**c**) third frequency; (**d**) fourth frequency.

Figure 7 depicts variations of the first four frequencies with the rotating plate in the case of different porosity coefficients. Obviously, the frequencies of the plate are decreased with larger porosity coefficients, which means that the core layer has more pores. It can significantly reduce the weight, and the impact on the vibration frequency of the plate is relatively small. So, it is necessary to choose the porous core to achieve weight reduction.

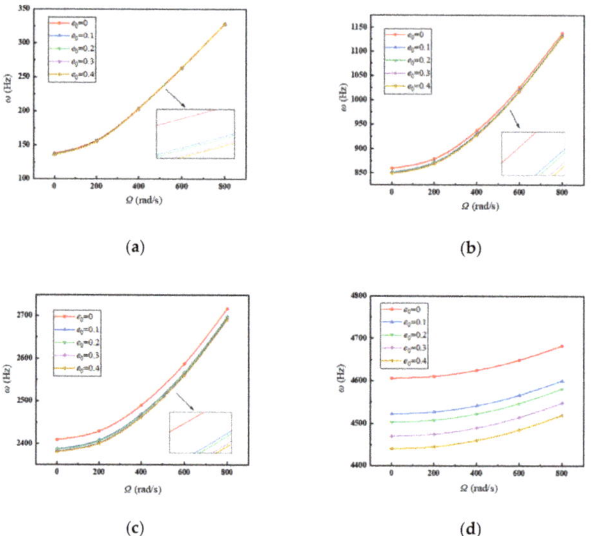

Figure 7. Variations of frequencies with rotating speed under different porosity coefficients. (**a**) First frequency; (**b**) second frequency; (**c**) third frequency; (**d**) fourth frequency.

Variations of the first four frequencies with the rotating plate in the case of different ratios of surface-thickness and core-thickness are exhibited in Figure 8. As the ratios continue to increase, frequencies of the plate increase significantly. It tells those thicker surfaces give a hand in enhancing the structural stiffness.

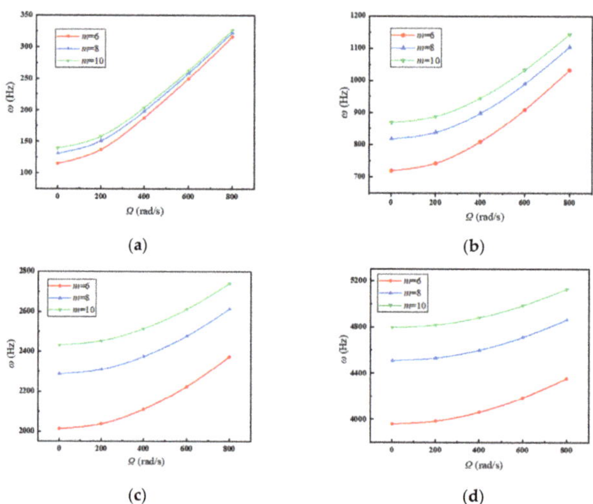

Figure 8. Variations of frequencies with rotating speed under different ratios of core layer thickness and surface layer thickness. (**a**) First frequency; (**b**) second frequency; (**c**) third frequency; (**d**) fourth frequency.

Figure 9 displays variations of the first four frequencies with the rotating plate in the case of different GPL distribution patterns. The plate with GPL distribution pattern X has the highest natural frequencies. To obtain better mechanical performance, adding more GPLs around the surfaces is a good choice.

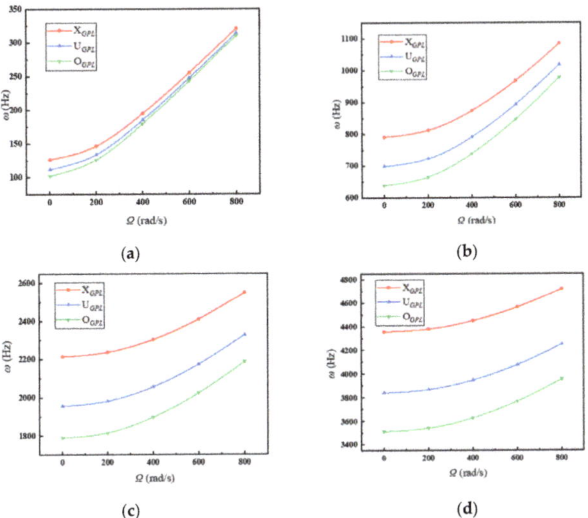

Figure 9. Variations of frequencies with rotating speed under different GPL distribution patterns. (**a**) First frequency; (**b**) second frequency; (**c**) third frequency; (**d**) fourth frequency.

Figure 10 shows variations of the first four frequencies with the rotating plate in the case of different porosity distribution patterns. It is obvious that porosity distribution pattern X provides the greater frequencies than the other two porosity distribution patterns. One can tell that setting more pores around the edges and arranging larger pores in the middle plane are conducive to achieve better structural stiffness.

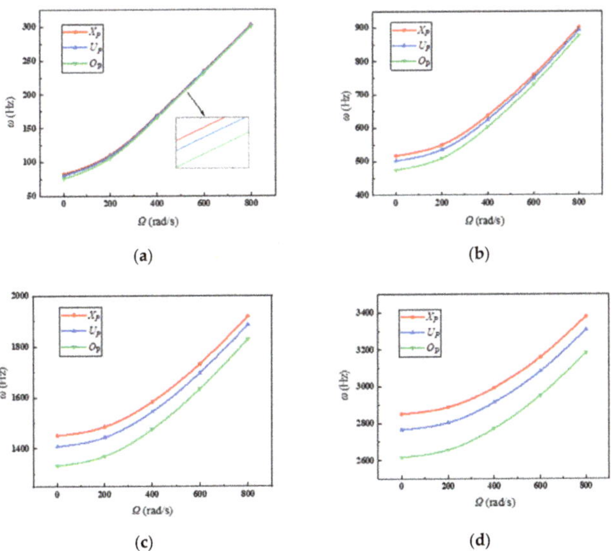

Figure 10. Variations of frequencies with rotating speed under different porosity distribution patterns. (**a**) First frequency; (**b**) second frequency; (**c**) third frequency; (**d**) fourth frequency.

Variations of the first four frequencies with the rotating plate in the case of length-to-thickness ratio of the plate are given in Figure 11, where the blade length is constant. Lower length-to-thickness ratio of the plate shows greater frequencies. It indicates that thinner blades should be designed in rotating machines for better mechanical performance.

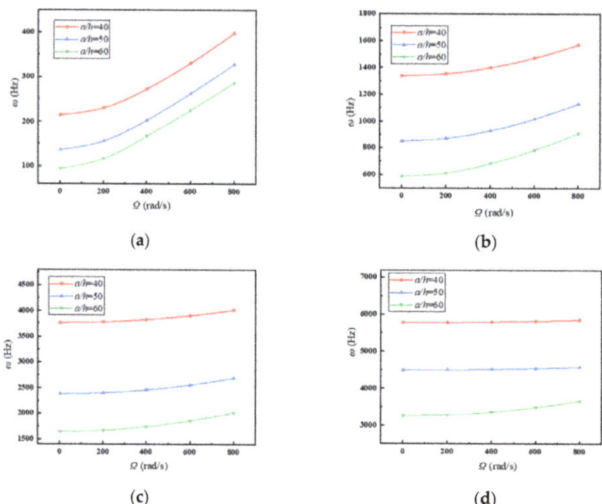

Figure 11. Variations of frequencies with rotating speed under different length-to-thickness ratio of the plate. (**a**) First frequency; (**b**) second frequency; (**c**) third frequency; (**d**) fourth frequency.

Figure 12 plots variations of the first four frequencies with the rotating plate in the case of different length-to-width ratio of the plate, where the blade width is constant. One can see that frequencies decrease dramatically with increase of the length-to-width ratio of the plate. It can be told that the blade length should be closer to the blade width to enhance the structural performance of the plate.

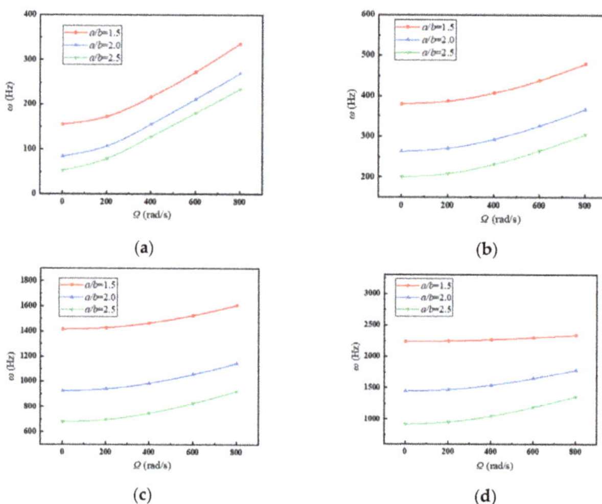

Figure 12. Variations of frequencies with rotating speed under different length-to-width ratio of the plate. (**a**) First frequency; (**b**) second frequency; (**c**) third frequency; (**d**) fourth frequency.

Figure 13 depicts variations of the first four frequencies with the rotating plate in the case of different pre-twist angles. Increasing the pre-twist angle of the plate tends to reduce the frequencies. It should be noted that the blade should be flatter in the absence of additional requirements.

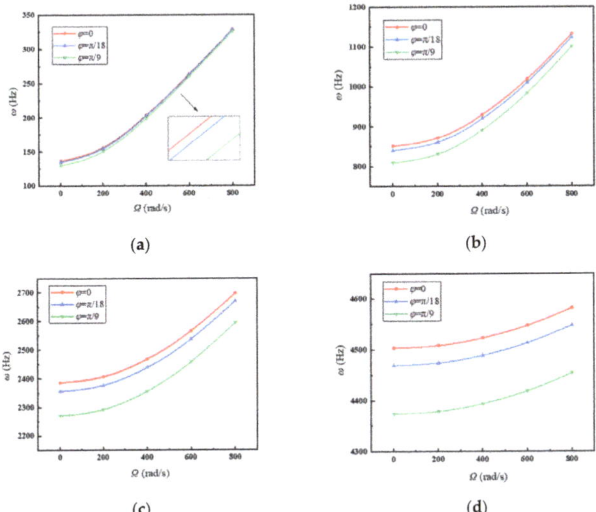

Figure 13. Variations of frequencies with rotating speed under different pre-twist angles. (**a**) First frequency; (**b**) second frequency; (**c**) third frequency; (**d**) fourth frequency.

Figure 14 shows variations of the first four frequencies with the rotating plate in the case of different setting angles. Visibly, raising the setting angle will increase the frequencies of the plate. We can know that the blade with larger setting angle contributes to improve the structural performance.

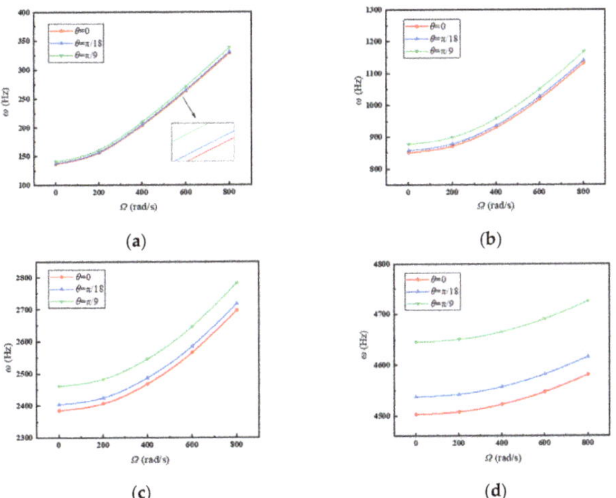

Figure 14. Variations of frequencies with rotating speed under different setting angles. (**a**) First frequency; (**b**) second frequency; (**c**) third frequency; (**d**) fourth frequency.

6. Conclusions

This paper studies free vibration analysis of a rotating sandwich porous blade reinforced with GPLs. The effective material parameters of the sandwich plate are obtained by the mixing law and the Halpin–Tsai model. In addition, the frequencies can be calculated based on the Hamilton principle and the method of hypothesis modes. Plus, the present results are verified by the finite element method. Some useful conclusions have been drawn as follows:

(1) Better mechanical performance can be achieved by adding more GPLs into the surface layer in a small content and making more GPLs on the edges of the plate.
(2) Setting less pores in the core layer and arranging more smaller pores around edges can enhance the structural stiffness.
(3) Applying thinner core layer contributes to better structural stiffness of the sandwich structure.
(4) Shorter and thinner blade should be designed to obtain better mechanical properties.
(5) Appropriately increasing setting angle and reducing pre-twist angle can is a good choice to obtain better structural stiffness.

Author Contributions: Conceptualization, J.P. and T.Z.; Funding acquisition, L.Z. and T.Z.; Investigation, J.P., L.Z. and T.Z.; Methodology, J.P. and L.Z.; Supervision, T.Z.; Writing—original draft, J.P.; Writing—review & editing, T.Z. All authors have read and agreed to the published version of the manuscript.

Funding: This research was funded by the Major Project of Aeroengine and Gas Turbine of China (HT-J2019-IV-0016-0084), the National Natural Science Foundation of China (No. 51805076, No. U1708255 and No. 52005086), the National Science and Technology Major Project of China (J2019-I-0008-0008) and the Fundamental Research Funds for the Central Universities of China (N2105013).

Conflicts of Interest: The authors declare no conflict of interest in preparing this article.

References

1. Mohammad, R.P.; Amir, R.M. Hygro-thermo-elstic nonlinear analysis of functionally gaded porous composite thin and moderately thick shallow panels. *Mech. Adv. Mater. Struct.* **2022**, *29*, 594–612.
2. Zhao, T.Y.; Ma, Y.; Zhang, H.Y.; Pan, H.G.; Cai, Y. Free vibration analysis of a rotating graphene nanoplatelet reinforced pre-twist blade-disk assembly with a setting angle. *Appl. Math. Model.* **2021**, *93*, 578–596. [CrossRef]
3. Zhao, T.Y.; Yan, K.; Li, H.W.; Wang, X. Study on theoretical modeling and vibration performance of an assembled cylindrical shell-plate structure with whirl motion. *Appl. Math. Model.* **2022**, *110*, 618–632. [CrossRef]
4. Zhao, T.Y.; Cui, Y.S.; Pan, H.G.; Yuan, H.Q.; Yang, J. Free vibration analysis of a functionally graded graphene nanoplatelet reinforced disk-shaft assembly with whirl motion. *Int. J. Mech. Sci.* **2021**, *197*, 106335. [CrossRef]
5. Zhao, T.Y.; Cui, Y.S.; Wang, Y.Q.; Pan, H.G. Vibration characteristics of graphene nanoplatelet reinforced disk-shaft rotor with eccentric mass. *Mech. Adv. Mater. Struct.* **2021**. [CrossRef]
6. Zhao, T.Y.; Li, K.; Ma, H. Study on dynamic characteristics of a rotating cylindrical shell with uncertain parameters. *Anal. Math. Phys.* **2022**, *12*, 97. [CrossRef]
7. Zhao, T.Y.; Wang, Y.X.; Pan, H.G.; Yuan, H.Q.; Cai, Y. Nonlinear forced vibration analysis of spinning shaft-disk assemblies under sliding bearing supports. *Math. Methods Appl. Sci.* **2021**, *44*, 12283–12301. [CrossRef]
8. Zhang, W.; Li, X.; Ma, H.; Luo, Z.; Li, X. Transfer learning using deep representation regularization in remaining useful life prediction across operating conditions. *Reliab. Eng. Syst. Saf.* **2021**, *211*, 107556. [CrossRef]
9. Xu, H.; Wang, Y.Q.; Zhang, Y.F. Free vibration of functionally graded graphene platelet-reinforced porous beams with spinning movement via differential transformation method. *Arch. Appl. Mech.* **2021**, *12*, 4817–4834. [CrossRef]
10. Wang, Y.Q.; Zu, J.W. Vibration behaviors of functionally graded rectangular plates with porosities and moving in thermal environment. *Aerosp. Sci. Technol.* **2017**, *69*, 550–562. [CrossRef]
11. Liu, G.; Chen, G.F.; Cui, F.S. Nonlinear vibration analysis of composite blade with variable rotating speed using Chebyshev polynomials. *Eur. J. Mech.* **2020**, *82*, 103976. [CrossRef]
12. Avramov, K.V.; Pierre, C. Flexural-flexural-torsional Nonlinear Vibrations of Pre-twisted Rotating Beams with Asymmetric Cross-sections. *J. Vib. Control* **2007**, *13*, 329–364. [CrossRef]
13. Mcgee, O.G. On the three-dimensional vibration analysis of simultaneously skewed and twisted cantilevered parallelepipeds. *Int. J. Numer. Methods Eng.* **1992**, *33*, 1388–1411. [CrossRef]
14. Yao, M.H.; Ma, L.; Zhang, W. Nonlinear dynamics of the high-speed rotating plate. *Int. J. Aerosp. Eng.* **2018**, *2018*, 56109151. [CrossRef]
15. Xu, X.P.; Han, Q.K.; Chu, F.L. Nonlinear vibration of a rotating cantilever beam in a surrounding magnetic field. *Int. J. Non-Linear Mech.* **2017**, *95*, 59–72. [CrossRef]
16. Wang, F.X.; Zhang, W. Stability analysis of a nonlinear rotating blade with torsional vibrations. *J. Sound Vib.* **2012**, *331*, 5755–5773. [CrossRef]
17. Hashemi, S.H.; Farhadi, S.; Carra, S. Free vibration analysis of rotating thick plates. *J. Sound Vib.* **2009**, *323*, 366–384. [CrossRef]
18. Li, L.; Zhang, D.G. Free vibration analysis of rotating functionally graded rectangular plates. *Compos. Struct.* **2016**, *136*, 493–504. [CrossRef]

19. Shakour, M. Free vibration analysis of functionally graded rotating conical shells in thermal environment. *Compos. Part B* **2019**, *163*, 574–584. [CrossRef]
20. Qin, Y.; Wang, L.; Li, Y.H. Coupled vibration characteristics of a rotating composite thin-walled beam subjected to aerodynamic force in hygrothermal environment. *Int. J. Mech. Sci.* **2018**, *140*, 260–270. [CrossRef]
21. Oh, Y.; Yoo, Y.H. Vibration analysis of a rotating pre-twisted blade considering the coupling effects of stretching, bending, and torsion. *J. Sound Vib.* **2018**, *431*, 20–39. [CrossRef]
22. Yang, B.; Ding, H.J. Elasticity solutions for a uniformly loaded rectangular plate of functionally graded materials with two opposite edges simply supported. *Acta Mech.* **2009**, *207*, 245258. [CrossRef]
23. Arumugam, A.B.; Rajamohan, V. Vibration analysis of rotating delaminated non-uniform composite plates. *Aerosp. Sci. Technol.* **2017**, *60*, 172–182.
24. Tuzzi, G.; Schwingshackl, C.W. Study of coupling between shaft bending and disc zero nodal diameter modes in a flexible shaft-disc assembly. *J. Sound Vib.* **2020**, *479*, 115362. [CrossRef]
25. Sun, J.; Kari, L.; Arteaga, I.L. A dynamic rotating blade model at an arbitrary stagger angle based on classical plate theory and the Hamilton's principle. *J. Sound Vib.* **2013**, *332*, 1355–1371. [CrossRef]
26. Bellucci, S.; Balasubramanian, C.; Micciulla, F. CNT composites for aerospace applications. *J. Exp. Nanosci.* **2007**, *2*, 193–206. [CrossRef]
27. Gauvin, F.; Robert, M. Durability study of vinylester/silicate nanocomposites for civil engineering applications. *Polym. Degrad. Stab.* **2015**, *121*, 359–368. [CrossRef]
28. Shi, G.; Araby, S.; Gibson, C.T. Graphene platelets and their polymer composites: Fabrication, structure, properties, and applications. *Adv. Funct. Mater.* **2018**, *28*, 1706705. [CrossRef]
29. Zhao, T.Y.; Wang, Y.X. Analytical solution for vibration characteristics of rotating graphene nanoplatelet-reinforced plates under rub-impact and thermal shock. *Adv. Compos. Lett.* **2020**, *29*, 1–15. [CrossRef]
30. Zhao, T.Y.; Jiang, L.P. Coupled free vibration of a functionally graded pre-twisted blade-shaft system reinforced with graphene nanoplatelets. *Compos. Struct.* **2021**, *262*, 113362. [CrossRef]
31. Zhao, T.Y.; Yang, Y.F. Free vibration analysis of a spinning porous nanocomposite blade reinforced with graphene nanoplatelets. *J. Strain Anal.* **2021**, *56*, 574–586. [CrossRef]
32. Li, Q.Y.; Wu, D. Nonlinear vibration and dynamic buckling analyses of sandwich functionally graded porous plate with graphene platelet reinforcement resting on Winkler–Pasternak elastic foundation. *Int. J. Mech. Sci.* **2018**, *148*, 596–610. [CrossRef]
33. Yang, J.; Chen, D. Buckling and free vibration analyses of functionally graded graphene reinforced porous nanocomposite plates based on Chebyshev-Ritz method. *Compos. Struct.* **2018**, *193*, 281294. [CrossRef]
34. Chen, D.; Yang, J. Elastic buckling and static bending of shear deformable functionally graded porous beam. *Compos. Struct.* **2015**, *133*, 54–61. [CrossRef]
35. Wu, H.L.; Yang, J. Parametric instability of thermo-mechanically loaded functionally graded graphene reinforced nanocomposite plates. *Int. J. Mech. Sci.* **2018**, *135*, 431–440. [CrossRef]
36. Lei, Z.; Liew, K. Free vibration analysis of functionally graded carbon nanotube-reinforced composite plates using the element-free kp-Ritz method inthermal environment. *Compos. Struct.* **2016**, *106*, 128–138. [CrossRef]
37. Yang, J.; Wu, H.L. Buckling and postbuckling of functionally graded multilayer graphene platelet-reinforced composite beams. *Compos. Struct.* **2017**, *161*, 111–118. [CrossRef]
38. Wang, Y.; Feng, C.; Zhao, Z.; Yang, J. Eigenvalue buckling of functionally graded cylindrical shells reinforced with graphene platelets (GPL). *Compos. Struct.* **2018**, *202*, 38–46. [CrossRef]
39. Zhao, T.Y.; Jiang, L.P.; Yu, Y.X.; Wang, Y.Q. Study on theoretical modeling and mechanical performance of a spinning porous graphene nanoplatelet reinforced beam attached with double blades. *Mech. Adv. Mater. Struct.* **2022**. [CrossRef]
40. Yang, B.; Kitipornchai, S.; Yang, Y.F. 3D thermo-mechanical bending solution of functionally graded graphene reinforced circular and annular plates. *Appl. Math. Model.* **2017**, *49*, 69–86. [CrossRef]
41. Ye, C.; Wang, Y.Q. Nonlinear forced vibration of functionally graded graphene platelet-reinforced metal foam cylindrical shells: Internal resonances. *Nonlinear Dyn.* **2021**, *3*, 2051–2069. [CrossRef]

 *mathematics*

Article

Deep Learning-Based Remaining Useful Life Prediction Method with Transformer Module and Random Forest

Lefa Zhao [1,*], Yafei Zhu [2] and Tianyu Zhao [3,*]

[1] School of General Education, Shenyang Sport University, Shenyang 110115, China
[2] International Engineering College, Shenyang Aerospace University, Shenyang 110136, China
[3] Key Laboratory of Structural Dynamics of Liaoning Province, College of Sciences, Northeastern University, Shenyang 110819, China
* Correspondence: larry2012@syty.edu.cn (L.Z.); zhaotianyu@mail.neu.edu.cn (T.Z.)

Abstract: This paper focuses on the prognosis problem in manufacturing of the electronic chips for devices. Electronic devices are of great importance at present, which are popularly applied in daily life. The basis of supporting the electronic device is the powerful electronic chip and its manufacturing technology. Chip manufacturing has been one of the most important technologies in recent years. The etching machine is the key equipment in the etching process of the wafers in chip manufacturing. Due to the high demands for precise manufacturing, monitoring the health state and predicting the remaining useful life (RUL) of the etching system is quite important. However, the task is very hard because of the lack of knowledge of exact onset of failure or degradation and the multiple operating conditions, etc. This paper proposes a novel deep learning-based RUL prediction method for the etching system. The transformer module and random forest are integrated in the methodology to identify the health state of the machine and predict its RUL, through training with the complex data of the etching machine's sensors and exploring its underlying features. The experiments are based on the subject of the 2018 PHM Data Challenge—for estimating time-to-failure or RUL of Ion Mill Etching Systems in an online fashion using data from multiple sensors. The results indicate the proposed method is promising for the real applications of the prognosis of the etching system for electronic devices.

Keywords: deep learning; remaining useful life prediction; transformer; random forest

MSC: 68T01

Citation: Zhao, L.; Zhu, Y.; Zhao, T. Deep Learning-Based Remaining Useful Life Prediction Method with Transformer Module and Random Forest. *Mathematics* **2022**, *10*, 2921. https://doi.org/10.3390/math10162921

Academic Editor: Yolanda Vidal

Received: 10 July 2022
Accepted: 10 August 2022
Published: 13 August 2022

1. Introduction

In recent years, deep learning technology has made a great breakthrough in image recognition, natural language processing, etc. In industry, machine condition monitoring has benefited well from deep learning [1–3]. Many researchers have used the deep learning algorithm to monitor the operating situation of all kinds of equipment and investigate the problem of remaining useful life (RUL) prediction, such as the pipeline system of a nuclear power station [4]. Traditionally, researchers could resolve the related problems for some simple structures through mechanical modeling [5,6], but the complexity of more equipment, such as the ion mill etching system, is far beyond the ability of traditional technique.

In daily life, electronic devices such as computers and personal smartphone require the high performance of electric hardware. Electronic chip manufacturing technology has become a nation's core strategy of science and technology. Professional equipment is highly dependent on the electronic chips. For instance, the sensors with chips for training athletes and evaluating their performance require high-level electronic chips. Examples of the electronic devices are shown in Figure 1. The etching machine is one of the most important systems in electronic chip manufacturing. Due to the complex working system of the etching machine, it is difficult to monitor its health state and predict the RUL.

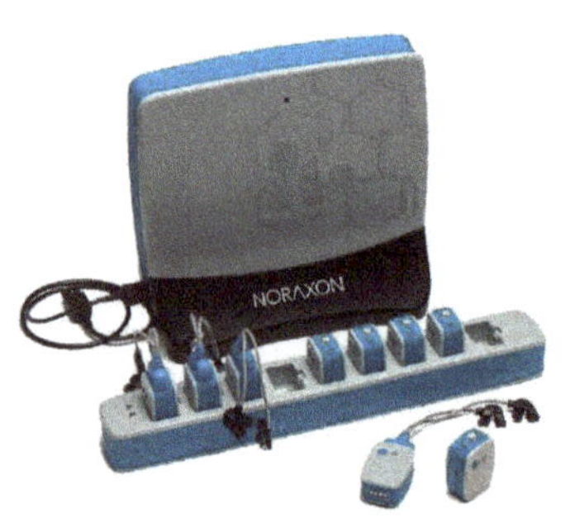  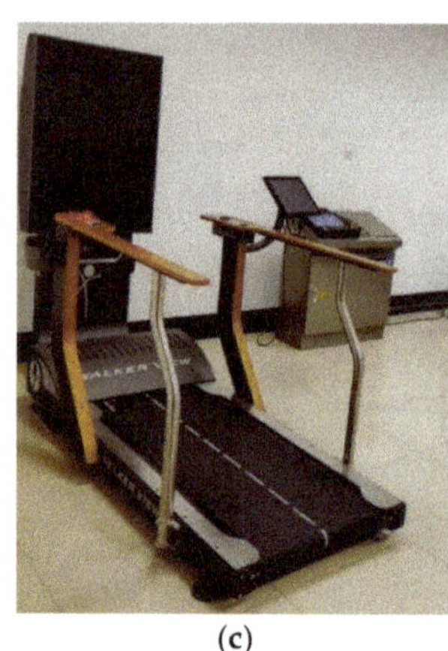

(a)　　　　　　　　　　　(b)　　　　　　　　　　　(c)

Figure 1. Examples of electronic devices with chips in athlete training. (**a**) Signal measurement device for electromyography. (**b**) Intelligent running training device. (**c**) Digital monitoring device for running.

In the current literature, LSTM (long-short-term memory network) of RNN (recurrent neural network) [7] have been popularly used for the RUL prediction problem. Other kinds of machine learning methods have also been used on this issue [8–11]. However, more and more researchers have addressed the related problem by using LSTM [12–14]. For investigating time series data problems, the LSTM network has a good learning capability [15]. The etching machine condition is also a time series data analysis problem.

In the deep learning-based studies, researchers adopted the Attention Model to solve the disappearance of long-short-term memory network gradients [16–18]. Although the attention machine successfully solved the gradient disappearance issue of LSTM, it also increased more computation to the learning task. Therefore, researchers further proposed the self-attention mechanism, which removes the structure of the long-short-term memory network and uses the attention machine directly to establish a network. In this way, the network can learn the relevance of information in time. Additionally, it can further overlay the network structure into a multi-head self-attention module block. Afterwards, the researchers created a new deep learning module with the structure of an auto-encoder network, which is named as the Transformer network.

Since the Transformer network was proposed, it has shown excellent learning in natural language [19–21], and compared with the basic CNN and RNN networks, the Transformer network outperforms them in the related problems. In addition, the Transformer network could not cause gradient vanishing or gradient exploding as easily as the RNN.

This paper proposes a novel deep learning-based method for the RUL prediction problem of the etching system. The Transformer module is integrated with the random forest algorithm to improve the learning capability of the model for processing the condition-monitoring time series data. Experiments on the real etching machine data are carried out for validations. The results of the experiments show that the proposed method is promising for the RUL prediction problem in real industries.

Section 2 presents the data set and the pre-processing of it. Section 3 introduces the methodologies proposed in this paper. Section 4 provides the experimental results for validations. We close the paper with conclusions in Section 5.

2. Data Set

2.1. Data Set

The data set used in this study is from the competition topic of the 2018 PHM Data Challenge. The data set is provided by the competition, including the training set and the prediction task data set. Additionally, it includes three kinds of data of 20 etching machines: physical information of etching machine operation, fault occurrence operation and fault occurrence countdown. The prediction task data set includes 5 data of etching machines, and it has only 2 categories: physical information of the etching machine operation and the countdown to the occurrence of the fault as the predicted answer. Etching machine failures are divided into three parts:

1.   FlowCool Presser Dropped Below Limit;
2.   FlowCool Presser Too High Check FlowCool Pump;
3.   FlowCool Leak.

The sensor that collects physical information of etching machine operation contains the contents shown in the following Table 1.

Table 1. Operation susceptor of etching machine.

ID#	Parameter Name	Type	Description
S1	time	Numeric	time
S2	Tool	Categorical	tool id
S3	stage	Categorical	processing stage of wafer
S4	Lot	Categorical	wafer id
S5	runnum	Numeric	number of times tool has been run
S6	recipe	Categorical	describes tool settings used to process wafer
S7	recipe_step	Categorical	process step of a recipe
S8	IONGAUGEPRESSURE	Numeric (Sensor)	pressure reading for the main process chamber when under vacuum
S9	ETCHBEAMVOLTAGE	Numeric	voltage potential applied to the beam plate of the grid assembly
S10	ETCHBEAMCURRENT	Numeric	ion current impacting the beam grid determining the amounts of ions accelerated through the grid assembly to the wafer
S13	FLOWCOOLFLOWRATE	Numeric	rate of flow of helium through the flowcool circuit, controlled by mass flow controller
S14	FLOWCOOLPRESSURE	Numeric (Sensor)	resulting helium pressure in the flowcool circuit
S15	ETCHGASCHANNEL1-READBACK	Numeric	rate of flow of argon into the source assembly in the vacuum chamber
S16	ETCHPBNGAS-READBACK	Numeric	rate of flow of argon into the PBN assembly in the chamber
S17	FIXTURETILTANGLE	Numeric	wafer tilt angle setting
S18	ROTATIONSPEED	Numeric	wafer rotation speed setting
S19	ACTUALROTATION-ANGLE	Numeric (Sensor)	measure wafer rotation angle
S20	FIXTURESHUTTER-POSITION	Numeric	open/close shutter setting for wafer shielding
S21	ETCHSOURCEUSAGE	Numeric	counter of use for the grid assembly consumable
S22	ETCHAUXSOURCE-TIMER	Numeric	counter of the use for the chamber shields consumable
S23	ETCHAUX2SOURCE-TIMER	Numeric	counter of the use for the chamber shields consumable
S24	ACTUALSTEPDURATION	Numeric (Sensor)	measured time duration for a particular step

The physical information of the etching machine operation is collected every four seconds, but there are also many irregular collection points. Every data set has a different size, but all of them are above 70 million seconds. The data set file of the time of failure contains the time of occurrence and category of failure.

The fault occurrence countdown file contains countdown time points for multiple occurrence points of three types of faults, and these points correspond to the time points collected by physical information of the etching machine.

In the training network, we use the information collected by all numerical type sensors except S1: time. Among them, the information collected by the water fixture position sensor (S20: FIXTURESHUTTER-POSITION) is the position of the water on the platform during the etching process. There are four different positions, which are represented by five numbers—they are 0,1,2,3,225. To facilitate the study, we change the five positions into a one-hot code represented by a binary vector. Other vectors which were selected in the data set have been normalized by the provider and they are suitable for further study.

Strictly speaking, the time point recorded by the fault occurrence time data set is not an accurate time of fault occurrence. Instead, the time point is when the etching machine shuts down due to the failure. The actual failure should be much earlier than these time points.

2.2. Pre-Process

There are three types of etching machine failures. This study assumes that the three types of failure are independent of each other. In the training model, the data is processed into three data sets based on the three types of failure, and three learning networks are trained for each of the three failures.

The etching machine used has running data up to tens of millions of seconds, and among these data, data which is too early can be considered to be in a healthy state. However, the occurrence of failure or shutdown should originate at a later point in time than abnormal operation. So, to directly learn the early data has no meaning for the remaining prediction of efficient life, and it will occupy a significant amount of time and resources of calculation. Therefore, we should train a random forests model which is used to monitor the time point when abnormal operation occurs.

At present, since there are no relatively abnormal operations and scientific theory on the concerned data, the references of the related study set the period at more than 5500 s from shutdown as a healthy time, and considers the period less than 5000 s as the time of abnormal operation. The data between the two steps of time will not be used.

However, the data of healthy time is far more than abnormal time. Such an uneven data set can cause the random forests, which we would use in the methodology, to have difficulty studying the characteristic of abnormal time. Hence, we should obtain the interpolation and fit for the abnormal time data, and then the original data is about sampling 1000 times the number of samples (different data sets have different and uneven numbers of failures, so they need to be adjusted according to the situation) to form new abnormal time data. Furthermore, among the data of healthy time and abnormal data, we choose smaller data, respectively, as a sample. Finally, we merge them into the training set of random forests, with 20% of them as the test set.

For the Transformer, as in random forest, the data set is processed into three data sets based on three failures for model training. To predict the RUL, it is necessary to input a time sequence. To reduce the amount of calculation, the data will be down-sampled. According to the prediction strategy, the Transformer network of this subject only learns from the data of the abnormal running time.

In down-sampling, for a sequence of failures, taking the downtime as the starting point, retrospective sampling is carried out. One sample point is taken for each R point, and M sample points are taken for one sampling. After one sampling, the first sample point after the starting point is moved to the starting point is repeated the above operation, and the operation is repeated N times. In this way, the sampling will overlap the same piece of fault information, but there is a certain degree of difference, which enhances the learning information and gives the trained model a certain degree of robustness.

During the experiment, the data set exposed some problems. For example, when the data pre-processing adopts the sampling method of R = 15, M = 300, N = 15, theoretically, the method M × R + N = 4515 requires retrospective sampling from the location of the failure, and it is required to be able to collect data points, which represents a time series of $4515 \times 4 = 18{,}060$ s. However, in actual operation, it is found that a lot of time is skipped in the time before the data set is close to the fault location. In other words, the time point before the fault location is not evenly collected at the frequency of collecting a data point every 4 s. The overall span of some samples can reach more than 30,000 s, and the maximum can reach 80,000 s, which is far greater than 18,060 s. Therefore, in order to ensure that there are sufficient and effective samples, in the actual data pre-processing, the data can only be required to include as many data points as possible within 18,000 s according to the specific conditions of the data set. Taking the data pre-processing of the failure type of "coolant pressure falling below the limit" in the data of the etching machine training set numbered 03_M01_DC as an example, in this training set, such failures occurred 43 times in total. According to the collection scheme described above, when the requirement is within 18,000 s, it contains 2000 data points, and 255 samples can be obtained.

3. Methodology

3.1. Overall Structure

Because early operating time can be considered as healthy running time, this stage has no relationship with the eventual failure. To strengthen efficiency, this study first uses the random forest algorithm to examine the abnormal operation time point in the operation of the etching machine, and then the data in the abnormal operation stage is used to predict the RUL.

In the stage of RUL, the Transformer network is used. However, the original Transformer network is faced with the problem of processing natural language and a complex structure and a huge amount of calculation. Based on referring to the improved network of the existing Transformer, only the original Transformer can be used in the part of enclosed code. After being improved, it will be used in the prediction tasks. The detailed process is shown in Figure 2, where X_t is a high-dimension input data at time t, while w and n represent the time steps.

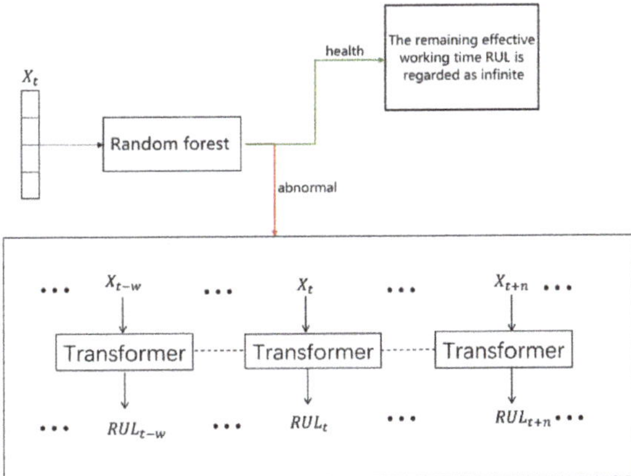

Figure 2. The overall process of random forest detection of abnormal running time and Transformer prediction of RUL.

3.2. Random Forest

In this paper, because the Transformer leads to a huge calculation amount for every input time-series data, we cannot input all the fragments of the raw data. Additionally, the fragments of the raw data could be divided into two kinds, such that one is the health data and the other one is the abnormal data. In addition, just the abnormal fragments would cause the reduction in the machine's RUL. Therefore, the Transformer could just train with the abnormal fragments of the raw data.

In order to identify the healthy state of the etching machine, the random forest is used to process the raw data [22–24], which is one of the most popular and efficient machine learning methods. Although the machine learning methods are not as effective as the deep learning methods for many tasks with complex data, their simple structures are more efficient than the deep learning methods. So, a machine learning method should always be used to pre-process data before a complicated deep learning method.

The random forest method is based on the decision tree method, and the random forest, simply speaking, is a combination of many decision trees [25,26]. As the basic machine learning method, it has three kinds, including ID3, C4.5 and CART (Classification and Regression Tree). The main difference between them is the different algorithm for the split of every node. Generally, CART has the best effect, which is selected in this paper.

Random forest is an integrated learning method in machine learning, which connects many decision trees. An intuitive explanation is that a decision tree is a classifier, and then n decision trees will have n classification results. Random forest is to integrate the classification results of these n trees. If the result of the decision tree is regarded as a vote for a certain category, the category with the most votes is finally selected as the result.

The study uses scikit-learn library in Python 3.8 to build a random forest algorithm which can be used to detect the abnormal running time point. Additionally, the MAE (Mean Absolute Error) can be used to calculate the correct rate in the testing phase, which is shown as Equation (1).

$$MAE = \frac{1}{n}\sum_{i=1}^{n}|\widehat{y}_i - y_i| \tag{1}$$

In Equation (1), y_i represents the true value of data category, $\widehat{y}_i$ is category which is predicted by the random forest, and n is the number of samples.

3.3. Transformer

The Transformer is a powerful and advanced method of deep learning, which is an important technology of artificial intelligence. Additionally, deep learning can be roughly classified into three categories according to the structure of deep artificial neural networks, includes convolution neural networks (CNN), recurrent neural network (RNN) and auto-encoder (AE). They have great success in resolving the problems with time-series data, such as natural language processing tasks, video identification problems and instrument diagnosis [27–29]. The panorama of Transformer structure is displayed in Figure 3. It is obvious that the kernel of the Transformer network is the multi-headed self-attention mechanism.

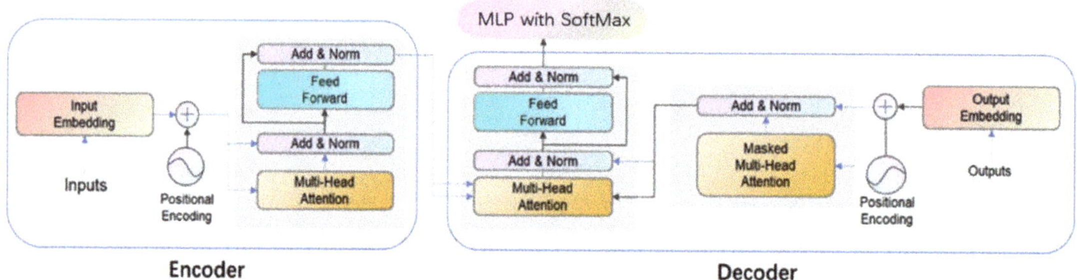

Figure 3. Transformer network structure.

The multi-head attention structure is a stacked self-attention mechanism. Additionally, self-attention is a variant of the attention mechanism. It reduces dependence on external information and is better at capturing the internal correlation of data. Its calculation includes three vectors, Q, K, V, named query, key, value, respectively, which have the same dimensions. They are obtained by Equation (2). The matrix $X = \{x_1, x_2, \cdots, x_n\}$

represents a sample of input data for the Transformer, and every x_i is one of the points in the time-series data, which contains the signals of the etching machine's sensors and means its dimension is 20 in the study. Additionally, the Q, K, V are the information about X in three kinds of state, which are the X itself in other words. In the way of the attention mechanism, which is the source of the self-attention mechanism, the Q means what we want to know, the K means the crucial information we already have, and V is the raw information where we want to explore some underlying content. In the attention mechanism, the three matrixes could come from different information; however, in the self-attention mechanism, they all come from the X mechanism, which means what we explore is the X itself. In addition, the three matrixes could be defined as $Q = \{q_1, q_2, \cdots, q_n\}$, $K = \{k_1, k_2, \cdots, k_n\}$ and, $V = \{v_1, v_2, \cdots, v_n\}$, where n is the number of time steps in the sequence and equals to 2000 in the study. In Equation (2), W_Q, W_K, W_V are three trainable parameter matrixes.

$$\begin{aligned} Q &= X^T \cdot W_Q \\ K &= X^T \cdot W_K \\ V &= X^T \cdot W_V \end{aligned} \tag{2}$$

Then, the calculation of the self-attention mechanism can be expressed as Equation (3), and the d_k is the dimension of the three matrixes Q, K, V, which depends on the dimension of input data and the head number of multi-headed self-attention mechanism. The multi-head self-attention mechanism is averagely dividing the d_k into few parts then continuing the calculation of the self-attention mechanism for each part.

$$Self\text{-}Attention(Q, K, V) = softmax\left(\frac{(Q \cdot K^T)}{\sqrt{d_k}}\right) \cdot V \tag{3}$$

The early Transformer networks' task is natural language processing [30–33]. Their input training data and label data language sentences with rich meanings, so we should encode the training data information by encoder and decode label data information. However, the task in this study is to predict the RUL of the etching machine based on the physical information sequence running. The input training data is the physical information of the working condition with rich information, but the label data is only a countdown sequence to the downtime, and it has no profound information.

After referring to the structure of the Vision Transformer (VIT), only the encoder part of the original Transformer network will be used, and the word vector-encoding part will be removed [34–37]. This study uses TensorFlow and Keras library in Python 3.8 to achieve the encoder part of the predictive network, which also means the original Transformer network. The Hyperparameters that the network needs to determine include the number of training times, the number of heads of the multi-head attention mechanism, the number of layers superimposed by the autoencoder, and the dimensions of the Feed Forward network. The structure of our proposed method is showed in Figure 4.

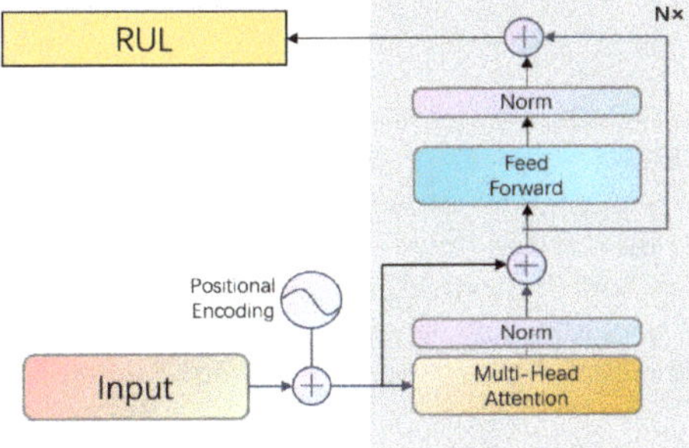

Figure 4. The improved Transformer structure used in this study.

The model uses Adam optimizer as the loss function. Take 80% of the data as training data, 20% as testing data. In the test, the mean absolute error is used to calculate the error between the true value and the predicted value of the proposed method [38].

4. Experimental Results

4.1. Study on the Number of Decision Trees in Random Forest

In the random forest algorithm, the most important parameter is the number of decision trees in random forest. Too few decision trees will impact the accuracy of the category, and many more algorithms will waste time and calculation resources. Due to the failure of each data set and the number of differences being huge, some of the data sets are too small, and thus, this study chooses the data of Number 03_M01_DC, which is in the etching training data regarding the drop in cooling fluid pressure to below the limit failure types of data. Random forest uses it to train algorithms to determine the number of decision trees. In that training set, such faults occurred a total of 40 times, with a large number of occurrences and abundant available data. After pre-processing, we obtained 151,500 samples, half of which are healthy data points, while the others are abnormal data points. Additionally, we then disorder them randomly. The preset numbers of decision trees are 1, 2, 3, 5, 10, 15, 20, 25, 50, 100, 200 and 500, and then, we conduct several experiments, respectively. Finally, the MAE of the trained random forest algorithm in the validation set is recorded under these parameters. The results are shown in Figure 5.

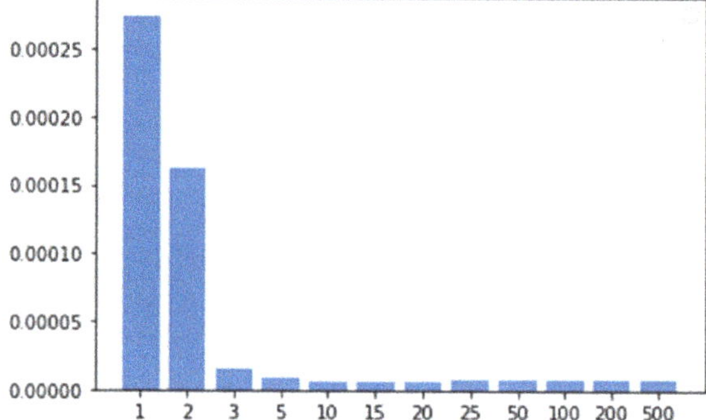

Figure 5. The relationship between the accuracy of random forest classification and the number of decision trees.

The horizontal axis is the number of decision trees, and the vertical axis is the average absolute error of the random forest algorithm corresponding to the number of decision trees in the verification set. We can see intuitively that when the number of decision trees is less than or equal to 10, the average decision error of the random forest algorithm reaches the lowest level, and the average absolute error is 0.000006. Additionally, we can ensure that the number of random forest decisions is 10.

4.2. Correlation Analysis of Data Set Multidimensional Variables and Abnormal Working Conditions

After the random forest has learned the training set, according to the structure of the decision tree, the various dimensional variables of the input data can be analyzed, and the correlation between each dimension and the learning result can be obtained. After learning all 20 etching machine training sets and combining the results of 20 random forest algorithms, the correlation between the input data and the learning results is shown in Figure 6.

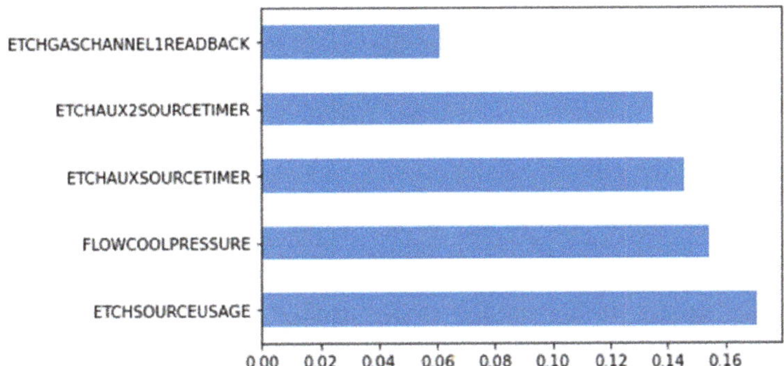

Figure 6. The 5 variables with the highest correlation between input data and results.

The vertical axis is the five variables with the highest correlation with the learning results, and the horizontal axis is the correlation score corresponding to the five variables in deep learning. According to this score, follow-up manual research on the law of the relationship between etching machine failure and working conditions, or related research on maintenance work, can refer to this evaluation, focusing on variables with high correlation scores.

4.3. Research on Hyperparameters of Transformer Prediction Model

In this section, using the training set of the etching machine numbered 03_M01_DC obtained in Section 2.2, we first simply set up the network: we set the number of hearts of the multi-head attention mechanism to 1, the number of layers superimposed by the auto-encoder is set to 1, and the dimension of the feed-forward network is set to 8. At this time, the prediction network has a simple structure, and low computational complexity. It is used only to determine whether the prediction network is effective when learning the data set. We take reading all samples as one learning, and observe whether the prediction network loss function drops and converges. The result is displayed in Figure 7.

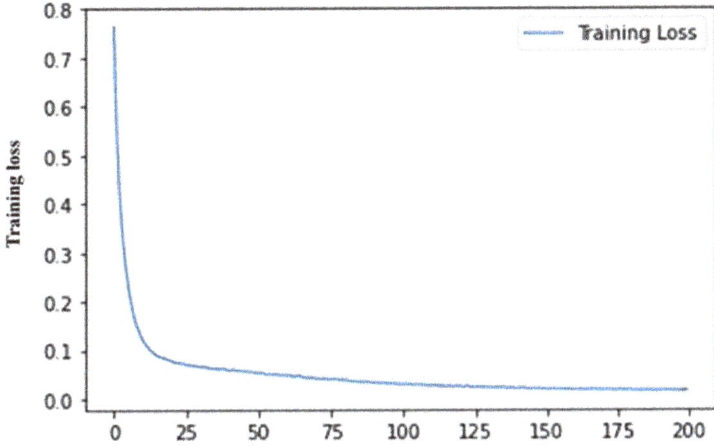

Figure 7. Forecasting the network loss function to change with the number of training steps.

As shown in Figure 7, it is obvious that the loss function of the prediction network has dropped significantly in the first 25 training steps, and its loss function gradually decreases and tends to be flat with the increase in the number of training times. It can be seen that the prediction network has effectively learned the data set.

According to the results, the number of training times is determined to be 100 times, and only the number of heads of the multi-head attention mechanism is changed to explore the influence of the number of heads of the multi-head attention mechanism on the predictive network learning effect. When setting the head number of the multi-head attention mechanism, it must be set as a factor of the input data dimension. In this experiment, the input data dimension is 20, so the head number of the multi-head attention mechanism can only be set to 1, 2, 4, 5, 10, or 20. The average absolute error of the prediction network in the test is observed under six different parameters.

As shown in Table 2, when the number of hearts of the multi-head attention mechanism is 2, the average absolute error of the prediction network is the lowest. After determining the number of hearts of the multi-head attention mechanism as 2, and then exploring the influence of predicting the dimension of the feed-forward neural network of the network, according to various Transformer research recommendations, the dimension of the feed-forward neural network should be set to the power of 2 as much as possible. The experimental results are as follows in Table 3.

Table 2. The number of heads of the multi-head attention mechanism and the average absolute error of the prediction network.

Number of Heads of Multi-Head Attention Mechanism	Mean Absolute Error (Unit: Second)
1	2840.07
2	2561.87
4	3598.99
5	2807.26
10	3042.27
20	2971.62

Table 3. The number of heads of the multi-head attention mechanism and the average absolute error of the prediction network.

Feedforward Neural Network Dimensions	Mean Absolute Error (Unit: Second)
8	5716.82
16	4076.40
32	3736.63
64	3892.85
128	3786.88
256	2844.60
512	2248.19
1024	2968.11
2048	3006.22

According to the current research experience of various Transformer networks, when the dimension of the feed-forward neural network is slightly larger than the length of the input sequence, the learning effect of the Transformer network is the best. The input sequence length in this experiment is 300 steps of time, as shown in Table 3. When the feed-forward neural is 512 dimensions, the training effect is the best, which is consistent with this experience. Finally, the influence of the number of auto-encoder stacks on the learning effect of the prediction network is studied. The results are shown in Table 4. When the number of auto-encoder stacks is 4, the average error is the lowest.

Table 4. The number of superimposed layers of the auto-encoder and the average absolute error of the prediction network.

Number of Superimposed Layers of Autoencoder	Mean Absolute Error (Unit: Second)
1	4832.86
2	2615.82
3	2235.90
4	2138.53
5	2452.54

4.4. The Complete Network Performs Prediction Tasks

In this experiment, three sets of training sets were obtained by pre-processing part of the training set data of the etching machine numbered 03_M01_DC concerning the three types of failures, in which 204 training samples and 51 test samples were obtained for the "Flow Cool Pressure Dropped Below Limit" fault type, 60 training samples and 15 test samples were obtained for "Flow cool Pressure Too High Check Flow cool Pump" fault type, the Transformer model of this study was used for training, and 120 training samples and 30 test samples were obtained for the "Flow cool leak" fault type. Figures 8–10 show the prediction results of the RUL of a certain sample of the corresponding fault type test sample after the model has learned the three training sample data sets. The red broken line "RUL_GT" is the actual RUL, and the blue broken line "RUL_PRE" is the RUL predicted by the model.

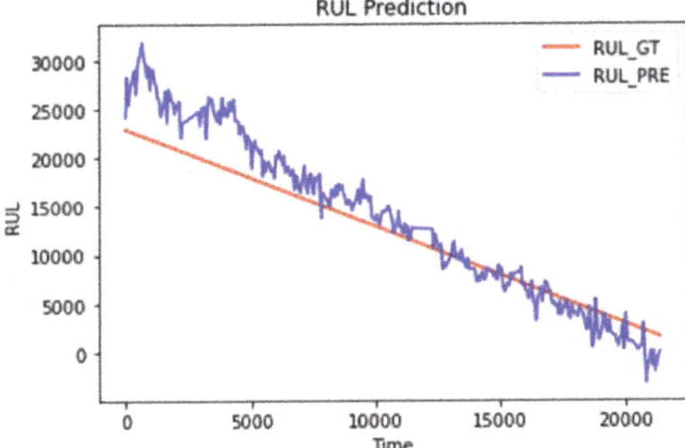

Figure 8. Prediction of RUL of the "Coolant pressure drops below the limit" fault type.

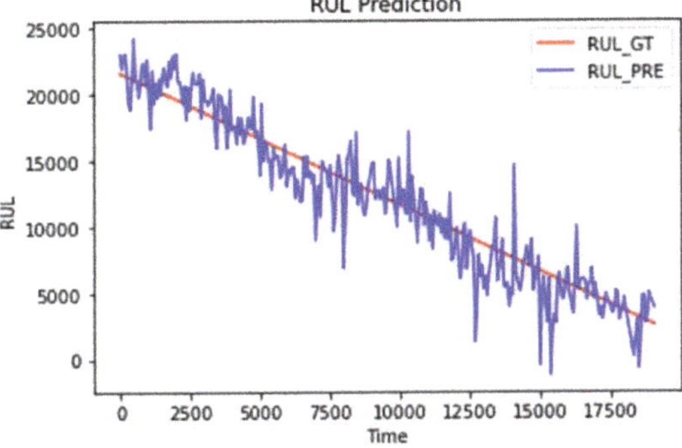

Figure 9. Prediction of RUL of "cooling pressure too high" fault type.

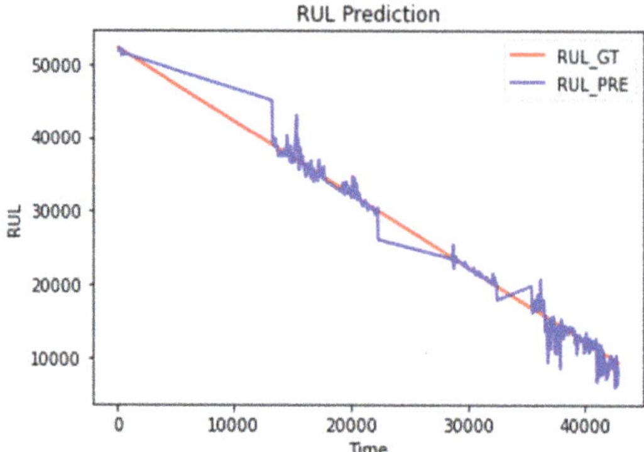

Figure 10. Prediction of RUL of "coolant leakage" fault type.

It can be seen from the following three figures that although the same sampling method is used, the period of the samples is very different, which directly reflects that the original data sampling is not sampled once and evenly every four seconds. It also brings great difficulties to the learning task. It can be seen from the three graphs that the blue line representing the predicted value still fluctuates tightly along the red line representing the true value, which shows that the model used in this topic has better prediction ability.

This paper randomly selects three sequences about the failure type "Flow Cool Pressure Dropped Below Limit" from any etching machine as the data set of the complete network prediction task. The specific operation is to detect the occurrence point of the abnormal operation in the data by the trained random forest model, and then use the occurrence point as the starting point. The sampling is started along the time direction of the data, and the Transformer model is used as input to predict the RUL until the stop point is repeated. The Data Challenge provides two scoring methods for prediction tasks, as in Tables 5 and 6:

Table 5. Scoring method 1.

Ground Truth RUL (GT)	Submission RUL (SUB)	Score
Number	Number	$\lvert GT - SUB \rvert \times \exp(-0.001GT)$
NaN	Number	$\lvert SUB \rvert \times \exp(-0.001SUB)$
Number	NaN	$\lvert GT \rvert \times \exp(-0.001GT)$
NaN	NaN	0

Table 6. Scoring Method 2.

Ground Truth RUL (GT)	Submission RUL (SUB)	Score
Number	Number	$0.1 \times (GT - SUB)2$
NaN	Number	$5/(\lvert SUB \rvert + 3)$
Number	NaN	$20 \times \exp[-1\lvert/(GT\rvert + 0.1)]$
NaN	NaN	0

The sum of the two is the total score, and the smaller score means better. To visually demonstrate the effect of the method of this subject, a single-layer simple recurrent neural network, a double-layer simple recurrent neural network, a single-layer long-term memory network, and a double-layer long-term memory network are added to the experiment to conduct prediction experiments after training on the same data set; according to the scoring rules, the effects of the method of this subject and the comparison method can be obtained as shown in Table 7 below:

Table 7. Comparison of prediction results with common deep learning methods.

Method	Total Score	Mean Absolute Error (Unit: Second)
Single-layer RNN	5.90×10^{15}	6843
Double-layer RNN	6.22×10^{15}	7632
Single-layer LSTM	5.96×10^{15}	6500
Double-layer LSTM	5.67×10^{15}	6753
Proposed Method	1.77×10^{15}	2240

As shown in the table, the total score of the ordinary single-layer long-term and short-term memory network is much higher than the method used in this subject, which proves that the method proposed in this subject has a good effect on predicting the RUL of the multi-dimensional time series. It is worth noting that the average absolute error in the prediction of the method used in this topic is much lower than that of other methods. It can be seen that the prediction results of the method in this topic have better accuracy. In addition, during the experiment, the training time of the contrast method used was more than one hour, while the training time of the method used in this topic was only about half an hour, and the computational efficiency was greatly enhanced.

5. Conclusions

In this paper, two models of random forest and transformer are constructed to solve the task of predicting the RUL of the etching machine. The random forest model is used to detect the time point of abnormal operation of the etching machine during operation, and the Transformer model is used to predict the abnormal operation stage until shutdown.

In the experiment, the random forest shows ultimate efficiency, and when we use it to identify the health state of the machine, it is very fast. Additionally, the transformer method is obviously better than the compared methods. The effect of the Transformer would be significantly improved when the rise of the parameters of the Transformer method, but the calculated amount of it also increases rapidly, which means the training needs more time or better devices. Therefore, the method would be labored when it faces tasks with a high dimension and long-length data, and we would reform the method based on the short-length data in the future.

From the experimental results, both models have achieved the preset functions, which proves the feasibility of the prediction method of this subject, but it is worth reflecting that in this method, the three types of failures are separately trained when predicting the RUL. That is, it is assumed that the three are independently affecting the downtime of the etching machine. However, in practice, it is usually not the case. Therefore, in follow-up research, the RUL labels of the three faults can be combined for learning, and the relationship between faults and the RUL can be further studied.

In summary, the method proposed in this topic achieves a good effect on predicting the RUL of the etching machine, which is well suited for practical applications. For instance, the proposed method is promising for manufacturing the electronic chips of the sport devices for training athletes and evaluating their performance. It can be also used for other areas such as the aerospace industry, automation, etc.

Author Contributions: Formal analysis, L.Z.; Methodology, Y.Z.; Project administration, T.Z. All authors have read and agreed to the published version of the manuscript.

Funding: This study was funded by the Key R&D Plan of China for Winter Olympics (2021YFF0306401) and the Key Special Project of the National Key Research and Development Program "Technical Winter Olympics" (2018YFF0300502 and 2021YFF0306400).

Institutional Review Board Statement: Not applicable.

Informed Consent Statement: Not applicable.

Data Availability Statement: Data is contained within the article.

Conflicts of Interest: The authors declare no conflict of interest.

References

1. Smith, W.A.; Randall, R.B. Rolling element bearing diagnostics using the Case Western Reserve University data: A benchmark study. *Mech. Syst. Signal Process.* **2015**, *64*, 100–131. [CrossRef]
2. Zhang, W.; Li, X.; Li, X. Deep learning-based prognostic approach for lithium-ion batteries with adaptive time-series prediction and on-line validation. *Measurement* **2020**, *164*, 108052. [CrossRef]
3. Li, X.; Li, X.; Ma, H. Deep representation clustering-based fault diagnosis method with unsupervised data applied to rotating machinery. *Mech. Syst. Signal Process.* **2020**, *143*, 106825. [CrossRef]
4. Li, X.; Fu, X.-M.; Xiong, F.-R.; Bai, X.-M. Deep learning-based unsupervised representation clustering methodology for automatic nuclear reactor operating transient identification. *Knowl.-Based Syst.* **2020**, *204*, 106178. [CrossRef]
5. Zhao, T.; Li, K.; Ma, H. Study on dynamic characteristics of a rotating cylindrical shell with uncertain parameters. *Anal. Math. Phys.* **2022**, *12*, 97. [CrossRef]
6. Zhao, T.Y.; Yan, K.; Li, H.W.; Wang, X. Study on theoretical modeling and vibration performance of an assembled cylindrical shell-plate structure with whirl motion. *Appl. Math. Model.* **2022**, *110*, 618–632. [CrossRef]
7. Li, X.; Zhang, W.; Ma, H.; Luo, Z.; Li, X. Domain generalization in rotating machinery fault diagnostics using deep neural networks. *Neurocomputing* **2020**, *403*, 409–420. [CrossRef]
8. Li, X.; Zhang, W.; Ma, H.; Luo, Z.; Li, X. Data alignments in machinery remaining useful life prediction using deep adversarial neural networks. *Knowl.-Based Syst.* **2020**, *197*, 105843. [CrossRef]
9. Li, X.; Zhang, W.; Ma, H.; Luo, Z.; Li, X. Partial transfer learning in machinery cross-domain fault diagnostics using class-weighted adversarial networks. *Neural Netw.* **2020**, *129*, 313–322. [CrossRef]
10. Zhang, W.; Li, X.; Ma, H.; Luo, Z.; Li, X. Transfer learning using deep representation regularization in remaining useful life prediction across operating conditions. *Reliab. Eng. Syst. Saf.* **2021**, *211*, 107556. [CrossRef]
11. Li, X.; Zhang, W.; Ma, H.; Luo, Z.; Li, X. Degradation alignment in remaining useful life prediction using deep cycle-consistent learning. *IEEE Trans. Neural Netw. Learn. Syst.* **2021**. [CrossRef] [PubMed]
12. Hsu, C.-S.; Jiang, J.-R. Remaining useful life estimation using long short-term memory deep learning. In Proceedings of the 2018 IEEE International Conference on Applied System Invention, Chiba, Japan, 13–17 April 2018; IEEE: Piscataway, NJ, USA, 2018; pp. 58–61.
13. Yuan, M.; Wu, Y.; Lin, L. Fault diagnosis and remaining useful life estimation of aero engine using LSTM neural network. In Proceedings of the 2016 IEEE International Conference on Aircraft Utility Systems, Beijing, China, 10–12 October 2016; IEEE: Piscataway, NJ, USA, 2016; pp. 135–140.
14. Zhang, J.; Wang, P.; Yan, R.; Gao, R.X. Long short-term memory for machine remaining life prediction. *J. Manuf. Syst.* **2018**, *48*, 78–86. [CrossRef]
15. Malhotra, P.; Vig, L.; Shroff, G.; Agarwal, P. Long short-term memory networks for anomaly detection in time series. *Proceedings* **2015**, *89*, 89–94.
16. Zhang, G.; Bai, X.; Wang, Y. Short-time multi-energy load forecasting method based on CNN-Seq2Seq model with attention mechanism. *Mach. Learn. Appl.* **2021**, *5*, 100064. [CrossRef]
17. Wang, X.; Tang, M.; Yang, T.; Wang, Z. A novel network with multiple attention mechanisms for aspect-level sentiment analysis. *Knowl.-Based Syst.* **2021**, *227*, 107196. [CrossRef]
18. Wang, Y.; Huang, M.; Zhao, L.; Zhu, X. Attention-based LSTM for aspect-level sentiment classification. In Proceedings of the 2016 Conference on Empirical Methods in Natural Language Processing, Austin, TX, USA, 1–5 November 2016; pp. 606–615.
19. Li, Z.H.; Zhang, Y.; Abu-Siada, A.; Chen, X.; Li, Z.; Xu, Y.; Zhang, L.; Tong, Y. Fault diagnosis of transformer windings based on decision tree and fully connected neural network. *Energies* **2021**, *14*, 1531. [CrossRef]
20. Yun, H.; Kang, T.; Jung, K. Analyzing and controlling inter-head diversity in multi-head attention. *Appl. Sci.* **2021**, *11*, 1548. [CrossRef]
21. Savini, E.; Caragea, C. Intermediate-task transfer learning with BERT for sarcasm detection. *Mathematics* **2022**, *10*, 844. [CrossRef]
22. Wang, N.; Fan, X.; Fan, J.; Yan, C. Random forest winter wheat extraction algorithm based on spatial features of neighborhood samples. *Mathematics* **2022**, *10*, 2206. [CrossRef]
23. Kovalnogov, V.; Fedorov, R.; Klyachkin, V.; Generalov, D.; Kuvayskova, Y.; Busygin, S. Applying the random forest method to improve burner efficiency. *Mathematics* **2022**, *10*, 2143. [CrossRef]
24. Pal, M. Random forest classifier for remote sensing classification. *Int. J. Remote Sens.* **2005**, *26*, 217–222. [CrossRef]
25. Shinkevich, A.I.; Ershova, I.G.; Galimulina, F.F.; Yarlychenko, A.A. Innovative mesosystems algorithm for sustainable development priority areas identification in industry based on decision trees construction. *Mathematics* **2021**, *9*, 3055. [CrossRef]
26. Al Hamad, M.; Zeki, A.M. Accuracy vs. cost in decision trees: A survey. In Proceedings of the 2018 International Conference on Innovation and Intelligence for Informatics, Computing and Technologies, Sakhier, Bahrain, 18–20 November 2018; IEEE: Piscataway, NJ, USA, 2018; pp. 1–4.
27. Zhang, W.; Li, X.; Ma, H.; Luo, Z.; Li, X. Universal domain adaptation in fault diagnostics with hybrid weighted deep adversarial learning. *IEEE Trans. Ind. Inform.* **2021**, *17*, 7957–7967. [CrossRef]

28. Zhang, W.; Li, X. Data privacy preserving federated transfer learning in machinery fault diagnostics using prior distributions. *Struct. Health Monit.* **2022**, *21*, 1329–1344. [CrossRef]
29. Zhang, W.; Li, X. Federated transfer learning for intelligent fault diagnostics using deep adversarial networks with data privacy. *IEEE/ASME Trans. Mechatron.* **2021**, *27*, 430–439. [CrossRef]
30. Vaswani, A.; Shazeer, N.; Parmar, N.; Uszkoreit, J.; Jones, L.; Gomez, A.N.; Kaiser, Ł.; Polosukhin, I. Attention is all you need. In Proceedings of the 31st Conference on Neural Information Processing Systems (NIPS 2017), Long Beach, CA, USA, 4–7 December 2017; Volume 30.
31. Dai, Z.; Yang, Z.; Yang, Y.; Cohen, W.W.; Carbonell, J.; Le Quoc, V.; Salakhutdinov, R. Transformer-XL: Language modeling with longer-term dependency. In Proceedings of the ICLR 2019, New Orleans, LA, USA, 6–9 May 2019.
32. Dai, Z.; Yang, Z.; Yang, Y.; Carbonell, J.; Le, Q.; Salakhutdinov, R. Transformer-XL: Attentive language models beyond a fixed-length context. *arXiv* **2019**, arXiv:1901.02860.
33. Yang, Z.; Dai, Z.; Yang, Y.; Carbonell, J.; Salakhutdinov, R.R.; Le Quoc, V. XLNet: Generalized autoregressive pretraining for language understanding. In Proceedings of the NeurIPS 2019, Vancouver, BC, Canada, 8–14 December 2019; Volume 32.
34. Arnab, A.; Dehghani, M.; Heigold, G.; Sun, C.; Lučić, M.; Schmid, C. ViViT: A video vision transformer. In Proceedings of the IEEE/CVF International Conference on Computer Vision 2021, Montreal, QC, Canada, 10–17 October 2021; IEEE: Piscataway, NJ, USA, 2021; pp. 6836–6846.
35. Liu, Z.; Lin, Y.; Cao, Y.; Hu, H.; Wei, Y.; Zhang, Z.; Lin, S.; Guo, B. Swin Transformer: Hierarchical vision transformer using shifted windows. In Proceedings of the IEEE/CVF International Conference on Computer Vision 2021, Montreal, QC, Canada, 10–17 October 2021; IEEE: Piscataway, NJ, USA, 2021; pp. 10012–10022.
36. Sun, Z.; Liu, C.; Qu, H.; Xie, G. A novel effective vehicle detection method based on Swin Transformer in hazy scenes. *Mathematics* **2022**, *10*, 2199. [CrossRef]
37. Ju, X.; Zhao, X.; Qian, S. TransMF: Transformer-based multi-scale fusion model for crack detection. *Mathematics* **2022**, *10*, 2354. [CrossRef]
38. Qi, J.; Du, J.; Siniscalchi, S.M.; Ma, X.; Lee, C.-H. Analyzing upper bounds on mean absolute errors for deep neural network-based vector-to-vector regression. *IEEE Trans. Signal Process.* **2020**, *68*, 3411–3422. [CrossRef]

Article

A Deep Learning Approach for Predicting Two-Dimensional Soil Consolidation Using Physics-Informed Neural Networks (PINN)

Yue Lu and Gang Mei *

School of Engineering and Technology, China University of Geosciences (Beijing), Beijing 100083, China
* Correspondence: gang.mei@cugb.edu.cn

Abstract: The unidirectional consolidation theory of soils is widely used in certain conditions and approximate calculations. The multidirectional theory of soil consolidation is more reasonable than the unidirectional theory in practical applications but is much more complicated in terms of index determination and solution. To address the above problem, in this paper, we propose a deep learning method using physics-informed neural networks (PINN) to predict the excess pore water pressure of two-dimensional soil consolidation. In the proposed method, (1) a fully connected neural network is constructed; (2) the computational domain, partial differential equation (PDE), and constraints are defined to generate data for model training; and (3) the PDE of two-dimensional soil consolidation and the model of the neural network are connected to reduce the loss of the model. The effectiveness of the proposed method is verified by comparison with the numerical solution of PDE for two-dimensional consolidation. Moreover, the FEM and the proposed PINN-based method are applied to predict the consolidation of foundation soils in a real case of Sichuan Railway in China, and the results are quite consistent. The proposed deep learning approach can be used to investigate large and complex multidirectional soil consolidation.

Keywords: engineering geology; soil consolidation; excess pore water pressure; deep learning; physics-informed neural network (PINN)

MSC: 35-04

Citation: Lu, Y.; Mei, G. A Deep Learning Approach for Predicting Two-Dimensional Soil Consolidation Using Physics-Informed Neural Networks (PINN). *Mathematics* **2022**, *10*, 2949. https://doi.org/10.3390/math10162949

Academic Editors: Xiang Li, Shuo Zhang and Wei Zhang

Received: 5 July 2022
Accepted: 12 August 2022
Published: 16 August 2022

Publisher's Note: MDPI stays neutral with regard to jurisdictional claims in published maps and institutional affiliations.

1. Introduction

Soil deformation and stability problems associated with soil consolidation occur during the construction of large infrastructures such as highways, embankments, and airports. Soil consolidation laws are complex and depend not only on the type and properties of the soil but also on its boundary conditions, drainage conditions, and types of loading [1,2]. Therefore, to ensure the safety of infrastructures, the study of multidirectional soil consolidation theory, which is closer to the actual working conditions, has broad application prospects and economic value.

There is much research work on soil consolidation. Terzaghi [3] in his seminal work on soil mechanics presented his consolidation theory for soil in 1925 as part of his comprehensive theory of soil mechanics. Biot [4] proposed his consolidation theory based on the effective stress principle, soil continuity, and equilibrium equation under the condition of considering the relationship between pore pressure and the soil skeleton deformation during soil consolidation. Schiffman [5] investigated the consolidation equation for the case of a linear increase in load with time and presented an analytical solution for one-dimensional soil consolidation under this situation. Indraratna [6] proposed a method for the radial consolidation of clays using a compression index and varying horizontal permeability.

Currently, most consolidation problems are analyzed using finite element analysis. The finite element method (FEM) is one of the most typical mesh-based numerical methods, which is quite powerful and widely used in various science and engineering applications. However, when dealing with complex study areas or domains, the mesh generation in FEM is quite computationally expensive. Notably, in some cases, high-quality meshes cannot be achieved, thus leading to unsatisfactory computational accuracy [7,8]. Moreover, finite element analysis requires detailed material parameters of the study areas or domains. In some cases, detailed and accurate values of martial parameters are not easy to obtain.

Currently, there are two problems that occur when analyzing two-dimensional or three-dimensional soil consolidation. (1) The modeling process of traditional numerical methods is quite complicated for high-dimensional problems. (2) In general, traditional numerical methods are computationally quite inefficient when investigating multidimensional soil consolidation.

To address the above problems, in this paper, we propose a data-free deep learning method to predict two-dimensional soil consolidation using PINNs. In the proposed method, the prediction of excess pore water pressure is demonstrated for different boundary conditions: drainage at the top boundary and drainage at the top and bottom boundaries. First, we use DeepXDE [9], a library in Python, to define the computational domain, PDEs, constraints, and the number of training and testing data generated under these conditions for two-dimensional soil consolidation. Then, we construct the neural network. Finally, we connect the PDE of two-dimensional soil consolidation and the model of the neural network to reduce the loss of the model. Using this method, the excess pore water pressure of the soil can be predicted simply and efficiently.

A physics-informed neural network (PINN) is a type of neural network for solving PDEs using physical equations as operational constraints [10]. The idea behind a PINN is to convert physical constraints as additional loss functions in deep neural networks [11]. More details about the PINN will be introduced in Section 2.2.

The rest of this paper is organized as follows. Section 2 describes the details of this proposed method. Section 3 verifies this proposed method in two simple examples and analyses the results. In Section 4, the FEM and the proposed PINN-based method are applied to predict the consolidation of foundation soils in a real case of Sichuan Railway in China and make a comparative analysis. Section 5 discusses the advantages and shortcomings of the proposed deep learning method and points out future work. Finally, Section 6 concludes the paper.

2. Methods

2.1. Overview of the Proposed Deep Learning Method

In this paper, we propose a deep learning approach using PINN to predict the excess pore water pressure of two-dimensional soil consolidation (see Figure 1). First, we construct a fully connected neural network. Second, we define the PDE, time domain, and initial and boundary conditions for two-dimensional soil consolidation in DeepXDE, a Python library. Third, we connect the PDE to the neural network and tune the parameters to reduce the model loss. Finally, we employ the trained model to predict the excess pore water pressure. We verify this proposed method with two simple examples: two-dimensional consolidation for drainage at the top boundary and drainage at the top and bottom boundaries.

2.2. Background and Theory of PINN

In this section, we introduce how to employ PINN to solve the PDE.

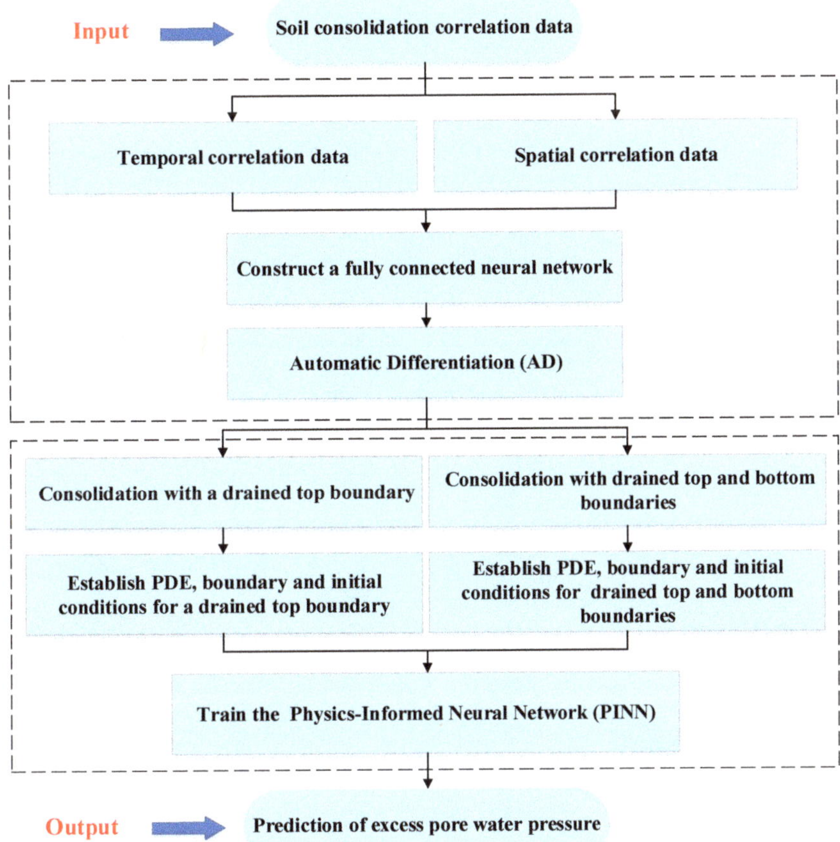

Figure 1. Flowchart of the proposed deep learning method.

2.2.1. Background of PINN

The idea of applying prior knowledge to deep learning was first proposed by Owhadi [12]. Subsequently, Raissi et al. [13,14] used Gaussian process regression to establish a representation of linear operator generalization to present uncertainty estimates for various physical problems, introducing and illustrating the PINN method for solving nonlinear PDEs [10]. Karniadakis et al. [15] proposed physics-informed machine learning as an algorithm that combines incomplete data with physical prior knowledge and discussed its various applications in forward and inverse problems.

Currently, PINNs have been increasingly used in various engineering problems, such as fluid mechanics [16–19]. For example, Bandai et al. [20] proposed the constitutive relation and soil water flux density for volumetric water content measurement based on a physical information neural network. Zhang, Z. [21] used a physics-informed neural network to simulate and predict the transient Darcy flow of unlabeled data in heterogeneous reservoirs. Bekele [22] used a PINN to solve forward and inverse problems of one-dimensional consolidation of soils.

2.2.2. Theory of PINN

A PINN combines PDEs and physics-informed constraints into the computation of a loss function to constrain the neural network and reduce the training loss, replacing the actual observed data of the model, i.e., a "data-free" neural network. It approximates the PDE solution by training the neural network to minimize the loss function, including terms along the boundary of the space-time domain reflecting the initial and boundary conditions and residuals of PDEs at selected points in the domain. By combining values in the input domain with physical information, PINN generates an estimated solution to the point differential equation after training.

The process of solving the PDE requires the derivative of the input values. There are four methods for calculating derivatives: hand-coded, symbolic, numerical, and automatic. However, it is impractical to calculate the derivatives manually in the face of complex equations. The automatic differentiation (AD) used in a PINN uses exact expressions with floating-point values rather than symbolic strings, and there is no approximation error [23]. Undoubtedly, the prediction accuracy and efficiency are improved.

A PINN is composed of physical information, neural networks, and feedback mechanisms [24]. First, the physics-informed model is used to calculate the partial derivatives of the functions and to determine the loss of the equation terms. Then, the model is trained by connecting the two modular neural networks through a differentiation algorithm. Finally, continuous feedback adjustments are made to minimize the training losses. The PINN workflow schematic is illustrated in Figure 2.

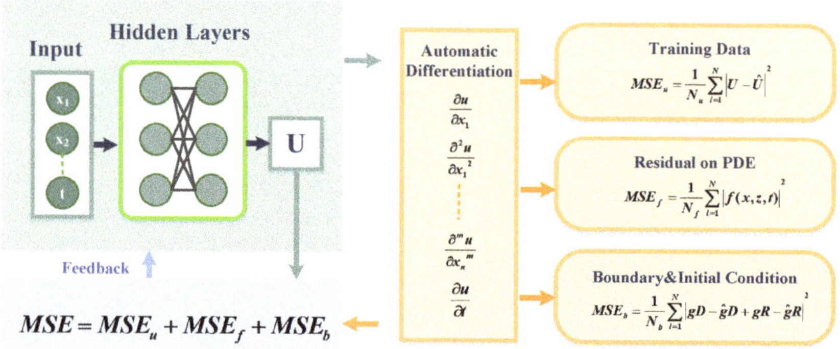

Figure 2. Illustration of a PINN algorithm for solving partial differential equations. This method uses AD technology to analyze and derive the integer derivative, and the obtained MSE is fed back to the neural network.

Physics-informed neural networks learn by minimizing the loss of the mean squared error. The mean square error formula of the neural network model is described in Equation (1) [10,25].

$$MSE = MSE_u + MES_f + MSE_b \tag{1}$$

where

$$MSE_u = \frac{1}{N_u}\sum_{i=1}^{N_u}|u(x,z,t) - \hat{u}(x,z,t)|^2 \tag{2}$$

$$MSE_f = \frac{1}{N_f}\sum_{i=1}^{N_f}|f(x,z,t)|^2 \tag{3}$$

$$MSE_b = \frac{1}{N_b}\sum_{i=1}^{N_b}|g_D(x,z,t) - \hat{g_D}(x,z,t) + g_R(x,z,t) - \hat{g_R}(x,z,t)|^2 \tag{4}$$

Here, (x,z,t) is the input to the training of a neural network model. In the proposed method, training points are randomly generated based on the physical constraints of the governing PDE. $g_D(x, z, t)$ represents the initial training points, and $g_R(x, z, t)$ represents the boundary training points.

In this paper, we use the Python library DeepXDE to solve practical applications with PINNs. Solving differential equations with DeepXDE uses built-in modules to specify problems, including computational domains (geometry and time), PDEs, boundary/initial conditions, and neural network architecture [9]. The workflow of DeepXDE is shown in Figure 3. Furthermore, four boundary conditions (Dirichlet, Neumann, Robin, and periodic) are provided by this library. Initial conditions can be defined by IC modules. For example, the loss type, metric, optimizer, learning rate table, initialization, and regularization can be adjusted and selected by themselves according to different needs.

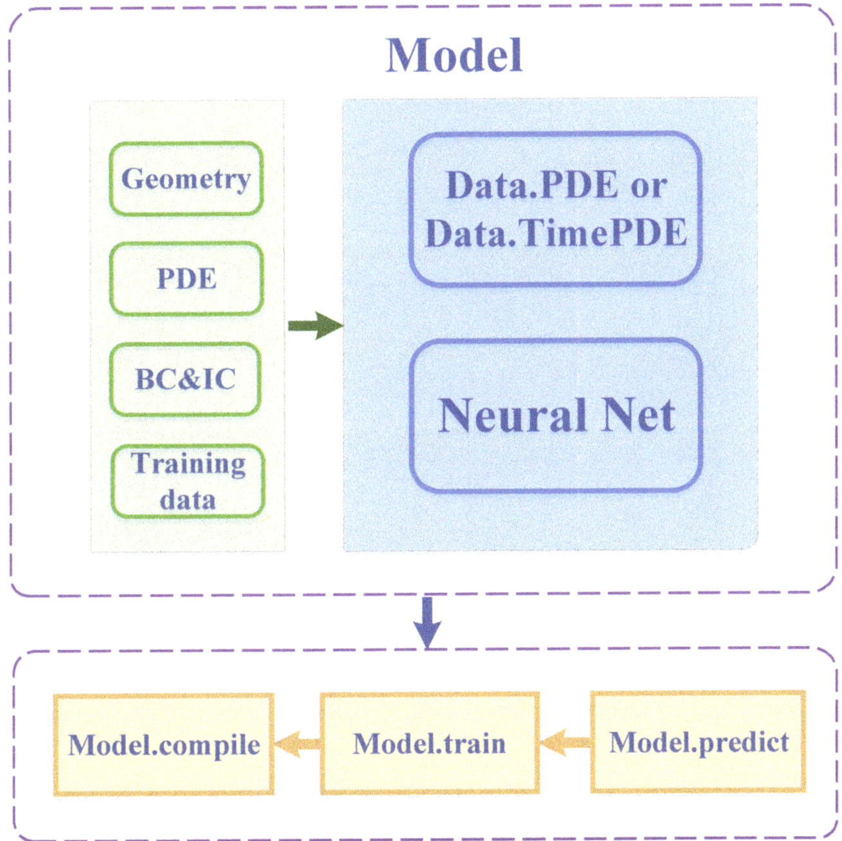

Figure 3. The workflow of DeepXDE. The green modules define the PDE and the training hyperparameters. The blue modules combine the PDE and training hyperparameters. The yellow modules are the three steps to solve the PDE.

2.3. Problem 1: Two-Dimensional Soil Consolidation for Drainage at Top Boundary

In this section, we introduce how to employ the deep learning approach to solve the problem of two-dimensional consolidation for drainage at a top boundary.

Rendulic [26] extended the one-dimensional consolidation theory to two or three dimensions and proposed the Terzaghi–Rendulic theory, assuming that the sum of normal stresses at any point in soil under constant external loads is a constant in consolidation. Therefore, the consolidation problem is the same as the thermal diffusion problem of consolidation, and its mathematical expression is also called the diffusion equation (see Equation (5)).

$$\frac{\partial u}{\partial t} - C_v\left(\frac{\partial^2 u}{\partial x^2} + \frac{\partial^2 u}{\partial z^2}\right) = 0 \tag{5}$$

where u represents the excess pore water pressure, C_v represents the soil consolidation coefficient, and x and z represent the horizontal and vertical directions of the soil layer, respectively.

For two-dimensional consolidation of drainage at the top boundary, it is assumed that the bottom boundary is impervious. The excess pore water pressure dissipates only at the top boundary. The top boundary satisfies the Dirichlet boundary condition $u(x) = 0$, and the bottom boundary satisfies the Neumann boundary condition $\frac{\partial u}{\partial z} = 0$. A schematic diagram of consolidation for drainage at a top boundary is displayed in Figure 4. Assume that the initial excess pore water pressure distribution is q, and the initial excess pore pressure is uniformly distributed and equal to the surface overload. We set the thickness of the soil layer as H. The boundary conditions are mathematically expressed as Equation (6).

$$\begin{cases} u = 0 & (at\ \Gamma_b, t > 0) \\ \frac{\partial u}{\partial z} = 0 & (at\ \Gamma_t, t > 0) \\ u|_{x=|A|} = 0 & (t > 0) \end{cases} \tag{6}$$

In the proposed method, we use the PDE, boundary, and initial conditions of consolidation for drainage at a top boundary to generate training data, and then the trained model is applied to predict the excess pore water pressure.

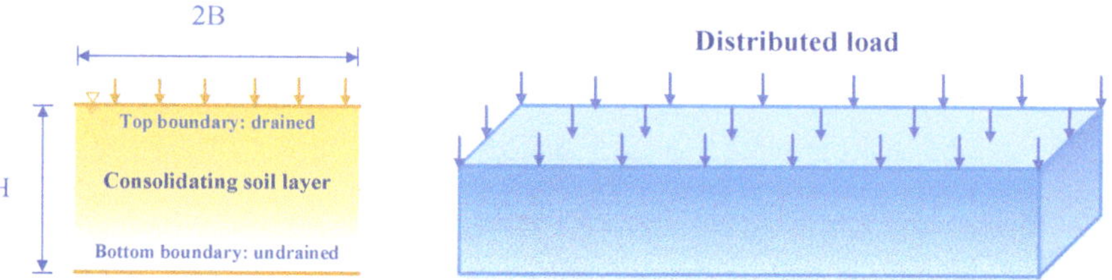

Figure 4. Schematic diagram of two-dimensional soil consolidation for drainage at a top boundary.

2.4. Problem 2: Two-Dimensional Soil Consolidation for Drainage at Top and Bottom Boundaries

In this section, we introduce how to employ the deep learning approach to solve the problem of two-dimensional soil consolidation for drainage at the top and bottom boundaries.

When both the top and bottom of the foundation are drainable boundaries, the excess pore water pressure is dissipated by both boundaries. The top and bottom boundaries satisfy the Dirichlet boundary condition $u(x) = 0$. A schematic diagram of consolidation drained at the top and bottom boundaries is displayed in Figure 5. Mathematically, this condition of soil consolidation for drainage at the top and bottom boundaries is expressed as Equation (7).

$$\begin{cases} u = 0 & (at\ \Gamma_t \cup \Gamma_b, t > 0) \\ u|_{x=|A|} = 0 & (t > 0) \end{cases} \tag{7}$$

Similarly, we set the initial excess pore pressure distribution as q. However, the maximum drainage distance for consolidation for drainage at the top and bottom boundaries is taken as half the thickness of the soil layer. Therefore, the thickness of the soil layer is set to double the drained thickness at the top boundary, i.e., 2H. We use the PDE, boundary, and initial conditions to generate training data, and then the trained model is applied to predict the excess pore water pressure.

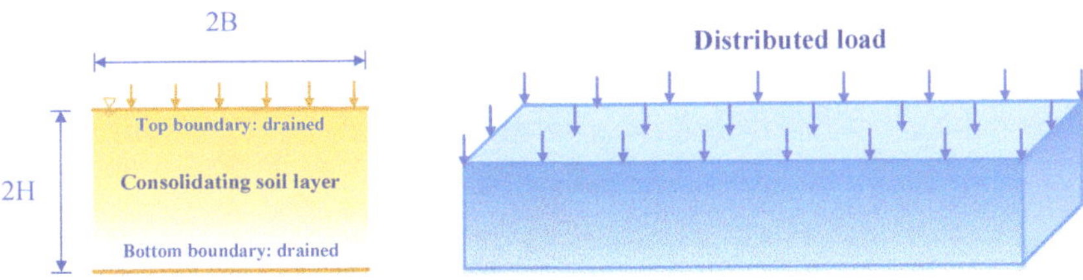

Figure 5. Schematic diagram of two-dimensional soil consolidation for drainage at the top and bottom boundaries.

3. Validation of the Proposed Deep Learning Approach

In this section, to verify the effectiveness of the proposed deep learning approach, we applied this proposed method with simple data to different boundary conditions and compared the results predicted by our approach with the numerical solutions obtained by the improved weighted residual method.

3.1. Experimental Environment

The experiments were conducted on a laptop with an NVIDIA GeForce RTX3070 laptop GPU and an AMD Ryzen 7 5800H with Radeon graphics. In order to obtain a better quantification of the machine, we tested the computer with CineBench R23, which resulted in a CPU (multi core) of 10920 and a CPU (single core) of 1392. The library used to implement the PINN was DeepXDE version 0.13.6.

3.2. Results of Consolidation with Drained Top Boundary

According to the weighted residual method, we assumed that there is drainage sand well at the center of the substrate (load) and considered its influence range in the horizontal direction to be limited, which is shown by the numerical analysis as $A = 2B$. Since there is usually no drainage sand well at the center of the load in actual projects, the numerical solution was obtained after excluding this condition (Equation (8)).

$$u = \frac{16q}{\pi^2} \sum_{m=1,3,5...}^{\infty} \frac{1}{m^2} \sin(\frac{\pi m}{2A}(x+A)) \sin(\frac{\pi m}{2H}Z) e^{-(\frac{1}{A}+\frac{1}{4H^2})^2 C_v m^2 \pi^2 t} \tag{8}$$

For a numerical example of a drained top boundary, we set the soil layer thickness to $H = 1$ m, and the soil consolidation coefficient was $C_v = 0.01$ cm^2/s. In addition, we assumed that the foundation was subjected to a distributed load $q = 10$ kN/m^2 and that the load level affects the range $A = 1$ m. The numerical solution Equation (8) was used as the reference solution for the training results. The geometry module of this example was Rectangle $[-1,0]$ $[1,1]$. Soil consolidation is a time-dependent PDE problem, and the time domain calculated in this experiment ranged from 0 to 1. Finally, the input of the PDE system and the construction of the physical information model were completed. The residuals were tested by sampling 100 points in the domain, initial and boundary conditions and using 1000 points to test the PDE residuals.

Here, we used a fully connected neural network of depth 6 (i.e., 5 hidden layers) and width 32. Temporal and spatial partial derivatives of excess pore water pressure were determined by AD in this neural network. Values of (x, z, t) were used as the input of the neural network, where this model predicts the excess pore water pressure as the output. The Adam optimizer was chosen to train 10,000 epochs for this experiment, and the time required was approximately 15 s. The time spent on model training was proportional to the number of hidden units, hidden layers, and training epochs, and we tuned the parameters depending on the desired accuracy.

On the established soil consolidation for the drained top boundary model, 100 points were randomly selected, the numerical solution and the predictive solution were entered, and the color maps of the numerical solution and the predictive solution at different times were obtained by interpolation, as shown in Figure 6.

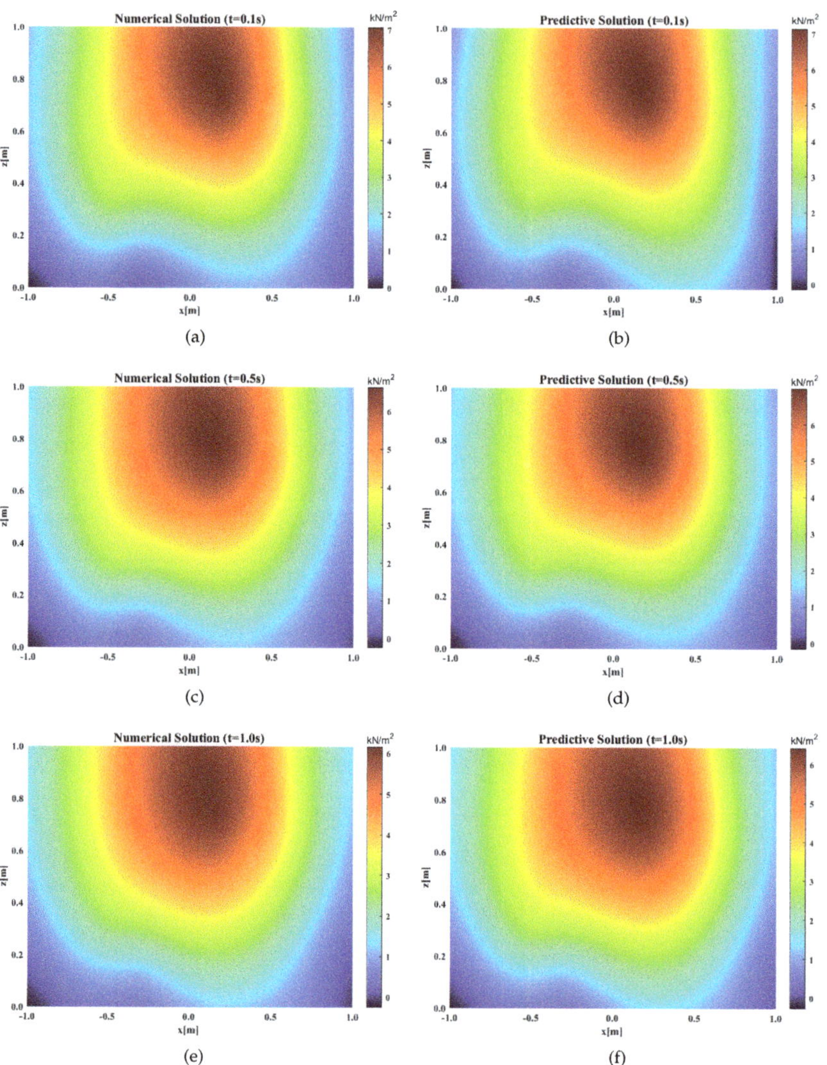

Figure 6. Color maps for numerical solution and predicted solution of two-dimensional soil consolidation for drainage at a top boundary at different times. (**a**) Numerical solution (t = 0.1 s); (**b**) Predictive solution (t = 0.1 s); (**c**) Numerical solution (t = 0.5 s); (**d**) Predictive solution (t = 0.5 s); (**e**) Numerical solution (t = 1.0 s); (**f**) Predictive solution (t = 1.0 s).

The color maps of the numerical solution and the predictive solution of consolidation with drained top boundary are illustrated in Figure 6. We can observe the excellent consistency between the numerical solution and the predictive solution at different times. The excess pore water pressure is at its maximum at the intersection of the load center and the bottom of the soil layer and dissipates gradually with time.

The final train loss and test loss of this two-dimensional soil consolidation for drainage in the top boundary model are displayed in Figures 7 and 8.

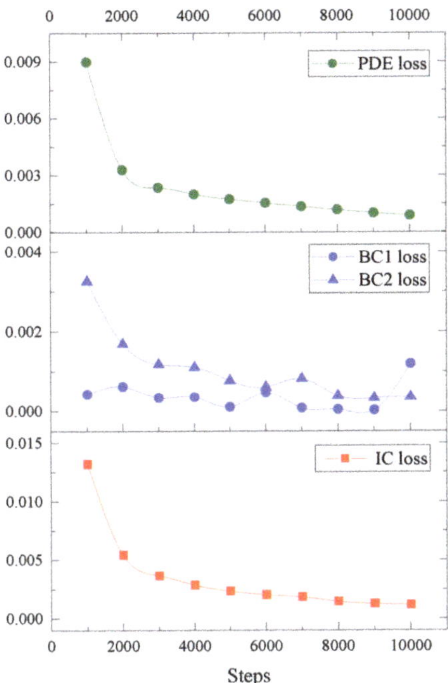

Figure 7. Training results for two-dimensional consolidation model of drainage at a top boundary.

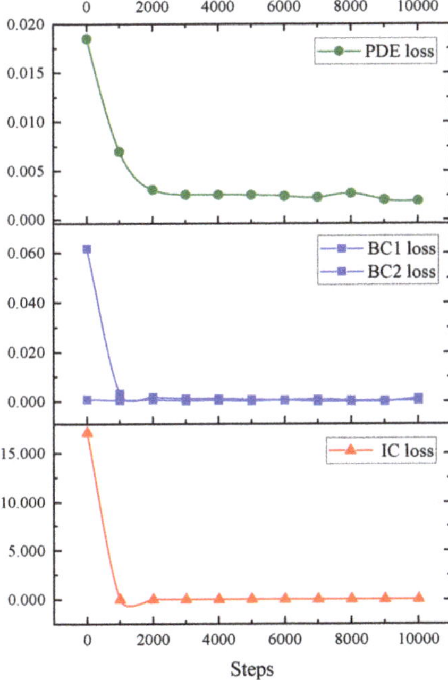

Figure 8. Testing results for two-dimensional consolidation model of drainage at a top boundary.

According to Figures 7 and 8, it is observed that the loss of PDE, boundary, and initial conditions of this model in training and testing has a good downward trend and gradually tends to be stable after 2000 epochs of training.

The test measure in this experiment is the ratio of training loss to the numerical solution, which better reflects the training results of the model (see Equation (9)). The final mean squared error loss and test metric of a drained top boundary model with two-dimensional consolidation are displayed in Figure 9.

$$test\ metric = \frac{u - \hat{u}}{u} \tag{9}$$

In this case, the training loss drops to 2.64×10^{-3}, the test loss drops to 3.67×10^{-3}, and the test metric drops to 6.82×10^{-2}.

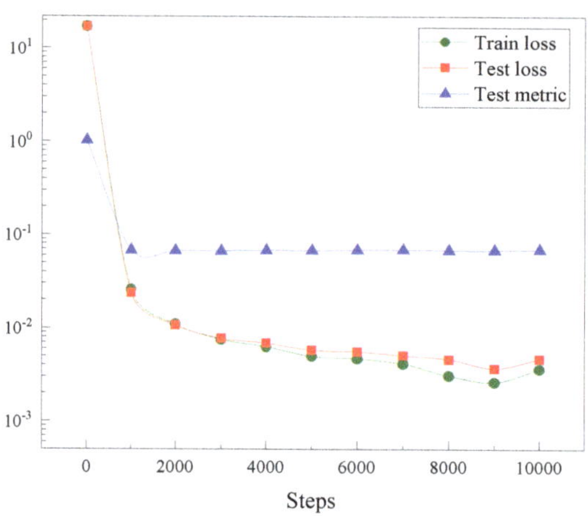

Figure 9. Mean squared error loss and test metric for two-dimensional consolidation model of drainage at a top boundary.

3.3. Results of Consolidation for Drained Top and Bottom Boundaries

For two-dimensional consolidation drained at the top and bottom boundaries, we contemplated using the same neural network model as described in Section 3.2. However, the excess pore water pressure in this condition was permitted to dissipate through both boundaries, corresponding to the absence of pore water in the center of the soil layer. For comparison, we set the soil layer thickness to 2H = 2 m, and the geometry module of this example was Rectangle [−1,0] [1,2]. The other constraints were the same as those in Section 3.2.

Similarly, we used a fully connected neural network of depth 6 (i.e., 5 hidden layers) and width 32. The temporal and spatial partial derivatives of excess pore water pressure were determined by AD in this neural network. Values of (x, z, t) were used as the input of the neural network, where this model predicts the excess pore water pressure as the output. The Adam optimizer was chosen to train 10,000 epochs for this experiment. Since the boundary constraints of double-sided drainage are simpler than those of single-sided drainage, the training time of the model was shorter.

On the established soil consolidation for the drainage at the top and bottom boundary models, 100 points were randomly selected, the numerical solution and the predictive solution were entered, and the color maps of the numerical solution and the predictive solution at different times were obtained by interpolation, as displayed in Figure 10.

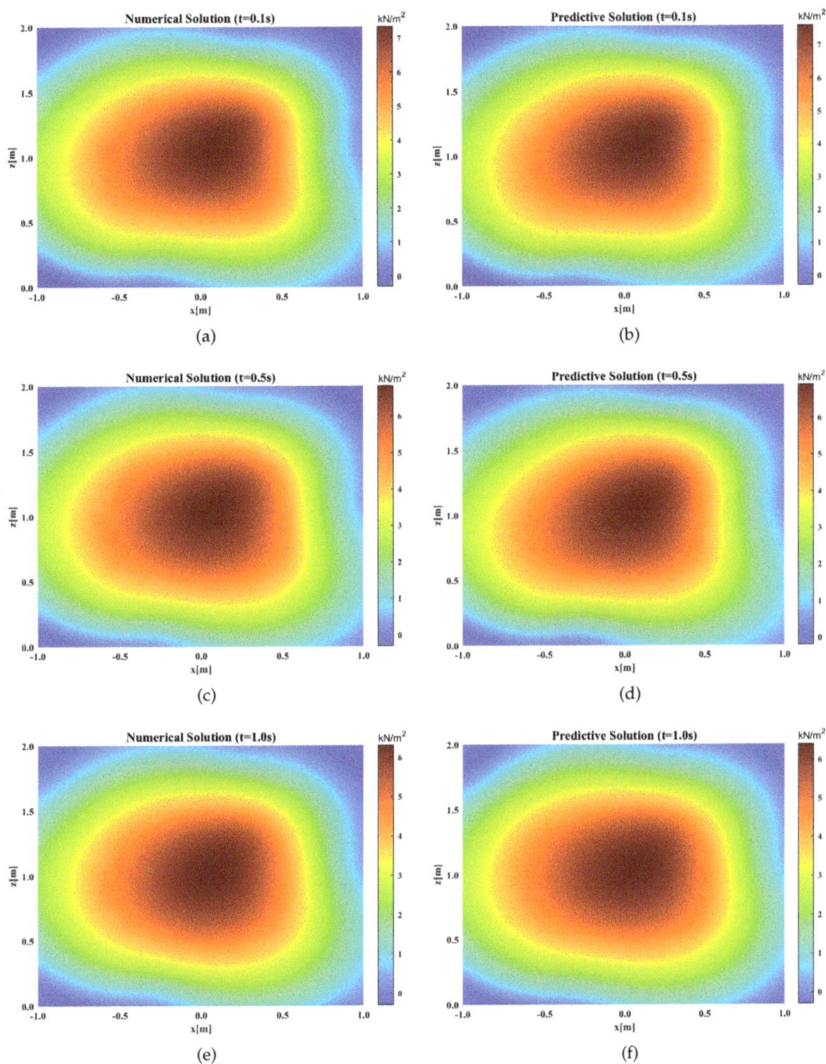

Figure 10. Color maps for numerical solution and predicted solution of two-dimensional soil consolidation for drainage at the top and bottom boundaries at different times. (**a**) Numerical solution (t = 0.1 s); (**b**) Predictive solution (t = 0.1 s); (**c**) Numerical solution (t = 0.5 s); (**d**) Predictive solution (t = 0.5 s); (**e**) Numerical solution (t = 1.0 s); (**f**) Predictive solution (t = 1.0 s).

The color maps of the numerical solution and the predictive solution of consolidation with drained top and bottom boundaries are illustrated in Figure 10. We can observe the excellent consistency between the numerical solution and the predictive solution at different times. The excess pore water pressure is at its maximum at the intersection of the load center and the middle of the soil layer and dissipates gradually with time.

The final train loss and test loss of this two-dimensional soil consolidation for drained at the top and bottom boundary models are displayed in Figures 11 and 12.

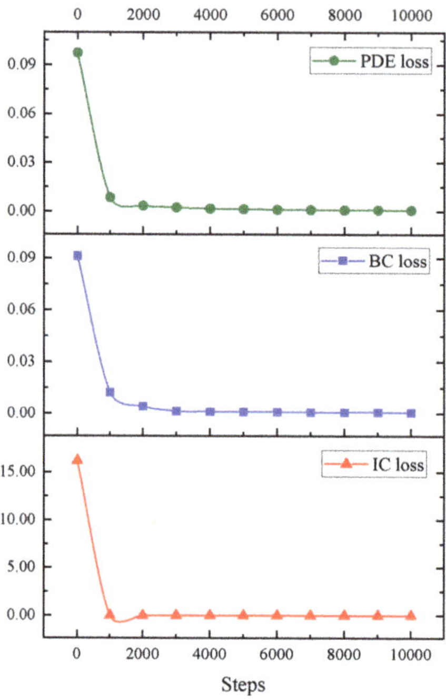

Figure 11. Training results for two-dimensional consolidation model of drainage at the top and bottom boundaries.

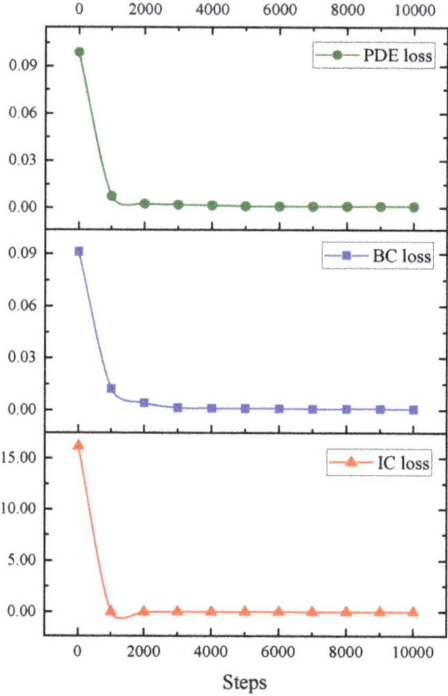

Figure 12. Testing results for two-dimensional consolidation model of drainage at the top and bottom boundaries.

According to Figures 11 and 12, it is observed that the loss of PDE, boundary, and initial conditions of this model in training and testing have a good downward trend and gradually tend to be stable after 2000 epochs of training.

The final mean squared error loss and test metric of two-dimensional consolidation for drainage at the top and bottom boundaries are displayed in Figure 13.

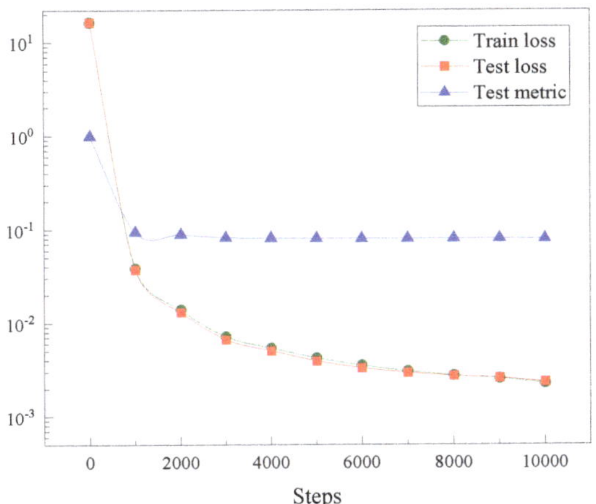

Figure 13. Mean squared error loss and test metric for two-dimensional consolidation model of drainage at the top and bottom boundaries.

In this case, the training loss drops to 2.27×10^{-3}, the test loss drops to 2.34×10^{-3}, and the test metric drops to 7.96×10^{-2}. We observed the great performance of the PINN models in predicting excess pore water pressure.

4. Application of the Proposed Deep Learning Approach

In this section, the proposed deep learning approach was used to predict the excess pore water pressure of soil layers in a real case. Details of the application are introduced as follows.

4.1. Engineering Background

The case we studied was a railway subgrade. The railway runs from Chengdu West Station to Pujiang Station, passing through the Sichuan Basin, the western part of the Sichuan Plain, and the hilly edge of the basin, with an altitude of 500~600 m. We selected one section of the railway. The length of this line is 182.6 m in the territory of Dayi D3K51 + 901 ~ D3K52 + 083.6 m section. For the parameters of the soil, see Table 1.

Table 1. Parameters of the soil.

Parameter	γ_{unsat} (kN/m^3)	γ_{sat} (kN/m^3)	k_x (m/day)	k_y (m/day)	E (kN/m^2)	c (kN/m^2)	φ (°)	ψ (°)	μ
Clay	15	18	1×10^{-4}	1×10^{-4}	1000	2	24	0	0.33
Peat	8	11	2×10^{-3}	2×10^{-3}	350	5	20	0	0.35
Sand	16	20	1	1	3000	1	30	0	0.30

The shape of the subgrade was trapezoidal, filled with sand, with a width of 16 m and a height of 4 m. The soil layers were peat and clay layers. For the geological profile of the subgrade, see Figure 14.

The layered construction scheme was used in this case study area. Stage 1 involved filling 2 m of the embankment and then consolidating the soil layers for 200 days. Stage

2 involved filling 2 m of the embankment, and the soil layers will be consolidated for a long time.

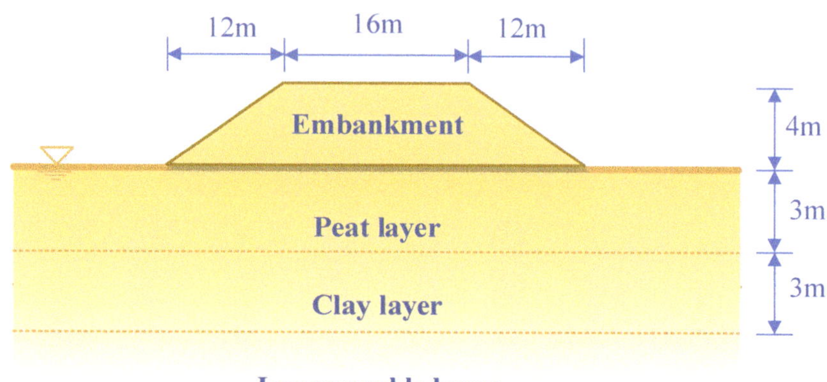

Figure 14. Schematic diagram of geological section of the subgrade.

4.2. Results of Finite Element Analysis

To further verify the accuracy of the PINN results, PLAXIS software (https://www.bentley.com/en/products/brands/plaxis, accessed on 1 August 2022) was used to numerically investigate the above engineering problems. The Mohr–Coulomb model was used in PLAXIS. Due to the symmetry of the geometric model, the right half of the model was intercepted for analysis. The plane strain model was selected and analyzed. The boundary conditions are defined by standard fixed boundaries in the PLAXIS. The consolidation control standard for this case is maximum excess pore water of less than 1 kN/m^2.

By selecting a point in the middle of the soft soil layer near the left boundary to reflect the development of excess pore water pressure under the subgrade during the construction of the subgrade, the change process of excess pore water pressure is illustrated in Figure 15. It can be observed that the excess pore water pressure rises rapidly with the filling of the subgrade and decreases gradually with time during the consolidation period. It takes approximately 650 days from the start of stage 1 to the complete consolidation of the soil layers of the subgrade. The distribution of excess pore water pressure at 650 days is illustrated in Figure 16. It can be observed that the excess pore water pressure under the center of the subgrade is maximum and less than 1 kN/m^2.

4.3. Results of PINN-Based Method

In this section, the proposed PINN approach was employed to predict the excess pore water pressure of the subgrade in this case study area. The bottom of the foundation was the impervious layer. This model was constructed in the same way as described in Section 2.3.

The load covered the range A = 20 m, and the thickness of the foundation soil layer was H = 6 m. Therefore, the geometry module of the case study area was a Rectangle [0,−6] [20,0]. Two different prediction models were developed based on the consolidation coefficients of different soil layers. The residuals were tested by sampling 1000 points in the domain, initial and boundary conditions and using 1000 points to test the PDE residuals. Similarly, a fully connected neural network of depth 6 (i.e., 5 hidden layers) and width 32 was used. The Adam optimizer was chosen to train 50,000 epochs for this experiment.

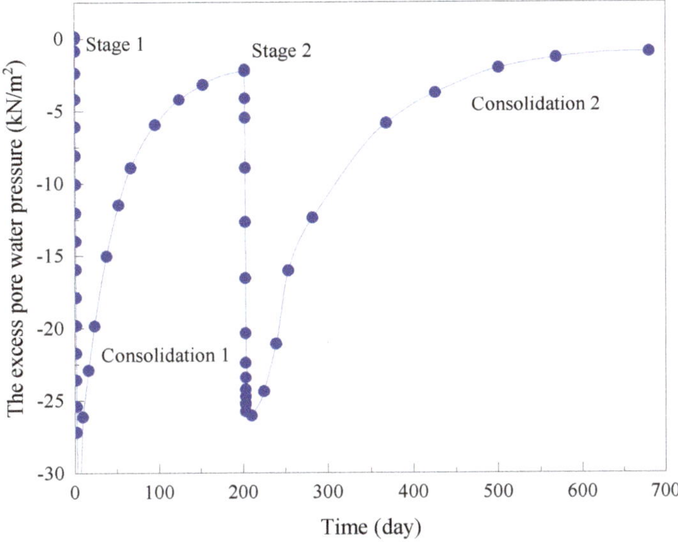

Figure 15. Line chart of excess water pressure change process during consolidation.

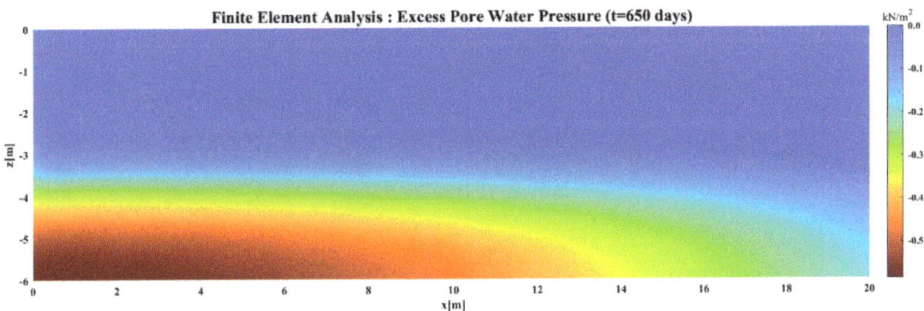

Figure 16. Color map of excess pore water pressure based on the finite element analysis.

After the training of the constructed model above, the excess pore water pressure in the soil reaches a desirable value at approximately 650 days. The distribution of excess pore water pressure at 650 days is illustrated in Figure 17.

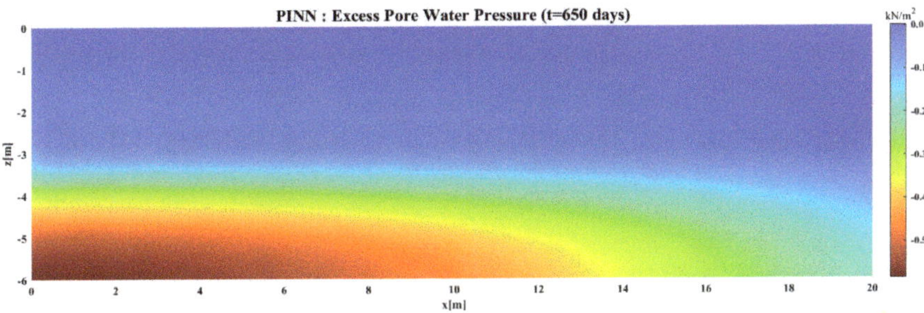

Figure 17. Color map of excess pore water pressure based on the proposed PINN-based method.

4.4. Comparative Analysis

As illustrated in Figure 15, it was obtained that the consolidation control standard was achieved after 600 days, and for comparison, the excess pore water pressure distribution within the soil layer at 650 days was plotted separately using two methods (i.e., the FEM and the proposed PINN-based method).

The results obtained from the finite element analysis and the PINN-based method are shown in Figures 16 and 17. The color plots are obtained by interpolation of the nearest excess pore pressure values from the actual grid points and are chosen here only for visualization.

Under the same conditions, the excess pore water pressure prediction by FEM and the PINN-based method was compared, and the results were quite consistent. The consistency between the FEM results and the PINN-based results indicates that the deep learning model reasonably predicts the excess pore pressure based on the initial and boundary training data alone. Moreover, the PINN-based method does not require generating meshes, and it does require fewer detailed material parameters of the study area or domain than that of the FEM. Therefore, using this method, the excess pore water pressure of the soil can be predicted simply and efficiently. This demonstrates the remarkable accuracy of the physical constraints and the potential of the PINN-based method applied to numerically investigate the geotechnical consolidation under more complex conditions.

5. Discussion

5.1. Advantages of the Proposed Method

There are two advantages of the proposed deep learning approach.

(1) Compared with traditional methods, the proposed method is computationally simple. In the proposed PINN method, the physical information including partial differential equations, initial conditions, and boundary conditions of soil consolidation is defined without having actual data, and the data in the computational domain are randomly and automatically generated for model training.

(2) Compared with traditional methods, the proposed method is computationally efficient. In the proposed PINN method, defined physical information is loosely coupled. The prediction of excess pore water pressure in two-dimensional soil consolidation can be adjusted and is highly adaptable to consolidation problems in different engineering environments without the need for remodeling.

5.2. Shortcomings of the Proposed Method

The proposed method is proposed based on PINN. PINN has good performance in solving two-dimensional soil consolidation, but complex high-dimensional PDEs usually have no precise solutions, and there is no completely accurate reference value to judge the training accuracy of the PINN training model. In addition, for complex engineering problems, stronger boundary conditions are needed to improve the fit to the engineering problems. Therefore, for some high-dimensional problems with weak boundary conditions, deep neural networks, as a general function approximator, can only obtain an approximate solution to the problem by minimizing the loss of the training model. How to further improve the computational accuracy is the current problem with PINN.

5.3. Outlook and Future Work

In future work, we will consider various constraints to improve the training accuracy of the neural network as much as possible and assess the applicability of this proposed deep learning approach using PINN to other engineering geology problems.

There are several strategies to improve the accuracy of neural network model training results. Adding more data is a good idea for ordinary models, but this idea does not apply to complex geological engineering problems with a lack of observation data. At present, the most effective method for PINN is algorithm optimization. It is well understood that deep learning algorithms are driven by parameters that mainly affect the learning process results. In the future, we plan to combine several algorithms to build high-precision models. However, the choice of algorithm is difficult, and this intuition comes from experience and practice. Therefore, all relevant models should be applied, and comparative performance should be checked.

The advantage of PINN in solving geotechnical problems is the use of prior knowledge and logic to discover the characteristics of the problem, but it lacks the ease of consistency with real data [27]. Further research is needed to achieve a perfect combination of physical knowledge and neural networks. Many improvements to the methods currently proposed are still possible, and some theoretical problems remain unresolved. There is still potential for development in optimizing training PINNs and expanding PINNs to solve multiple equations.

We present a simple PINN problem for predicting the excess pore water pressure of two-dimensional consolidation, but this method can be extended to many large and complex multidirectional soil consolidation problems. The combination of deep learning models and physical laws is a new trend in the development of engineering geology, which is still in the initial stage of research and has not yet been widely applied to practical engineering. In the future, such as in foundation deformation monitoring of large facilities, the monitoring and early warning of landslides can be attempted using the proposed deep learning method.

6. Conclusions

In this paper, we propose a deep learning method using a PINN to predict the excess pore water pressure of two-dimensional soil consolidation. The essential idea behind the proposed method is to implement data-free model training with physics-informed constrained neural networks. In the proposed method, we present two simple examples of how to predict soil excess pore water pressure with different boundary conditions. In the proposed method, (1) a fully connected neural network is constructed, (2) the computational domain, partial differential equation (PDE), and constraints are defined to generate data for model training, and (3) the PDE of two-dimensional soil consolidation and the model of the neural network is connected to reduce the loss of the model. The effectiveness of the method is verified by comparing it with the numerical solution of the PDE for two-dimensional consolidation. Moreover, the excess pore water pressure prediction by FEM and the PINN- based method is compared, and the results are quite consistent. The consistency between the FEM results and the PINN-based results indicates that the deep learning model reasonably predicts the excess pore pressure based on the initial and boundary training data alone. In the future, the proposed deep learning approach can be used to investigate large and complex multi-directional soil consolidation.

Author Contributions: Conceptualization, Y.L. and G.M.; methodology, Y.L. and G.M.; software, Y.L. and G.M.; validation, Y.L. and G.M.; formal analysis, Y.L. and G.M.; investigation, Y.L. and G.M.; resources, Y.L. and G.M.; data curation, Y.L. and G.M.; writing—original draft preparation, Y.L.; writing—review and editing, Y.L. and G.M.; visualization Y.L. and G.M.; supervision, G.M.; project administration, G.M.; funding acquisition, G.M. All authors have read and agreed to the published version of the manuscript.

Funding: This research was jointly supported by the National Natural Science Foundation of China (Grant Nos. 11602235), and the Major Program of Science and Technology of Xinjiang Production and Construction Corps (2020AA002). The authors would like to thank the editor and the reviewers for their helpful comments and suggestions.

Institutional Review Board Statement: Not applicable.

Informed Consent Statement: Not applicable.

Data Availability Statement: Not applicable.

Acknowledgments: The authors would like to thank the editor and the anonymous reviewers for their valuable comments.

Conflicts of Interest: The authors declare no conflict of interest.

References

1. Lo, W.C.; Sposito, G.; Lee, J.W.; Chu, H. One-dimensional consolidation in unsaturated soils under cyclic loading. *Adv. Water Resour.* **2016**, *91*, 122–137. [CrossRef]
2. Pham, B.T.; Nguyen, M.D.; Bui, K.T.T.; Prakash, I.; Chapi, K.; Bui, D.T. A novel artificial intelligence approach based on Multi-layer Perceptron Neural Network and Biogeography-based Optimization for predicting coefficient of consolidation of soil. *Catena* **2019**, *173*, 302–311. [CrossRef]
3. Terzaghi, K. *Erdbaumechanik auf Bodenphysikalischer Grundlage*; Deuticke: Leipzig, Germany, 1925.
4. Biot, M.A. General Theory of Three-Dimensional Consolidation. *J. Appl. Phys.* **1941**, *12*, 155–164. [CrossRef]
5. Schiffman, R.L.; Stein, J.R. One-Dimensional Consolidation of Layered Systems. *J. Soil Mech. Found. Div.* **1970**, *96*, 1499–1504. [CrossRef]
6. Indraratna, B.; Rujikiatkamjorn, C.; Sathananthan, I. Radial consolidation of clay using compressibility indices and varying horizontal permeability. *Can. Geotech. J.* **2005**, *42*, 1330–1341. [CrossRef]
7. Ng, A.K.L.; Small, J.C. Use of coupled finite element analysis in unsaturated soil problems. *Int. J. Numer. Anal. Methods Geomech.* **2000**, *24*, 73–94. [CrossRef]
8. Yarushina, V.M.; Podladchikov, Y.Y. (De)compaction of porous viscoelastoplastic media: Model formulation. *J. Geophys. Res. Solid Earth* **2015**, *120*, 4146–4170. [CrossRef]
9. Lu, L.; Meng, X.; Mao, Z.; Karniadakis, G.E. DeepXDE: A Deep Learning Library for Solving Differential Equations. *SIAM Rev.* **2021**, *63*, 208–228. [CrossRef]
10. Raissi, M.; Perdikaris, P.; Karniadakis, G.E. Physics-informed neural networks: A deep learning framework for solving forward and inverse problems involving nonlinear partial differential equations. *J. Comput. Phys.* **2019**, *378*, 686–707. [CrossRef]
11. Blechschmidt, J.; Ernst, O.G. Three ways to solve partial differential equations with neural networks—A review. *GAMM-Mitteilungen* **2021**, *44*, e202100006. [CrossRef]
12. Owhadi, H. Bayesian Numerical Homogenization. *Multiscale Model. Simul.* **2015**, *13*, 812–828. [CrossRef]
13. Raissi, M.; Perdikaris, P.; Karniadakis, G.E. Inferring solutions of differential equations using noisy multi-fidelity data. *J. Comput. Phys.* **2017**, *335*, 736–746. [CrossRef]
14. Raissi, M.; Perdikaris, P.; Karniadakis, G.E. Machine learning of linear differential equations using Gaussian processes. *J. Comput. Phys.* **2017**, *348*, 683–693. [CrossRef]
15. Karniadakis, G.E.; Kevrekidis, I.G.; Lu, L.; Perdikaris, P.; Wang, S.; Yang, L. Physics-informed machine learning. *Nat. Rev. Phys.* **2021**, *3*, 422–440. [CrossRef]
16. Raissi, M.; Yazdani, A.; Karniadakis, G.E. Hidden fluid mechanics: Learning velocity and pressure fields from flow visualizations. *Science* **2020**, *367*, 1026–1030. [CrossRef] [PubMed]
17. Tartakovsky, A.M.; Marrero, C.O.; Perdikaris, P.; Tartakovsky, G.D.; Barajas-Solano, D. Physics-Informed Deep Neural Networks for Learning Parameters and Constitutive Relationships in Subsurface Flow Problems. *Water Resour. Res.* **2020**, *56*, e2019WR026731. [CrossRef]
18. Almajid, M.M.; Abu-Al-Saud, M.O. Prediction of porous media fluid flow using physics informed neural networks. *J. Pet. Sci. Eng.* **2022**, *208*, 109205. [CrossRef]
19. Depina, I.; Jain, S.; Mar Valsson, S.; Gotovac, H. Application of physics-informed neural networks to inverse problems in unsaturated groundwater flow. *Georisk Assess. Manag. Risk Eng. Syst. Geohazards* **2021**, *16*, 21–36. [CrossRef]
20. Bandai, T.; Ghezzehei, T.A. Physics-Informed Neural Networks with Monotonicity Constraints for Richardson-Richards Equation: Estimation of Constitutive Relationships and Soil Water Flux Density from Volumetric Water Content Measurements. *Water Resour. Res.* **2021**, *57*, e2020WR027642. [CrossRef]
21. Zhang, Z. A physics-informed deep convolutional neural network for simulating and predicting transient Darcy flows in heterogeneous reservoirs without labeled data. *J. Pet. Sci. Eng.* **2022**, *211*, 110179. [CrossRef]
22. Bekele, Y.W. Physics-informed deep learning for one-dimensional consolidation. *J. Rock Mech. Geotech. Eng.* **2021**, *13*, 420–430. [CrossRef]
23. Waheed, U.b.; Haghighat, E.; Alkhalifah, T.; Song, C.; Hao, Q. PINNeik: Eikonal solution using physics-informed neural networks. *Comput. Geosci.* **2021**, *155*, 104833. [CrossRef]
24. Cuomo, S.; Di Cola, V.S.; Giampaolo, F.; Rozza, G.; Raissi, M.; Piccialli, F. Scientific Machine Learning Through Physics–Informed Neural Networks: Where we are and What's Next. *J. Sci. Comput.* **2022**, *92*, 88. [CrossRef]
25. Haghighat, E.; Raissi, M.; Moure, A.; Gomez, H.; Juanes, R. A physics-informed deep learning framework for inversion and surrogate modeling in solid mechanics. *Comput. Methods Appl. Mech. Eng.* **2021**, *379*, 113741. [CrossRef]
26. Rendulic, L. Porenziffer und Porenwasserdruck in Tonen. *Bauingenieur* **1936**, *17*, 559–564.
27. Garnelo, M.; Shanahan, M. Reconciling deep learning with symbolic artificial intelligence: Representing objects and relations. *Curr. Opin. Behav. Sci.* **2019**, *29*, 17–23. [CrossRef]

 *mathematics*

Article

SemG-TS: Abstractive Arabic Text Summarization Using Semantic Graph Embedding

Wael Etaiwi * and Arafat Awajan

Princess Sumaya University for Technology, Amman 11941, Jordan
* Correspondence: w.etaiwi@psut.edu.jo

Abstract: This study proposes a novel semantic graph embedding-based abstractive text summarization technique for the Arabic language, namely SemG-TS. SemG-TS employs a deep neural network to produce the abstractive summary. A set of experiments were conducted to evaluate the performance of SemG-TS and to compare the results to those of a popular baseline word embedding technique called word2vec. A new dataset was collected for the experiments. Two evaluation methodologies were followed in the experiments: automatic and human evaluations. The Rouge evaluation measure was used for the automatic evaluation, while for the human evaluation, Arabic native speakers were tasked to evaluate the relevancy, similarity, readability, and overall satisfaction of the generated summaries. The obtained results prove the superiority of SemG-TS.

Keywords: abstractive text summarization; semantic graph; semantic graph embedding; Arabic text summarization

MSC: 68T50; 68T07

Citation: Etaiwi, W.; Awajan, A. SemG-TS: Abstractive Arabic Text Summarization Using Semantic Graph Embedding. *Mathematics* **2022**, *10*, 3225. https://doi.org/10.3390/math10183225

Academic Editor: Xiang Li, Shuo Zhang and Wei Zhang

Received: 10 August 2022
Accepted: 29 August 2022
Published: 6 September 2022

Publisher's Note: MDPI stays neutral with regard to jurisdictional claims in published maps and institutional affiliations.

1. Introduction

Due to the rapid increase in the number of electronic documents, articles, and pages on the Internet, the need to summarize their content has emerged [1]. When online content rises at a fast pace, finding relevant information becomes a more difficult mission. Users can get distracted and thus miss catching and reading valuable and interesting material. There is therefore a need for a text summarization solution. Text summarization compresses a large volume of texts from various sources (such as documents, web sites, and comments) into a shorter length and concise summary [2,3]. The automatic extraction or creation of a summary of a given text is called text summarization. Several challenges have been identified while summarizing documents [4], such as: (1) Redundancy, which can lead to the final summary including redundant information. (2) Irrelevancy, in which the final summary may contain irrelevant information. (3) Coverage loss, in which a key detail is missed in the final summary. In addition, (4) the final summary may not be readable if it comprises unrelated words. Text summarization could be categorized into many ways and according to many factors [1].

- According to the number of documents, text summarization is categorized into single or multi-document summarization. The task of multi-document summarization is more difficult and has many additional challenges and issues that should be considered and solved, such as content redundancy.
- Text summarization is categorized into two main types based on the output summary: extractive and abstractive. In extractive text summarization, the summary is generated by ranking and selecting the most relevant text components (such as sentences) from the original text. In abstractive text summarization, the summary is produced from scratch, including words and expressions that may not exist in the original text.

Therefore, an abstractive summary preserves the main ideas in the original text and re-interprets them into a different form by using varying words and phrases. Abstractive text summarization is much more sophisticated than extractive text summarization since it needs to employ extensive Natural Language Processing (NLP) processes.

- Based on the total number of statements in an output summary, text summarization is divided into two major groups. When the final summary comprises a single sentence at most, it is considered a single-statement summarization. Otherwise, it is called a multi-statement summarization.

The summarization of English texts has been the subject of several studies in the field of text summarization. However, challenges with text summarization have highlighted the need for more studies in order to increase the efficacy of current text summary techniques for languages other than English. For instance, according to Al Saleh, summarizing Arabic texts is more difficult than summarizing English texts. As a result, Arabic text summarizing techniques have not made as much progress as those used for other languages due to Arabic's distinctive characteristics. Few studies have been proposed to produce Arabic text summary methods [5]. This is primarily due to the Arabic language's complexity both in terms of syntax and morphology, the Arabic diglossia, the language's high levels of ambiguity, and its highly derivational and inflectional nature. Many of the proposed solutions for text summarization have concentrated on extracting text summarization rather than abstracting text summarization; this is because extractive text summarization is much simpler than abstractive text summarization [6]. In an extractive text summary, the extracted summary includes the most relevant statements in the original text, which may be long, complex, and difficult to understand. Although abstractive text summarization is more complex and challenging than extractive text summarization, it is needed to produce simple and human-friendly statements that describe the most important ideas of the original text.

Semantic representation is used by a number of Natural Language Processing (NLP) applications to improve outcomes in the field of computer linguistics (e.g., machine translation and question answering). The main goal of semantic representation is to create detailed notations of the text that accurately convey its meaning. Huge and complicated data structures are represented and formalized in a standard and formal fashion using graphs. Compared with other text representation schemes such as predicate logic representation, frame representation, and rule-based representation, the graph model is more efficient because it is characterized by its ability to represent the semantic relations between the words in a text [7].

The method of semantic representation that has been used most frequently is the semantic graph [8–11]. A semantic graph is a network that reflects the semantic relationship between different concepts (e.g., terms, and sentences). Graph vertices are concepts, while graph edges are semantic relationships between concepts. The semantic graph is used to encode plain text and represent its context as a graph. Semantic preservation is a difficult task in semantic graph representation because semantic relationships differ depending on the language of the text, and because they are hard to capture in some languages.

Text summarization employs several text features for sentences, paragraphs, and words. Traditional methods require the use of hand-crafted features [12], which takes time and effort to manually extract the useful features. However, deep learning makes it possible to generate useful features from training data. Instead of using hand-crafted features, which mostly rely on the prior expertise of designers and are extremely challenging to utilize with a massive amount of data, deep learning automatically learns features from the existing data.

Owing to the aforementioned challenges, a new framework for abstractive Arabic text summarization using Arabic semantic graph representation is required. The proposed framework is called SemG-TS. The morphological and syntactical characteristics of the Arabic language should be taken into consideration when creating the semantic graph and when learning it. Thus, the SemanticGraph2Vec model is used to preserve the semantic relationships between words in the text graph. Since deep learning has had positive results in several different fields of AI and in data mining problems [13], it is used to produce a text summary output. Finally, in order to evaluate the proposed SemG-TS, a new text summarization dataset is created based on well-written and published news articles. Furthermore, two evaluation methodologies are followed in the experiments: automatic and human evaluations.

The remainder of this paper is organized as follows. In Section 2, a brief review of the related work on text summarization for the Arabic language is presented. The proposed model is described in Section 3. The dataset used in the experiments is described in Section 4. In Section 5, the experiments and evaluation results are discussed. The conclusions are summarized in Section 6.

2. Related Work

Text summarization is more than fifty years old; the research community is very active in this area [1]. Researchers continue to improve the performance of current text summarization approaches or propose novel summarization approaches to enhance the quality of the output summary. However, the output of current text summarization models is still at a moderate level.

Due to the Arabic language's intrinsic complexity, both in terms of structure and morphology, methods and approaches for summarizing Arabic texts are still immature and insufficient [5,14]. Arabic text summarization approaches are classified into three main groups: graph-based approaches, deep learning-based approaches, and genetic algorithm and machine learning-based approaches.

- Graph-based approaches: Belkebir and Guessoum [15] used a multi-graph to decompose the original text into a set of sentence subsets. The Bell Numbers Theory was used to calculate the number of subsets. Graph vertices represented sentences, while the edges between the sentences represented the relationships between the sentences. Each layer of the multi-graph represented a semantic relationship between the sentences of the document. A machine learning approach was used to pick the most appropriate (highly probable) operation for each layer (partition). The list of operations used in the experiments included: sentence extraction using the AdaBoost machine learning technique, concept generalization and fusion for abstractive sentence generation, and sentence compression. The TALAA-ASC corpus [16] was used to evaluate the proposed model in terms of precision, recall, F-score, and ROUGE. In another study, an Arabic text summarization approach for a single document in Arabic was proposed by Azmi and Altmami [17]. The proposed approach relied on an extractive approach that produced the highly ranked sentences to be included in the final summary. Subsequently, a rule-based reduction technique was used to reduce the size of the extracted sentences and to reshape their structure. The authors referred to this approach as an abstractive text summarization approach, which is not accurate. The abstractive summary should contain new terms that do not exist in the original text, and this was not applied in the proposed approach. The proposed approach was evaluated on a set of 150 news articles. The results were analyzed manually by two human experts who scored the output summary out of a maximum score of five. The average score was between 4.53 and 1.92.
  Elbarougy et al. [18] proposed an extractive graph-based Arabic text summarization technique. The proposed model represented the original text as a graph, where the vertices of the graph were the sentences. Each sentence (vertex) was initially ranked by the total number of nouns in the sentence. The weights of the graph edges were calculated using the cosine similarity between the sentences. The proposed model consisted of three main stages: The first stage was the pre-processing stage, which included normalization, tokenization, stop word removal, stemming, and morphological analysis. The next stage was the feature extraction and graph construction stage, in which the graph was constructed and features were extracted. The last stage was the application of the Modified PageRank algorithm and the extraction of the final

summary. The PageRank algorithm was used with a different number of iterations in order to get the number of iterations that would produce the best results. The Essex Arabic Summaries Corpus (EASC) containing 153 documents was used to evaluate the proposed model in terms of precision, recall, and F-score.

In another study, Elbarougy et al. [19] proposed a graph-based extractive Arabic text summarization approach using multi-morphological analysis. This proposed approach transformed the original text into a graph. The sentences were represented as vertices, and the relationships between the sentences were calculated using the cosine similarity between the sentences based on Term Frequency–Inverse Document Frequency (TF-IDF) and the mutual nouns between the connected sentences. Three morphological analyzer algorithms were used to improve the efficiency of the proposed text summarization approach: Buckwalter Arabic Morphological Analyzer (BAMA) [20], Safar Alkhalil [21], and Stanford Natural Language Processing (NLP) [22]. The experimental results of the Essex Arabic Summaries Corpus (EASC) showed that the Safar Alkhalil morphological analyzer performed better than the other three analyzers.

- Deep learning-based approaches: Alami et al. [23] proposed a new extractive Arabic text summarization method. Auto-encoder models were used by the authors to learn a feature space from high-dimensional input data. Many inputs were discussed in the proposed research, including: term frequency, local vocabulary, and global vocabulary. The input sentences were ranked on the basis of the representation provided by the auto-encoder model. Two description methods were used in the proposed model to study the impact of the auto-encoder model: graph-based text summarization and query-based text summarization. Two separate datasets were used in the experiments: the EASC and the authors' dataset, which included 42 news articles. The authors concluded that the auto-encoder using the Term Frequency–Inverse Document Frequency (TF-IDF) representation of global vocabularies provides a more discriminative feature space and increases the recall of other models for both graph-based and query-based summarization approaches.

  Qaroush et al. [24] proposed an extractive single document summary approach aimed at optimizing content coverage and consistency between sentences in the summary. The proposed approach satisfied the two opposing semantic goals of coverage and diversity by evaluating each sentence based on a combination of the most informative statistics and semantic properties. Two text summarization techniques were used to determine the appropriateness of the statistical and semantic features: score-based and supervised machine learning. The EASC dataset was used in the experiments in order to demonstrate the effectiveness of the proposed method. The proposed approach was domain-independent and did not include any domain-specific information or features. The experimental results showed the efficacy of the proposed approach in terms of precision, recall, and F-score.

- Genetic algorithms and machine learning-based approaches: Belkebir and Guessoum [25] turned the task of summarizing Arabic text into a process of prediction. They used a machine learning-based approach (called AdaBoost) to determine whether or not the sentence would appear in the output summary. The authors collected their dataset from news websites, including 20 manually summarized articles. The experimental results indicated that the proposed machine learning approach overcame the other approaches in terms of precision, recall, and F-score.

  Several researchers have used optimization algorithms for text summarization purposes. The extractive Arabic text summarization approach proposed by Al-Abdallah and Al-Taani [26] used the Firefly algorithm. The proposed approach consisted of four main steps: (1) Text pre-processing, including segmentation, tokenization, stop word removal, and stemming. (2) Calculating similarity scores using the structural feature of a sentence, including title similarity, sentence length, sentence location, and term TF-IDF weight. (3) Building a graph of candidate solutions, where vertices represent the sentences in the original document, and the edges represent the similarity between sentences. (4) Using the Firefly algorithm to select sentences included in the summary. The proposed approach was evaluated on the EASC corpus in terms of the Recall-Oriented Understudy for Gisting Evaluation (ROUGE) metrics. Another hybrid approach proposed by Al-Radaideh et al. [27] combined domain knowledge, statistical features, and genetic algorithms to extract the essential parts of political documents. The proposed approach consisted of three main steps: document pre-processing, sentence scoring, and summary generation. The pre-processing step included the segmentation and tokenization of sentences, removed stop words, and extracted domain keywords, part-of-speech tagging, and stemming. After that, in the sentence scoring step, every sentence in the original document was assessed to determine its importance. The score of the sentence was based on several features, such as the presence of domain-specific keywords in the sentence, the frequency of words, the sentence length, the sentence position, and others. In the third step, the final summary was produced using sentence scores, cosine similarity, and genetic algorithms. The experiments were performed on two corpora: KALIMAT and EASC. The results of the proposed approach were compared to another three state-of-the-art approaches in terms of ROUGE metrics.

As shown in Table 1, much of the work reviewed concentrated on the use of extractive text summarization rather than abstractive text summarization. However, abstractive text summarization is more challenging than extractive text summarization since it refers to a new version of the original text, while extractive text summarization aims to extract the most important sentences from the original text. In the case of Arabic, fewer works on abstractive text summarization have been proposed. Al-Saleh and Menai [5] reported the following in their survey published in 2015: 'To the best of our knowledge, there exists no Arabic summarization system that can generate abstractive summaries'. After that, a very limited amount of research was proposed in this field. Most Arabic summarization approaches used graph theory and machine learning. Furthermore, hybrid approaches were proposed more frequently in Arabic rather than English. In addition, the majority of the articles reviewed were used to extract text from single documents instead of multi-documents. The EASC corpus was the most commonly used dataset for evaluating Arabic text summarization. Finally, ROUGE was the metrical assessment tool that was used the most to evaluate text summarization approaches.

Table 1. Recently proposed Arabic text summarization approaches.

Ref	Year	Technique	Number of Documents	Summarization Type	Dataset	Evaluation Metrics
[25]	2015	Machine Learning	Single documents	Extractive	20 documents	precision, recall, F-score
[15]	2017	Graph-based	Single documents	Extractive, Abstractive	TALAA-ASC corpus	precision, recall, F-score, ROUGE
[27]	2018	Genetic algorithms	Single documents	Extractive	KALIMAT, EASC	ROUGE
[17]	2018	Ranking and rule-based	Single documents	Extractive, Abstractive	150 documents	precision, recall, F-score, ROUGE-N
[23]	2019	Auto-encoder	Single documents	Extractive	EASC and 42 documents	ROUGE
[24]	2019	Score-based and Machine Learning	Single documents	Extractive	EASC	precision, recall, F-score, ROUGE
[18]	2019	Graph-based	Single documents	Extractive	EASC	precision, recall, F-score, ROUGE
[26]	2019	Graph-based and Firefly algorithm	Single documents	Extractive	EASC	precision, recall, F-score
[19]	2020	Graph-based	Single documents	Extractive	EASC	precision, recall, F-score

3. SemG-TS: Semantic Graph-Based Text Summarization

The overall structure of the proposed abstractive single-statement Arabic text summarization model is shown in Figure 1. It starts with the representation of the original text as a semantic graph based on the proposed approach in [28], which took into account the characteristics of the Arabic language. Then, the graph embedding method is used to produce structural information from the semantic graph based on the SemanticGraph2Vec graph embedding approach proposed in [29]. The Arabic language semantic features that are stored in the semantic graph direct the semantic walks to generate appropriate Arabic-language vectors. After that, the output vectors are transferred to the deep neural network (NN) to produce the final text summary.

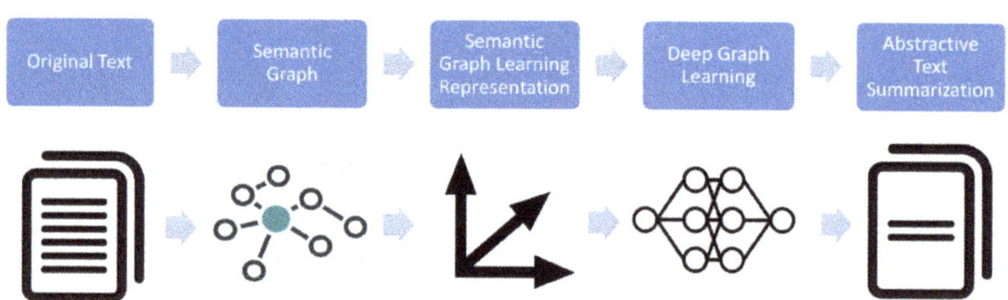

Figure 1. Proposed framework.

The SemG-TS consists of the following steps:

1. Data Representation: The semantic presentation of the original text becomes a main step in the proposed model, as the produced text summary focuses on retaining the main ideas of the original text. It is common knowledge that the semantic representation of the text is susceptible to the text language represented; thus, a semantic Arabic text representation graph is used in SemG-TS to consider the characteristics of the Arabic language during the construction stage of the semantic graph. A rooted acyclic semantic graph is used to represent the semantic relationships between words in the original text [28]. To the best of our knowledge, Etaiwi and Awajan [28] presented the only graph-based text representation method for Arabic language that considered the Arabic language characteristics during the text representation. Each word in the original text is represented as a vertex in the semantic graph, and the semantic relationships between the words are represented as semantic edges. Based on a set of Arabic language resources, tools, and concepts such as Arabic dependency relations, Arabic part-of-speech tags, extraction of Arabic name entities, Arabic language patterns, and predefined linguistic rules of the Arabic language, the semantic relations are extracted. Three steps comprise the building of the semantic graph: (1) Identify the word's relationships that are interdependent in the original text. (2) Use Arabic language resources to ascertain possible relationships between words (e.g., POS taggers). (3) Establish the semantic relationships between words and produce the final semantic graph in accordance with predetermined rules. A sample of the semantic graph representation is shown in Figures A1 and A2, which are listed in the Appendix A.

2. Graph Embedding: A semantic graph embedding technique is used in the graph embedding stage to preserve the semantic relationships during the graph embedding. The primary objective of graph embedding is to learn the low-dimensional representations of a graph or any of its components, such as vertices and edges, while preserving the graph's structure. However, in the application of text summarization, preserving semantic relationships becomes an important factor that can affect the final quality of the summary. During the semantic graph embedding, the SemanticGraph2Vec model referred to in [29] is used at this stage to consider the semantic relationships between words. The SemanticGraph2Vec model is a random walk-based technique

that explores the semantic graphs according to semantic priorities. The semantic relationships in SemanticGraph2Vec are dynamically sorted by frequency in accordance with their appearance in the text. As a result, the semantic relationship that is employed the most frequently will be given top priority. For instance, because it appears in texts the most, the "subject" relationship gets the lowest rank (highest priority). Finally, the high-priority relationships are more likely to be included in the walks generated.

3. Abstractive text summarization: The deep NN model is applied at this phase since deep learning outperforms other machine learning techniques in a number of NLP applications, including named entity recognition and machine translation [30,31]. The main goal of this stage is to learn the low-dimensional vectors generated from the previous stage in order to generate the text summary. The efficiency of deep learning is significantly improved by the use of the mechanisms of sequence-to-sequence learning and attention. The efficiency of statistical learning and local representations of words and phrases is evaluated in machine translation by the use of distributed word embedding in deep learning [31]. These mechanisms can also be extended to other NLP activities such as text summarization and question answering. Therefore, in the proposed model, sequence-to-sequence learning and attention mechanism were applied.

4. Dataset

For the Arabic language, there are no high-quality datasets that could be used to simultaneously compare the researchers' work. Most researchers in the Arabic language translated the English datasets into Arabic to validate their work, such as [32]. Few Arabic datasets are available for text summarization, such as KALIMAT [33], EASC [34], and Arabic Gigaword [35]. However, all these resources suffer from several limitations, such as the dataset's size, the dataset orientation, and the limited abstraction. For example, the EASC dataset contains only 153 documents, while the KALIMAT dataset was designed for extractive text summarization. Because academics prefer to gather their own information, the lack of Arabic standard datasets has made the evaluation process more challenging and even subjective in some instances [5]. Summary evaluation is a difficult task because there is no specific ideal summary for a given text.

Due to the limitations stated, there is a need for a large dataset for Arabic text summarization. High-quality databases with a small amount of grammatical errors may be found widely on reliable websites such as AlJazeera.net and CNN-Arabic news. Such websites contain thousands of well-written Arabic articles with single-line summaries (title and highlights). For our experiments, articles were collected from the AlJazeera.net website to build our dataset for abstractive text summarization. To evaluate the proposed abstractive single-statement Arabic text summarizer, a total of 8385 documents are used. The dataset consisted of 3,419,057 words, with an average of 5.5 characters per word. The total number of paragraphs was 16,770, with an average of 204 words in each paragraph. The titles of the articles were considered their summaries.

The articles were selected on the basis of a predefined list of keywords. The articles that were published in the last five years were considered. Keywords were carefully chosen so that they would cover a variety of different categories of articles (for example, political, sport, economy, and art). The keywords are listed in Table 2.

Table 2. Keywords used to build the dataset.

Keyword	Number of Articles
"مصر" (Egypt)	2492
"سلام" (Peace)	2299
"عرب" (Arab)	2202
"اوروبا" (Europe)	1000
"رئيس" (President)	392
Total	8385

5. Experiments and Evaluation

In order to evaluate the proposed SemG-TS model, the experiments were divided into three main parts: building the semantic graph, embedding the semantic graph, and applying deep learning for abstractive single-statement Arabic text summarization. In the first two parts, a standalone workstation with Intel Xeon Silver 4114 2.20 HHz CPU, 64 GB RAM, and Nvidia Quadro P5000 was used. In the third part, a standalone workstation with 64 GB RAM, Dual Intel Xeon E5-2620v4 CPU clocked at 2.10 GHz, and Nvidia GTX 1080 was used.

- Building the semantic graph: The first part of the experiments aimed to represent the given dataset as a semantic graph. As mentioned in [28], the process of building the semantic graph consists of two main steps:

  1. Identify the possible relationships between the words. The Farasa Segmenter is used in this step to break up the original sentence into words. In order to find subjects, objects, and adjective relations, the Farasa Part-of-Speech (POS) tagger is used. The Farasa Named entity recognizer is used to extract person and location name entities. The word's root is taken out using the Tashaphyne Arabic Light Stemmer. The original word is then compared to its root to identify the pattern of the original word.
  2. Apply predefined rules to identify the semantic relationship between words and to build the final semantic graph.

- Embedding the semantic graph: The second part of the experiments attempted to embed the semantic graph in low-dimensional vectors, in which each vertex was interpreted as a vector. SemanticGraph2vec, a customized random-walk based approach, was used to explore the semantic graph. Semantic walks were derived by the priority semantic relationship. Then, the vertices' representation was learned by optimizing the semantic neighborhood objective with the use of Stochastic Gradient Descent (SGD) with negative sampling.

- Applying deep learning for abstractive Arabic text summarization: In this part, three sets of experiments were performed. Abstractive Arabic text summarization models were trained separately on the dataset mentioned above. Seven-fold cross-validation was performed to determine the efficiency of the summarization. Essentially, the dataset was divided randomly into seven subsets of equal size. The model was trained on 6/7 of the dataset and tested on the remaining subset. Evaluation measures were stated as an average over the seven-fold validation span. The first experiment used SemanticGraph2Vec as a graph embedding method, while the second and third experiments used two versions of Word2vec. The deep learning network used in the experiments consisted of Long Short-Term Memory (LSTM) in the Encoder, LSTM BasicDecoder for training, and BeamSearchDecoder for inference. BahdanauAttention with weight normalization was used as an attention mechanism. The network had the following parameters: two hidden layers, 200 hidden units, beam width of 10, embedding size of 128, the total number of epochs was 30, learning rate of 0.005, batch size of 128, and a keep probability of 0.80. These parameters were selected on the basis of the following sensitivity analysis.

5.1. Sensitivity Analysis

In a separate series of experiments, the sensitivity of the deep learning network parameters was evaluated and tested. The purpose of the sensitivity analysis was to assess the efficiency of the deep NN with respect to the parameter being examined. In the experiments, the dataset was split randomly into two parts: the training dataset containing 90% of the data and the testing dataset containing 10% of the data. The loss value was considered an evaluation measure. Several values for each parameter were examined in a variety of experiments in which all other parameters were fixed. The sensitivity analysis included the following parameters:

- Learning Rate: Three separate experiments were performed to determine the most effective learning rate. Other parameters were set, as shown in Table 3. Three different learning rate values were examined: 0.010, 0.005, and 0.001. The loss values shown in Table 4 indicate that the lower loss value was obtained using a learning rate of 0.005.

Table 3. Experiment parameters for the learning rate sensitivity analysis.

Parameter Name	Parameter Value
Number of units	200
Number of hidden layers	2
Beam width	10
Embedding size	128
Number of epochs	10
Batch size	128
Keep probability	0.80

Table 4. Sensitivity analysis results for learning rate (loss value).

Epoch Number	Learning Rate = 0.010	Learning Rate = 0.005	Learning Rate = 0.001
1	65.19	63.55	63.79
2	55.09	51.83	56.79
3	53.00	48.12	53.65
4	47.70	42.82	51.76
5	45.60	38.00	48.51
6	42.52	35.27	44.72
7	37.25	30.44	44.80
8	34.44	32.48	40.47
9	31.73	23.16	35.11
10	28.14	19.96	31.40

- Beam width: Three separate experiments were performed to determine the most effective beam width. Other parameters were set, as shown in Table 5. Three different beam width values were examined: 5, 10, and 15. The loss values shown in Table 6 indicate that a lower loss value was obtained using a beam width of 10.

Table 5. Experiment parameters for beam width sensitivity analysis.

Parameter Name	Parameter Value
Number of units	200
Number of hidden layers	2
Embedding size	128
Number of epochs	10
Learning rate	0.005
Batch size	128
Keep probability	0.80

Table 6. Sensitivity analysis results for beam width (loss value).

Epoch Number	Beam Width = 5	Beam Width = 10	Beam Width = 15
1	62.87	63.55	64.17
2	52.38	51.83	53.32
3	49.38	48.12	48.78
4	43.18	42.82	45.36
5	41.95	38.00	41.01
6	39.19	35.27	38.05
7	33.89	30.44	31.45
8	30.01	32.48	28.11
9	29.19	23.16	24.70
10	25.07	19.96	21.11

- Batch size: Three separate experiments were performed to determine the most effective batch size. Other experiment parameters were set, as shown in Table 7. Three different batch size values were examined: 128, 64, and 32. The loss values shown in Figure 2 indicate that the lower loss value was obtained using a batch size of 32.

Table 7. Experiment parameters for batch size sensitivity analysis.

Parameter Name	Parameter Value
Number of units	200
Number of hidden layers	2
Beam width	10
Embedding size	128
Number of epochs	20
Learning rate	0.005
Keep probability	0.80

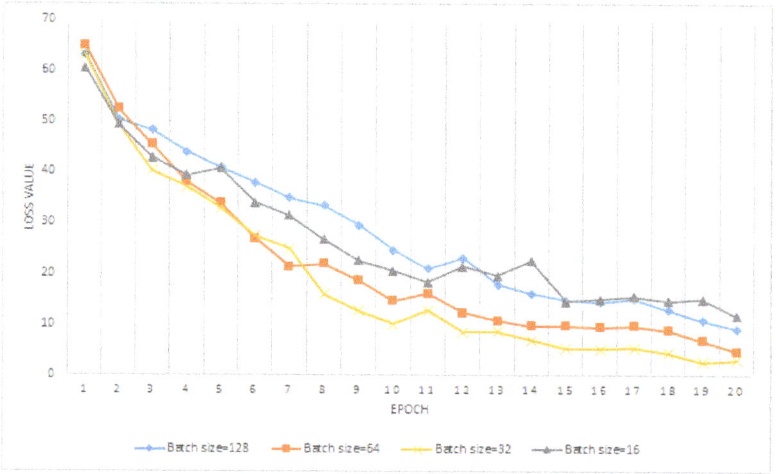

Figure 2. Sensitivity analysis results for batch size on the testing dataset.

- Number of units: Three separate experiments were performed to determine the most effective number of units in the deep neural network. Other experiment parameters were set, as shown in Table 8. Three different values of the number of units were examined: 100, 200, and 300. The loss values shown in Figure 3 indicate that the lower loss value was obtained using 200 units.

Table 8. Experiment parameters for number of units sensitivity analysis.

Parameter Name	Parameter Value
Number of hidden layers	2
Beam width	10
Embedding size	128
Number of epochs	20
Learning rate	0.005
Batch size	32
Keep probability	0.80

- Number of epochs: Three separate experiments were performed to determine the most effective number of epochs in the deep neural network. Other experiment parameters were set, as shown in Table 9. Three different values of the number of epoch were examined: 10, 20, and 30. The loss values shown in Figure 4 indicate that the loss value continued to decrease after 10 and 20 epochs, whereas it was almost constant after 30 epochs. This means that the deep neural network stopped learning after 30 epochs, and any additional epochs did not increase learning. The loss value did not decrease. Therefore, 30 epochs of experiments resulted in better outcome as the network continued to learn until the 26th epoch.

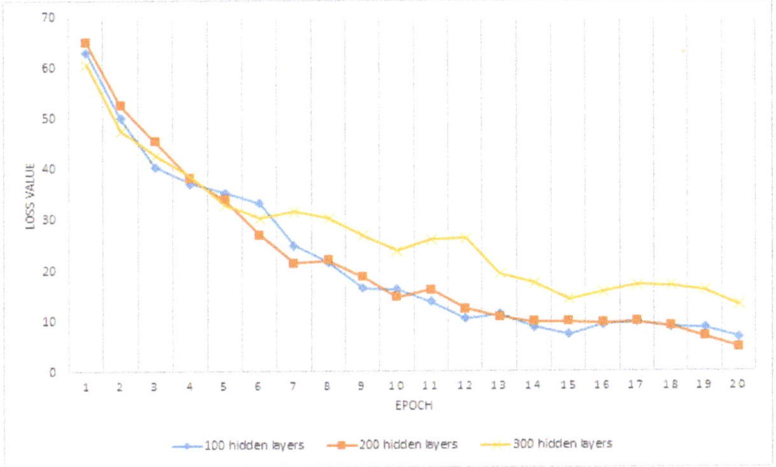

Figure 3. Sensitivity analysis results for number of units on the testing dataset.

Table 9. Experimental parameters for number of epochs sensitivity analysis.

Parameter Name	Parameter Value
Number of units	200
Number of hidden layers	2
Beam width	10
Embedding size	128
Learning rate	0.005
Batch size	32
Keep probability	0.80

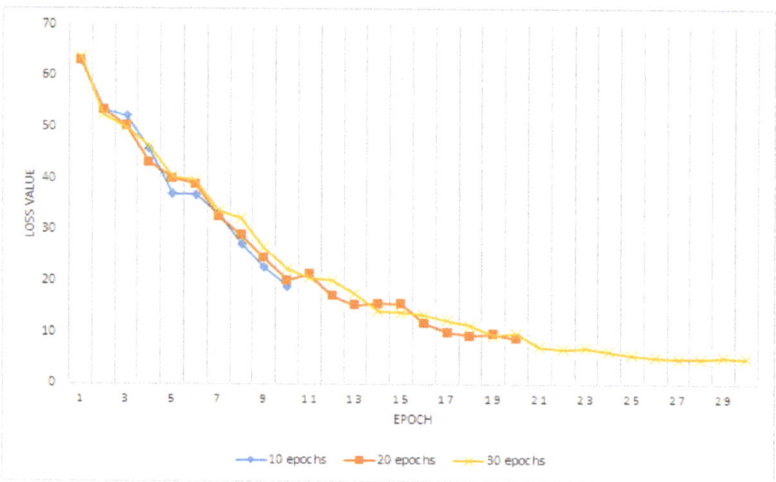

Figure 4. Sensitivity analysis results for number of epochs.

5.2. Evaluation

The results of all experiments are summarized in this section. In addition, the findings collected are discussed and used to compare the proposed SemG-TS (using semantic-Graph2Vec) with the baseline word embedding model (word2vec) in terms of their ability to enhance the quality of the abstractive Arabic text summarization. Two different types of evaluation were used: automatic evaluation and manual evaluation. The ROUGE evaluation measure was used to perform an automatic evaluation of the produced summary.

A standard automatic evaluation of summaries called ROUGE was proposed by Lin et al. [36]. It compares the produced summary (typically by the proposed models) against a set of reference summaries (typically produced by humans). ROUGE is measured based on the similarity of n-grams (an n-gram is a subsequence of n words) [37]. Several variants of ROUGE are used to evaluate text summarization models, such as ROUGE-N, ROUGE-L, and ROUGE-S. ROUGE-1, for instance, addresses the similarity of the unigrams in the final summary and the reference summary. The similarity of the bigrams in the produced summary and the reference summary is referred to as ROUGE-2. ROUGE-N, in general, evaluates how comparable the produced summary is to the reference summary in terms of unigram, bigram, trigram, and higher order n-grams.

Examples 1. *Consider the following system summary and reference summary:*

System summary: "جلس العصفور فوق غصن الشجرة" *(The bird sat on the branch of the tree).*

Reference summary: "جلس العصفور فوق الشجرة" *(The bird sat atop the tree).*

When considering individual words, the number of overlapping words between the system summary and the reference summary is four. The recall is defined as follows:

$$Recall = \frac{number\,of\,overlapping\,words}{total\,number\,of\,words\,in\,the\,reference\,summary} = \frac{4}{4} \tag{1}$$

However, four out of five words in the system summary are needed or relevant. Thus, the precision is determined as follows:

$$Precision = \frac{number\,of\,overlapping\,words}{total\,number\,of\,words\,in\,the\,system\,summary} = \frac{4}{5} \tag{2}$$

In the automatic evaluation in this paper, ROUGE-1 was considered.

Furthermore, manual evaluations were used to evaluate the produced summary by human experts. Since few works have been proposed in the field of abstractive Arabic text summarization, the experiments aimed to compare the proposed approach results with the original word2vec word embedding. The following subsections go through both evaluations in detail.

The state-of-the-art word2vec embedding model is used to compare the performance of the proposed semantic graph embedding in creating a relevant and high-quality summary. Word2vec was introduced by the Google Research Team in 2013 [38]. It is a two-layer NN that processes text and "vectorizes" words. The word2vec input is a text corpus, and the output is a set of vectors that represent the words in that corpus. The purpose of word2vec is to group vectors of similar words in vector-space. That is, it mathematically detects similarities between words. The word2vec output is a vocabulary in which each word has an attached vector that can be fed into a deep-learning network to detect the relationship between the represented words [38]. Representing words using vectors is very important for most NLP applications [39]. Thus, word2vec is used in many applications, such as sentiment analysis [40] and plagiarism detection [41].

5.2.1. The Automatic Evaluation

The performance of the proposed SemG-TS model is automatically compared with the performance of two versions of word2vec on the testing dataset detailed in Section 4. The first version was trained on the above dataset in order to produce the initial vectors for the text summarization, and the second version had uniform random initial vectors assigned to each word for the text summarization. The ROUGE evaluation measure was used. The three models were evaluated on the same dataset above, and the results are shown in Table 10. Clearly, the SemG-TS model, on average, surpassed the two word2vec models in all the evaluation measures. In other words, the best results of the SemG-TS model were 15.8%, 29.5%, and 21.4% better than the best version of word2vec (random-based) in terms of precision, recall, and F-measure, respectively.

Table 10. Automatic evaluation using ROUGE.

	Word2Vec (Pretrained)	Word2Vec (Random)	SemG-TS
Precision	2.26×10^{-2}	3.92×10^{-2}	4.54×10^{-2}
Recall	2.42×10^{-2}	3.92×10^{-2}	5.08×10^{-2}
F-measure	2.30×10^{-2}	3.87×10^{-2}	4.70×10^{-2}

Although the three models had a low ROUGE performance, it can be noted that SemG-TS surpassed the baseline word embedding model (word2vec) in both versions, which satisfies the main goal of the experiments. These results might be improved by a number of methods, such as: (1) Use more data for training. This is merely an effect of the amount of data in any deep learning model [42,43]. (2) Improve the quality of the dependency parser used to create a semantic graph so it can have more accurate dependency relationships between words. (3) Use a collection of more semantic relationships that enrich the semantic representation.

The loss values of the three experiments are shown in Figure 5. Loss values will continue to decrease with more epochs, which will decrease until they are stable. Therefore, the loss value was almost constant in the last three epochs.

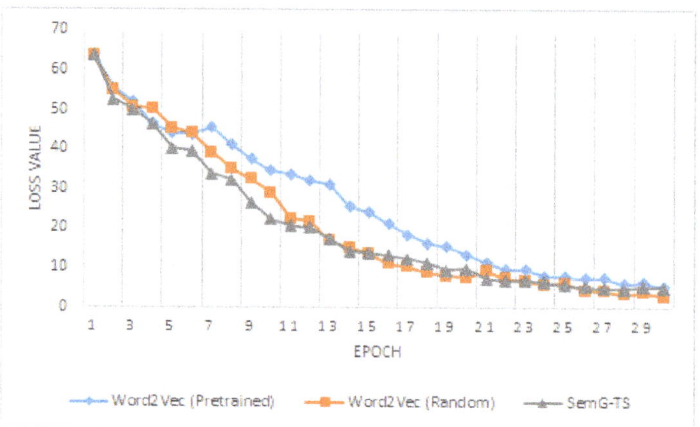

Figure 5. Loss values for experiment with 30 epochs.

5.2.2. The Manual Evaluation

The ROUGE evaluation measures compute the frequency of the overlapping n-grams of the summary produced and the reference summary; thus, the abstractive text summary may not contain the same words that were used in the reference summary, which makes the ROUGE evaluation method irrelevant for this type of application. The proposed abstractive text summarization model was therefore evaluated manually by human experts. The evaluators were required to assess both the proposed summary and the summary produced by the baseline algorithm. The original text and the two summaries were provided on the main screen of a customized application, and four main questions maintained the relevance, similarity, readability, and overall satisfaction of the evaluated summary.

A simple desktop application was built for the assessment of an evaluator, as the correct way to know whether the proposed summary is relevant and appropriate is to receive feedback directly from a human being. A sample screenshot of the evaluation screen is shown in Figure 6, and more samples are listed in the Appendix B. Element number 1 refers to the article ID and the article title, element number 2 refers to the article body. Suggested summaries are shown in element number 3. Finally, the evaluation questions are set out in element 4.

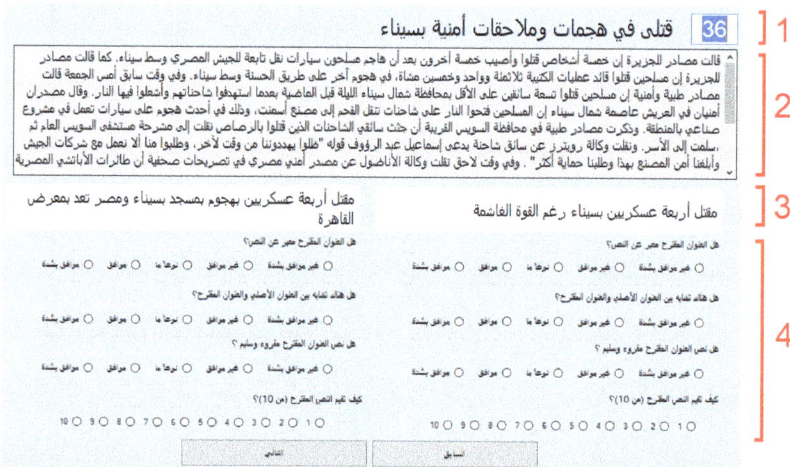

Figure 6. Screenshot of manual assessment application.

Every text summarization model was set to produce its summary for the article displayed. The order in which the two summaries appeared below the article was randomized. As a result, the evaluator did not know which model the summary being shown was referring to.

Next to the article body, four assessment questions were listed in order to get feedback about the relevancy of the summary, similarity between the suggested summary and the original summary, the suggested summary's readability and quality, and overall satisfaction. Evaluators were also provided with five radio buttons to indicate the relevancy, similarity, and readability of the suggested summary: (a) I totally agree, (b) I agree, (c) Maybe, (d) I disagree, and (e) I totally disagree. However, a scale of 1–10 was used to indicate the overall satisfaction of the evaluator with the suggested summary, with a higher value indicating more satisfaction. The questions on the assessment screen were the following:

1. Does the proposed summary express the text? This question refers to the relevance of the proposed summary to the original text. It should consider the similarity of the domain, the semantic similarity, and the principal similarity of the main ideas expressed in the article.
2. Is the proposed summary similar to the title of the article? This question measures the similarity of the title of the article and the suggested summary in terms of domain, content, and keyword similarities.
3. Is the proposed summary readable and logical? This question evaluates the consistency of the suggested summary in terms of linguistic integrity and logical validity.
4. What is your overall level of satisfaction with the suggested summary? This question measures the overall satisfaction of the evaluator with the suggested summary.

Evaluators were selected based on several conditions, such as: The mother tongue of the evaluator should be the Arabic language, the evaluator should hold a post-graduate degree, and also should be from different scientific backgrounds. In addition, 605 articles were chosen randomly from the dataset, and three evaluators submitted their feedback on both suggested summaries.

Figure 7 shows the results of the frequency of summary relevancy, similarity, readability, and overall satisfaction. Looking at these raw data, SemG-TS and word2vec are similar to each other in terms of relevancy and how near their summaries are to the reference summary. However, in terms of readability and overall satisfaction, SemG-TS has more fragmented data at all levels than word2vec. In comparison, word2vec has more rank-1 (lower rank) than SemG-TS.

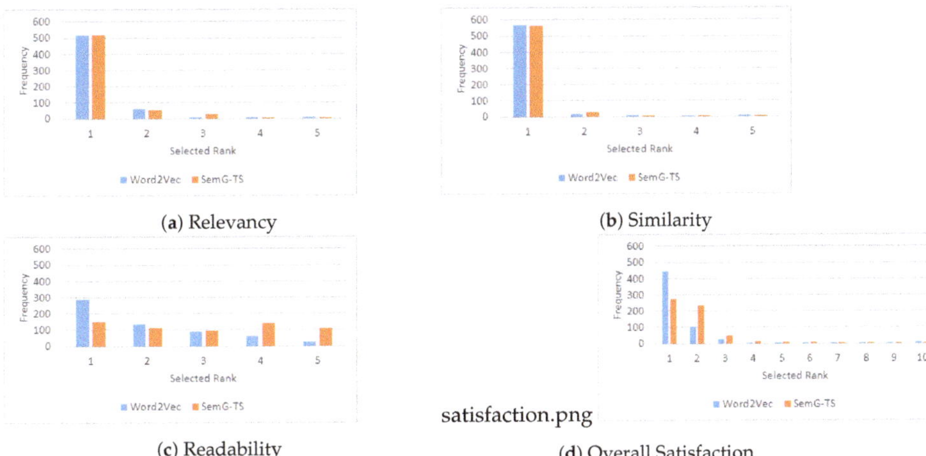

Figure 7. The frequencies of the evaluators' responses.

Table 11 summarizes the basic statistics of the summary assessment from the evaluators. The mean scores in relevancy and similarity are slightly higher for the SemG-TS model, while the mean scores in readability and overall satisfaction are significantly higher for the SemG-TS model. However, considering the scales of the ratings, the SemG-TS manages to increase readability significantly with marginal sacrifices in relevancy.

Paired-sample t-tests were conducted to compare the means between the summary produced by the proposed model and the summary produced by the baseline model. There was a significant difference in the relevancy scores of SemG-TS and word2vec; $t(604) = -1.64$, $\alpha = 0.05$. There was also a significant difference in the readability scores of SemG-TS and word2vec; $t(604) = -10.47$, $\alpha = 0.05$. According to the overall satisfaction score, there was also a significant difference in the overall satisfaction scores for SemG-TS and word2vec; $t(604) = 4.72$, $\alpha = 0.05$. However, there was no significant difference in similarity, with $t(604) = -0.35$, $\alpha = 0.05$.

As the distribution of data was chi-squared, as seen in Figure 7, the chi-squared test was used to evaluate the likely of the frequency of the evaluation results for SemG-TS and word2vec to be substantially different. The chi-squared test showed that there was a significant difference between the two models in terms of readability and overall satisfaction, with 978.18 and 701.3 chi-square values ($\alpha = 0.05$) for SemG-TS and word2vec, respectively. Conversely, the chi-squared test showed no significant difference between the two models in terms of relevancy and similarity, because the chi-square values were 196.58 and 157.68 ($\alpha = 0.05$), respectively, for SemG-TS and word2vec.

Table 11. Basic statistics of the manual evaluation.

	Relevancy		Similarity	
	SemG-TS	Word2Vec	SemG-TS	Word2Vec
Count	605	605	605	605
Mean	1.23	1.23	1.11	1.14
STD	0.65	0.70	0.48	0.62
Percentage	4.7%	4.7%	2.1%	2.8%
	Readability		Overall Satisfaction	
	SemG-TS	Word2Vec	SemG-TS	Word2Vec
Count	605	605	605	605
Mean	2.91	2.01	1.89	1.55
STD	1.45	1.20	1.35	1.44
Percentage	38.2%	20.3%	18.9%	15.5%

6. Conclusions

In this research, SemG-TS, an abstractive single-statement Arabic text summarization model is proposed. The proposed model consists of three main steps: the construction of a semantic graph, the embedding of a semantic graph, and the production of a final summary. The semantic random-walk-based approach, called SemanticGraph2vec, was applied in the embedding step, and then deep NN was used to produce the final summary. A new dataset consists of news articles that had been collected from the Al-Jazeera.Net website was used in the experiments. Two different types of evaluation were used: automated evaluation and manual evaluation. The ROUGE evaluation measure was used for automatic assessment. Conversely, a manual evaluation was carried out by human experts to measure the relevancy, similarity, readability, and overall satisfaction of the proposed summaries. The results were compared to the word embedding model, word2vec. The experimental results show that the proposed SemG-TS model surpasses word2vec in terms of ROUGE, relevancy, readability, and overall satisfaction.

Author Contributions: Conceptualization, W.E.; Methodology, W.E.; Project administration, A.A.; Resources, W.E.; Software, W.E.; Supervision, A.A.; Validation, W.E.; Writing—original draft, W.E.; Writing—review & editing, A.A. All authors have read and agreed to the published version of the manuscript.

Funding: This research received no external funding.

Institutional Review Board Statement: Not applicable.

Informed Consent Statement: Not applicable.

Data Availability Statement: Not applicable.

Conflicts of Interest: The authors declare no conflicts of interest.

Appendix A. Semantic Graph Representation Samples

In this appendix, different examples and test cases of the used semantic graph are illustrated and discussed. The first example represents the sentence:

"اغتيال مدير هيئة العدالة والمسائلة في بغداد"

("The assassination of the director of Justice and Accountability Commission in Baghdad"). There is no verb in this sentence. It contains the location noun "بغداد" (Baghdad) and the conjunction word "و" (and). Each word in the sentence is represented as a distinct vertex, as seen in Figure A1. The location is represented by an extra concept vertex.

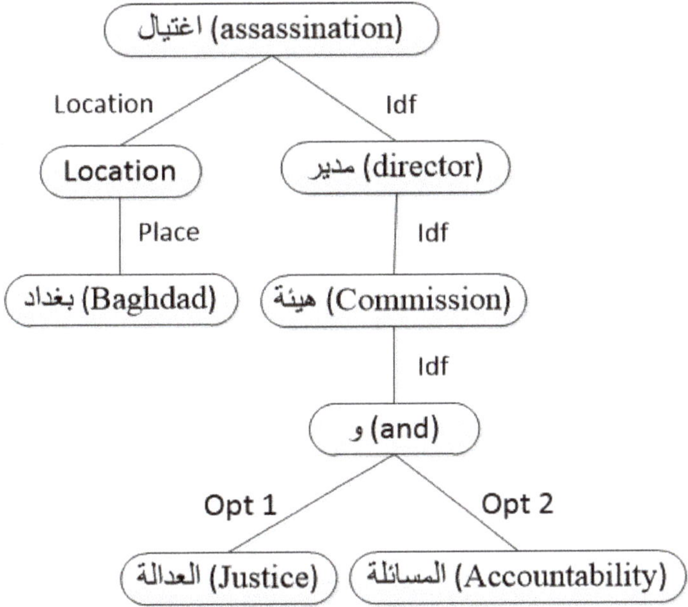

Figure A1. Semantic representation sample number 1.

The second example, illustrated in Figure A2, represents the sentence:

"قرر الجيش الأمريكي خفض عدد قواته في الباكستان خلال العام المقبل"

("The US military has decided to reduce the number of its troops in Pakistan during next year"). The semantic graph in this example is expanded to include vertices for the location and date/time concepts. A verb and its properties are present in the sentence (subject and object).

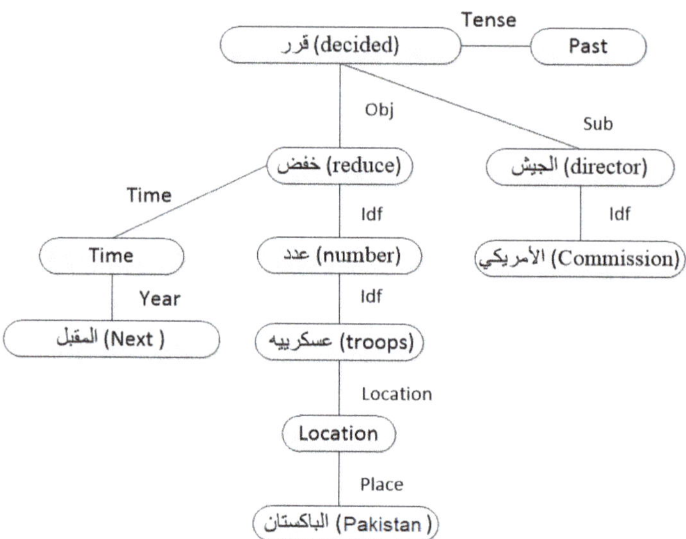

Figure A2. Semantic representation sample number 2.

Appendix B. Produced Summary Samples

Examples of the summaries that were created using the proposed approach and the word2vec word embedding model are shown in this appendix. Screenshots of the manual evaluation application's home screen are shown in Figures A3–A8. The original text and the two summaries are shown in random order on each screenshot.

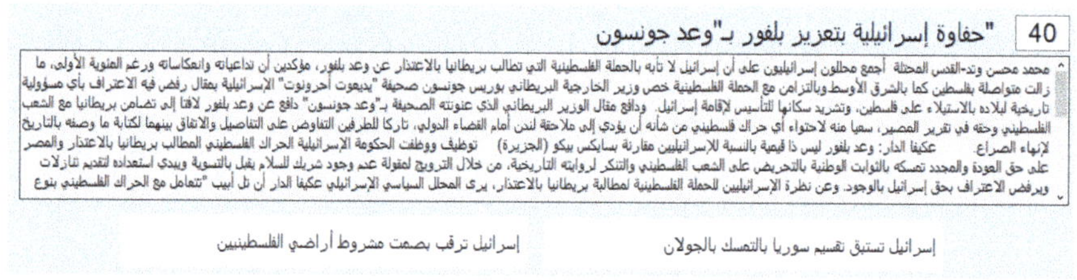

Figure A3. Sample number 1.

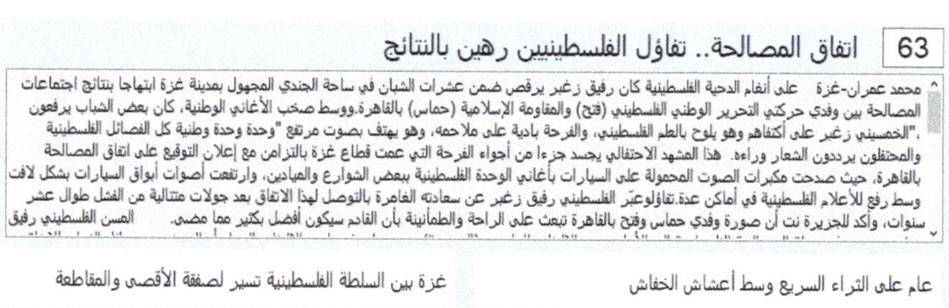

Figure A4. Sample number 2.

| 303 | الأردن يستضيف المنتدى الاقتصادي العالمي |

أكمل الأردن استعداداته لاستضافة فعاليات المنتدى الاقتصادي العالمي لمنطقة الشرق الأوسط وشمال أفريقيا تحت شعار "تمكين الأجيال نحو المستقبل". ويشارك في المنتدى الذي يستمر ثلاثة أيام بالبحر الميت أكثر من ألف شخصية عربية وعالمية. واختارت لجنة متخصصة مئة شركة من المنطقة العربية للمشاركة في المنتدى تضم رواد أعمال. وتعتمد هذه الشركات في منتجاتها على التكنولوجيا الحديثة لتلبية احتياجات أساسية في قطاعات النقل والاتصالات وعمليات الدفع الإلكتروني وخدمات الرعاية الصحية. وتشمل الشركات العربية المئة الناشئة نماذج ريادية من الأردن وسوريا ولبنان وفلسطين والعراق والكويت والإمارات والبحرين والسعودية وعمان واليمن ومصر وليبيا والجزائر والمغرب. هذا وكان المنتدى الاقتصادي العالمي بدأ فعالياته غير الرسمية بجلسة نقاشية خصصت لموضوع الابتكار كأحد أبرز العوامل التنافسية. وذكر بيان صادر عن المنتدى أن اجتماعه لهذا العام، وهو التاسع في الأردن والسادس عشر على مستوى المنطقة، يركز على محاور رئيسية تشمل تحفيز الريادة والإبداع عبر التقنية الحديثة، وبناء اقتصادات تضمن مشاركة الجميع والجهود الإغاثية والدبلوماسية الضرورية لمواجهة تحديات

| آلاف الوظائف ونصف مليار دولار لليمن | الأردن يستضيف المنتدى الاقتصادي |

Figure A5. Sample number 3.

| 81 | لماذا يهتم بوتين بالشرق الأوسط؟ |

قال كاتب بصحيفة تايمز البريطانية إن أغلب أهداف الرئيس الروسي فلاديمير بوتين في الشرق الأوسط وشمال أفريقيا قصيرة المدى، وتتراوح بين بيع الأسلحة والحصول على قروض مالية والتوصل لاتفاقات حول أسعار النفط. إلى السعي لتهدئة المنطقة وإجهاض الثورات المحتملة. وأوضح الكاتب مايكل بيرلي في مقال له بصحيفة تايمز البريطانية إن بوتين وزير خارجيته سيرغي لافروف يتمنعان بشهرة واسعة في المنطقة، والأهم من ذلك أن الحكام بالمنطقة على على بيع المروحيات والمقاتلات والدبابات والغواصات فقط، بل تمتد لتصل إلى السعي لتهدئة المنطقة. وأضاف أنه رغم أن روسيا كانت عامل قلق في منطقة البلطيق وجورجيا وأوكرانيا وأوروبا بدعمها لليمين "المتطرف" في فرنسا وألمانيا، فإنها في الشرق الأوسط ترفض التدخل الغربي والثورات الداخلية بهدف حماية نفسها من تأثير التغيرات بالمنطقة، بالإضافة إلى منع ما يُقدر بـ 3200 مقاتل من الجهاديين الروس للعودة لبلاده. سياسة تهدئة وقال بيرلي إن ما يُذاع في الغرب من روح انتقامية يتصف بها بوتين لا تجد ما يؤكدها في سياسته بالشرق الأوسط، فعندما أسقطت تركيا المقاتلة الروسية التي جنحت ودخلت حدودها، وعندما قتل شرطي تركي السفير الروسي بأنقرة، وعندما تعرض المبعوث الروسي إلى دولة قطر لمضايقات، كان الرد الروسي أقل كثيرا مما هو

| لأول مرة مصر تبيع سندات دولية بملياري يورو | دبلوماسية التجنيس جواز السفر الروسي لمواطني دول عربية |

Figure A6. Sample number 4.

| 90 | دراسة إسرائيلية: مصالحة حماس وفتح بطريقها للفشل |

لم تستبعد دراسة إسرائيلية أن تلقى المصالحة الداخلية التي أقدمت عليها حركة المقاومة الإسلامية حماس مع حركة التحرير الوطني الفلسطينية "فتح" المصير نفسه الذي عرفته الاتفاقات السابقة المبرمة بين الطرفين وهو الفشل. وأضافت الدراسة التي نشرها معهد أبحاث الأمن القومي التابع لجامعة تل أبيب، أن فتح وحماس وقعتا سابقا سلسلة اتفاقات عديدة كان مصيرها "الفشل الذريع"، ومن بينها ما تم التوقيع عليه في مكة 2007، وصنعاء 2008، والقاهرة 2011، والدوحة 2012، والشاطئ 2014، ولذلك ليس مستبعد -تقول الدراسة- أن "تؤدي الظروف الحالية إلى النتيجة ذاتها من الإخفاق". وعن أسباب إعلان حماس خطوتها الأخيرة، ترى الدراسة أن ضغوطا متلاحقة على الحركة -التي تفرض سيطرتها على غزة- دفعتها إلى حل اللجنة الإدارية في القطاع، مشيرة إلى أن "الطريق للمصالحة الفلسطينية لا يزال طويلا جدا". وضمن هذا السياق، قال جلعاد شير، أحد المشاركين في الدراسة وهو الرئيس السابق لدائرة المفاوضات مع الفلسطينيين، إن المصالحة الأخيرة جاءت في وقت يعيش فيه قطاع غزة ضائقة صحية وبطالة مرتفعة وأزمة إنسانية، في حين تعوض حماس منذ وقت طويل معركة بقاء سياسي في ظل التطورات الإقليمية الأخيرة وتبدل شبكة التحالفات السياسية للحركة بين دول المنطقة. وأضاف شير، الجنرال الإسرائيلي المتقاعد الذي سبق له أن تقلد مناصب عسكرية مرموقة في الجيش الإسرائيلي، أن استجابة حماس للمصالحة بحل اللجنة الإدارية وضمت عباس رئيس السلطة الفلسطينية محمود عباس في معضلة صعبة

| جمعة الحرية والحياة تختبر تهدئة غزة | السيسي يكشف الارتجال الاقتصادي مع حماس |

Figure A7. Sample number 5.

| 318 | ملك الأردن يصل إلى القاهرة في زيارة رسمية |

وصل الملك الأردني عبد الله الثاني اليوم الأربعاء إلى العاصمة المصرية القاهرة، في زيارة رسمية قصيرة لعقد مباحثات قبيل القمة العربية الإسلامية الأميركية المقررة في العاصمة السعودية الرياض. واستقبل الرئيس المصري عبد الفتاح السيسي ملك الأردن لدى وصوله إلى مطار القاهرة الدولي. وبحسب تقارير إعلامية محلية، فإن الزيارة التي تُستغرق ساعات قليلة تشمل مباحثات مع السيسي حول الجهود المصرية والعربية لكسر الجمود القائم في عملية السلام في الشرق الأوسط خاصة قبل القمة العربية الإسلامية الأميركية. وتعد زيارة الملك عبد الله الثاني إلى مصر الثانية خلال ثلاثة أشهر، حيث زار القاهرة في 21 فبراير/شباط الماضي. وأجرى مباحثات رسمية تطرقت إلى عدد من القضايا وشملت العلاقات الثنائية والقضية الفلسطينية.

| الملك سلمان سوداني جديدة رسمية ولا تقلق | ملك الأردن يصل الخرطوم |

Figure A8. Sample number 6.

References

1. Gambhir, M.; Gupta, V. Recent automatic text summarization techniques: A survey. *Artif. Intell. Rev.* **2017**, *47*, 1–66. [CrossRef]
2. Yang, C.C.; Wang, F.L. Hierarchical summarization of large documents. *J. Am. Soc. Inf. Sci. Technol.* **2008**, *59*, 887–902. [CrossRef]
3. Harabagiu, S.; Lacatusu, F. Using topic themes for multi-document summarization. *ACM Trans. Inf. Syst. (TOIS)* **2010**, *28*, 1–47. [CrossRef]
4. Verma, P.; Verma, A. A Review on Text Summarization Techniques. *J. Sci. Res.* **2020**, *64*, 251–257. [CrossRef]
5. Al-Saleh, A.B.; Menai, M.E.B. Automatic Arabic text summarization: A survey. *Artif. Intell. Rev.* **2015**, *45*, 203–234. [CrossRef]
6. Gupta, V.; Lehal, G.S. A Survey of Text Summarization Extractive Techniques. *J. Emerg. Technol. Web Intell.* **2010**, *2*, 258–268. [CrossRef]
7. Abdulsahib, A.K.; Kamaruddin, S.S. Graph based text representation for document clustering. *J. Theor. Appl. Inf. Technol.* **2015**, *76*, 1–13.

8.   Banarescu, L.; Bonial, C.; Cai, S.; Georgescu, M.; Griffitt, K.; Hermjakob, U.; Knight, K.; Koehn, P.; Palmer, M.; Schneider, N. Abstract Meaning Representation for Sembanking. In Proceedings of the 7th Linguistic Annotation Workshop and Interoperability with Discourse, Sofia, Bulgaria, 8–9 August 2013; Association for Computational Linguistics: Stroudsburg, PL, USA, 2013; pp. 178–186.

9.   Abend, O.; Rappoport, A. Universal Conceptual Cognitive Annotation (UCCA). In Proceedings of the 51st Annual Meeting of the Association for Computational Linguistics (Volume 1: Long Papers), Sofia, Bulgaria, 4–9 August 2013; Association for Computational Linguistics: Stroudsburg, PL, USA, 2013; pp. 228–238.

10.   Alansary, S.; Nagi, M.; Adly, N. The universal networking language in action in English-Arabic machine translation. In Proceedings of the 9th Egyptian Society of Language Engineering Conference on Language Engineering, (ESOLEC 2009), Cairo, Egypt, December 2009; pp. 23–24.

11.   Ismail, S.S.; Aref, M.; Moawad, I.F. Rich semantic graph: A new semantic text representation approach for arabic language. In Proceedings of the 7th WSEAS European Computing Conference (ECC '13), Dubrovnik, Croatia, 25–27 June 2013; pp. 97–102.

12.   Liang, H.; Sun, X.; Sun, Y.; Gao, Y. Text feature extraction based on deep learning: A review. *EURASIP J. Wirel. Commun. Netw.* **2017**, *2017*, 9287489. [CrossRef]

13.   Dang, H.T. DUC 2005: Evaluation of Question-Focused Summarization Systems. In Proceedings of the Workshop on Task-Focused Summarization and Question Answering, Sydney, Australia, 23 July 2006; SumQA '06; Association for Computational Linguistics: Stroudsburg, PL, USA, 2006; pp. 48–55.

14.   Qassem, L.M.A.; Wang, D.; Mahmoud, Z.A.; Barada, H.; Al-Rubaie, A.; Almoosa, N.I. Automatic Arabic Summarization: A survey of methodologies and systems. *Procedia Comput. Sci.* **2017**, *117*, 10–18. [CrossRef]

15.   Belkebir, R.; Guessoum, A. TALAA-ATSF: A Global Operation-Based Arabic Text Summarization Framework. In *Intelligent Natural Language Processing: Trends and Applications*; Springer International Publishing: Berlin/Heidelberg, Germany, 2017; pp. 435–459.

16.   Belkebir, R.; Guessoum, A. TALAA-ASC: A sentence compression corpus for Arabic. In Proceedings of the 2015 IEEE/ACS 12th International Conference of Computer Systems and Applications (AICCSA), Marrakech, Morocco, 17–20 november 2015; IEEE: Piscataway, NJ, USA, 2015; pp. 1–8.

17.   Azmi, A.M.; Altmami, N.I. An abstractive Arabic text summarizer with user controlled granularity. *Inf. Process. Manag.* **2018**, *54*, 903–921.

18.   Elbarougy, R.; Behery, G.; Khatib, A.E. Extractive Arabic Text Summarization Using Modified PageRank Algorithm. *Egypt. Inform. J.* **2020**, *21*, 73–81. [CrossRef]

19.   Elbarougy, R.; Behery, G.; Khatib, A.E. Graph-Based Extractive Arabic Text Summarization Using Multiple Morphological Analyzers. *J. Inf. Sci. Eng.* **2020**, *36*, 347–363.

20.   Buckwalter, T. Issues in Arabic orthography and morphology analysis. In Proceedings of the Workshop on Computational Approaches to Arabic Script-Based Languages, Geneva, Switzerland, 28 August 2004; Association for Computational Linguistics: Stroudsburg, PL, USA, 2004; pp. 31–34.

21.   Jaafar, Y.; Bouzoubaa, K. Benchmark of Arabic morphological analyzers challenges and solutions. In Proceedings of the 2014 9th International Conference on Intelligent Systems: Theories and Applications (SITA-14), Rabat, Morocco, 7–8 May 2014; IEEE: Piscataway, NJ, USA, 2014; pp. 1–6.

22.   Manning, C.; Surdeanu, M.; Bauer, J.; Finkel, J.; Bethard, S.; McClosky, D. The Stanford CoreNLP Natural Language Processing Toolkit. In Proceedings of the 52nd Annual Meeting of the Association for Computational Linguistics: System Demonstrations, Baltimore, ML, USA, 23–24 June 2014; Association for Computational Linguistics: Stroudsburg, PL, USA, 2014; pp. 55–60.

23.   Alami, N.; En-nahnahi, N.; Ouatik, S.A.; Meknassi, M. Using Unsupervised Deep Learning for Automatic Summarization of Arabic Documents. *Arab. J. Sci. Eng.* **2018**, *43*, 7803–7815. [CrossRef]

24.   Qaroush, A.; Farha, I.A.; Ghanem, W.; Washaha, M.; Maali, E. An efficient single document Arabic text summarization using a combination of statistical and semantic features. *J. King Saud Univ. -Comput. Inf. Sci.* **2019**, *33*, 677–692. [CrossRef]

25.   Belkebir, R.; Guessoum, A. A Supervised Approach to Arabic Text Summarization Using AdaBoost. In *New Contributions in Information Systems and Technologies*; Springer International Publishing: Berlin/Heidelberg, Germany, 2015; pp. 227–236.

26.   Al-Abdallah, R.Z.; Al-Taani, A.T. Arabic Text Summarization using Firefly Algorithm. In Proceedings of the 2019 Amity International Conference on Artificial Intelligence (AICAI), Dubai, United Arab Emirates, 4–6 February 2019; IEEE: Piscataway, NJ, USA, 2019; pp. 61–65.

27.   Al-Radaideh, Q.A.; Bataineh, D.Q. A Hybrid Approach for Arabic Text Summarization Using Domain Knowledge and Genetic Algorithms. *Cogn. Comput.* **2018**, *10*, 651–669. [CrossRef]

28.   Etaiwi, W.; Awajan, A. Graph-based Arabic text semantic representation. *Inf. Process. Manag.* **2020**, *57*, 102183.

29.   Etaiwi, W.M.A. Semantic Graph Learning for Abstractive Arabic Text Summarization. Ph.D. Thesis, Princess Sumaya University for Technology, Amman, Jordan, 2020.

30.   Young, T.; Hazarika, D.; Poria, S.; Cambria, E. Recent Trends in Deep Learning Based Natural Language Processing. *IEEE Comput. Intell. Mag.* **2018**, *13*, 55–75. [CrossRef]

31.   Deng, L.; Liu, Y. (Eds.) *Deep Learning in Natural Language Processing*; Springer: Singapore, 2018.

32.   Fejer, H.N.; Omar, N. Automatic multi-document Arabic text summarization using clustering and keyphrase extraction. *J. Artif. Intell.* **2015**, *8*, 1–9. [CrossRef]

33. El-Haj, M.; Koulali, R. KALIMAT a multipurpose Arabic Corpus. In Proceedings of the Second Workshop on Arabic Corpus Linguistics (WACL-2), Lancaster, UK, 22–26 July 2013; pp. 22–25.

34. El-Haj, M.; Kruschwitz, U.; Fox, C. Using mechanical Turk to create a corpus of Arabic summaries. In Proceedings of the Language Resources (LRs) and Human Language Technologies (HLT) for Semitic Languages workshop held in conjunction with the 7th International Language Resources and Evaluation Conference (LREC 2010), Valletta, Malta, 17 May 2010; pp. 36–39.

35. Napoles, C.; Gormley, M.; Van Durme, B. Annotated gigaword. In Proceedings of the Joint Workshop on Automatic Knowledge Base Construction and Web-Scale Knowledge Extraction, Montreal, QC, Canada, 7–8 June 2012; Association for Computational Linguistics: Stroudsburg, PL, USA, 2012; pp. 95–100.

36. Hovy, E.; Lin, C.Y.; Zhou, L. Evaluating duc 2005 using basic elements. In Proceedings of the DUC, Sydney, Australia, 9–10 October 2005; Citeseer: Princeton, NJ, USA, 2005; Volume 2005.

37. Steinberger, J.; Ježek, K. Evaluation measures for text summarization. *Comput. Inform.* **2012**, *28*, 251–275.

38. Mikolov, T.; Chen, K.; Corrado, G.S.; Dean, J.A. Computing Numeric Representations of Words in a High-Dimensional Space. U.S. Patent 9,037,464, 22 August 2017.

39. Suleiman, D.; Awajan, A. Comparative Study of Word Embeddings Models and Their Usage in Arabic Language Applications. In Proceedings of the 2018 International Arab Conference on Information Technology (ACIT), Werdanye, Lebanon, 28–30 November 2018; IEEE: Piscataway, NJ, USA, 2018; pp. 1–7.

40. Alayba, A.M.; Palade, V.; England, M.; Iqbal, R. Improving Sentiment Analysis in Arabic Using Word Representation. In Proceedings of the 2018 IEEE 2nd International Workshop on Arabic and Derived Script Analysis and Recognition (ASAR), London, UK, 12–14 March 2018; IEEE: Piscataway, NJ, USA, 2018, pp. 13–18.

41. Suleiman, D.; Awajan, A.; Al-Madi, N. Deep Learning Based Technique for Plagiarism Detection in Arabic Texts. In Proceedings of the 2017 International Conference on New Trends in Computing Sciences (ICTCS), Amman, Jordan, 11–13 October 2017; IEEE: Piscataway, NJ, USA, 2017; pp. 216–222.

42. Barbedo, J.G.A. Impact of dataset size and variety on the effectiveness of deep learning and transfer learning for plant disease classification. *Comput. Electron. Agric.* **2018**, *153*, 46–53. [CrossRef]

43. Foody, G.; Mcculloch, M.B.; Yates, W.B. The effect of training set size and composition on artificial neural network classification. *Int. J. Remote Sens.* **1995**, *16*, 1707–1723. [CrossRef]

 *mathematics*

Review

Sensor-Based Prognostic Health Management of Advanced Driver Assistance System for Autonomous Vehicles: A Recent Survey

Izaz Raouf [1], Asif Khan [2], Salman Khalid [1], Muhammad Sohail [1], Muhammad Muzammil Azad [1] and Heung Soo Kim [1,*]

[1] Department of Mechanical, Robotics and Energy Engineering, Dongguk University–Seoul, 30 Pildong-ro 1-gil, Jung-gu, Seoul 04620, Korea

[2] Faculty of Mechanical Engineering, Ghulam Ishaq Khan Institute of Engineering and Science and Technology, Topi, Swabi 23460, Khyber Pakhtunkhwa, Pakistan

* Correspondence: heungsoo@dgu.edu; Tel.: +82-2260-8577; Fax: +82-2-2263-9379

Abstract: Recently, the advanced driver assistance system (ADAS) of autonomous vehicles (AVs) has offered substantial benefits to drivers. Improvement of passenger safety is one of the key factors for evolving AVs. An automated system provided by the ADAS in autonomous vehicles is a salient feature for passenger safety in modern vehicles. With an increasing number of electronic control units and a combination of multiple sensors, there are now sufficient computing aptitudes in the car to support ADAS deployment. An ADAS is composed of various sensors: radio detection and ranging (RADAR), cameras, ultrasonic sensors, and LiDAR. However, continual use of multiple sensors and actuators of the ADAS can lead to failure of AV sensors. Thus, prognostic health management (PHM) of ADAS is important for smooth and continuous operation of AVs. The PHM of AVs has recently been introduced and is still progressing. There is a lack of surveys available related to sensor-based PHM of AVs in the literature. Therefore, the objective of the current study was to identify sensor-based PHM, emphasizing different fault identification and isolation (FDI) techniques with challenges and gaps existing in this field.

Keywords: autonomous vehicle; prognostic health management; sensor-based fault detection; data-driven approaches; perception sensors

MSC: 68T01

Citation: Raouf, I.; Khan, A.; Khalid, S.; Sohail, M.; Azad, M.M.; Kim, H.S. Sensor-Based Prognostic Health Management of Advanced Driver Assistance System for Autonomous Vehicles: A Recent Survey. *Mathematics* **2022**, *10*, 3233. https://doi.org/10.3390/math10183233

Academic Editors: Xiang Li, Shuo Zhang and Wei Zhang

Received: 11 August 2022
Accepted: 3 September 2022
Published: 6 September 2022

Publisher's Note: MDPI stays neutral with regard to jurisdictional claims in published maps and institutional affiliations.

1. Introduction

Recently, automation in the automobile industry has been evolving with significant development. Autonomous vehicles (AVs) with advanced driver assistance systems (ADASs) provide significant benefits to drivers, while also providing new transportation use scenarios and implementations [1]. Localization, perception, planning, vehicle control, and system management are the five fundamental capabilities for AVs to drive without human involvement. The ADAS system of AVs is the electronic system that executes the driving operations [2]. The automation offered by ADAS to AVs is a significant feature for the safety of the modern vehicle. The demand for the ADAS system is increasing daily, because of its intelligent safety development toward customer requirements [3]. Over the years, various researchers have identified safety-related issues in AV technology [4]. For example, Yu and Biswas [5] proposed a unique dedicated short-range communication (DSRC)-based medium access control (MAC) framework for intervehicle communication (IVC). Furthermore, the distributed power control method is suggested to control a load of periodic messages on the channel [6]. Bi et al. [7] introduced a cross-layer broadcast protocol for efficient and dependable message delivery in IVC systems. Palazzi et al. [8]

proposed an innovative IVC framework that adjusts its features and functionality to deliver implementations efficiently. Tabatabaei et al. [9] improved simpler network topologies for simulation models by enhancing ray-tracing-derived wireless propagation models.

The ADAS is composed of various sensors. The primary purpose of these sensors is to improve the safety of passengers and the vehicle itself, which is the primary justification for developing AVs [10]. The AV localization consists of different sensors: vision sensors (cameras), LiDAR, RADAR, ultrasonic sensors, GPS/GNN, etc. [11,12]. These sensors of the ADAS system can be affected by various malfunctions that lead to the failure of these components. For instance, camera quality can be affected by multiple factors, such as lens occlusion or soiling, environmental and weather conditions, optical faults, and visibility distance [13]. Similarly, LiDAR failure occurs due to read position data, short-circuit and overvoltage, misalignment of the optical receiver, and fault in the optical filter mirror motor [14]. In addition, various reasons have been listed that have led to RADAR failures, such as cyberattack [15] and environmental conditions [16]. Ultrasonic sensor performance can be degraded via vehicle corner error [16], temperature variation and relative humidity [17], false echoes caused by turbulence [18], and acoustic or electric noise [19]. Faults in GPS/GNN occur due to anomalies in different segments of the positioning sensors, i.e., receiver malfunction in the user segment, clock anomalies in the space segment, and satellite broadcast anomalies due to the control segment [20].

Sensor-based PHM in AV technology is indeed evolving, and different studies world-wide are proposing their ideas. Recently, different researchers have proposed various PHM strategies employing sensor-based fault detection. Mori et al. [21] presented a Kalman filter-based FDI for various sensors, including camera sensors. Tadjine et al. [22] proposed a self-diagnosis approach for a camera-based ADAS system to identify and assess these visual warnings. Duran et al. [14] enlisted various kinds of faults in the LiDAR system, along with the severity level of fault occurrence in any particular component of the LiDAR system. In addition, signal processing challenges were described for the RADAR in AVs to justify the updated integration and technology trends [23]. Park et al. [24] proposed a multi-sliding mode observer for the fault detection of the sensor to ensure the longitudinal control of the AVs. Similarly, Oh and Yi [25] proposed a sliding mode algorithm for the fault detection of AV sensors. Lyu et al. [26] proposed fault prediction based on reliability data, prediction parameter monitoring, cumulative damage model, and early warning in a RADAR system as a function of the system's physical characteristics. Lim et al. [27] highlighted some of the undesirable situations of ultrasonic sensors. The transducer of the ultrasonic sensor was modified to minimize the width of the beam [28]. The multiple echo signal processing method was applied to reduce vehicle corner error [16]. In addition, Changle Li et al. [29] classified GPS errors into three main categories: GPS satellites, signal propagation, and error at the end of the receiver.

This paper provides comprehensive insight into the development and future research possibilities of sensor-based PHM systems in AV technology. PHM for AV technology is still evolving with multiple research scopes. However, grasping the overall shape of technology and its trajectory is extremely difficult. The majority of studies defined problems in a very narrow range, with several limitations. However, this is the very first attempt to review the overall sensor-based PHM for AVs. AVs are composed of different sensors such as RADAR, cameras, ultrasonic sensors, and LiDAR. The impacts of sensor malfunctioning and sensor uncertainty on the PHM are described. In the present paper, the abovementioned sensors are summarized in detail along with the fault-detection approaches associated with ADAS. Furthermore, the issues associated with the PHM of AVs are highlighted. This paper also covers the safety concerns of AV technology and future industry trends for further developments. This review is divided into three different sections. Section 2 provides an overview of PHM, AVs, and faults associated with sensors. In Section 3, different PHM approaches for different sensors of ADAS for AVS are discussed. Section 4 summarizes the limitations/challenges in the field of AVs and sensor-based PHM for AVs.

2. Overview of PHM, ADAS in AVs, and Sensor Faults

2.1. Overview of PHM Technology

PHM was used for the first time in the 1990s during the Joint Strike Fighter (JSF) project by the US army. PHM provides tangible tools to facilitate carrying out necessary decisions in a timely manner. The PHM cycle is composed of eight steps as shown in Figure 1 and Table 1. Initially, a physical sensor is used to sense soft system performance attributes in the form of a variable of the system. Afterward, sensor data are collected from the system using a data acquisition system such as an internal monitor, data bus, or PC. In the data manipulation state, the data preprocessing techniques can be acquired. In the state of detection, whether the system is normal or abnormal can be proposed on the basis of system condition indicators. In the health assessment state, a set of information can be presented to acquire the state of health (SOH) of the system. The prognostic assessment gives future SOH and remaining useful life (RUL) prediction [30,31]. The advisory generation function gives applicability to operate and repair the system. The final stage of health management uses information for advisory generation when the system is unable to operate normally (healthy state). Prognostic assessment is considered the most critical step in the PHM process where the RUL of the system can be predicted on the basis of available data and current operational condition.

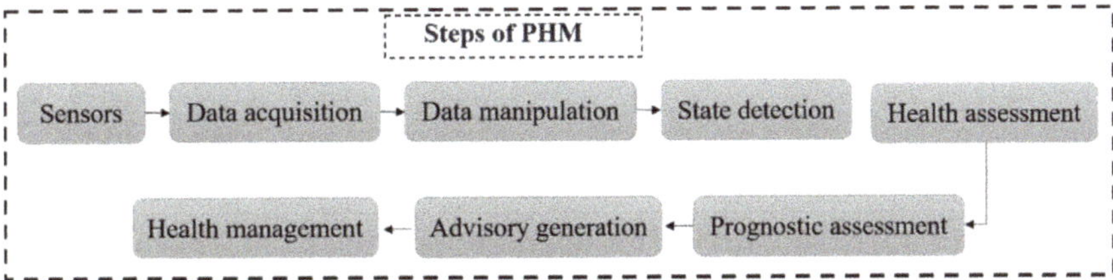

Figure 1. Steps involved in the prognostic health management (PHM) process.

2.2. Autonomous Vehicle and Advanced Driver Assistance System

Recently, autonomous vehicles have gained public interest due to their potential for enhancing road traffic productivity and capability. The advanced driver assistance system (ADAS) is the electronic system that controls driving and parking operations [32]. The automated system provided by ADAS to autonomous vehicles is a prominent characteristic for protecting the modern automobile. The safety systems are categorized into two classes of passive and active. Passive safety systems protect vehicle occupants from injuries during and after a crash, e.g., airbags, padded dashboards, and seat belts. At the same time, the active system includes various features, such as lane keeping, automatic braking, and adaptive cruise control [33]. Due to the growing client demand for smart safety systems, some of the critical purposes for manufacturers involve developing the ADAS. Moreover, with the increasing number of electronic control units and the combination of multiple sensors, there are now sufficient computing aptitudes in the car to support ADAS deployments. Various sensors enable various ADAS solutions, such as RADAR, cameras, ultrasonic sensors, and LiDAR. The vision-based ADAS, which principally manages cameras as vision sensors, is prevalent in the modern automobile [34]. Figure 2 shows the locations of various sensors in AVs. Figure 3 shows the proposed taxonomy of the ADAS based on the model of sensors used. The vision system is composed of various cameras such as monocular, stereo, and infrared cameras. The RADAR can be long-, short-, or medium-range.

2.3. Sensor Malfunctioning in AVs

A fault is an undesirable deviation from the normal state of a system's characteristic, property, or parameter [36,37]. The fault can be categorized into sensor, actuator, and component-level faults [38]. While the sensor fault focuses more on input module problems, the actuator faults focus on output module concerns. Furthermore, the sensor fault is categorized into hard and soft faults [39]. In hard faults, the sensor data abruptly shift from the usual situation to a faulty one; complex faults appear in stepwise format. In contrast, soft faults occur as slow degradations in the sensor output with respect to time. Soft faults are more difficult to detect and eliminate, because sensor data take time to leave a confidence limit. In addition, component or process faults occur in the complete module of the system. For the AV, the fault is usually caused because of the sensors. There are various faults in the sensors, such as a faulty transmitter or receiver, or a fault in the processing system. On the other hand, scratches, cracks, holes, and sensor covers are considered mechanical faults. A film on the sensor cover, such as water, ice, dust, snow, or salt, can prevent objects from being detected (false negatives), from being seen (false positives), or from being correctly classified [40,41]. In addition, inaccurate data injection by another active electromagnetic source leads the system to an electronic hack via a wired or wireless connection to the sensor [42]. Furthermore, when exposed to unfavorable environmental conditions, the perception sensor holds constraints that reduce the field of view. Crosstalk from other active perception sensors may cause a fault in the sensor. Figure 4 shows various faults associated with sensors [43].

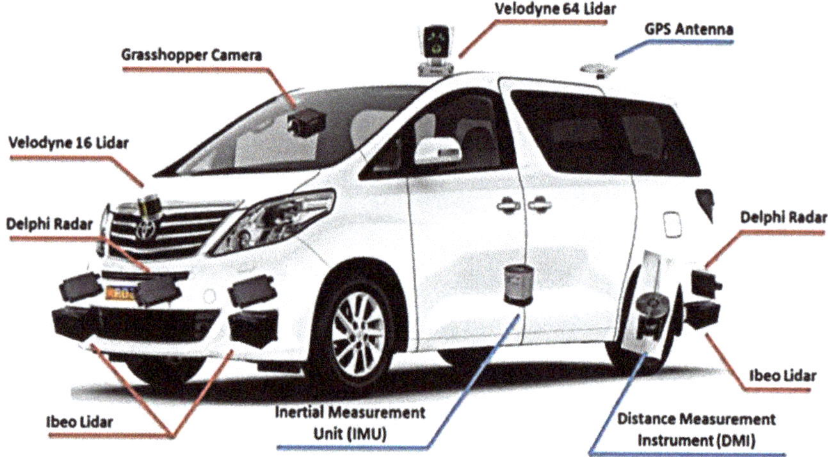

Figure 2. Demonstrations of various sensors in an autonomous vehicle (AV) [35].

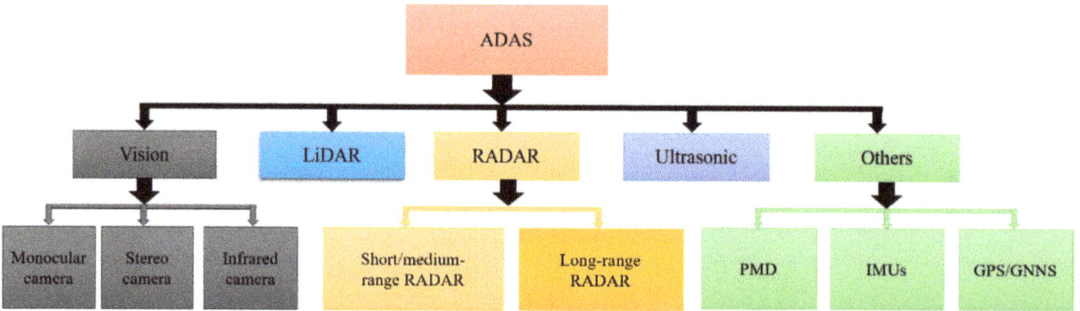

Figure 3. Taxonomy of advanced driver assistance systems (ADASs) based on the model of sensors.

Fault diagnosis consists of three steps: fault detection, fault isolation, and fault identification. Hence, sensor fault detection and isolation (FDI) for the localization system of autonomous vehicles is one of the most critical tasks. Localization systems consist of external sensors such as camera systems (vision), LiDAR, RADAR, ultrasonic sensor, and global navigation satellite systems, which are significantly affected by weather conditions and geographic variances [44]. Various faults, such as erratic, spike, hard-over, and stuck are examples of sensor faults [45]. Even if the sensor is fully functioning, it is critical to detect the performance degradation of various components. Hence, fault detection of the multiple sensors without prior knowledge is one of the most significant tasks for the safety of autonomous cars. Furthermore, preventive maintenance is an effective practice for reducing the sensor failure rate [46]. The next section comprehensively summarizes the PHM of ADAS sensors.

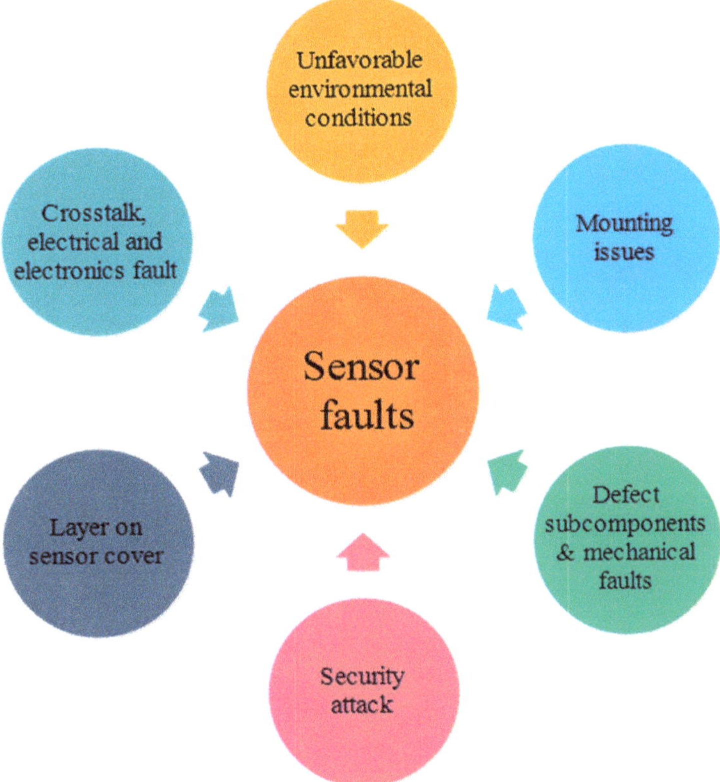

Figure 4. Demonstration of various sensor faults.

2.4. Sensors Uncertainty and PHM

PHM requires a high-performance sensor system to determine the health monitoring of the system and maintain a certain level of uncertainty. In a previous study [47], the various sources of prognostic uncertainties were investigated, and it was discovered that measurement inaccuracy by the sensor system is one of the primary sources of uncertainty in PHM applications. Recognizing the performance characteristics of different sensors can assist in identifying the degree of uncertainty induced by different sensors and in adjusting the uncertainty of the PHM implementation. Failed sensor systems generate inaccurate or incomplete data, causing PHM to generate incorrect detections and estimations. The adverse effects on PHM can be more serious if the sensor system is used to measure a vital attribute or is installed in a restricted access position. The reliability of the sensors reflects the ability of a sensor system to perform an essential role under defined conditions for a specific duration. Nevertheless, sensor system manufacturers very seldom describe reliability information such as the mean time between failures (MTBF) and failure rate under specific environmental and operating conditions. However, the reliability of the sensors can be improved by using numerous sensors (redundancy) for monitoring the same system. As a result, the probability of data loss due to sensor system uncertainty is reduced. Several other techniques, such as sensor validation, can improve sensor reliability. Sensor validation is used to evaluate the authenticity of a sensor system and adjust or correct it as needed [48]. This operation examines signal quality and ensures that the sensor system is operating properly by detecting and eliminating the impact of systematic errors. When choosing a sensor system, the client can also look at whether it includes validation capabilities [49].

3. Sensor-Based PHM for ADAS System

In this section, various kinds of ADAS sensors are introduced according to the working principles. Various faults associated with different sensors such as cameras, RADAR, ultrasonic sensors, and LiDAR are highlighted. Furthermore, various PHM techniques are described for aforementioned sensors with fault types, techniques, and consequences. Lastly, the challenges related to each sensor are mentioned.

3.1. PHM of Vision Sensors

The vision-based ADAS relies on images from the cameras and uses computer vision systems to obtain essential information. This system includes various cameras, such as monocular, stereo, and infrared cameras. Figure 5 shows the workflow of the vision system. Firstly, in image acquisition, a frame is captured from videos, consisting of pixel data and three-channel information, such as red, green, and blue (RGB) sets of pixels. Secondly, preprocessing consists of denoising, color improvement, color space transformation, and image stabilization. The features are then separated in the segmentation process that helps divide these features into various recognizable objects, such as road, footpath, crosswalk, and sky. The method of classifying an object in an image, e.g., an object ahead of a vehicle or any obstacle, can be determined in object detection. Depth estimation estimates the distance of an object relative to the camera. Lastly, the control system interprets the vision data from the previous layers.

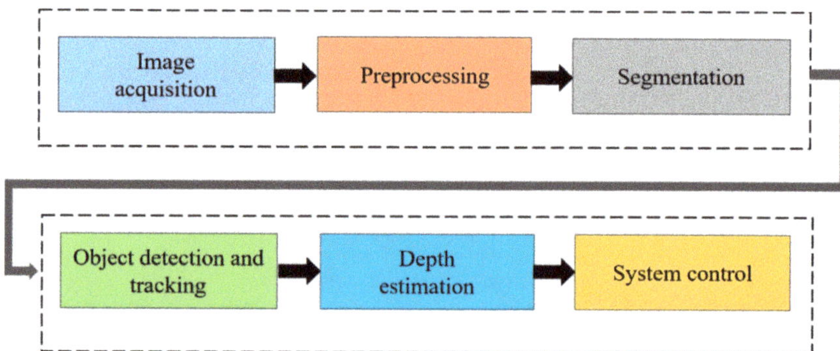

Figure 5. Vision data flow of an advanced driver assistance system (ADAS).

Through the adoption of a camera-based ADAS system, handy opportunities have evolved to support autonomous driving systems. Figure 6 shows object detection of the camera images infused with LiDAR mapping for AV applications. The in-vehicle multi-purpose cameras and exterior fish-eye parking cameras assist in extending the knowledge of drivers in several circumstances, such as identifying pedestrians, other cars, and road signs or generating a bird's-eye view. In addition to the ability to visualize, human visual perception is constricted by visibility conditions. However, in actual scenarios, various conditions influence the degradations of camera sightedness. Camera quality can be affected by multiple factors, such as lens occlusion or soiling, environmental and weather conditions, optical faults, sensor faults, and visibility distance. Hence, these factors affect the camera performance via blocking, blurring, range reduction, or misalignment of view. Table 1 summarizes various kinds of faults and factors that influence the visual system.

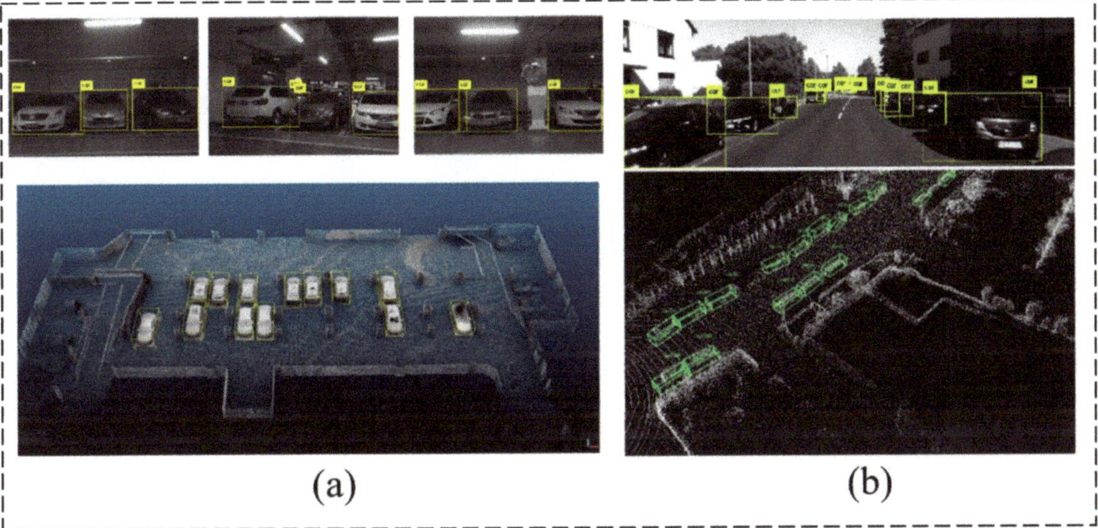

Figure 6. Object detection via camera and LiDAR infusion for an autonomous vehicle (AV) using simultaneous localization and mapping (SLAM) technique: (**a**) 2D object detection; (**b**) 3D object detection [50].

Table 1. Demonstration of the various factors that influence the performance of cameras [51].

S. No	Camera Faults	Detailed Description of Camera Malfunctioning
1	Lens occlusion or soiling	Covering of the lens by solid or fluid
2	Weather condition	Rain/snow Icing of camera Fogging of camera
3	Environmental condition	Time (dawn or dust) Crossing by tunnel or over a bridge Inner-city roads or motorways
4	Optical faults	Lens occupied by dust Lens loss Interior fogging Damage or stone impact of the lens
5	Sensor faults	Smear Image element defect (black or white marks) Thermal disturbance
6	Visibility distance	Range of distance to detect a clear image

Tremendous research work has been carried out to perform the FDI of AV camera sensors. For that purpose, various FDI techniques are utilized for AV sensor fault detection. Table 2 demonstrates various kinds of faults for the camera of the AV and the FDI techniques, along with the advantages of the proposed techniques. Kalman filter is one of the leading-edge techniques that can be used for FDI using multiple sensor data. Each Kalman filter is designed on the basis of a specific hypothesis for detecting a particular sensor fault. The state covariance matrix estimated from each filter can be compared for FDI analysis of sensors [52,53]. Mori et al. [21] presented a Kalman filter-based FDI for various sensors, including camera sensors. The sensor data are affected by multiple factors, such as climate, humidity, smog and fog, topography, and even network communications. In the proposed methodology, to tackle these issues, sensors filters are evaluated by Hoteling's test to obtain the outcomes and their covariance. Hence, the FDI of the sensor is assessed by correlating the generated within the sensor. In another study, the Kalman filter and discrete wavelet transform were proposed as rain removal algorithms using the You Only Look Once (YOLOv3) methodology for the camera FDI of AVs [54]. Realpe et al. [55] proposed a sensor fusion framework that integrates data from a unified configuration with sensor weight provided in a real-time FDI using the SVM algorithm to reduce the impact of sensor faults. Although Google, GM, BMW, and Tesla are trying and testing various AVs, multiple issues, such as bugs in traditional software, are a challenging task to fix, when compared with the DNN-based software [56]. Hence, DeepTest-based algorithms are implemented to detect the erroneous behavior that leads to fatal crashes. The presented study automatically generated test cases on the basis of real-world variations in driving states, such as lighting, fog, and rain. Tadjine et al. [22] presented a self-diagnosis approach for a camera-based ADAS system that identifies and assess these visual warnings. To overcome the camera failures because of the weather conditions, such as heavy rain and snow, Sprinnker et al. [57] presented a camera-based fog detection mechanism by analyzing the power spectrum slope (PSS) of a small image frame near the vanishing point, resulting in quick differentiation of fog-free and fog-filled street scenes.

Table 2. Demonstration of fault types and prognostic health management (PHM) analysis for an autonomous vehicle (AV) camera.

Fault Type	Technique	Advantages
Noise in sensor data due to weather or geographical changes [21]	Unscented Kalman filter	Decreasing computational cost
Displacements in sensor data [55]	Support vector machine (SVM) algorithm	Reducing uncertainties using sensor fusion
Sensor data due to various environmental conditions (rain, fog, lighting) [58]	Deep neural network (DNN) driven	Reducing software complexities using DNN-based model
Camera-based fog detection [57]	Power spectrum slope	Self-diagnosis mechanism to warn the system against critical conditions
Possible defects (blooming, smear, picture element defects, thermal noise) [22]	Edge analysis of consecutive frames	Proposed techniques work under diverse weather conditions
Misalignment [14]	Bayesian belief network approach	The presented model shows good performance and overall navigation can predict accurately

3.2. PHM of Light Detection and Ranging (LiDAR) Sensor

The LiDAR system combined with the vision system can be used as a fundamental technology for the optical system of AVs. Automotive LiDAR sensors are supposed to perform blind-spot monitoring, pedestrian identification, obstacle detection [35], and landscape mapping [59] to ensure reliability and safety during driving operations. LiDAR sensors are currently being used by various companies, such as Google [60], BMW, and Volvo [61], to develop autonomous vehicles. Figure 7 shows the application of the LiDAR sensor in a real driving environment [62]. Usually, the LiDAR unit comprises various parts: power regulator, receiver, lens filter, laser, rotating mirror, onboard processors, and position encoder. A complex aggregate of synchronizing hardware (including precision motors and position encoders) and onboard processing capabilities is used to detect motion. Despite being designed for outdoor use, advanced LiDAR systems are extremely precise, making the mechanical components and optics vulnerable to shock. It is critical to keep the device in a safe, strategic position around the vehicle at all times. LiDAR must be equipped in places with high ground clearance and few vehicle parts, to avoid possible obstruction of the field of view. To maintain the device, precautions should be taken. Device failure could be caused by foreign object impact, shock, or vibrations caused by crashes or rough terrain navigation. One of the most crucial components of the device is the LiDAR optical filter. Any damage to the filter will have a negative impact on the reliability of the measurements. To prevent or reduce effects and scratches from vegetation, the LiDAR filter should be protected with a shroud. Table 3 lists the various LiDAR subsystem fault conditions and hazards [14].

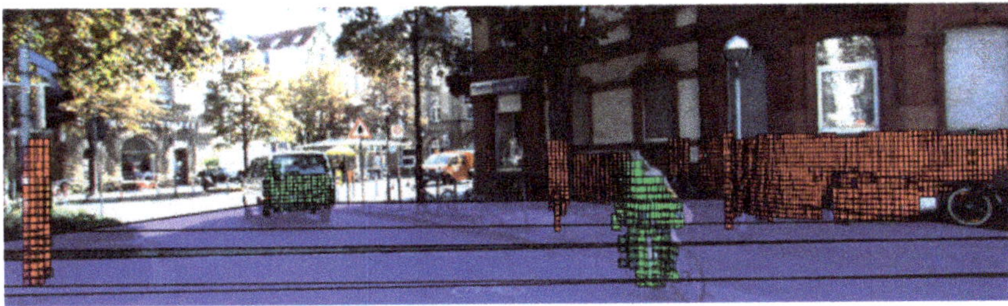

Figure 7. Demonstration of LiDAR application in a real environment for an autonomous vehicle (AV). The mapping of various object is identified (blue color represents the plane up to a certain extent; red color represents a static object; green color indicates a moving object) [62].

Table 3. Possible faults of light detection and ranging (LiDAR) sensor and their impact [14].

Subsystem of LiDAR	Fault Conditions	Hazards
Position encoder	Failure to read position data	Malfunction of mirror motor
Electrical	Short-circuit and overvoltage	Electrical component failure
Optical receiver	Misalignment	Error in the optical receiver
Optical filter	Damage	Error in the optical receiver
Mirror motor	Malfunction	LiDAR failure

Table 4 shows the research work carried out for LiDAR technology PHM. It is divided into various categories, such as fault, FDI, and sensor recovery. The proposed drafts of fault categories and, notably, typical faults are by no means exhaustive. Nevertheless, they are intended to incorporate all significant issues that must be addressed to progress to the next level of reliable environment perception. Adverse climatic circumstances have been intensively studied for LiDAR sensors outside of our specified fault classes, primarily due to their frequency and significant influence on LiDAR perceptual theory. Faults can be categorized according to the underlying science in an alternative classification method. This could allow for standardized fault detection, isolation, and recovery techniques across fault classification. Comprehensive research work has been reviewed for fault detection, isolation, and recovery for LiDAR used as an automotive perception sensor [43]. Scattering and multiple scattering methods can be used for various faults caused by rain, smoke, snow, dust, or fog. More explicitly, the pertinent interpretation is evaluated by the particle size-to-laser wavelength relationship. The wavelength varies in the range 0.8–1.5 μm according to the laser source. Mie scattering can be applied if the particle is of a similar size to the wavelength [43]. Rayleigh scattering is to be applied when the particle is much smaller than the laser wavelength. Alternatively, non-scattering and absorption formulations are appropriate unless the particle is much larger than the wavelength, as in the case of hail. Scattering and absorption are essential not just for precipitation, but primarily for sensor protector issues. In sensor FDI, the residuals between the sensor output and various sources are correlated. In the next paragraph, various FDI techniques are presented for the LiDAR of the AV. In the recovery class, various parameters, such as software, hardware, and temperature, are adjusted according to the specification of the manufacturer.

Table 4. Details of light detection and ranging (LiDAR) prognostic health management (PHM).

PHM Category	Description/References
Fault category	Subcomponent failure [63,64] Mechanical fault of the sensor protector [65] Coating on the sensor protector [65,66] Escalating problem [67,68] Security breach [69–71] Adverse climatic circumstance [65,71] Intermodulation distortion [72,73]
FDI category	Correlation with sensor framework [43] Output of the monitoring sensor [63] Correlation to passive ground truth [43] Correlation to active ground truth [43] Correlation to another similar sensor [43] Correlation to another and different sensor [43] Matching of various interfaces [43]
Recovery category	Software adjustment [74] Hardware adjustment [67] Temperature adjustment [75] Mopping of sensor shield [75]

The PHM for the LiDAR of the AVs is an underdeveloped field; however, various researchers have recently been trying to develop various algorithms for the LiDAR PHM to avoid road accidents. Table 5 summarizes research work carried out for the LiDAR PHM. For example, Mori et al. [21] presented a model based on Student's *t*-distribution using the Kalman filter that correlates the data within the sensor for accurate FDI analysis. Simulation and an experiment on a highway scenario confirm the robustness and accuracy of the localization and measurement noise estimation. The Velodyne LiDAR sensor allows a file containing correction factors for the alignment of the data collected by its lasers to resolve statistical anomalies (biases) in sensor readings. On the other hand, in practice, those parameters are not very specific. For example, even after applying Velodyne's correction factors and distance offset calibrated using readings from another reference LiDAR sensor, points with uncertainties of the order of 30 cm were noted [76]. A sensor fusion design that utilizes a support vector machine (SVM) technique to integrate data from a federalized fusion framework with sensor weight feedback data provided in real-time by the fault detection and diagnosis module was used to reduce the impact of sensor faults [55]. Duran et al. [14] enlisted various kinds of faults in the LiDAR system, along with the severity level of fault occurrence in any particular component of the LiDAR system. The Bayesian belief network (BBN) algorithm was proposed to incorporate a predictive safety system.

Table 5. Demonstration of fault types and prognostic health management (PHM) analysis for the light detection and ranging (LiDAR).

Fault Type	Technique
Noise in data due to weather condition [21]	Unscented Kalman filter
Displacements in sensor data [55]	Support vector machine (SVM) algorithm
Various faults (failure to read data, short-circuit, overvoltage, or misalignment) [14]	Bayesian belief network approach
Sensor data due to various environmental conditions (rain, fog, or lighting) [58]	Deep neural network driven

3.3. Radio Detection and Ranging (RADAR)

Radio detection and ranging (RADAR) radiates radio waves to be reflected by an obstacle, and then measures the signal runtime; it is used to approximate the object's radial velocity with the help of the Doppler effect phenomenon. RADARs are robust against several lighting and weather conditions; however, due to the poor resolution of RADAR, it is challenging to categorize objects. RADAR sensors can operate at a number of frequencies. Nevertheless, vehicular applications appear to be standardizing on 24 and 77 GHz, with a few very-short-range sensors operating at 5.8 or 10.5 GHz [77]. They are often used in adaptive cruise control (ACC), in traffic jam assistance systems, and to assess distance and angle information about traffic objects [78,79]. The RADAR system's operating mechanism is that it emits radio waves and collects echoes reflected off the objects.

RADAR is more economical than LiDAR and cameras, yet it can accurately estimate target range and velocity effectively. Modern RADARs both observe the target and measure distances, and they have the potential to locate, image, and identify targets [80]. As a result, the prime purpose of the RADAR in autonomous driving is the replacement of human driver vision, providing consistent, reliable information on a moving vehicle's surroundings to enable a prompt response in constantly changing circumstances, as well as threats to and from the driven vehicle. The RADAR sensor is usually the most common in the ADAS accommodated in modern road vehicles. These systems are devised to provide different cruise control functions, as well as collision detection. These sensors can also detect the relative velocity of detected targets [81]. However, the main obstacle for the automotive RADAR system is to yield high-resolution information in an environment that incorporates several dynamic objects in an immensely clustered automotive scene with a high update rate [82,83]. Figure 8 presents a typical situation as an example of pedestrian and AV RADAR.

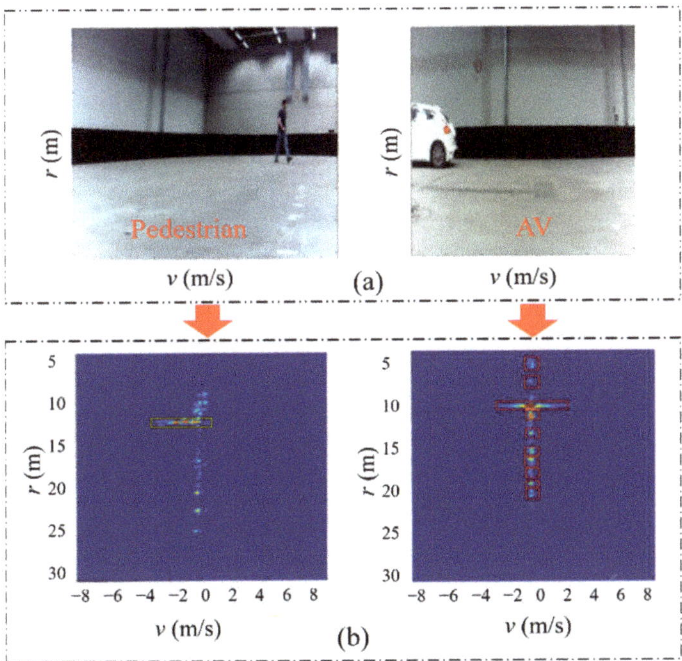

Figure 8. Demonstration of a particular scenario of a pedestrian and a moving autonomous vehicle (AV). (**a**) Digital images; (**b**) RADAR information of the scene using support vector machine (SVM) and multi-objective optimization [84].

The RADAR sensor is used to measure information regarding the environment, and internal AV sensors measure acceleration, velocity, and position; the steering angle of autonomous vehicles and their speed are then evaluated on the basis of these parameters [85]. For example, a Mercedes-Benz S-Class vehicle equipped with almost six RADAR sensors was introduced in 2013, almost covering the complete 360° angular near and far range of the environment on each side of the vehicle. In normal traffic, the vehicle can cover almost 100 km, totally autonomously, from Mannheim to Pforzheim, Germany [86]. However, if sensors fail due to some fault, the autonomous vehicle cannot manage steering angle and speed adequately, resulting in catastrophic accidents. As a result, several studies on fault detection, isolation, and tolerance control have been carried out. The reliability of the RADAR system depends on the exploration of well-grounded approaches to detect faults, such as communication between vehicles, the geographical database of predefined roadside RADAR targets, the recognition of abrupt failures with the help of fuzzy logic and knowledge of the vehicle acceleration abilities, and the use of an unnecessary sensor that is fairly inexpensive but of poor quality. An experimental study showed an inexpensive redundant sensor coupled with a specifically designed nonlinear filter to be the most reliable solution for RADAR health monitoring [87]. Even when intervehicle communication is not available in a realistic highway environment, this approach would still work effectively. Figure 9 demonstrates the semiautonomous adaptive cruise controller (ACC), where both a RADAR sensor and an intervehicle communication system are present. Therefore, an intelligent system must be able to keep track of the health condition of both the intervehicle communication channel and the RADAR sensor [88].

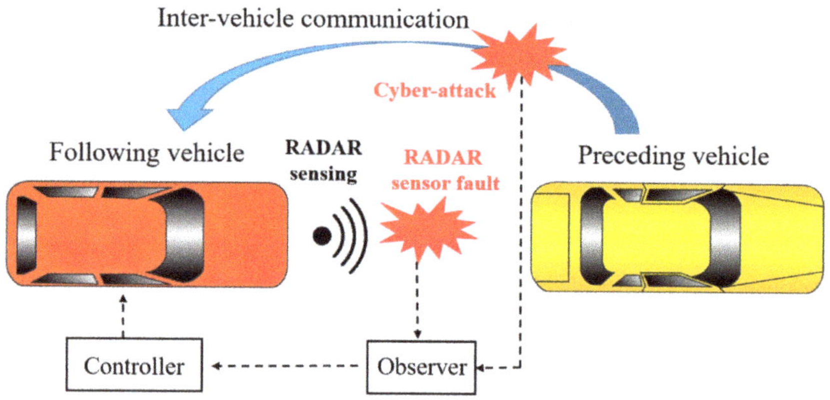

Figure 9. Fault diagnostics for radio detection and ranging (RADAR) and intervehicle communication system.

To prevent collisions and assure safety on the road, the automotive RADAR must be fault proof, and its reliability and performance should be tested repeatedly, which requires proper diagnostic of well-functioning RADAR, so that the AV may participate in traffic. Calibration in relevant service stations is one way to test the performance of automotive RADAR. In contrast to offline calibration in service stations, the other way to diagnose the adequate functioning of automotive RADAR would be by means of monitoring the state, i.e., the health of the RADAR in real time [89]. If any changes occur in the performance of RADAR unit components, the fault prediction of the RADAR system is used to monitor those changes. As a result, it should dynamically monitor and control impacts on the performance of RADAR unit components, identify and manage the occurrence and progression of the fault, and provide sufficient time and decision-making basis for fault prevention and clearance. It should also be able to forecast the state of the RADAR in the future, determine the remaining life, plan maintenance, and ensure supply. Fault prediction based on reliability data, prediction parameter monitoring, cumulative damage model, and early warning circuit are some of the methods used to predict faults on the basis of the physical characteristics of RADAR [26]. Eventually, the objective of RADAR system PHM is to coordinate and rationally deploy maintenance support resources, as well as automatically develop and implement the maintenance strategy. Table 6 describes the research work that outlines the faults in RADAR and strategies utilized by various researchers to resolve them in the AV.

Table 6. Demonstration of radio detection and ranging (RADAR) fault types and the fault detection mechanism.

Fault/Problem	Technique	Consequence
Probabilistic fault for an acceleration sensor and RADAR [90]	A longitudinal kinematic model-based probabilistic fault detection and diagnostic algorithm	Unsafe longitudinal control of the AV
Fault in the range rate signal (mobility of vehicle) [87]	Redundant sensor combined with a specially designed nonlinear filter	Continuously monitors the RADAR sensor, and detects a failure when it happens
Acceleration sensor fault diagnosis [25]	Using a sliding mode observer, a probabilistic fault diagnosis algorithm is developed	Inaccurate relative displacement and velocity measurement
Fault in the sensor used for longitudinal control [91]	Multi-sliding mode observer-based predictive fault detection algorithm	Faulty measurements from the environment sensors
Fault in the sensor used for longitudinal control [24]	Multi-sliding mode observer	Acceleration of the ego vehicles and inaccurate data from the forward objects
Continuous diagnostics of external factors, such as water layer or dirt on the bumper [16]	Statistical model for RADAR cross-section (RCS) of repetitive targets	Can significantly affect RADAR performance
A cyberattack on a transmission medium and RADAR health monitoring for a connected vehicle both happening at the same time [15]	Observer-based controller in connected ACC Vehicles	Detect a cyber-attack or a fault in the velocity measurement RADAR channel
Both RADAR sensor failure and cyber-attack linked to the presence of two unknown inputs [88]	Sensor fault detection and cyber-attack detection observer	Unsmooth operation of ACC vehicles
Signal processing of RADAR [23]	Multi-input multi-output and cognitive RADAR	Inaccurate detection of still or moving objects, and measurement of their motion parameters
RADAR fault signal reconstruction [92]	A failsafe architecture that focuses on fault reconstruction, detection, and tolerance control	Insecure functional safety of autonomous vehicle

3.4. Ultrasonic Sensors

An ultrasonic sensor (also called sonar) is a device that makes use of the echolocation phenomenon to determine if an object is in the domain of the sensor. Figure 10 depicts the typical ultrasonic echolocation of the sensor [27]. The ultrasonic sensor can also determine the target distance by tracing the time for a signal to return to the ultrasonic sensor after it has been emitted. On the other hand, ultrasonic sensors have interference due to noise and blind zones in close proximity, which can lead to inaccurate readings [27]. Materials with high sonic wave absorption coefficients and damping capabilities, such as acoustic foam, might also affect ultrasonic sensor readings [93].

Numerous AVs use ultrasonic sensors on the market to identify obstacles and aid in driving and parking. This section discusses the importance of ultrasonic sensors in giving comprehensive information about objects surrounding the vehicle. These sensors are mostly placed in vehicle bumpers, and operate at frequencies in the range 25–50 kHz [94]. They also provide additional useful information, such as the speed of the vehicle and the number of vehicles in a given distance [95]. However, they are highly sensitive to temperature and environment. Ultrasonic sensors are economical and have a straightforward installation method; they are extensively used in intelligent parking systems to locate available parking spaces [96–98]. Ultrasonic sensor-based autonomous vehicle detection and ZigBee-based communication between detection sensors were used to achieve the smart parking solution using a RabbitCore microcontroller by Idris et al. [99]. While entering and exiting the parking lot, they employed the shortest path algorithm to identify the closest parking place and exit position near the current car location. The Smart Parking System (SPS) needs specific directions to be followed by drivers in a certain way, and any deviation would lead toward failure. Another innovation is Park Assist, which utilizes an ultrasonic sensor to identify obstacles and find optimal steering angles for parking [100,101]. The information from the backup camera is combined with readings of the sensor to provide driver data about the parking. This distinct feature is only accessible when the vehicle is progressing at slow speed; despite this, there are typically secure mechanisms to prevent the wheel from overturning. Tesla has also merged such attributes in its vehicle, recognized as the Summon self-parking feature [102]. Similarly, the ultrasonic sensors were used by Kianpisheh et al. to locate vehicles in multilevel parking lots [95]. However, additional horizontal sensors installed on the walls of parking were used to spot inappropriate parking, and an alarm was triggered to report improper parking position to the driver. In this method, smart parking using three sensors was achieved; nevertheless, three sensors per parking place are not feasible, and more cost-effectiveness research studies should be carried out. Hence, to overcome the shortcomings of the existing method, Ma et al. proposed a multi-sensor-based parking space recognition method [103]. In this method, LiDAR is used to detect the edge points of parking spaces. A camera is also employed to extract the contours of parking spaces edges. In addition, it integrates the length of the library detected by the LiDAR with the contours of the parking space edges extracted from image, to decide whether the parking space matches the requirements. This technique can enhance parking space resources by identifying parking spots in more complex situations.

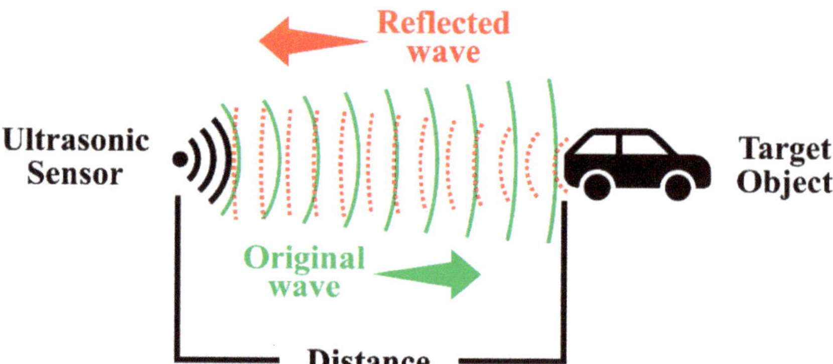

Figure 10. Echolocation used by ultrasonic sensors.

Although ultrasonic sensors have significantly contributed to the AV sector, fault detection and PHM of ultrasonic-based devices are very important to reduce severe roadside impacts. Lim et al. highlighted some of the undesirable situations of ultrasonic sensors [27]. The scenario involved blind-spot range, which is altered by the exposed exterior obstacle area; covering the ultrasonic transmitter and/or receiver can compromise the accuracy of detection. The specific target material may also cause inaccurate reading of the ultrasonic sensor, and sensor readings can be altered if any secondary sensor or sound wave device causes interference to the primary sensor output. Vehicle corner detection is another problem related to the ultrasonic sensor in AVs. To detect vehicle corners precisely, various designs are used. Two types of approaches are commonly employed to reduce the vehicle error of corner detection. In the first approach, the ultrasonic sensor's transducer is modified to minimize the width of the beam [28]. In the second approach, multiple echo signal processing methods are applied to reduce vehicle corner error [16]. Table 7 presents some other faults associated with ultrasonic sensors, along with their consequences.

Table 7. Demonstration of ultrasonic sensor fault types and their detection mechanism.

Fault/Problem	Techniques	Consequence
Acoustic and electronic noise [19]	Levenberg–Marquardt backpropagation artificial neural network (LMBP-ANN) architecture using mean squared error (MSE) and R-values	Major effect on ultrasonic sensor operation and distance measurements
Vehicle corner error [104]	Parallel parking assist system (PPAS)	The corners of the vehicle are not regular right angles; hence, the ultrasonic sensor has a large error at the corner of the vehicle during the measurement process
Vehicle corner error [16]	Combined ultrasonic sensors and three-dimensional vision sensors to detect parking spaces	This method uses a vision sensor to make up for the inaccurate measurement of the ultrasonic at the corner of the vehicle.
Performance degradation under bright ambient light [105]	Processing the data acquired by the three-dimensional time-of-flight (ToF) camera and reconstructing objects around the vehicle	Results in shadows and brightness in the image, which limits the detection of low-reflective objects, such as dark cars
Cross echoes (direction of sensor) [106]	Error detection model	Unreliable and non-robust sensor assessment
False echoes caused by turbulence [18]	Signal processing, such as filtering or Hilbert transform	Prevent vehicle collision with pedestrians and other obstacles
Fault, such as cross-eyed, dreaming, and blind sensor errors [107]	Fault detection based on Grid Map	Sensor calibration error
Simulated fault in the ultrasonic sensor [108]	Fault detection by statistical estimations	Inaccurate ultrasonic sensor-based parking operation
Obstacle avoidance [109]	Artificial neural network with supervised learning	Unsuitable classification and pattern recognition of data collected by an ultrasonic sensor
Obstacle detection and avoidance [110]	Policy-free, model-free Q-learning-based RLalgorithm with the multilayer perceptron neural network (MLP−NN)	Optimal vehicle future action based on the current state of the vehicle through better obstacle prediction

3.5. Positioning Sensors

Whether aerial, land, or sea-based, all kinds of autonomous vehicles require a positioning system to locate their position. The global navigation satellite system (GNSS) is the most widespread technology used for this purpose. The GNSS relies on satellites orbiting the Earth at approximately 20,000 km from the Earth's surface. The GNSS system emits a signal, and a receiver decodes this signal to extract the information of the receiver's position, time, and speed. The Global Positioning System (GPS) is the most common GNSS system freely available to be used in any part of the world [111]. In addition to GPS, other commonly available GNSSs are GLONASS, GALILEO, and BEIDOU. Each requires input signals from at least four of the 12 available GNSS satellites to provide an accurate 3D position (x, y, z) information, along with the time-of-flight between transmitter satellites and receiver [112,113]. Changle Li et al. classified GPS errors into three main categories: GPS satellites, signal propagation, and error at the receiver's end [29]. These categories were further elaborated by Sara et al. to monitor the GPS accuracy for AVs. In addition to the aforementioned errors, the refraction of the GPS signal in the atmospheric layer was mentioned to be a cause of error in GPS signal [114]. Figure 11 illustrates this phenomenon [114,115]. The same phenomenon was used by Catherine et al. for motion planning of AVs [115].

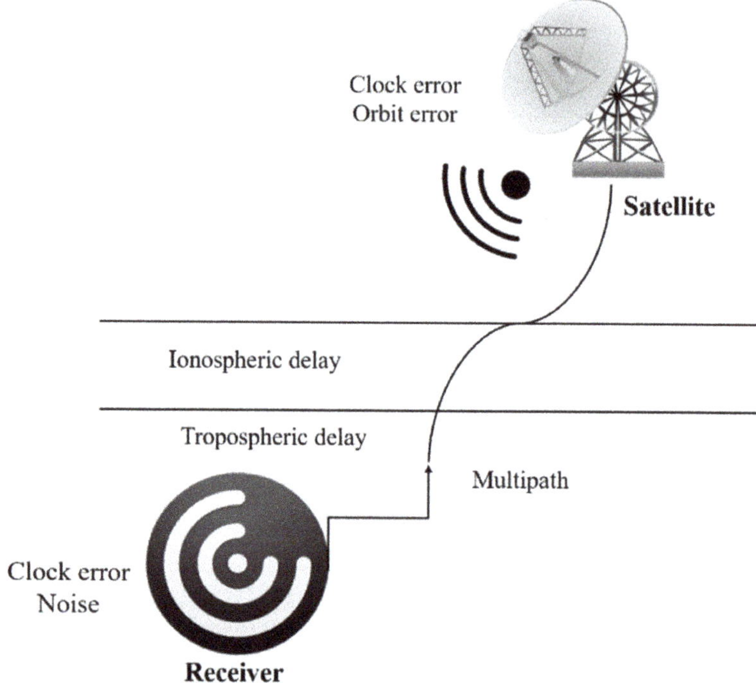

Figure 11. Principal Global Positioning System (GPS) errors.

Due to the involved damage in testing the developed GPS algorithms, researchers prefer applying their proposed methodologies on prototypes; for example, Wan Rahiman et al. tested their proposed algorithm on a prototype vehicle that reaches its destination in three steps, using input from GPS [116]. The major drawback of GPS for AVs is degradation in its accuracy when there is no direct line of sight between satellite (transmitter) and vehicle (receiver), e.g., inside a tunnel or near tall buildings [116]. Hence, during the past few decades, many researchers have tried adding other positioning systems and GPS to improve the AV's overall positioning accuracy. Kojima et al. used a laser system and GPS to track the positioning of a vehicle and determine its surrounding objects [117]. Elsewhere, Zein et al. applied a mechatronic system, which enabled the GPS tracking system to remember routes taken during supervised driving [118]. A positioning system developed by Quddus et al. relies on digital road map and machine vision to determine the surroundings to ensure vehicle safety [119].

Assessing the probability of GNSS satellite fault is a well-formulated framework in the context of autonomous applications. However, autonomous vehicles operate in unpredictable conditions, which leads to additional challenges [120]. Some of the major challenges described in [121] include static infrastructure, such as buildings and thick foliage, and dynamic obstacles, such as traffic and pedestrians. Various faults, such as satellite faults and received signal faults, have been identified for the GNSS system. Satellite faults [20] occur due to anomalies in different GNSS segments, i.e., receiver malfunction in the user segment, clock anomalies in the space segment, and satellite broadcast anomalies due to the control segment. Table 8 summarizes the different fault types and techniques of the GNSS.

Table 8. Summary of global navigation satellite system (GNSS) system fault detection and isolation.

Fault Type/Faulty Data	Technique	Advantages
Jumps in GPS observation and noise due to drift in state evaluation [122]	Kalman filter	Minimize chances of undetected faults
Disturbance in data due to various traffic (hazardous, risky, and safe events) [123]	Markov blanket (MB) algorithm	Evaluation of the proposed approach in real application of hazardous environmental situation
Injected error in the GPS sensor via log file [124]	Pseudo-code on inference algorithm	Robust model for timely fault detection and autonomous fault recovery system for sensors
Satellite and received signal faults [125]	Simultaneous localization and mapping (Graph-SLAM) framework	Applicability in AVs for urban areas
Sensor data with and without curbs on the roadsides [126]	Unscented Kalman filter (UKF)	Apply to urban areas by improving performance of previous methods for UKF
Sensor fault (current and voltage), environment (such as skidding, heating up, missing the trace) [127]	Sensor redundancy fault detection model	Evaluating the system in the real environment with experimental testing

In addition to the error due to the signal disappearance of GPS satellites, there can be other kinds of errors in the positioning of AVs. During the testing of positioning systems, most researchers prefer indoor or controlled environments. Bader et al. proposed a fault-tolerant approach in multi-sensor data fusion, relying on the duplication–comparison method. The value of their method was explained using a case study using real data and fault injection implemented with Kalman filter for the positioning of a mobile robot. Figure 12 describes the basic working of the proposed architecture. Here, the results of both fusion blocks are compared with each other. The deviation between the compared results indicates the presence of error in the system. Using the remaining values from fusion and output of the sensor, it can be determined whether the source of error is software- or hardware-based. In a case study, an actual vehicle was localized using the data from the accelerometer, gyrometer, and odometer, feeding them to a Kalman filter and taking data from another odometer and GPS, before providing them to another Kalman filter. Lastly, the fault tolerance of the considered vehicles was evaluated using experimental data and fault injection, and the objective of their work was presented in terms of fault detection and system recovery [128].

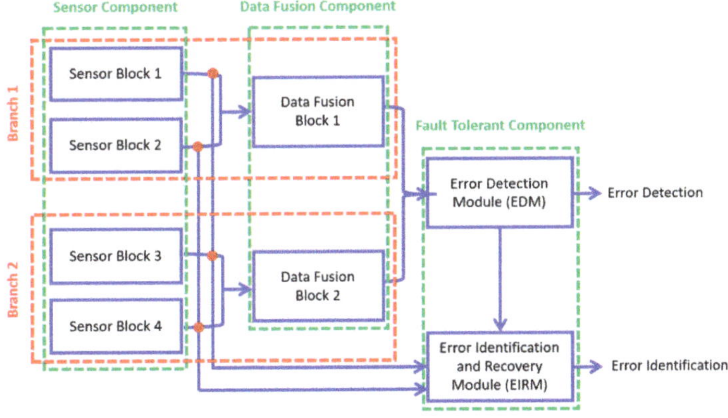

Figure 12. Duplication–comparison architecture for fault tolerance in multisensory perception.

Bijjahalli et al. [129] presented a hierarchical approach at a component level along with hybrid Bayesian networks for the detection of a fault in GPS sensors, particularly multipath or antenna masking problems for GPS. The proposed method deals with GPS issues, such as multipath of signal, complete loss of signal, and antenna masking. The modern world requirement of real-time positions, particularly with high accuracy, led to the emergence of the real-time kinematic GPS (RTK GPS) strategy because of its easy implementation and productivity. RTK GPS, like all GPS techniques, is susceptible to multipath errors. Notwithstanding, RTK GPS, like all GPS techniques, has imperfections and inconsistencies. A multipath error appears if GPS signals are reflected from the ground or other objects together around the receiver, likely to result in a systematic error in the simulation of the range between both the satellite and the receiver. The GPS monitor shown in Figure 13 takes care of the sensor's real-time kinematic (RTK) correction status, the number of active satellites, and the covariance of data provided by the sensor.

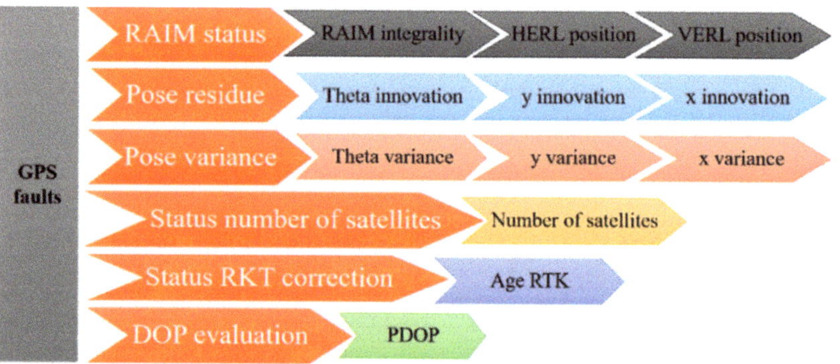

Figure 13. Global positioning system (GPS) diagnostic hybrid Bayesian network.

3.6. Discussion

The PHM process can be affected by variations in the domain such as car type, onboard sensor configurations, and sensor algorithms. To elaborate, it is one of the key challenges to developing a globalized PHM model that would be capable of working under various kinds of conditions such as different types of cars. Moreover, the PHM technology has a discrepancy in adaptation from the lab scale to the real environmental conditions. In view of that, the outside environmental conditions such as external interference and noise can affect the sensor data, which ultimately affects the PHM process. The generalization capabilities can be affected when applying the developed model from one type of AV to another. In addition, for an effective PHM model, the onboard sensor suites are key for real-time PHM analysis. However, some physical obstacles restrict the onboard processing for the PHM process. Firstly, if the processing requires extensive computation and high speeds, this would consume substantially more energy. Secondly, the availability of memory constraints, such as running complex software necessitates a significant amount of memory. Because of these two constraints, embedding complex algorithms into onboard processing units is a complicated task. Other constraints include access to the most suitable sensing regions due to limited sensing environments or uninhabitable or toxic surroundings. To sum up, these are the important issues when developing a PHM strategy for AV technology [49].

4. Challenges and Future Perspectives AVs and Its PHM

The autonomous vehicle is an underdeveloped technology, and extensive research potential exists to develop the AVs. Hence, various researchers are testing AV technology for real-world implementation. However, multiple challenges have been identified during the testing phases of the AVs. Table 9 shows some of the crashes during the testing phase. In addition, various issues are involved in the development phases of the AVs, such as environmental and traffic safety aspects, legal aspects, and moral and ethical aspects [130]. Knowledge of the environment continues to be the most challenging obstacle to dependable, smooth, and safe driving [131]. Customer acceptance, social and economic impacts, telecommunication, ethical considerations, planning, guidelines, and policy are just a few of the research questions that must be addressed [132]. Software concerns, such as system security and reliability, have also emerged as significant issues that need to be acknowledged. There are a series of policy implications and difficulties that policymakers have in optimizing and governing a diverse range of vehicles with varying operational limitations. Policymakers must also ensure that drivers are aware of the capabilities of these vehicles and can operate them safely. One of the challenges is connecting several smart cars to the facilities that require big data. This term refers to the processing and analysis of large datasets [133].

Table 9. Various accidents during the development of autonomous vehicle (AV) technology.

Type of Car	Reason/Consequence	Remarks
Hyundai autonomous car [134]	Raining/crashed during testing	The sensors failed to detect street signs, lane markings, and even pedestrian crossings due to the angle of the car switching in the rain, and the orientation of the sun.
Tesla autonomous car [135]	Image contrast/the driver was killed	Failure of camera and confusion of white truck with clear sky.
Google autonomous car [136]	Speed estimation failure/collision with bus while lane changing	The car assumed that the bus would stop while merging with the traffic.

As mentioned above, the PHM for AV technology is still progressing, with a wide range of research objectives. However, understanding the overall shape of technology and its trajectory is incredibly challenging. The majority of the work defines problems within a very narrow range, with numerous constraints. Most of the available literature could not cover the overall sensor assessment of the AVs, which is a complicated task in terms of data handling. Real-time PHM is needed for the AV technology under real environmental scenarios. Furthermore, it is a quite challenging task to develop a PHM system for the AV that works under different operating conditions. It is a complicated process to compensate for the lab-scale model in real environmental conditions because of the complex working conditions in real-time applications. The data collection system makes the working environment bulkier in actual scenarios. These are key issues to be addressed in a real-time PHM of AVs. AVs are composed of different kinds of sensors. Complementary data from various sensors can be used to compensate for individual sensor inaccuracies and operating ranges. As a result, the overall information is accurate over an extensive range. However, it is challenging to propose an FDI algorithm that simultaneously diagnoses the fault in individual sensors. Similarly, it is complicated to deal with overall "big data" for all sensors collectively. In addition, it is a comparatively easy task to detect and eliminate hard faults. However, soft faults are more difficult to detect and eliminate because sensor data take time to leave a confidence limit [58]. While Google, GM, BMW, and Tesla will each experiment and test various AVs, traditional software bugs are more difficult to fix than DNN-based software bugs [56]. The Kalman filter variants have widespread application among existing quantitative model-based methods due to their simplicity and ability to handle reasonable uncertainties and nonlinearities. However, the presence of Gaussian noise complicates fault diagnosis [21]. In addition, controlling external light, which acts as noise during image processing, is one of the key issues for AVs [59].

AV safety is one of the most crucial features that require special attention at all stages of the vehicle's lifetime. Software failures can be costly in terms of recalls, and they can even be fatal. The failure or malfunction of an automotive system can cause serious injuries or death. Hence, the overall safety of AVs can be improved in various aspects such as passive, active, or functional safety. Safety-related intervehicle communication (IVC) is one of the crucial hazards in AV technology. However, the reliability of dedicated short-range communication (DSRC) performance is inadequate to guarantee vehicle stability execution in such circumstances. Over the years, various approaches have been proposed to resolve IVC-based safety. For instance, Yu and Biswas [5] proposed a unique DSRC-based medium access control (MAC) framework for IVC that comprised a self-configuring time division of numerous guidelines with short and deterministic time lag-linked capabilities. Furthermore, the distributed power control method was suggested to control a load of periodic messages on the channel [6]. Bi et al. [7] introduced a cross-layer broadcast protocol for efficient and dependable message delivery in IVC systems. Palazzi et al. [8] proposed an innovative IVC framework that adjusts its features and functionality to deliver implementations efficiently by rapidly perpetuating their communications across a vehicular network. Tabatabaei et al. [9] improved simpler network topologies for simulation models by enhancing ray-tracing-derived wireless propagation models.

Various issues are concerns to adopt the AV technology on a large scale such as legal obligations, ethical implications, confidentiality issues, data protection and hacking, and the massive cost of vehicles and related technologies. On the other hand, the future of AV technology is brighter because of its peculiar features such as the pervasive utilization of AVs on highways resulting in fewer traffic accidents, efficiency in terms of fuel usage, and increased productivity. Hence, it appears that the gradual substitution of conventional vehicles with AVs will take place, with the main factor being society's adjustment to this type of innovation and corresponding features. Researchers and specialists anticipate that AVs will be widely adopted in the coming 20 to 25 years. According to the surveys, depending on the level of advancement, the AV technology can be adopted until 2030–2040 in well-developed nations with decent infrastructure [137].

5. Conclusions

Recent years have seen a rise in self-driving autonomous vehicles (AVs), where the advanced driver assistance system (ADAS) plays a critical role. It is imperative for traffic safety and higher driving efficiency to carry out timely diagnosis (detection, quantification, and isolation of faults) and prognosis (future evaluation of defects) of the main components of ADAS in the framework of prognostic health management (PHM). This article provided an extensive review of the main features of ADAS, the types of faults in each different sensor, and the research efforts related to PHM from the published literature.

The detailed discussion of the possible shortcomings and commonly occurring defects, as well as the PHM efforts, are summarized for different ADAS components below.

- For the LiDAR system, the sensor-based faults are malfunction of mirror motor, damage to optical filter, misalignment of the optical receiver, security breach, adverse climatic circumstances, intermodulation distortion, and short-circuit and overvoltage of electrical components. Some representative PHM efforts for LiDAR are correlation with sensor framework, output of the monitoring sensor, correlation to passive ground truth, correlation to active ground truth, correlation to another similar sensor, and correlation to a different sensor.
- RADAR is more economical than LiDAR and cameras, and it works on the principle of the Doppler effect. The primary failure modes of RADAR are fault in the range rate signal and sensor fault. Some preventive and corrective measures for RADAR are calibration in relevant service stations, sliding mode observer, sensor fault detection, cyberattack detection observer, and the LSTM-based deep learning approach.
- The ultrasonic sensors used to determine an object in the domain of the sensors are susceptible to acoustic/electronic noise, performance degradation under bright ambient light, vehicle corner error, and cross echoes, among others. Common approaches for detecting faults and corrective measures in ultrasonic sensors are artificial neural networks, parallel parking assist systems, combined ultrasonic sensors and three-dimensional vision sensors, and grid maps.

- The positioning sensors and systems employed to locate the position of AVs are prone to jumps in GPS observation, satellite and received signal faults, and sensor data with/without curbs on the roadsides. The techniques employed for the fault detection and isolation of positioning sensors and systems are the Kalman filter, Markov blanket (MB) algorithm, and sensor redundancy fault detection model.

The AVs and the PHM of its main components are not yet fully developed, and a great deal of research is needed to fully develop reliable autonomous driving. This article discussed the existing research efforts to highlight the current techniques, as well as identified potential research gaps. To sum up, the current review paper is a first attempt at highlighting the fault detection for the overall sensors of the ADAS for AVs, which provides insight to readers on the current progress and potential research gaps in this field. The current study identified different faults in various sensors using fault diagnosis techniques, which can motivate readers toward further research to overcome the existing challenges in this field.

Author Contributions: Conceptualization, H.S.K. and I.R.; methodology, I.R.; formal analysis, I.R.; investigation, I.R., A.K. and S.K.; resources, H.S.K.; writing—original draft preparation, I.R., A.K., S.K., M.S. and M.M.A.; writing—review and editing, H.S.K., A.K. and S.K.; visualization, I.R. and H.S.K.; supervision, H.S.K.; project administration, H.S.K.; funding acquisition, H.S.K. All authors have read and agreed to the published version of the manuscript.

Funding: This work was supported by the Ministry of Trade, Industry, and Energy (MOTIE) and the Korea Institute for Advancement of Technology (KIAT) through the International Cooperative R&D program (Project No. P0011923), as well as by a National Research Foundation of Korea (NRF) grant, funded by the Korea government (MSIT) (No. 2020R1A2C1006613).

Conflicts of Interest: The authors declare no conflict of interest.

References

1. Meyer-Waarden, L.; Cloarec, J. "Baby, You Can Drive My Car": Psychological Antecedents That Drive Consumers' Adoption of AI-Powered Autonomous Vehicles. *Technovation* **2022**, *109*, 102348. [CrossRef]
2. Nowicki, M.R. A Data-Driven and Application-Aware Approach to Sensory System Calibration in an Autonomous Vehicle. *Measurement* **2022**, *194*, 111002. [CrossRef]
3. Jain, S.; Ahuja, N.J.; Srikanth, P.; Bhadane, K.V.; Nagaiah, B.; Kumar, A.; Konstantinou, C. Blockchain and Autonomous Vehicles: Recent Advances and Future Directions. *IEEE Access* **2021**, *9*, 130264–130328. [CrossRef]
4. Reid, T.G.; Houts, S.E.; Cammarata, R.; Mills, G.; Agarwal, S.; Vora, A.; Pandey, G. Localization Requirements for Autonomous Vehicles. *arXiv* **2019**, arXiv:1906.01061. [CrossRef]
5. Yu, F.; Biswas, S. Self-Configuring TDMA Protocols for Enhancing Vehicle Safety with DSRC Based Vehicle-to-Vehicle Communications. *IEEE J. Sel. Areas Commun.* **2007**, *25*, 1526–1537. [CrossRef]
6. Torrent-Moreno, M.; Mittag, J.; Santi, P.; Hartenstein, H. Vehicle-to-Vehicle Communication: Fair Transmit Power Control for Safety-Critical Information. *IEEE Trans. Veh. Technol.* **2009**, *58*, 3684–3703. [CrossRef]
7. Bi, Y.; Cai, L.X.; Shen, X.; Zhao, H. Efficient and Reliable Broadcast in Intervehicle Communication Networks: A Cross-Layer Approach. *IEEE Trans. Veh. Technol.* **2010**, *59*, 2404–2417. [CrossRef]
8. Palazzi, C.E.; Roccetti, M.; Ferretti, S. An Intervehicular Communication Architecture for Safety and Entertainment. *IEEE Trans. Intell. Transp. Syst.* **2009**, *11*, 90–99. [CrossRef]
9. Tabatabaei, S.A.H.; Fleury, M.; Qadri, N.N.; Ghanbari, M. Improving Propagation Modeling in Urban Environments for Vehicular Ad Hoc Networks. *IEEE Trans. Intell. Transp. Syst.* **2011**, *12*, 705–716. [CrossRef]
10. You, J.-H.; Oh, S.; Park, J.-E.; Song, H.; Kim, Y.-K. A Novel LiDAR Sensor Alignment Inspection System for Automobile Productions Using 1-D Photodetector Arrays. *Measurement* **2021**, *183*, 109817. [CrossRef]
11. Kala, R.; Warwick, K. Motion Planning of Autonomous Vehicles in a Non-Autonomous Vehicle Environment without Speed Lanes. *Eng. Appl. Artif. Intell.* **2013**, *26*, 1588–1601. [CrossRef]
12. Correa-Caicedo, P.J.; Barranco-Gutiérrez, A.I.; Guerra-Hernandez, E.I.; Batres-Mendoza, P.; Padilla-Medina, J.A.; Rostro-González, H. An FPGA-Based Architecture for a Latitude and Longitude Correction in Autonomous Navigation Tasks. *Measurement* **2021**, *182*, 109757.
13. Duran, O.; Turan, B. Vehicle-to-Vehicle Distance Estimation Using Artificial Neural Network and a Toe-in-Style Stereo Camera. *Measurement* **2022**, *190*, 110732. [CrossRef]

14. Duran, D.R.; Robinson, E.; Kornecki, A.J.; Zalewski, J. Safety Analysis of Autonomous Ground Vehicle Optical Systems: Bayesian Belief Networks Approach. In Proceedings of the 2013 Federated Conference on Computer Science and Information Systems, Kraków, Poland, 8–11 September 2013; pp. 1419–1425.

15. Woongsun, J.; Ali, Z.; Rajesh, R. Resilient Control Under Cyber-Attacks in Connected ACC Vehicles. In Proceedings of the ASME 2019 Dynamic Systems and Control Conference, Park City, UT, USA, 8–11 October 2019.

16. Park, W.J.; Kim, B.S.; Seo, D.E.; Kim, D.S.; Lee, K.H. Parking Space Detection Using Ultrasonic Sensor in Parking Assistance System. In Proceedings of the 2008 IEEE Intelligent Vehicles Symposium, Eindhoven, The Netherlands, 4–6 June 2008; pp. 1039–1044. [CrossRef]

17. van Schaik, W.; Grooten, M.; Wernaart, T.; van der Geld, C. High Accuracy Acoustic Relative Humidity Measurement in Duct Flow with Air. *Sensors* **2010**, *10*, 7421–7433. [CrossRef]

18. Alonso, L.; Milanés, V.; Torre-Ferrero, C.; Godoy, J.; Oria, J.P.; de Pedro, T. Ultrasonic Sensors in Urban Traffic Driving-Aid Systems. *Sensors* **2011**, *11*, 661–673. [CrossRef]

19. Sahoo, A.K.; Udgata, S.K. A Novel ANN-Based Adaptive Ultrasonic Measurement System for Accurate Water Level Monitoring. *IEEE Trans. Instrum. Meas.* **2020**, *69*, 3359–3369. [CrossRef]

20. Blanch, J.; Walter, T.; Enge, P. A Simple Satellite Exclusion Algorithm for Advanced RAIM. In Proceedings of the 2016 International Technical Meeting of The Institute of Navigation, Monterey, CA, USA, 25–28 January 2016; pp. 239–244.

21. Mori, D.; Sugiura, H.; Hattori, Y. Adaptive Sensor Fault Detection and Isolation Using Unscented Kalman Filter for Vehicle Positioning. In Proceedings of the 2019 IEEE Intelligent Transportation Systems Conference (ITSC), Auckland, New Zealand, 27–30 October 2019; IEEE: Piscataway, NJ, USA, 2019; pp. 1298–1304.

22. Tadjine, H.; Anoushirvan, D.; Eugen, D.; Schulze, K. Optical Self Diagnostics for Camera Based Driver Assistance. In *Proceedings of the FISITA 2012 World Automotive Congress*; SAE-China, FISITA, Eds.; Lecture Notes in Electrical Engineering; Springer: Berlin/Heidelberg, Germany, 2013; Volume 197, pp. 507–518. ISBN 978-3-642-33804-5.

23. Saponara, S.; Greco, M.S.; Gini, F. Radar-on-Chip/in-Package in Autonomous Driving Vehicles and Intelligent Transport Systems: Opportunities and Challenges. *IEEE Signal Processing Mag.* **2019**, *36*, 71–84. [CrossRef]

24. Park, S.; Oh, K.; Jeong, Y.; Yi, K. Model Predictive Control-Based Fault Detection and Reconstruction Algorithm for Longitudinal Control of Autonomous Driving Vehicle Using Multi-Sliding Mode Observer. *Microsyst. Technol.* **2020**, *26*, 239–264. [CrossRef]

25. Oh, K.; Yi, K. A Longitudinal Model Based Probabilistic Fault Diagnosis Algorithm of Autonomous Vehicles Using Sliding Mode Observer. In Proceedings of the ASME 2017 Conference on Information Storage and Processing Systems, San Francisco, CA, USA, 29–30 August 2017; American Society of Mechanical Engineers: New York, NY, USA, 2017; pp. 1–3.

26. Lyu, Y.; Pang, Z.; Zhou, C.; Zhao, P. Prognostics and Health Management Technology for Radar System. *MATEC Web Conf.* **2020**, *309*, 04009. [CrossRef]

27. Lim, B.S.; Keoh, S.L.; Thing, V.L.L. Autonomous Vehicle Ultrasonic Sensor Vulnerability and Impact Assessment. In Proceedings of the IEEE World Forum on Internet of Things (WF-IoT), Singapore, 5–8 February 2018; pp. 231–236. [CrossRef]

28. Bank, D. A Novel Ultrasonic Sensing System for Autonomous Mobile Systems. *Proc. IEEE Sens.* **2002**, *1*, 1671–1676. [CrossRef]

29. Li, C.; Fu, Y.; Yu, F.R.; Luan, T.H.; Zhang, Y. Vehicle Position Correction: A Vehicular Blockchain Networks-Based GPS Error Sharing Framework. *IEEE Trans. Intell. Transp. Syst.* **2021**, *22*, 898–912. [CrossRef]

30. Hu, J.; Sun, Q.; Ye, Z.-S.; Zhou, Q. Joint Modeling of Degradation and Lifetime Data for RUL Prediction of Deteriorating Products. *IEEE Trans. Ind. Inf.* **2021**, *17*, 4521–4531. [CrossRef]

31. Ye, Z.-S.; Xie, M. Stochastic Modelling and Analysis of Degradation for Highly Reliable Products: Z.-S. YE AND M. XIE. *Appl. Stochastic Models Bus. Ind.* **2015**, *31*, 16–32. [CrossRef]

32. Ng, T.S. ADAS in Autonomous Driving. In *Robotic Vehicles: Systems and Technology*; Springer: Berlin/Heidelberg, Germany, 2021; pp. 87–93.

33. Li, X.; Lin, K.-Y.; Meng, M.; Li, X.; Li, L.; Hong, Y. Composition and Application of Current Advanced Driving Assistance System: A Review. *arXiv* **2021**, arXiv:2105.12348.

34. Choi, J.D.; Kim, M.Y. A Sensor Fusion System with Thermal Infrared Camera and LiDAR for Autonomous Vehicles and Deep Learning Based Object Detection. *ICT Express*, 2022, *in press*. [CrossRef]

35. Wang, H.; Wang, B.; Liu, B.; Meng, X.; Yang, G. Pedestrian Recognition and Tracking Using 3D LiDAR for Autonomous Vehicle. *Robot. Auton. Syst.* **2017**, *88*, 71–78. [CrossRef]

36. Khan, A.; Khalid, S.; Raouf, I.; Sohn, J.-W.; Kim, H.-S. Autonomous Assessment of Delamination Using Scarce Raw Structural Vibration and Transfer Learning. *Sensors* **2021**, *21*, 6239. [CrossRef]

37. Raouf, I.; Lee, H.; Kim, H.S. Mechanical Fault Detection Based on Machine Learning for Robotic RV Reducer Using Electrical Current Signature Analysis: A Data-Driven Approach. *J. Comput. Des. Eng.* **2022**, *9*, 417–433. [CrossRef]

38. Habibi, H.; Howard, I.; Simani, S.; Fekih, A. Decoupling Adaptive Sliding Mode Observer Design for Wind Turbines Subject to Simultaneous Faults in Sensors and Actuators. *IEEE/CAA J. Autom. Sin.* **2021**, *8*, 837–847. [CrossRef]

39. Saeed, U.; Jan, S.U.; Lee, Y.-D.; Koo, I. Fault Diagnosis Based on Extremely Randomized Trees in Wireless Sensor Networks. *Reliab. Eng. Syst. Saf.* **2021**, *205*, 107284. [CrossRef]

40. Bellanco, I.; Fuentes, E.; Vallès, M.; Salom, J. A Review of the Fault Behavior of Heat Pumps and Measurements, Detection and Diagnosis Methods Including Virtual Sensors. *J. Build. Eng.* **2021**, *39*, 102254. [CrossRef]

41. Rajpoot, S.C.; Pandey, C.; Rajpoot, P.S.; Singhai, S.K.; Sethy, P.K. A Dynamic-SUGPDS Model for Faults Detection and Isolation of Underground Power Cable Based on Detection and Isolation Algorithm and Smart Sensors. *J. Electr. Eng. Technol.* **2021**, *16*, 1799–1819. [CrossRef]
42. Bhushan, B.; Sahoo, G. Recent Advances in Attacks, Technical Challenges, Vulnerabilities and Their Countermeasures in Wireless Sensor Networks. *Wirel. Pers. Commun.* **2018**, *98*, 2037–2077. [CrossRef]
43. Goelles, T.; Schlager, B.; Muckenhuber, S. Fault Detection, Isolation, Identification and Recovery (FDIIR) Methods for Automotive Perception Sensors Including a Detailed Literature Survey for Lidar. *Sensors* **2020**, *20*, 3662. [CrossRef] [PubMed]
44. Van Brummelen, J.; O'Brien, M.; Gruyer, D.; Najjaran, H. Autonomous Vehicle Perception: The Technology of Today and Tomorrow. *Transp. Res. Part C Emerg. Technol.* **2018**, *89*, 384–406.
45. Biddle, L.; Fallah, S. A Novel Fault Detection, Identification and Prediction Approach for Autonomous Vehicle Controllers Using SVM. *Automot. Innov.* **2021**, *4*, 301–314. [CrossRef]
46. Sun, Q.; Ye, Z.-S.; Zhu, X. Managing Component Degradation in Series Systems for Balancing Degradation through Reallocation and Maintenance. *IISE Trans.* **2020**, *52*, 797–810.
47. Gu, J.; Barker, D.; Pecht, M.G. Uncertainty Assessment of Prognostics of Electronics Subject to Random Vibration. In Proceedings of the AAAI Fall Symposium: Artificial Intelligence for Prognostics, Arlington, VA, USA, 9–11 November 2007; pp. 50–57.
48. Ibargüengoytia, P.H.; Vadera, S.; Sucar, L.E. A Probabilistic Model for Information and Sensor Validation. *Comput. J.* **2006**, *49*, 113–126. [CrossRef]
49. Cheng, S.; Azarian, M.H.; Pecht, M.G. Sensor Systems for Prognostics and Health Management. *Sensors* **2010**, *10*, 5774–5797. [CrossRef]
50. Gong, Z.; Lin, H.; Zhang, D.; Luo, Z.; Zelek, J.; Chen, Y.; Nurunnabi, A.; Wang, C.; Li, J. A Frustum-Based Probabilistic Framework for 3D Object Detection by Fusion of LiDAR and Camera Data. *ISPRS J. Photogramm. Remote Sens.* **2020**, *159*, 90–100. [CrossRef]
51. SAE-China; FISITA (Eds.) *Proceedings of the FISITA 2012 World Automotive Congress*; Springer: Berlin/Heidelberg, Germany, 2013; ISBN 3-642-33840-2.
52. Kobayashi, T.; Simon, D.L. Application of a Bank of Kalman Filters for Aircraft Engine Fault Diagnostics. In Proceedings of the ASME Turbo Expo 2003, Atlanta, GA, USA, 16–19 June 2003; Volume 1, pp. 461–470.
53. Salahshoor, K.; Mosallaei, M.; Bayat, M. Centralized and Decentralized Process and Sensor Fault Monitoring Using Data Fusion Based on Adaptive Extended Kalman Filter Algorithm. *Measurement* **2008**, *41*, 1059–1076. [CrossRef]
54. Köylüoglu, T.; Hennicks, L. Evaluating Rain Removal Image Processing Solutions for Fast and Accurate Object Detection. Master's Thesis, KTH Royal Institute of Technology, Stockholm, Sweden, 2019.
55. Realpe, M. Multi-Sensor Fusion Module in a Fault Tolerant Perception System for Autonomous Vehicles. *J. Autom. Control. Eng.* **2016**, *4*, 460–466. [CrossRef]
56. Sculley, D.; Holt, G.; Golovin, D.; Davydov, E.; Phillips, T.; Ebner, D.; Chaudhary, V.; Young, M. Machine Learning: The High Interest Credit Card of Technical Debt. 2014. Available online: https://blog.acolyer.org/2016/02/29/machine-learning-the-high-interest-credit-card-of-technical-debt/ (accessed on 10 August 2022).
57. Spinneker, R.; Koch, C.; Park, S.-B.; Yoon, J.J. Fast Fog Detection for Camera Based Advanced Driver Assistance Systems. In Proceedings of the 17th International IEEE Conference on Intelligent Transportation Systems (ITSC), Qingdao, China, 8–11 October 2014; IEEE: Piscataway, NJ, USA, 2014; pp. 1369–1374.
58. Tian, Y.; Pei, K.; Jana, S.; Ray, B. Deeptest: Automated Testing of Deep-Neural-Network-Driven Autonomous Cars. In Proceedings of the 40th International Conference on Software Engineering, Gothenburg, Sweden, 27 May–3 June 2018; pp. 303–314.
59. Hata, A.; Wolf, D. Road Marking Detection Using LIDAR Reflective Intensity Data and Its Application to Vehicle Localization. In Proceedings of the 17th International IEEE Conference on Intelligent Transportation Systems (ITSC), Qingdao, China, 8–11 October 2014; IEEE: Piscataway, NJ, USA, 2014; pp. 584–589.
60. Poczter, S.L.; Jankovic, L.M. The Google Car: Driving Toward A Better Future? *JBCS* **2013**, *10*, 7. [CrossRef]
61. Yoo, H.W.; Druml, N.; Brunner, D.; Schwarzl, C.; Thurner, T.; Hennecke, M.; Schitter, G. MEMS-Based Lidar for Autonomous Driving. *Elektrotech. Inftech.* **2018**, *135*, 408–415. [CrossRef]
62. Asvadi, A.; Premebida, C.; Peixoto, P.; Nunes, U. 3D Lidar-Based Static and Moving Obstacle Detection in Driving Environments: An Approach Based on Voxels and Multi-Region Ground Planes. *Robot. Auton. Syst.* **2016**, *83*, 299–311. [CrossRef]
63. Segata, M.; Cigno, R.L.; Bhadani, R.K.; Bunting, M.; Sprinkle, J. A Lidar Error Model for Cooperative Driving Simulations. In Proceedings of the 2018 IEEE Vehicular Networking Conference (VNC), Taipei, Taiwan, 5–7 December 2018; IEEE: Piscataway, NJ, USA, 2018; pp. 1–8.
64. Sun, X. Method and Apparatus for Detection and Ranging Fault Detection and Recovery. U.S. Patent 10,203,408, 12 February 2019.
65. Rivero, J.R.V.; Tahiraj, I.; Schubert, O.; Glassl, C.; Buschardt, B.; Berk, M.; Chen, J. Characterization and Simulation of the Effect of Road Dirt on the Performance of a Laser Scanner. In Proceedings of the 2017 IEEE 20th International Conference on Intelligent Transportation Systems (ITSC), Yokohama, Japan, 16–19 October 2017; IEEE: Piscataway, NJ, USA, 2017; pp. 1–6.
66. Trierweiler, M.; Caldelas, P.; Gröninger, G.; Peterseim, T.; Neumann, C. Influence of Sensor Blockage on Automotive LiDAR Systems. In Proceedings of the 2019 IEEE SENSORS, Montreal, QC, Canada, 27–30 October 2019; IEEE: Piscataway, NJ, USA, 2019; pp. 1–4.

67. Periu, C.F.; Mohsenimanesh, A.; Laguë, C.; McLaughlin, N.B. Isolation of Vibrations Transmitted to a LIDAR Sensor Mounted on an Agricultural Vehicle to Improve Obstacle Detection. *Can. Biosyst. Eng.* **2013**, *55*, 233–242. [CrossRef]
68. Hama, S.; Toda, H. Basic Experiment of LIDAR Sensor Measurement Directional Instability for Moving and Vibrating Object. In Proceedings of the IOP Conference Series: Materials Science and Engineering, Chongqing, China, 23–25 November 2018; IOP Publishing: Bristol, UK, 2019; Volume 472, p. 012017.
69. Choi, H.; Lee, W.-C.; Aafer, Y.; Fei, F.; Tu, Z.; Zhang, X.; Xu, D.; Deng, X. Detecting Attacks against Robotic Vehicles: A Control Invariant Approach. In Proceedings of the 2018 ACM SIGSAC Conference on Computer and Communications Security, Toronto, ON, Canada, 15–19 October 2018; pp. 801–816.
70. Petit, J.; Shladover, S.E. Potential Cyberattacks on Automated Vehicles. *IEEE Trans. Intell. Transp. Syst.* **2014**, *16*, 546–556. [CrossRef]
71. Shin, H.; Kim, D.; Kwon, Y.; Kim, Y. Illusion and Dazzle: Adversarial Optical Channel Exploits against Lidars for Automotive Applications. In Proceedings of the International Conference on Cryptographic Hardware and Embedded Systems, Santa Barbara, CA, USA, 17–19 August 2016; Springer: Berlin/Heidelberg, Germany, 2017; pp. 445–467.
72. Kim, G.; Eom, J.; Park, Y. An Experiment of Mutual Interference between Automotive LIDAR Scanners. In Proceedings of the 2015 12th International Conference on Information Technology-New Generations, Las Vegas, NV, USA, 13–15 April 2015; IEEE: Piscataway, NJ, USA, 2015; pp. 680–685.
73. Zhang, F.; Liu, Q.; Gong, M.; Fu, X. Anti-Dynamic-Crosstalk Method for Single Photon LIDAR Detection. In *LIDAR Imaging Detection and Target Recognition 2017*; International Society for Optics and Photonics: Washington, DC, USA, 2017; Volume 10605, p. 1060503.
74. Ning, X.; Li, F.; Tian, G.; Wang, Y. An Efficient Outlier Removal Method for Scattered Point Cloud Data. *PLoS ONE* **2018**, *13*, e0201280. [CrossRef]
75. McMichael, R.; Schabb, D.E.; Thakur, A.; Francisco, S.; Kentley-Klay, D.; Torrey, J.R. Sensor Obstruction Detection and Mitigation Using Vibration and/or Heat. U.S. Patent 11,176,426, 16 November 2021.
76. Bohren, J.; Foote, T.; Keller, J.; Kushleyev, A.; Lee, D.; Stewart, A.; Vernaza, P.; Derenick, J.; Spletzer, J.; Satterfield, B. Little Ben: The Ben Franklin Racing Team's Entry in the 2007 DARPA Urban Challenge. *J. Field Robot.* **2008**, *25*, 598–614. [CrossRef]
77. Fallis, A.G. Autonomous Ground Vehicle. *J. Chem. Inf. Modeling* **2013**, *53*, 1689–1699.
78. Kesting, A.; Treiber, M.; Schönhof, M.; Helbing, D. Adaptive Cruise Control Design for Active Congestion Avoidance. *Transp. Res. Part C Emerg. Technol.* **2008**, *16*, 668–683. [CrossRef]
79. Werneke, J.; Kleen, A.; Vollrath, M. Perfect Timing: Urgency, Not Driving Situations, Influence the Best Timing to Activate Warnings. *Hum. Factors* **2014**, *56*, 249–259. [CrossRef]
80. Li, H.-J.; Kiang, Y.-W. Radar and Inverse Scattering. In *The Electrical Engineering Handbook*; Elsevier: Amsterdam, The Netherlands, 2005; pp. 671–690.
81. Rohling, H.; Möller, C. Radar Waveform for Automotive Radar Systems and Applications. In Proceedings of the 2008 IEEE Radar Conference, RADAR, Rome, Italy, 26–30 May 2008; Volume 1. [CrossRef]
82. Bilik, I.; Longman, O.; Villeval, S.; Tabrikian, J. The Rise of Radar for Autonomous Vehicles. *IEEE Signal Process. Mag.* **2019**, *36*, 20–31. [CrossRef]
83. Campbell, S.; O'Mahony, N.; Krpalcova, L.; Riordan, D.; Walsh, J.; Murphy, A.; Ryan, C. Sensor Technology in Autonomous Vehicles: A Review. In Proceedings of the 29th Irish Signals and Systems Conference, ISSC, Belfast, UK, 21–22 June 2018; pp. 1–4. [CrossRef]
84. Severino, J.V.B.; Zimmer, A.; Brandmeier, T.; Freire, R.Z. Pedestrian Recognition Using Micro Doppler Effects of Radar Signals Based on Machine Learning and Multi-Objective Optimization. *Expert Syst. Appl.* **2019**, *136*, 304–315. [CrossRef]
85. Loureiro, R.; Benmoussa, S.; Touati, Y.; Merzouki, R.; Ould Bouamama, B. Integration of Fault Diagnosis and Fault-Tolerant Control for Health Monitoring of a Class of MIMO Intelligent Autonomous Vehicles. *IEEE Trans. Veh. Technol.* **2014**, *63*, 30–39. [CrossRef]
86. Dickmann, J.; Appenrodt, N.; Bloecher, H.L.; Brenk, C.; Hackbarth, T.; Hahn, M.; Klappstein, J.; Muntzinger, M.; Sailer, A. Radar Contribution to Highly Automated Driving. In Proceedings of the 2014 44th European Microwave Conference, Rome, Italy, 6–9 October 2014; pp. 412–415. [CrossRef]
87. Rajamani, R.; Shrivastava, A.; Zhu, C.; Alexander, L. *Fault Diagnostics for Intelligent Vehicle Applications*; Minnesota Department of Transportation: Saint Paul, MN, USA, 2001.
88. Jeon, W.; Xie, Z.; Zemouche, A.; Rajamani, R. Simultaneous Cyber-Attack Detection and Radar Sensor Health Monitoring in Connected ACC Vehicles. *IEEE Sens. J.* **2021**, *21*, 15741–15752. [CrossRef]
89. Yigit, E. *Automotive Radar Self-Diagnostic Using Calibration Targets That Are Embedded in Road Infrastructure*; Delft University of Technology: Delft, The Netherlands, 2021.
90. Oh, K.; Park, S.; Lee, J.; Yi, K. Functional Perspective-Based Probabilistic Fault Detection and Diagnostic Algorithm for Autonomous Vehicle Using Longitudinal Kinematic Model. *Microsyst. Technol.* **2018**, *24*, 4527–4537. [CrossRef]
91. Oh, K.; Park, S.; Yi, K. A Predictive Approach to the Fault Detection in Fail-Safe System of Autonomous Vehicle Based on the Multi-Sliding Mode Observer. In Proceedings of the ASME-JSME 2018 Joint International Conference on Information Storage and Processing Systems and Micromechatronics for Information and Precision Equipment, ISPS-MIPE, San Francisco, CA, USA, 29–30 August 2018; pp. 2018–2020. [CrossRef]

92. Song, T.; Lee, J.; Oh, K.; Yi, K. Dual-Sliding Mode Approach for Separated Fault Detection and Tolerant Control for Functional Safety of Longitudinal Autonomous Driving. *Proc. Inst. Mech. Eng. Part D J. Automob. Eng.* **2021**, *235*, 1446–1460. [CrossRef]
93. Cheek, E.; Khuttan, D.; Changalvala, R.; Malik, H. Physical Fingerprinting of Ultrasonic Sensors and Applications to Sensor Security. In Proceedings of the 2020 IEEE 6th International Conference on Dependability in Sensor, Cloud and Big Data Systems and Application, DependSys, Nadi, Fiji, 14–16 December 2020; pp. 65–72. [CrossRef]
94. Al-Turjman, F.; Malekloo, A. Smart Parking in IoT-Enabled Cities: A Survey. *Sustain. Cities Soc.* **2019**, *49*, 101608. [CrossRef]
95. Kianpisheh, A.; Mustaffa, N.; Limtrairut, P.; Keikhosrokiani, P. Smart Parking System (SPS) Architecture Using Ultrasonic Detector. *Int. J. Softw. Eng. Its Appl.* **2012**, *6*, 51–58.
96. Kotb, A.O.; Shen, Y.C.; Huang, Y. Smart Parking Guidance, Monitoring and Reservations: A Review. *IEEE Intell. Transp. Syst. Mag.* **2017**, *9*, 6–16. [CrossRef]
97. Taraba, M.; Adamec, J.; Danko, M.; Drgona, P. Utilization of Modern Sensors in Autonomous Vehicles. In Proceedings of the 12th International Conference ELEKTRO 2018, Mikulov, Czech Republic, 21–23 May 2018; pp. 1–5. [CrossRef]
98. Ma, Y.; Liu, Y.; Zhang, L.; Cao, Y.; Guo, S.; Li, H. Research Review on Parking Space Detection Method. *Symmetry* **2021**, *13*, 128. [CrossRef]
99. Idris, M.Y.I.; Tamil, E.M.; Razak, Z.; Noor, N.M.; Km, L.W. Smart Parking System Using Image Processing Techniques in Wireless Sensor Network Environment. *Inf. Technol. J.* **2009**, *8*, 114–127. [CrossRef]
100. Hanzl, J. Parking Information Guidance Systems and Smart Technologies Application Used in Urban Areas and Multi-Storey Car Parks. *Transp. Res. Procedia* **2020**, *44*, 361–368. [CrossRef]
101. Valasek, C. *A Survey of Remote Automotive Attack Surfaces*; Technical White Paper; IOActive: Washington, DC, USA, 2014; pp. 1–90.
102. Nourinejad, M.; Bahrami, S.; Roorda, M.J. Designing Parking Facilities for Autonomous Vehicles. *Transp. Res. Part B Methodol.* **2018**, *109*, 110–127. [CrossRef]
103. Ma, S.; Jiang, Z.; Jiang, H.; Han, M.; Li, C. Parking Space and Obstacle Detection Based on a Vision Sensor and Checkerboard Grid Laser. *Appl. Sci.* **2020**, *10*, 2582. [CrossRef]
104. Jeong, S.H.; Choi, C.G.; Oh, J.N.; Yoon, P.J.; Kim, B.S.; Kim, M.; Lee, K.H. Low Cost Design of Parallel Parking Assist System Based on an Ultrasonic Sensor. *Int. J. Automot. Technol.* **2010**, *11*, 409–416. [CrossRef]
105. Pelaez, L.P.; Recalde, M.E.V.; Munoz, E.D.M.; Larrauri, J.M.; Rastelli, J.M.P.; Druml, N.; Hillbrand, B. Car Parking Assistance Based on Time-or-Flight Camera. In Proceedings of the IEEE Intelligent Vehicles Symposium, Paris, France, 9–12 June 2019; pp. 1753–1759. [CrossRef]
106. Bank, D. An Error Detection Model for Ultrasonic Sensor Evaluation on Autonomous Mobile Systems. In Proceedings of the IEEE International Workshop on Robot and Human Interactive Communication, Berlin, Germany, 27 September 2002; pp. 288–293. [CrossRef]
107. Soika, M. Grid Based Fault Detection and Calibration of Sensors on Mobile Robots. *Proc. IEEE Int. Conf. Robot. Autom.* **1997**, *3*, 2589–2594. [CrossRef]
108. Abdel-Hafez, M.F.; Al Nabulsi, A.; Jafari, A.H.; Al Zaabi, F.; Sleiman, M.; Abuhatab, A. A Sequential Approach for Fault Detection and Identification of Vehicles' Ultrasonic Parking Sensors. In Proceedings of the 2011 4th International Conference on Modeling, Simulation and Applied Optimization, ICMSAO, Kuala Lumpur, Malaysia, 19–21 April 2011. [CrossRef]
109. De Simone, M.C.; Rivera, Z.B.; Guida, D. Obstacle Avoidance System for Unmanned Ground Vehicles by Using Ultrasonic Sensors. *Machines* **2018**, *6*, 18. [CrossRef]
110. Arvind, C.S.; Senthilnath, J. Autonomous Vehicle for Obstacle Detection and Avoidance Using Reinforcement Learning. In *Soft Computing for Problem Solving*; Springer: Berlin/Heidelberg, Germany, 2020; pp. 55–66.
111. Rosique, F.; Navarro, P.J.; Fernández, C.; Padilla, A. A Systematic Review of Perception System and Simulators for Autonomous Vehicles Research. *Sensors* **2019**, *19*, 648. [CrossRef]
112. Capuano, V.; Harvard, A.; Chung, S.-J. On-Board Cooperative Spacecraft Relative Navigation Fusing GNSS with Vision. *Prog. Aerosp. Sci.* **2022**, *128*, 100761. [CrossRef]
113. Gyagenda, N.; Hatilima, J.V.; Roth, H.; Zhmud, V. A Review of GNSS-Independent UAV Navigation Techniques. *Robot. Auton. Syst.* **2022**, *152*, 104069. [CrossRef]
114. Zermani, S.; Dezan, C.; Hireche, C.; Euler, R.; Diguet, J.-P. Embedded and Probabilistic Health Management for the GPS of Autonomous Vehicles. In Proceedings of the 2016 5th Mediterranean Conference on Embedded Computing (MECO), Bar, Montenegro, 12–16 June 2016; pp. 401–404.
115. Dezan, C.; Zermani, S.; Hireche, C. Embedded Bayesian Network Contribution for a Safe Mission Planning of Autonomous Vehicles. *Algorithms* **2020**, *13*, 155. [CrossRef]
116. Rahiman, W.; Zainal, Z. An Overview of Development GPS Navigation for Autonomous Car. In Proceedings of the 2013 IEEE 8th Conference on Industrial Electronics and Applications (ICIEA), Melbourne, Australia, 19–21 June 2013; pp. 1112–1118.
117. Kojima, Y.; Kidono, K.; Takahashi, A.; Ninomiya, Y. Precise Ego-Localization by Integration of GPS and Sensor-Based Odometry. *J. Intell. Connect. Veh.* **2008**, *3*, 485–490.
118. Zein, Y.; Darwiche, M.; Mokhiamar, O. GPS Tracking System for Autonomous Vehicles. *Alex. Eng. J.* **2018**, *57*, 3127–3137. [CrossRef]
119. Quddus, M.A.; Ochieng, W.Y.; Noland, R.B. Current Map-Matching Algorithms for Transport Applications: State-of-the Art and Future Research Directions. *Transp. Res. Part C Emerg. Technol.* **2007**, *15*, 312–328. [CrossRef]

120. Ercek, R.; De Doncker, P.; Grenez, F. Study of Pseudo-Range Error Due to Non-Line-of-Sight-Multipath in Urban Canyons. In Proceedings of the 18th International Technical Meeting of the Satellite Division of The Institute of Navigation (ION GNSS 2005), Long Beach, CA, USA, 13–16 September 2005; Citeseer: University Park, PA, USA, 2005; pp. 1083–1094.

121. Joerger, M.; Spenko, M. Towards Navigation Safety for Autonomous Cars. *Inside GNSS* **2017**, 40–49. Available online: https://par.nsf.gov/biblio/10070277 (accessed on 10 August 2022).

122. Sukkarieh, S.; Nebot, E.M.; Durrant-Whyte, H.F. Achieving Integrity in an INS/GPS Navigation Loop for Autonomous Land Vehicle Applications. In Proceedings of the 1998 IEEE International Conference on Robotics and Automation (Cat. No. 98CH36146), Leuven, Belgium, 20–24 May 1998; IEEE: Piscataway, NJ, USA, 1998; Volume 4, pp. 3437–3442.

123. Yan, L.; Zhang, Y.; He, Y.; Gao, S.; Zhu, D.; Ran, B.; Wu, Q. Hazardous Traffic Event Detection Using Markov Blanket and Sequential Minimal Optimization (MB-SMO). *Sensors* **2016**, *16*, 1084. [CrossRef]

124. Khalid, A.; Umer, T.; Afzal, M.K.; Anjum, S.; Sohail, A.; Asif, H.M. Autonomous Data Driven Surveillance and Rectification System Using In-Vehicle Sensors for Intelligent Transportation Systems (ITS). *Comput. Netw.* **2018**, *139*, 109–118. [CrossRef]

125. Bhamidipati, S.; Gao, G.X. Multiple Gps Fault Detection and Isolation Using a Graph-Slam Framework. In Proceedings of the 31st International Technical Meeting of the Satellite Division of the Institute of Navigation, ION GNSS+ 2018, Miami, FL, USA, 24–28 September 2018; Institute of Navigation: Manassas, VA, USA, 2018; pp. 2672–2681.

126. Meng, X.; Wang, H.; Liu, B. A Robust Vehicle Localization Approach Based on Gnss/Imu/Dmi/Lidar Sensor Fusion for Autonomous Vehicles. *Sensors* **2017**, *17*, 2140. [CrossRef]

127. Bikfalvi, P.; Lóránt, I. Combining Sensor Redundancy for Fault Detection in Navigation of an Autonomous Mobile Vehicle. *IFAC Proc. Vol.* **2000**, *33*, 843–847. [CrossRef]

128. Bader, K.; Lussier, B.; Schön, W. A Fault Tolerant Architecture for Data Fusion: A Real Application of Kalman Filters for Mobile Robot Localization. *Robot. Auton. Syst.* **2017**, *88*, 11–23. [CrossRef]

129. Bijjahalli, S.; Ramasamy, S.; Sabatini, R. A GNSS Integrity Augmentation System for Airport Ground Vehicle Operations. *Energy Procedia* **2017**, *110*, 149–155. [CrossRef]

130. Barabás, I.; Todoruţ, A.; Cordoş, N.; Molea, A. Current Challenges in Autonomous Driving. In *IOP Conference Series: Materials Science and Engineering*; IOP Publishing: Bristol, UK, 2017; Volume 252, p. 012096.

131. Anderson, J.M.; Nidhi, K.; Stanley, K.D.; Sorensen, P.; Samaras, C.; Oluwatola, O.A. *Autonomous Vehicle Technology: A Guide for Policymakers*; Rand Corporation: Perth, Australia, 2014; ISBN 0-8330-8437-2.

132. Maddox, J.; Sweatman, P.; Sayer, J. Intelligent Vehicles+ Infrastructure to Address Transportation Problems—A Strategic Approach. In Proceedings of the 24th international technical conference on the enhanced safety of vehicles (ESV), Gothenburg, Sweden, 8–11 June 2015.

133. Sivaraman, S. *Learning, Modeling, and Understanding Vehicle Surround Using Multi-Modal Sensing*; University of California: San Diego, CA, USA, 2013; ISBN 1-303-38570-8.

134. Lavrinc, D. This Is How Bad Self-Driving Cars Suck in Rain; Technology Report. 2014. Available online: https://jalopnik.com/ (accessed on 10 August 2022).

135. McFarland, M. Who's Responsible When an Autonomous Car Crashes. Available online: https://www.scientificamerican.com/article/who-s-responsible-when-a-self-driving-car-crashes/ (accessed on 10 August 2022).

136. Davies, A. *Google's Self-Driving Car Caused Its First Crash*; Wired: London, UK, 2016.

137. Stoma, M.; Dudziak, A.; Caban, J.; Droździel, P. The Future of Autonomous Vehicles in the Opinion of Automotive Market Users. *Energies* **2021**, *14*, 4777. [CrossRef]

Article

Non-Contact Detection of Delamination in Composite Laminates Coated with a Mechanoluminescent Sensor Using Convolutional AutoEncoder

Seogu Park [1], Jinwoo Song [1], Heung Soo Kim [1],* and Donghyeon Ryu [2]

[1] Department of Mechanical, Robotics and Energy Engineering, Dongguk University–Seoul, 30 Pildong-ro 1-gil, Jung-gu, Seoul 04620, Republic of Korea
[2] Department of Mechanical Engineering, New Mexico Tech, Socorro, NM 97229, USA
* Correspondence: heungsoo@dgu.edu; Tel.: +82-2-2260-8577; Fax: +82-2-2263-9379

Abstract: Delamination is a typical defect of carbon fiber-reinforced composite laminates. Detecting delamination is very important in the performance of laminated composite structures. Structural Health Monitoring (SHM) methods using the latest sensors have been proposed to detect delamination that occurs during the operation of laminated composite structures. However, most sensors used in SHM methods measure data in the contact form and do not provide visual information about delamination. Research into mechanoluminescent sensors (ML) that can address the limitations of existing sensors has been actively conducted for decades. The ML sensor responds to mechanical deformation and emits light proportional to mechanical stimuli, thanks it can provide visual information about changes in the physical quantity of the entire structure. Many researchers focus on detecting cracks in structures and impact damage with the ML sensor. This paper presents a method of detecting the delamination of composites using ML sensors. A Convolutional AutoEncoder (CAE) was used to automatically extract the delamination positions from light emission images, which offers better performance compared to edge detection methods.

Keywords: composite materials; Convolutional AutoEncoder (CAE); delamination; Mechanoluminescent (ML) sensor; non-contact sensing; structural health monitoring

MSC: 65-04

Citation: Park, S.; Song, J.; Kim, H.S.; Ryu, D. Non-Contact Detection of Delamination in Composite Laminates Coated with a Mechanoluminescent Sensor Using Convolutional AutoEncoder. *Mathematics* **2022**, *10*, 4254. https://doi.org/10.3390/math10224254

Academic Editors: Xiang Li, Shuo Zhang and Wei Zhang

Received: 4 October 2022
Accepted: 10 November 2022
Published: 15 November 2022

Publisher's Note: MDPI stays neutral with regard to jurisdictional claims in published maps and institutional affiliations.

1. Introduction

Recently, fiber-reinforced composite laminates have been widely used in the aerospace, mobility, and shipping industries due to their excellent specific strength, stiffness, and fatigue resistance [1–7]. However, fiber-reinforced composite laminates fabricated by laminating the fiber layers have several defects at the interface between the laminated layers [2,8]. In the case of defects, delamination is a typical defect of laminated composites [3,9]. Delamination reduces the strength and stiffness of composite materials [2,3,10]. Thus, it is very important to detect delamination in the performance of composite laminates [11–18]. Structural Health Monitoring (SHM) methods using the latest sensors, such as piezoelectric (PZT) sensors [19,20], carbon nanotube (CNT) sensors [21], and fiber Bragg grating (FBG) sensors [22], were proposed for detecting delamination in laminated composite structures. However, most sensors used in SHM measure data in a contact manner [23,24]. These sensors do not provide visual information about delamination, which can be a quick and instinctive sensor signal to detect delamination.

To solve these limitations of the aforementioned contact sensors, the wavefield image scanning technique was proposed as a non-contact technique for damage detection [25,26]. The wavefield image scanning method is a technique for obtaining a guided wavefield of a target structure excited by an excitation source as an image using a laser Doppler vibrometer (LDV). This technique proved to be highly effective in the non-contact detection of delamination in composite structures [25,26]. However, their efficiency depends on the surface treatment of the control structure and the inspection time of the entire structure [25,26]. In addition, a high-power laser beam used for inspection could affect the condition of the structure in the long term [25].

To overcome this problem, research has been actively pursued over the past few decades to develop non-contact sensors using mechanoluminescent (ML) materials. The ML sensor was fabricated in the form of a thin film by spraying a mixture of inorganic ML microparticles and transparent resin onto the substrate [27]. The airbrush allows the ML thin films to be freely coated onto complex surfaces. ML particles embedded in the ML sensor coating are subjected to mechanical stimuli, experienced by the ML sensor coating and consequently emit light. The ML light intensity was shown to vary in tandem with the extent of the mechanical stimuli, such as tension, fracture, impact, and pressure [28]. The ML light sensor signal can be measured in a real time to produce optical images with a camera. Accordingly, the ML sensor coating emits visual non-contact sensing information in the ML light, which can be used to understand the physical phenomena on ML-coated structural surfaces [29]. To harness the unique multi-physics ML characteristics, many different physical sensors were developed using ML materials, such as a strain sensor [30], a stress distribution sensor [23,24,31], an impact sensor [32], a torque sensor [33], and vibration sensor [34]. Further, there are several researchers who have investigated the use of ML materials for crack detection because the ML light intensity is much brighter at the crack tip to generate a high signal-to-noise ratio [27,35–39]. The research was conducted in order to detect the cracks propagation and delamination in the adhesive layer of the double cantilever beam (DCB) using the unique ML feature [29]. However, relatively less attention has been paid to the use of ML to detect delamination between the laminated fiber layers of the composites.

As part of this research, we studied the non-contact sensing capabilities of the ML sensor coating to detect delamination occurring between the fiber membranes of the composite material using the visualized ML light sensor signal. The three specific objectives to achieve the general objective are as follows: (i) the ML sensor system is constructed as a simple non-contact sensor system consisting of ML sensors that are thinly coated on the surface of composite laminates, (ii) the light emitted by the ML sensor on the delaminated interface of the composite laminates was captured with a high-speed camera to record video to export the images, (iii) an image processing technique is applied to automatically extract the delamination locations on the ML images. Convolutional AutoEncoder (CAE) was applied to automatically extract delamination locations from the obtained light emission images. The CAE results were compared with those of the edge detection method.

2. Background on Convolutional AutoEncoder (CAE)

2.1. Motivations on CAE

The measurement data of the ML sensor is in the form of an image, unlike other contact sensors. Therefore, the application of image processing techniques is very important for extracting spatial information from ML sensor data. In this study, it is only necessary to segment the delamination position, that is, the light-emitting part in the ML sensor image. A representative image segmentation technique is the thresholding method which divides the objects to be segmented from the rest using a threshold value of pixels [40]. However, it is very difficult to automatically define the threshold value in low-contrast and noisy images in this way. To overcome these limitations, researchers performed automatic image crack detection using deep learning techniques, Convolutional Neural Network (CNN) [41–43], Fully Convolutional Network (FCN) [44], and Convolutional AutoEncoder(CAE) [45,46]. Among them, the CAE anomaly detection study of concrete structures motivated us to use CAE in our research for the following four reasons: (i) other types of autoencoder are designed for learning time series data, whereas CAE is designed for learning image data, (ii) CAE anomaly detection does not require labelled data as required by other deep learning techniques, (iii) CAE is designed to produce reconstructed images of the input images as results, and therefore, the CAE automatically learns the features of the training images, and iv) CAE trained by only the input images does not correctly reconstruct images with properties different than the input images and the detection of anomalies in pixel units is possible by using these CAE characteristics [45].

2.2. Architecture of CAE for Anomaly Detection

CAE is a network composed of an encoder, a latent space, and a decoder. The encoder extracts the representative features of the images through convolutional layers and the compressed features are encoded in the latent space, which is smaller in dimension than the input images [45]. The encoded features pass through the decoder and the decoder, which is composed of transposed convolutional layers, reconstructs the features as close to the original images as possible. In other words, CAE optimizes a huge number of parameters to best reconstruct the training image dataset.

Figure 1 shows the overall CAE architecture. CAE consists of encoder and decoder parts. the CAE input images are normalized images ranging from 0 to 1 with a size of 50×50 pixels, and the images are normal images with no light emission. In the encoder, representative features of the input images are extracted, and the feature dimensions are reduced as the images pass through the three modules, which are two convolutional layers and one max pooling layer. In order to minimize information loss caused by the dimensionality reduction, the number of channels of the convolutional layers are doubled every time it passes through the modules. After passing through the last module's max pooling layer, the features pass through one additional convolutional layer and the features are compressed into 128 dimensions in the latent space. In the decoder, the encoded features are reconstructed into the input image. The reconstruction process involves the passage of the three modules which are one transposed convolutional layer and two convolutional layers. The number of channels of the transposed convolutional layers are reduced as half. After passing through the last convolutional layer of the decoder, the input images are reconstructed by one additional transposed convolutional layer. For training of the CAE, Mean Squared Error (MSE) was adopted as a loss function and the Adam optimizer was used to minimize the loss function. MSE can be calculated by dividing the sum of the reconstruction errors of all images by the total number of images. MSE can be defined as follows:

$$\textit{Mean Squared Error (MSE)} = \frac{1}{N} \sum_{n=1}^{N} \left\{ p(r, c) - p(r, c)^{reconstructed} \right\}^2 \tag{1}$$

where p is the pixel value of the input image, $p^{reconstructed}$ is the pixel value of the reconstructed image, r is the image row index, c is the image column index, and N is the total number of images.

After the training, CAE has the optimal parameters to reproduce normal images as well as possible, and these parameters make it difficult to restore defective images.

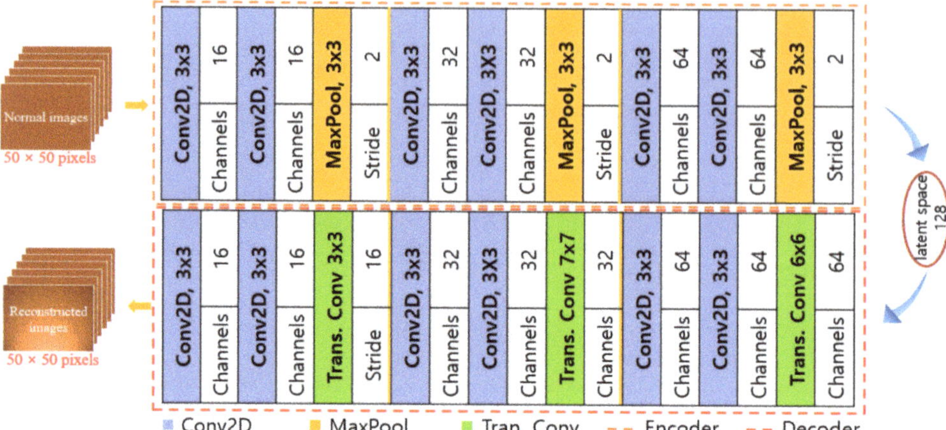

Figure 1. Model of the architecture of a convolutional autoencoder for segmentation of light emission.

3. Methodology

The proposed method of ML image-based delamination detection is divided into the data acquisition process, including the fabrication of ML coated composite laminates and image processing of the acquired data. Figure 2 is a brief diagram of the ML image-based delamination detection method, which consists of three steps. In the first step, ML coated composite laminates are fabricated and images are obtained with a camera when a bending load is applied to the composite. In the second stage, feature extraction is performed on the images without light emission using Convolutional AutoEncoder (CAE). Then, the light-emitted images are entered into the trained CAE model, and the reconstruction error images are calculated by obtaining images that are not well reconstructed as results. In the third step, a threshold value of reconstruction error is extracted from the reconstruction error images and a binary classification is carried out for each pixel based on the threshold value. After classification, the location of the composite delamination is extracted by merging the classified images.

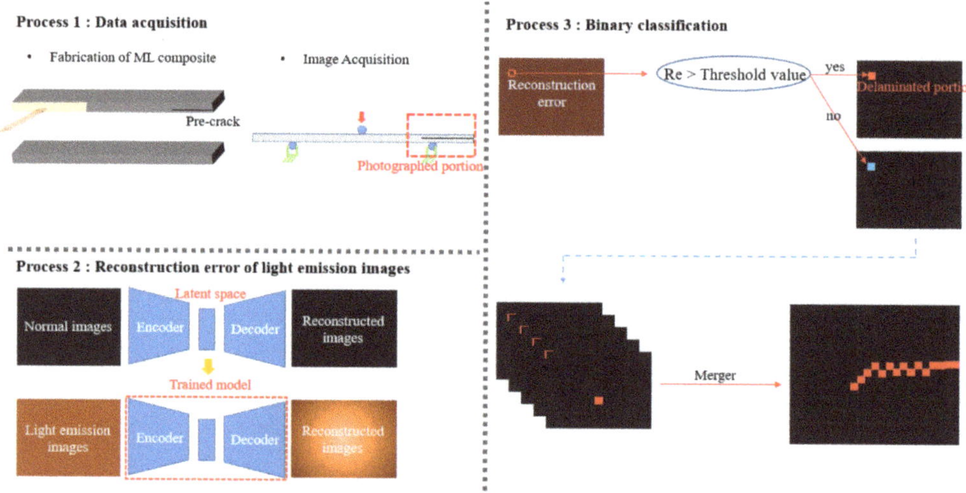

Figure 2. Methodology of the proposed ML image-based delamination detection.

4. Experimental Details

4.1. Preparation of Test Specimens

Data acquisition consists of the ML composite fabrication and acquisition of light emission images by means of a camera. ML composite refers to a composite bonded to an ML compound that emits light in response to mechanical deformation. As shown in Figure 3, ML coated composite laminates are manufactured in the following steps: (1) ML compound is made by mixing inorganic particles and a compound of resin material and hardener, (2) composite laminates are coated with an ML compound on the laminate side. In the first step, polydimethylsiloxane (PDMS; product #:Sylgard 184 kit) and silicone elastomer curing agent (product #:Sylgard 184 kit) are mixed in a weight ratio of 10:1. The mixed compound is blended with copper doped zinc sulfide (ZnS:Cu) particles in a weight ratio of 3:7 to complete ML compound. In the second stage, two carbon fiber reinforced composite (CFRP) plates are made by a Vacuum Assisted Resin Transfer Molding (VARTM) process. Both plates are manufactured by laminating 20 carbon fiber prepregs (Fiber glass product #:2069-C), and one of them, polytetrafluoroethylene (PTFE), is inserted between the 10th and 11th layers to initiate delamination under load. After fabrication, the two specimens are cut identically to length, width and thickness of 17.78 cm, 2.54 cm, and 3.81 mm. In the specimen with pre-crack inserted, the length of the pre-crack is 2.08 cm from the end of the specimen. The ML composite is then completed after coating ML compound on the side of the specimens with a wooden stick and heating in an oven at 80 °C for 2 h.

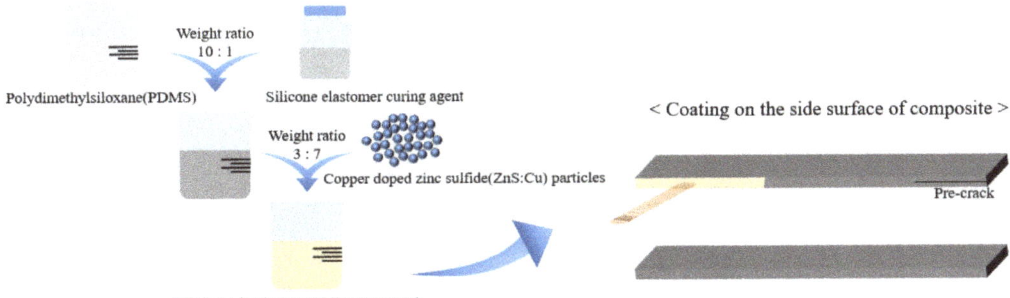

Figure 3. Fabrication of ML coated composite laminates.

4.2. Test Setup

Figure 4 is a schematic diagram relating to the ML sensor system configuration and the image acquisition process. The ML sensor system consists of ML coated composite laminates, a high speed camera for measuring light emission images, and a computer as a data acquisition device. In this study, a 3-point bending test was performed to trigger delamination of CFRP composite laminates under bending load. For comparison of two specimens, 3-point bending tests were performed on both specimens under certain load conditions. The specific load condition is 10 cycles of the same specification with a minimum displacement of 6mm and a load rate of 1500 mm/min. Image acquisition from both experiments was performed in a dark room to minimize ambient light sources and was recorded with a highspeed camera (Shimadzu HPV-X HyperVision camera). The result was a thousand images for each specimen at 120 frames per second (fps), corresponding to five cycles and one load cycle. The images were stored as 16-bit gray scale images on the computer. Figure 5 shows an experimental setup of an ML sensor system.

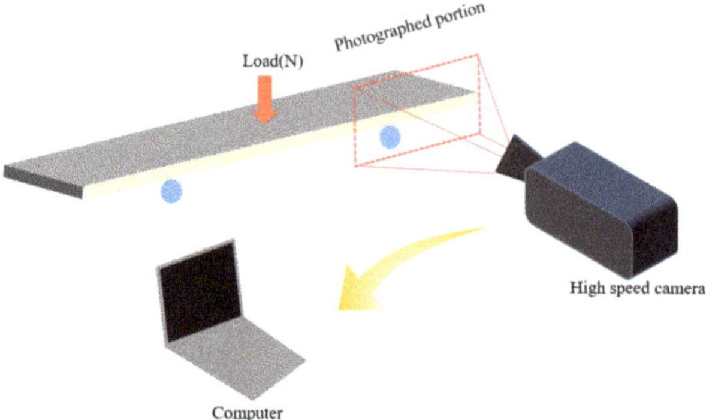

Figure 4. ML sensor system configuration and image acquisition.

Figure 5. Experimental setup for the 3-point bending test of ML coated composite laminates.

4.3. Reconstruction Error of Light Emission Images

The measurement data of the ML sensor is in the form of an image, unlike other contact sensors. Therefore, the application of image processing techniques is very important for extracting spatial information from ML sensor data. In this study, it is only necessary to segment the delamination position, that is, the light-emitting part in the ML sensor image. A representative image segmentation technique is the thresholding method which divides the objects to be segmented from the rest using a threshold value of pixels [40]. However, it is very difficult to automatically define the threshold value in low-contrast and noisy images in this way. To overcome these limitations, researchers performed automatic image crack detection using deep learning techniques, Convolutional Neural Network (CNN) [41–43], Fully Convolutional Network (FCN) [44], and Convolutional AutoEncoder(CAE) [45]. Among them, the CAE anomaly detection study of concrete structures motivated us to use CAE in our research for the following three reasons: (i) CAE anomaly detection does not require labelled data as required by other deep learning techniques, (ii) CAE is designed to produce reconstructed images of the input images as results, and therefore, the CAE automatically learns the features of the training images, and (iii) CAE trained by only the input images does not correctly reconstruct images with properties different than the input images and the detection of anomalies in pixel units is possible by using these CAE characteristics [45].

CAE is a network composed of an encoder, a latent space, and a decoder. The encoder extracts the representative features of the images through convolutional layers and the compressed features are encoded in the latent space, which is smaller in dimension than the input images [45]. The encoded features pass through the decoder and the decoder, which is composed of transposed convolutional layers, reconstructs the features as close to the original images as possible. In other words, CAE optimizes a huge number of parameters to best reconstruct the training image dataset. Thus, the trained CAE model does not adequately restore images that are non-uniform from the trained images, leading to a high reconstruction error of the defective part. In this study, the parts with high reconstruction error indicate that light is emitted, and therefore parts signify that delamination is occurring in these parts.

Figure 6 shows the process of obtaining reconstruction error images that indicate portions of light emission. The process of acquiring reconstruction error images consists of four steps. In the first step, the original 250×450-pixel images obtained with the camera are cropped into images of the same 50×50-pixel size. This is to increase the number of images and divide the original images into square images suitable for CAE training. Through this process, 1000 images obtained from each of the two specimens are augmented to 40,000 images with a size of 50×50 pixels for each specimen. In the second step, the cropped 16-bit grayscale images, which consist of pixel values in the range 0 and $2^{16} - 1$, are normalized to the range 0 and 1 for efficient computation. In the third step, CAE training takes place with the use of a prepared data set. The training dataset consists of 40,000 images of a normal specimen, and this is to learn the optimal parameters of the CAE model to reconstruct images that do not emit light. The model trained in this way produces a high reconstruction error for images in which light is emitted. The pixel reconstruction error is defined as follows [45].

$$reconstruction\ error = \left\{ p(r,\ c) - p(r,\ c)^{reconstructed} \right\}^2 \tag{2}$$

where p is the pixel value of the input image, $p^{reconstructed}$ is the pixel value of the reconstructed image, r is the image row index and c is the image column index.

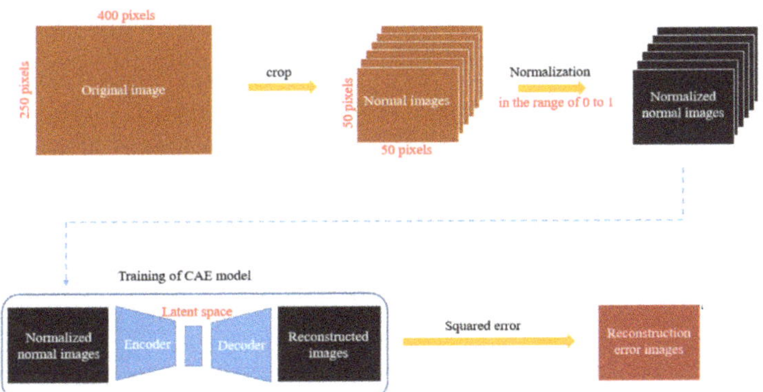

Figure 6. Schematic process of obtaining reconstruction error images.

In the fourth step, the reconstruction error images are finally obtained by calculating the reconstruction error in pixel units between the reconstructed images and the input images. In other words, 40,000 reconstruction error images are obtained where each pixel value consists of the reconstruction error.

4.4. Binary Classification

Figure 7 shows a simplified flowchart of the binary classification in pixel units which is required for segmenting only the light emission part of the light emission image.

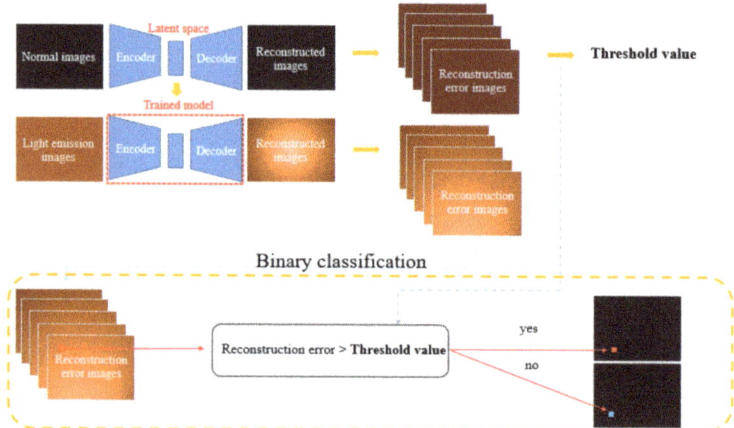

Figure 7. Schematic process of binary classification using the threshold value.

The binary classification proceeds in two steps. In the first step, a threshold value is determined based on the reconstruction error images obtained in Section 2.2, and this threshold value determines whether the pixel is emitting light. The threshold value is entirely user-defined and is carefully defined based on whether the light-emitting part is properly segmented when removing noise from an image. In the second step, the CAE model is used to create the reconstruction error images of the defective images, and the reconstruction error images are obtained in the same process as in Section 2.2. After that, all pixels of the reconstruction images are classified based on a predefined threshold value. As a result, pixels that are larger than the threshold have the same value of 1 at their respective positions, and the remaining pixels are mapped to 0.

The classified images are 50×50 pixels in size. The cropped images must be merged after binary classification and restored to the original image size to specify the delamination location in the original image. Figure 8 shows a schematic process for combining classified images. The 40 images from one original image, which is 250×400 pixels, are returned to their respective cropped positions, and the combined image as a result of this process becomes a binary classification image that determines the location of the delamination in the original image. The merged image is an image in which the pixels corresponding to the delamination location have a pixel value of 1, and the rest of the pixels have a pixel value of 0.

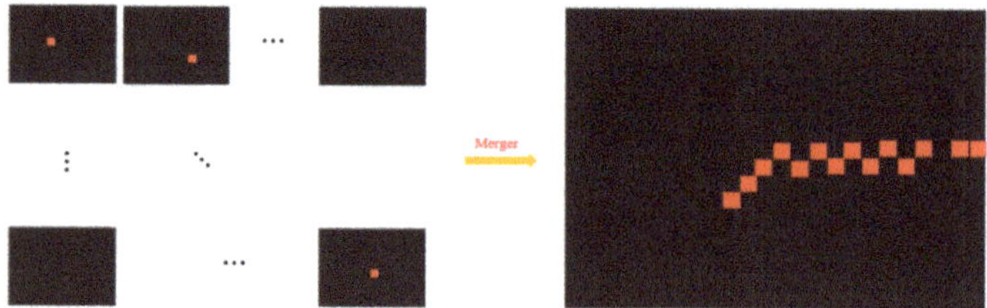

Figure 8. Schematic flow chart of classified images connection.

5. Results

This section begins by confirming whether the ML sensor is emitting light due to delamination. That is verified by comparing the mean pixel value (MPV) of the images from the experiments. Then, this paper shows the segmentation results of the light emission images that are classified by CAE. To validate the effectiveness of the segmentation method, the results are compared with the detection results using the Canny edge detection method.

5.1. MPV Changes

MPV is the average value of all pixels in the image. It is used as an indicator of light emission in images for the following reasons: (i) all images are acquired in an experimental environment without exposure to light, and the image datasets consist of a normal dataset and a defective dataset with the same number of images, (ii) the only experimental variable is the presence of pre-crack in the specimen, and (iii) therefore, the obvious MPV difference between the two datasets indicates that the difference is caused by light emission from the delamination location.

Figure 9 is a graph comparing the change in the Mean Pixel Value (MPV) of 1000 images each obtained from the two specimens in Section 2.1. In Figure 9, the blue line shows the MPV for 1000 images obtained from a normal specimen and the red line shows the MPV for defective images obtained from another specimen. MPV can be defined as follows:

$$Mean\ Pixel\ Value\ (MPV) = \frac{sum\ of\ all\ pixel\ values}{the\ number\ of\ pixels} \tag{3}$$

MPV can be calculated by dividing the sum of all pixel values by the number of pixels and MPV is between 0 and $2^{16} - 1$ because all images are 16-bit grayscale images. As shown in Figure 9, the MPV of the defective images is confirmed to have several peak values that cannot be observed in the normal images. Since the presence of pre-crack is the experimental variable, several peaks show that the ML sensor repeatedly emits light during the loading and unloading cycle at the delamination location.

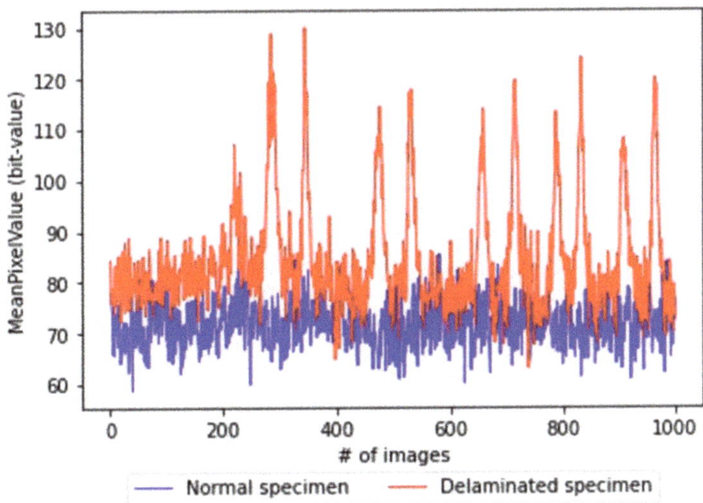

Figure 9. MPV of images obtained from the experiments.

Figure 10 is a gray color image of the acquired 221st image, which was acquired in a first loading cycle. The clustered pixels showed the light emission locations.

Figure 10. A gray color image of the 221st defective image.

5.2. Pixel-Level Segmentation CAE

Many variables affect the pixel values distribution, including the position of the camera, the shooting angle and the state of the lens. Therefore, it is essential to incorporate image processing techniques to efficiently analyze images from the ML sensor. In this study, pixel-level segmentation was performed to extract the delamination locations on defective images using Convolutional AutoEncoder (CAE).

Based on the CAE characteristics the reconstruction error images were obtained as described in Section 2.2, among which the reconstruction error images for the normal dataset were used to extract a reconstruction error threshold value that can classify the pixel light emission. Figure 11 shows the maximum reconstruction errors of the reconstruction error images for each dataset. As can be seen in Figure 11, it is confirmed that the maximum reconstruction errors of defective images have several peaks that cannot be detected in normal images. The peaks are analogous to the MPV peaks in Figure 8. It can be analyzed that the trained CAE shows high reconstruction errors for the light emission images. To classify light emission in pixel units, the threshold value was selected from the maximum reconstruction errors of normal images in Figure 11. In this study, the threshold value was set with an increase from the mean value of the maximum reconstruction errors for normal images to their maximum value. Finally, the threshold value was set to 1.5 times the mean value, which can eliminate noise while detecting pixels with low light intensity. After selecting the threshold value, the reconstruction error images of the defective images were classified in pixel units, and pixels with reconstruction errors greater than the threshold value were classified as 1, and the remaining pixels were classified as 0. Then, the classified 40,000 images were merged to their original size to finally obtain a total of 1000 classified images.

Figure 12 shows some of the CAE classification results, and the classified images are six consecutive images when the first load is applied to the pre-fracture specimen k. The clustered pixels of the classified images indicate the location and start time of delamination. Furthermore, the classified images show that only the delamination portions are segmented during noise removal by a threshold value extracted from CAE. Figure 13 shows the sequence of six consecutive images when the first unload is applied to the specimen. More pixels are classified in the first unload cycle because sufficient delamination has already occurred. These results show the CAE characteristics where the reconstruction error is increased in the defective portions of the image.

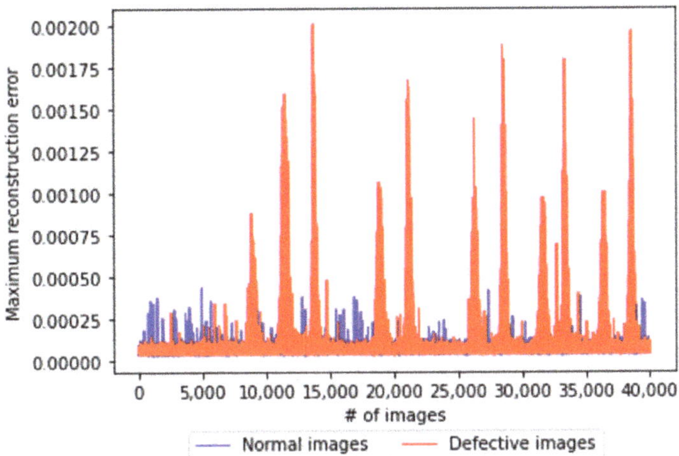

Figure 11. Maximum reconstruction error of the images from the experiments.

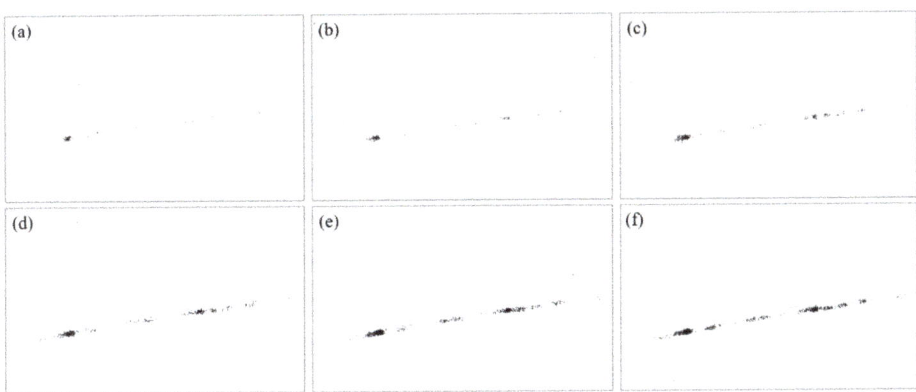

Figure 12. Some representative classified images in the first load cycle: (**a**) 212th; (**b**) 213th; (**c**) 214th; (**d**) 215th; (**e**) 216th; (**f**) 217th.

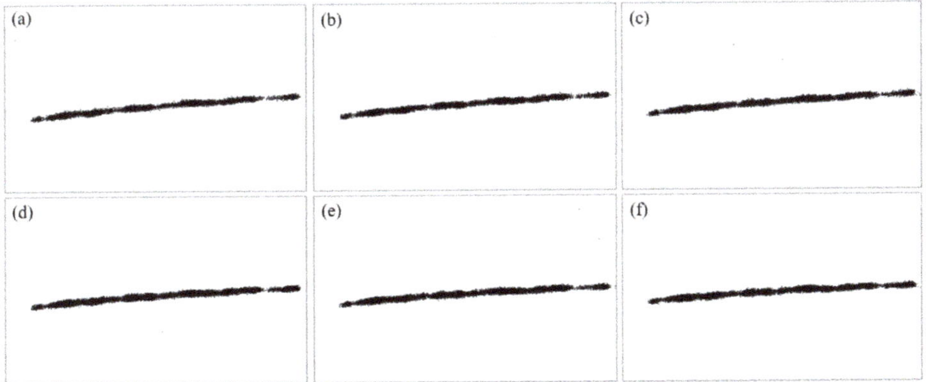

Figure 13. Some representative classified images in the first unload cycle: (**a**) 282th; (**b**) 283th; (**c**) 284th; (**d**) 285th; (**e**) 286th; (**f**) 287th.

5.3. Comparision of CAE Results to Canny Edge Detection Results

This section conducted a comparative study comparing the results obtained with CAE and the Canny edge detection algorithm. Canny edge detection is a widely used and robust algorithm among various edge detection methods [47]. Edge detection was selected for the performance comparison because light emission is the part where the light intensity changes rapidly and can therefore be considered the edge of the image.

Figure 14 shows the comparative results of the different detection methods. In Figure 14, the numbers in the first row are the gray images for the four consecutive original images in the second load cycles. The images in the second and third rows are the result images obtained by CAE and Canny edge detection, respectively. As can be seen in Figure 13, the gray images for the original images demonstrate the relative pixel intensities at the delamination location, showing that non-contact detection of composite delamination is feasible using an ML sensor. However, the delamination location in the images can be manually identified by a person and the use of image processing techniques is essential to build an automated detection system. Canny edge detection method results show good performance in detecting edges in light-emitting portions while removing noise from the original image. However, the results show that light-emitting parts can only be detected as multiple edges. For that reason, edge detection detects all pixels with larger gradients as edges. Therefore, in the edge detection method, the undetected pixels exist between edges in the light emission part. Whereas, it can be seen that the results using CAE minimized the number of undetected pixels by showing the spatial information of the light emission portions as a cluster. In addition, CAEs show good performance in eliminating noise from the original images.

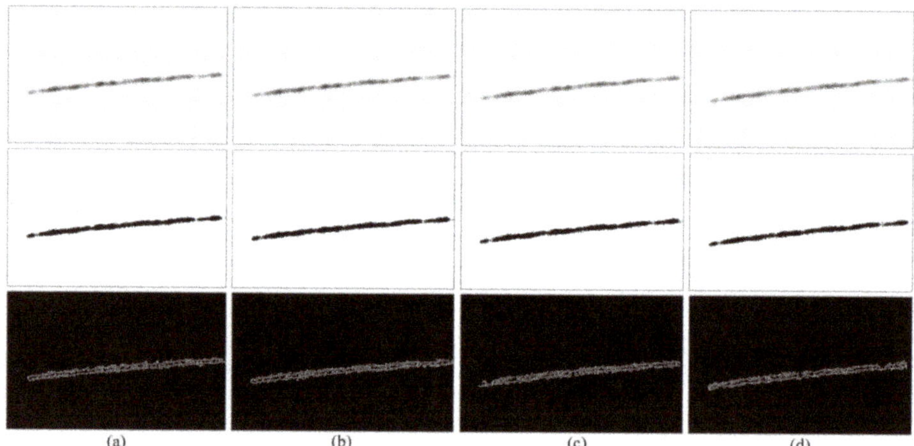

Figure 14. Comparative results—top: gray image for the original image, middle: CAE, bottom: Canny edge detection: (**a**) 344th; (**b**) 345th; (**c**) 346th; (**d**) 347th.

6. Discussions

We investigated the non-contact detection of delamination in composite laminates using ML sensors. In the Section 5.1, it was confirmed that when the composite is loaded, repetitive light is emitted from the delamination location. Furthermore, no light is emitted even under load as long as there is no delamination. These results show that the delamination of composite laminates can be detected in a non-contact manner with the ML sensor.

In addition, we applied image processing technique to extract the delamination portions in the ML images. Convolutional AutoEncoder (CAE) was selected as the image processing technique, and the CAE classified the images in a pixel unit using the threshold value of the reconstruction errors. In the Section 5.2, the results indicate that the reconstruction error used for the pixel-level classification is sufficient as an indicator of light emission. In the Section 5.3, we compared the performance of CAE and Canny edge detection on the same images. Canny edge detection did not properly detect pixels between many edges, whereas CAE extracted more accurate delamination locations by minimizing the number of undetected pixels. Additionally, CAE has superior performance compared to other network models [41–44,48] in the following two aspects: (i) the image labeling task is not required for CAE training, which can reduce the huge amount of time to prepare data which are required for training CAE and FCN models, and (ii) the detection resolution of CNN is limited to the training image size, whereas CAE can improve the detection resolution in a pixel unit by using a simple static threshold value.

7. Conclusions

Little research has been carried out to date on detecting delamination in composite laminates using ML sensors, and image processing techniques have rarely been applied to ML sensor images. In this study, we confirmed the applicability of the ML sensor for detecting delamination in composite laminates. In addition, delamination locations were automatically extracted from ML images using CAE, which shows that the application of an image processing technique enables real-time composite delamination of composite to be detected. However, the ML sensor may be limited in an environment where external light sources are exposed because the ML sensor is a light-emitting sensor. The light intensity of the ML sensor has a broad peak in the visible light wavelength band. Therefore, visible light can be noise in the ML images. Thus, more sophisticated image processing techniques should be applied to analyze ML images exposed to external light sources. This will limit the application of the ML sensor in the actual field. To deal with future limitations, we will evaluate the adaptability of the ML sensor to detect delamination of composites when light sources are exposed. In addition, the CAE will be verified as to whether it is also effective for ML images acquired in an environment with external light sources. Another limitation is the versatility of the ML sensor system about internal delamination of composite laminates. This study showed that the ML sensor system is effective as a non-contact sensor for visible delamination such as cracks. However, future studies should focus on various internal defects of composite laminates for the application of the ML sensor system in the actual field.

Author Contributions: Conceptualization, H.S.K., D.R. and S.P.; methodology, S.P. and J.S.; formal analysis S.P. and J.S.; investigation, S.P.; resources, H.S.K.; writing—original draft preparation, S.P., J.S., D.R. and H.S.K.; writing—review and editing, H.S.K., J.S. and D.R.; visualization, S.P.; supervision, H.S.K. and D.R.; project administration, H.S.K.; funding acquisition, H.S.K. All authors have read and agreed to the published version of the manuscript.

Funding: This research was supported by the MOTIE (Ministry of Trade, Industry, and Energy) in Korea, under the Fostering Global Talents for Innovative Growth Program (P0017307) supervised by the Korea Institute for Advancement of Technology (KIAT).

Data Availability Statement: Not applicable.

Conflicts of Interest: The authors declare no conflict of interest.

References

1. Prashanth, S.; Subbaya, K.M.; Nithin, K.; Sachhidananda, S. Fiber Reinforced Composites—A Review. *J. Mater. Sci. Eng.* **2017**, *06*, 2–6. [CrossRef]
2. Khan, S.U.; Kim, J.-K. Impact and Delamination Failure of Multiscale Carbon Nanotube-Fiber Reinforced Polymer Composites: A Review. *Int. J. Aeronaut. Space Sci.* **2011**, *12*, 115–133. [CrossRef]
3. Camanho, P.P.; Davila, C.G.; De Moura, M.F. Numerical Simulation of Mixed-Mode Progressive Delamination in Composite Materials. *J. Compos. Mater.* **2003**, *37*, 1415–1438. [CrossRef]
4. An, H.; Youn, B.D.; Kim, H.S. Reliability-based Design Optimization of Laminated Composite Structures under Delamination and Material Property Uncertainties. *Int. J. Mech. Sci.* **2021**, *205*, 106561. [CrossRef]

5. Khan, A.; Kim, H.S. A Brief Overview of Delamination Localization in Laminated Composites. *Multiscale Sci. Eng.* **2022**, *4*, 102–110. [CrossRef]

6. Huang, B.; Wang, J.; Kim, H.S. A stress function based model for transient thermal stresses of composite laminates in various time-variant thermal environments. *Int. J. Mech. Sci.* **2020**, *180*, 105651. [CrossRef]

7. Khalid, S.; Kim, H.S. Recent Studies on Stress Function-Based Approaches for the Free Edge Stress Analysis of Smart Composite Laminates: A Brief Review. *Multiscale Sci. Eng.* **2022**, *4*, 73–78. [CrossRef]

8. Khan, A.; Raouf, I.; Noh, Y.R.; Lee, D.; Sohn, J.W.; Kim, H.S. Autonomous assessment of delamination in laminated composites using deep learning and data augmentation. *Compos. Struct.* **2022**, *290*, 115502. [CrossRef]

9. Bolotin, V.V. Delaminations in composite structures: Its origin, buckling, growth and stability. *Compos. Part B Eng.* **1996**, *27*, 129–145. [CrossRef]

10. Khalid, S.; Kim, H.-S.; Kim, H.S.; Choi, J.-H. Inspection Interval Optimization for Aircraft Composite Tail Wing Structure Using Numerical-Analysis-Based Approach. *Mathematics* **2022**, *10*, 3836. [CrossRef]

11. Khan, A.; Kim, N.; Shin, J.K.; Kim, H.S.; Youn, B.D. Damage assessment of smart composite structures via machine learning: A review. *JMST Adv.* **2019**, *1*, 107–124. [CrossRef]

12. Khan, A.; Ko, D.-K.; Lim, S.C.; Kim, H.S. Structural vibration-based classification and prediction of delamination in smart composite laminates using deep learning neural network. *Compos. Part B Eng.* **2019**, *161*, 586–594. [CrossRef]

13. Khan, A.; Kim, H.S. Assessment of delaminated smart composite laminates via system identification and supervised learning. *Compos. Struct.* **2018**, *206*, 354–362. [CrossRef]

14. An, H.; Youn, B.D.; Kim, H.S. A methodology for sensor number and placement optimization for vibration-based damage detection of composite structures under model uncertainty. *Compos. Struct.* **2022**, *279*, 114863. [CrossRef]

15. Khan, A.; Khalid, S.; Raouf, I.; Sohn, J.-W.; Kim, H.-S. Autonomous Assessment of Delamination Using Scarce Raw Structural Vibration and Transfer Learning. *Sensors* **2021**, *21*, 6239. [CrossRef] [PubMed]

16. Khalid, S.; Lee, J.; Kim, H.S. Series Solution-Based Approach for the Interlaminar Stress Analysis of Smart Composites under Thermo-Electro-Mechanical Loading. *Mathematics* **2022**, *10*, 268. [CrossRef]

17. Khan, A.; Kim, H.S. Classification and prediction of multidamages in smart composite laminates using discriminant analysis. *Mech. Adv. Mater. Struct.* **2022**, *29*, 230–240. [CrossRef]

18. An, H.; Youn, B.D.; Kim, H.S. Optimal Sensor Placement Considering Both Sensor Faults Under Uncertainty and Sensor Clustering for Vibration-Based Damage Detection. *Struct. Multidiscip. Optim.* **2022**, *65*, 102. [CrossRef]

19. Sohn, H.; Park, G.; Wait, J.R.; Limback, N.P.; Farrar, C.R. Wavelet-based active sensing for delamination detection in composite structures. *Smart Mater. Struct.* **2004**, *13*, 153–160. [CrossRef]

20. Tan, P.; Tong, L. Delamination Detection of Composite Beams Using Piezoelectric Sensors with Evenly Distributed Electrode Strips. *J. Compos. Mater.* **2004**, *38*, 321–352. [CrossRef]

21. Abot, J.L.; Song, Y.; Vatsavaya, M.S.; Medikonda, S.; Kier, Z.; Jayasinghe, C.; Rooy, N.; Shanov, V.N.; Schulz, M.J. Delamination detection with carbon nanotube thread in self-sensing composite materials. *Compos. Sci. Technol.* **2010**, *70*, 1113–1119. [CrossRef]

22. Takeda, S.; Okabe, Y.; Takeda, N. Delamination detection in CFRP laminates with embedded small-diameter fiber Bragg grating sensors. *Compos. Part Appl. Sci. Manuf.* **2002**, *33*, 971–980. [CrossRef]

23. Xu, C.-N.; Watanabe, T.; Akiyama, M.; Zheng, X.-G. Direct view of stress distribution in solid by mechanoluminescence. *Appl. Phys. Lett.* **1999**, *74*, 2414–2416. [CrossRef]

24. Xu, C.-N.; Zheng, X.-G.; Akiyama, M. Dynamic visualization of stress distribution by mechanoluminescence image. *Appl. Phys. Lett.* **2000**, *76*, 179–181. [CrossRef]

25. Park, B.; An, Y.-K.; Sohn, H. Visualization of hidden delamination and debonding in composites through noncontact laser ultrasonic scanning. *Compos. Sci. Technol.* **2014**, *100*, 10–18. [CrossRef]

26. Sohn, H.; Dutta, D.; Yang, J.Y.; Park, H.J.; DeSimio, M.; Olson, S.; Swenson, E. Delamination detection in composites through guided wave field image processing. *Compos. Sci. Technol.* **2011**, *71*, 1250–1256. [CrossRef]

27. Terasaki, N.; Xu, C.-N. Historical-Log Recording System for Crack Opening and Growth Based on Mechanoluminescent Flexible Sensor. *IEEE Sens. J.* **2013**, *13*, 3999–4004. [CrossRef]

28. Timilsina, S.; Kim, J.S.; Kim, J.; Kim, G.-W. Review of state-of-the-art sensor applications using mechanoluminescence microparticles. *Int. J. Precis. Eng. Manuf.* **2016**, *17*, 1237–1247. [CrossRef]

29. Terasaki, N.; Fujio, Y.; Horiuchi, S.; Akiyama, H. Mechanoluminescent studies of failure line on double cantilever beam (DCB) and tapered-DCB (TDCB) test with similar and dissimilar material joints. *Int. J. Adhes. Adhes.* **2019**, *93*, 102328. [CrossRef]

30. Sohn, K.-S.; Timilsina, S.; Singh, S.P.; Lee, J.-W.; Kim, J.S. A Mechanoluminescent ZnS:Cu/Rhodamine/SiO$_2$/PDMS and Piezoresistive CNT/PDMS Hybrid Sensor: Red-Light Emission and a Standardized Strain Quantification. *ACS Appl. Mater. Interfaces* **2016**, *8*, 34777–34783. [CrossRef]

31. Terasaki, N.; Fujio, Y.; Sakata, Y.; Uehara, M.; Tabaru, T. Direct Visualization of Stress Distribution Related to Adhesive through Mechanoluminescence. *ECS Trans.* **2017**, *75*, 9. [CrossRef]

32. Ryu, D.; Castano, N.; Vedera, K. Mechanoluminescent Composites Towards Autonomous Impact Damage Detection of Aerospace Structures. In Proceedings of the Structural Health Monitoring 2015, Stanford, CA, USA, 1–3 September 2015; Destech Publications: Lancaster, PA, USA, 2015.

33. Kim, J.S.; Kim, G.-W. New non-contacting torque sensor based on the mechanoluminescence of ZnS:Cu microparticles. *Sens. Actuators Phys.* **2014**, *218*, 125–131. [CrossRef]
34. Chen, B.; Peng, D.-F.; Lu, P.; Sheng, Z.-P.; Yan, K.-Y.; Fu, Y. Evaluation of vibration mode shape using a mechanoluminescent sensor. *Appl. Phys. Lett.* **2021**, *119*, 094102. [CrossRef]
35. Timilsina, S.; Bashnet, R.; Kim, S.H.; Lee, K.H.; Kim, J.S. A life-time reproducible mechano-luminescent paint for the visualization of crack propagation mechanisms in concrete structures. *Int. J. Fatigue* **2017**, *101*, 75–79. [CrossRef]
36. Fujio, Y.; Xu, C.-N.; Terasawa, Y.; Sakata, Y.; Yamabe, J.; Ueno, N.; Terasaki, N.; Yoshida, A.; Watanabe, S.; Murakami, Y. Sheet sensor using SrAl2O4:Eu mechanoluminescent material for visualizing inner crack of high-pressure hydrogen vessel. *Int. J. Hydrogen Energy* **2016**, *41*, 1333–1340. [CrossRef]
37. Fujio, Y.; Xu, C.-N.; Sakata, Y.; Ueno, N.; Terasaki, N. Invisible crack visualization and depth analysis by mechanoluminescence film. *J. Alloys Compd.* **2020**, *832*, 154900. [CrossRef]
38. Kim, W.J.; Lee, J.M.; Kim, J.S.; Lee, C.J. Measuring high speed crack propagation in concrete fracture test using mechanoluminescent material. *Smart Struct. Syst.* **2012**, *10*, 547–555. [CrossRef]
39. Timilsina, S.; Lee, K.H.; Kwon, Y.N.; Kim, J.S. Optical Evaluation of In Situ Crack Propagation by Using Mechanoluminescence of $SrAl_2O_4 : Eu^{2+}, Dy^{3+}$. *J. Am. Ceram. Soc.* **2015**, *98*, 2197–2204. [CrossRef]
40. Raju, P.D.R.; Neelima, G. Image Segmentation by using Histogram Thresholding. *Int. J. Comput. Sci. Eng. Technol.* **2012**, *2*, 776–779.
41. Zhang, L.; Yang, F.; Daniel Zhang, Y.; Zhu, Y.J. Road crack detection using deep convolutional neural network. In Proceedings of the 2016 IEEE International Conference on Image Processing (ICIP), Phoenix, AZ, USA, 25–28 September 2016; IEEE: Phoenix, AZ, USA, 2016; pp. 3708–3712.
42. Li, S.; Zhao, X. Image-Based Concrete Crack Detection Using Convolutional Neural Network and Exhaustive Search Technique. *Adv. Civ. Eng.* **2019**, *2019*, 6520620. [CrossRef]
43. Cha, Y.-J.; Choi, W.; Büyüköztürk, O. Deep Learning-Based Crack Damage Detection Using Convolutional Neural Networks: Deep learning-based crack damage detection using CNNs. *Comput.-Aided Civ. Infrastruct. Eng.* **2017**, *32*, 361–378. [CrossRef]
44. Dung, C.V.; Anh, L.D. Autonomous concrete crack detection using deep fully convolutional neural network. *Autom. Constr.* **2019**, *99*, 52–58. [CrossRef]
45. Chow, J.K.; Su, Z.; Wu, J.; Tan, P.S.; Mao, X.; Wang, Y.H. Anomaly detection of defects on concrete structures with the convolutional autoencoder. *Adv. Eng. Inform.* **2020**, *45*, 101105. [CrossRef]
46. Tang, W.; Vian, C.M.; Tang, Z.; Yang, B. Anomaly detection of core failures in die casting X-ray inspection images using a convolutional autoencoder. *Mach. Vis. Appl.* **2021**, *32*, 102. [CrossRef]
47. Ding, L.; Goshtasby, A. On the Canny edge detector. *Pattern Recognit.* **2001**, *34*, 721–725. [CrossRef]
48. Dung, C.V.; Sekiya, H.; Hirano, S.; Okatani, T.; Miki, C. A vision-based method for crack detection in gusset plate welded joints of steel bridges using deep convolutional neural networks. *Autom. Constr.* **2019**, *102*, 217–229. [CrossRef]

 *mathematics*

Article

Improved Large Covariance Matrix Estimation Based on Efficient Convex Combination and Its Application in Portfolio Optimization

Yan Zhang [1], Jiyuan Tao [2], Zhixiang Yin [1] and Guoqiang Wang [1,*]

[1] School of Mathematics, Physics and Statistics, Shanghai University of Engineering Science, Shanghai 201620, China
[2] Department of Mathematics and Statistics, Loyola University Maryland, Baltimore, MD 21210, USA
* Correspondence: guoq_wang@hotmail.com

Abstract: The estimation of the covariance matrix is an important topic in the field of multivariate statistical analysis. In this paper, we propose a new estimator, which is a convex combination of the linear shrinkage estimation and the rotation-invariant estimator under the Frobenius norm. We first obtain the optimal parameters by using grid search and cross-validation, and then, we use these optimal parameters to demonstrate the effectiveness and robustness of the proposed estimation in the numerical simulations. Finally, in empirical research, we apply the covariance matrix estimation to the portfolio optimization. Compared to the existing estimators, we show that the proposed estimator has better performance and lower out-of-sample risk in portfolio optimization.

Keywords: covariance matrix estimation; shrinkage transformations; rotation-invariant estimator; portfolio optimization

MSC: 90C25; 62P05; 62P20

Citation: Zhang, Y.; Tao, J.; Yin, Z.; Wang, G. Improved Large Covariance Matrix Estimation Based on Efficient Convex Combination and Its Application in Portfolio Optimization. *Mathematics* **2022**, *10*, 4282. https://doi.org/10.3390/math10224282

Academic Editors: Xiang Li, Shuo Zhang and Wei Zhang

Received: 24 October 2022
Accepted: 13 November 2022
Published: 16 November 2022

Publisher's Note: MDPI stays neutral with regard to jurisdictional claims in published maps and institutional affiliations.

1. Introduction

With the development of information technology, the covariance matrix estimation plays a crucial role in multivariate statistics analysis, and it is used widely in many fields, such as finance, wireless communications, biology, chemometrics, social networks, health sciences, etc. [1–5]. In particular, due to the high noise of the sample covariance matrix, the properties of financial data are not characterized by multivariate normality and stationarity [6]. As an essential input to many financial models, it is vital to remove the sample noise to improve the estimation accuracy of the covariance matrix in asset allocation and risk management [4,7,8]. It is known that the sample covariance matrix is no longer a good estimator of the population covariance matrix when the dimension of the matrix is close to or larger than the sample size. In fact, the sample covariance matrix becomes a singular matrix in high-dimensional data. The so-called "high dimensions" mainly include large orders of 30 in magnitude and high data dimensions [1–3]. So far, some popular ways used to obtain a good estimator are the shrinkage estimation methods without prior information, sparse estimation methods with prior information, the factor model [9,10], the rank model [11], etc.

The shrinkage method, proposed by Stein [12], is one without prior information for estimating the covariance matrix. The essential idea of this method is to pull extreme eigenvalues of the sample covariance matrix toward the mean of the eigenvalues by shrinking the eigenvalues when the dimension of the matrix is close to the sample size. Ledoit and Wolf showed that the shrinkage estimation methods have an improvement over the sample covariance matrix. Specifically, they proposed the shrinkage estimation methods provide good solutions to deal with the overfitting of the sample covariance matrix [8,13,14].

Since the linear shrinkage method is the first-order approximation to a nonlinear problem, as the dimension of the matrix becomes high, it is no longer suitable for the improvement of the sample covariance matrix. Thus, they proposed the nonlinear shrinkage method [15], which has better performance for high-dimensional asymptotics. Recently, Ledoit and Wolf proposed optimal nonlinear shrinkage estimators [16], which are decision-theoretically optimal within a class of nonlinear shrinkage estimators. For more details on the shrinkage methods, refer to [2,3,17,18].

The sparse estimation with prior information is another one for estimating the covariance matrix, which estimates the sparse matrix directly and its inverse indirectly. In the case of direct estimation, Bickel and Levina [19] showed that the estimation can be obtained by the threshold methods under the hypothesis of the sparseness of the true covariance matrix. In the case of no assumption of the sparse pattern, Rothman et al. [20] proposed a new class of generalized threshold estimators to obtain the sparse estimation by inducing sparsity and imposing the norm penalty. Theoretically, these methods are shown to be superior, and the generalized thresholding estimators are consistent with a large class of approximate sparse covariance matrices. In fact, the resulting estimators are not always positive-definite. In order to guarantee the positive definiteness of the covariance matrix estimation, Rothman et al. [21] built a convex optimization model based on the quadratic loss function under the Frobenius norm (*F*-norm) and studied the estimation of the high-dimensional covariance matrix. Subsequently, some convex optimization models with penalty functions such as the L_1 function were proposed [22,23], and some nonconvex penalty functions were used to achieve both sparsity and positive definiteness [24,25]. However, since the changes of the variance and covariance over time are not considered, they are affected by dimensional disasters and large noise problems. For more details about optimization algorithms and inverse matrix estimation methods, refer to the literature [7,26–31] and the references therein.

In addition, Bun et al. [32] introduced the rotation-invariant estimation in which they assumed that the estimator of the population correlation matrix shares the same eigenvectors as the sample covariance matrix itself. The experiments' results demonstrated that the rotation-invariant estimator is more suitable for dealing with large dimension datasets than the eigenvalue clipping methods and can be significantly improved over the sample covariance matrix as the data size grows, but it did not perform well on a small sample data. In a recent paper [33], Deshmukh et al. combined the shrinkage transformation with the eigenvalue clipping to obtain the estimator of the covariance matrix for the convex combination of the optimal parameters. This estimator can achieve less out-of-sample risk in portfolio optimization for small datasets.

The research in this paper was mainly motivated by [32,33], and the novelties of this study are as follows:

1. A new large covariance matrix estimator is proposed by constructing a convex combination of the linear shrinkage estimation and the rotation-invariant estimator under the Frobenius norm.
2. Our new covariance matrix estimator improves the impact of the sample noise on the covariance matrix by adjusting the parameters of the convex combination in financial data.
3. The proposed estimator has better performance and lower out- of-sample risk in portfolio optimization.

The rest of this paper is organized as follows: Section 2 describes the related work of covariance matrix estimation. Section 3 introduces our new proposed estimator and its application. Section 4 implements the numerical simulation and empirical research. Section 5 gives the conclusions.

2. Preliminaries

2.1. The Rotation-Invariant Estimator

First, we briefly introduce the basic idea of the rotation-invariant estimator. For more details, we refer to [32].

Let $r = (r_1, r_2, ..., r_N)$ denote a $T \times N$ matrix of T independent and identically distributed (iid) observations on a system of N random variables with mean vector μ. N and T denote the number of variable and the size of the variable, respectively. In this case, the sample covariance matrix is given by

$$\Sigma_{SCM} = (\sigma_{ij}) = \frac{1}{N-1} \sum_{i=1}^{N} (r_i - \mu)(r_i - \mu)', \tag{1}$$

Let N and T be asymptotic in the high-dimensional regime, i.e.,

$$N \asymp T. \tag{2}$$

In addition, the concentration ratio is given by

$$c = \frac{N}{T}. \tag{3}$$

The construction steps of the rotation-invariant estimator are as follows:

- **Step 1**: Calculate the Stieltjes transform of the empirical spectral measure of S_1 from

$$s(z) = \frac{1}{T} Tr(S_1 - z)^{-1} \tag{4}$$

where z denotes the spectral parameter and

$$S_1 = \frac{1}{N-1} \sum_{i=1}^{N} (r_i - \mu)' (r_i - \mu), \tag{5}$$

The function (4) contains all the information about the eigenvalues of the matrix S_1, which has the same nonzero eigenvalues as Σ_{SCM}.

- **Step 2**: Update (4) based on the nonzero eigenvalues of $Y'Y$ and YY', i.e.,

$$s(z) = \frac{1}{T} Tr(S_1 - z)^{-1}, \tag{6}$$

where $y_i = r_i - \mu$, $Y = (y_1, y_2, ..., y_N)$, and λ_i denotes the ith eigenvalue of the sample covariance matrix Σ_{SCM}.

- **Step 3**: Calculate the function $\widehat{\delta}_i$ of the ith eigenvalue of S from

$$\widehat{\delta}_i = \frac{1}{\lambda_i |s(\lambda_i + i\eta)|^2}. \tag{7}$$

where $s(\cdot)$ is the empirical Stieltjes transform from (6) and parameter $\eta = T^{-\frac{1}{2}}$.

- **Step 4**: Output the resulting covariance matrix estimator Σ_{RIE} from

$$\Sigma_{RIE} = U_N \widehat{D}_N U_N', \tag{8}$$

where

$$\widehat{D}_N = Diag(\widehat{\lambda}_1, \widehat{\lambda}_2, ..., \widehat{\lambda}_N), \tag{9}$$

U_N is an orthogonal matrix, whose columns $[u_1, u_2, ..., u_N]$ are the corresponding eigenvectors, with the eigenvalue of the rotation-invariant estimator defined by

$$\widehat{\lambda}_i = \frac{\sum\limits_{i=1}^{N} \lambda_i}{\sum\limits_{i=1}^{N} \widehat{\delta}_i} \widehat{\delta}_i. \tag{10}$$

One can easily verify that

$$\sum_{i=1}^{N} \widehat{\lambda}_i = \sum_{i=1}^{N} \lambda_i. \tag{11}$$

This implies that the estimator Σ_{RIE} has the same trace as the sample covariance matrix. More literature reviews on rotation-invariant estimators are presented in the Table 1.

Table 1. The related literature review.

Author	Brief Introduction	Ref.
Ledoit, O., Wolf, M.	Under the assumption of the large dimension asymptotic, Ledoit and Wolf kept the eigenvectors of the sample covariance matrix and shrunk the inverse sample eigenvalues to construct a rotation-invariant estimator of the large covariance matrix.	[34]
Donoho et al.	Based on spiked covariance and the rotation-invariant estimator, Donoho et al. demonstrated that the optimal estimation of the population covariance matrix is related to the best shrinker, which acts as an element of the sample eigenvalues.	[35]
J. Bun et al.	J. Bun et al. established the asymptotic global law estimate model for three general classes of noisy matrices using the replica method and introduced how to "clean" the noisy eigenvalues of the noisy observation matrix.	[36]
Debashis Paul, Alexander Aue	Debashis Paul and Alexander Aue summarized the random matrix theory (RMT) and described how the development of high-dimensional statistical inference theory and practice is affected by the corresponding development in the RMT field.	[37]

2.2. Improved Covariance Estimator Based on Eigenvalue Clipping

Deshmukh et al. [33] introduced an improved estimation based on eigenvalue clipping, which takes the optimal parameters in the convex combination of the sample covariance matrix Σ_{SCM}, the shrinkage target Σ_F

$$\Sigma_F = (f_{ij}), \tag{12}$$

with

$$f_{ij} = \begin{cases} \dfrac{2\sqrt{\sigma_{ii}\sigma_{jj}}}{N(N-1)} \sum\limits_{i=1}^{N-1} \sum\limits_{j=i+1}^{T} \dfrac{\sigma_{ij}}{\sigma_{ii}\sigma_{jj}}, & i \neq j, \\ \sigma_{ii}, & i = j, \end{cases} \tag{13}$$

and the matrix Σ_{MP} obtained by applying eigenvalue clipping.

Let $y_i = r_i - \bar{r}_i$ be independent, identically distributed, random variables with finite variance σ. The Marchenko–Pastur density $\rho_{\Sigma_{SCM}}(\lambda)$ of the eigenvalues of Σ_{SCM} is defined by

$$\rho_{\Sigma_{SCM}}(\lambda) = \frac{1}{N}\frac{dn(\lambda)}{d\lambda}. \tag{14}$$

where $n(\lambda)$ is the number of eigenvalues of the sample covariance matrix Σ_{SCM} less than λ.

In the condition of the limit $N \to \infty$, $T \to \infty$, and $\frac{1}{c} \geq 1$, the density follows from (14):

$$\rho_{\Sigma_{SCM}}(\lambda) = \frac{1}{2\pi c\sigma^2}\frac{\sqrt{(\lambda_{max} - \lambda)(\lambda - \lambda_{min})}}{\lambda}, \tag{15}$$

where

$$\lambda_{max} = \sigma^2(1 + c + 2\sqrt{c}), \quad \lambda_{min} = \sigma^2(1 + c - 2\sqrt{c}). \tag{16}$$

$[\lambda_{min}, \lambda_{max}]$ represents the MP law bounds. In this case, the covariance matrix can be cleaned by scaling the eigenvectors of Σ_{SCM} with these new eigenvalues. Σ_{MP} is obtained by this method.

Let Σ be the population covariance matrix; the optimal parameters in convex combination can be found from the following optimization problem [33].

$$\min_{\theta,\phi} \quad ||\Sigma - \Sigma_{est}||_F \tag{17}$$

$$\text{s.t.} \begin{cases} \Sigma_{est} = \phi(\theta\Sigma_F + (1 - \theta)\Sigma_{MP}) + (1 - \phi)\Sigma_{SCM}, \\ 0 \leq \theta \leq 1, 0 \leq \phi \leq 1. \end{cases} \tag{18}$$

where θ and ϕ are the parameters of the convex combination.

Usually, the eigenvectors of the sample covariance matrix deviate from those of the population covariance matrix under large-dimensional asymptotics. Correcting the deviation of the eigenvalues of the sample covariance matrix can improve the performance of the large covariance matrix. Although the estimation can adapt to changing the sampling noise conditions by performing parameter optimization, the performance of the estimation outperforms other estimations only for small-dimensional problems.

3. Proposed Estimator and Application in Portfolio Optimization

3.1. Proposed Estimator

For further improve the performance of the large covariance matrix, we replaced the eigenvalues falling inside Marchenko–Pastur (MP) law bounds with the rotation-invariant estimator Σ_{RIE} and applied the linear shrinkage estimation to shrink the eigenvalues falling outside the MP law bounds in this paper. Our new estimation is presented below.

$$\min_{\theta,\phi} \quad ||\Sigma - \Sigma_{est}||_F \tag{19}$$

$$\text{s.t.} \begin{cases} \Sigma_{est} = \phi(\theta\Sigma_F + (1 - \theta)\Sigma_{RIE}) + (1 - \phi)\Sigma_{SCM}, \\ 0 \leq \theta \leq 1, 0 \leq \phi \leq 1, \end{cases} \tag{20}$$

Thus, the estimation of the covariance matrix is given by

$$\Sigma^* = \phi^*(\theta^*\Sigma_F + (1 - \theta^*)\Sigma_{RIE}) + (1 - \phi^*)\Sigma_{SCM}. \tag{21}$$

where θ^* and ϕ^* are the optimal parameters of the optimization problem given by (19) and (20).

It is well known that the financial data are heavy-tailed and non-normal [7,33]. However, the existing covariance matrix estimation methods generally requires the assumption of normality [32,38]. For overcoming this drawback, we propose a new estimator, which is a convex combination of the linear shrinkage estimation and the rotation-invariant estimator under the Frobenius norm. One advantage of the new estimation is that we can remove the noise caused by the bulk eigenvalues and the extreme eigenvalues in the financial data. Furthermore, we set five-fold cross-validation $k = 5$ to implement the simulation and empirical research for improving the accurate estimation of the covariance matrix.

The detailed steps of our new estimation are as follows.

- **Step 0**: Input the sample data $r = (r_1, r_2, ..., r_N)$, and set $k = 1$.
- **Step 1**: Calculate Σ_{SCM}, Σ_F, and Σ_{RIE} from (5), (12), and (8), respectively.
- **Step 2**: Calculate Σ_{est} from (20), and denote $\Sigma_{est}^{(\theta_i, \phi_j)}$ for $\theta_i, \phi_j, i = 1, 2, ..., M, j = 1, ..., P$, where M and P are the numbers of θ and ϕ taken between 0 and 1, respectively.
- **Step 3**: Calculate the error:

$$\Delta_k^{(\theta_i, \phi_j)} = ||\Sigma_{est}^{(\theta_i, \phi_j)} - \Sigma||_F,$$

for $\theta_i, \phi_j, i = 1, 2, ..., M, j = 1, ..., P$, and let $k = k + 1$.
- **Step 4**: Repeat **Steps 1–3** in the cross-validation until the folds $k = 5$.
- **Step 5**: Find the optimal parameters θ^* and ϕ^* in the convex combination from the corresponding smallest error sum Δ_{sum} given by

$$\Delta_{sum} = \sum_{k=1}^{5} \sum_{i=1}^{M} \sum_{j=1}^{P} \Delta_k^{(\theta_i, \phi_j)}.$$

- **Step 6**: Output the proposed estimation Σ^* from (21).

3.2. Minimum Variance Portfolio Optimization

According to Markowitz's theory [39], we included an additional return constraint in the portfolio because even a risk-averse investor would expect a minimal positive return. The classic portfolio optimization model that satisfies the minimum expected return is defined by

$$\min_{x} \quad x'\Sigma x \tag{22}$$

$$\text{s.t.} \begin{cases} 1'x = 1, \\ r'x \geq r_{min}, \\ x \geq 0, \end{cases}$$

where x, r, and r_{min} represent the weight of portfolio optimization, daily return, and the minimum daily expected return, respectively. It is well known that the portfolio selection is widely used in the financial field, which is a convex quadratic programming problem [39].

In the portfolio optimization, the weight of each asset is closely related to the covariance matrix. An accurate covariance matrix can achieve a more reasonable weight distribution and better portfolio effect. Due to the heavy-tailed nature of financial data and the availability of limited samples [8], many studies started concentrating on the global minimum variance (GMV) portfolio. To improve the performance of the sample covariance matrix in the portfolio optimization, DeMiguel [40] added the additional constraint and regularizing asset weight vector into the minimum variance portfolio and showed that the estimator always leads the constructed portfolio to achieve a smaller variance and a higher Sharpe ratio than other portfolios. Furthermore, Ledoit and Wolf [18] applied the estimation to the portfolio optimization to overcome the dimension and noise problems of a high-dimensional covariance matrix, and the results were better than the linear shrinkage estimation [13]. Moreover, due to the influence of financial market information on covariance matrix estimation, the time-varying covariance matrix or the correlation matrix also have practical significance in portfolio optimization. For more details, refer to [41] and the references therein.

In this paper, we divided the sample data into in-sample data and out-of-sample data, which were used for the estimation and prediction of the covariance matrix, respectively. To measure the out-of-sample performance of the estimation of the covariance matrix in portfolio optimization, we used the out-of-sample risk, the average return, and the Sharpe ratio as the criteria of the measurement. The average return was annualized by multiplying it by 252 (252 trading days per year), and the standard deviation was annualized by multiplying it by $\sqrt{252}$. The out-of-sample performance of the portfolio model was evaluated through the following procedure.

- **Step 0:** Input the returns of the current in-sample r_{in} and out-of-sample data r_{out}, the expected return r_{min}, and the estimation of the covariance matrix Σ^*.
- **Step 1:** Set $r := r_{in}$, and solve the optimal weight vector x^* from Model (22) by the quadratic optimizer called quadprog in Matlab.
- **Step 2:** Calculate the out-of-sample $\widehat{\Sigma}^*$ from (21), and obtain the out-of-sample standard deviation:

$$\sigma_{out} = var((x^*)' r_{out}),$$

the average return:

$$r_{ave} = E((x^*)' r_{out}),$$

and the Sharpe Ratio:

$$SR = \frac{r_{ave} - r_f}{\sigma_{out}}$$

where x^* and r_f represent the optimal weight vector and the risk-free interest, respectively.

4. Numerical Simulation and Empirical Research

4.1. Numerical Simulation

In the simulation, we used the simulation data of Engle et al. [41], and the mean return ranged between -0.0031 and 0.0036. We divided the dataset into in-sample data and out-of-sample data, and both the sample sizes were $T = 500$. In pursuit of accuracy, we implemented the five-fold cross-validation, and the parameter selection criterion was the F-norm of the estimator and the population covariance matrix. We set three dimensions for the return series, which were $N = 100, 200$, and 400, respectively. The maximum concentration ratio is

$$c = \frac{N}{T} = \frac{400}{500} = 0.80. \tag{23}$$

To measure the performance of the estimators, we compared the error between each estimator and the population covariance matrix. The six estimators are shown in Table 2.

Table 2. The estimators for comparison.

The Formulation of Estimation	Ref.
$\Sigma_{SCM} = \frac{1}{N-1} \sum_{i=1}^{N} (r_i - \mu)(r_i - \mu)'$	[42]
$\Sigma_{Identity} = I$	[8,38]
$\Sigma_L = \widehat{\rho}\Sigma_{SCM} + (1 - \widehat{\rho})\Sigma_F$	[13]
$\Sigma_{NL} = U_N D_N^{or} U_N^*, \ \lambda_i^{or} = \frac{\lambda_i}{\lvert 1 - c - c\lambda_i \widehat{m}_F(\lambda_i) \rvert}$	[15,18,43]
$\Sigma_D = \phi(\theta\Sigma_F + (1 - \theta)\Sigma_{MP}) + (1 - \phi)\Sigma_{SCM}$	[33]
$\Sigma^* = \phi(\theta\Sigma_F + (1 - \theta)\Sigma_{RIE}) + (1 - \phi)\Sigma_{SCM}$	/

In the five-fold cross-validation, we obtained the error between the proposed estimation and the population covariance matrix for the different parameters θ and ϕ under three asset dimensions. In Figures 1–3, the horizontal and longitudinal axis represent the different values of θ and ϕ, respectively, and the vertical axis represents the sum of the error. It is obvious that there are two optimal parameters to minimizing the error between the proposed estimator and the population covariance matrix for all θ and ϕ. The results are shown in Table 3. To some degree, this ensures the effectiveness of the proposed estimation.

Table 4 shows that the F-norm error of our new estimation is the smallest in the ones of the six estimations. Under this premise, we calculated the portfolio variance in the minimum variance portfolio that satisfies the minimum 0.0015 expected return. The results are shown in Table 5. Figures 4–6 show the mean return of out-of-sample data ranging from the 1st asset to the 400th asset. We mark individual points on the graph. The horizontal and longitudinal axis represent the order of assets in the total assets and the mean return of this asset, respectively. We can see that the mean return of the point that is marked is relatively high. Generally speaking, higher asset returns will also face relatively large investment risks. To understand the following description, we divided the return into three asset risk grades: high ($r_{min} \geq 0.001$), middle ($0.0005 \leq r_{min} \leq 0.001$), and low ($r_{min} < 0.0005$), respectively. In Table 5, it is obvious that the variance of $\Sigma_{Identity}$ is the largest in all asset dimensions. In the case of $N = 200$, the asset weights of the portfolio model corresponding to $\Sigma_{Identity}$ are distributed on the 15th, 51st, 71st, 75th, and 138th assets in Figure 7, respectively, with 87% high-risk assets and 13% medium assets. However, in the case of $N = 400$, the asset weights of the portfolio model corresponding to $\Sigma_{Identity}$ are distributed on twenty assets, with 60% high-risk assets, 39.5% medium assets, and only 0.5% low-risk assets, and we can see that the high-risk and medium-risk assets account for the vast majority of the 20 assets. Instead, the portfolio model corresponding to our new estimator Σ^* distributed the weights on high-risk assets and medium-risk assets as 69% and 26.12%, respectively, to achieve the 0.0015 expected return. The remaining 5% was distributed on low-risk assets to reduce investment risk. The corresponding results are shown in Figures 8 and 9. Overall, the reasonable distribution of asset weights on high-, medium, and low-risk assets can appropriately decrease investment risks. As the number of the assets increased, the performance of our new estimator Σ^* became better. At the same time, the proposed estimation in the minimum variance portfolio was more dispersed on the allocation of the assets.

Table 3. The optimal parameters θ and ϕ in convex combination and the sum of the corresponding error.

N	θ	ϕ	Error
100	0.3333	0.3636	0.0273
200	0.3434	0.3939	0.0515
400	0.3939	0.4040	0.1080

Table 4. The error between each estimator and the population covariance matrix under the optimal parameter.

N	Σ_{SCM}	$\Sigma_{Identity}$	Σ_L	Σ_{NL}	Σ_D	Σ^*
100	0.0132	9.9927	0.0121	0.0128	0.0117	0.0055
200	0.0291	14.1313	0.0261	0.0282	0.0256	0.0103
400	0.0580	19.9842	0.0508	0.0560	0.0498	0.0216

Table 5. The variance comparison of six estimations in the minimum variance portfolio.

N	Σ_{SCM}	$\Sigma_{Identity}$	Σ_L	Σ_{NL}	Σ_D	Σ^*
100	0.0011	0.9694	0.0011	0.0010	8.0298 *	7.0942 *
200	7.8576 *	0.3956	7.9096 *	7.7615 *	6.7529 *	5.9007 *
400	3.8828 *	0.1077	4.2676 *	3.8435 *	3.7395 *	3.1368 *

* denotes the unit is 10^{-4}.

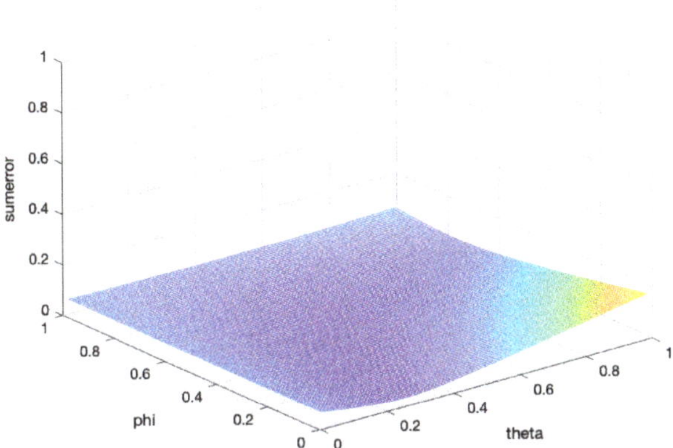

Figure 1. The sum of the error of five-fold cross-validation between the proposed estimation and the population covariance matrix under the different θ and ϕ for $N = 100$.

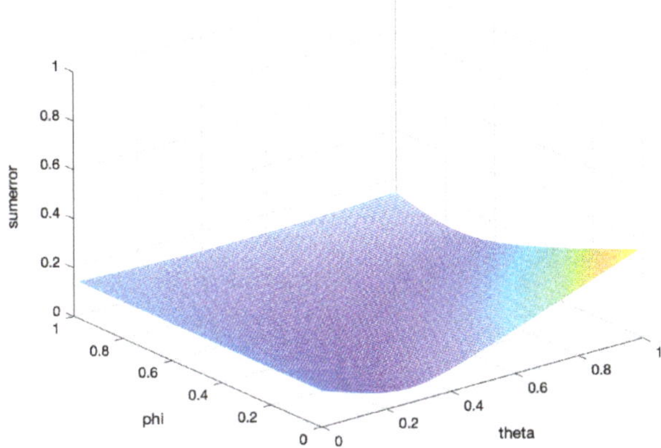

Figure 2. Thesum of the error of the five-fold cross-validation between the proposed estimation and the population covariance matrix under the different θ and ϕ for $N = 200$.

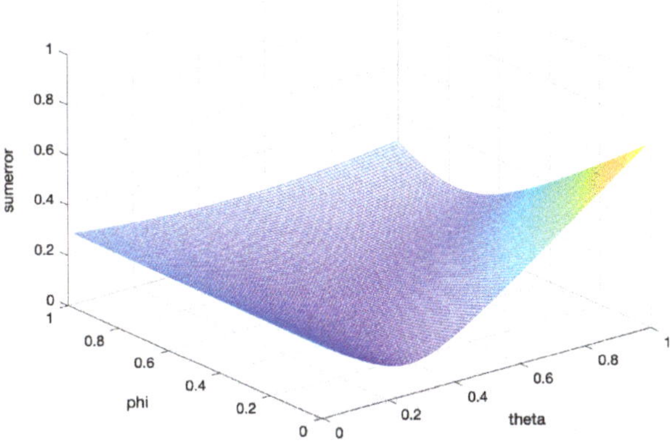

Figure 3. The sum of the error of the five-fold cross-validation between the proposed estimation and the population covariance matrix under the different θ and ϕ for $N = 400$.

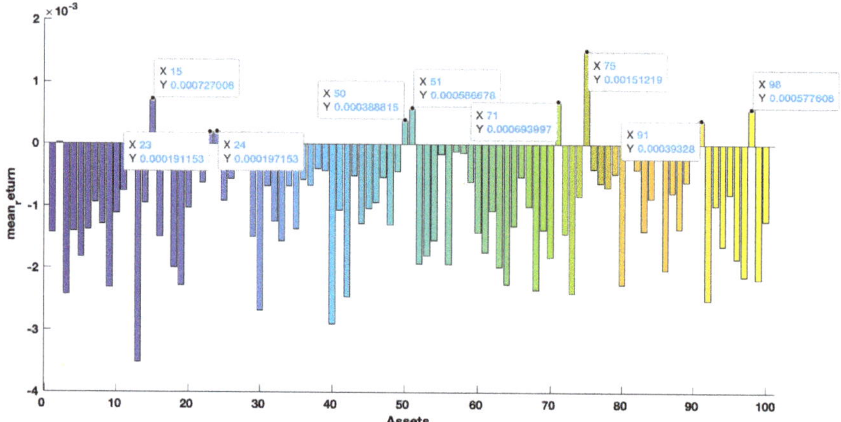

Figure 4. The mean return of the out-of-sample data for $N = 100$.

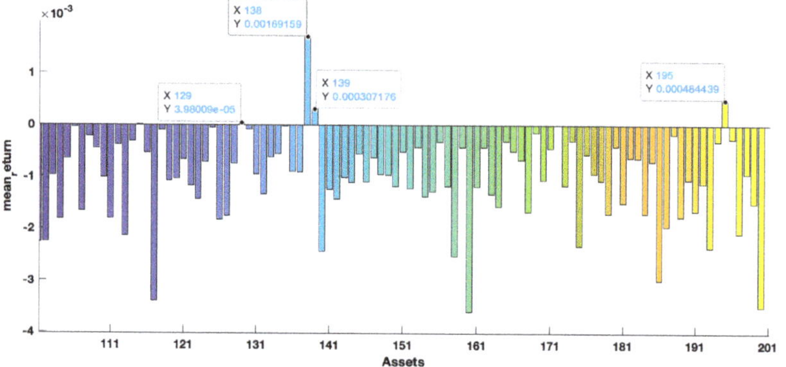

Figure 5. The mean return of the out-of-sample data range from the 101st asset to the 200th asset.

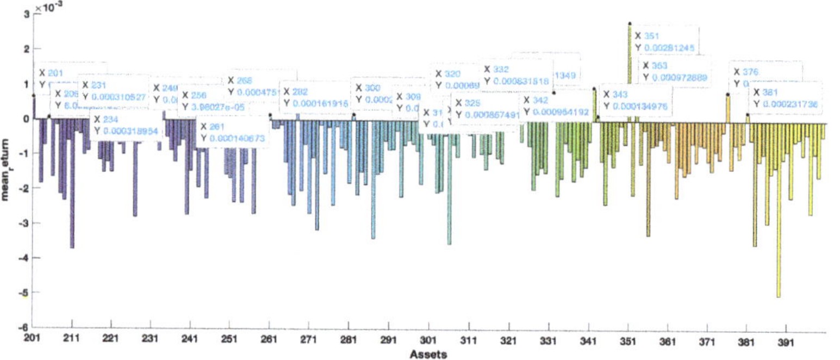

Figure 6. The mean return of the out-of-sample data range from the 201st asset to the 400th asset.

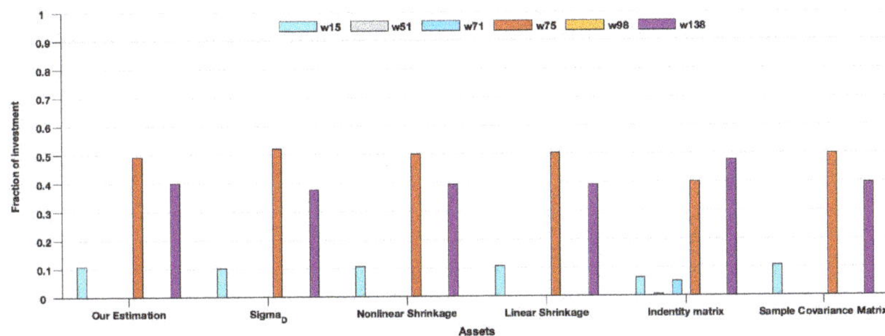

Figure 7. The assets' weights of each estimation under the out-of-sample data $N = 200$.

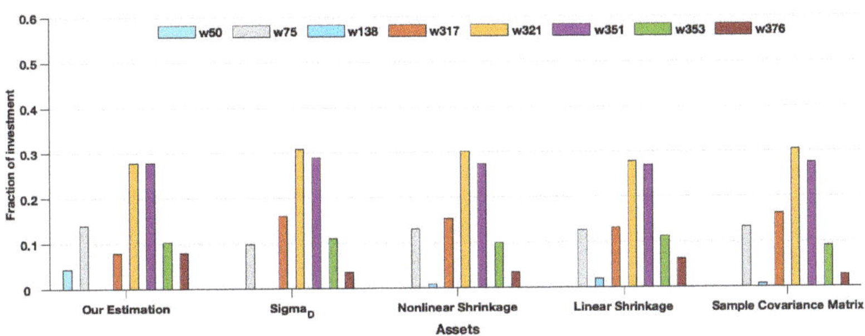

Figure 8. The assets' weights of each estimation under the out-of-sample data for $N = 400$.

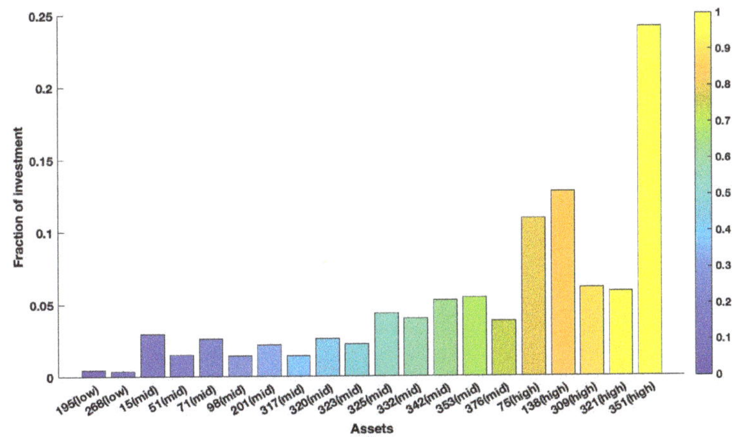

Figure 9. The assets' weights of the identity matrix under the out-of-sample data $N = 400$.

4.2. Empirical Research

The data of this paper came from the component stock of CSI500, HS300, and SSE50 on the tushare financial website. The whole period of the samples was from 24 May 2017 to 1 July 2021. Removing the missing data of the samples from transaction, we finally obtained 426 component stocks of CSI500, 218 component stocks of HS300, and 41 component stocks of SSE50.

In this paper, we set $T_1 = 500$ and $T_2 = 500$ as the window of estimation and prediction, respectively. The maximum concentration ratio is

$$c = \frac{N}{T_1} = \frac{426}{500} = 0.852. \tag{24}$$

We used the log return as we studied the object and divide all samples into two parts for estimation and prediction. We constructed six portfolio optimization models by using the estimator in Table 2. The procedures of estimation and prediction are as follows.

- **Step 0**: Input the sample data; divide the data into in-sample data $T_1 = 500$ and out-of-sample data $T_2 = 500$.
- **Step 1**: Calculate Σ_F, Σ_{RIE}, and Σ_{SCM} based on the in-sample data.
- **Step 2**: Set five-fold cross-validation; calculate the Σ_{est} from (20) for parameters between 0 and 1; implement the minimum variance portfolio (22), where r_{min} takes a value from the minimum to maximum mean return; solve the corresponding weight vector x by multiple times of iteration over the values of both θ and ϕ in the convex optimization.
- **Step 3**: Calculate the standard deviation based on the out-of-sample data, and record the out-of-sample risk σ_{out} in each iteration.
- **Step 4**: Calculate the optimal parameters θ^*, ϕ^* when the sum of σ_{out} of the five-fold cross-validation achieves the minimum.
- **Step 5**: Implement the minimum variance portfolio (22) to obtain the assets' weights, the average return r_{ave}, and the out-of-sample risk σ_{risk} when satisfying the minimum 0.002 return constraints under the θ^* and ϕ^*.
- **Step 6**: Calculate the Sharpe ratio, where the risk-free interest is set as 1.75%.

In portfolio optimization, the reduction of volatility at the first decimal place is also considered to be quite significant [13,33]. Tables 6 and 7 show the performance of the six portfolio optimization model based on the different asset dimensions. For out-of-sample data, we used the standard deviation as the performance metric. Furthermore, we calculated the average return and the Sharpe ratio in the portfolio optimization model (22) and the risk-free interest was set to 1.75%.

Tables 6–8 show that the average returns of each estimator are equal. Table 6 shows that the standard deviation of the portfolio optimization model corresponding to $\Sigma_{Identity}$ is only 27.53%, which is the smallest in each estimator. The standard deviation of the portfolio optimization model corresponding to our new estimator Σ^* is 27.97%, and its performance ranks fourth among all estimators.

Table 7 shows the performance of the portfolio optimization model corresponding to each estimator with 218 assets. It can be seen that the performance of the estimator $\Sigma_{Identity}$ becomes weak. In this case, $\Sigma_{Identity}$ is the worst estimator, which is expected as it assumes zero correlations among stocks, and Σ_{SCM} is the second-worst. The Sharpe ratio of the portfolio optimization corresponding to Σ_{NL} is the highest in each estimator followed by the one of Σ_D. At the same time, the performance of our new estimator Σ^* ranks third among all estimators. Comparing to the case of $N = 218$, the performance of our new estimator improved as the asset dimension increased.

Table 8 compares the performance of each model with the number of assets of 426. The result shows that the portfolio optimization model corresponding to our new estimator Σ^* obtaining the smallest standard deviation leads to the highest Sharpe ratio. Obviously, compared with other estimators, especially with $\Sigma_{Identity}$, our new estimator has a significant decrease in the out-of-sample standard deviation. Meanwhile, this also implies that the performance of our new estimator Σ^* is superior to the ones of the other five estimators as the asset dimension increases.

The homogeneity of the variance test is a metric to measure whether the variances of the two investment strategies are equal, and we used the improved bootstrap inference [44] to test the significant variance difference between Σ^* and other estimations excess returns.

Table 9 shows that the test between Σ^* and the alternative methods all reject the null hypothesis of equal variances. Moreover, the sample variance of the excess return generated corresponding to our new estimator Σ^* is significantly lower than the other portfolio optimization models as the number of assets increases. Therefore, our new estimation Σ^* is superior to other estimations.

Table 6. The out-of-sample performance comparison between each estimator of the 41 assets in SSE50.

Index	Average Return *	Standard Deviation *	Sharpe Ratio
Σ_{SCM}	50.40	27.98	1.7390
$\Sigma_{Identity}$	50.40	27.53	1.7399
Σ_L	50.40	28.00	1.7375
Σ_{NL}	50.40	27.95	1.7400
Σ_D	50.40	27.96	2.7399
Σ^*	50.40	27.97	1.7391

* denotes the unit is %.

Table 7. The out-of-sample performance comparison between each estimations of the 218 assets in HS300.

Index	Average Return *	Standard Deviation *	Sharpe Ratio
Σ_{SCM}	50.40	18.69	2.6031
$\Sigma_{Identity}$	50.40	20.28	2.3990
Σ_L	50.40	18.70	2.6017
Σ_{NL}	50.40	17.79	2.7340
Σ_D	50.40	17.81	2.7314
Σ^*	50.40	18.68	2.6044

* denotes the unit is %.

Table 8. The out-of-sample performance comparison between each estimations of the 426 assets in CSI500.

Index	Average Return *	Standard Deviation *	Sharpe Ratio
Σ_{SCM}	50.40	21.25	2.2899
$\Sigma_{Identity}$	50.40	23.04	2.1115
Σ_L	50.40	21.24	2.2909
Σ_{NL}	50.40	21.22	2.2927
Σ_D	50.40	21.18	2.2970
Σ^*	50.40	20.87	2.3315

* denotes the unit is %.

Table 9. The difference in the out-of-sample variance between Σ^* and the alternative estimation with all assets (the significance level is 5%).

Number of Assets	Σ_{SCM}	$\Sigma_{Identity}$	Σ_L	Σ_{NL}	Σ_D
41	-0.0001	0.0350	-0.0019	0.0011	0.0010
218	-0.0000	-0.1607	-0.0010	0.0986	0.0966
426	-0.0363	-0.1979	-0.0350	-0.0342	-0.0303

5. Conclusions

In this paper, we proposed a new estimator for the covariance matrix, which is a convex combination of the linear shrinkage estimation and the rotation-invariant estimator under the F-norm. We first obtained the optimal parameters through considerable numerical operations, and then, we focused on the accuracy of the model and ignored the complexity of the calculation. Moreover, we demonstrated the effectiveness of the model in the simulation. Finally, we applied our estimation to the minimum variance portfolio optimization and showed that the performance of the proposed estimator is superior to the other five existing estimators in the portfolio optimization for high-dimensional data.

In addition, we only considered the sample noise on the covariance matrix in this article, but in the financial field, the covariance matrix estimation will vary with time due to the influence of market information, and the covariance matrix estimation will be affected by the market information. Therefore, the performance of our new estimation in the dynamic conditional correlation model [41] can be investigated as part of future work for a large-dimensional covariance matrix.

Author Contributions: Conceptualization, Y.Z.; Fund acquisition, G.W. and Z.Y.; methodology, Y.Z. and J.T.; supervision, G.W. and Z.Y.; writing—original draft preparation, Y.Z.; writing—review and editing, Y.Z., J.T. and G.W. All authors have read and agreed to the published version of the manuscript.

Funding: This research was funded by the National Natural Science Foundation of China (Nos. 11971302 and 12171307).

Informed Consent Statement: Not applicable.

Data Availability Statement: The data of this paper came from the component stock of CSI500, HS300, and SSE50 on the tushare financial website accessed on 1 July 2021: https://www.tushare.pro.

Conflicts of Interest: The authors declare no conflict of interest.

References

1. Hu, J.; Bai, Z.D. A review of 20 years of naive tests of significance for high-dimensional mean vectors and covariance matrices. *Sci. China Math.* **2016**, *59*, 2281–2300. [CrossRef]
2. Tong, T.; Wang, C.; Wang, T. Estimation of variances and covariances for high-dimensional data: A selective review. *Wiley Interdiscip. Rev. Comput. Stat.* **2014**, *6*, 255–264. [CrossRef]
3. Engel, J.; Buydens, L.; Blanchet, L. An overview of large-dimensional covariance and precision matrix estimators with applications in chemometrics. *J. Chemom.* **2017**, *31*, e2880. [CrossRef]
4. Sun, R.; Ma, T.; Liu, S.; Sathye, M. Improved covariance matrix estimation for portfolio risk measurement: A review. *J. Risk Financ. Manag.* **2019**, *12*, 48. [CrossRef]
5. Fan, J.; Liao, Y.; Liu, H. An overview of the estimation of large covariance and precision matrices. *Econom. J.* **2016**, *19*, C1–C32. [CrossRef]
6. Rachev, S.T. *Handbook of Heavy Tailed Distributions in Finance*; Elsevier: North Holland, The Netherlands, 2003.
7. Yuan, X.; Yu, W.Q.; Yin, Z.X.; Wang, G.Q. Improved large dynamic covariance matrix estimation with graphical lasso and its application in portfolio selection. *IEEE Access* **2020**, *8*, 189179–189188. [CrossRef]
8. Ledoit, O.; Wolf, M. Improved estimation of the covariance matrix of stock returns with an application to portfolio selection. *J. Empir. Financ.* **2003**, *10*, 603–621. [CrossRef]
9. Fan, J.; Fan, Y.; Lv, J. High dimensional covariance matrix estimation using a factor model. *J. Econ.* **2008**, *147*, 186–197. [CrossRef]
10. Xu, F.F.; Huang, J.C.; Wen, Z.W. High dimensional covariance matrix estimation using multi-factor models from incomplete information. *Sci. China Math.* **2015**, *58*, 829–844. [CrossRef]
11. Liu, H.; Han, F.; Yuan, M.; Lafferty, J.; Wasserman, L. High-dimensional semiparametric Gaussian copula graphical models. *Ann. Stat.* **2012**, *40*, 2293–2326. [CrossRef]
12. Stein, C. Lectures on the theory of estimation of many parameters. *J. Sov. Math.* **1986**, *34*, 1373–1403. [CrossRef]
13. Ledoit, O.; Wolf, M. Honey, I shrunk the sample covariance matrix. *J. Portfolio Manag.* **2004**, *30*, 110–119. [CrossRef]
14. Ledoit, O.; Wolf, M. A well-conditioned estimator for large-dimensional covariance matrices. *J. Multivar. Anal.* **2004**, *88*, 365–411. [CrossRef]
15. Ledoit, O.; Wolf, M. Nonlinear shrinkage estimation of large-dimensional covariance matrices. *Ann. Stat.* **2012**, *40*, 1024–1060. [CrossRef]
16. Ledoit, O.; Wolf, M. Optimal estimation of a large-dimensional covariance matrix under stein's loss. *Bernoulli* **2018**, *24*, 3791–3832. [CrossRef]
17. Ledoit, O.; Wolf, M. The power of (non-) linear shrinking: A review and guide to covariance matrix estimation. *J. Financ. Econ.* **2022**, *20*, 187–218. [CrossRef]
18. Ledoit, O.; Wolf, M. Nonlinear shrinkage of the covariance matrix for portfolio selection: Markowitz meets Goldilocks. *Rev. Financ. Stud.* **2017**, *30*, 4349–4388. [CrossRef]
19. Bickel, P.J.; Levina, E. Covariance regularization by thresholding. *Ann. Stat.* **2008**, *36*, 2577–2604. [CrossRef]
20. Rothman, A.; Levina, E.; Zhu, J. Generalized thresholding of large covariance matrices. *J. Am. Stat. Assoc.* **2009**, *104*, 177–186. [CrossRef]

21. Rothman, A.J. Positive definite estimators of large covariance matrices. *Biometrika* **2012**, *99*, 733–740. [CrossRef]
22. Zhou, S.L.; Xiu, N.H.; Luo, Z.Y.; Kong, L.C. Sparse and low-rank covariance matrix estimation. *J. Oper. Res. Soc. China* **2015**, *3*, 231–250. [CrossRef]
23. Xue, L.Z.; Ma, S.Q.; Zou, H. Positive-definite l1-penalized estimation of large covariance matrices. *J. Am. Stat. Assoc.* **2012**, *107*, 1480–1491. [CrossRef]
24. Liu, H.; Wang, L.; Zhao, T. Sparse covariance matrix estimation with eigenvalue constraints. *Comput. Graph. Stat.* **2014**, *23*, 439–459. [CrossRef] [PubMed]
25. Wen, F.; Yang, Y.; Liu, P.; Qiu, R.C. Positive definite estimation of large covariance matrix using generalized non-convex penalties. *IEEE Access* **2016**, *4*, 4168–4182. [CrossRef]
26. Friedman, J.; Hastie, T.; Tibshirani, R. Sparse inverse covariance estimation with the graphical lasso. *Biostatistics* **2008**, *9*, 432–441. [CrossRef]
27. Finegold, M.; Drton, M. Robust graphical modeling of gene networks using classical and alternative t-distributions. *Ann. Appl. Stat.* **2011**, *5*,1057–1080. [CrossRef]
28. Yuan, X.M. Alternating direction method for covariance selection model. *J. Sci. Comput.* **2012**, *51*, 261–273. [CrossRef]
29. Li, P.L.; Xiao, Y.H. An efficient algorithm for sparse inverse covariance matrix estimation based on dual formulation. *Comput. Stat. Data Anal.* **2018**, *128*, 292–307. [CrossRef]
30. Yuan, M.; Lin, Y. Model selection and estimation in the Gaussian graphical model. *Biometrika* **2007**, *94*, 19–35. [CrossRef]
31. Yang, J.F.; Sun, D.F.; Toh, K.C. A proximal point algorithm for log-determinant optimization with group lasso regularization. *SIAM J. Optim.* **2013**, *23*, 857–893. [CrossRef]
32. Bun, J.; Bouchaud, J.-P.; Potters, M. Cleaning large correlation matrices: Tools from random matrix theory. *Phys. Rep.* **2017**, *666*, 1–9. [CrossRef]
33. Deshmukh, S.; Dubey, A. Improved covariance matrix estimation with an application in portfolio optimization. *IEEE Signal Process. Lett.* **2020**, *27*, 985–989. [CrossRef]
34. Ledoit, O.; Wolf, M. Quadratic shrinkage for large covariance matrices. *Bernoulli* **2022**, *28*, 1519–1547. [CrossRef]
35. Donoho, D.; Gavish, M.; Johnstone, I. Optimal shrinkage of eigenvalues in the spiked covariance model. *Ann. Stat.* **2018**, *46*, 1742–1778. [CrossRef] [PubMed]
36. Bu, J.; Allez, R.; Bouchaud, J.P.; Potters, M. Rotational invariant estimator for general noisy matri-ces. *IEEE Trans. Inf. Theory* **2016**, *62*, 7475–7490.
37. Paul, D.; Aue, A. Random matrix theory in statistics: A review. *J. Stat. Plan. Inference* **2014**, *150*, 1–29. [CrossRef]
38. Haff, L.R. Empirical Bayes estimation of the multivariate normal covariance matrix. *Ann. Stat.* **1980**, *8*, 586–597. [CrossRef]
39. Markowitz, H. Portfolio Selection. *J. Finance* **1952**, *7*, 77–91.
40. DeMiguel, V.; Garlappi, L.; Nogales, F.J.; Uppal, R. A generalized approach to portfolio optimization: Improving performance by constraining portfolion norms. *Manag. Sci.* **2009**, *55*, 798–812. [CrossRef]
41. Engle, R.F.; Ledoit, O.; Wolf, M. Large dynamic covariance matrices. *J. Bus. Econom. Stat.* **2019**, *37*, 363–375. [CrossRef]
42. Bollerslev, T.R.; Engle, R.; Nelson, D. A captial asset pricing model with time varying covariances. *J. Polit. Econ.* **1988**, *96*, 116–131. [CrossRef]
43. Ledoit, O.; Peche, S. Eigenvectors of some large sample covariance matrix ensembles. *Probab. Theory Relat. Fields* **2011**, *151*, 233–264. [CrossRef]
44. Ledoit, O.; Wolf, M. Robust performances hypothesis testing with the variance. *Wilmott* **2011**, *2011*, 86–89. [CrossRef]

 *mathematics*

Article

Important Arguments Nomination Based on Fuzzy Labeling for Recognizing Plagiarized Semantic Text

Ahmed Hamza Osman * and Hani Moaiteq Aljahdali

Department of Information System, Faculty of Computing and Information Technology in Rabighn, King Abdulaziz University, Jeddah 21911, Saudi Arabia
* Correspondence: ahoahmad@kau.edu.sa

Abstract: Plagiarism is an act of intellectual high treason that damages the whole scholarly endeavor. Many attempts have been undertaken in recent years to identify text document plagiarism. The effectiveness of researchers' suggested strategies to identify plagiarized sections needs to be enhanced, particularly when semantic analysis is involved. The Internet's easy access to and copying of text content is one factor contributing to the growth of plagiarism. The present paper relates generally to text plagiarism detection. It relates more particularly to a method and system for semantic text plagiarism detection based on conceptual matching using semantic role labeling and a fuzzy inference system. We provide an important arguments nomination technique based on the fuzzy labeling method for identifying plagiarized semantic text. The suggested method matches text by assigning a value to each phrase within a sentence semantically. Semantic role labeling has several benefits for constructing semantic arguments for each phrase. The approach proposes nominating for each argument produced by the fuzzy logic to choose key arguments. It has been determined that not all textual arguments affect text plagiarism. The proposed fuzzy labeling method can only choose the most significant arguments, and the results were utilized to calculate similarity. According to the results, the suggested technique outperforms other current plagiarism detection algorithms in terms of recall, precision, and F-measure with the PAN-PC and CS11 human datasets.

Keywords: similarity; plagiarism; semantic; SRL; fuzzy labeling

MSC: 68P20; 68P10; 63E72; 68U15

Citation: Osman, A.H.; Aljahdali, H.M. Important Arguments Nomination Based on Fuzzy Labeling for Recognizing Plagiarized Semantic Text. *Mathematics* **2022**, *10*, 4613. https://doi.org/10.3390/math10234613

Academic Editors: Xiang Li, Shuo Zhang and Wei Zhang

Received: 20 October 2022
Accepted: 30 November 2022
Published: 5 December 2022

Publisher's Note: MDPI stays neutral with regard to jurisdictional claims in published maps and institutional affiliations.

1. Introduction

The evolution of, and rapid access to information through, the Internet has contributed to various data protection and ethical problems. "The act of using another person's words or ideas without giving credit to that person" is known as plagiarism. It can generally be considered as anything from basic copy-paste, in which information is simply copied, to higher levels of complexity, in which the text is distorted by sentences, translations, idea adoptions, etc. [1]. Plagiarism could be considered to be more versatile than simple, and more nuanced than trivial copying and pasting. There have typically been the following different forms of plagiarism: straight-line plagiarism, basic footnote pestilence, nuanced footnote plagiarism, plagiarism, quotation-free plagiarism and paraphrasing. The plagiarism problem includes plagiarized media, magazines and Internet tools. Longitudinal research has been undertaken in order to show students' secret patterns of plagiarism, and to analyze academics' experiences of plagiarism. On the other hand, detection of plagiarism tasks can narrowly be divided into two, namely extrinsic detection and intrinsic detection [2–4]. In extrinsic detection, the suspected document is compared with a sample that is either offline or online, whereas if the suspected document is detected internally, structural and stylometric information is used to evaluate this document, which is inserted into a report without any record of a reference source. Many online plagiarism inspectors use a method that normally consists of World Wide Web surveys, and studies indicate that the most commonly available tools to detect plagiarism cannot detect structural changes and common paraphrases imposed by the users who plagiarise [3]. Our empirical research has shown that university teachers want computerized approaches to detect the plagiarism of ideas. The quality of various academic activities, including theses, dissertations, journal articles, congresses, essays, assignments and so on, is crucial to assess.

A method called paraphrasing may be used to change the organization of a statement or swap some of the original words with synonyms. It is also plagiarism if there are no any correct citations or quotation marks. Due to the changes in fingerprints between the original and copied documents, the approaches utilized in existing detection technologies are unable to identify the use of plagiarism. These cases are far more difficult to identify, since semantic plagiarism is frequently a blurry process that is challenging to find and even more challenging to curtail. One of the key problems in the field of plagiarism detection is how to effectively and efficiently distinguish between plagiarized and non-plagiarized papers [5–7].

Some pirated studies such as [8] at least mention the original version. However, manually checking for plagiarism in a suspicious paper is a very challenging and time-consuming task involving various source materials [9]. It is therefore thought of as a big advance in this regard to use computer systems that can perform the procedure with the least amount of user interaction. The technologies for detecting plagiarism that have been proposed so far are highly capable of catching various types of plagiarism; however, detecting whether plagiarism is present in a text relies on human monitoring [10].

Comparing the copied document with the original document is a common practice in plagiarism detection approaches. Character-matching strategies can be used to identify either completely or partially identical strings. The currently used technique for paraphrasing acquisition uses machine learning and crowdsourcing [11]. This approach focuses on the following two issues: gathering data through crowdsourcing and gathering samples at the passage level. The crowdsourcing paradigm is ineffective without automatic quality assurance and, without crowdsourcing, the cost of building test corpora is too high for practical use. Additionally, a citation-based approach is applied. This technique is employed to detect academic texts that have been read and utilized without citation [11]. The current work offers a method for human semantic plagiarism detection based on conceptual matching and arguments nomination using a fuzzy labeling method, which detects plagiarism through copy-and-paste, rewording or synonym replacement, changing word structure in sentences, and changing sentences from the passive to the active voice and vice versa.

Research addressing the automated detection of suspected plagiarism instances falls under the category of plagiarism detection methods. Methods for examining textual similarity at the lexical, syntactic, and semantic levels, as well as the similarity of non-textual content elements such as citations, illustrations, tables, and mathematical equations, are frequently presented in studies. Research that addresses the evaluation of plagiarism detection algorithms, such as by offering test sets and reporting on performance comparisons, was also examined, as it focuses mostly on gap filling. Studies on the prevention, detection, prosecution, and punishment of plagiarism in educational institutions fall under the category of plagiarism policy. This research analyzed the occurrence of plagiarism at institutions, examined student and teacher attitudes about plagiarism, and discussed the effects of institutional rules.

This research is interrelated and necessary to conduct a thorough analysis of the phenomenon of academic plagiarism. Without a strong structure that directs the investigation and documentation of plagiarism, using plagiarism detection tools in practice will be useless. Research and development efforts for enhancing plagiarism detection methods and systems are guided by the information gained from examining the application of plagiarism detection systems in practice.

In order to keep up with the behavior shifts that plagiarists typically demonstrate when faced with a higher chance of getting caught due to improved detection technologies and harsher techniques, ongoing study is required. Thishis study is one of the methods used to bridge the research gaps in the field of text theft and plagiarism.

The remainder of the sections are as follows: the above-described study on plagiarism detection is described in Section 2. Fuzzy logic is the subject of Section 3. Section 4 provides a detailed explanation of the method's basic concept. In our suggested strategy, we employed an experimental design that is described in Section 5. Section 6 presents the corpus and dataset, as well as similarity detection, and the results and discussion are in Section 7.

2. Related Works

There are two stages to detecting plagiarism: source document retrieval (also known as candidate retrieval) and comprehensive comparison between the source document and the document under examination. In the last five years, many researchers have focused on the retrieval of sources and presented solutions for it, because of the recent breakthroughs in plagiarism detection.

Recently, two approaches to recognizing extrinsic plagiarism were suggested by Arabi and Akbari [12]. Both approaches use two steps of filtering, based on the bag of words (BoW) technique at the document and sentence levels, and plagiarism is only looked into in the outputs of these two stages, in order to reduce the search space. Semantic matrices and two structural are created using a mix of the WordNet ontology and the weighting TF–IDF methodology, as well as the pre-trained network method of words embedding Fast Text. Then, the TF–IDF weighting method is used in the second technique to detect similarities in suspicious documents and sentences.

Research [13] has found that accessing plagiarism sources using external knowledge base sources increased semantic similarity and contextual importance. Other than examples where the text had been duplicated verbatim, the researchers employed a closest neighbor search and support vector machine to find potential candidates for other sorts of plagiarism. Using encoded fingerprints to create queries, a researcher has presented candidate retrieval for Arabic text reuse from online pages and provided the optimal selection of source documents [14]. Cross-lingual candidate retrieval utilizing two-level proximity information was suggested, in addition to prior work on candidate retrieval from the same language. With the suspect (or query) document segmented using a topic-based segmentation algorithm, the researchers next utilized a proximity-based model to find sources related to the segmented portions of the suspicious document. There is still room for improvement in the second phase of plagiarism detection, according to a study of the current trends in plagiarism detection research [12,15,16]. More languages and machine learning approaches need to be explored in the field of cross-language plagiarism detection, as shown by recent studies [17–19].

The detection of disguised plagiarism has been the subject of many studies [20–22]. WordNet-combined semantic similarity metrics were utilized to identify highly obfuscated plagiarism instances in handwritten paraphrases and simulated plagiarism cases [5–7,23–25]. Adding an intermediary phase between candidate retrieval and comprehensive analysis allowed for visual assessment of highly obfuscated plagiarisms, and this additional step included an expanded Jaccard measure to deal with synonyms/hypernyms in text fragments [5]. Studies have examined and evaluated approaches using both content-based and citation-based plagiarism detection in academic writing [26]. Citations and references were shown to be an effective addition to existing plagiarism detection techniques. Document plagiarism detection has been studied as a binary classification task in recent works [27]. Naive Bayes (NB), support vector machine (SVM), and decision tree (DT) classifiers have been used to determine whether or not suspicious-source document pairings included plagiarism [28]. Part of speech (POS) and chunk features were used to extract monolingual features from text pairings, concentrating on modest yet effective syntax-based features.

When compared to traditional baselines, the suggested classifiers were shown to be more accurate in detecting plagiarism in English texts [28]. Genetic algorithms (GA) were utilized to identify disguised plagiarism in the form of summary texts using syntactic and semantic aspects. An algorithm based on the GA method was used to extract concepts at the sentence level [29,30]. Syntactic and semantic elements from the WordNet lexical database were used to include two detection levels, document-level and passage-level [30]. It was shown that a combined syntactic–semantic metric that incorporates additional characteristics such as chunking and POS tagging, as well as semantic role labeling (SRL) and its POS tagging variant, may better distinguish between various kinds of plagiarism. When it comes to spotting veiled plagiarism in a monolingual situation, deeper linguistic traits take center stage.

Paraphrasing is a technique that modifies or replaces some of the original words by their synonym, by changing the structure of the sentence. It is also considered to be plagiarism without a correct citation or quotation marks. Due to variation in the finger printouts between the original and plagiarism files, methods used in existing detection tools cannot be detected as described above. Such cases are much more difficult for people to spot, as linguistic plagiarism is often a smooth process that is difficult to find and more difficult to stop, as it often crosses international borders. Due to the plagiarism issue, there have been a number of arguments, including intellectual property (IP), ethics, legal restrictions and copyright. Intellectual property (IP) is a legal right to the production of the mind, creative and economic, as well as relevant legal fields. In particular, plagiarism is deemed wrong in a moral context, because the plagiarist takes the original author's ideas and contents and tries to deny the author's contribution, by failing to include proper citations or quotations. More legal restrictions are therefore necessary if the original author is to be able to claim their specific rights in respect of their new invention or function. There are many kinds of plagiarism, including copying and pasting, reprocessing and paraphrasing the text, plagiarism of ideas and plagiarism by converting one language to another. Plagiarism is one of the serious problems in education. The discrepancies in fingerprints between the original and the plagiarized material prevent existing detection technologies from detecting plagiarism. Semantic plagiarism is typically a hazy process that is hard to look for and even more difficult to stop, since it generally crosses international borders. The number of arguments picked up by using the fuzzy inference system(FIS) is greater than that detected using the argument weight method in [31]. Fuzzy logic may also tackle the issue of uncertainty in argument selection that affects plagiarized users. One of the most difficult challenges in the world of plagiarism detection is accurately distinguishing between plagiarized and non-plagiarized content. Plagiarism detection software currently uses character matching, n-grams, chunks, and keywords to find inconsistencies. A novel approach of detecting plagiarism is proposed in this paper. Based on semantic role labeling and fuzzy logic, these approaches will be likely to be used in the future.

Natural language processing approaches such as semantic role labeling (SRL), text clustering [32] and text classification [33] have all made use of SRL [34]. Osman et al. have proposed an improved plagiarism detection method based on SRL [5]. The suggested approach was taught to examine the behavior of the plagiarized user using an argument weighting mechanism. Plagiarism detection is not affected by all arguments. Using fuzzy rules and fuzzy inference systems, we are trying to identify the most essential points in a plagiarized text. Fuzzy logic, a kind of approximation reasoning, is a strong tool for decision support and expert systems. It is possible that most of human thinking is based on fuzzy facts, fuzzy connectives, and fuzzy rules of inference [2]. The *t*-test significance procedure was used to demonstrate the validity of the findings acquired utilizing the new method's fuzzy inference system.

The main contributions and goal of the proposed method is a thorough plagiarism detection technique that focuses on many types of detection, including copy–paste plagiarism, rewording or synonym replacement, changing word structure in sentences, and switching from the passive to the active voice and vice versa. The SRL was utilized to perform semantic analysis on the sentences. The concepts or synonyms for each word in the phrases were extracted using the WordNet thesaurus. These three points are the main differences between our proposed method and other techniques. The second aspect is the comparison process. Whereas prior approaches have concentrated on conventional comparison techniques such as character-based and string matching, our suggested method uses the SRL as a method of analysis and comparison to capture plagiarized meaning of a text. The crucial aspect of this variation is an increase in our suggested method's similarity score employing the fuzzy logic algorithm, where none of the proposed approaches have ever been employed before.

3. Fuzzy Logic System

Many prediction and control systems, fuzzy knowledge management systems, and decision support systems have shown success with the fuzzy logic system [35–37]. For confusing and obscure information, it is often utilized. The connection between inputs and intended outputs of a system may be determined using this technique. Assumptions and approximations may be taken into account while making a choice using it. A defuzzification method and a set of predetermined rules are part of a fuzzy inference system.

Mamdani employed fuzzy logic to regulate a modest laboratory steam engine, which was first described by Zadeh [38]. It is possible to obtain decision-making models in linguistic terms, thanks to an assumption in mathematics about ambiguous reasoning. For many applications and complex control systems, fuzzy logic has recently emerged as one of the most effective methods. More than 1000 industrial commercial fuzzy applications have been successfully created in the last several years, according to Munakata and Jani [39]. Fuzzy logic's distinctive properties are at the heart of the curreendeavour.

The theory of fuzzy sets offers a foundation for the use of fuzzy logic. It became necessary to adapt traditional logic to cope with partial truths, because of its inability to deal with just two values, true and false (neither completely true nor completely false). Thus, the fuzzy logic is an extension of classical logic by generalizing the classical logic inference rules, which are capable of handling approximate reasoning. Each member of a "fuzzy set" has a degree of membership in that set, which is defined by a membership function, which is an extension of the standard "crisp set." Members of the target set are assigned a membership degree between zero and one by the membership function, which allocates a membership degree to each member of the target set [35]. Based on a set of fuzzy "IF–THEN" principles, the computer can convert language statements into actions. Conditions are linked with actions in "if A then B" fuzzy IF–THEN rules, with "if A then B" being the most common version. In the construction and modification of fuzzy logic, the rules are easily understood and simple to alter, to add new rules or to delete current rules.

By applying a membership function to the fuzzy sets of linguistic words, input values are converted into degrees of membership (in the (0;1) range). As shown in Equation (1), the equation concerning $x_i k(x_i)$ may be represented by a fuzzy set, which is obtained by holding certain variables constant μ_i and then transforming that set into a fuzzy one [40].

$$A = \frac{\mu_i k}{x_i} x_i \in X \tag{1}$$

There are fuzzy sets A and X in the world of discourse, and values vary from 1 to 0 in the fuzzy set.

In the context of fuzzification, $k(\ )$ is referred to as the kernel. "A" is the fuzzified version of "A".

$$A = \mu_1 k(x_1) + \mu_2 k(x_2) + \ldots + \mu_n k(x_n) \tag{2}$$

To execute fuzzy reasoning, the inference element of a fuzzy system combines facts collected via the fuzzification process with a set of production rules [40]. The FIS shown in Figure 1.

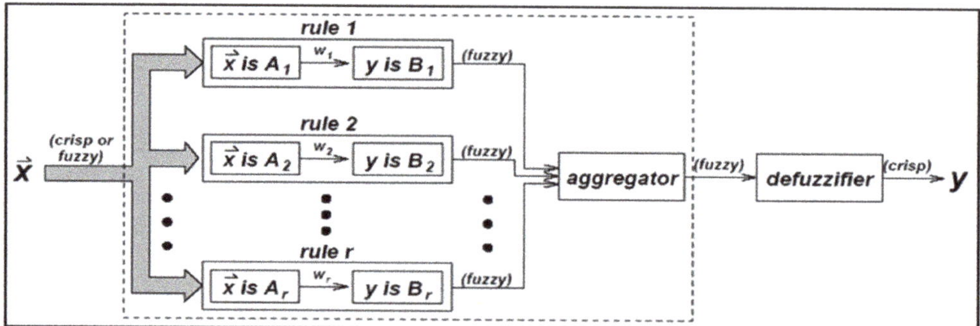

Figure 1. The fuzzy inference system phases.

Figure 1 depicts the fuzzy inference system (FIS) phases. The initial stage in the FIS is to use membership functions contained in the fuzzy knowledge base to transform explicit input into linguistic variables. The fuzzy input is then transformed into a fuzzy output by using an IF–THEN type of fuzzy rule. The final step converts the fuzzy output of the inference engine into a clean output using a membership function similar to that used by fuzzers.

4. Proposed Method

The following are the four key phases of the suggested procedure:

- The first step in data preparation is called pre-processing.
- Segmentation, stop words removal, and stemming
- Extraction of semantic role labeling
- Extraction of concepts
- The fourth step is fuzzy SRL

Figure 2 depicts the suggested method's overall design.

The next sections contain more information on each of these stages.

4.1. Data Preparation

Preparation of the data included text segmentation, stop word removal, and word stemming. Text was segmented into sentences using text segmentation software [41]. To eliminate pointless words, the stop words removal technique was used. Prefixes and suffixes were also removed using the stemming technique to uncover the base word of a term. These words were culled from the text and the rest were discarded. As a result, there may have been a decrease in the similarity of papers.

Text Segmentation: Natural language processing (NLP) relies heavily on pre-processing. Simple text segmentation is a sort of pre-processing in which text is divided into meaningful chunks. Separating text into individual phrases, words, or themes is a common practice. Steps such as information extraction, semantic role labels, syntax parsing, machine translations, and plagiarism detection all rely heavily on this stage. Boundary detection and text segmentation are used to conduct sentence segmentation. This is the most common way to denote the end of a phrase, using a period (.), exclamation point (!), or question mark (?) [42]. The first phase in our suggested text segmentation approach was sentence-based text segmentation, in which the original and comparison texts were broken down into sentence units. Due to our suggested technique's goal of comparing suspicious text with the source, we decided to utilize this method.

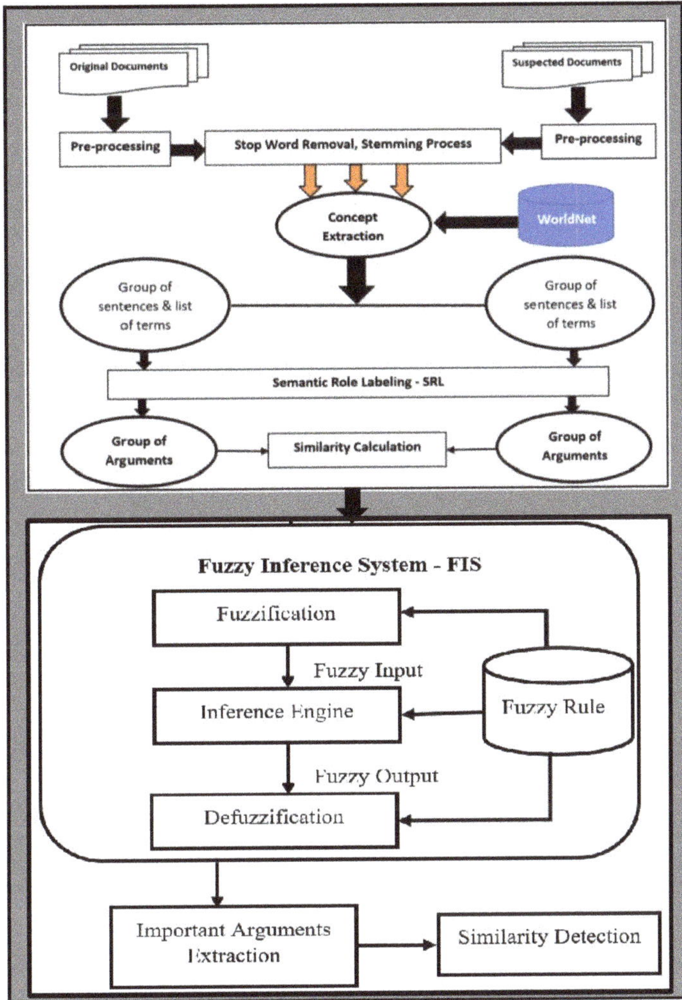

Figure 2. Fuzzy semantic approach to detecting plagiarism.

Stop Words Removal and Stemming Process: Stop words are common occurrences in written materials. Words such as "the", "and", and "a" are examples. As a result of their omission from the index, these keywords have no hint values or meanings associated with their content [43]. According to Tomasic and Garcia-Molina [44], these words account for 40% to 50% of the total text words in a document collection. Automatic indexing may be sped up and index space saved by eliminating stop words, which does not affect retrieval effectiveness [45]. There are a variety of methods for determining stop words, and each has its own advantages and disadvantages. There are a number of English stop word lists now in use in search engines. To make the system work faster, we devised a solution that eliminated all the text's stop words. The SMART information retrieval system at Cornell University, employing the Buckley stop words list [46], is the basis for our suggested technique.

Stemming is another text pre-processing step. Currently, there are several English-language stemmers to choose from that are comprehensive and in-depth. The well-known English stemmers, such as Nice Stemmer, Text Stemmer, and Porter Stemmer, are only a few examples. A term's inflectional and derivationally related forms are reduced to a generic base form, using the Porter Stemming method. As an example, consider the following:

am, is, are ⇒ be article, articles, article's, articles' ⇒ article

Information retrieval challenges such as word form variations may be addressed with stemming (Lennon et al., 1981). It is not uncommon for a word to be misspelled or a phrase to be shortened or abbreviated, for a variety of reasons.

The stemming process produces a different word n-gram set, which is then used for similarity matching between texts using the proposed method.

4.2. Extraction of Arguments and Semantic Role Labeling

Semantic role labeling is a technique for identifying and classifying arguments in a piece of writing. Essentially, a semantic analysis of a text identifies all of its other concepts' arguments. In addition to determining "subject", "object", "verb", or "adverb", it may also be used to characterize elements of speech. Each word in the suspected and source sentences is labeled with its matching role throughout the roles labeling procedure. As a result of this research, semantic role labeling based on the sentence level was offered as a unique plagiarism detection approach.

Using semantic role labeling (SRL), a method for comparing the semantic similarity of two papers, one may determine whether the ideas in both documents are arranged similarly. In this research, ideas were labeled with role labels and gathered into groups. Groups were employed in this manner to as a fast guide to collect the suspicious portion of the text. An example of a plagiarized situation is found here:

Example (1):

Chester kicked the ball. (Original), the ball was kicked by Chester. (Suspected)

By using the Online Demo of SRL (http://cogcomp.cs.illinois.edu/page/research, accessed on 22 July 2022), the produced arguments are:

An original ("Chester kicked the ball") and suspected ("The ball was kicked by Chester") phrases analysis using SRL are shown in Figures 3 and 4:

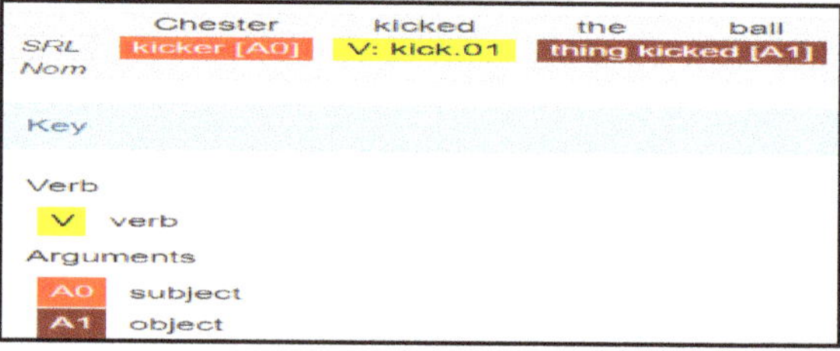

Figure 3. An analysis of the original phrase based on SRL.

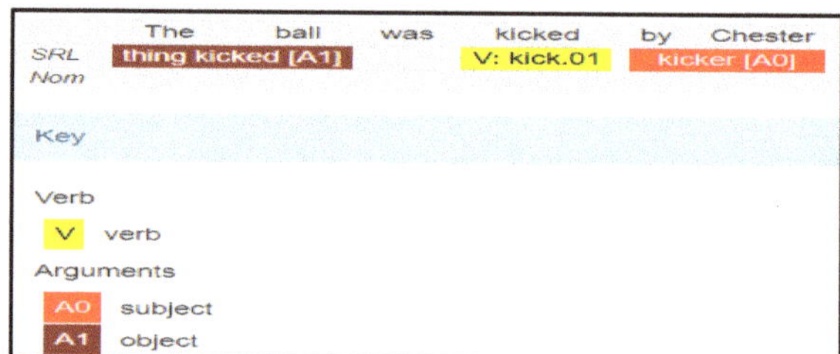

Figure 4. An analysis of the suspected phrase based on SRL.

The syntax of the two phrases above may alter depending on whether the active or passive voice is employed if synonyms and antonyms are utilized. In fact, the semantics of these two phrases are quite similar. In spite of the labels being moved about inside the sentences, the SRL still manages to capture the arguments (subject, object, verb, and indirect object) for a sentence. Our suggested approach of plagiarism detection, based on a comparison of the sentence's arguments, is supported by this capture.

According to the SRL scheme of similarity [47], original and suspected papers were checked for similar keywords. When two words are found to be the same, we go straight to the argument label and compare the phrases in which they are conveyed. After identifying potential plagiarized phrases, this phase compares the argument labels of those sentences with the argument labels of the original phrases. In order to make an accurate comparison, the words must be compared correctly. The plagiarism ratio may be incorrect if we compare the phrases in Arg0 (subject) in the suspected text with all other arguments in the original text. For example, comparing the subject with the adjective argument (Arg–Adj) to the subject with the time argument (Arg–TMP) is an unfair general-purpose argument (Arg–O).

String matching [48,49] and n-gram [15] are two examples of approaches that compare each word in a suspected sentence to the original phrase. The terms "ball", "kicked", and "Chester" will be compared. Aside from the fact that this comparison is incorrect, it also consumes comparison time. Our technique compares the reasons in the suspected sentence phrase to those in the original phrase to see whether they are comparable. Subject to subject comparisons, verb to verb comparisons, etc., are all possible with our suggested SRL technique. This will reduce the number of comparisons we have to make. No comparison will be made between arguments in questionable papers and arguments from the actual source materials. When comparing original and suspected phrases, we can see that active and passive synonyms have different structures and term positions when compared to their passive counterparts, as seen in this example. These two phrases are, in fact, semantically interchangeable. The researchers have found that, despite altering synonyms within phrases, their technique managed to capture the semantic meaning of a statement. Using the WordNet concept extraction, our suggested approach of plagiarism detection may be supported.

4.3. Concept Extraction

The extraction of concepts is an important part of our detection process. WordNet [50] is used in this research as a source of synonyms and related words. It is one of the lexical semantic connections, which are relationships between words. The WordNet system quantifies semantic similarity, since the closer two words are to one another, the more similar is the structure of their connection, and the more frequent are the lexical units shared between them. Using WordNet Thesaurus as a starting point, we begin the process of identifying key concepts. The following are the steps in the procedure: Using the WordNet synset (synonym set) from the words used in the text of the document, the document's terms are mapped onto the WordNet Thesaurus database. WordNet is structured, based on the concept of synsets. A synonym set is a collection of words or phrases that have the same meaning in a certain context. Using an example of a synset from the WordNet Thesaurus database, we can better illustrate what have said so far regarding idea extraction.

Figure 5 demonstrates a synsets extraction from the terms "Canine" and "Chap" [paper: A semantic approach for text clustering using WordNet and lexical chains] and [paper title: Comparative cluster labeling involving external text sources].

In the above example, the synset of terms "Canine" and "Chap", the phrase "canine" for example, may refer to a variety of different things depending on the context: feline, carnivore, automobile, mammal, placental, and many more. The hyponymy (between specialized and more general ideas) and meronymy (between parts and holes) are examples of semantic interactions that might connect synsets together. Figure 5 provides an example of synset relations using WordNet database.

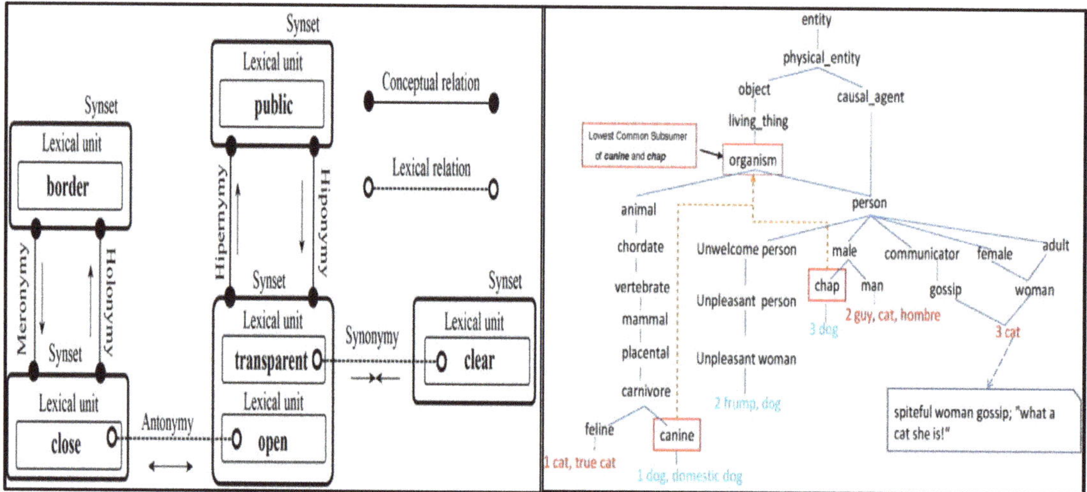

Figure 5. Terms synsets extraction.

5. Fuzzy SRL

Semantic role labeling is a method for detecting plagiarism by comparing two phrases' semantic similarities. In this section, the concept of the suggested approach is detailed.

The SRL similarity metric introduced and explained in [28] is used to determine the argument similarity score. For plagiarism detection, fuzzy is utilized as an argument selection technique to choose the most relevant arguments.

Using a fuzzy decision-making framework, Vieira [34] suggested a fuzzy criterion for feature selection. Classical multi-objective optimization has the challenge of balancing the weights of many objectives; our technique does not have that problem. Fuzzy logic elements were used into our system to determine the degree of resemblance between the suspect and the source documents. In the FIS system, we created a feature vector for each sentence (S) as follows: S = A F1, A F2,..., where A F1 represents the first argument feature, and so on. By comparing the documents, we may infer their values. Following the fuzzy logic approach, the arguments score is formed, and then a final set of high-scoring arguments is selected to combine with the similarity detection based on the comparison. Algorithm 1 below outlines the phases of our new technique.

Stemming, on the other hand, is a text pre-processing technique. Stemming is a solution to the issue of word form variation in information retrieval [34]. Spelling mistakes, alternative spellings, multi-word constructions, transliteration, affixes, and abbreviations are the most prevalent kinds of variation. Matching algorithms suffer from a lack of efficiency because of the wide range of word forms used in the information retrieval process. Using root words in pattern matching improves information retrieval significantly. This phase was completed using a Porter stemming strategy [35]. Extracting the most important words from a piece of text is an important part of our suggested technique. Because of this, our suggested method's ability to detect similarity between papers may suffer.

Algorithm 1 An improved plagiarism detection method based on fuzzy logic.

Step	Main Process	Process Detail
1	*Read original document O and suspected documents S:*	Read the original document O and suspected documents S, O and S = {Title, S1,S2,S3, … ,Sn}
2	*Apply SRL cross the original document O and suspected documents S:*	Extract all the arguments for each sentence. Collect all the similar argument in separated node.
3	*Preprocessing:*	Extract the individual sentences of the documents. Then, remove stop words. The last step for preprocessing is word stemming.
4	*Arguments similarity score calculation:*	Calculate the similarity between each corresponding argument (Verb with Verb, Subject with Subject … etc)
5	*Perform sentence score using Fuzzy Logic Method:*	
	A. *Construct the membership function as fuzzification:*	Define the meaning (linguistic variable) of input/output terms and determine fuzzy set used in the fuzzy inference system as described in Section 7.
	B. *Construct the fuzzy IF-THEN rules:*	Define the possible fuzzy IF-THEN rules as described in Section 7.
	C. *Defuzzification:*	Convert the fuzzy output from the inference system into a crisp output (the high score more than 0.5).
	6. Test the results before and after optimization.	Use T-test significant test to show if there is a significant improvement or not.

5.1. Membership Functions and Inference System

A fuzzy system relies on the ability to make inferences. In order to perform fuzzy reasoning, the data gathered through the fuzzification process are combined with a sequence of production rules [34]. To translate numerical data into linguistic variables and execute reasoning, fuzzy expert systems and fuzzy controllers need preset membership functions and fuzzy inference rules [35]. The magnitude of each input's involvement is represented graphically by the membership function.

Fuzzy logic-based plagiarism detection was implemented with different inputs, using a similarity score between individual arguments of original sentences and suspected sentences and one output value of y, which is a similarity score between all arguments of the original and suspected sentences. This was done in order to implement our proposed method. To demonstrate Mamdani's fuzzy inference given a collection of fuzzy rules, the goal is to provide an example. To represent each individual linguistic variable, there are many kinds of "membership functions" on the inputs and outputs in this system. The linguistic variables for x and y, for example, comprise significant and insignificant components that must be considered. These functions are shown in Figure 6.

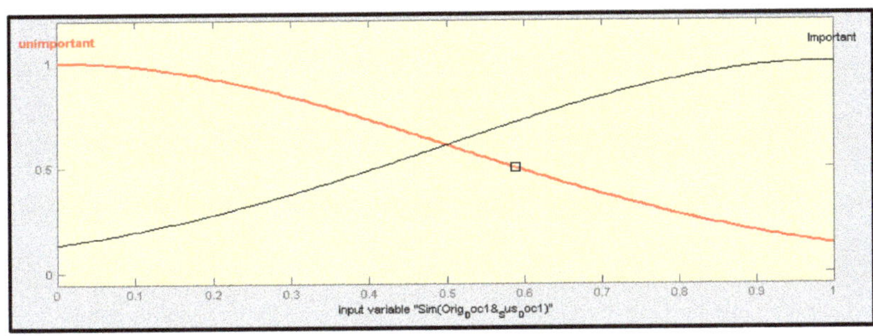

Figure 6. Input MF for fuzzy model.

There were two linguistic values assigned to each input in the suggested method, "important" and "unimportant". Similarity scores were calculated for input and output using the fuzzy membership function, which yielded important and unimportant scores, depending on whether the score was larger or smaller than 0.5. FIS Toolbox in MATLAB was used to calculate the membership function. Using this toolkit, non-linear processes with fuzzy rules created automatically in the FIS environment may be perfectly modelled. All of this information was entered into a computer program that determined the answer. Each rule in the system was seen as crucial to the generation of numerical forecasts. Although each argument's similarity score was used to reflect its input value, an overall score was used to show how similar each argument was to other likely suspect phrases. Section 5 explains how the arguments' similarity was determined.

5.2. Fuzzy IF–THEN Rules Construction

When dealing with an inference engine, a good understanding of the fuzzification rules is critical. The fuzzification rules base comprising the IF–THEN rules generates the linguistic parameters for the middle and yield variables outlined above. This set of IF–THEN rules extracts the most significant arguments based on our criterion. Based on the input characteristics, a popular approach for constructing rules was used to extract and create all available rules. The following equation was used to obtain the total number of rules:

$$R = f^n \tag{3}$$

where R denotes the rules; f denotes the features input; n signifies the rule's logic of possibility.

For example, in a a five-input system with two logic outputs for each input (true and false), the total number of rules created is 32. All potential rules to help the inference system to distinguish between significant and unimportant arguments were generated by Equation (3) using our suggested technique.

Our suggested technique was put to the test with over 1000 papers, yielding a massive number of rules. Although it was difficult to capture all of the created rules in the fuzzy system, it was a crucial concern. It was imperative that the number of rules created could be reduced. This issue was addressed using a mix of rule reduction techniques [34]. These rules reflect the membership function's inputs and outputs. There were around 1000 papers that were considered to be relevant arguments in the training data set for the proposed technique. Figure 7 depicts the three-dimensional fuzzy rule graphs of our suggested technique.

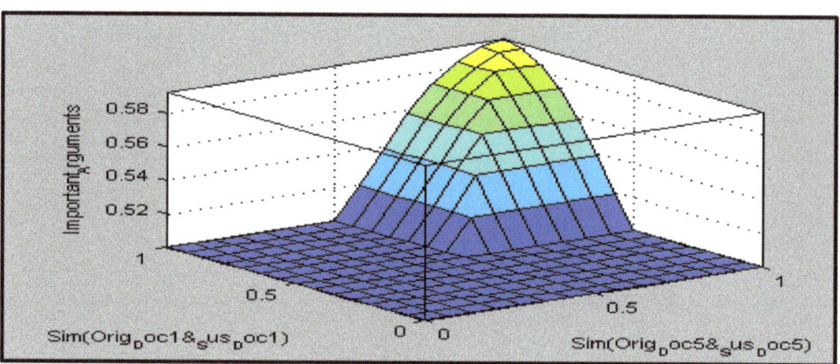

Figure 7. Important argument similarity using fuzzy model.

In order to improve the detection of similarities, the suggested method aims to choose only the strongest reasons that may have a significant impact on the plagiarism process. The fuzzy IF–THEN rule base is an important part of FIS. Prior to reducing the number of rules, all available rules were retrieved. The most essential arguments were chosen for the second round of testing comparisons. Arguments that were deemed insignificant by the FIS were not taken into consideration. After deciding on the arguments, a test was carried out. The degree of similarity relies on the number of reasons retrieved from the sentences, therefore lowering the insignificant arguments leads to an increase in the similarity score, as was discovered when comparing the findings from the first test. The CS11 human plagiarism corpus was used to obtain the matching score. In the next sections, the calculation of similarity is detailed.

5.3. Defuzzification

Defuzzification is the final phase in the fuzzy logic procedure. A final score is assigned to each argument during defuzzification, based on the inference system findings. A fuzzy set's aggregate output is utilized as the input and the outcome is a single value. Defuzzification must be finished before a single value output may be generated. According to Mogharreban [34], there are several defuzzification methods. Fuzzy reasoning systems benefit from our usage of the maximum mean defuzzification approach.

The maximum mean: The mean of maxima is computed using the distribution of output to get a single value. The equation below shows how this is done:

$$\frac{\sum_{j-1}^{q} Z_j u_c(Z_j)}{\sum_{j-1}^{q} u_c(Z_j)} \tag{4}$$

$$\sum_{j-1}^{1} \frac{Z_j}{j} \tag{5}$$

where I is the time when the distribution output hits the maximum level of $z\,j$, z is the mean of maximum, and $z\,j$ is the membership function's maximum point.

6. Experimental Design and Dataset

Experiments were conducted to determine how many sentences from the original papers were found to be plagiarized. The tests were carried out on a PAN-PC dataset [2]. According to the PAN-PC dataset [2], each of these texts was based on one or more original parts. It was decided to use the new method by looking for allegedly suspicious original texts. There were many groupings of texts, each with a particular quantity of types. When comparing the two groups, and the number of texts for each group, the first set consisted of five texts. Then, five more texts were added to the initial group, followed by 10, 20, 40, 100, and 1000. Grouping is a useful technique [5] for identifying how a plagiarized argument performs under various conditions. A total of 1000 documents were used in the studies after analyzing the arguments' behavioral patterns. As input variables in FIS, each group and each argument was selected. This results in a tally of how closely these individuals are related to one another. The input variable's values are a similarity score for each pair of arguments that are comparable. As part of the data training, the trials were carried out on the PAN-PC dataset. After that, it was put to the test on a large sample size of 1000 documents. It was discovered that important arguments may be picked using FIS. After the arguments were picked, a second round of testing was conducted. The degree of similarity was discovered to be dependent on the number of reasons retrieved from the sentences, and by lowering the unimportant arguments, the similarity score was found to be higher, as was the case with the initial testing. It was subsequently determined that the PAN-PC dataset was utilized to cross-check the results. Below, we explain how that number was determined.

The CS11 human corpus was used in an additional experiment. The problem with the PAN-PC corpus is that most of the plagiarism instances were intentionally manufactured. There are 100 instances of plagiarism in the CS11 people short answer questions corpus, according to Clough and Stevenson [36]. Examples of plagiarized texts of varying degrees of plagiarization may be found in this resource. Since the Clough and Stevenson corpus was created and built by real people rather than computer programs, it provides a more realistic picture of the actions of people who have copied work. Each document in the corpus has at least one suspiciously copied section, as well as five original sentences taken from Wikipedia. Native and non-native speaking students were asked to respond to five questions, based on the original materials. Answers were based on the instructions provided by the corpus designers, with the exception of non-plagiarized examples, and were based on actual texts with varying degrees of text overlap. Average word counts for the short sections were in the tens of words (200–300). Near-copy (19), heavy revision (19), and light revision (19) instances were found in 57 samples, while the remaining 38 samples were found to be plagiarism-free. The following are examples of questionable documents:

- Near-copy: it focuses on copying and pasting from the source text
- Light-revision: Minor alterations to the original text, such as substituting synonyms for phrases and introducing grammatical changes
- Heavy-revision: editing and rewriting in original material with restructuring and paraphrasing
- Non plagiarism: participant information was included into the writings without altering the originals

The matching arguments and the arguments included in the sentences are both taken into account when determining similarity. When comparing the two documents, the first variable identifies arguments that are similar in both, while the second identifies arguments that do not appear in either text. The Jaccard coefficient was used to determine the matching among the arguments in the original and the suspected texts.

$$similarity(C_i(ArgT_j, ArgT_k)) = \frac{C(ArgT_j) \cap C(ArgT_k)}{C(ArgT_j) \cup C(ArgT_k)} \tag{6}$$

where $Ci\ (ArgTk)$ = ideas of the original document's argument text; $C(ArgTj)$ = concepts of the suspected document's argument text.

Using the following equation, we estimated similarity between the original and the suspicious texts:

$$TS(txt1, txt2) = \sum_{i=1,l} \sum_{\substack{j=1,m \\ k=1,n}} SimC_i(ArgT_j, ArgT_k) \tag{7}$$

where TS is the total similarity score, m = the number of arguments text in the original document, n = the number of arguments text in the suspected document, and i = the matching between the arguments text in the original text with concept i and the suspected text with that concept, along with the number of concepts.

7. Results and Discussion

Plagiarized materials were copied and pasted, synonyms were changed, and sentences were restructured in a variety of ways (paraphrasing). Three typical testing measures for plagiarism detection were utilized as described in the Equations (8)–(10).

$$Recall = \frac{(No\ of\ detected\ args)}{(Total\ no\ of\ args)} \tag{8}$$

$$Precision = \frac{(No\ of\ plagirized\ Args)}{(No\ of\ detected\ Args)} \tag{9}$$

$$F - \text{measure} = \frac{(2 \times \text{Recall} \times \text{Precision})}{(\text{Recall} + \text{precision})} \tag{10}$$

Using the collection of documents we chose, we ran the tests shown in Figure 8, which displays the findings. For the similarity computation, a set of documents is represented by a row.

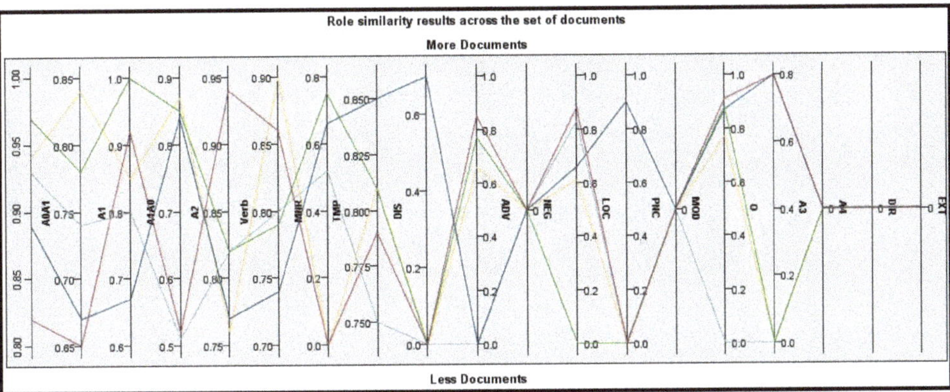

Figure 8. Role similarity scores across the set of documents.

The SRL was employed to break down the text into different arguments, examples of which are shown in Table 1 below.

Table 1. Argument types and their descriptions.

Type	Description
Arg0	agent
Arg1	direct object/theme/patient
Arg2–5	not fixed
V	verb
MNR	manner
TMP	time
DIS	discourse connectives
ADV	adjective
NEG	negation marker
LOC	location
PNC	purpose
MOD	modal verb
O	general purpose
DIR	direction
EXT	extent

Experiments employed a variety of argument types and descriptions, as shown in Table 1.

Each pair of documents is represented in Table 2 by the percentage of similarity between the suspected and original documents. Recall, precision, and F-measures all have scores over 0.58, whereas all recall measures have scores above 0.80. Table 2 shows that the scores are all larger than 0.5, which indicates that the findings are excellent, but it was still possible to enhance these scores to obtain better similarity values.

Table 2. Ranking of SRL arguments using FIS.

Fuzzy Result	O	LOC	Verb	A0	A2	A1	TMP	MNR	A0A1	PNC	A1A0	DIR	ADV	DIS	NEG	MOD	A3	A4
Fuzzy Result of 5 Documents	0.6403	0.6332	0.6278	0.6277	0.6254	0.6065	0.6009	0.597	0.5936	0.5	0.4866	0.3935	0.3614	0.3591	0.3591	0.3591	0.3591	0.3591
Fuzzy Result of 10 Documents	0.6403	0.6332	0.6277	0.6254	0.6065	0.6009	0.597	0.5936	0.5	0.5	0.4866	0.3935	0.3614	0.3591	0.3591	0.3591	0.3591	0.3591
Fuzzy Result of 20 Documents	0.5287	0.5251	0.5233	0.5186	0.5143	0.5082	0.5	0.5	0.5	0.5	0.5	0.4541	0.4411	0.4411	0.4411	0.4364	0.4357	0.4324
Fuzzy Result of 40 Documents	0.5409	0.5361	0.5359	0.5353	0.5347	0.5309	0.526	0.5252	0.5194	0.5078	0.4948	0.4749	0.4675	0.4671	0.4671	0.466	0.4632	0.4616
Fuzzy Result of 100 Documents	0.5068	0.5057	0.5055	0.5046	0.5045	0.5044	0.5041	0.5039	0.5038	0.5	0.5	0.4941	0.494	0.4922	0.4919	0.4919	0.4919	0.4918
Fuzzy Result of 1000 Documents	0.5017	0.5012	0.5012	0.5011	0.5011	0.501	0.501	0.5	0.4998	0.4996	0.4985	0.4985	0.498	0.4979	0.4979	0.4979	0.4979	0.4978
Rank	significant	significant	significant	significant	significant	significant	significant	significant	Not significant	Not significant	Not significant	Not significant	Not significant	Not significant	Not significant	Not significant	Not significant	Not significant

FIS has shown that the writer who plagiarizes does not concentrate on all of the reasons in a statement, therefore certain arguments are left out. Arguments like this are said to be insignificant. Table 2 shows the outcomes of the FIS cross SRL sentences.

Table 2 shows the ranking of the SRL arguments using FIS. In order to test our method, we used a variety of groupings of documents (5, 10, 20, 40, 100 and 1000). These allegedly plagiarized texts used a variety of plagiarism strategies, including copying and pasting, swapping certain phrases for their counterparts, and altering sentence structure (paraphrasing). There are two kinds of arguments. Both types of arguments have a similarity score larger than 0.5; however, the first form of argument is considered significant while the second type is considered irrelevant. Similarity scores were calculated for input and output using the fuzzy membership function, which yielded important and unimportant scores, depending on whether the score was larger or smaller than 0.5. The comparison step of the proposed technique uses a Jaccard similarity measure [37] with a threshold value of 0.5 [38–40]. For this reason, we chose 0.5 as our cutoff value. In order to enhance the similarity score, the FIS method chose the most essential reasons. On the other hand, the similarity score was reduced by minor arguments. Unimportant arguments were discarded to minimize the general resemblance of the original and suspected texts. To determine the degree to which two arguments are similar, the SRL similarity measure, developed by Osman et al. [28], is used. A table titled the "similarity scores table" shows all of the similarity ratings between the various arguments. An input to the FIS is the similarity score table. Features include the arguments and overall similarity between them, as well as the amount of original and suspected texts in the dataset that were utilized in its construction. This system's goal is to increase the similarity scores in plagiarism detection by generating many key arguments.

A common approach used by those who plagiarize is to concentrate on key phrases and then adapt their work to include them. Only the most crucial points that have a significant impact on the reader would be reworked. There are a number of target selection approaches available, all of which aim to anticipate as accurately as possible the essential objectives of the data. FIS is one of these approaches. Statistical significance test (*t*-test) results were used to demonstrate the benefits of the new strategy. These findings are shown in Table 3 and demonstrate the statistical significance of the suggested approach.

Table 3. Statistical significance testing using the *t*-test.

	Mean	Std. Deviation	Std. Error Mean	95% Confidence Interval of the Difference		Sig. (2-tailed)
				Lower	Upper	
Recall-1–Recall-2	9.542×10^{-2}	3.348×10^{-2}	1.367×10^{-2}	6.028×10^{-2}	0.1306	0.000928
Precision-1–Precision-2	0.2238	5.402×10^{-2}	2.206×10^{-2}	0.1671	0.2805	0.000159
F-measure-1–Fmeasure-2	0.1521	3.661×10^{-2}	1.494×10^{-2}	0.1137	0.1906	0.000156

There are many metrics in Table 3 that may be compared using the pair of variables before and after optimization using the FIS-SRL approach, as well as their significance, using the paired samples *t*-test process. Comparing the means of two variables representing the same group at various points in time is done using the paired samples *t*-test technique. In the pair of variables statistics table, the mean values of the two variables ((Recall-1, Recall-2); (Precision-1, Precision-2); and (F-measure-1, F-measure-2)) are shown. As a paired samples *t*-test examines two variables' mean values, it is important to know their averages. The *t*-test may be used to determine whether there is a significant difference between two variables if the significance value is less than 0.05. For example, it was found that the suggested technique had significant recall (0.000928), precision (0.000159), and F-measure results in the significance field of Table 3 (Sig. (2-tailed)). This suggests that the proposed method had significant results in all three areas. The fact that the confidence interval for the mean difference does not include 0 shows that the difference is, likewise, significant. There is also a lack of statistical significance in the F-measure, recall, and precision. Comparison of the outcomes before and after optimization indicates that there is considerable difference.

The PAN-PC dataset evaluates and compares the presented solution with other plagiarism detection systems. Figure 9 shows the comparison findings.

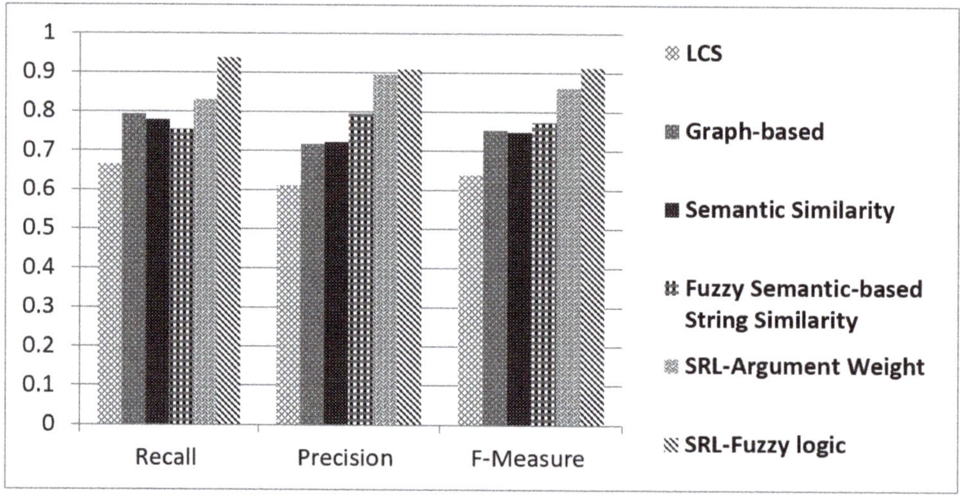

Figure 9. Contrast between the current text-based similarity detection methods.

A comparison of SRL fuzzy logic with string-similarity, LCS, graph-based methods, semantic similarity methods, and SRL argument weight methods is shown in Figure 9 [29,30,34–36]. The similarity results were shown to be improved with our new technique.

Our suggested technique was compared to Chong's naive Bayes classifier [51] with a set of all features, best features, and ferret baseline method in the Tables 4–6 for the similarity classes (heavy-revision, light-revision, and near-copy). Table 4 shows the heavy-revision plagiarism class.

Table 4. Heavy plagiarism class.

Plagiarism Detection Method	Average Recall	Average Precision	Average *F*-Measure
Naïve-Bayes Method with all features	0.333	0.211	0.258
Naïve-Bayes Method with the best features	0.667	0.526	0.588
Naïve-Bayes Method with Ferret Baseline	0.615	0.421	0.5
Fuzzy-SRL-Method	0.713	0.796	0.746

Table 5. Light plagiarism class.

Plagiarism Detection Method	Average Recall	Average Precision	Average *F*-Measure
Naïve-Bayes Method with all features	0.44	0.579	0.5
Naïve-Bayes Method with the best features	0.55	0.579	0.564
Naïve-Bayes Method with Ferret Baseline	0.419	0.684	0.52
Fuzzy-SRL-Method	0.725	0.809	0.760

Table 6. Cut-and-paste plagiarism class.

Plagiarism Detection Method	Average Recall	Average Precision	Average F-Measure
Naïve-Bayes Method with all features	0.267	0.211	0.235
Naïve-Bayes Method with the best features	0.5	0.474	0.486
Naïve-Bayes Method with Ferret Baseline	0.5	0.211	0.296
Fuzzy-SRL-Method	0.935	0.741	0.827

Table 5 compares the proposed technique to previous methods, based on a mild plagiarism class. Recall, precision, and F-measure were all found to be the best for the suggested technique. Table 5 shows the results for the light-revision plagiarism class.

Table 6 shows an assessment of the suggested approach and other methods on the on copy-and-paste class. We observed that the suggested technique had the highest scores for F-measure, recall, and precision.

In addition, the amount of time it takes to complete a task is also taken into consideration. This metric is often used to evaluate the effectiveness of algorithms. The temporal complexity of the suggested approach was used to assess its suitability. The suggested method was found to be in the same class as the rest of the methods. There are several plagiarism detection methods in this class, according to research by Maxim Mozgovoy and JPlag [34,35]. Even so, they observed that certain plagiarism detection algorithms have a time complexity of O(f(n)N2), where f(n) is the time it takes to compare a pair of files with a length of n and N is the collection size (number of files). Time-consuming techniques, such as fuzzy semantic comparison and semantic-based string similarity, were compared. It was demonstrated that semantic-based string similarity, LCS, and semantic-based similarity all have the same level of temporal complexity as the proposed method. Table 7 displays the results, in terms of how long each type of method takes.

Table 7. Time complexity comparison.

Algorithm	Time Complexity
Fuzzy Semantic-based String Similarity	$O(n^2)$
Longest Common Subsequence (LCS)	$O(n^3)$
Semantic-based Similarity	$O(n^2)$
SRL-Argument Weight	$O(n^2)$
Graph-based Method	$O(V + E)$
Sentence-based Natural Language	$O(n^2)$
SRL-Fuzzy Logic	$O(n^2)$

On the other hand, the string similarity-based fuzzy semantic method, semantic similarity, the similarity based on SRL method, the similarity based on graph-based representation method, and similarity based on sentence-NLP all have higher temporal complexity than ours, as shown in Table 7. The findings reveal that the suggested technique falls within a category of detection algorithms that is generally recognized. There are three major differences between our suggested approach and previous methods:

When it comes to copying and pasting, rewording or replacing words, changing the voice of a phrase from active to passive or vice versa, or changing the word structure in phrases, are all instances of plagiarism that may be caught using the method we provide.

In contrast to earlier methods, which focused on more traditional comparison techniques like character-based and string matching, the SRL is used as a comparison mechanism to analyze and compare text to identify instances of plagiarism. According to our results on the PAN PC-09 dataset, we are able to outperform other methods for detecting plagiarism, such as longest common subsequence [52], graph-based method [31], fuzzy semantic-based string similarity [49], and semantic-based similarity [53]., Additionally, we found that our technique outperforms other methods described by Chong [51], including naive Bayes classifier and ferret baseline, on CS11 corpora.

8. Conclusions and Future Work

The current study offers a plagiarism detection system that includes the following steps: the first and second documents are uploaded into a database, where the text is processed to be segmented into sentences, stop words are eliminated, and words are stemmed to their original forms. Next, the processed text is parsed in each document to find any arguments within, and then each argument found is represented as a member of a group, to determine how similar the groups of text are to one another. To select the best arguments from the text, the FIS has been applied. For plagiarism detection, semantic role labeling may be utilized by extracting the arguments of sentences and comparing the arguments. A FIS has been used to choose the arguments that have the most impact. When performing the similarity calculation, only the most essential reasons were taken into consideration, thanks to the use of FIS. The standard datasets for human plagiarism detection (CS-11) have been tested. In comparison to fuzzy semantic-based string similarity, LCS, and semantic-based approaches, the suggested approach has been proven to perform better.

A common approach used by those who plagiarize is to concentrate on key phrases and then adapt their work to include them. The proposed method proved that crucial points that have a significant impact on the reader should be reworked. The study aimed to anticipate, as accurately as possible, the essential objectives of the data. The results of statistical significance tests demonstrated the impact and benefits of the new strategy, compared with methods of plagiarism detection based on other strategies.

The limitation of this research must also be emphasized. This research did not cover some types of plagiarism, such as the similarity of non-textual content elements, citations, illustrations, tables, and mathematical equations, and these types are frequently discussed in studies.

To conclude, the methods of paraphrase type identification suggested in this research can be used and improved in a wide range of academic contexts. This involves not only support in identifying plagiarism, but also a focus on upholding ethical academic conduct. Genetic algorithms may be used to improve the results that can be produced, by employing the FIS in future. In addition, the above-mentioned limitation of this study is still considered as a research gap, which will be filled in the future.

Author Contributions: Conceptualization, A.H.O. and H.M.A.; methodology, A.H.O.; validation, A.H.O. and H.M.A.; formal analysis, A.H.O.; investigation, A.H.O.; resources, A.H.O.; data curation, A.H.O. and H.M.A.; writing—original draft preparation, A.H.O. and H.M.A.; writing—review and editing, A.H.O. and H.M.A.; visualization, A.H.O.; supervision, A.H.O.; project administration, A.H.O.; funding acquisition, A.H.O. All authors have read and agreed to the published version of the manuscript.

Funding: This research work was funded by the Institutional Fund Projects under grant no. (IFPIP: 481-830-1443). The authors gratefully acknowledge the technical and financial support provided by the Ministry of Education and King Abdulaziz University, DSR, Jeddah, Saudi Arabia.

Institutional Review Board Statement: Not applicable.

Informed Consent Statement: Not applicable.

Data Availability Statement: Not applicable.

Acknowledgments: This research work was funded by the Institutional Fund Projects under grant no. (IFPIP: 481-830-1443). The authors gratefully acknowledge the technical and financial support provided by the Ministry of Education and King Abdulaziz University, DSR, Jeddah, Saudi Arabia.

Conflicts of Interest: The authors declare no conflict of interest. The funders had no role in the design of the study; in the collection, analyses, or interpretation of data; in the writing of the manuscript; or in the decision to publish the results.

References

1. Potthast, M.; Stein, B.; Barrón-Cedeño, A.; Rosso, P. An evaluation framework for plagiarism detection. In *Coling 2010: Posters*; Coling 2010 Organizing Committee: Beijing, China, 2010.
2. Potthast, M.; Stein, B.; Eiselt, A.; Barron-Cedeno, A.; Rosso, P. Overview of the 1st International Competition on Plagiarism Detection. In Proceedings of the PAN-09 3rd Workshop on Uncovering Plagiarism, Authorship and Social Software Misuse and 1st International Competition on Plagiarism Detection, San Sebastian, Spain, 10 September 2009; Available online: CEUR-WS.org (accessed on 18 June 2022).
3. Mozgovoy, M.; Kakkonen, T.; Cosma, G. Automatic Student Plagiarism Detection: Future Perspectives. *J. Educ. Comput. Res.* **2010**, *43*, 511–531. [CrossRef]
4. Kakkonen, T.; Mozgovoy, M. An Evaluation of Web Plagiarism Detection Systems for Student Essays. In Proceedings of the Sixteenth International Conference on Computers in Education, Taipei, Taiwan, 27–31 October 2008.
5. Osman, A.H.; Salim, N.; Binwahlan, M.S.; Alteeb, R.; Abuobieda, A. An improved plagiarism detection scheme based on semantic role labeling. *Appl. Soft Comput.* **2012**, *12*, 1493–1502. [CrossRef]
6. Osman, A.H.; Barukab, O.M. SVM significant role selection method for improving semantic text plagiarism detection. *Int. J. Adv. Appl. Sci.* **2017**, *4*, 112–122. [CrossRef]
7. Osman, A.H.; Salim, N.; Elhadi, A.A.E. A tree-based conceptual matching for plagiarism detection. In Proceedings of the 2013 International Conference on Computing, Electrical and Electronic Engineering, Khartoum, Sudan, 26–28 August 2013.
8. Foltýnek, T.; Meuschke, N.; Gipp, B. Academic plagiarism detection: A systematic literature review. *ACM Comput. Surv. CSUR* **2019**, *52*, 1–42. [CrossRef]
9. Lovepreet, V.G.; Kumar, R. Survey on Plagiarism Detection Systems and Their Comparison. In *Computational Intelligence in Data Mining: Proceedings of the International Conference on ICCIDM 2018*; Springer: Odisha, India, 2019.
10. Gillam, L.; Vartapetiance, A. From English to Persian: Conversion of Text Alignment for Plagiarism Detection. In Proceedings of the Working notes of FIRE 2016—Forum for Information Retrieval Evaluation, Kolkata, India, 7–10 December 2016.
11. Burrows, S.; Potthast, M.; Stein, B. Paraphrase acquisition via crowdsourcing and machine learning. *ACM Trans. Intell. Syst. Technol.* **2013**, *4*, 1–21. [CrossRef]
12. Arabi, H.; Akbari, M. Improving plagiarism detection in text document using hybrid weighted similarity. *Expert Syst. Appl.* **2022**, *207*, 118034. [CrossRef]
13. Alzahrani, S.; Aljuaid, H. Identifying cross-lingual plagiarism using rich semantic features and deep neural networks: A study on Arabic-English plagiarism cases. *J. King Saud Univ. Comput. Inf. Sci.* **2022**, *34*, 1110–1123. [CrossRef]
14. Lulu, L.; Belkhouche, B.; Harous, S. Candidate document retrieval for Arabic-based text reuse detection on the web. In Proceedings of the 2016 12th International Conference on Innovations in Information Technology (IIT), Abu Dhabi, United Arab Emirates, 28–30 November 2016.
15. Yalcin, K.; Cicekli, I.; Ercan, G. An external plagiarism detection system based on part-of-speech (POS) tag n-grams and word embedding. *Expert Syst. Appl.* **2022**, *197*, 116677. [CrossRef]
16. Chang, C.-Y.; Lee, S.-J.; Wu, C.-H.; Liu, C.-F.; Liu, C.-K. Using word semantic concepts for plagiarism detection in text documents. *Inf. Retr.* **2021**, *24*, 298–321. [CrossRef]
17. Bohra, A.; Barwar, N. A Deep Learning Approach for Plagiarism Detection System Using BERT. In *Congress on Intelligent Systems. Lecture Notes on Data Engineering and Communications Technologies*; Springer: Singapore, 2022.
18. Alotaibi, N.; Joy, M. English-Arabic Cross-language Plagiarism Detection. In Proceedings of the International Conference on Recent Advances in Natural Language Processing (RANLP 2021), Online, 1–3 September 2021.
19. Roostaee, M.; Fakhrahmad, S.M.; Sadreddini, M.H. Cross-language text alignment: A proposed two-level matching scheme for plagiarism detection. *Expert Syst. Appl.* **2020**, *160*, 113718. [CrossRef]
20. Al-Shamery, E.S.; Gheni, H.Q. Plagiarism Detection using Semantic Analysis. *Indian J. Sci. Technol.* **2016**, *9*, 1–8. [CrossRef]
21. Cader, J.M.A.; Cader, A.J.M.A.; Gamaarachchi, H.; Ragel, R.G. Optimization of Plagiarism Detection using Vector Space Model on CUDA Architecture. *Int. J. Innov. Comput. Appl.* **2022**, *13*, 232–244. [CrossRef]
22. Guillén-Nieto, V. Plagiarism Detection: Methodological Approaches. In *Language as Evidence*; Springer: Berlin/Heidelberg, Germany, 2022; pp. 321–372.
23. Osman, A.H.; Aljahdali, H.M. Role Term-Based Semantic Similarity Technique for Idea Plagiarism Detection. *Int. J. Adv. Comput. Sci. Appl.* **2018**, *9*, 475–484. [CrossRef]
24. Osman, A.H.; Salim, N. An improved semantic plagiarism detection scheme based on chi-squared automatic interaction detection. In Proceedings of the 2013 International Conference on Computing, Electrical and Electronic Engineering (ICCEEE), Khartoum, Sudan, 26–28 August 2013.
25. Osman, A.H.; Salim, N.; Binwahlan, M.; Twaha, S.; Kumar, Y.J.; Abobieda, A. Plagiarism detection scheme based on semantic role labeling. In Proceedings of the 2012 International Conference on Information Retrieval & Knowledge Management, Kuala Lumpur, Malaysia, 24–26 July 2012.
26. Gipp, B. Citation-Based Document Similarity. In *Citation-Based Plagiarism Detection*; Springer: Wiesbaden, Germany, 2014; pp. 43–55.
27. Luo, L.; Ming, J.; Wu, D.; Liu, P.; Zhu, S. Semantics-based obfuscation-resilient binary code similarity comparison with applications to software and algorithm plagiarism detection. *IEEE Trans. Softw. Eng.* **2017**, *43*, 1157–1177. [CrossRef]

28. Amini, P.; Ahmadinia, H.; Poorolajal, J.; Amiri, M.M. Evaluating the High Risk Groups for Suicide: A Comparison of Logistic Regression, Support Vector Machine, Decision Tree and Artificial Neural Network. *Iran. J. Public Health* **2016**, *45*, 1179–1187.

29. Pajić, E.; Ljubović, V. Improving plagiarism detection using genetic algorithm. In Proceedings of the 2019 42nd International Convention on Information and Communication Technology, Electronics and Microelectronics (MIPRO), Opatija, Croatia, 20–24 May 2019.

30. Vani, K.; Gupta, D. Detection of idea plagiarism using syntax–semantic concept extractions with genetic algorithm. *Expert Syst. Appl.* **2017**, *73*, 11–26.

31. Osman, A.H.; Salim, N.; Binwahlan, M.; Hentably, H.; Ali, A.M. Conceptual similarity and graph-based method for plagiarism detection. *J. Theor. Appl. Inf. Technol.* **2011**, *32*, 135–145.

32. Krishna, S.M.; Bhavani, S.D. An efficient approach for text clustering based on frequent itemsets. *Eur. J. Sci. Res.* **2010**, *42*, 385–396.

33. Suanmali, L.; Salim, N.; Binwahlan, M.S. Automatic Text Summarization Using Feature-Based Fuzzy Extraction. *J. Teknol. Mklm.* **2009**, *2*, 105–155.

34. Shehata, S.; Karray, F.; Kamel, M.S. An Efficient Model for Enhancing Text Categorization Using Sentence Semantics. *Comput. Intell.* **2010**, *26*, 215–231. [CrossRef]

35. Baruah, H.K. The theory of fuzzy sets: Beliefs and realities. *Int. J. Energy Inf. Commun.* **2011**, *2*, 1–22.

36. Guribie, F.L.; Owusu-Manu, D.-G.; Badu, E.; Edwards, D.J. Fuzzy synthetic evaluation of the systemic obstacles to personalizing knowledge flows within and across projects. *Constr. Innov.* **2022**. [CrossRef]

37. Jiskani, I.M.; Cai, Q.; Zhou, W.; Lu, X.; Shah, S.A.A. An integrated fuzzy decision support system for analyzing challenges and pathways to promote green and climate smart mining. *Expert Syst. Appl.* **2021**, *188*, 116062. [CrossRef]

38. Zadeh, L.A. Fuzzy sets. *Inf. Control.* **1965**, *8*, 338–353. [CrossRef]

39. Munakata, T.; Jani, Y. Fuzzy systems: An overview. *Commun. ACM* **1994**, *37*, 68–76. [CrossRef]

40. Ibrahim, A. *Fuzzy Logic for Embedded Systems Applications*; Newnes: Oxford, UK; Elsevier: Berkeley, CA, USA, 2004.

41. Ma, W.; Tran, D.; Sharma, D. A novel spam email detection system based on negative selection. In Proceedings of the 2009 Fourth International Conference on Computer Sciences and Convergence Information Technology, Seoul, Republic of Korea, 24–26 November 2009.

42. Mikheev, A. Tagging sentence boundaries. In Proceedings of the 1st Meeting of the North American Chapter of the Association for Computational Linguistics, Seattle, WA, USA, 29 April–4 May 2000.

43. van Rijsbergen, C.J. A New Theoretical Framework for Information Retrieval. *ACM SIGIR Forum* **2017**, *51*, 44–50. [CrossRef]

44. Tomasic, A.; Garcia-Molina, H. Query processing and inverted indices in shared-nothing text document information retrieval systems. *VLDB J.* **1993**, *2*, 243–275. [CrossRef]

45. Frakes, W. Information Retrieval: Data Structures and Algorithm. Baeza-Yates, R., Ed.; Pearson College Div: London, UK, 1992.

46. Buckley, C.; Salton, G.; Allan, J.; Singhal, A. *Automatic Query Expansion Using SMART: TREC 3*; NIST Special Publication sp; Department of Computer Science, Cornell University: Ithaca, NY, USA, 1995; p. 69.

47. Palmer, M.; Gildea, D.; Kingsbury, P. The Proposition Bank: An Annotated Corpus of Semantic Roles. *Comput. Linguist.* **2005**, *31*, 71–106. [CrossRef]

48. Shivaji, S.K.; Prabhudeva, S. Plagiarism detection by using karp-rabin and string matching algorithm together. *Int. J. Comput. Appl.* **2015**, *115*, 37–41.

49. Alzahrani, S.; Salim, N. Fuzzy Semantic-Based String Similarity for Extrinsic Plagiarism Detection. In Proceedings of the CLEF 2010 LABs and Workshops, Notebook Papers, Padua, Italy, 22–23 September 2010.

50. Miller, G.A. WordNet: A lexical database for English. *Commun. ACM* **1995**, *38*, 39–41. [CrossRef]

51. Chong, M.; Specia, L.; Mitkov, R. Using natural language processing for automatic detection of plagiarism. In Proceedings of the 4th International Plagiarism Conference (IPC-2010), Newcastle upon Tyne, UK, 21–23 June 2010.

52. Kent, C.; Salim, N. Features Based Text Similarity Detection. *J. Comput.* **2010**, *2*, 53–57.

53. Kent, C.K.; Salim, N. Web Based Cross Language Plagiarism Detection. In Proceedings of the Second International Conference on Computational Intelligence, Modelling and Simulation, Bali, Indonesia, 28–30 September 2010; pp. 199–204.

Article

Designing the Architecture of a Convolutional Neural Network Automatically for Diabetic Retinopathy Diagnosis

Fahman Saeed [1], Muhammad Hussain [2,*], Hatim A. Aboalsamh [2], Fadwa Al Adel [3] and Adi Mohammed Al Owaifeer [4]

[1] Department of Computer Science, Imam Mohammad Ibn Saud Islamic University (IMSIU), Riyadh 11432, Saudi Arabia
[2] Department of Computer Science, King Saud University, Riyadh 11543, Saudi Arabia
[3] Department of Ophthalmology, College of Medicine, Princess Nourah bint Abdulrahman University, Riyadh 11671, Saudi Arabia
[4] Ophthalmology Unit, Department of Surgery, College of Medicine, King Faisal University, Al-Ahsa 31982, Saudi Arabia
* Correspondence: mhussain@ksu.edu.sa

Abstract: Diabetic retinopathy (DR) is a leading cause of blindness in middle-aged diabetic patients. Regular screening for DR using fundus imaging aids in detecting complications and delays the progression of the disease. Because manual screening takes time and is subjective, deep learning has been used to help graders. Pre-trained or brute force CNN models are used in existing DR grading CNN-based approaches that are not suited to fundus image complexity. To solve this problem, we present a method for automatically customizing CNN models based on fundus image lesions. It uses k-medoid clustering, principal component analysis (PCA), and inter-class and intra-class variations to determine the CNN model's depth and width. The designed models are lightweight, adapted to the internal structures of fundus images, and encode the discriminative patterns of DR lesions. The technique is validated on a local dataset from King Saud University Medical City, Saudi Arabia, and two challenging Kaggle datasets: EyePACS and APTOS2019. The auto-designed models outperform well-known pre-trained CNN models such as ResNet152, DenseNet121, and ResNeSt50, as well as Google's AutoML and Auto-Keras models based on neural architecture search (NAS). The proposed method outperforms current CNN-based DR screening methods. The proposed method can be used in various clinical settings to screen for DR and refer patients to ophthalmologists for further evaluation and treatment.

Keywords: classification; deep learning; DeepPCANet; diabetic retinopathy; medical imaging; PCA; AutoML; NAS

MSC: 68T07

Citation: Saeed, F.; Hussain, M.; Aboalsamh, H.A.; Al Adel, F.; Al Owaifeer, A.M. Designing the Architecture of a Convolutional Neural Network Automatically for Diabetic Retinopathy Diagnosis. *Mathematics* **2023**, *11*, 307. https://doi.org/10.3390/math11020307

Academic Editors: Xiang Li, Shuo Zhang and Wei Zhang

Received: 3 November 2022
Revised: 25 December 2022
Accepted: 28 December 2022
Published: 6 January 2023

1. Introduction

Diabetes is a leading global health dilemma. One of its serious complications is diabetic retinopathy (DR), which has a prevalence of 34.6% worldwide and is considered a primary cause of blindness among middle-aged diabetic patients [1,2]. A patient has a high DR risk if he or she has had diabetes for a long time or is poorly managed. The DR treatment at its early stage slows down the retinal microvascular degeneration process. Graders manually screen fundus images to detect DR prognosis, which is time-consuming and subjective [3–5]. On the other hand, screening a large number of diabetic patients for the possible prevalence of DR puts a heavy load on graders and reduces their efficiency. It necessitates intelligent systems for DR screening, and many ML-based systems have been proposed that show good results on public data sets. However, their performance is not certain in real DR screening programs, where there are different ethnicities, and the retinal fundus images are captured using different cameras. These factors affect these systems' performance and remain a challenge in their widespread use [6].

Deep CNN has shown remarkable results in many applications [7–11] and has been employed in DR screening [2,12–15]. A CNN model usually involves a large number of parameters and needs a large amount of data for training. A brute force approach, which has been widely used for DR screening, is to adopt a highly complex CNN model designed for object recognition and pre-trained on the ImageNet dataset and fine-tune them using fundus images [16–19]. As the ImageNet dataset consists of natural images, and the structural patterns of natural images and fundus images are entirely different, the architectures of the fine-tuned models do not adequately encode the fundus images. In addition, the complexity of pre-trained models is very high and not customized to DR screening from fundus images.

Instead, CNN models are manually designed from scratch. The design process starts with a CONV layer of a small width (i.e., the number of filters) and increases the widths of CONV layers by a fixed ratio as the network goes deeper [16–18]. There is no way to know what the depth should be (i.e., the number of layers) of a CNN model; a hit–trial strategy is used to fix the depth. In addition, CNN models are trained using iterative optimization algorithms such as stochastic gradient descent algorithms, and their convergence heavily depends on the initial guess of learnable parameters. Different data-independent [20,21] and data-dependent [22,23] approaches have been proposed to initialize them.

Alternatively, automated machine learning (AutoML) has developed into a significant area of research due to the widespread application of machine learning techniques [24]. AutoML's purpose is to make machine-learning models accessible to those with limited machine-learning prior knowledge. Some of the most commonly used methods for employing machine learning (ML) are easily available and may be used with just one or two lines of code. These systems include Auto-WEKA, Hyperopt-Sklearn, TPOT, Auto-Sklearn, and Auto-Keras [25–32]. Efforts have been made to automate the model selection and tuning hyper-parameters automatically, and so forth. Within the perspective of profound NAS stands for learning, neural architecture search [33], which aims to determine the optimal neural network architecture for a given learning task and dataset, has evolved into a highly effective computational tool for AutoML [34,35]. It achieved competitive performance on the CIFAR-10 and Penn Treebank benchmarks by utilizing a reinforcement learning-based search strategy; consequently, NAS became a mainstream research topic in the machine learning community. NAS is prohibitively expensive and time-consuming in terms of computation [36]. Zoph and Le [33] utilize massive computational resources (800 GPUs for three to four weeks) to achieve their result.

The preceding discussion demonstrates that developing an AutoML-customized lightweight CNN model for DR screening that uses a small subset of the target dataset and consumes fewer resources in a variety of clinical settings is difficult; it entails answering three design questions: (i) what must be the depth of the model, (ii) what must be the width of each of its convolutional (CONV) layer, i.e., the number of its kernels, and (iii) how to initialize the learnable parameters. To address these questions, we propose a constructive data-dependent approach for designing CNN models for DR screening under diverse clinical settings that automatically determine the depth of the model and the width of each CONV layer and initialize the learnable parameters. A custom-designed model takes a fundus image as input and grades it into normal or DR levels. We validated the proposed approach on three datasets: a local DR dataset from King Saud University Medical City, Saudi Arabia, and two benchmark Kaggle datasets: EyePACS [37] and APTOS2019 [38]. Specifically, the main contributions of the paper are as follows:

- We proposed a constructive data-dependent AutoML approach to design lightweight CNN models customized to DR screening under various clinical settings. It automatically determines the depth of the model, and the width of each COVN layer and initializes the learnable parameters using the fundus images dataset.

- To corroborate the usefulness of the proposed approach, we applied it to build an AutoML custom-designed lightweight CNN architecture for three datasets.
- We performed extensive experiments to show that the custom-designed lightweight CNN models compete well with the pre-trained models such as ResNet [17], DenseNet [18], ResNeSt [39], an AutoML NAS method, and other state-of-the-art methods for DR screening.

The layout of the rest of the paper is as follows: the literature view is presented in Section 2, datasets are described in Section 3, the detail of the proposed method is given in Section 4, the detail of experiments and the results are presented in Section 5, and finally, Section 6 concludes the paper.

2. Previous Work

Different methods have been introduced for automatic DR screening; an extensive literature review is given in [40–43]. There are some efforts to compress and reduce the complexity of existing pre-trained CNN models by weights pruning [44,45] or filters pruning [46–48]. First, we provide an overview of the previous work on building a deep model and initializing its weights and then give an overview of the state-of-the-art techniques for DR diagnosis.

2.1. Data-Dependent and Auto-Deep Models

Different researchers employed principal component analysis (PCA) in various ways to build deep networks. Chan et al. [49] created an unsupervised two-layer model (PCANet). It is not an end-to-end model and is used only for feature extraction. Philipp et al. [22] used PCA to re-initialize pre-trained CNN models to avoid vanishing or exploding gradient problems. Suau et al. [23] used PCA and correlation to compress the filters of pre-trained CNN models. Seuret et al. [50] employed PCA to initialize the layers of stacked auto-encoders (SAEs). The above PCA-based methods have been employed for designing a CNN-like model for feature extraction, data-dependent re-initialization of the pre-trained models, or compressing their weights to reduce their complexity, but not for the data-dependent design of end-to-end CNN models.

Zhong et al. [51] introduced a method to build a BlockQNN module automatically using the block-wise setup, Q-Learning paradigm, and epsilon-greedy exploration and stacked them to obtain the automatic CNN model. They evaluated their method using CIFAR-10, CIFAR-100, and ImageNet. It needs a lot of computational resources. They used 32 GPUs and got the best CNN model with BlockQNN after three days and Faster BlockQNN after 20 h.

AutoML's initial effort was led by academia and machine learning practitioners, followed by startups and Auto-Weka (2013) [52] from the Universities of British Columbia (UBC). Following that, the University of Freiburg published Auto-Sklearn (2014) [53]. TPOT was created by the University of Pennsylvania [27] in (2015). Following the success of Zoph and Le in [33] in performing comparably to the CIFAR-10 and Penn Treebank benchmarks, other recent efforts to develop NAS have been made [54,55], they incorporate modern design elements previously associated with handcrafted architectures, such as skip connections, which enable the construction of complex, multi-branch networks. To maximize efficiency, state-of-the-art systems employ cell-search spaces [56], which involves configuring only repeated cell architectures rather than the global architecture, and employ gradient-based optimization [57]. Since 2013, Bayesian optimization has achieved several early successes in NAS, resulting in state-of-the-art vision architectures [58]. Google Cloud AutoML based on NAS method is one of the famous auto deep learning models' auto-generation [59]. It utilizes transfer learning and NAS to determine the optimal network architecture and hyper-parameter configuration for that architecture that minimizes the model's loss function [60]. Another method for autoML-based NAS for generating deep learning models is Auto-Keras (2017) [29] from Texas A&M University, which runs on top of Keras, Tensorflow, and Scikit-learn

2.2. DR Screening Methods

Clinical DR screening categorizes a patient based on fundus images into different grades: level 0 (normal), level 1 (mild), level 2 (moderate), level 3 (severe), and level 4 (proliferative). In the state-of-the-art on DR screening, various deep learning-based methods have been proposed, which address mainly three image-level DR grading scenarios: (i) scenario 1 (SC1): normal and different levels of DR severity—a multi-class problem, (ii) scenario 2 (SC2): normal (level 0) vs. DR (levels 1~4)—a two-class problem, (iii) scenario 3 (SC3): non-referral (level 0 and 1) vs. referral (levels 2–4)—a two-class problem. In the following paragraphs, we give an overview of the state-of-the-art best methods. Islam et al. [61] built a hand-designed CNN model consisting of 18 layers and 8.9 million learnable parameters and got on the EyePACS dataset a sensitivity of 94.5%, a specificity of 90.2% for SC2, a sensitivity of (98%) and a specificity of (94%) for SC3. Li et al. [62] introduced two hand-designed CNN models with 11 and 14 layers for feature extraction from the EyePACS dataset. The features from both models are fused and classified using an SVM classifier. They achieved an accuracy of 86.17% for SC1 and an accuracy of 91.05%, a sensitivity of 89.30%, and a specificity of 90.89% for SC2 using five-fold cross-validation. Challa et al. [63] built a CNN model consisting of 10 layers for the EyePACS dataset and obtained an accuracy of 86% for SC1. Tymchenko et al. [64] built an ensemble of 20 CNN models. The ensemble used five versions of each of four pre-trained models: SE-ResNetXt50 with input sizes of 380 × 380 and 512 × 512, EfficientNet-B4, and EfficientNet-B5. It was fine-tuned using the APTOS2019 dataset. They got an accuracy of 91.9%, a sensitivity of 84%, a specificity of 98.1%, and a Kappa of 96.9% for SC1 on the APTOS2019 dataset. Sikder et al. [65] used an ensemble learning algorithm called ET classifier to classify the colored information of the fundus images from the APTOS2019 dataset. They filtered the dataset by removing many noisy samples and achieved an accuracy of 91% and a recall of 89.43% for SC1. DR categorization was performed manually by Sikder et al. (2021) [66]. They conducted significant preprocessing to fundus pictures before extracting the histogram and GLCM features. The APTOS2019 dataset was utilized to validate the procedures, with 75% used for training and 25% for testing. The XGBoost algorithm was used to fine-tune and pick the best features for optimal performance. Classification accuracy for DR (five classes) was 94.20% (95% CI: 93.88–94.51%) for the whole set of features and 93.70% (95% CI: 93.48–93.93%) for the subset.

The above overview of the state-of-the-art methods shows that some used hand-designed CNN models, and others employed pre-trained models and fine-tuning. For creating hand-designed models, the architectures of CNN models were fixed empirically using the hit-and-trial approach. In the case of fine-tuning, the complexity of the pre-trained models is very high and is not customized to the structures of fundus images.

3. Materials

We developed and validated custom-designed CNN models using two Kaggle challenge datasets: EyePACS [37] and APTOS2019 [38], and one local dataset collected at King Saud University Medical City (KSU-DR). Each dataset was preprocessed and augmented using the procedure described in Section 4.2.1. KSU-DR and EyePACS were divided into training (80%), validation (10%), and testing (10%). APTOS2019 consists of two sets: public training and public testing; 90% of the public training data was used for training and the remaining 10% for validation and public testing for testing.

3.1. KSU-DR

The data were collected after obtaining approval from King Saud University Medical City's local Institutional Review Board committee. The samples were collected randomly from fundus images of diabetic patients acquired during their routine endocrinologist's appointment at the funduscopic screening clinic. Fundus images were captured with a non-mydriatic fundus camera (3D-OCT-1-Maestro non-mydriasis fundus camera); a 45-degree fundus photo was captured from each eye. All patients were from Saudi Arabia, 44% were males, and 56% were females. The mean patient age was 53 years; 17% had type 1 diabetes, and 83% had type 2 diabetes. The mean duration of diabetes was 18 years (ranging from 4–42 years). Random samples of 1750 images were selected and graded by two expert ophthalmologists; 1024 were graded as normal, 477 as mild non-proliferative DR, 222 as moderate non-proliferative DR, 20 as severe non-proliferative DR, and 7 as proliferative DR (PDR).

3.2. EyePACS

EyePACS [37] consists of 88,702 color retinal fundus images with varying resolutions up to about 3000 × 2000 pixels [63], collected from 44,351 subjects, but only 35,126 labeled images are available in the public domain; most of the researchers used this set for the proposal of new algorithms [61,67]. We also used 35,126 labeled images to design and evaluate the custom-designed CNN model. The images are graded into normal and 4 DR classes—mild, moderate, severe, and proliferative.

3.3. APTOS2019

APTOS2019 dataset [38] was published by the Asia Pacific Tele-Ophthalmology Society on the Kaggle competition website. Clinical experts graded the images into normal and 4 DR levels (mild, moderate, severe, and proliferative). The public domain version of this database contains 3662 fundus images for training and 1928 fundus images for testing.

4. Proposed Method

4.1. Problem Formulation

The problem is to predict whether a subject has normal vision or suffering from DR (with different levels of severity) using his/her retinal fundus images. Formally, let $R^{h \times w \times 3}$ be the space of color retinal fundus images with resolution $h \times w$ and $P = \{1, 2, \ldots, C\}$ be the set of labels where C is the number of classes, which represent different DR grades; in case of two grades (i.e., normal and DR), $C = 2$, such that $c = 1$ means normal and $c = 2$ stands for DR; when there are five grades, $C = 5$, and $c = 1, 2, 3, 4, 5$ are the labels for normal, mild, moderate, severe, proliferative DR, respectively. To predict the grade of a patient, we need to define a mapping $\phi : R^{h \times w \times 3} \rightarrow P$ that takes a fundus image $x \in R^{h \times w \times 3}$ and associates it to a label $c \in P$, i.e., $\phi(x) = c$. We model the mapping function ϕ using a custom-designed CNN model.

4.2. Custom-Designed CNN Model

The main constituent layer of a CNN model is the CONV layer, and the widely adopted CNN models contain a large number of CONV layers, e.g., VGGNet [68] contains 13 CONV layers. The number of layers (depth) and the number of filters in each layer (width) are fixed manually, keeping in view the ImageNet challenge dataset [69], without following any formal procedure. Retinal fundus images have complex small-scale structures, which form discriminative patterns and are entirely different from those of the natural images in the ImageNet dataset. We design an AutoML CNN model for the DR problem by drawing its architecture from the fundus images; we determine the depth of a model and the widths of its CONV layers in a customized way using the discriminative information in fundus images specific to different DR levels. In this direction, the first design decision is about specifying the search space and extracting discriminatory information. For this purpose, first, we reduce the search space and select the most representative fundus images from the available DR dataset using the K-medoids clustering algorithm [70] and then apply PCA [71] to determine the widths of CONV layers and initialize them. The next design decision is about the depth (i.e., the number of CONV layers). We control the depth using the ratio of the between-class scatter matrix S_b to the within-class scatter matrix S_w. Finally, motivated by the design strategy of ResNet [17], we add global pooling layers that follow the last CONV layer, and their outputs are fused and fed directly to a softmax layer. These layers control the drastic increase in the number of learnable parameters (which cause overfitting). The design process is described in detail below, and its overview is shown in Figure 1.

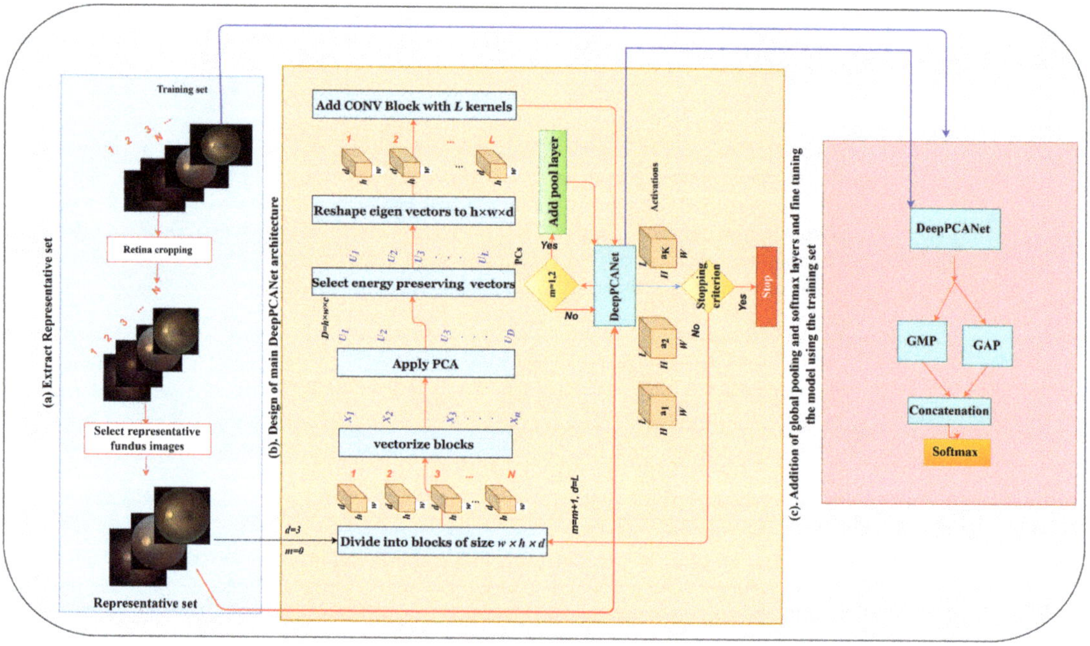

Figure 1. Design procedure of DeepPCANet.

4.2.1. Preprocessing

The retinal fundus images are usually not calibrated and are surrounded by a black area, as shown in Figure 1a. To center the retina and remove the black area around it, firstly, the retina circle is cropped, and the background is removed using the method presented in [65], and then it is resized to 512×512 pixels. Usually, the DR datasets are imbalanced, i.e., the numbers of images of different classes are significantly different; we increase the data of minority classes using data augmentation. We apply affine transformations to randomly rotate the image with an angle $\theta \in (-180, 180)$.

4.2.2. Selection of Representative Fundus Images

Using the EyePACS training dataset, we choose the most representative fundus images using (K-means [72] and K-medoids [70], and random samples) selection methods to customize a DeepPCANet model and then test it. The discriminative features are extracted from training fundus images for clustering using the efficient LGDBP descriptor proposed in [73]. The number K of clusters for K-means and K-medoids is specified using the gap statistic method [74].

As indicated in Table 1, the K-medoids gave the best results and are the most precise. Due to the fact that K-means gives mean feature vectors as cluster centers, it is inadequate at selecting representative fundus images, and outliers are a serious concern. On the other hand, because the K-medoids algorithm selects representative fundus images as cluster centers, using representative fundus images is appropriate. Both K-medoids and K-means outperform the random fundus image model.

Table 1. Comparison between clustering methods based on Eyepacs (SC1).

Dataset	Model	ACC %	SE %
Eye PACS	Random fundus images	85.12	81.33
	K-means	89.32	83.45
	K-medoids	**94.22**	**86.56**

4.2.3. Designing the Main DeepPCANet Architecture

The design of the AutoML customized architecture of DeepPCANet needs to address two questions, i.e., (i) what should be the depth of the model and (ii) what should be the width of each CONV layer? These questions are addressed by an iterative algorithm, incrementally adding CONV layers, and stopping when a specific criterion is satisfied. It is based on the idea of exploiting discriminative information of fundus images to select the number of kernels in a CONV layer and initialize them. It takes representative fundus images RI_j, $j = 1, 2, 3, \ldots, K$ as input and divides them into patches of size 7×7. The patches are vectorized and used to determine the number of kernels and initialize them. One possible idea is to cluster the patches and select the cluster centers as kernels, but the issue is choosing the number of clusters. We go for a simple and effective procedure, i.e., we employ PCA because it reduces the redundancy and helps to determine the kernels and their number, exploiting the discriminative information in the patches. The principal components (PCs), i.e., the eigenvectors along which the maximum energy is preserved, serve as kernels of the first layer. After computing the PCs, the DeepPCANet is initialized with an input layer and a CONV block (BN+ReLU+CONV) with kernels equal to the number of PCs; the kernels are initialized by reshaping the PCs. Please note that we fix the size of patches to 7×7 so that the size of kernels of the first CONV layers is 7×7 following the convention of most of the existing CNN models such as Inception [16], ResNet [17], and DenseNet [18]. Using the current architecture of DeepPCANet, activations a_j, $j = 1, 2, 3, \ldots,$ K of representative fundus images RI_j, $j = 1, 2, 3, \ldots, K$ are calculated. Inspired by the Fisher ratio [75], using these activations, the ratio of the trace (TR) of between-class scatter matrix S_b to the trace of within-class scatter matrix S_w is calculated $TR = \frac{Trace(Sb)}{Trace(Sw)}$ and is used to decide whether to stop or add another CONV block. The new CONV blocks continue to be added as long as TR continues to increase. This criterion ensures that the features generated by DeepPCANet have large inter-class variation and small intra-class scatter. To add a CONV block, the above procedure is repeated with activations a_j, $j = 1, 2, 3, \ldots, K$. To reduce the size of feature maps for computational efficiency, pooling layers are added after the first and second CONV blocks. As the kernels and their number are determined from the fundus images, each layer can have a different number of filters. The detail of the design procedure is elaborated in Algorithm 1. It is to be noted that the PCs (u_i), which are used to specify the kernels of a CONV layer, are orthogonal and capture most of the variability in input fundus images, without redundancy, in the form of independent features. The PCs are selected so that the maximum energy is preserved. The energy is measured in terms of the corresponding eigenvalues, i.e., $Energy = \frac{\sum_{l=1}^{L} \lambda_l}{\sum_{j=1}^{D} \lambda_j}$ [23,76] and a threshold value is used to ensure that a certain percentage of energy (e.g., 99%) is preserved. The threshold value of 99% preserves the maximum energy with 209 (L) PCs for CONV1 in the EyePACS dataset, as shown in Figure 2. The depth of the AutoML CNN model and the width of each layer are important factors determining the model complexity. Step 7 of Algorithm 1 adaptively determines the best number of kernels that ensure the preservation of the maximum energy of the input image. Step 9 initializes the kernels to be suitable for the DR domain. The selected kernels extract the features from fundus images (five classes) so that the variability of the structures in fundus images is maximally preserved. It is also essential that the features must be discriminative, i.e., have large inter-class variance and small intra-class scatter as we go deeper in the network; it is ensured using the trace ratio

$TR = \frac{Trace(Sb)}{Trace(Sw)}$, the larger the value of the trace ratio, the larger the inter-class variance, and the smaller the intra-class scatter [75]. Step 13 in Algorithm 1 allows adding CONV layers as long as TR increases and determines the data-dependent depth of DeepPCANet. As shown in Figure 3, the maximum ratio is at layers 4, 5, and 16 for KSU-DR, APTOS2019, and EyePACS, respectively. It means that the suitable depth of the DeepPCANet model for the KSU-DR dataset is four layers (Figure 3a), for APTOS2019 it is five layers ((Figure 3b), and for the EyePACS dataset it is sixteen layers (Figure 3c). The model for EyePACS is deeper because it contains many poor quality fundus images, and there is the possibility of label noise because only one expert graded each image in this dataset. Each dataset was collected from a different region and under different conditions using different cameras, so the architecture of the DeepPCANet model is different for each dataset.

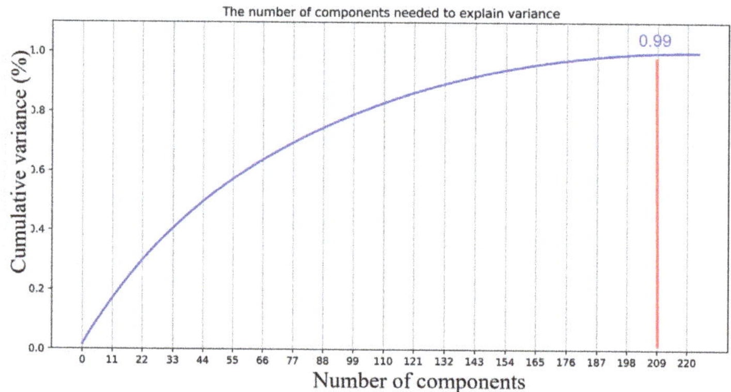

Figure 2. Selecting the best threshold. The appropriate threshold is (0.99) and the number of eigenvectors is 209.

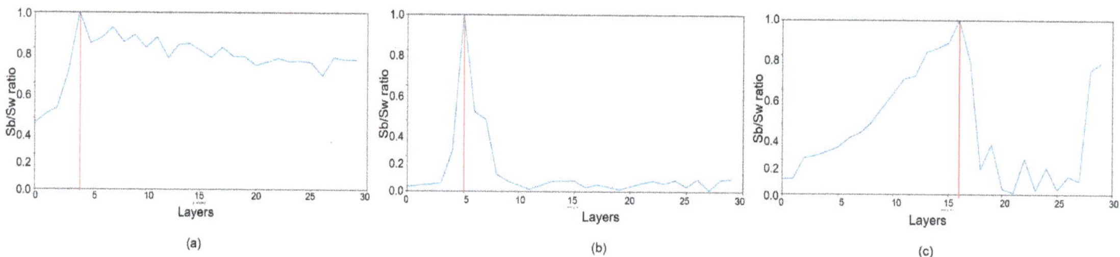

Figure 3. Trace ratio between class scatter and within class scatter. The depth for (**a**) APOTS2019 dataset is 4 layers, (**b**) KSU-DR dataset is 5 layers, and (**c**) EyePACS dataset is 16 layers.

Algorithm 1. To design the main DeepPCANet Architecture.

Input: Representative fundus images: $RI_j, j = 1, 2, \ldots, K$ of size $W \times H$ and the class labels $c = 1, 2, \ldots, C$; Energy threshold ε
Output: The main architecture of DeepPCANet Architecture
Processing
Step 1: Initialize DeepPCANet with an input layer and set $w = 7, h = 7, d = 3, m = 0$ (*number of layers*)
Step 2: Set $a_j = RI_j, j = 1, 2, 3, \ldots, K$, and TRP (*previous TR*) = 0.
Step 3: Divide $a_j, j = 1, 2, 3, \ldots, K$, into blocks $b_{ij}, i = 1, 2, 3, \ldots, B, j = 1, 2, 3, \ldots, K$, of size $w \times h \times d$, where d is the number of channels (feature maps) in a_j and B is the number of blocks created from each a_j.
Step 4: Flatten b_{ij} into vectors $x_i \in R^D$, $i = 1, 2, \ldots M$, where $M = K \times B$, and $D = w \times h \times d$.
Step 5: Compute zero-center vectors $\phi_i, i = 1, 2, \ldots M$ such that $\phi_i = x_i - \bar{x}$, where $\bar{x} = \frac{1}{M} \sum_{i=1}^{M} x_i$.
Step 6: Compute the covariance matrix $C = AA^T$, where $A = [\phi_1 \, \phi_2 \ldots \phi_M]$. Calculate the eigenvalues λ_j and eigenvectors u_j $(j = 1, 2, \ldots, D)$ of the covariance matrix C.
Step 7: Select L eigenvectors u_i $i = 1, 2, \ldots, L$ $(L < D)$ corresponding to the L largest eigenvalues such that $\frac{\sum_{l=1}^{L} \lambda_l}{\sum_{j=1}^{D} \lambda_j} \geq \varepsilon$, where ε determines the level of energy to be preserved (e.g., $\varepsilon = 0.99$, for 99% energy preservation).
Step 8: The eigenvectors corresponding to the $\frac{\sum_{l=1}^{L} \lambda_l}{\sum_{j=1}^{D} \lambda_j} < \varepsilon$ are summed up to form a single eigenvector, and then stacked at the end of the L eigenvectors.
Step 9: Reshape u_i, $i = 1, 2, \ldots, L+1$ to kernels of size $W \times H \times D$ and add the CONV block to DeepPCANet; Update $m = m + 1$.
Step 10: If $m = 1$ or 2, add max pool layers with a pooling window of size 2×2 and stride 2 to DeepPCANet.
Step 11: Compute the activations $a_j, j = 1, 2, 3, \ldots, K$ of representative fundus images $RI_j, j = 1, 2, 3, \ldots, K$ such that $a_j = $ DeepPCANet (RI_j).
Step 12: Compute the trace ratio between scatter between matrix (S_b) and within matrix (S_w) as
$TR = \frac{Trace(Sb)}{Trace(Sw)}$ where $S_w = \sum_{i=1}^{C} \sum_{j=1}^{n_i} \left(x_j - \mu_i \right) \left(x_j - \mu_i \right)^T$ and $S_b = \sum_{i=1}^{C} n_i \left(\mu_i - \mu \right) \left(\mu_i - \mu \right)^t$.
Step 13: If TRP (*previous TR*) $\leq TR$, *set* $TRP = TR, W = 3, H = 3, D = L$, and go to Step 3, stop otherwise.

4.2.4. Addition of Global Pool and Softmax Layers

The dimension of the activation of the last CONV block is $W \times H \times L$. If it is flattened and passed to a fully connected (FC) layer, the number of learnable weights and biases of the FC becomes excessively large, which leads to overfitting. To overcome this issue, the activation of the last CONV block is passed simultaneously to global average pooling (GAP), and global max-pooling (GMP) layers [77], which extract the mean and largest feature from each feature map, and these features are fused using a concatenation layer. Both GAP and GMP help to reduce the number of learnable parameters and extract discriminative features from the activation. Finally, a softmax layer is introduced as a classification layer, and the output of the concatenation layer is passed to this layer, as shown in Figure 1c. A dropout layer is also added after the last CONV layer to overcome the overfitting problem.

4.2.5. Finetuning the DeepPCANet Model

After determining the architecture of AutoML's custom-designed DeepPCANet, it is fine-tuned using the training and validation sets. Fine-tuning involves various hyper-parameters: the optimization algorithm, learning rate, batch size, activation function, and dropout probability. We employed the Optuna optimization algorithm [78] to determine the best values of the hyper-parameters. We tested three optimizers (Adam, SGD, and RMSprop), a learning rate between 1e-5 and 1e-1, four batch sizes (5, 10, 15, 20), three activation functions (ReLU, LReLU, and Sigmoid), and dropout probability between 0.25 and 0.50. After training for ten epochs, the Optuna returned the best hyper-parameters for each dataset, as shown in Table 2. The number of kernels in each layer of each model is based on an energy threshold of 0.99. The models for APTOS2019, KSU-DR, and EyePACS datasets (five classes each) are DeepPCANet-4, DeepPCANet-5, and DeepPCANet-16, respectively, and their specifications are shown in Figure 4. Each dataset has different AutoML architecture because each one is from different ethnicities; the EyePACS dataset is from the USA, APTOS2019 is from India, and KSU-DR is from KSA, as well as the use of retinal images captured using different cameras. To confirm the distinct architectures for the three DR datasets, we combined the extracted K-medoids fundus images into a single dataset, generated a custom DeepPCANet, and tested it on the three datasets. As illustrated in Table 3, the outcome is not as good as that obtained using the customized DeepPCANet for each DR dataset, as illustrated in Tables 4 and 5. Each dataset is from different ethnicities; the EyePACS dataset is from the USA, APTOS2019 is from India, and KSU-DR is from KSA; as well as the use of different retinal images captured using different cameras, so each dataset has a different custom-designed model. After fixing the hyper-parameters, each model is fine-tuned using training and validation sets for 100 epochs. The fine-tuned model is tested using the testing set.

Table 2. The best hyper parameters found using Optuna algorithm (SC1).

Dataset	Activation Function	Learning Rate	Patch's Size	Optimizer	Dropout
KSU-DR	LReLU	0.0001	10	RMSprop	0.50
EyePACS	LReLU	0.0055	10	RMSprop	0.38
APTOS2019	LReLU	0.0007	5	RMSprop	0.40

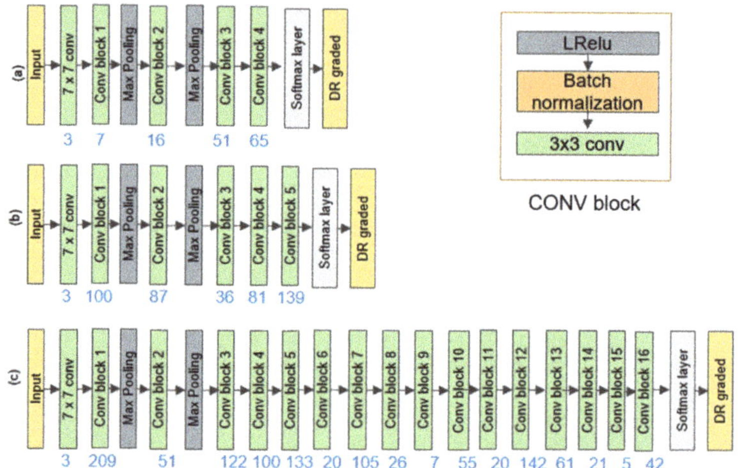

Figure 4. DeepPCANet architecture for (**a**) APOTS2019, (**b**) KSU-DR, and (**c**) EyePACS datasets.

Table 3. Customize the DeepPCANet by combining the extracted K-medoids fundus images to confirm the distinct architectures for the three DR datasets.

Dataset	Model	Performance (%)			
		ACC	SE	SP	Kappa
EyePACS (SC1)		73	28	83	8
APTOS2019 (SC1)	PCANet model (mixed dataset)	88	36	91	51
KSU-DR (SC2)		80	81	81	59

Table 4. Comparison between DeepPCANet models and the pretrained models for SC1 scenario, M and K stand for millions and thousands.

Dataset	Model	#FLOPs	# Parameters	ACC %	SE %	SP %	Kappa %
APTOS2019	ResNet152	5.6 M	60.19 M	95.25	88.22	96.97	88.15
	DenseNet121	1.44 M	7.98 M	96.58	91.55	97.82	89.22
	ResNeSt50	5.39 M	27.5 M	97.11	92.29	98.2	90.82
	DeepPCANet-4	**1.36 M**	**63.7 K**	**98.21**	**95.29**	**98.9**	**94.32**
EyePACS	ResNet152	5.6 M	60.19 M	92.25	80.74	94.9	75.16
	DenseNet121	1.44 M	7.98 M	91.14	80.07	95	74.84
	ResNeSt50	5.39 M	27.5 M	93.12	82.33	95.21	78
	DeepPCANet-16	**2.11 M**	**557.68 K**	**94.22**	**86.56**	**96.30**	**81.64**

Table 5. Comparison between DeepPCANet model and the pretrained models for SC2 scenario.

Dataset	Model	#FLOPs	# Parameters	ACC %	SE %	SP %	Kappa %
KSU-DR dataset	ResNet152	5.6 M	60.19 M	97.98	97.83	97.83	95.75
	DenseNet121	1.44 M	7.98 M	98.51	96.06	98.86	96.4
	ResNeSt50	5.39 M	27.5 M	99.47	99.46	99.46	98.93
	DeepPCANet-5	**1.375 M**	**73.66 K**	**99.5**	**99.5**	**99.5**	**98.99**
APTOS2019	ResNet152	5.6 M	60.19 M	95	94.44	94.44	89.80
	DenseNet121	1.44 M	7.98 M	99.32	98.8	98.8	98.73
	ResNeSt50	5.39 M	27.5 M	98.33	96.54	96.53	94.22
	DeepPCANet-4	**1.36 M**	**63.7 K**	**99.7**	**99.44**	**99.44**	**99.3**
EyePACS	ResNet152	5.6 M	60.19 M	91.36	90.94	92.25	82.53
	DenseNet121	1.44 M	7.98 M	91.51	91.75	91.75	82.72
	ResNeSt50	5.39 M	27.5 M	90.53	90.92	90.92	79.04
	DeepPCANet-16	**2.11 M**	**557.68 K**	**94.44**	**94.28**	**94.28**	**88.71**

5. Experiments and Results

This section first describes the evaluation protocol and the experiments performed to evaluate the proposed method and then presents the results.

5.1. Evaluation Protocol

We determined the architecture of the DeepPCANet for each DR dataset and fine-tuned it using the training set of the corresponding DR database; the detail is given in Section 3. After that, the performance of each model was evaluated using the test set of the related database. To validate the usefulness and the superiority of the model design technique, we compared custom-designed models with the widely used state-of-the-art pre-trained CNN models such as ResNet [17], DenseNet [18], and ResNeSt [39], which have shown outstanding performance for various computer vision applications. Additionally, we compared it with AutoML models (Google Cloud AutoML) and Auto-Keras. We fine-tuned the competing models using the same procedure employed for DeepPCANet on each dataset.

For evaluation, we adopted three scenarios SC1 [62,63], SC2 [61,62], and SC3, as described in Section 5.1. We evaluated the AutoML custom-designed models using SC1 and SC2 on APTOS2019 and EyePACS and SC3 in EyePACS. However, the evaluation of the KSU-DR dataset was performed using SC2 because the number of images for five classes is not enough. In addition, we used four commonly used metrics in medical application and deep learning models: accuracy (ACC), sensitivity (SE), specificity (SP), and Kappa [13,79–82].

5.1.1. Five Class Problem (SC1)

Using the APTOS2019 and EyePACS datasets, we built DeepPCANet-4 and DeepPCANet-16 models, respectively, for SC1 using the respective training sets and fined-tuned them using the corresponding training and validation sets (see detail in Section 3). After fine-tuning, the models were evaluated on test datasets of EyePACS and APTOS2019; the results are shown in Table 4. The results of the ResNet152, DenseNet121, and ResNeSt50 models, fine-tuned using the same training set and evaluated using the same testing set as for from EyePACS and APTOS2019, are also shown in Table 4. The results show that DeepPCANet-4 and DeepPCANet-16 outperform ResNet152, DenseNet121, and ResNeSt50 on both datasets in terms of all metrics; in particular, in both cases, the sensitivity and Cohen's Kappa are higher than those of ResNet152, DenseNet12, and ResNeSt50, Cohen's Kappa is considered a more robust statistical measure than accuracy [83,84]. The DeepPCANet-4 has the lowest number of FLOPs (1.36 M) and learnable parameters (63.7 K) among all competing models, as shown in Table 4.

DeepPCANet-16 has fewer learnable parameters than the pertained ResNet152, DenseNet121, and ResNeSt50 and has fewer FLOPs than ResNet152 and ResNeSt50 models, but slightly greater than DenseNet121. In contrast, it has the best performance in terms of metrics on the EyePACS dataset. ResNeSt50 has better performance than ResNet152 and DenseNet121. To compare the AutoML DeepPCANet to the state-of-the-art AutoML methods, we use the most DR-intensive dataset available, the EyePACS, based on scenario SC1. According to the NAS method [24], we test two AutoML methods; the Google Cloud (vision) AutoML [43] and Auto-Keras [23]. We set up and generated the AutoML using Auto-Keras methods locally using the same device and based on the representative set, fine-tuned the generated CNN model using a training and validation set; then, it was evaluated using the test set as with DeepPCANet-16. For Google Cloud AutoML, we upload the representative, training, validation, and test sets to the Google cloud storage and follow the same evaluation procedure. DeepPCANet-16 outperformed the Google Cloud AutoML, and Auto-Keras has fewer number FLOPs, as shown in Table 6, but its performance is lower than both models. The FLOPs and number of parameters of Google Cloud AutoML are hidden, showing only the precision (PR) and recall (SE) metrics. NAS algorithms are time-consuming and resource-intensive; they typically look for the cell structure, including the topology of the connections and the operation (transformation) that connects each cell. After that, the resulting cell is replicated to construct the neural network [85]. We used a basic simple cell structure throughout our AutoML DeepPCANet (LReLU, batch normalization layer, and CONV layer). The filters in the CONV layers are derived automatically from fundus' lesions and require less time. They optimized both the search architecture and hyper-parameters in NAS algorithms. In contrast, we first derived the optimal DeepPCANet architecture and then used Optuna to optimize the hyper-parameters, as shown in Table 2.

Table 6. Comparison between DeepPCANeT-16 and AutoML methods.

Dataset	Model	#FLOPs	# Parameters	ACC %	SE %	PR %
EyePACS	**Auto-Keras**	0.31 M	15 M	73	73	53
	Google-AutoML	Hidden	Hidden	–	71.43	79.1
	DeepPCANet-16	2.11 M	**557.68 K**	**94.44**	**94.28**	**96.12**

5.1.2. Two Class Problem (SC2)

We validated the DeepPCANet models' performance using the three datasets for SC2. The custom-designed models DeepPCANet-5, DeepPCANet-4, and DeepPCANet-16 for KSU-DR, APTOS2019, and EyePACS, respectively, which were designed and fine-tuned using only fundus images, outperform the highly complex CNN models such as ResnNet152, DenseNet121, and ResNeSt50, which were trained using ImageNet dataset and fine-tuned using fundus images, in terms of all metrics, as shown in Table 5. Though DenseNet121 outperforms ResNet152 and ResNeSt50 on the three datasets, its performance is not better than the custom-designed models. DeepPCANet-5 involves 1.375 M FLOPs, which is smaller than the number of FLOPs of ResNet152, DenseNet121, and ResNeSt50. The number of learnable parameters of DeepPCANet-5 is 73.66K which is much smaller than those of the pre-trained models ResNet152 (60.19 M), DenseNet121 (7.98 M), and ResNeSt50 (27.5 M). In Figure 5, we provide illustrations of the ROC curves on the three datasets using the four models (customized DeepPCANet, ResNet152, DenseNet121, and ResNeSt50). It indicates that the DeepPCANet models' performance is better than the three pre-trained models on the three datasets.

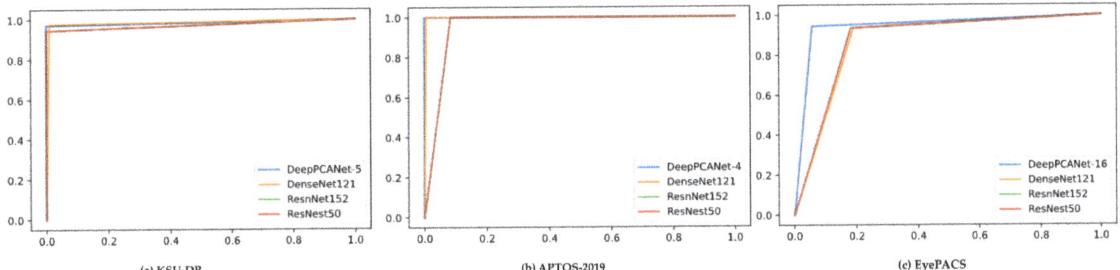

Figure 5. ROC curve for custom-designed DeepPCANet and the pretrained models for SC2 scenario and datasets: (**a**) KSU-DR, (**b**) APTOS-2019, (**c**) EyePACS.

5.2. Visualization

To understand the decision-making mechanism of the custom-designed CNN models, we created the visual feature maps using the gradient-weighted class activation mapping (GradCam) visualization method [86]. The visual feature maps of two random fundus images generated by the DeepPCANet-5 model customized for the local KSU-DR dataset are shown in Figure 6d,h. The same fundus images were given blindly to two expert ophthalmologists at King Khalid Hospital of KSU, and they independently specified the lesion regions manually. Though there is a slight difference in the annotations of both experts, they agreed on most of the lesions, as shown in Figure 6b,c for the fundus image Figure 6a from class moderate and Figure 6f,g for the fundus image Figure 6e from class PDR. The visual features maps of the DeepPCANet-5 model highlight the lesions annotated by both experts, as shown in Figure 6d,h. The yellow and orange splatter in Figure 6d,h indicates that the DeepPCANet-5 model makes decisions based on the features learned from the lesion regions.

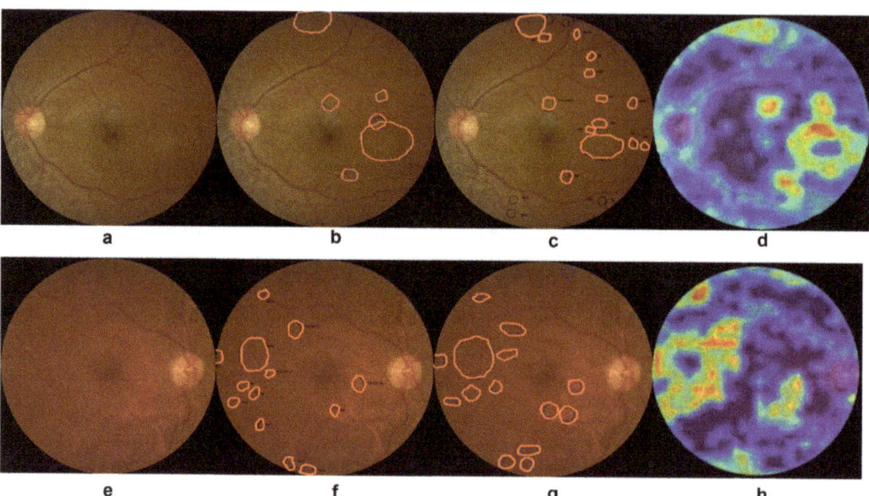

Figure 6. Visualization of the decision-making mechanism of DeepPCANet-5 model. (**a**) Fundus image from class moderate, (**b**,**c**) lesions specified by experts 1 and 2, respectively, (**d**) DeepPCANet-5 map (**e**) fundus image from class PDR, (**f**,**g**) lesions specified by experts 1 and 2, respectively, (**h**) DeepPCANet-5 map.

6. Discussions

This study proposed a technique to auto-custom-design a DeepPCANet model for a target DR dataset. The depth of the model and the width of each layer is not specified randomly or by exhaustive experiments. The custom-designed DeepPCANet models for DR screening have small depths and varying widths of CONV layers and involve a small number of learnable parameters. The results of the AutoML DeepPCANet models customized for the KSU-DR, APTOS2019, and EyePACS datasets (presented in Tables 4–6) demonstrate that it outperforms the well-known highly complex pre-trained models ResNet152, DenseNet121, and ResNeSt50, as well as AutoML from Google and Auto-Keras that was fine-tuned using the same DR datasets. Generally, the DeepPCANet got competitive performance with a small number of layers and parameters. As shown in Table 4, the custom-designed DeepPCANet models for the three datasets have a small number of parameters in thousands against that number in millions of ResNet152, DenseNet121, and ResNeSt50. DeepPCANet-4 and DeepPCANet-5 have fewer FLOPs than all pre-trained models and have better performance. The DeepPCANet-16 has fewer FLOPs than that of ResNet152 and ResNeSt50 and also has better performance. Though DenseNet121 has fewer FLOPs than DeepPCANet-16, it has the least performance and a large number of parameters. The reason for the lightweight structures and superior performance of custom-designed DeepPCANet models is that their architectures have been directly drawn from the fundus images, unlike the state-of-the-art CNN models, which are mainly designed for object detection. In addition to comparing the custom-designed DeepPCANet models with famous pre-trained models, it is essential to validate their effectiveness in DR screening by comparing them to the state-of-the-art methods on two challenging datasets (APOTS2019 and EyePACS). DeepPCANet-4 generated for SC1 on the APTOS2019 dataset outperforms the state-of-the-art methods on the same dataset in terms of accuracy, sensitivity, specificity, and Kappa, as shown in Table 7. The DeepPCANet-4 based on the five-class problem (SC1) and APTOS2019 dataset outperforms the method presented in Sikder et al. (2021), which used handcrafted features and needs a long processing time for fundus image preprocessing and extracting features. Though the method by Tymchenko et al., 2020 [64] outperforms the DeepPCANet-4 in the Kappa score for the five-class problem (SC1), it has less accuracy, sensitivity, and specificity, and it is based on a highly complex ensemble of 20 CNN models.

For the same scenario, the DeepPCANet-16 designed for EyePACS outperforms the existing methods in accuracy and specificity. The method by Islam et al., 2018 [61] obtained higher sensitivity, but their model is more complex, and it was tested on 4% of the dataset, as shown in Table 7. For the SC2 (normal vs. DR levels), DeepPCANet-4 outperforms the method by Tymchenko et al. [64] in all metrics on APTOS2019. In this scenario, on the EyePACS dataset, as shown in Table 7, the DeepPCANet-16 is better than other methods in accuracy, sensitivity, and specificity; the method by Islam et al., 2018 [61] is slightly better than DeepPCANet-16 in sensitivity, but it was tested only on 4% of the EyePACS dataset. The method of Chetoui et al., 2020 [87] is better than DeepPCANet-16, whereas they used transfer learning based on Inception-Resnet-v2, which has high complexity and a large number of parameters. It consists of five convolutional layers, each followed by batch normalization, two pooling layers, forty-three inception modules, three residual connections, the pooling of global averages, and the use of two fully connected layers in conjunction with the rectified linear unit (ReLU); whereas, DeepPCANet-16 is a 16-layer structure that employs the basic CONV setup. The DeepPCANet-16, based on the EyePACS dataset for the SC3 (0 and 1 vs. DR levels), obtained less accuracy than Colas et al. [67] and Islam et al. [61] but obtained higher sensitivity and specificity, which are more important and robust than accuracy in the medical applications [88].

Table 7. Comparison between DeepPCANet models and state-of-the-art methods.

Paper	Method	Dataset	Performance (%)			
			ACC	SE	SP	Kappa
Five classes (SC1)						
Sikder et al., 2019 [65]	Colored features extraction using ensemble	APTOS2019	91	89.54	-	-
Tymchenko et al., 2020 [64]	An ensembled models with 3 CNN architectures fficientNet-B4, EfficientNet-B5, and SE-ResNeXt50	APTOS2019	91.9	84	98	96.9
Shorfuzzaman et al., 2021 [89]	CNN-based transfer learning ensemble	aptos2019	96.2	94.00	-	-
Sikder et al. (2021)	Histogram and GLCM features tuning using XGBoostand genetic algorithm.	aptos2019	94.20	-	-	-
DeepPCANet-4	**DeepPCANet model customized for APTOS2019 dataset**	**APTOS2019 (test: 40% of public dataset)**	**98.21**	**95.28**	**98.85**	**94.32**
Lahmar et al., 2021 [90]	Transfer learning (MobileNet V2)	APTOS2019 (SC1)	93.09	89.27	92.69	-
Islam et al., 2018 [61]	A CNN model consisting of 18 layers with 3×3 and 4×4 kernels	EyePACS (test: 4% of dataset)		94.5	90.2	
Li et al., 2019 [62]	Deep learning model based on DCNN	EyePACS (test: 10% of dataset)	86.17	-	-	-
DeepPCANet-16	**DeepPCANet model customized for EyePACS dataset**	**EyePACS (test: 10% of public dataset)**	**94.22**	**89.56**	**96.30**	**81.64**

Table 7. *Cont.*

Paper	Method	Dataset	Performance (%)			
			ACC	SE	SP	Kappa
Normal vs. DR (all DR levels) (two classes) (SC2)						
Tymchenko et al., 2020 [64]	Ensembled models with 3 CNN architectures EfficientNet-B4, EfficientNet-B5, and SE-ResNeXt50	APTOS2019	99.3	99.3	99.3	98.6
DeepPCANet-4	**DeepPCANet model customized for APTOS2019 dataset**	**APTOS2019 (test: 10% of public dataset)**	**99.7**	**99.44**	**99.44**	**99.3**
Islam et al., 2018 [61]	A CNN model consisting of 18 layers with 3×3 and 4×4 kernels	EyePACS (test: 4% of public dataset)		94.5	90.2	-
Li et al., 2019 [62]	Features extraction using deep learning model based on DCNN and SVM classification	EyePACS	91.05	89.30	90.89	-
Chetoui et al., 2020 [87]	Pretrained Inception-Resnet-v2 DCNN	EyePACS (SC2)	97.9	95.8	97.1	98.6
DeepPCANet-16	DeepPCANet model customized for EyePACS dataset	EyePACS (test: 10% of public dataset)	94.44	94.28	94.28	88.71
Non-referral (Normal and DR grad 1) vs. referral (DR grade 2 to highest grade) (two classes) (SC3)						
Colas et al., 2016 [67]	A CNN model. End to end training.	EyePACS (train: 89%, test: 11%)	96.2	66.6	94.6	
Islam et al., 2018 [61]	A CNN model	EyePACS (train: 96%, test: 4%)	98	94		
DeepPCANet-16	DeepPCANet model derived from EyePACS dataset	EyePACS (test: 10% of public dataset)	94.59	94.86	94.87	89.02

7. Conclusions

We introduced an approach to building an AutoML data-dependent CNN model (DeepPCANet) customized for DR screening automatically. This approach tackles the limitations of the available annotated DR datasets and the problem of a vast search space and a huge number of parameters in a deep CNN model. It bauto-lightweightghtweight CNN model customized for a target DR dataset using k-medoid clustering, principal component analysis (PCA), and inter-class and intra-class variations. The DeepPCANet model is data-dependent, and each DR dataset has its appropriate AutoML architecture. The customized models, DeepPCANet-5 for the local KSU-DR dataset, DeepPCANet-4 for APTOS2019, and DeepPCANet-16 for the EyePACS dataset outperform the pre-trained very deep and highly complex ResNet152, DenseNet121, and ResNeSt50 models fine-tuned using the same datasets and procedure. The performance, complexity, and number of parameters of the customized DeepPCANet models are significantly less than ResNet152 and ResNeSt50. Though DenseNet121 has fewer FLOPs than DeepPCANet-16, it has the least performance and a large number of parameters. On the EyePACS dataset, compared to the Google Cloud AutoML and Auto-Keras, DeepPCANet-16 based on SC1 obtained better performance with fewer parameters. Using the EyePACS dataset, DeepPCANet-16 also compared to the state-of-the-art methods (for SC2 and SC3), the DeepPCANet-16 has less complexity and parameters and has competitive performance. The DeepPCANet fails to predict DR grade from fundus images, which have poor quality. It could not correctly grade some poor quality fundus images from the EyePACS dataset; each image in this dataset was graded by only one expert from the geographic region of California, which can potentially lead to annotation bias. How the DeepPCANet can reliably predict the DR grade from poor quality fundus images is a subject of future work. Additionally, how the DeepPCANet can be generalized with different fundus datasets is a subject of future work.

Author Contributions: Conceptualization, F.S. and M.H.; data curation, F.S., F.A.A. and A.M.A.O.; formal analysis, F.S., F.A.A. and A.M.A.O.; funding acquisition, methodology, F.S. and M.H.; project administration, M.H. and H.A.A.; resources, M.H. and H.A.A.; software, F.S.; supervision, M.H. and H.A.A.; validation, F.S.; visualization, F.S.; writing original draft, F.S.; writing—review and editing, M.H. All authors have read and agreed to the published version of the manuscript.

Funding: The authors extend their appreciation to the Deputyship for Research and Innovation, Ministry of Education in Saudi Arabia for funding this research work through the project no. (IFKSURG-2-108).

Data Availability Statement: Public domain datasets were used for experiments.

Conflicts of Interest: The authors declare no conflict of interest.

References

1. Yau, J.W.Y.; Rogers, S.L.; Kawasaki, R.; Lamoureux, E.L.; Kowalski, J.W.; Bek, T.; Chen, S.-J.; Dekker, J.M.; Fletcher, A.; Grauslund, J.; et al. Global Prevalence and Major Risk Factors of Diabetic Retinopathy. *Diabetes Care* **2012**, *35*, 556–564. [CrossRef] [PubMed]
2. Quellec, G.; Charrière, K.; Boudi, Y.; Cochener, B.; Lamard, M. Deep image mining for diabetic retinopathy screening. *Med. Image Anal.* **2017**, *39*, 178–193. [CrossRef] [PubMed]
3. Sreejini, K.; Govindan, V. Retrieval of pathological retina images using Bag of Visual Words and pLSA model. *Eng. Sci. Technol. Int. J.* **2019**, *22*, 777–785. [CrossRef]
4. Hemanth, D.J.; Deperlioglu, O.; Kose, U. An enhanced diabetic retinopathy detection and classification approach using deep convolutional neural network. *Neural Comput. Appl.* **2020**, *32*, 707–721. [CrossRef]
5. Stolte, S.; Fang, R. A Survey on Medical Image Analysis in Diabetic Retinopathy. *Med. Image Anal.* **2020**, *64*, 101742. [CrossRef]
6. Ting, D.S.W.; Pasquale, L.R.; Peng, L.; Campbell, J.P.; Lee, A.Y.; Raman, R.; Tan, G.S.W.; Schmetterer, L.; Keane, P.A.; Wong, T.Y. Artificial intelligence and deep learning in ophthalmology. *Br. J. Ophthalmol.* **2019**, *103*, 167–175. [CrossRef]
7. Gu, J.; Wang, Z.; Kuen, J.; Ma, L.; Shahroudy, A.; Shuai, B.; Liu, T.; Wang, X.; Wang, G.; Cai, J.; et al. Recent advances in convolutional neural networks. *Pattern Recognit.* **2018**, *77*, 354–377. [CrossRef]
8. Grigorescu, S.; Trasnea, B.; Cocias, T.; Macesanu, G. A survey of deep learning techniques for autonomous driving. *J. Field Robot.* **2020**, *37*, 362–386. [CrossRef]
9. Abou Arkoub, S.; Hajjam El Hassani, A.; Lauri, F.; Hajjar, M.; Daya, B.; Hecquet, S.; Aubry, S. Survey on Deep Learning Techniques for Medical Imaging Application Area. In *Machine Learning Paradigms*; Springer: Cham, Switzerland, 2020; pp. 149–189.
10. Mohamadou, Y.; Halidou, A.; Kapen, P.T. A review of mathematical modeling, artificial intelligence and datasets used in the study, prediction and management of COVID-19. *Appl. Intell.* **2020**, *50*, 3913–3925. [CrossRef]
11. Zhu, H.; Shu, S.; Zhang, J. FAS-UNet: A Novel FAS-Driven UNet to Learn Variational Image Segmentation. *Mathematics* **2022**, *10*, 4055. [CrossRef]
12. Lam, C.; Yu, C.; Huang, L.; Rubin, D. Retinal lesion detection with deep learning using image patches. *Investig. Ophthalmol. Vis. Sci.* **2018**, *59*, 590–596. [CrossRef] [PubMed]
13. Gao, Z.; Li, J.; Guo, J.; Chen, Y.; Yi, Z.; Zhong, J. Diagnosis of Diabetic Retinopathy Using Deep Neural Networks. *IEEE Access* **2019**, *7*, 3360–3370. [CrossRef]
14. Shaik, N.S.; Cherukuri, T.K. Hinge attention network: A joint model for diabetic retinopathy severity grading. *Appl. Intell.* **2022**, *52*, 15105–15121. [CrossRef]
15. Gao, Z.; Jin, K.; Yan, Y.; Liu, X.; Shi, Y.; Ge, Y.; Pan, X.; Lu, Y.; Wu, J.; Wang, Y.; et al. End-to-end diabetic retinopathy grading based on fundus fluorescein angiography images using deep learning. *Graefe's Arch. Clin. Exp. Ophthalmol.* **2022**, *260*, 1663–1673. [CrossRef] [PubMed]
16. Szegedy, C.; Liu, W.; Jia, Y.; Sermanet, P.; Reed, S.; Anguelov, D.; Erhan, D.; Vanhoucke, V.; Rabinovich, A. Going deeper with convolutions. In Proceedings of the IEEE Conference on Computer Vision and Pattern Recognition, Boston, MA, USA, 7–12 June 2015; pp. 1–9.
17. He, K.; Zhang, X.; Ren, S.; Sun, J. Deep residual learning for image recognition. In Proceedings of the 2016 IEEE Conference on Computer Vision and Pattern Recognition, Las Vegas, NV, USA, 27–30 June 2016; pp. 770–778.
18. Huang, G. Densely connected convolutional networks. CVPR 2017. *arXiv* **2016**, arXiv:1608.06993.
19. Saini, M.; Susan, S. Diabetic retinopathy screening using deep learning for multi-class imbalanced datasets. *Comput. Biol. Med.* **2022**, *149*, 105989. [CrossRef]
20. Glorot, X.; Bengio, Y. Understanding the difficulty of training deep feedforward neural networks. In Proceedings of the Thirteenth International Conference on Artificial Intelligence and Statistics, Sardinia, Italy, 13–15 May 2010; pp. 249–256.
21. He, K.; Zhang, X.; Ren, S.; Sun, J. Delving deep into rectifiers: Surpassing human-level performance on imagenet classification. In Proceedings of the IEEE International Conference on Computer, Santiago, Chile, 7–13 December 2015; Volume 22, pp. 1026–1034.

22. Krähenbühl, P. Data-dependent initializations of convolutional neural networks. *arXiv* **2015**, arXiv:1511.06856.
23. Suau, X.; Apostoloff, N. Filter Distillation for Network Compression. In Proceedings of the IEEE Winter Conference on Applications of Computer Vision (WACV), Piscataway, NJ, USA, 1–5 March 2020; pp. 3129–3138.
24. Singh, V.K.; Joshi, K. Automated Machine Learning (AutoML): An overview of opportunities for application and research. *J. Inf. Technol. Case Appl. Res.* **2022**, *24*, 75–85. [CrossRef]
25. Thornton, C. Auto-WEKA: Combined selection and hyperparameter optimization of classification algorithms. In Proceedings of the 19th ACM SIGKDD International Conference on Knowledge Discovery and Data Mining, New York, NY, USA, 11–14 August 2013; pp. 847–855.
26. Komer, B.; Bergstra, J.; Eliasmith, C. Hyperopt-sklearn: Automatic hyperparameter conTableuration for scikit-learn. In *ICML Workshop on AutoML*; Citeseer: Austin, TX, USA, 2014; Volume 9.
27. Olson, R.S.; Bartley, N.; Urbanowicz, R.J.; Moore, J.H. Evaluation of a tree-based pipeline optimization tool for automating data science. In Proceedings of the Genetic and Evolutionary Computation Conference, Denver, CO, USA, 20–24 June 2016; pp. 485–492.
28. Feurer, M.; Springenberg, J.; Hutter, F. Initializing bayesian hyperparameter optimization via meta-learning. In Proceedings of the AAAI Conference on Artificial Intelligence, Austin, TX, USA, 25–30 January 2015; Volume 29. No. 1.
29. Jin, H.; Song, Q.; Hu, X. Auto-keras: An efficient neural architecture search system. In Proceedings of the 25th ACM SIGKDD International Conference on Knowledge Discovery & Data Mining, New York, NY, USA, 4–8 August 2019; pp. 1946–1956.
30. Doke, A.; Gaikwad, M. Survey on Automated Machine Learning (AutoML) and Meta learning. In Proceedings of the 2021 12th International Conference on Computing Communication and Networking Technologies (ICCCNT), Kharagpur, India, 6–8 July 2021; IEEE: Piscataway, NJ, USA, 2021.
31. Stojadinovic, M.; Milicevic, B.; Jankovic, S. Improved predictive performance of prostate biopsy collaborative group risk calculator when based on automated machine learning. *Comput. Biol. Med.* **2021**, *138*, 104903. [CrossRef]
32. Aloraini, T.; Aljouie, A.; Alniwaider, R.; Alharbi, W.; Alsubaie, L.; AlTuraif, W.; Qureshi, W.; Alswaid, A.; Eyiad, W.; Al Mutairi, F.; et al. The variant artificial intelligence easy scoring (VARIES) system. *Comput. Biol. Med.* **2022**, *145*, 105492. [CrossRef]
33. Zoph, B.; Le, Q.V. Neural architecture search with reinforcement learning. *arXiv* **2016**, arXiv:1611.01578.
34. Domhan, T.; Springenberg, J.T.; Hutter, F. Speeding up automatic hyperparameter optimization of deep neural networks by extrapolation of learning curves. In Proceedings of the Twenty-fourth International Joint Conference on Artificial Intelligence, Buenos Aires, Argentina, 25–31 July 2015.
35. Tan, R.Z.; Chew, X.; Khaw, K.W. Neural Architecture Search for Lightweight Neural Network in Food Recognition. *Mathematics* **2021**, *9*, 1245. [CrossRef]
36. Liu, H. Hierarchical representations for efficient architecture search. *arXiv* **2017**, arXiv:1711.00436.
37. Kaggle. Diabetic Retinopathy Detection (Kaggle). 2019. Available online: https://www.kaggle.com/c/diabetic-retinopathy-detection/data (accessed on 26 September 2021).
38. Kaggle. APTOS Blindness Detection. 2019. Available online: https://www.kaggle.com/c/aptos2019-blindness-detection (accessed on 26 September 2021).
39. Zhang, H. Resnest: Split-attention networks. *arXiv* **2020**, arXiv:2004.08955.
40. Mateen, M.; Wen, J.; Hassan, M.; Nasrullah, N.; Sun, S.; Hayat, S. Automatic Detection of Diabetic Retinopathy: A Review on Datasets, Methods and Evaluation Metrics. *IEEE Access* **2020**, *8*, 48784–48811. [CrossRef]
41. Soomro, T.A.; Afifi, A.J.; Zheng, L.; Soomro, S.; Gao, J.; Hellwich, O.; Paul, M. Deep learning models for retinal blood vessels segmentation: A review. *IEEE Access* **2019**, *7*, 71696–71717. [CrossRef]
42. Asiri, N.; Hussain, M.; Al Adel, F.; Alzaidi, N. Deep learning based computer-aided diagnosis systems for diabetic retinopathy: A survey. *Artif. Intell. Med.* **2019**, *99*, 101701. [CrossRef]
43. Bhandari, S.; Pathak, S.; Jain, S.A.; Deshmukh, V. A Review on Swarm intelligence & Evolutionary Algorithms based Approaches for Diabetic Retinopathy Detection. In Proceedings of the 2022 IEEE World Conference on Applied Intelligence and Computing (AIC), Sonbhadra, India, 17–19 June 2022; IEEE: Piscataway, NJ, USA, 2022.
44. Han, S.; Mao, H.; Dally, W.J. Deep compression: Compressing deep neural networks with pruning, trained quantization and huffman coding. *arXiv* **2015**, arXiv:1510.00149.
45. He, Y.; Zhang, X.; Sun, J. Channel pruning for accelerating very deep neural networks. In Proceedings of the IEEE International Conference on Computer Vision, Venice, Italy, 22–29 October 2017; pp. 1389–1397.
46. Howard, A.G.; Zhu, M.; Chen, B.; Kalenichenko, D.; Wang, W.; Weyand, T.; Andreetto, M.; Adam, H. Mobilenets: Efficient convolutional neural networks for mobile vision applications. *arXiv* **2017**, arXiv:1704.04861.
47. Jiang, C.; Li, G.; Qian, C.; Tang, K. Efficient DNN Neuron Pruning by Minimizing Layer-wise Nonlinear Reconstruction Error. In Proceedings of the Twenty-Seventh International Joint Conference on Artificial Intelligence (IJCAI-18), Stockholm, Sweden, 13–19 July 2018; Volume 2018, pp. 2298–2304.
48. Choudhary, T.; Mishra, V.; Goswami, A.; Sarangapani, J. A transfer learning with structured filter pruning approach for improved breast cancer classification on point-of-care devices. *Comput. Biol. Med.* **2021**, *134*, 104432. [CrossRef]
49. Chan, T.H.; Jia, K.; Gao, S.; Lu, J.; Zeng, Z.; Ma, Y. PCANet: A simple deep learning baseline for image classification? *IEEE Trans. Image Process.* **2015**, *24*, 5017–5032. [CrossRef] [PubMed]

50. Seuret, M.; Alberti, M.; Liwicki, M.; Ingold, R. PCA-initialized deep neural networks applied to document image analysis. In Proceedings of the 2017 14th IAPR International Conference on Document Analysis and Recognition (ICDAR), Kyoto, Japan, 9–15 November 2017; IEEE: Piscataway, NJ, USA, 2017.

51. Zhong, Z.; Yang, Z.; Deng, B.; Yan, J.; Wu, W.; Shao, J.; Liu, C.L. Blockqnn: Efficient block-wise neural network architecture generation. *IEEE Trans. Pattern Anal. Mach. Intell.* **2020**, *43*, 2314–2328. [CrossRef] [PubMed]

52. Kotthoff, L.; Thornton, C.; Hoos, H.H.; Hutter, F.; Leyton-Brown, K. Auto-WEKA. In *Automated Machine Learning*; Springer: Cham, Switzerland, 2019; pp. 81–95.

53. Feurer, M.; Klein, A.; Eggensperger, K.; Springenberg, J.; Blum, M.; Hutter, F. Auto-sklearn: Efficient and robust automated machine learning. In *Automated Machine Learning*; Springer: Cham, Switzerland, 2019; pp. 113–134.

54. Real, E.; Aggarwal, A.; Huang, Y.; Le, Q.V. Regularized evolution for image classifier architecture search. In Proceedings of the AAAI Conference on Artificial Intelligence, Palo Alto, CA, USA, 22 February–1 March 2022; No. 01. Volume 33.

55. Zoph, B.; Vasudevan, V.; Shlens, J.; Le, Q.V. Learning transferable architectures for scalable image recognition. In Proceedings of the IEEE Conference on Computer Vision and Pattern Recognition, Salt Lake City, UT, USA, 18–23 June 2018.

56. Pham, H.; Guan, M.; Zoph, B.; Le, Q.; Dean, J. Efficient neural architecture search via parameters sharing. In Proceedings of the International Conference on Machine Learning, Stockholm, Sweden, 10–15 July 2018; PMLR 80. pp. 4095–4104.

57. Liu, H.; Simonyan, K.; Yang, Y. Darts: Differentiable architecture search. *arXiv* **2018**, arXiv:1806.09055.

58. Bergstra, J.; Yamins, D.; Cox, D. Making a science of model search: Hyperparameter optimization in hundreds of dimensions for vision architectures. In Proceedings of the International Conference on Machine Learning, Atlanta, GA, USA, 17–19 June 2013; PMLR 28. pp. 115–123.

59. Bisong, E. Google AutoML: Cloud vision. In *Building Machine Learning and Deep Learning Models on Google Cloud Platform*; Springer: Berkeley, CA, USA, 2019; pp. 581–598.

60. Bisong, E. *An Overview of Google Cloud Platform Services. Building Machine Learning and Deep Learning Models on Google Cloud Platform*; Springer: Berkeley, CA, USA, 2019; pp. 7–10.

61. Islam, S.M.S.; Hasan, M.M.; Abdullah, S. Deep Learning based Early Detection and Grading of Diabetic Retinopathy Using Retinal Fundus Images. *arXiv* **2018**, arXiv:1812.10595.

62. Li, Y.-H.; Yeh, N.-N.; Chen, S.-J.; Chung, Y.-C. Computer-assisted diagnosis for diabetic retinopathy based on fundus images using deep convolutional neural network. *Mob. Inf. Syst.* **2019**, *2019*, 6142839. [CrossRef]

63. Challa, U.K.; Yellamraju, P.; Bhatt, J.S. A Multi-class Deep All-CNN for Detection of Diabetic Retinopathy Using Retinal Fundus Images. In Proceedings of the International Conference on Pattern Recognition and Machine Intelligence, Tezpur, India, 17–20 December 2019; Springer: Cham, Switzerland, 2019; pp. 191–199.

64. Tymchenko, B.; Marchenko, P.; Spodarets, D. Deep Learning Approach to Diabetic Retinopathy Detection. *arXiv* **2020**, arXiv:2003.02261.

65. Sikder, N.; Chowdhury, M.S.; Arif, A.S.M.; Nahid, A.A. Early Blindness Detection Based on Retinal Images Using Ensemble Learning. In Proceedings of the 2019 22nd International Conference on Computer and Information Technology (ICCIT), Dhaka, Bangladesh, 18–20 December 2019; IEEE: Piscataway, NJ, USA, 2019.

66. Sikder, N.; Masud, M.; Bairagi, A.K.; Arif, A.S.M.; Nahid, A.A.; Alhumyani, H.A. Severity classification of diabetic retinopathy using an ensemble learning algorithm through analyzing retinal images. *Symmetry* **2021**, *13*, 670. [CrossRef]

67. Colas, E.; Besse, A.; Orgogozo, A.; Schmauch, B.; Meric, N.; Besse, E. Deep learning approach for diabetic retinopathy screening. *Acta Ophthalmol.* **2016**, *94*. [CrossRef]

68. Simonyan, K.; Zisserman, A. Very deep convolutional networks for large-scale image recognition. *arXiv* **2014**, arXiv:1409.1556.

69. Deng, J.; Dong, W.; Socher, R.; Li, L.J.; Li, K.; Fei-Fei, L. Imagenet: A large-scale hierarchical image database. In Proceedings of the 2009 IEEE Conference on Computer Vision and Pattern Recognition, Miami, FL, USA, 20–25 June 2009; IEEE: Piscataway, NJ, USA, 2009.

70. Zhang, Q.; Couloigner, I. A new and efficient k-medoid algorithm for spatial clustering. In Proceedings of the International Conference on Computational Science and Its Applications, Singapore, 9–12 May 2005; Springer: Berlin/Heidelberg, Germany, 2005; pp. 181–189.

71. Wold, S.; Esbensen, K.; Geladi, P. Principal component analysis. *Chemom. Intell. Lab. Syst.* **1987**, *2*, 37–52. [CrossRef]

72. Likas, A.; Vlassis, N.; Verbeek, J.J. The global k-means clustering algorithm. *Pattern Recognit.* **2003**, *36*, 451–461. [CrossRef]

73. Saeed, F.; Hussain, M.; Aboalsamh, H.A. Method for Fingerprint Classification. U.S. Patent 9530042, 13 June 2016.

74. Tibshirani, R.; Walther, G.; Hastie, T. Estimating the number of clusters in a data set via the gap statistic. *J. R. Stat. Soc. Ser. B (Stat. Methodol.)* **2001**, *63*, 411–423. [CrossRef]

75. Mika, S.; Ratsch, G.; Weston, J.; Scholkopf, B.; Mullers, K.R. Fisher discriminant analysis with kernels. In *Neural Networks for Signal Processing IX: Proceedings of the 1999 IEEE Signal Processing Society Workshop (Cat. No. 98TH8468), Madison, WI, USA, 25 August 1999*; IEEE: Piscataway, NJ, USA, 1999.

76. Al Asbahi, A.A.M.H.; Gang, F.Z.; Iqbal, W.; Abass, Q.; Mohsin, M.; Iram, R. Novel approach of Principal Component Analysis method to assess the national energy performance via Energy Trilemma Index. *Energy Rep.* **2019**, *5*, 704–713. [CrossRef]

77. Cook, A. Global Average Pooling Layers for Object Localization. 2017. Available online: https://alexisbcook.github.io/2017/global-average-pooling-layers-for-object-localization (accessed on 23 November 2022).

78. Akiba, T.; Sano, S.; Yanase, T.; Ohta, T.; Koyama, M. Optuna: A next-generation hyperparameter optimization framework. In Proceedings of the 25th ACM SIGKDD International Conference on Knowledge Discovery & Data Mining, New York, NY, USA, 4–8 August 2019; pp. 2623–2631.

79. Yu, M.; Wang, Y. Intelligent detection and applied research on diabetic retinopathy based on the residual attention network. *Int. J. Imaging Syst. Technol.* **2022**, *32*, 1789–1800. [CrossRef]

80. Chowdhury, A.R.; Chatterjee, T.; Banerjee, S. A Random Forest classifier-based approach in the detection of abnormalities in the retina. *Med. Biol. Eng. Comput.* **2019**, *57*, 193–203. [CrossRef]

81. Zhang, W.; Zhong, J.; Yang, S.; Gao, Z.; Hu, J.; Chen, Y.; Yi, Z. Automated identification and grading system of diabetic retinopathy using deep neural networks. *Knowl.-Based Syst.* **2019**, *175*, 12–25. [CrossRef]

82. Zebin, T.; Rezvy, S. COVID-19 detection and disease progression visualization: Deep learning on chest X-rays for classification and coarse localization. *Appl. Intell.* **2021**, *51*, 1010–1021. [CrossRef]

83. Ben-David, A. Comparison of classification accuracy using Cohen's Weighted Kappa. *Expert Syst. Appl.* **2008**, *34*, 825–832. [CrossRef]

84. Fernández-Fuentes, X.; Mera, D.; Gómez, A.; Vidal-Franco, I. Towards a fast and accurate eit inverse problem solver: A machine learning approach. *Electronics* **2018**, *7*, 422. [CrossRef]

85. Shu, Y.; Wang, W.; Cai, S. Understanding architectures learnt by cell-based neural architecture search. *arXiv* **2019**, arXiv:1909.09569.

86. Selvaraju, R.R.; Cogswell, M.; Das, A.; Vedantam, R.; Parikh, D.; Batra, D. Grad-Cam: Visual explanations from deep networks via gradient-based localization. In Proceedings of the IEEE International Conference on Computer Vision, Venice, Italy, 22–29 October 2017; pp. 618–626.

87. Shorfuzzaman, M.; Hossain, M.S.; El Saddik, A. An Explainable Deep Learning Ensemble Model for Robust Diagnosis of Diabetic Retinopathy Grading. *ACM Trans. Multimed. Comput. Commun. Appl. (TOMM)* **2021**, *17*, 1–24. [CrossRef]

88. Lahmar, C.; Idri, A. On the value of deep learning for diagnosing diabetic retinopathy. *Health Technol.* **2021**, *12*, 89–105. [CrossRef]

89. Chetoui, M.; Akhloufi, M.A. Explainable end-to-end deep learning for diabetic retinopathy detection across multiple datasets. *J. Med. Imaging* **2020**, *7*, 044503. [CrossRef] [PubMed]

90. Reynolds, C.R.; Fletcher-Janzen, E. *Handbook of Clinical Child Neuropsychology*; Springer: Boston, MA, USA, 2013; ISBN 978-0-387-70708-22.

MDPI

St. Alban-Anlage 66

4052 Basel

Switzerland

Tel. +41 61 683 77 34

Fax +41 61 302 89 18

www.mdpi.com

Mathematics Editorial Office

E-mail: mathematics@mdpi.com

www.mdpi.com/journal/mathematics